The Prose of JOHN MILTON

Selected and Edited from the Original Texts with Introductions, Notes, Translations, & Accounts of All of His Major Prose Writings

General Introduction by J. Max Patrick, Editor

ANCHOR BOOKS
DOUBLEDAY & COMPANY, INC.
GARDEN CITY, NEW YORK
1967

The Anchor Seventeenth-Century Series
is published by Doubleday Anchor Books
under the General Editorship of
Professor J. Max Patrick
New York University

This edition has been specially prepared for Anchor Books
and has never appeared before in book form

Library of Congress Catalog Card Number 67–15390

Printed in the United States of America
First Edition

CONTENTS

Abbreviations xi

Introduction BY J. MAX PATRICK xiii

Chronology of Milton's life xxxiii

The Prolusions, *Prolusiones Quaedam Oratoriae*, Some Academic Exercises, 1628–1632, EDITED AND TRANSLATED BY THOMAS R. HARTMANN 1

Foreword 3

Prolusion VII, A Speech in Defense of Learning 15

The Anti-Prelatical Tracts, 1641–1642, EDITED BY EVERETT H. EMERSON 29

Foreword 31

Of Reformation, May 1641 41

Summary with extracts of:

Of Prelatical Episcopacy, June or July 1641 93

Animadversions, July 1641 97

The Reason of Church-Governement, January or February 1642 103

An Apology Against a Pamphlet, April 1642 115

A Note on the "Postscript" in Smectymnuus, *An Answer*, 1641, BY J. MAX PATRICK 123

The Divorce Tracts, 1643–1645, EDITED BY J. MAX PATRICK AND ARTHUR M. AXELRAD 125

Foreword 127

Extracts from:

The Dedicatory Address to Parliament in *Doctrine and Discipline*, second edition, February 1644 135

The Doctrine and Discipline of Divorce, first edition, August 1643 143

Summary with extracts of:

The Judgement of Martin Bucer, August 1644 203

Tetrachordon, March 1645 209

Colasterion, March 1645 213

The Tractate on Education, 1644, EDITED BY THOMAS R. HARTMANN 217
Foreword 219
Of Education, June 1644 229

The Tract for Liberty of Publication, 1644, EDITED BY J. MAX PATRICK 245
Foreword 247
Areopagitica, November 1644 265

The Anti-Monarchical Tracts, 1649, EDITED BY JOHN T. SHAWCROSS 335
Foreword 337
The Tenure of Kings and Magistrates, first edition, February 1649 347
Summary with extracts, BY J. MAX PATRICK, of:
Observations upon the Articles of Peace, May 1649 383
Eikonoklastes, October 1649 389

The Defenses, 1651–1655, EDITED AND TRANSLATED BY JOHN R. MULDER 399
Foreword 401
Selections from:
Pro Populo Anglicano Defensio: "The First Defense," February 1651 403
Pro Populo Anglicano Defensio Secunda: "The Second Defense," May 1654 409
Pro se Defensio: The Defense of Himself: "The Third Defense," August 1655 433

The Political and Religious Tracts of 1659–1660, EDITED BY BARBARA KIEFER LEWALSKI 437
Foreword 439
A Treatise of Civil Power, February 1659 443
Considerations Touching the Likeliest Means to Remove Hirelings, August 1659, EDITED BY WILLIAM B. HUNTER, JR. 475
Foreword with accounts of: 519
Letter to a Friend, October 1659
Proposals of Certain Expedients, October–December 1659
The Present Means (Letter to Monk), March 1660
Brief Notes upon a Late Sermon, April 1660
The Readie and Easie Way to Establish a Free Commonwealth, second edition, ca. April 1660 527

The Historical Writings, The Commonplace Book, and The State Papers, EDITED BY J. MAX PATRICK 559

Summaries with extracts of:

The History of Britain, composed ca. 1646–ca. 1666, published 1670, including the digression or *Character of the Long Parliament* 561

A Brief History of Moscovia, written ca. 1648, published 1682 573

The *Commonplace Book,* 1630?–1665? 577

Literae Pseudo-Senatus Anglicani, 1676; *Republican-Letters,* 1682; *Letters of State,* 1694; the Skinner and Columbia Manuscripts, and other State Papers, composed 1649–1660 583

The Familiar Letters, 1627–1666, EDITED AND TRANSLATED BY JOHN T. SHAWCROSS 591

Foreword 593

Selected Familiar Letters 597

Christian Doctrine, *De Doctrina Christiana,* 1640–1673? EDITED BY J. MAX PATRICK 627

Foreword 629

Summary of *Christian Doctrine* 637

Bibliography 671

ABBREVIATIONS

EETS	*Early English Text Society*
ELN	*English Language Notes*
HLQ	*Huntington Library Quarterly*
JEGP	*Journal of English and Germanic Philology*
JHI	*Journal of the History of Ideas*
MLN	*Modern Language Notes*
MLQ	*Modern Language Quarterly*
MLR	*Modern Language Review*
MP	*Modern Philology*
PBSA	*Papers of the Bibliographical Society of America*
PQ	*Philological Quarterly*
QJS	*Quarterly Journal of Speech*
RES	*Review of English Studies*
SAMLA	*South Atlantic Modern Language Association*
SB	*Studies in Bibliography*
SEL	*Studies in English Literature*
SP	*Studies in Philology*
UTQ	*University of Toronto Quarterly*

INTRODUCTION

Resourcefulness, industry, and marriage to Sarah Jeffrey (who possessed both virtue and wealth), enabled John Milton senior to overcome the rigidities of the English social system. He derived from an undistinguished Roman Catholic Oxfordshire family, became an Anglican, went to London (probably as a musician), rose to some prominence in the business world as a scrivener engaged in legal and financial affairs, and gained social status as a gentleman by acquiring a coat of arms. He also won some recognition as a composer: his eight-part choral work for the King of Poland has not survived, but his hymns are still sung in the Church of England. He brought up his children, Anne, John, and Christopher, in a cultured, comfortable, pious, tolerant London household, encouraging John to become an Anglican priest and Christopher to enter the field of law.

The future poet was born on December 9, 1608, five years after James I succeeded Queen Elizabeth I, eight years before the deaths of Shakespeare and Cervantes. Like the royal family, Milton senior had his sons tutored by a Scot–Thomas Young. In 1620, the year when the Pilgrims settled New Plymouth, twelve-year-old John entered St. Paul's School. There he received an admirable humanistic education which greatly influenced the program of studies later propounded in *Of Education*. In 1625 Charles I came to the throne and, at a somewhat older age than was customary, John enrolled in Christ's College, Cambridge. A disagreement with his tutor led to his rustication or temporary expulsion, but he returned, displayed his virtuosity in the Prolusions or Academic Exercises which he published in his old age, and received his B.A. in 1629, two years before the death of John Donne.

By this time Milton had composed a number of short poems in Latin and English. In 1634 his *Mask* (better known as *Comus*) entertained the aristocratic Bridgewater family; it was published without his name and without Henry Lawes' music for it, about three years later. *Lycidas,* a pastoral elegy occasioned by the drowning of a college acquaintance, was printed in a volume of poems in memory of Edward King.

About 1638 Milton went on a tour of France and Italy but did not reach Greece, as he had intended, because of the social, political, economic, and religious crisis in England. Tensions had become acute on a political level between king and parliament and, inside the Church of England, between conservatives who felt that the Reformation had gone far enough—or too far—and others, loosely called "Puritans," who wanted forms of faith and worship more Protestant than those established by law. These oppositions were exacerbated by problems of inflation, taxation, obsolete institutions and vested interests, increasing population, and the advance of capitalism.

"Puritan," as ordinarily understood today, is a misleading term to apply to Milton senior or either of his sons. They were a moderate Church of England family; the boys attended a school whose services were Anglican; and John subscribed to the Thirty-Nine Articles when he entered Christ's College. If the Miltons sang psalms, they also warbled madrigals; and their home was frequented by musicians, many of them Roman Catholics and Royalists. Indeed, Christopher Milton supported the king and the established church and ultimately became a Roman Catholic judge under James II. Art and literature were regarded with favor in the Milton home; and the fact that John somehow managed to get a poem of tribute to Shakespeare into the second folio suggests the broad and up-to-date cultural interests of his family. Nor should it be forgotten that John wrote and never disowned poems honoring the Anglican bishop, Joseph Andrewes, and the Roman Catholic Marchioness of Winchester. Indeed, had John died in 1640, he would probably have been classed with Robert Herrick, George Herbert, and Abraham Cowley as an Anglican poet who wrote charming masques for the aristocracy, memorialized a young man who would have become a Church of England pastor, composed a number of excellent elegiac poems, and celebrated festivals of the Anglican church year. The urbane seriousness of *L'Allegro* and *Il Penseroso* can hardly be called puritanical.

Even the Milton who wrote the prose works in the present collection cannot unreservedly be called a Puritan: *Protestant* is a more apt term. Like the more advanced Anglicans and unlike many, probably most, of the Presbyterians, Baptists, and Congregationalists of the revolutionary period, Milton rejected the Calvinistic doctrine of predestination and believed in free will. His teachings on divorce horrified most Christians of all kinds. And had he published *Christian Doctrine,* its heresies would likewise have shocked most Englishmen of his times. On the other hand, Protestants in general, including High Anglicans, have found his epics and *Samson Agonistes* to be Christian, not distinctively Puritan, poems.

The same cannot be said for some of his prose tracts. Certainly he opposed episcopacy—government of the church by a hierarchy of bishops who claimed and exercised powers beyond what the Bible (as interpreted by Milton) seemed to justify, powers such as the exclusive right to ordain priests. Indeed, Milton rejected the doctrine of apostolic succession and regarded bishops as no more than presbyters (ministers or priests). He regarded the bishops' assumption and exercise of control over preaching, publication, doctrine, ritual, and interpretation of the Bible as a tyranny, one based on what he viewed as man-made traditions, worldliness, self-interest, alliance with secular powers, and either ignorance or deliberate falsification of what Holy Scripture and Right Reason teach. He felt that the bishops and their supporters were not only hindering but preventing the continued reformation of God's church in England. In Milton's opinion, God had shown special favor to his Englishmen when Wycliffe initiated the movement toward Scripture-based Protestantism. Under the Tudors, papal power in England had been broken and doctrinal and administrative reforms had gone a long way to remove "Popery" from English religion. Nevertheless, it seemed obvious to Milton that despite what he believed to be the finger of God pointing to the removal of episcopacy, the Reformation had remained incomplete in England and lagged behind what was accomplished in other Protestant countries. In attacking the bishops, Milton took what seemed to be the most obvious step toward freeing religion from man-imposed tyranny.

Milton did not initiate the attack on the prelates. Archbishop Laud, who had tried to regularize the Church of England in what seemed to Milton a step backward to Romanism, was impeached in 1640, the year of the Root and Branch Petition against government of the church by bishops. Taking these as a cue for literary action, Milton published *Of Reformation, Of Prelatical Episcopacy,* and *Animadversions upon the Remonstrants Defence* in 1641, and

The Reason of Church-Government and *An Apology against a Pamphlet,* in 1642, all in the cause of religious liberty.

Meanwhile he had set up a household of his own and partly occupied himself with teaching. Among his few pupils were John and Edward Phillips, sons of his sister Anne. This activity brought in some money, but Milton lived chiefly on wealth derived from his father. For example, he held a mortgage against some land owned by Richard Powell of Oxfordshire. The Powells and Miltons were old friends and had long been involved in such transactions. It is, accordingly, not improbable that John made the acquaintance of Richard's daughter Mary and chose her as his possible bride long before 1642, when he won her hand. They were married about May, when he was thirty-three and she was little more than half his age. Though women grew to responsible maturity earlier in those days, this teen-age girl seems to have had some difficulty in adjusting to a household that included the Phillips boys and offered less gaiety and social activities than she was accustomed to. On the other hand, when Milton consented to her visiting her father's home, about July 1642, there was apparently no severe tension between them, for he confidently expected her return and was surprised when she did not come back. External factors probably made the crucial difference: the civil war erupted; the Powells were Royalists; and Milton's anti-prelatical tracts had identified him with the rebels. Prospects for a parliamentary success may have looked slim when viewed from Oxfordshire; and the Powells may well have decided that the prudent course was to avoid identification with the losing side. On the other hand, if the Royalists lost, the marriage tie would still hold good, and the Powells perhaps presumed on what eventually happened—that Milton's good nature and decency would lead him to take back a repentant wife who put the blame on her mother. Moreover, the Powells were in royalist territory, and communications and travel to parliamentary London were difficult and dangerous.

Milton tried to get Mary to return, but not to the heroic extent of disguising himself and penetrating into enemy territory to reclaim her. Instead, within a year of her failure to return, he made that return somewhat difficult by publishing *The Doctrine and Discipline of Divorce* in August 1643, following it with an enlarged edition six months later, and with three other tracts, *The Judgement of Martin Bucer* (August 1644) and *Tetrachordon* and *Colasterion*

(March 1645): all of them urged that divorce be allowed for incompatibility, their central point being that the essence of Christian marriage lies in the rational and spiritual union of what is highest in humanity, thus distinguishing it from animals. He thought that a couple who are joined contractually and carnally but lack higher marital love and are naturally incompatible in mind and temperament should not be forced by church or state to remain yoked. He advocated that if a couple made a sincere effort over a reasonable period of time to iron out difficulties and find harmony and companionship, it should be recognized that there had never been a true marriage. The greater part of Milton's tracts on the subject tried to demonstrate that such views were in accord with the Bible.

Inasmuch as remarkably little is known about Milton's personal relationship with his wife and his attitude toward her, it is unfair to them to assume that they were seriously and permanently incompatible or that he was embittered by this experience throughout his life. What is obvious is that their few months together after the marriage did not amount to a sincere effort to find harmony over a reasonable period of time. There is no evidence that they did not find compatibility after her return. Mary remained with him till her death and bore him several children. It is also noteworthy that the experience did not stop Milton from entering upon two subsequent marriages.

The divorce tracts had a larger purpose than private aims. Milton regarded them as part of a program for religious, domestic, and political freedom in which he successively attacked the tyranny of bishops, the oppression of canon law as it persisted in the regulations governing marriage and divorce, and the tyranny of kings and state-controlled religion. All were aspects of his effort to continue the Reformation. His tractate *Of Education* (June 1644) dealt with another aspect of domestic freedom and was part of his larger attack against the tyrannies of custom, tradition, and thought control. Throughout his writings he particularly opposed the domination of education, theology, and thinking by the Schoolmen—the divines and philosophers in the degenerated tradition of medieval scholasticism. Their methods and Milton's earliest attacks on them are discussed below in the section on Milton's *Prolusions*.

Having attacked the bishops, Milton recognized that what he regarded as tyranny was still repugnant when its powers were merely transferred to, and exercised by others. So he continued to attack abuses of authority, institutions which enabled them, and doctrines and traditions which supported them. Thus his divorce pamphlets attacked canon law, the courts and institutions to which its powers had been transmitted, and, above all, the doctrines and customs which prevented the establishment of what he believed to be a better discipline of marriage and divorce. Criticisms of the enslaving force of custom are reiterant in his tracts. They may also be viewed as part of a struggle over the means of controlling men's ideas and actions—the pulpit, the press, and educational institutions. Traditionally these had largely been controlled by the church—that is, ultimately by the bishops, though the ecclesiastics were themselves often subject to state control.

In 1640, the eve of the civil war, when those symbols of secular and ecclesiastical tyranny Laud and Strafford were being impeached, the system of censorship, which was largely under the bishops' control, had broken down. Thus the printing presses were opened to those who, like Milton, wanted to advance the Reformation in England. But in 1643 the Long Parliament instituted a system whereby books, pamphlets, newspapers, and even posters could not be published legally without a license of approval obtained prior to publication from any one of a small group of officials appointed for that purpose. This put a major means of influencing men's ideas into the hands of mediocre men and those who appointed them.

What most disturbed Milton was that such censorship would prevent a free discussion and search for truth among the adherents of Bible-based Protestantism. He was not unwilling to curb Roman Catholics and Anglicans to the extent that they held church tradition as an authority complementary to Holy Scripture; for in Milton's judgment, traditions, when not clearly grounded on the Bible, were man-made and violated what he interpreted as scriptural injunctions against adding one jot or tittle to the completeness of God's Word. In short, he saw this Licensing Order as an effort to prevent the Reformation from continuing beyond what Calvin and other Protestant reformers had taught. And in Milton's view, although man should not add to what the Bible taught as necessary to salvation, Christians were nevertheless obliged to study and discuss it; for by so doing they could discover new riches and insights, could clarify what was previously not fully or properly understood, and could thus continue to advance the Reformation. Thus his title to the first divorce tract proclaimed that he had restored the doctrine and discipline of divorce "From the Bondage of Canon Law, and Other Mistakes, to the True Meaning of Scripture." By preventing publication of such truth-discovering tracts, Parliament, instead of furthering the Reformation, was stopping it and acting as tyrannically as the bishops and the monarchy.

Accordingly Milton composed *Areopagitica,* his most famous and most influential pamphlet. In it he made a powerful case against prepublication censorship, though he granted that if books, authors, and printers broke known laws (against libel, blasphemy, and the like), the books could be destroyed and those responsible for them punished. Perhaps the most powerful—certainly the most characteristic—of his numerous arguments was that, even as prelatical tyranny could prevent men from exercising their highest and distinctive rationality, and even as yoking an incompatible man and woman denied them the harmonious union of their highest human faculties, so censorship was an attempt to stifle man's essential rationality, thus thwarting his proper humanity.

In 1645 Milton also published his *Poems . . . both English and Latin, Compos'd at Several Times;* and it was in that year that he received Mary back as his wife. In 1646 their daughter Anne was born.

Meanwhile, on the national scene, the army was remodeled, King Charles surrendered to the Scots, the first civil war came to an end, the abolition of episcopacy was completed, and Presbyterianism was officially decreed but imperfectly established in England. In 1647 Milton's father died, and in the next year another daughter, Mary, was born. The king escaped and, in 1648, made a treaty with the Scots, with the result that the second civil war began. When the Royalists had been defeated and a republican Commonwealth established, Milton, who had been tutoring, writing a history of Britain, and otherwise engaged in private studies, took the occasion of Charles I's beheading to publish *The Tenure of Kings and Magistrates* (February 1649), in which he justified the overthrow of tyrants and denounced the Presbyterians for having turned from advancing the Revolution in the first civil war to supporting Charles in the second. Having denounced ecclesiastics and their laws and practices for thwarting men's responsible exercise of choice and reason and discussion, and having condemned censorship which prevented the right use of humanity's distinctive powers, and having inveighed against education and customs which warp healthy development of those powers, Milton now asserted that any ruler who arrogates himself above the human condition and derogates his subjects to the status of beasts or vermin thereby forfeits not only his claim to rule but also his right to live.

In 1650 second editions of *The Tenure* and *Eikonoklastes* appeared, Oliver Cromwell succeeded Lord Fairfax as commander of the armed forces and defeated the Scots at Dunbar, and Milton was kept busy writing letters of state to foreign powers in his capacity as Secretary for Foreign Tongues. But in answer to a royalist apology for Charles I, he managed to find time to write *Pro Populo Anglicano Defensio* (February 1651), which later became known as his "First Defense of the English People." Since it was intended for an international audience, it was written in Latin. Meanwhile, personal afflictions bore heavy on Milton: in 1652 he became completely blind; and, although this misfortune was alleviated by the birth of a son in 1651, it was followed in the next year not only by the death of the infant John but by the deaths of his wife Mary and daughter Deborah.

Considering that his light was spent, that it was a kind of death to hide his talent, but that an omnipotent God had no need of man's services, Milton recognized that men who only stand and wait also serve Him through their obedience and through their refusal to lie down under the burden of affliction. Accordingly he stood ready to perform whatever providence indicated, whenever and however his talents were called upon. After Oliver Cromwell became Lord Protector in 1653, Milton continued to perform his duties as Secretary; as such, he had some share in the negotiations that ended the first Anglo-Dutch war (1652–54). Moreover, in May 1654, he published his "Second Defense of the English People," *Pro Populo Anglicano Defensio Secunda,* a reply to an apology for Charles I which Milton believed to be the work of Alexander More, though its author was in fact Pierre du Moulin. *Pro Populo* is now read chiefly for the autobiographical passages and the account of Oliver Cromwell, which are printed below. Milton followed it, in August 1655, with his "Third Defense," *Pro se Defensio,* in which he answered his detractors. In 1656 he married Katherine Woodcock, who bore him a daughter in the following year. But both the mother and little Katherine died in 1658.

Also in 1658 Richard Cromwell succeeded his father. Milton took the occasion to publish, in February and August, complementary tracts against the evils of state-controlled religion and a nationally supported clergy. The times were turbulent, but with great flexibility, as governments changed from Protector to Rump Parliament to army and re-restored Rump, Milton continued his work as Secretary for Foreign Tongues and did what little he could to prevent restoration of the monarchy. To this end he published *The Readie and Easie Way to Establish a Free Commonwealth* in March 1660, revising it for a second edition about April. But his advocacy of a self-perpetuating senate on the Venetian model was ineffective.

The restoration of Charles II in 1660 meant that Milton's life and property were in danger; for he had been a major propagandist in justifying the execution of the new king's father. But thanks to influential friends and his blindness, he was spared. After the Act of Oblivion he was allowed to return to the obscurity of private life.

Though this enforced retirement faced him with many difficulties, it was fortunate for English poetry. Over many years Milton had planned to write on the fall of man; indeed, he wrote part of a drama on the theme before he decided to couch it as an epic. Because he believed that God had given the English an exceptional opportunity to lead an ever-advancing reformation of church and state, he had gladly served both his God and his country. But Englishmen failed to use their opportunity properly; and, as a result, he turned to a task which was difficult for one whose hopes and efforts had been frustrated by the Restoration—the task of justifying the ways of God and asserting his eternal providence—a providence which took account even of the Restoration.

Gradually Milton adjusted himself to life in defeat. In 1663 he married Elizabeth Minshull, who was much his younger: she survived him into the eighteenth century. The plague of 1665 drove them to take refuge in Chalfont St. Giles; and it was there that Milton allowed his friend Thomas Ellwood to read a manuscript of *Paradise Lost*. Publication was delayed by the Great Fire of 1666. The first edition, in ten books, appeared in 1667 and was followed in 1671 by *Paradise Regain'd*, accompanied by *Samson Agonistes*.

Meanwhile he published a number of prose works he had probably written in whole or part previously: *Accidence Commenc't Grammar* (June 1669) was followed by *The History of Britain* (1670) and a treatise on the art of logic, *Artis Logicae Plenior*

Institutio (1672—the year of the first production of William Wycl erley's *The Country Wife*). A newly written tract, *Of True Religio* reached print about May 1673; and in the autumn of that year th second edition of *Poems* was accompanied by *Of Education.* Pub lication of the familiar letters and college prolusions in May 167 was followed in July by the second edition of *Paradise Lost,* i twelve books, and by Milton's death which probably occurred o November 8. He was buried, as his father had been before hin with Church of England rites in the chancel of the Church of St Giles in Cripplegate.

Milton's chief posthumous works were his State Papers in Lati (1676) and in a translation by Edward Phillips (1694); *A Brie History of Moscovia* (1682), and *De Doctrina Christiana* (1825) translated by Charles R. Sumner as *Of Christian Doctrine.*

Although the notion has little historical basis, the name of Milto often evokes a symbol of austere, prescriptive and proscriptive narrow, harsh Puritanism. This misconception derives partly from distorting propagandist attacks made against the rebels during and after the Revolution. It is rather difficult to find anyone in the seventeenth century who approximates the fictional Puritan that writers like Samuel Butler in *Hudibras* built up by congregating traits and alleged traits of many different rebels into one fictitious monster. Those who come nearest to this fiction of a Puritan are Presbyterians like William Prynne. Such men were in fact on the Royalist side in the second civil war. Although it is true that at one stage Milton gave cautious support to a moderate Presbyterianism, he resisted the rigidities of Calvinism and powerfully denounced the Presbyterians in several of his tracts.

One major influence that contributed to the harsh misconception of Milton was the distorting life of the poet written by Samuel Johnson in the eighteenth century. Johnson was too honest a critic not to see some of the merits of Milton's poetry; but as an ardent supporter of the monarchy and the established church, he went out of his way to collect and twist facts and myths about the man in order to discredit him; and the apparent common sense and honesty of Johnson's approach made plausible what otherwise should have been doubted by any intelligent reader.

But the picture of Milton drawn by Johnson differs from the popular, modern misconception. Johnson saw him as a rebel, a radical, a sort of libertine who threatened the sanctities of monarchy, episcopacy, and marriage. Since then Milton has been somehow identified with the Puritans in *The Scarlet Letter,* with harsh notions about men like Cotton Mather, and with the more rigid Presbyterians of the seventeenth century; and this composite has been further overlaid by a perverse notion of Milton as a symbol of the more unpleasant aspects of Victorianism and Victorian religion, so that he emerges almost unrecognizably as a symbol of authoritarianism, austerity, and intolerance, a sour and dour enemy of joy and pleasure, a sort of mid-nineteenth-century father figure. With a strange perversity, some men, in reaction to Victorian parents, the Victorian God, and constrictive forces of various kinds, have centered their antipathies on a seventeenth-century radical who denounced prepublication censorship, attacked constrictive authority in church and state, advocated divorce for incompatibility, brought up his nephews and daughters so that they dared to disagree with him and think for themselves, taught that a liberal deity had given men free will, and fought against established customs, education, laws, institutions, and just about everything else that interfered with the right of the individual to responsible freedom and independent reasonable judgment.

The myth of Milton as the Victorian authority figure is not the only one which has encumbered his reputation. Pictures of him as an extreme liberal, as a romantic on the side of Satan, as an advocate of unlimited free speech and publication, as a supporter of free love, and as a great democrat likewise involve varying degrees of distortion.

The truth is that the real Milton kept himself partially hidden and that his numerous autobiographical passages present a public image rather than a truly personal one. He barely mentions his mother and gives only a glimpse of his father; and it is easy to forget that he had a brother, Christopher. He discloses almost nothing about his wives, nephews, and daughters. As a result, lacking factual information, critics have relied overmuch on rumor, gossip, and inadequate evidence. Even Milton's personal letters tend to have the decorum of maintaining a public image. Compared with John Evelyn's account of his voyage to Italy, Milton's relation of his European tour is amazingly spare in personal observations and reactions. We lack answers to hosts of intriguing questions: Did he ever attend a performance of a Shakespeare play? Was he ever present when John

Donne preached a sermon? What were his attitudes toward his mothers-in-law?

We do know that he had good friends such as Andrew Marvell, that he was esteemed by men of culture such as Sir Henry Wotton and Henry Lawes, that Edward Phillips sympathized with the Royalists but remained loyal to the uncle who educated him, and that young men such as Thomas Ellwood sought him out. Furthermore, we learn from his own writings that he recognized that it would be both natural and proper for a husband to admit an intellectually superior wife's right to supremacy in a marriage; also, that Milton regarded the relationship between husband and wife as akin to that between God and man, involving justice, love, and reciprocal responsibility, and barring anything tyrannical or unreasonable. And we know that he not only took back the wife who deserted him but also generously gave a haven in his household to her family.

That Milton had personal frailties and that he shared some of the faults of his age are not to be denied. Certainly the account of him given by his "anonymous" seventeenth-century biographer (Cyriack Skinner?) needs to be taken with a grain of salt, for it was written in that vein of eulogistic overstatement which characterizes Walton's life of George Herbert. Nevertheless, it may serve as a corrective to false judgments concerning Milton:

> He had naturally a sharp wit, and steady judgment; which helps toward attaining learning he improved by an indefatigable attention to his study; and he was supported in that by a temperance, always observed by him, but in his youth even with great nicety. Yet did he not reckon this talent but as entrusted with him; and therefore dedicated all his labors to the glory of God and some public good. . . . And he was so far from being concerned in the corrupt designs of his masters . . . that he took care all along strictly to define and persuade to true liberty, and . . . denounced the punishments due to abusers of that specious name. And as he was not linked to one party by self interest, so neither was he divided from the other by animosity; but was forward to do any of them good offices . . . he was not sparing to buy good books . . . and was generous in relieving the wants of his friends. . . .
>
> He was of a moderate stature, and well proportioned, of a ruddy complexion, light brown hair, and handsome features. . . . His deportment was sweet and affable; and his gait erect and manly, bespeaking courage and undauntedness . . . on which account he wore a sword while he had his sight, and was skilled in using it.

He had an excellent ear and could bear a part both in vocal and instrumental music. His moderate estate left him by his father was, through his good economy, sufficient to maintain him. . . .

He rendered his studies and various works more easy and pleasant by allotting them to their several portions of the day. . . . The youths that he instructed from time to time served him often as amanuenses, and some elderly persons were glad for the benefit of his learned conversation, to perform that office. . . . He died in a fit of the gout, but with so little pain or emotion that the time of his expiring was not perceived by those in the room.

The thought in most of Milton's prose works is strikingly modern. His insistence that mental-spiritual harmony and love are the *sine qua non* of marriage anticipates the twentieth-century emphasis on the importance of compatibility in marriage. To some readers his unwavering adherence to the authority of the Bible may seem old-fashioned; on the other hand, his refusal to subscribe to intricate creedal formulas propounded by dogmatic theologians, if he could not find warrant for them in Holy Scripture, has more than one echo in radical modern theology. He would have understood the current death-of-God discussion as a dramatic way of saying that the traditional orthodox definition of the Trinity as three coequal, coeternal Persons who are one God, rather than helping some Christians to understand and love the God revealed in the Bible, prevents them from having a meaningful idea of him and thus, in a sense, kills the concept of deity. Rather than demanding blind faith in formulas that seemed more verbal than significant, Milton preferred the modesty of not presuming to go beyond what was explicit or could be clearly inferred from the Scriptures. But this did not mean that he was satisfied to be static in interpretation; for he viewed the teachings of God as dynamic, open to increasing clarification and discovery. In such avoidance of excessive literalism and in such refusal to idolize formulations that need reinterpretation if they are to be vital for believers, Milton has many affinities with modern seekers after richer and clearer truths.

Milton is also modern in his attack on blind custom and its idols, in his emphasis on responsible individualism, and in his advocacy of separation of church and state. Though his application of toleration had practical limitations imposed by historical circumstances, his theories about it and about freedom of publication and fertile discussion are so pertinent to twentieth-century circumstances that his words are almost inevitably quoted when such freedoms and rights need defense. And his opposition to tyranny and obscurantism in all their forms, whether in ideas, politics, religion, society, or the home, still has manifold pertinence.

Milton also offers a corrective to some of the weaknesses of modern life: for example, his distinction between liberty and license; his analyses of why and how progressive movements fail; and his personal example of dedication to liberty, self-sacrifice, courage in the face of extreme adversity, and extraordinary achievements despite extraordinary handicaps.

Milton was a consummate master of the art of prose—a fact too easily overlooked by journalistic critics who pay too much attention to his metaphor that he wrote his prose with his left hand. The inspiration for both figurative hands, whether he wrote in prose or verse, came from the same inspired intellect, from a mind trained in the techniques of rhetoric, oratory, debate, exposition, and poetry, a mind ready to exploit all their features with lively flexibility, whether he was writing a tract in verse to justify God's ways or in the passionate advocacy of prose to justify unlicensed printing, the abolition of episcopacy, recognition of mental harmony as essential to marriage, or the execution of tyrants.

Too often Milton's prose is approached with false expectations and judged as if he aimed for the lucidity of *Gulliver's Travels* or the clarity, simplicity, balance, and precision which Matthew Arnold demanded. Arnold's other dictum, that we see the object as it really is, without preconceptions, points to a sounder approach to Milton's complex, often difficult, involved prose artistry.

The reader who approaches the intricate, involuted style of metaphysical poetry with the expectation that he will find in it the same kind of beauty and easy comprehension that he discovers in Housman or Herrick or Wordsworth is going to condemn it as most nineteenth-century critics did, blinded by prejudices. Milton's prose, the product of the same period as metaphysical poetry, must likewise be approached with the expectation that it will be challenging, that it will sometimes require painstaking explication, that it will be fascinating and moving and powerful and artistic—but not in the manner of Pater, Huxley, Newman, and Macaulay. Milton did not scorn the charms of cadence, the felicities of imagery and diction, or the graces of assonance and consonance in prose. But his aims were less the gain of mere clarity or lulling harmony than the achievement of maximum, appropriate expressivity, powerful persuasion, passionate advocacy, and effective indoctrination. In his best prose works, almost everything is vital, in process, undergoing transformation and development, except when the immediate need is for close argument, point-by-point refutation of an opponent, or careful explanation of complex ideas.

In reading Milton's prose, it is well to forget modern rules for punctuation and spelling and to imagine an orator speaking or Milton himself dictating to a secretary. His marks of punctuation usually indicate where and to what extent he paused during delivery. Though his pauses are thus, in a sense, "natural," his style is a consciously artificial one based on awareness of orthodox Ciceronianism but strongly influenced by Silver Age Latin authors and by that rebellion against the rigidities of conventional Ciceronian style which was a European movement led by Montaigne, Muret, and Lipsius. These writers had a full awareness of, and training in, the rigidly periodic style which was attributed to Cicero; and they were masters of it, as was Milton, when they chose to use it. However, working in this tradition, they exploited it with dislocations, twistings, deliberate wrestings and meaningful distortions, above all with virtuosity, with prodigious technical skill and artistry. The so-called "Ciceronian" sentence (Cicero himself used a variety of styles) was a work of art, an idea written out not during the thinking but after its completion. The idea achieved by the mind in progress was recollected, reordered, and reformulated as an afterthought characterized by control, balance, and periodicity. The alternative method of writing ideas as they occur and develop, letting them ramify and diverge, results in a sentence expressive of the mind thinking, not of the mind having thought. Such is the form usually adopted by Milton—to express thought in action, with its turns and twistings, ellipses, anacolutha, sudden breaks and departures, wordplay, and reversals of direction. Most of these are indicated by his punctuating for pauses in oral delivery. The effect is that of an intellect in operation—immediate, flexible, inspired, and vital.

But the reader must not be deceived by this flexibility, this readiness to depart from stylistic conventions, this willingness to bend the language to fit the developing, changing idea. For in the ultimate analysis this style is not as spontaneous as it seems: it is conscious and deliberate—as consciously thought out and constructed as the more conventional Ciceronian period—probably more consciously so. Milton strives for the *effect* of a mind developing ideas spontaneously, flexibly, and freely (except where the nature of his material dictates a duller and less dramatic approach). In fact, he exploits the techniques and devices of both Ciceronians and anti-Ciceronians to achieve this effect. The result is a double source of appreciation for the reader: he feels that he is thinking along with Milton, developing ideas and feelings with him, participating in the dynamics of his thought. But on reflection and analysis the reader becomes aware of the incredible virtuosity, the mastery of varied styles, the artistic and persuasive skill of a master rhetorician; and he thus derives a second kind of pleasure—appreciation of that incredible virtuosity, that transcendent artistry—but only if he is prepared to see and accept it—not if he expects it to conform to the pedantic rigorism of grammarians and other prescribers.

There are many more aspects of Milton's prose to relish: his skill as a debater, persuader, and reasoner; his mastery of the total architecture of a work; his talent for insinuating his viewpoints; his recurrent image patterns; and his ideas and subject matter. For most modern readers the ideas propounded in such a work as *Areopagitica* are welcome ones, confirmation and clarification of principles already cherished and of reasons already embraced or readily acceptable. But Milton propounds other ideas which may distress modern readers. Some will find his doctrine of divorce unacceptable —though they need to approach it without prejudice lest they be among the thousands who have misunderstood it. Many will deplore that in a tract against repressive censorship, Milton saw fit not to tolerate "Popery," though they need to remember that he was not referring to the Roman Catholicism of the twentieth century. Terminology is likely to be a barrier to the understanding of Milton or of any other seventeenth-century writer. For example, when Bacon attacked "Aristotelianism," he was opposing far less what Aristotle taught than what his followers alleged that he taught.

One key to Milton's thought which has been emphasized above is his stress on the importance of keeping reason—reason rightly and responsibly used—dominant over the other human faculties. He objected to the tyranny of king, prelate, presbyterian, licenser, teacher, custom, or law which denied to individuals the right to use their reason. His position was that if men are to grow in knowledge of truth and in virtue—roughly equivalent to what today is called *character*—they must be free to make choices; and such freedom includes the privilege of making mistakes and learning from them. But more important for such growth is freedom of reading, publication, and discussion; for they are forms of experience on a verbal level where the harm they can do is limited; indeed, they provide their own interplay of corrective ideas. Toleration is essential for such fertile discussion and growth.

When Milton argues for a particular point, which he believes is based on reason and consonant with the Bible, he uses every available resource to persuade his reader. He appeals to emotions, even to prejudices; he exploits his readers' weaknesses; he understates arguments unfavorable to his position and damns the position he opposes, not only by means of rational arguments but also by associating the opposition and its viewpoints with what is ridiculous, ugly, and unpleasing. There is something close to unscrupulousness in such a method. For example, in *Of Prelatical Episcopacy*, when he wants to belittle the authority of a bishop about whom almost nothing is known, he alleges that a later figure who bore the same name was untrustworthy, thus endowing the first one with unreliability by mere arbitrary association.

This is the traditional persuasive method of rhetoricians, the method pervasive in Milton's times and still widely used, especially by politicians, preachers, and lawyers. It sometimes amounts to an exploitation of the irrational in order to lift men to acceptance of what is reasonable. Cicero uses it in his orations; Shakespeare's Antony resorts to it in his speech on Caesar; and Sir Philip Sidney employs it in his *Apology for Poetry*. Its justification is a practical one: argument, to be persuasive, must be adjusted to the weaknesses and strengths of those who are being persuaded. A purely reasonable case will hardly convince those who are unreasonable. They can be most effectively brought to comprehension of what is true and rational through appeals adjusted to them not as they ought to be but as they are, complete with prejudices and frailties. Milton was rhetorician enough to adapt his pleading to his readers or auditors, to argue in their terms. Thus in *Areopagitica*, where his immediate aim was to persuade members of Parliament to abolish a system of prepublication licensing, Milton, being aware that most of them did not share his belief in separation of church and state, carefully refrains from mentioning that doctrine or basing arguments on it.

In other words, most of Milton's tracts are to be read not as philosophical treatises or as exercises in pure reasoning, but as debaters' speeches adjusted to special occasions and special audiences, yet not staying on the level of those audiences but calculated to raise them to sounder and more reasonable positions. Part of the method of such persuasion is often to sneak up on readers by writing in terms of their assumptions and then, almost imperceptibly, moving them on to other positions. Sometimes the most effective method is for the author to seem absolutely confident and assured, to assume that all reasonable men agree with his conclusions.

Because Milton frequently assumes such an air of assurance and finality for rhetorical purposes, it comes rather as a surprise to recognize that on many matters his thought is characterized by modesty and restraint. This modesty, this holding back, is particularly noticeable in his writings on religion. Taking the position that God has revealed in his book as much as is proper for men to know about his truths, Milton, though eager to explore and discuss and develop the meaning and implications of what is revealed, is nevertheless ready to stop where the Bible stops and will not have the presumption to add to it.

Some features of this edition and its selections need explanation and comment. The original spelling and punctuation have been retained because they are functional and enable the reader, once he adjusts to them, to follow Milton's meaning better than any awkward recasting into the Procrustean bed of modern usages could allow. There are, however, some exceptions—passages where the original punctuation may prove a barrier. In some instances of this kind, punctuation has been added in brackets or the passage has been paraphrased in the notes. Other changes are made silently throughout the text: *u* and *v*, *i* and *j* are regularized in accordance with modern practice, as are *then* and *than;* and abbreviations are usually expanded. For most of the tracts, page numbers of the editions used are put in brackets *preceding* the texts for those pages (not following, as in the *Yale Milton*). Obvious typographical errors, broken letters, etc., are silently corrected.

The tracts are not edited in a uniform manner but are intended to illustrate different editorial approaches. Difficult opening sections of some of the pamphlets are rather heavily annotated to enable the reader to get the "feel" of the work; after which, he will need less assistance. The tracts most likely to be selected and read by those not inclined to read the whole volume—*Areopagitica,* for example —are copiously furnished with explanatory notes and some interpretations of difficult passages so that the reader who is unfamiliar with the complexities of Miltonic style will be able to proceed without difficulty. Except in the case of the *Areopagitica,* glosses appear on the text page and explanatory notes, signified by numbers in the text, appear immediately after each pamphlet or tract. In the case of the summaries, the footnotes appear on the page.

The introduction and forewords in this volume constitute a guide to Milton's prose works. The editing is directed in part to students and scholars but is particularly intended for intelligent readers who have specialized in subjects other than English and who wish to read Milton's major prose outside the classroom but require some assistance in doing so. However, as the retention of original spelling and punctuation indicates, this is not a work of popularization; it is intended to be a means whereby the reader can follow, appreciate, and understand what Milton wrote.

The contributors have taken advantage of the progress made in recent decades in editing and scholarship, taking note especially of the Yale edition of Milton's prose works. But they have based their texts on the originals and in several instances have provided readings that are demonstrably superior to those found elsewhere. Many new insights are incorporated into the introductions and annotations. Preference has been given to tracts Milton wrote in English.

This collection, published while the three-hundredth anniversary of the first edition of *Paradise Lost* is being celebrated, serves as a reminder of the breadth of Milton's genius. He is unique among the world's great writers of epics for having also written poetic dramas, lyrics, and a large body of prose, some of it artistically comparable to the excellence of his two epics.

J. Max Patrick

January 1967

CHRONOLOGY OF MILTON'S LIFE

1608: John Milton born on Dec. 9, Bread St., Cheapside, London.
1618–1620: Tutored by Thomas Young.
1620?–1624: Attended St. Paul's School, under Alexander Gill.
1625: Admitted to Christ's College, Cambridge, Feb. 12; matriculated April 9.
1626: Rusticated, Lent term through spring vacation.
1628?–1632: Delivered *Prolusiones* (published, 1674); Bachelor's degree, Mar. 26, 1629; Master's degree, July 3, 1632; began *Commonplace Book* about 1630 (published, 1876).
1632 July–1635: Resided with family at Hammersmith; *A Mask* (*Comus*) performed, Sept. 29, 1634.
1635?–1638: Lived with family at Horton, Buckinghamshire, but went frequently to London after his mother's death on April 3, 1637; published *A Mask* in 1637/8? and *Lycidas* in 1638.
1638 April?–1639 Aug.?: Toured France and Italy.
1639 Autumn: Tutored (until about 1647).
1641: May have written the "Postscript" in Smectymnuus, *An Answer to a Booke entituled, An Humble Remonstrance,* March; *Of Reformation,* May?; *Of Prelatical Episcopacy,* June or July; *Animadversions,* July.
1642: *Reason of Church-Governement,* Jan. or Feb.; *Apology against a Pamphlet,* April. Married Mary Powell, May?, who returned to her family about July.
1643: Milton's father came to live with him in April; 1st ed. of *Doctrine and Discipline of Divorce,* about August.
1644: Second edition enlarged of *Doctrine and Discipline,* Feb.; *Of Education,* June; *The Judgement of Martin Bucer,* Aug.; *Areopagitica,* Nov.; sight failing.
1645: *Tetrachordon* and *Colasterion,* Mar.; 1st ed. of *Poems,* autumn? Wife returned, summer?
1646: Daughter Anne born on Oct. 25.
1649: Appointed Secretary for the Foreign Tongues, Mar. 15 (continued until at least Oct. 22, 1659); completed four books of *History of Britain,* about March, and the digression on the Long Parliament possibly earlier (both may have been revised later); 1st ed. of *The Tenure of*

Kings and Magistrates, Feb.; *Observations upon the Articles of Peace,* May; 1st ed. of *Eikonoklastes,* Oct., in answer to *Eikon Basilike,* about Feb.

1650: Second edition of *Tenure,* enlarged, Feb.; 2nd ed. enlarged of *Eikonoklastes.* Probably lost sight of left eye.

1651: *Pro Populo Anglicano Defensio* ("First Defense of the English People"), Feb., in answer to Salmasius, *Defensio regia pro Carolo I,* which appeared in England by May 1649; revision of "First Defense," Oct. 1658. Son John born Mar. 16; nephew John Phillips published *Responsio ad Apologiam Anonymi* toward the end of the year in answer to John Rowland's attack on "First Defense," *Pro Rege et Populo Anglicano Apologia.*

1652: Totally blind by Feb.; daughter Deborah born, May 2; wife Mary died about May 5 and son John about June 16.

1654: *Pro Populo Anglicano Defensio Secunda* ("Second Defense"), May, in answer to Pierre du Moulin's attack on the Commonwealth, *Regii Sanguinis Clamor,* Aug.?

1655: *Pro se Defensio* ("Defense of Himself"), Aug., in answer to Alexander More, *Fides Publica,* Oct.

1656: Married Katherine Woodcock, Nov. 12.

1657: Daughter Katherine born, Oct. 19.

1658: Wife died, Feb. 3, and daughter Katherine, Mar. 17; edition of Sir Walter Raleigh, *The Cabinet-Council,* May?

1659: *A Treatise of Civil Power,* Feb.; *Considerations Touching the Likeliest Means to Remove Hirelings,* Aug.; *A Letter to a Friend, Concerning the Ruptures of the Commonwealth,* written by Oct. 20 (published by John Toland in 1698); Milton may have written "Proposalls of certaine expedients for the preventing of a civill war now feard, and the settling of a firme government," in the autumn (published in the *Columbia Milton*).

1660: Harassed and imprisoned. *The Readie and Easie Way to Establish a Free Commonwealth,* Mar.; 2nd ed. revised, about April; *The Present Means, and Brief Delineation of a Free Commonwealth,* known also as "Letter to General Monk," was written after Mar. 3 (published by Toland in 1698); *Brief Notes upon a Late Sermon,* April. Escaped the death penalty under the Act of Oblivion, Aug. 29; jailed, Oct.?–Dec. 15, after books by him were burned.

1663: Married Elizabeth Minshull, Feb. 24.

1665: At Chalfont St. Giles to escape the plague, June?–Feb. 1666?

1667: First edition of *Paradise Lost,* Aug.?; further issues in 1668 and 1669.

1669: *Accidence Commenc't Grammar,* June?

1670: *The History of Britain,* Nov.?

1671: *Paradise Regain'd* and *Samson Agonistes,* early in the year; 2nd ed. 1680.

1672: *Artis Logicae Plenior Institutio,* May?

1673: *Of True Religion,* May?; 2nd ed. enlarged of *Poems,* with *Of Education,* 2nd ed., Nov.?

1674: *Epistolarum Familiarium Liber Unus,* with the Prolusions, May; 2nd ed. revised of *Paradise Lost,* July; *A Declaration, or Letters Patent,* July?. Died about Nov. 8; buried in St. Giles, Cripplegate, Nov. 12.

Posthumous: *Literae Pseudo-Senatus Anglicani,* Oct.? 1676, was inaccurately translated into English in 1682, and more reliably translated by Edward Phillips in *Letters of State,* 1694, with four sonnets and a life of Milton; *A Brief History of Moscovia,* Feb.? 1682; *De Doctrina Christiana,* 1825, with a translation by Charles R. Sumner.

THE PROSE OF JOHN MILTON

THE PROLUSIONS

Prolusiones Quaedam Oratoriae

Some Academic Exercises, 1628–1632

EDITED AND TRANSLATED BY THOMAS R. HARTMANN

Foreword

Prolusion VII
A Speech in Defense of Learning

FOREWORD

The *Seventh Prolusion* "may be arrogant in parts, and it may be too rhetorical for modern tastes, but it is one of Milton's major works and one of the noblest expressions of the enthusiasm for Learning that held men's minds in the full tide of the Renaissance."[1] After such a judgment by no less a Miltonist than E. M. W. Tillyard, it would be rash for anyone interested in Milton and Renaissance literature to bypass the *Seventh Prolusion* on the grounds that it is merely an academic exercise. Unfortunately, this remarkable speech has, until now, remained buried in the unhappy category of Milton's college writings that includes six other, more typically undergraduate assignments. For, although it was composed while Milton was still at Cambridge, he was then a graduate student about to receive his master of arts degree. The *Seventh Prolusion* stands apart from the others as Milton's first mature prose composition.

The *Prolusiones Quaedam Oratoriae* (Some Oratorical Exercises) were first published with some of Milton's familiar letters in 1674, some forty-five years after they were composed at Christ's College, Cambridge. These prolusions are Latin exercises which Milton delivered orally to satisfy some of the requirements for the bachelor's and master's degrees, although the sixth one is a comic parody of such requirements, probably written during summer vacation. Since Milton preserved these early writings and then authorized their publication, he no doubt thought they had some value, if only biographical.[2] He did not, however, date any of these exercises, and the order in which they were published may not even indicate their

[1] E. M. W. Tillyard, *Milton: Private Correspondence and Academic Exercises,* trans. Phyllis B. Tillyard (Cambridge, 1932), Introduction, p. xxxix; hereafter cited as *Private Correspondence.* Tillyard's commentary on the *Prolusions* is reprinted in his *Studies in Milton* (London, 1955), pp. 113–36. Mrs. Tillyard's translation is edited by Kathryn A. McEuen in the *Yale Milton,* I, 211–306.

[2] For the circumstances of their late publication, see David Masson, *The Life of John Milton* (7 vols.; Cambridge, 1875–94), I, 273; hereafter cited as Masson.

relative time of composition. Most probably the *Seventh Prolusio* was delivered not long before Milton left Cambridge in July 163 at the age of twenty-three.

As a group the prolusions fall into two genres: disputations an declamations, exercises in logical argumentation and exercises i rhetorical persuasion. Only two of Milton's prolusions are disputa tions, the *Fourth* and *Fifth* ones, and they deal with philosophica problems that would easily exasperate a student: "In the Destruc tion of Any Substance There Can Be No Resolution into Firs Matter" and "There Are No Partial Forms in an Animal in Additio to the Whole." In the *Fourth Prolusion,* Milton turned his obviousl unpleasant assignment in logical argument into a literary exercis by manipulating his philosophical material. He borrowed materia from the scholastic philosopher Francis Suarez,[3] and then sur rounded and interrupted Suarez' serious discussion with comment of his own, such as "I cannot tell whether I have bored you, bu I have certainly bored myself to extinction." The prolusion becam a satire on the very method Milton was assigned to employ. On the other hand, the *Fifth Prolusion* is much more serious, perhaps be- cause it was delivered before the assembled body of the university. In the *Fourth Prolusion* Milton borrowed his arguments from the Jesuit Suarez only to mock them, but in the *Fifth* he openly cites the Dominican Chrysostom Javello as his source and criticizes this philosopher only for his style. Milton accepts Javello's arguments, and revises them so thoroughly that they become his own. Thus, the *Fifth Prolusion,* Milton's single pure disputation, shows that no mat- ter how strongly he may have objected to practicing his logic in this kind of exercise, when he was called upon to do so, he did rather well.

The other five prolusions are declamations in which Milton put into practice what he learned from the classical rhetoricians Aris- totle, Cicero, and Quintilian. He openly avows their influence and assumes that his success or failure will be judged in terms of their prescriptions. In each of these prolusions Milton was assigned to persuade either the members of his college or the assembled uni-

[3] Milton took so many short passages from Suarez' *Disputationes metaphysicae* (1597), including some inaccurate references to Aristotle, that there seems to be no doubt about his borrowings. For a complete correlation of the arguments in the *Fourth Prolusion* and Suarez' *Disputationes,* see Thomas R. Hartmann, "Milton's *Prolusions:* A Study" (dissertation, New York University, 1962), pp. 58–73, and the appendix to ch. III.

versity that one side of a question is more convincing than the other; the other side was assigned to one of his fellow students, so that the whole procedure amounted to a debate.

In terms of subject matter, which was predetermined, and rhetorical style, which was not, the *First Prolusion* seems to be one of Milton's earliest exercises. He was asked to persuade his fellow students in college that Day is more excellent than Night. Obviously a debate over such a question is meaningless; Milton's use of the classical rhetorical prescriptions is not very impressive either, for he engages in a sarcastic defense of himself that could only alienate his audience.[4] But this rhetorical mistake does allow us a brief glimpse of Milton's early life at Cambridge: he was at odds with his fellow students and probably not very happy. The topic of the *Second Prolusion*, "the Harmony of the Spheres," was clearly more to his taste. Here he uses irony to defend the Pythagorean-Platonic doctrine by making fun of Aristotle's objections. This speech deserves to be compared with the *Nativity Ode;* they may have been composed about the same time, about 1629.[5]

Milton may have hated logical disputations, but he certainly seems to have enjoyed most of his rhetorical exercises in declamation. His *Third* and *Seventh Prolusions* reveal a young man exulting in his newly discovered powers of persuasion. Where the *Third Prolusion* exhibits his ability to attack and to devastate, the *Seventh* exhibits his ability to defend and to praise. Although less perfect than the *Seventh,* the *Third Prolusion* has a richness and subtlety often missed by commentators. For instance, they are too quick to assume that since Milton is attacking scholastic philosophy, he must also be attacking Aristotle's philosophy, as Bacon did.[6] Milton's denunciation of scholastic method is indeed passionate, elaborate, and rich in figures of speech:

> . . . what pleasure can there possibly be in these petty disputations of sour old men, which reek, if not of the cave of Trophonius, at any

[4] Milton recognized this himself: "I fear I shall have to say something contrary to all the rules of oratory, and be forced to depart from the first and chief duty of an orator" (*Yale Milton,* I, 219).

[5] See A. S. P. Woodhouse, "Notes on Milton's Early Development," *UTQ,* XIII (1943), 93–94; and Tillyard, *Private Correspondence,* pp. xxviii–xxix.

[6] Although in the Renaissance "the philosophical revolt against scholasticism involved Aristotle in an associated discredit" (R. McKeon, *The Basic Works of Aristotle* [New York, 1941], p. xii), Milton recognized that views of Aristotle differed considerably.

> rate of the monkish cells in which they were written, exude the gloomy severity of their writers, bear the traces of their author's wrinkles, and in spite of their condensed style produce by their excessive tediousness only boredom and distaste; and if they are read at length, provoke an altogether natural aversion and an utter disgust in their readers.[7]

But in the heart of this long emotional speech, Milton shows that he is not an indiscriminate lampooner, for he distinguishes "that philosophy which was once cultured and well-ordered and urbane" from the "hideous" mess the medieval writers made of it.[8] And, after an urgent plea for the study of nature, Milton tells his audience to "take as your instructor him who is already your delight—Aristotle, who has recorded all these things with learning and diligence for our instruction."[9] It is surprising how many readers, swept along by his rhetorical power, have failed to notice how carefully Milton delineates the object of his attack.[10] Only David Masson seems to have recognized what Milton was aiming at.[11]

It is impossible for a modern reader to appreciate fully the *Sixth Prolusion* because it is a parody of an elaborate university ceremony that no longer exists and that is difficult to re-create from the meager historical evidence. The full-dress Acts Ceremony, as it was called, was performed on Commencement Day each year and on special occasions, such as visits to the university by the king and his royal party. The highlight of the day's proceedings was a logical demonstration or disputation in which one of the students defended a philosophical thesis and answered objections raised by another student. Although this kind of debate was the center of interest, the disputant's thesis was introduced and embellished by other students who would argue for or against it, using methods that were not primarily logical, but rhetorical, poetical, and even nonsensical. Thus, the students during Milton's time at Cambridge were called upon to participate in the Acts Ceremony in five different ways. They were asked to compose and deliver orally (1) declamations, such as Milton's *Second* and *Third Prolusions,* (2) "praevaricators'" speeches, which were humorous and often vulgar, (3) verses,

[7] *Yale Milton,* I, 241.
[8] *Yale Milton,* I, 245.
[9] *Yale Milton,* I, 247–48.
[10] E.g., James Holly Hanford, *A Milton Handbook* (New York, 1946), pp. 73, 356, 362–63; and Tillyard, *Private Correspondence,* p. xxiii.
[11] Masson, I, 282.

ch as "Naturam non pati senium," which Milton wrote for one of s fellows, and "De Idea Platonica quemadmodum Aristoteles in- llexit," which he may have delivered himself, (4) disputations, ce the *Fifth Prolusion,* and (5) objections, which the defendant ıd to answer. Since each of these roles obliged the students to scuss a single assigned thesis, they were able to exercise their lents in logic, rhetoric, poetry, and humorous parody, while the ıdience was presented with the difficult philosophical thesis in variety of popular modes before they were asked to consider it ientifically in the demonstration.[12]

The *Sixth Prolusion* seems clearly to be designed as a comic ver- on of the Acts Ceremony. The "thesis" that unites its three parts ıight be formulated thus: Students should be allowed to poke fun t their philosophical studies. The first section, labeled "Oration," written in the form of a declamation in favor of lighthearted ecreation and against its suppression. In its relation to the speech hat follows, the "oratio" should also be considered as a preliminary peech similar to the ones that preceded the disputation in the Acts. Finally, it is a real parody of the declamation or preliminary speech because it borrows its structure from these speeches and makes fun of them. For instance, in his exordium Milton indulges in flattery ınd bombast, addressing his audience with such hyperbolic compli- nents that they must have delighted in his mockery of the first rule of rhetoric—that the speaker must win the good will of the audience. The second section, labeled "Prolusio,"[13] is a typical prevaricator's speech, in which Milton reduces the question under discussion to the limits of impropriety, employing language that has embarrassed some of his editors,[14] and recites an almost interminable list of jibes at members of the university. "At a Vacation Exercise in Col- lege" is the third section; it is a fragment of a dramatic poem that Milton designed as a parody of the formal disputation. Although this burlesque was acted out by Milton and ten of his fellow stu- dents, only the lines spoken by Milton himself, and probably not all of these, were published by him. After a noteworthy prologue

12 This brief discussion of the "Acts" and Milton's contribution differs from D. L. Clark's version in "Milton's Rhetorical Exercises," *QJS*, XLVI (1960), 297–301.

13 Apparently in Milton's day *prolusio* was used loosely to indicate any type of writing or essay.

14 E.g., McEuen in *Yale Milton*, I, 265, and Mrs. Tillyard, who left untrans- lated certain offensive lines, in *Private Correspondence*, p. 94.

in praise of his godlike "native Language," Milton mocks the for and content of the philosophical disputation in a playlet on th subject of Aristotle's Ten Categories.

The *Seventh Prolusion* belongs to a great and long tradition, th tradition of celebrating and defending intellectual activity as th essential part of human life. The tradition reaches back to Plat and Aristotle. It was continued by the great Roman educators Ci ero and Quintilian; by English writers such as Alfred and Chauce who turned Boethius' *Consolation of Philosophy* into Old and Mi dle English; by the early Renaissance educators; and finally, b Francis Bacon, Milton's nearest great predecessor. With this illu trious tradition behind him, Milton understandably complained o the "abundance of material" and the "multiplicity of things to say. Since he was exposed to so much of this tradition at St. Paul' School and at Cambridge, one cannot mention all the works tha possibly influenced the *Seventh Prolusion*. But some of the majo sources of Milton's ideas and spirit deserve to be highlighted; the are at least these four: Plato's *Symposium*, Aristotle's *Nicomachea Ethics*, Cicero's *Pro Archia Poeta*, and Bacon's *Advancement o Learning*. Milton's glorification of knowledge and his descriptio of the supreme happiness that results from study and contemplatio have been linked with the *Symposium;*[15] his account of the importance of knowledge for virtue and moral behavior has been associated with the *Pro Archia Poeta;*[16] and his zealous concern for the dignity of learning, his attacks on medieval philosophy and its residual influence on the universities, and his use of specific examples, such as Alexander, have been cited as echoes of the *Advancement of Learning*.[17] Aristotle's influence, on the other hand, has been overlooked; perhaps it is merely taken for granted, since much of the curriculum at Cambridge was devoted to the study of his works and commentaries on them.[18] Those unacquainted with that curriculum should be careful to notice that Milton's discussion of happiness in relation to virtue, to friendship, and especially to contemplation, and his emphasis on leisure as a prerequisite for

[15] See Irene Samuel, *Plato and Milton* (Ithaca, N.Y., 1947), pp. 103–4, and Tillyard, who mentions the *Phaedrus*, in *Private Correspondence*, pp. xxxiii–xxxiv.

[16] See McEuen, *Yale Milton*, I, 288.

[17] Ibid., p. 287.

[18] See Masson, I, 263–64, and W. T. Costello, S.J., *The Scholastic Curriculum at Early Seventeenth-Century Cambridge* (Cambridge, Mass., 1958).

ontemplation, correspond to some of the major points in the *Jicomachean Ethics*.[19]

In defense of his claim that it is "one of Milton's major works," 'illyard wrote an illuminating commentary on the *Seventh Prolu- ion*.[20] He rests his case principally on three arguments: that the vork reveals much about Milton's aspirations for his future, that it mbodies "much of the Miltonic philosophy" that appears in his ater works, and that it is an excellent piece of rhetorical art.[21] These are certainly good reasons, and they deserve even more at- ention than Tillyard gives them, with perhaps a different kind of mphasis.

Tillyard rightly stresses their biographical value. All of the pro- usions are important for the hints and direct information they offer about Milton's early life and his education, and the *Seventh Prolu- sion* especially is a rich source of biographical knowledge. If read with care, this postgraduate composition can help us understand why Milton was so impatient with his college and university education; why he secluded himself after graduation for almost six years at the prime of his life, and what he intended to accomplish during this time; and why twelve years after leaving Cambridge he proposed to eliminate the kind of schools from which he graduated and to establish a new system of secondary and college education. Most of all, the *Seventh Prolusion* reveals better than any other of Milton's works the motives that prompted his lifelong devotion to study and contemplation, and to their fruits in public service and controversial writing. Finally, since Milton did devote a decade of his life to teaching, this prolusion gives us a picture of the magnificent goals he set before the minds of his students and the persuasive power with which he urged young men to study. Perhaps his nephews and the other students heard daily his stirring call to study: "I have given the battle cry. You rush forth to battle!"

Tillyard perceptively observes that "it is remarkable how many ideas, well known in Milton's later works, are found fully formed or in embryo in this *Prolusion*."[22] He cites two specific examples, one from *Lycidas* and one from *Paradise Lost*.[23] Every reader who

19 See especially *Ethics*, X, 7–8, and cf. *Seventh Prolusion*, note 8.
20 *Private Correspondence*, pp. xxxii–xxxix (cf. note 1, above).
21 *Private Correspondence*, p. xxxiii.
22 Ibid.
23 *Private Correspondence*, p. xxxix; see *Seventh Prolusion*, notes 21 and 30.

is familiar with Milton's later writings will no doubt recognize a great many more. He will recognize, for instance, how frequently Milton's objections to the educational practices of his day and his proposals for reform in the *Seventh Prolusion* foreshadow what he wrote twelve years later in the more detailed tract *Of Education*. The two works complement each other and show a consistent point of view; Milton the graduate student and Milton the mature teacher were of one mind on the central issues, and several peripheral ones, of education.[24]

Finally, Tillyard has unreserved praise for Milton's prose style. The *Seventh Prolusion*, he says, "is a superb piece of writing. The Latin has disengaged itself from the trammels of academic rhetoric and rises and falls with the ease and sweep of accomplished eloquence."[25] Underneath the apparently artless movement of this speech, however, a basic pattern can be found, a pattern Milton learned from the classical rhetoricians. First, Milton takes full advantage of the three means of persuasion emphasized by Aristotle, Cicero, and Quintilian: the character of the speaker, the argument, and the feelings of the audience.[26] Right from the start, he shows his awareness of the first and last means, for he compliments his audience and establishes his own character as particularly suited to praise learning, since he was so reluctant to leave his studies. Secondly, the arrangement of his argument (*dispositio*) contains the five parts of a speech outlined by the classical rhetoricians: *exordium, narratio, confirmatio, refutatio,* and *peroratio*.[27] After establishing himself as a devotee of learning in his *exordium*, Milton gives his first *narratio* when he cites the fact that learning has an overabundance of arguments in her favor, while ignorance must borrow from her every part of its defense. This is followed by a *confirmatio*, or first proof, in which he argues that since man's soul is an immortal spirit destined by God for happiness in an eternal life, men must be made aware of this end by knowledge and study,

[24] See the Foreword to *Of Education* for a more detailed account of these similarities.

[25] *Private Correspondence*, p. xxxiii.

[26] Aristotle, *Rhetoric*, I, 2, 1356a 1–4. D. L. Clark, in his *Rhetoric in Greco-Roman Education* (New York, 1957), points out the same division in Cicero (p. 69) and Quintilian (p. 223).

[27] See, for example, Cicero, *De oratore*, I, xxxi, 137–43; cf. McEuen, *Yale Milton*, I, 217, and Milton's own concern for rhetorical rules in all the prolusions, e.g., note 4, above.

ѕing their higher faculties to perceive the divine significance in ıtural phenomena. Next is the *refutatio,* in which he answers the ͻjection that since moral goodness is necessary for happiness, igɔrant men can achieve happiness without learning; Milton admits ıis is possible, but he insists that learning adds power to goodness, dds power even "to lead a whole nation to moral excellence." This ıoves him to a short *peroratio* or flourish that ends this first main ıovement of the speech: where Virtue and Learning "are joined ɔgether into one joyful union . . . knowledge . . . claims excelɜnce and recognition and majesty very nearly divine." The reıainder of the speech is made up of these same parts, joined ɔgether in an amazing variety of ways to arouse and bring to rest, ınd then arouse again with more intensity the emotions of the audiɜnce. Milton ends his speech with a long *refutatio,* in which he ıttacks ignorance directly, personifying it only to reduce its "person" gradually down the scale of nature to the absurd position of nonɔeing; then in a short *peroratio,* he urges his "intelligent listeners" ɔo fight on the side of learning against ignorance.

It is important to remember that Milton was greatly influenced by the classical rhetoricians, not only so that one can appreciate how masterfully he can work within their rules, how he can control rather than be controlled by them, but also to guard against making incautious judgments about what he is saying. If there is a flaw in Tillyard's treatment, it is simply that he is not sufficiently aware of the rhetorical nature of the *Seventh Prolusion;* this oversight allows him to read into certain passages a biographical literalness that may not be there at all.

For instance, Tillyard cites one of Milton's boldest flourishes:

> Gentlemen, when universal learning shall once complete its cycle, the spirit of man, no longer imprisoned in its gloomy reformatory, will stretch far and wide until its godlike greatness fills the whole world and the void beyond. Then suddenly the circumstances and consequences of events will come to light for the man who holds the stronghold of wisdom. Nothing in his life will happen unexpectedly or by chance. He will certainly be one whose power and authority the stars, the earth, and the sea will obey. The winds and tempests will serve him; Mother Nature herself will surrender like a goddess relinquishing the empire of the world. She will entrust the world's rights, its laws, and its administration to him as governor.

This might well be construed as the speech of a youth ambitiou to become another Prospero, or even another Faust; and this is ex actly how Tillyard construes it:

> Such was the quality of Milton's ambition. The passage is an amazing outburst of *hubris*, and, one would think, the product of a man inevitably doomed to disaster, obsessed by the illusions of the tragic hero. . . .[28]

So Tillyard chooses Faust rather than Prospero. But is it necessar to make such a choice at all? Is the passage necessarily autobio graphical? Or is it simply an exemplary execution of rhetorical arti

Milton's speech in praise of learning belongs to the genre which in classical rhetoric is called oratory of display, or, in the opening words of the *First Prolusion*, the "demonstrative" style of oration. Aristotle specified that the device of amplification in particular should be used in this genre:

> It is only natural that methods of "heightening the effect" should be attached particularly to speeches of praise; they aim at proving superiority over others, and any such superiority is a form of nobleness.
>
> And, in general, of the lines of argument which are common to all speeches, this "heightening of effect" is most suitable for declamations. . . .[29]

Quintilian also "agrees that the proper business of such speeches is to amplify and embellish."[30] Since Milton's role as imitator of classical rhetoric required that he employ above all the device of amplification or "heightening of effect," his use of this device should hardly be construed as "an amazing outburst of *hubris*." Thus, rather than agreeing with Tillyard's conclusion, it might be more to the point to say, as Aristotle does, that "it is only natural that methods of 'heightening the effect' should be attached particularly to speeches of praise."

The present translation is based on the Latin text of the first edition in the New York Public Library, *KC 1674; the *Prolusiones* are bound with the *Familiar Letters* under the title: *Joannis Miltonii*

[28] *Private Correspondence*, p. xxxvii.
[29] *Rhetoric*, I, 9, 1356a 22–28.
[30] Clark, *Rhetoric in Greco-Roman Education*, p. 135.

Angli, Epistolarum Familiarium Liber Unus: Quibus Accesserunt, Ejusdem, jam olim in Collegio Adolescentis, Prolusiones Quaedam Oratoriae. Londini, Impensis *Brabazoni Aylmeri* sub Signo *Trium Columbarum,* Via vulgo Cornhill dicta, An. Dom. 1674. Consideration was also given to the Latin text of the *Seventh Prolusion* reproduced, along with an unsatisfactory translation, in the *Columbia Milton,* XII, 246–84.

THE SEVENTH PROLUSION

A Speech in Defense of Learning Delivered in the College Chapel

LEARNING MAKES MEN HAPPIER THAN IGNORANCE[1]

Gentlemen, to me nothing is more delightful than the appearance of you, an ardent group of men in academic robes, nor more desirable than this honorable task of speaking, which I have performed gratefully one or more times before. Nevertheless, I should mention something which is a fact, and always seems to be so: even though my nature and my course of studies are not opposed to this oratorical activity, I hardly ever undertake to speak of my own free will. If it were in my own power to do so, I would gladly have avoided this evening's task. For I have learned from books and sayings of the most learned men that nothing common or mediocre can be tolerated in an orator, or in a poet, and that anyone who wishes to be a true orator and to be recognized as one must be equipped with a solid foundation: he must have learned and digested all the arts and all the sciences.[2] Since I am too young to have done this so far, I have chosen rather to build up that foundation in myself, to struggle by long and strenuous study for true recognition, than to snatch false praise with a hasty and premature style of writing.

Excited and enflamed every day by these thoughts and plans, I find no impediment or hindrance more serious than these frequent interruptions. Truly, nothing has nourished more the power and good health of my mind, despite discomfort to my body, than studious and liberal leisure. I consider this leisure to be the divine sleep of Hesiod, Endymion's nocturnal meetings with the moon, and the elevated solitude of Prometheus, led by Mercury to Mount Caucasus where he became the wisest of gods and men. Prometheus became so wise, in fact, that Jupiter himself is said to have consulted him about the marriage of Thetis.[3] I myself call to witness the woods and rivers and the lovely village elms under whose shade just last summer (if I may speak of the secrets of goddesses) I enjoyed such high favor with the Muses that even the memory of it delights me. There in the country and in remote forests, in a kind of secluded life, I seemed to have the power to grow.[4]

Here too I might have hoped for the same opportunity to seclude myself, had not this annoying task of speaking been imposed upon me entirely at the wrong time.[5] This so cruelly prevented my divine sleep; so tormented my mind, fixed on other things; and so blocked and burdened me in the immediate difficulties of my studies, that, having lost all hope of finding peace, I began to think with sadness about how far removed I was from that tranquillity which learning had at first promised me. I understood how bitter my life would be among these ragings and tossings and even considered abandoning my studies completely. And so, hardly in control of myself, I made the rash decision of praising Ignorance, which does not suffer at all from these disturbances. I proposed the following question for debate: Has Learning or Ignorance bestowed greater blessings on its followers?

I do not know what it was, but either my fate or my own disposition prevented me from giving up my early love of the Muses. Indeed, even blind chance itself, as if suddenly given prudence and foresight, seemed to be against it. Before I knew what happened, Ignorance found her champion, and the defense of Learning was left to me. I am quite glad that I was deluded in this way, nor am I ashamed that it was blind Fortune who restored my sight. On the contrary, I am grateful to her. Now at least I am permitted to praise Learning, from whose arms I have been torn, and in a sense to console myself for her absence by speaking about her. Now this speech is obviously not an interruption, for who would say he interrupts by praising and defending what he loves, what he admires, and what he wants to follow with all his heart?

At the same time, gentlemen, I do think that the power of eloquence shines most splendidly when it illuminates topics not particularly worthy of praise. Those topics most worthy of praise can hardly be done justice within the limits of a speech, for the very abundance of material is cumbersome, and the multiplicity of things to say confines and suppresses the expanding flow of eloquence. Such wealth of possible arguments now oppresses me; my very strength renders me helpless, and my very arms leave me unarmed. I must, therefore, make a selection; otherwise, my speech would be more truly a catalogue than a presentation of arguments. And, unlike arguments, a catalogue cannot provide the strong supports that will establish our case as firm and secure.

Right now it seems to me that one point must be stressed: I

must show how and to what degree Learning and Ignorance can carry us toward the happiness which we are all seeking. Within this framework my speech will move easily because I do not think I need fear objections Stupidity can bring against Knowledge, nor those Ignorance can bring against Learning. For this very power which objects, which makes speeches, which opens her lips in this famous and learned assembly, all of this power is had only by asking or rather by begging from Learning.

Gentlemen, I believe it is well known and generally accepted that the great Creator of the world, while making all other things changeable and corruptible, infused into man, besides what was mortal, a certain divine spirit, a part of Himself, as it were, immortal, imperishable, and free from death and destruction. After wandering on the earth for some time like a guest from heaven, chaste and holy, this divine spirit in man is supposed to fly to its celestial home above and return to its rightful throne and country. Therefore, nothing deserves to be called a cause of our happiness unless it somehow takes into account that everlasting life, as well as this life on earth.

Now, almost everyone agrees that contemplation alone is a cause sufficient to lead the mind, drawn into its own sphere, and without the help of the body, from which the mind is aloof, to imitate with incredible joy the eternity of the immortal gods. Yet without Learning the mind is completely sterile, joyless, and indeed nothing. For who can worthily look upon and contemplate the Ideas of things[6] human and divine, about which he can know almost nothing, unless he possesses a mind enriched and perfected through knowledge and study? Thus, every entrance to the happy life seems to be closed to the man who lacks Learning. It would seem as if our souls, which have the capacity and the almost insatiable desire for the highest wisdom, were given by God in vain, or for our suffering, unless He wanted us seriously to strive for the sublime, for the lofty knowledge of those things for which He has instilled a natural thirst in the human soul.

Examine the whole world in every way you can, and you will find that the great Artificer constructed it for His own glory. The more deeply we investigate the extraordinary design, the immense structure, the wonderful variety of creation—which it is not possible to do without Learning—the more we are filled with admiration and praise for the Author, and the more we seek to give Him honor, which we are firmly convinced He will be pleased to accept. Can we believe, gentlemen, that the immense space of the sky was illumined and adorned with eternal fires, was made to support amazingly rapid motions, and to accomplish vast distances in its revolutions for the sole purpose of providing lamps for ignorant and lazy men?[7] Are the heavens meant only to supply torches for us, for the idle and sluggish here below? And is there no more meaning in the luxurious growth of fruits and herbs than the frail beauty of the new blossoms? Really, we will be quite unfair judges of the values of things if we follow nothing but what is felt by our lowest senses. We will bear ourselves not merely basely and slavishly, but unjustly and maliciously toward the generosity of God. Through our own lack of action and through our ill-will, much of the honor and veneration due His mighty power will go unpaid. Therefore, if Learning introduces and leads us to happiness, and if it is commanded and approved by almighty God and contributes to His praise, certainly those who are devoted to it will not fail to gain the greatest blessings.[8]

I am quite aware, gentlemen, that this contemplation through which we strive for what is most desired cannot result in our true happiness without integrity of life and purity of conduct. Many men distinguished for their learning have been wicked: they have given themselves to wrath, hatred, and perverse desires. On the other hand, many ignorant men have been honorable and virtuous. What does this prove? That Ignorance is more blessed? Not in the least. For it so happens, gentlemen, that even though some eminent scholars have been lured into evil by the corrupt morals of their countries or by mobs of illiterate men, the influence of a single wise and prudent man has held to their duty many human beings who were without Learning. Undoubtedly, one family, even one man, endowed with Learning and Wisdom, the great gifts of God, may be sufficient to lead a whole nation to moral excellence. But where no Arts flourish, where all study is abandoned, there you will find no trace of good men: savagery and horrible barbarity will be rampant.

To prove this, I cite not one state or province or race but a fourth part of the whole world, Europe as a whole. There, some centuries ago, all worthy Learning perished, and for a long time all the universities of that age were abandoned by the Muses who had presided over them. Blind slothfulness pervaded and possessed everything. In the schools nothing was heard but the insipid dogmas of stupid monks; and on the empty public platforms, in the pulpits, even in the deserted professional chairs, that profane and deformed monster Ignorance displayed herself dressed in formal robes.[9] Then for the first time Piety went into mourning and Religion choked and sank to the ground. Even today, after a long and painful period of neglect, Learning has barely recovered from her grievous wounds.

Truly, gentlemen, it is an ancient and fixed maxim of philosophy that the knowledge of all the arts and sciences belongs to the intellect, while the home and shrine of honesty and virtue is the will. Since, however, as everyone agrees, the human intellect shines above the other mental faculties as their lord and governor, it controls and illuminates the will itself. Otherwise, the will would be blind and in darkness, for, like the moon, it shines with another's light.[10] Thus, even though we grant and freely admit that Virtue without Learning is more conducive to happiness than Learning without Virtue, yet where Virtue and Learning are joined together in one joyful union, as they certainly ought to be, and often are, then immediately, with an upright and lofty aspect, Knowledge shines forth and shows herself superior by far. She takes her high place with her king and emperor Intellect and looks down upon the unaided efforts of the will as lowly and beneath her feet; finally, Knowledge claims excellence and recognition and majesty very nearly divine.

Come, let us now descend to our life in this world and observe what can be gained both in private and public life. I need not even mention that Learning is the fairest distinction of youth, the firm defense of manhood, the glory and comfort of old age. I will also pass over the fact that many among the nobility, even the rulers of the Roman people,[11] after performing extraordinary deeds and receiving glory for great performances, turned from competition and ambition to the study of literature as to a harbor and sweet place of rest. Undoubtedly these honored old men understood that the remainder of their lives should be spent in the most profitable way. They were the highest among men; through literary study they hoped to be not least among gods. They once sought worldly honors, and now they sought immortality. Fighting against the enemies of the empire, they employed much different methods; now as they contended with death, the greatest enemy of the human race, notice what weapons they took up, what legions they drafted, and what provisions they chose.

Real happiness in this life nearly always involves a society of men and the formation of friendships. Many people, however, complain that the learned often are hard to please, rude, poorly trained in manners, and lacking in agreeable speech to win men's souls. I admit that a man who is for the most part alone and absorbed in his studies is much more inclined to converse with gods than with men, either because he dwells among divine things almost perpetually and among human things so seldom as to seem a stranger among them, or because his mind, apparently enlarged by continuous thinking about things divine, and finding it difficult to act within the strict confinement of the body, is less suited for the finer conventions of social behavior. But when true and worthy friendships can be made, no one cultivates them more carefully than the learned man. For what can we imagine more joyful, what more blessed, than conversations between wise and serious men? For instance, consider those the divine Plato is said to have had so often under the well-known plane tree;[12] those certainly were worthy of being heard with ecstatic silence by the whole human race. But to make dull chatter and to encourage one another in luxury and sensuality, that is friendship of ignorance, or really ignorance of friendship.

Moreover, if the greatest happiness of a man in society does consist in the noble and free joys of his mind, then his greatest pleasure will be found in Wisdom and Learning. What does it mean to grasp the nature of the heavens and of the stars, to comprehend all the motions and changes of the atmosphere, which terrify ignorant minds with the tremendous roll of thunder or with flaming comets, which freeze the snow and hail, or which let fall softly and gently the rain and dew? What does it mean to understand perfectly the changing winds and all the gases and vapors which the earth and the sea bring forth; to experience the hidden powers of plants and metals; to know the nature and, if possible, the feelings of every living creature; to have exact knowledge of the human body's anatomy and of medicine; and, lastly, to possess a godlike power and vigor of soul and any knowledge we can gain about those beings called spirits, genii, and demons?[13] There are infinite mysteries, many of which might well be solved before I could enumerate them all.

Gentlemen, when universal learning shall once complete its cycle, the spirit of man, no longer imprisoned in its gloomy reformatory,[14] will stretch far and wide until its godlike greatness fills the whole world and the void beyond. Then suddenly the circumstances and consequences of events will come to light for the man who holds the stronghold of wisdom. Nothing in his life will happen unexpectedly or by chance. He will certainly be one whose power and authority the stars, the earth, and the sea will obey. The winds and tempests will serve him; Mother Nature herself will surrender like a goddess relinquishing the empire of the world. She will entrust the world's rights, its laws, and its administration to him as governor.[15]

Furthermore, what great joy is given to the mind that soars through the histories and geographies of every country observing the condition and changes of kingdoms, nations, cities, and peoples in order to acquire practical wisdom and morals. Gentlemen, this is to participate in every age as if one were living in it, as if he were born a contemporary of time itself. Certainly, while we have looked into the future for the glory of our name, this present study is intended to extend and stretch our life backwards to the beginning and to wrest from reluctant Fate a certain immortality in the past.

Can I pass over what is incomparable? To be the oracle of many nations, to have a home honored as a temple, to be invited before kings and governments, to be visited by neighbors and strangers flocking together, and by others who will glory in the good fortune of seeing a wise man even once—these are the rewards of study. These are the gifts Learning can and often does confer on her followers in private life.

But what about public life? It is true that a reputation for learning has elevated few men to majestic heights and a reputation for virtue not many more. Without a doubt, such men in themselves enjoy a kingdom far more glorious[16] than any earthly reign, and who can strive for a double reign without incurring the infamy of ambition? I will add this: there have been only two men who have possessed the entire world and who beyond all kings and rulers have shared an empire equal to the gods themselves, namely Alexander the Great and Augustus Caesar, both of whom were students of philosophy.[17] In this, we seem to have an example set by God for men to follow, a guide to the kind of man the helm or reins of government ought to be entrusted.

Still, many countries even without learning have gained fame by their deeds and their wealth. Among the Spartans few are remembered for undertaking the study of the arts, and the Romans received philosophy within the walls of their city only at a late date. But the Spartans possessed a lawmaker in Lycurgus, who was both a philosopher and so ardent a student of poetry that he collected for the first time and with great care the writings of Homer, which were scattered throughout Ionia.[18] The Romans, hardly able to sustain themselves after various uprisings and riots in the city, had to send ambassadors to Athens, where the study of the arts flourished greatly, to beg for the Decemviral Laws, which have also been called the Twelve Tables.[19]

What shall we say if our opponents object to us that at the present time the Turks have an extensive mastery over the wealthy kingdoms of Asia and they are ignorant of all literary arts? Indeed, in that state (if, however, that should still be labeled a "state" whose rule was seized through violent and murderous acts of most cruel men, men united by their common choice of evil) I have heard of nothing exemplary. The provision of the necessities of life and the maintenance of our possessions, we owe to Nature, not to Art; wanton invasion of other countries, joint efforts in plundering, and evil conspiracy, we owe to a perversion of Nature. While other virtues are lacking, Justice of a sort is exercised among them, which is not surprising, for Justice, like a queen, commands her own reverence. Even the most unjust societies would quickly be dissolved without her. I must not, however, omit the fact that the Saracens, who were virtually the founders of the Turkish state, increased their empire not more by arms than by the study of arts and letters.

If we turn back to ancient times, we will find states that were not only regulated by, but also often founded on Learning. The earliest inhabitants of every nation are said to have wandered in forests and mountains, seeking proper food in the manner of wild animals, with heads erect but bodies bent over; except for their dignified forms, you might have thought they were beasts. The same caves and the same hollows sheltered both man and brute from wind and rain and the cold of winter. At that time no cities, no buildings of marble, no altars or temples of the gods could be seen; at that time no divine laws or even human laws were announced in the marketplace. There was no torch for weddings, no chorus, no song at the joyful feast, no mourning; there were no funeral rites, and hardly even a mound of dirt honored the dead. There were no banquets, no games, no sounds of music. At that time all these things were lacking, things which today provide many hours of idle luxury. Then suddenly the Arts and Sciences, like gods, breathed into the savage breasts of men, made men aware of themselves and drew them together within the walls of cities. Therefore, since through the Arts and Sciences cities first were founded, then made firm by laws, and later fortified by public assemblies, with these same directors they will be able to maintain themselves for a long time in great happiness.

Now what can be said of Ignorance? I see, gentlemen, that she gropes in the darkness, that she is senseless, that she stands far from us, that she looks about for an escape, and that she complains that life is short and Art is long. But if we, on the contrary, remove the two great impediments to our studies, first our poor way of teaching the Arts,[20] and secondly our own laziness, we will find that, with all due reverence to Galen or whomever it was,[21] the opposite is the case: life is long and Art is short. There is nothing more excellent than Art, or more difficult; there is nothing more sluggish than ourselves, or more languid. We allow ourselves to be shamed by the laborers and farmers who work from before dawn to late in the night. They are more diligent in the lowly business of cultivating common food than are we in the most noble business of cultivating the happy life. Even though we aspire to the highest and the best in human life, we are not able to carry the burden of study nor the dishonor of idleness; indeed, we are ashamed to be what we would consider it unworthy not to be.[22]

Notice how we guard our health against late hours and hard study. It is shameful to admit that we neglect to cultivate our minds while we are so afraid for our bodies. Who would not permit the strength of his body to diminish in order to acquire much more for his soul? Certainly those who argue against this are worthless men who have abandoned all concern for their time, for their talents, and for their health, and who eat and drink like whales and spend their nights among prostitutes and gamblers; they never complain that *these* things have made them any worse. Since, therefore, they have disposed and accustomed themselves to pursue every kind of ugly activity with such vigor and alacrity, but every virtuous and reasonable activity with weakness and sluggishness, they falsely and unjustly shift the blame to Nature and the brevity of life. But if we choose to live modestly and temperately, and to control the basic impulses of unbridled youth with reason and continuous devotion to study, preserving the divine power of our minds pure and free from every stain and defilement, it will seem incredible to us, my friends, looking back after some years, what a great distance we have covered and what a vast sea of learning we have so easily sailed.

On this voyage an excellent short cut can be used if one knows how to choose both the useful arts and what is useful in these arts.[23] First, how much contemptible nonsense comes from the grammarians and the rhetoricians? When they teach their arts you may hear the latter speak like barbarians and the former like babies. What about logic? She is indeed the queen of the arts if she is treated according to her true worth. But, alas, how much folly there is in reason! Here there are no men, only finches feeding on thorns and thistles. "O strong stomachs of reapers!"[24] And what shall I say about that subject which the Peripatetics call metaphysics?[25] It is not an art, even though the authority of great men tells me it is a most profitable one. I say it is not an art for the most part, but a pile of shameful rocks, a Lernaean bog of sophisms,[26] devised for shipwreck and destruction. These are the wounds that gowned Ignorance inflicts, as I mentioned earlier. This same disease of the hooded ones[27] has even penetrated deeply into natural philosophy.

The mathematicians are disturbed by the silly little glories of their demonstrations. When all of these things which have no value for the future are denounced and cut away, it will be amazing how many whole years we will gain.

And what about this! Jurisprudence in particular is made unintelligible by disordered methods of teaching, and—I can think of nothing worse—legal speech is American Indian or not even human.[28] Frequently, when I have heard our petty lawyers ranting, I happened to doubt whether those who did not seem to have a human mouth and a human language could possess any human feelings. I am indeed afraid that sacred Justice will find it impossible to look down upon us; I am afraid that she will never understand our complaints and wrongs because they are voiced in a language she does not know.

Gentlemen, if from childhood we allow no day to pass without lessons and diligent study, if we wisely omit from our curriculum what is unsuitable, superfluous, and useless, we shall, before reaching the age of Alexander the Great, certainly conquer something much greater and more glorious than his earthly world. Also we shall be so far from blaming the shortness of life and the slowness of art that I believe we shall be more inclined to weep and mourn, as Alexander did at one time, because there are no more worlds for us to conquer.

Ignorance is now giving her last breath. Behold her dying struggle and her final effort: "Mankind is moved chiefly by glory. A long series of successive years brought fame to the illustrious men of ancient times, but we live in an old and decrepit world, and we are checked by the impending destruction of all things. If we leave behind anything worthy of everlasting praise, our name will live only within narrow limits, for there will be almost no posterity to remember us. It is frustrating to produce so many books and shining monuments of knowledge now, for the approaching conflagration of the world will consume them all."[29]

I am not convinced that this may happen. Still, not to think of glory when you have done well is above all glory. Indeed, those famous men of ancient times can receive no benefit from the empty praise of men, for no pleasure and knowledge can come to those who are dead and gone. We, however, may hope for eternal life, which in no way will diminish the memory of our good works on earth. If we have earned any praise here, we shall be present to hear it in eternal life. According to many serious philosophers, those who lived most moderately in this life and devoted all their time to wholesome studies, and through their studies have helped mankind, will be rewarded in eternity with a wisdom that is unique and the greatest of all.[30]

Let those lazy men stop scoffing at what is uncertain or perplexing to us in our studies. These difficulties must be attributed not to learning but to the weakness of men. It is this weakness, gentlemen, that refutes or mitigates or compensates for the ignorance of Socrates and the timid hesitation of the Sceptics.[31]

Now then, what kind of happiness does Ignorance offer? To care only for oneself; to be hurt by nobody; to be above all anxiety and trouble; to live, as far as possible, a secure and quiet life—truly this is the life of a beast. This is the life of a bird that for security builds its little nest in the most secret depths of the forests and as close to the sky as possible, raises its young there, flies about for food without fear of the hunter, and sings its sweet melodies at dawn and at dusk. With these things, why should one desire that divine power of the mind? Let Ignorance lay aside her human shape, let her be given Circe's cup,[32] and let her go forth stooping to the beasts.

To the beasts, did I say? But even they do not want to receive so dishonorable a guest. If beasts either participate in some lower form of reasoning, as many argue, or have knowledge through some powerful instinct, they can use the Arts, or something like the Arts, among themselves. Plutarch tells us that dogs are not ignorant of logic when they are hunting wild animals, for if they happen to come to a fork in the path, they obviously use the disjunctive syllogism.[33] Similarly, Aristotle notes that the nightingale is accustomed to teach its young certain rules of music.[34] Almost every animal is its own physician, and many of them have even given extraordinary medical techniques to man. The Egyptian ibis shows us the value of purging the stomach, the hippopotamus of letting blood. Who can say that those animals which so often give predictions of winds, heavy rains, floods, and fair weather have no knowledge of astronomy?[35] How prudent and strict are the ethics of the geese flying over Mount Taurus; they moderate their dangerous habit of talking all the time by stopping their mouths with pebbles![36] Domestic habits owe much to the ants, and civil habits to the bees; and military art acknowledges its debt to the cranes for the idea of posting sentries and of organizing a triangular battle line.[37] The beasts are too wise to believe that Ignorance is worthy of their gatherings and their society. They drive Ignorance down below them.

Where? To the level of trees and stones. But even the very trees, the bushes, and the whole woods pulled up their roots and rushed to the perfect songs of Orpheus.[38] Often, they were guardians of mysteries and gave forth divine oracles, as the oaks at Dodona did.[39] Rocks, too, respond with a kind of docility to the sacred voice of the poets. Will not these also drive Ignorance away? Therefore, since she is lower than every beast, lower than tree stumps and stones, lower than every level of Nature, will she be permitted to rest in the non-being of the Epicureans?[40] No, not even there, because it is necessary that what is worse, what is more vile, what is more wretched, and what is lowest, should be Ignorance.

I come now to you, my most intelligent listeners. Even if I myself had said nothing, I can see that you are on my side, that you are not arguments but spears which I shall hurl at Ignorance until she is destroyed. I have given the battle cry. You rush forth to battle! Drive this enemy away, and throw her from your porches and walks. If you allow her to survive, you yourselves will become, as you well know, the most miserable of all creatures. This is your own cause, and everyone's.

If I have perhaps spoken much longer than is customarily permitted in this place, even though the dignity of my subject itself demanded it, I believe you will forgive me, my judges, since you will understand much better my feelings toward you, how concerned I am for you, and what labors and what vigils I have undertaken for your good. I have spoken.

NOTES

1. The Latin title is "Beatiores reddit Homines Ars quam Ignorantia." Since "art" does not have the same meaning as *ars*, "learning" seems to be the best equivalent here; in a few other places, "study" and "art" seem preferable. In contrast to "nature" or abilities not acquired or learned, *ars* meant for Milton those abilities learned through the systematic study of principles and rules. See D. L. Clark, *John Milton at St. Paul's School* (New York, 1948), pp. 127–28, 131.

2. E.g., Aristotle taught that rhetoric depends upon other studies, such as dialectic, ethics, and politics because a good rhetorician must be able "to reason logically, to understand human character and goodness . . . and to understand the emotions" (*Rhetoric*, I, 2, 1356ª 21–25). Cf. Quintilian, *Institutio oratoria*, I, 10, 7.

3. Hesiod tells how he was inspired at the beginning of his *Theogony;* the story of Endymion was repeated by many Latin authors and was the basis for John Lyly's *Endimion* (1591); Hesiod relates the story of Prometheus in *Works and Days*, lines 42–105, and *Theogony*, lines 510–616.

4. See Familiar Letter 3, at the end of which Milton speaks of returning to a similar solitude, probably to Hammersmith or Horton. [Page 601 of this volume.]

5. Milton's reluctance to leave his studies echoes *Faerie Queene*, I, x, 49, where Contemplation is a character disturbed by the Red Cross Knight and

harissa: "At their first presence grew agrieued sore / That forst him lay his eauenly thoughts aside. . . ."

6. Plato's ideal or perfect forms of things; Milton wrote "Ideas" in Greek.

7. Tillyard (*Private Correspondence*, p. xxxiv) cites a similar sentence from Iontaigne's *Apology of Raymond de Sebonde.*

8. Milton's whole discussion of contemplation and happiness follows the last hapters of Aristotle's *Ethics*. E.g., compare his conclusion with Aristotle's: "he who exercises his reason and cultivates it seems to be both in the best state of nind and most dear to the gods" (1179^a 23–24).

9. Cf. Milton's attack on medieval scholasticism in *Prolusion III*, "Contra Philosophiam Scholasticam," and *Of Education*, p. 231.

10. "In the Middle Ages there was a dispute concerning the faculties of the soul, the question being which was the 'noblest' faculty. . . . Aquinas was convinced of the preeminent claims of the intellect. For he maintained that whereas the will tends toward its object the intellect possesses it in cognition, and possession is better than tending towards" (F. C. Copleston, *Aquinas* [Harmondsworth, 1955], pp. 178–79).

11. McEuen (*Yale Milton*, I, 295, note 7) suggests Cato the Censor as "an excellent example" of a famous public official who turned to study in his old age.

12. See *Phaedrus*, 229, where Socrates and Phaedrus discuss friendship under a plane tree.

13. Milton was probably speaking of "the secular or Platonistic angelology" although he "does not commit himself to its soundness. . . . He acknowledges by implication the great place and importance of information about daemons *if* we can get any" (R. H. West, *Milton and the Angels* [Athens, Ga., 1955], p. 100).

14. The body, the prison house of the soul, is limited in space and time. Cf. Shakespeare's Sonnets 44, 45, 146.

15. Cf. Prospero in *The Tempest*.

16. Cf. *Paradise Lost*, XII, 587, where Michael promises Adam "A Paradise within thee, happier far."

17. Alexander was Aristotle's pupil and later his patron; Augustus (Octavius Caesar) had a reputation for learning and was the patron of Virgil, Ovid, Livy, and Horace. See Plutarch's Life of Alexander and Suetonius' *Caesars*, II, lxxxv, lxxxix.

18. See Plutarch's Life of Lycurgus.

19. The Twelve Tables of Roman law were formulated in 451 B.C. by ten men (*decem viri*); hence "Decemviral."

20. This is one of Milton's basic objections to the education of his day in *Of Education*.

21. The aphorism *Ars longa, vita brevis* has been attributed to Hippocrates. Cf. the first line of Chaucer's *Parliament of Fowls*: "The lyf so short, the craft so long to lerne." Regarding the emphasis on laziness in the paragraph, Tillyard says: "This passage exhibits Milton's furiously active nature. It also foreshadows the main reason for the Fall in *Paradise Lost*. Eve ate the fruit not so much because she was greedy or disobedient as because she was too slack to realize the importance of the issue" (*Private Correspondence*, p. xxxix).

22. *Immo pudet esse id, quod non haveri nos indignamur*—i.e., we are ashamed to be called scholars [for we are so lazy], yet we think that not to be a scholar would be unworthy.

23. Cf. *Of Education* in which Milton's key proposals are to reduce the time of study and to reorganize the arts curriculum.

24. Horace, *Epodes*, III, 4.

25. Cf. *Of Education*, p. 233.

26. In order to seduce Io, Jupiter caused the land of Lerna to be covered with a dark cloud (Ovid, *Metamorphoses*, I, 590 ff.).

27. *The hooded ones* refer to the monks of medieval scholasticism.

28. Cf. *Of Education*, pp. 232, 233 and notes 10 and 14.

29. Milton directly attacked this pessimistic view not long before in his Latin poem "Naturam non pati senium."

30. Compare this whole paragraph with *Lycidas*, lines 78–84: "Fame is no plant that grows on mortal soil, / Nor in the glistering foil / Set off to th' world, nor in broad rumor lies, / But lives and spreads aloft by those pure eyes / And perfet witness of all-judging *Jove* / As he pronounces lastly on each deed, / Of so much fame in Heav'n expect thy meed."

31. See Plato, *Apology*, 21–22, for Socrates' discovery of ignorance in himself and other men. After Alexander's death in 323 B.C., scepticism, a philosophical school that renounced all speculation, was founded by Pyrrho (hence the name *Pyrrhonism*).

32. In *Odyssey*, X, Circe's potion turns men into swine.

33. Although Plutarch's essay "Beasts Are Rational" appears in Book XII of the *Moralia*, Milton's account of dog logic comes from the essay "Which are the Most Crafty, Water or Land Animals" in Book XIII.

34. Aristotle, *Historia animalium*, IV, 9, 536^b 16–17. McEuen (*Yale Milton*, I, 304, note 27) and M. Y. Hughes (*Complete Poems and Major Prose* [New York, 1957], p. 628, note 20) erroneously cite this work as *Historia naturalium*.

35. Pliny (*Natural History*, VIII, xl–xlii) mentions the hippopotamus' blood-letting, the purging ibis, and the animal astronomers.

36. For this example, Tillyard (*Private Correspondence*, p. 143) cites Stephen Gosson's *Schoole of Abuse* (1579).

37. Cicero (*De natura deorum*, II, xlix, 125) gives a long and interesting account of the activity of migrating cranes.

38. Cf. Ovid, *Metamorphoses*, XI, i.

39. The rustling of the oak leaves at Dodona was interpreted as oracles from Zeus (e.g., *Odyssey*, XIV, 328).

40. Perhaps the *void* in Epicurus' atomist view of the world.

THE ANTI-PRELATICAL TRACTS
1641–1642

EDITED BY EVERETT H. EMERSON

Foreword

Complete text of *Of Reformation* (May 1641)

Summary with extracts of:

Of Prelatical Episcopacy (June or July 1641)

Animadversions (July 1641)

The Reason of Church-Governement (January or February 1642)

An Apology against a Pamphlet (April 1642)

A Note on the "Postscript" in Smectymnuus, *An Answer* (1641)
BY J. MAX PATRICK

FOREWORD

Milton's first five published prose writings were all attacks on ıe system of government of the Church of England. The hierarchi-ıl system, which gave great power and dignity to bishops and rchbishops, was offensive to many Englishmen; antagonism to it nd to the secular powers that supported it contributed to the spirit f rebellion which created the civil wars of the 1640s.

Milton's first attack, *Of Reformation Touching Church-Discipline ı England*, was published in the spring of 1641; the second, *Of 'relatical Episcopacy*, appeared a month or two later, in June or uly; a third, *Animadversions*, was published in July; the fourth and ongest, *The Reason of Church-Governement*, made its appearance ix months later, in January; and the last work, *An Apology*, was ublished less than a year from the first, in April 1642. In these five vorks Milton gave support to the Puritan cause during its crucial ears; episcopacy was eliminated in 1643.

Puritanism began in England in the sixteenth century. In the years between 1533 and 1558, England had fluctuated between Prot-estantism and Roman Catholicism. Elizabeth sought to achieve a compromise early in her reign in order to keep as many within the church as possible, and thus saw to it that the church retained epis-copacy and such ornaments of worship as clerical vestments—to reconcile Catholics; but otherwise she gave the church a moderate Protestant position. Many Protestant leaders wanted the elimina-tion of episcopacy and all Roman Catholic practices; they sought the adoption of the pure Protestantism of Geneva and the Rhine-land. Though, at first, these Protestants persuaded themselves that the compromise was a temporary measure, some were soon con-vinced that they could not accept the settlement. They sought to purify the church and thus came to be called Puritans. This term, though frequently abused, is useful to refer both to those who sought major changes, such as the substitution of presbyterianism for epis-copacy, and to those who sought minor ones, such as the elimination of vestments. Those who withdrew from the church, which th found impure, have also been called Puritans. It seems best, ho ever, to distinguish these, and call them Separatists.

Puritan dissatisfaction with the Anglican Compromise created whole body of literature on the polity and operation of the Chur of England even before the climactic events of the 1640s broug John Milton into the pamphlet debate. The Puritans' attacks we variously learned, witty, satirical, and eloquent, though seldom we these qualities combined before Milton turned his attention to th controversy. The special qualities of Milton's prose become clear if we consider the character of earlier Puritan assaults on the Angl can establishment.

The first real debate in print over the form of the church, the so called Admonition controversy, took place in the early 1570s. Th Puritan position was set forth by Thomas Cartwright, former Lad Margaret Professor of Divinity at Cambridge, and Walter Traver later celebrated for his debate with Richard Hooker. Both wer ordained priests of the Church of England. Travers' notable *Eccles asticae Disciplinae . . . Explicatio*[1] declared (as Milton was to that the Church of England needed further reformation. It neede to eliminate episcopacy and substitute the presbyterian form o church government, which he believed to be prescribed by the Bible:

> Now whereas I affirm that Christ hath left us so perfect a rule and discipline,[2] I understand it of that discipline which is common and general to all the church, and perpetual for all times, and so necessary, that without it this whole society and company and Christian commonwealth cannot well be kept under their prince and king Jesus Christ. And surely we must needs either confess that Christ hath left us such an order to live by or else spoil him of his kingly office. For what doth more belong unto the name, office and duty of a king than to give laws unto his citizens and subjects, and to make such decrees and ordinances whereby all the parts of his kingdom may be maintained. (Pp. 9–10, spelling modernized.)

Though Puritans might disagree over what the rule and discipline were, they agreed that both were set forth, as Travers said, in the New Testament.

[1] Translated by Cartwright as *A full and plaine declaration of Ecclesiastical Discipline* (1574).

[2] A system of basic rules and obligations, and the enforcement of the rules by stated methods of correction.

But the dignified and scholarly labors of Travers and Cartwright came to naught, despite substantial support from Parliament.[3] A very different kind of attack, perhaps made more out of frustration than of hope, was launched in 1588. The humorously long title of the first of the works of "Martin Marprelate" indicates the technique of the series of tracts: *Oh read over D. John Bridges, for it is worthy worke: Or an epitome of the fyrste Booke, of that right worshipfull volume, written against the Puritanes, in the defence of the noble cleargie, by as worshipfull a prieste, John Bridges, Presbyter, Priest or elder, doctor of Divillitie, and Deane of Sarum. Wherein the arguments of the puritans are wisely prevented,*[4] *that when they come to answere M. Doctor, they must needes say some-thing that hath bene spoken. Compiled for the behoofe and overthrow of the unpreaching Parsons, Fyckers,*[5] *and Currats, that have lernt their Catechismes, and are past grace: By the reverend and worthie Martin Marprelat gentleman, and dedicated by a second Epistle to the Terrible Priests. In this Epitome, the foresaide Fickers, etc. are very insufficiently furnished, with notable inabilitie of most vincible reasons, to answere the cavill of the puritanes. And lest M. Doctor should thinke that no man can write without sence but his selfe, the senceles titles of the several pages, and the handling of the matter throughout the Epitomie, shew plainely, that beetleheaded ignoraunce, must not live and die with him alone.*

Martin attempted to appeal to a wider audience than his many Puritan predecessors by combining humorous buffoonery, serious analyses of the defects of episcopacy, and vituperation. The combination is scarcely Miltonic, but the recognition that satire and wit were part of the Puritan tradition of attack helps readers to understand Milton's attack.

In Milton's time the warfare became even more heated. The Puritans' frustration, caused by their failure to eliminate either episcopacy or the "remnants of Romanism" (vestments, kneeling at Communion, the use of the sign of the cross in baptism, etc.), was aggravated by the successful efforts of Archbishop Laud to restore decency to the church, to establish sacramentalism, and to add to the dignity of the bishops. The physician John Bastwick expressed the Puritan distaste in his lively and bitter attack, *The Letany*

[3] A story well told by Sir John Neale in *Elizabeth I and her Parliaments* (2 vols.; New York, 1966).

[4] *prevented:* anticipated.

[5] *Fyckers:* Vicars.

(1637). He too used satire; his vocabulary is often learned, but his style lacks eloquence.

> And in those good *Pastors* and ministers places they have installed, foysted in and put PRIESTS SECUNDUM DIABOLI, for the most part, *such a generation of vipers proud ungratefull idle wicked and illiterate asses, and such profane scornes of all piety and goodnes, and so beastly lascivious, and lecherous as no piety wench can keepe her honesty for them* . . . (pp. 11–12).

In 1637 Milton was twenty-nine. The requirements for ordination to the ministry demanded an acceptance of the Anglican establishment; and though the ministry had been Milton's intended career, its lack of an effective discipline and the low moral standards of many clergymen prohibited him from accepting ordination. He had been, as he later put it, "church-outed by the Prelates." He found an outlet for his bitterness in the year of Bastwick's pamphlet in the greatest literary contribution to the attack on the prelates, the famous passage in *Lycidas*.

> Anow of such as for their bellies sake
> Creep and intrude, and climb into the fold?
> . . . .
> Blind mouthes! that scarce themselves know how to hold
> A sheep hook. . . .[6]

The very complex background of events surrounding the publication of Milton's Puritan attacks on the church cannot be fully rehearsed here.[7] The Long Parliament, which began its sessions in November 1640, had a host of grievances against Charles I and Archbishop Laud. In December fifteen thousand petitioners from London urged the abolition of episcopacy, and in January seven hundred clergymen pressed for its abolition. After publishing *Episcopacie by Divine Right* (1640), Bishop Joseph Hall came again to the defense of episcopacy, in January 1641, with *An Humble Remonstrance to the High Court of Parliament;* the defense referred

[6] *Poems* (1645).

[7] It is set forth in William Haller's *The Rise of Puritanism* (New York, 1938), in Arthur E. Barker's *Milton and the Puritan Dilemma* (Toronto, 1942), in Don M. Wolfe's introduction to the first volume of the *Complete Prose Works of John Milton* (New Haven, 1953), and in Will T. Hale's excellent edition of *Of Reformation* (New Haven, 1916).

episcopacy's long past, which Hall argued extended back to the primitive church.

Many pro-presbyterian debaters answered, among them the group of Puritan ministers who signed themselves SMECTYMNUUS, the initial letters of their names. The initials TY represent Thomas Young, Milton's boyhood tutor. Milton wrote a postscript for their work, *An Answer to a book, entitled, An Humble Remonstrance,* in which he surveyed the misdeeds of English bishops. It was published in March 1641.

Parliament in the meantime was debating the desirability of eliminating episcopacy. Among the defenders of the hierarchy was Lord George Digby, who delivered in early February an address published about the same time.[8] It was read with care by Milton, who had it before him in late May when he wrote *Of Reformation Touching Church-Discipline in England.* As George W. Whiting has shown, Milton's last pages are "directed chiefly, if not solely, at Digby's *Speech,* the points of which Milton follows in order and the phrases of which he sometimes quotes."[9]

The most interesting description of the circumstances of the composition of Milton's attacks on episcopacy is in his own *Pro Populo Anglicano Defensio Secunda* (1654). There he tells how he was engaged in literary pursuits when debate began over how the church was to be governed. Believing that the question was an important one,

> . . . I proceeded straightway, when I discovered that much sought true way towards liberty, towards the freeing of the whole life of man from servitude (since church discipline may influence the customs and manners of the state). I could not help knowing above all things the difference between divine and human law, since I had prepared myself with studies from adolescence. I could not in this crisis fail my fatherland (yea, indeed, the Church and my brothers) in the cause of the Gospel, since I had so trained myself that I could never be considered really useful if now I paid heed to other things. Since in this opportunity I had to prove useful, I determined to transfer all my strength and all my talent to this project. First of all, therefore, I wrote to a certain friend two books concerning the reformation of the Anglican Church. Then when two outstanding and distinguished bishops asserted their position against

8 *The Third Speech of the Lord George Digby.*
9 See *Milton's Literary Milieu* (Chapel Hill, 1939), p. 283.

> certain leading ministers, I responded. I thought that on these subjects, which I considered only because of my love of the truth and my responsibilities as a dutiful Christian, I should not write worse than those who debated for their own gain and unjust domination. I responded to one of the bishops with two books, one named concerning prelatical episcopacy and the other concerning the basis of ecclesiastical discipline; I responded to the other with certain animadversions and soon after an Apologia. And I brought help to the ministers, who could hardly endure their opponent's eloquence. . . .[10]

Students of early American history who see Puritanism as an essentially conservative force may have difficulty in understanding how the author of *Areopagitica* could ever have identified himself with the Puritans. In fact, as Milton suggests when he points to the desire for liberty as his motive in the debate, there were nontheological reasons why liberals supported the Puritan position. Arthur Barker has noted that the Smectymnuans emphasized the aristocratic element in presbyterianism; Milton, the democratic.[11] Other political, social, and economic reasons for supporting Puritanism have been described by Christopher Hill, who demonstrates, for example, that the church courts which Milton so roundly condemned were attempting to "enforce standards of conduct, which had been appropriate enough to an unequal agrarian society, long after large areas of England had left such a society behind."[12] Milton's dissatisfaction with the church, like his dissatisfaction with university education, was based to a considerable extent on his recognition that the times demanded change. It is significant that when episcopacy was restored in England, many of the features to which Milton objected, such as the powerful church courts, were no longer part of the ecclesiastical structure.

Although Milton's *Commonplace Book* shows that in the late 1630s he was reading widely in the church fathers, the early church historians, and such English historians as Stowe and Holinshed (all writers drawn on in the composition of his first tract), *Of Reformation* bears signs of hasty composition, particularly in its organization. Milton asserts, for example, that the three groups who oppose

[10] Editor's translation from the 1654 edition, pp. 88–89.

[11] *Milton and the Puritan Dilemma.*

[12] *Society and Puritanism in Pre-Revolutionary England* (New York, 1964), p. 309. This is a very fully documented study.

further reformation of the Church of England are "antiquitarians" (lovers of tradition for its own sake), libertines (those whose morals might be subject to ecclesiastical correction), and politicians. He then launches an extended attack on the first group. The libertines are referred to in only a few remarks made almost in passing. Finally Milton turns to the politicians, devoting the bulk of the second book to them. The attack on the antiquitarians is so long that one almost forgets that two other groups remain to be considered.

Though it may have been improvised in composition, *Of Reformation* is not without plan. The structure is not readily apparent, and thus a brief consideration of its organization may be helpful. Milton begins the work with a description of what Protestants regarded as the gradual degeneration of Christianity in the years between its establishment and the Reformation. This description suggests by implication that Laudian sacramentalism is of a piece with degenerate pre-Reformation Christianity. Milton next turns explicitly to England to consider why the English church was never completely reformed: he surveys English ecclesiastical history from the days of Edward VI through Elizabeth's reign in order to note the forces that prevented more radical purification. Next follows the attack on antiquitarians, opponents of reform closer to his own day. It is in four parts: a comparison of the attitude toward bishops in the early church and in Milton's day; a consideration of the chief corrupter of the early church, Constantine, and his contemporaries; an analysis of the church fathers' views on the church's source of authority; and finally a bitter attack on the pettiness and wrongheadedness of contemporary antiquitarianism.

After a few hasty stabs at the libertines' love of episcopal government, Milton turns to the second major theme of his book, an analysis of the advantages and disadvantages of presbyterianism and episcopacy to civil government. He first considers some current views of the relationship of church and state, then looks at some historical aspects of the relationship. In the course of this discussion, he notes that certain attitudes and practices of church authorities are particularly dangerous to the state; an attractively told fable illustrates the point.

The latter part of the second book is designed to show the advantages accruing to the state from the elimination of episcopacy and to demonstrate the danger of the bishops' growing power. Following the downfall of the hierarchical system, Milton foresees a glorious day. After a brief consideration of the objections brought against his position, Milton ends his essay with a powerful peroration, a prayer and a curse—a prayer that God will bring about a reformation of the church according to Milton's principles, and a curse upon the opponents of reform.

Milton's attacks on the bishops manifest the qualities that make his prose so great: an exploitation of the full resources of English from the poetic to the subliterary; striking imagery; concise, powerful, often highly sensuous phrases; packed, sprawling sentences. Though much has yet to be learned about the structure of Milton's prose, its vocabulary has been carefully studied by Joshua H. Neumann.[13] Two recent studies examine Milton's rhetoric and add to one's understanding of the context of Milton's first tract.[14]

The genius of Milton's prose, especially that of passages such as the much-admired prayer at the close of *Of Reformation,* is so great that one is tempted to adopt J. Milton French's contention that Milton's natural bent was toward prose, not poetry.[15] It is, perhaps, the great themes that make Milton's poems more obviously excellent than his prose. If the prose writings—at least the first great pamphlets—were less tied to events of the times, it would perhaps be easier to see their full worth.

The text of *Of Reformation* presented here is based on a study of six copies: a copy in the Houghton Library of Harvard University, *EC65/M6427/641 (A), and five copies in the British Museum: 105.b.42; 108.b.27; C.111.c.8; E.208 (3); and Ashley 1168. I have also taken advantage of the textual studies of Hale and Professor H. M. Ayres in the Columbia edition of Milton's works. Errata cited in the list published in the original edition have been corrected; all readings not supported by one of the 1641 copies examined are recorded in the notes.

A discussion of, and selections from, Milton's later anti-prelatical writings follow *Of Reformation.* The selections from *Of Prelatical Episcopacy, Animadversions,* and *The Reason of Church-Governe-*

13 *PMLA,* LX (1945), 102–20.

14 Thomas Kranidas, *The Fierce Equation: A Study of Milton's Decorum* (New York, 1966), and Robert F. Duvall, "Time, Place, Persons: The Background for Milton's *Of Reformation,*" in *SEL,* VII (1967), 107–18.

15 "Milton as a Historian," *PMLA,* L (1935), 469–79.

ment are based on Houghton Library copies; the selections from *An Apology* are from the copy in the University of Texas Library.

For help of various kinds I am indebted to the late Dr. William A. Jackson of Harvard; Mrs. June Moll of the University of Texas; the staff of the North Library of the British Museum; two former students, Miss Jane Ferguson and Miss Nancy Dawson; Mrs. A. F. Ruhland, and my wife Katherine.

OF REFORMATION TOUCHING CHURCH-DISCIPLINE IN ENGLAND: AND THE CAUSES THAT HITHERTO HAVE HINDRED IT.
TWO BOOKES, WRITTEN TO A FREIND.

Printed, for Thomas Underhill 1641.

[1]* OF REFORMATION IN ENGLAND
And the CAWSES that hitherto have hindred it

Sir,

Amidst those deepe and retired thoughts, which with every man Christianly instructed, ought to be most frequent, of *God,* and of his miraculous *ways,* and *works,* amongst men, and of our *Religion* and *Worship,* to be perform'd to him; after the story of our Saviour *Christ,* suffering to the lowest bent of weaknesse, in the *Flesh,* and presently triumphing to the highest pitch of *glory,* in the *Spirit,* which drew up his body also, till [2] we in both be united to him in the Revelation of his Kingdome: I do not know of any thing more worthy to take up the whole passion of pitty, on the one side, and joy on the other, than to consider first, the foule and sudden corruption, and then after many a tedious age, the long-deferr'd, but much more wonderfull and happy reformation of the *Church* in these latter dayes. Sad it is to thinke how that Doctrine of the *Gospel,* planted by teachers Divinely inspir'd, and by them winnow'd, and sifted, from the chaffe of overdated Ceremonies, and refin'd to such a Spirituall height, and temper of purity, and knowledge of the Creator, that the body, with all the circumstances of time and place, were purifi'd by the affections of the regenerat

* Numbers in brackets in this and subsequent complete texts denote page numbers in the original edition.

passion: emotion.
overdated Ceremonies: Old Testament rituals abandoned by Christians.
temper: quality brought about by tempering.
affections: mental tendencies.

Soule, and nothing left impure, but sinne; *Faith* needing not the weak, and fallible office of the Senses, to be either the Ushers, or Interpreters, of heavenly Mysteries, save where our Lord himselfe in his Sacraments ordain'd; that such a Doctrine should through the grossenesse, and blindnesse, of her Professors, and the fraud of deceivable traditions, drag so downwards, as to backslide one way into the Jewish beggery, of old cast rudiments, and stumble forward another way into the new-vomited Paganisme of sensuall Idolatry, attributing purity, or impurity, to things indifferent,[1] that they might bring the inward acts of the *Spirit* to the outward, and customary ey-Service of the body, as if they [3] could make *God* earthly, and fleshly, because they could not make themselves *heavenly*, and *Spirituall:* they began to draw downe all the Divine intercours, betwixt *God*, and the Soule, yea, the very shape of *God* himselfe, into an exterior, and bodily forme,[2] urgently pretending a necessity, and obligement of joyning the body in a formall reverence, and *Worship* circumscrib'd, they hallow'd it, they fum'd it, they sprincl'd it, they be deck't it, not in robes of pure innocency, but of pure Linnen, with other deformed, and fantastick dresses in Palls, and Miters, gold, and guegaw's fetcht from *Arons* old wardrope, or the *Flamins vestry:*[3] then was the *Priest* set to *con his motions*, and his *Postures* his *Liturgies*, and his *Lurries*, till the Soule by this meanes of over-bodying her selfe, given up justly to fleshly delights, bated her wing apace downeward: and finding the ease she had from her visible, and sensuous collegue the body in performance of *Religious* duties, her pineons now broken, and flagging, shifted off from her selfe, the labour of high soaring any more, forgot her heavenly flight, and left the dull, and droyling carcas to plod on in the old rode, and drudging Trade of outward conformity.[4] And here out of question from her pervers conceiting of *God*, and holy things, she had faln to beleeve no *God* at all, had not custome and the worme of conscience nipt her incredulity hence to all the duty's of evangelicall grace instead of the adop-[4]tive and cheerefull boldnesse which our new alliance with *God* requires, came Servile, and thral-like feare:[5] for in very deed, the superstitious man by his

Professors: those who merely profess.
deceivable: able to deceive.
Jewish beggery: borrowing Old Testament rituals. *old cast:* cast off.
new-vomited Paganisme: Laud's revival of rejected Roman practices, such as placing the Communion table in the former position of altars.
sprincl'd it: with holy water.
con his motions: memorize his ceremonial motions.
Lurries: something recited from memory, or a jumble of sounds.
droyling: sluggish.
conceiting: forming an idea.

good will is an Atheist; but being scarr'd from thence by the pangs, and gripes of a boyling conscience, all in a pudder shuffles up to himselfe such a *God,* and such a *worship* as is most agreeable to remedy his feare, which feare of his, as also is his hope, fixt onely upon the *Flesh,* renders likewise the whole faculty of his apprehension, carnall, and all the inward acts of *worship* issuing from the native strength of the SOULE, run out lavishly to the upper skin, and there harden into a crust of Formallitie. Hence men came to scan the *Scriptures,* by the Letter, and in the Covenant of our Redemption, magnifi'd the external signs more than the quickning power of the *Spirit,* and yet looking on them through their own guiltinesse with a Servile feare, and finding as little comfort, or rather terror from them againe, they knew not how to hide their Slavish approach to *Gods* behests by them not understood, nor worthily receav'd, but by cloaking their Servile crouching to all *Religious* Presentments, somtimes lawfull, sometimes Idolatrous, under the name of *humility,* and terming the Py-bald frippery, and ostentation of Ceremony's, *decency.*

Then was Baptisme chang'd into a kind of exorcism, and water Sanctifi'd by *Christs* institute, thought little enough to wash off the originall [5] Spot without the Scratch, or crosse impression of a Priests fore-finger: and that feast of free grace, and adoption to which *Christ* invited his Disciples to sit as Brethren, and coheires of the happy Covenant, which at that Table was to be Seal'd to them, even that Feast of love and heavenly-admitted fellowship, the Seale of filiall grace became the Subject of horror, and glouting adoration, pageanted about, like a dreadfull Idol: which sometimes deceve's wel-meaning men, and beguiles them of their reward, by their voluntary humility, which indeed, is fleshly pride, preferring a foolish Sacrifice, and the rudiments of the world, as Saint *Paul* to the *Colossians* explaineth,[6] before a savory obedience to *Christs* example. Such was *Peters* unseasonable Humilitie, as then his Knowledge was small, when *Christ* came to wash his feet; who at an impertinent time would needs straine courtesy with his Master, and falling troublesomly upon the lowly, alwise, and unexaminable intention of *Christ* in what he went with resolution to doe, so provok't by his

by his good will: voluntarily.
pudder: tumult.
decency: that which is proper; decorum.
exorcism: a ceremony to cast out demons preceded the baptismal washing with water.
originall Spot: original sin.
heavenly-admitted fellowship: the Lord's Supper.
glouting: looking attentively.

interruption the meeke *Lord,* that he threat'nd to exclude him from his heavenly Portion, unlesse he could be content to be lesse arrogant, and stiff neckt in his humility.[7]

But to dwell no longer in characterizing the *Depravities* of the *Church,* and how they sprung, and how they tooke increase; when I recall to mind at last, after so many darke Ages, wherein the huge overshadowing traine of *Error* had al-[6]most swept all the Starres out of the Firmament[8] of the *Church;* how the bright and blissfull *Reformation* (by Divine Power) strook through the black and settled Night of *Ignorance* and *Antichristian Tyranny,* me thinks a soveraigne and reviving joy must needs rush into the bosome of him that reads or heares; and the sweet Odour of the returning *Gospell* imbath his Soule with the fragrancy of Heaven. Then was the Sacred BIBLE sought out of the dusty corners where prophane Falshood and Neglect had throwne it, the *Schooles* opened, *Divine* and *Humane Learning* rak't out of the *embers* of *forgotten Tongues,* the *Princes* and *Cities* trooping a pace to the new erected Banner of *Salvation;* the *Martyrs,* with the unresistable *might* of *Weaknesse,* shaking the *Powers* of *Darknesse,* and scorning the *fiery rage* of the old *red Dragon.*[9]

The pleasing pursuit of these thoughts hath oft-times led mee into a serious question and debatement with my selfe, how it should come to passe that *England* (having had this *grace* and *honour* from God to bee the first that should set up a Standard for the recovery of *lost Truth,* and blow the first *Evangelick Trumpet* to the *Nations,* holding up, as from a Hill, the new Lampe of *saving light* to all Christendome,[10] should now be last, and most unsettl'd in the enjoyment of that *Peace,* whereof she taught the way to others; although indeed our *Wicklefs* preaching, at which all the succeeding *Reformers* more effectually ligh-[7]ted their *Tapers,* was to his Countrey-men but a short blaze soone dampt and stifl'd by the *Pope,* and *Prelates* for sixe or seven Kings Reignes;[11] yet me thinkes the *Precedencie* which God gave this *Iland,* to be the first *Restorer* of *buried Truth,* should have beene followed with more happy successe, and sooner attain'd Perfection; in which, as yet we are amongst the last: for, albeit in *purity* of *Doctrine* we agree with our Brethren; yet in Discipline, which is the *execution* and *applying* of *Doctrine* home, and laying the *salve* to the very *Orifice* of the *wound;* yea tenting and searching to the *Core,* without which *Pulpit Preaching* is but shooting at Rovers; in this we are no better than a *Schisme,* from all the *Reformation,* and a sore scandall to

successe: outcome.
at Rovers: at random, or at remote targets.

them; for while wee hold *Ordination* to belong onely to *Bishops*, as our *Prelates*[12] doe, wee must of necessity hold also their *Ministers* to be no *Ministers*, and shortly after their *Church* to be no *Church*. Not to speake of those sencelesse *Ceremonies* which wee onely retaine, as a dangerous earnest of sliding back to *Rome*, and serving meerely, either as a mist to cover nakednesse where true *grace* is extinguisht; or as an Enterlude to set out the *pompe* of *Prelatisme*. Certainly it would be worth the while therefore and the paines, to enquire more particularly, what, and how many the cheife causes have been, that have still hindred our *Uniforme Consent* to the rest of the *Churches* abroad, (at this time especially) when the *Kingdome* is in a good *propensity* thereto; and all Men in Pray-[8]ers, in Hopes, or in Disputes, either for or against it.

Yet will I not insist on that which may seeme to be the cause on Gods part; as his judgement on our sinnes, the tryall of his owne, the unmasking of Hypocrites; nor shall I stay to speake of the continuall eagernes and extreame diligence of the *Pope* and *Papists* to stop the furtherance of *Reformation*, which know they have no hold or hope of *England* their lost Darling, longer than the *government* of *Bishops* bolsters them out; and therefore plot all they can to uphold them, as may bee seene by the Booke of *Santa Clara* the Popish *Preist* in defence of *Bishops*, which came out piping hot much about the time that one of our own *Prelats* out of an ominous feare had writ on the same *Argument;* as if they had joyn'd their forces like good Confederates to support one falling *Babel*.

But I shall cheifly indeavour to declare those Causes that hinder the forwarding of *true Discipline*, which are among our selves. Orderly proceeding will divide our inquirie into our *Fore-Fathers dayes*, and into *our Times*. Henry the 8. was the first that rent this *Kingdome* from the *Popes* Subjection totally; but his Quarrell being more about *Supremacie*, than other faultinesse in *Religion* that he regarded, it is no marvell if hee stuck where he did. The next default was in the *Bishops*, who though they had renounc't the *Pope*, they still hugg'd the *Popedome*, and shar'd the Autho-[9]rity among themselves, by their sixe bloody Articles persecuting the *Protestants* no slacker than the *Pope* would have done. And doutles, when ever the *Pope* shall fall, if his ruine bee not like the sudden down-come of a Towre, the *Bishops*, when they see him tottering, will leave him, and fall to scrambling, catch who may, hee a Patriarch-dome, and

Booke . . . Bishops: Franciscus Sancta Clara, *Apologia Episcorum* (1640).
Prelats . . . Argument: Bishop Joseph Hall, *Episcopacie by Divine Right* (1640).
sixe . . . Articles: conservative statute passed in 1539.

another what comes next hand; as the French Cardinall of late, and the *See* of *Canterbury* hath plainly affected.

In *Edward* the 6. Dayes, why a compleate *Reform* was not effected, to any considerate man may appeare. First, he no sooner entred into his Kingdome, but into a Warre with *Scotland;* from whence the Protector returning with Victory had but newly put his hand to repeale the 6. *Articles,* and throw the Images out of *Churches,* but Rebellions on all sides stir'd up by obdurate Papists, and other Tumults with a plaine Warre in *Norfolke,* holding tack against two of the Kings *Generals,* made them of force content themselves with what they had already done. Hereupon follow'd ambitious Contentions among the *Peeres,* which ceas'd not but with the Protectors death, who was the most zealous in this point: and then *Northumberland* was hee that could doe most in *England,* who little minding *Religion,* (as his Apostacie well shew'd at his death),[13] bent all his wit how to bring the Right of the *Crowne* into his owne Line.[14] And for the *Bishops,* they were so far from any such worthy Attempts, as that they [10] suffer'd themselvs to be the common stales to countenance with their prostituted Gravities[15] every Politick Fetch that was then on foot, as oft as the Potent *Statists* pleas'd to employ them. Never do we read that they made use of their Authority and high Place of accesse, to bring the jarring Nobility to *Christian peace,* or to withstand their disloyall Projects; but if a Toleration for *Masse* were to be beg'd of the King for his Sister MARY, lest CHARLES the Fifth should be angry; who but the grave Prelates *Cranmer* and *Ridley* must be sent to extort it from the young King? But out of the mouth of that godly and Royall *Childe,* Christ himselfe return'd such an awfull repulse to those halting and time-serving *Prelates,* that after much bold importunity, they went their way not without shame and teares.[16]

Nor was this the first time that they discover'd to bee followers of this World; for when the Protectors Brother, Lord *Sudley,* the Admirall through private malice and mal-engine was to lose his life, no man could bee found fitter than Bishop *Latimer* (like another Doctor *Shaw*)[17] to divulge in his Sermon the forged Accusations laid to his charge, thereby to defame him with the People, who else was thought would take ill the innocent mans death, unlesse the

French Cardinall: Cardinal Richelieu.
See of Canterbury: Archbishop Laud.
holding tack: persisting.
common stales: prostitutes.
Politick Fetch: stratagem.
discover'd: either "were discovered" or "revealed themselves."
mal-engine: deceit.

Reverend *Bishop* could warrant them there was no foule play. What could be more impious than to debarre the Children of the King from their right to the Crowne? To comply with the ambitious [11] Usurpation of a Traytor; and to make void the last Will of HENRY 8. to which the Breakers had sworne observance? Yet Bishop *Cranmer*, one of the Executors, and the other *Bishops* none refusing, (lest they should resist the Duke of *Northumberland*) could find in their Consciences to set their hands to the disinabling and defeating not onely of Princesse MARY the *Papist*, but of ELIZABETH the *Protestant*, and (by the *Bishops* judgement) the Lawfull Issue of King HENRY.

Who then can thinke, (though these *Prelates* had sought a further *Reformation*) that the least wry face of a *Politician* would not have hush't them. But it will be said, These men were *Martyrs*: What then? Though every true Christian will be a *Martyr* when he is called to it; not presently does it follow that every one suffering for Religion, is without exception. Saint *Paul* writes, that A *man may give his Body to be burnt*, (meaning for Religion) *and yet not have Charitie:*[18] He is not therfore above all possibility of erring, because hee burnes for some Points of Truth.

Witnes the *Arians* and *Pelagians* which were slaine by the Heathen for *Christs* sake; yet we take both these for no true friends of *Christ*. If the *Martyrs* (saith *Cyprian*[19] in his 30. Epistle) decree one thing, and the *Gospel* another, either the *Martyrs* must lose their Crowne by not observing the *Gospel* for which they are *Martyrs;* or the [12] Majestie of the *Gospel* must be broken and lie flat, if it can be overtopt by the *novelty* of any other *Decree*.

And heerewithall I invoke the *Immortall* DEITIE *Reveler* and *Judge* of Secrets, That wherever I have in this BOOKE plainely and roundly (though worthily and truly) laid open the faults and blemishes of *Fathers, Martyrs,* or Christian *Emperors;* or have otherwise inveighed against Error and Superstition with vehement Expressions: I have done it, neither out of malice, nor list to speak evil, nor any vaine-glory; but of meere necessity, to vindicate the spotlesse *Truth* from an ignominious bondage, whose native worth is now become of such a low esteeme, that shee is like to finde small credit with us for what she can say, unlesse shee can bring a Ticket from *Cranmer, Latimer,* and *Ridley*; or prove her selfe a retainer to *Constantine,* and weare his *badge*. More tolerable it were for the *Church* of GOD that all these Names were utterly abolisht, like the *Brazen Serpent;*[20] than that mens fond opinion should thus idolize them, and the Heavenly *Truth* be thus captivated.

Now to proceed, whatsoever the *Bishops* were, it seemes they themselves were unsatisfi'd in matters of *Religion*, as they then stood, by that Commission granted to 8. *Bishops*, 8. other *Divines*, 8. *Civilians*, 8. *common Lawyers*, to frame *Ecclesiasticall Constitutions;*[21] which no wonder if it came to nothing; for (as *Hayward*[22] relates) both [13] their Professions and their Ends were different. Lastly, we all know by Examples, that exact *Reformation* is not perfited at the first push, and those unweildy Times of *Edward 6.* may hold some Plea by this excuse: Now let any reasonable man judge whether that *Kings Reigne* be a fit time from whence to patterne out the Constitution of a *Church Discipline*, much lesse that it should yeeld occasion from whence to foster and establish the continuance of Imperfection with the commendatory subscriptions of *Confessors* and *Martyrs*, to intitle and ingage a glorious *Name* to a grosse *corruption*. It was not *Episcopacie* that wrought in them the Heavenly Fortitude of *Martyrdome;* as little is it that *Martyrdome* can make good *Episcopacie:* But it was *Episcopacie* that led the good and holy Men through the temptation of the *Enemie*, and the snare of this present world to many blame-worthy and opprobrious *Actions*. And it is still *Episcopacie* that before all our eyes worsens and sluggs the most learned, and seeming religious of our *Ministers*, who no sooner advanc't to it, but like a seething pot set to coole, sensibly exhale and reake out the greatest part of that zeale, and those Gifts which were formerly in them, settling in a skinny congealment of ease and sloth at the top: and if they keep their Learning by some potent sway of Nature, 'tis a rare chance; but their *devotion* most commonly comes to that queazy temper of lukewarmnesse, that gives a Vomit to GOD himselfe.

[14] But what doe wee suffer mis-shapen and enormous *Prelatisme*, as we do, thus to blanch and varnish her deformities with the faire colours, as before of *Martyrdome*, so now of *Episcopacie?* They are not *Bishops*, GOD and all *good Men* know they are not, that have fill'd this Land with late confusion and violence; but a Tyrannicall crew and Corporation of Impostors, that have blinded and abus'd the World so long under that Name. He that inabl'd with *gifts* from *God*, and the lawfull and Primitive choyce of the *Church* assembl'd in convenient number, faithfully from that time forward feeds his Parochiall *Flock*, ha's his coequall and compresbyteriall Power to ordaine *Ministers* and *Deacons* by publique *Prayer*, and *Vote* of *Christs* Congregation in like sort as he himselfe was ordain'd, and is a true *Apostolick Bishop*. But when hee steps up into the Chayre of *Pontificall* Pride, and changes a moderate and exemplary House, for a mis-govern'd and haughty *Palace*, *spirituall Dignity* for

sluggs: makes sluggish.

carnall *Precedence,* and *secular high Office* and *employment* for the *high Negotiations* of his Heavenly *Embassage,* Then he *degrades,* then hee *un-Bishops* himselfe; hee that makes him *Bishop* makes him no *Bishop.* No marvell therfore if S. *Martin* complain'd to *Sulpitius Severus,*[23] that since hee was *Bishop* he felt inwardly a sensible decay of those *vertues* and *graces* that *God* had given him in great measure before; Although the same *Sulpitius* write that he was nothing tainted, or alter'd in his *habit, dyet,* or per-[15]sonall *demeanour* from that simple plainnesse to which he first betook himselfe. It was not therfore that thing alone which *God* tooke displeasure at in the *Bishops* of those times, but rather an universall rottennes, and gangrene in the whole *Function.*

From hence then I passe to Qu. ELIZABETH, the next *Protestant* Prince, in whose Dayes why *Religion* attain'd not a perfect reducement in the beginning of her Reigne, I suppose the hindring Causes will be found to bee common with some formerly alledg'd for King EDWARD 6. the greennesse of the Times, the weake Estate which Qu. MARY left the Realme in, the great Places and Offices executed by *Papists,* the *Judges,* the *Lawyers,* the *Justices* of Peace for the most part *Popish,* the *Bishops* firme to *Rome,* from whence was to be expected the furious flashing of Excommunications, and absolving the *People* from their Obedience. Next, her private *Councellours,* whoever they were, perswaded her (as *Camden*[24] writes) that the altering of *Ecclesiasticall Policie* would move sedition. Then was the *Liturgie* given to a number of moderate *Divines,* and Sir *Tho. Smith* a Statesman to bee purg'd, and Physick't: And surely they were moderate *Divines* indeed, neither hot nor cold; and *Grindall* the best of them, afterwards *Arch-Bishop* of *Canterbury* lost favour in the Court, and I think was discharg'd the goverment of his *See* for favouring the *Ministers,* though *Camden* seeme willing to finde another [16] Cause: therefore about her second Yeare in a *Parliament* of Men and Minds some scarce well grounded, others belching the soure Crudities of yesterdayes *Poperie,* those Constitutions of EDW. 6. which as you heard before, no way satisfi'd the men that made them, are now establish't for best, and not to be mended. From that time follow'd nothing but Imprisonments, troubles, disgraces on all those that found fault with the *Decrees* of the Convocation, and strait were they branded with the Name of *Puritans.* As for the Queene her selfe, shee was made beleeve that by putting downe *Bishops* her *Prerogative* would be infring'd, of which shall be spoken anon, as the course of Method brings it in. And why the *Prelats* labour'd it should be so thought, ask not them, but ask their Bellies. They had found a good Tabernacle, they sate under a spreading Vine, their Lot was fallen in a faire Inheritance. And these perhaps were the cheife impeachments of a more sound rectifying the *Church* in the Queens Time.

From this Period I count to begin our Times, which, because they concerne us more neerely, and our owne eyes and eares can give us the ampler scope to judge, will require a more exact search; and to effect this the speedier, I shall distinguish such as I esteeme to be the hinderers of *Reformation* into 3. sorts, *Antiquitarians* (for so I had rather call them than *Antiquaries,* whose labours are usefull and laudable) 2. *Libertines,* 3. *Politicians.*

[17] To the votarists of Antiquity I shall think to have fully answer'd, if I shall be able to prove out of Antiquity, First, that if they will conform our Bishops to the purer times, they must mew their feathers, and their pounces, and make but curttail'd Bishops of them; and we know they hate to be dockt and clipt, as much as to be put down outright. Secondly, that those purer times were corrupt, and their Books corrupted soon after. Thirdly, that the best of those that then wrote, disclaim that any man should repose on them, and send all to the Scriptures.

First therfore, if those that over-affect Antiquity, will follow the square thereof, their Bishops must be elected by the hands of the whole *Church.* The ancientest of the extant Fathers *Ignatius,*[25] writing to the Philadelphians saith, *that it belongs to them as to the Church of God to choose a Bishop.* Let no man cavill, but take the Church of *God* as meaning the whole consistence of Orders and Members, as S. *Pauls* Epistles expresse, and this likewise being read over: Besides this, it is there to be mark'd, that those Philadelphians are exhorted to choose a Bishop of *Antioch.* Whence it seems by the way that there was not that wary limitation of Dioces in those times, which is confirm'd even by a fast friend of Episcopacie, *Camden,* who cannot but love Bishops, as well as old coins, and his much lamented Monasteries for antiquities sake. He writes in his description of *Scotland, that over all the world Bishops had no* [18] *certaine Dioces, till Pope* Dionysius *about the yeare* 268. *did cut them out,* and *that the Bishops of* Scotland *executed their function in what place soever they came indifferently, and without distinction till King* Malcolm *the third, about the yeare* 1070. whence may be guest what their function was: was it to goe about circl'd with a band of rooking Officials, with cloke bagges full of Citations, and Processes

mew: shed.
pounces: powders.
square: pattern.
rooking: defrauding.

to be serv'd by a corporalty of griffonlike Promooters, and Apparitors? Did he goe about to pitch down his Court, as an Empirick does his banck, to inveigle in all the mony of the Countrey? no certainly it would not have bin permitted him to exercise any such function indifferently wherever he came. And verily some such matter it was as want of a fat Dioces that kept our Britain Bishops so poore in the Primitive times, that being call'd to the Councell of *Ariminum* in the yeare 359. they had not wherewithall to defray the charges of their journey, but were fed, and lodg'd upon the Emperors cost, which must needs be no accidentall, but usuall poverty in them, for the author *Sulp. Severus* in his 2 Booke of Church History praises them, and avouches it praise-worthy in a Bishop, to be so poore as to have nothing of his own. But to return to the ancient election of Bishops that it could not lawfully be without the consent of the people is so expresse in *Cyprian,* and so often to be met with, that to cite each place at large, were to translate a good part of the volume, therfore touching the [19] chief passages, I referre the rest to whom so list peruse the Author himselfe: in the 24. *Epist. If a Bishop* saith he, *be once made and allow'd by the testimony and judgement of his collegues, and the people, no other can be made.* In the 55. *When a Bishop is made by the suffrage of all the people in peace.* In the 68. marke but what he saies, *The people chiefly hath power, either of choosing worthy ones, or refusing unworthy:* this he there proves by authorities out of the old and new Testament, and with solid reasons, these were his antiquities.

This voyce of the people to be had ever in Episcopall elections was so well known, before *Cyprians* time, even to those that were without the Church, that the Emperor *Alexander Severus*[26] desir'd to have his governours of Provinces chosen in the same manner, as *Lampridius*[27] can tell: So little thought it he offensive to Monarchy; and if single authorities perswade not, hearken what the whole generall Council of *Nicaea* the first and famousest of all the rest determines, writing a Synodal *Epist.* to the African Churches, to warn them of Arrianisme, it exhorts them to choose orthodox Bishops in the place of the dead so they be worthy, and the people choose them, whereby they seem to make the peoples assent so necessary; that merit without their free choyce were not sufficient to make a Bishop. What would ye say now grave Fathers if you should wake and see unworthy Bishops, or rather no Bishops, but Egyptian taskmasters of Ceremonies thrust pur-[20]posely upon the groaning Church to the affliction, and vexation of *Gods* people? It was not of old that a Conspiracie of Bishops could frustrate and fob off the

Empirick does his banck: quack does his platform.

right of the people, for we may read how S. *Martin* soon after *Constantine* was made Bishop of *Turon* in *France* by the peoples consent from all places thereabout maugre all the opposition that the Bishops could make. Thus went matters of the Church almost 400. yeare after *Christ,* and very probably farre lower, for *Nicephorus Phocas* the Greek Emperour, whose reign fell neare the 1000. year of our Lord, having done many things tyrannically, is said by *Cedrenus*[28] to have done nothing more grievous and displeasing to the people, than to have inacted that no Bishop should be chosen without his will; so long did this right remain to the people in the midst of other palpable corruptions: Now for Episcopall dignity, what it was, see out of *Ignatius,* who in his Epistle to those of *Trallis* confesseth *that the Presbyters, are his fellow Counsellers, and fellow benchers.* And *Cyprian* in many places, as in the 6. 41. 52. Epist. speaking of *Presbyters,* calls them his *Compresbyters,* as if he deem'd himselfe no other, whenas by the same place it appeares he was a Bishop, he calls them Brethren; but that will be thought his meeknesse: yea, but the *Presbyters* and Deacons writing to him think they doe him honour enough when they phrase him no higher then Brother *Cyprian,* and deare *Cyprian* in the 26. Epist. For their Authority 'tis [21] evident not to have bin single, but depending on the counsel of the *Presbyters,* as from *Ignatius* was erewhile alledg'd; and the same *Cyprian* acknowledges as much in the 6 Epist. and addes therto that he had determin'd from his entrance into the Office of Bishop to doe nothing without the consent of his people, and so in the 31. Epist, for it were tedious to course through all his writings which are so full of the like assertions, insomuch that ev'n in the womb and center of Apostacy *Rome* it selfe, there yet remains a glimps of this truth, for the Pope himselfe, as a learned English writer notes well,[29] performeth all Ecclesiasticall jurisdiction as in Consistory amongst his Cardinals, which were originally but the Parish Priests of *Rome.* Thus then did the Spirit of unity and meeknesse inspire, and animate every joynt, and sinew of the mysticall body, but now the gravest, and worthiest Minister, a true Bishop of his fold shall be revil'd, and ruffl'd by an insulting, and only-Canon-wise Prelate, as if he were some slight paltry companion: and the people of *God* redeem'd, and wash'd with *Christs* blood, and dignify'd with so many glorious titles of Saints, and sons in the Gospel, are now no better reputed than impure ethnicks, and lay dogs; stones and Pillars, and Crucifixes have now the honour, and the almes due to *Christs* living members; the Table of Com-

maugre: despite.
ethnicks: heathens.

munion now become a Table of separation[30] stands like an exalted platforme upon the brow of the quire, fortifi'd with bulwark, and [22] barricado, to keep off the profane touch of the Laicks, whilst the obscene, and surfeted Priest scruples not to paw, and mammock the sacramentall bread, as familiarly as his Tavern Bisket. And thus the people vilifi'd and rejected by them, give over the earnest study of vertue, and godlinesse as a thing of greater purity than they need, and the search of divine knowledge as a mystery too high for their capacity's, and only for Churchmen to meddle with, which is that the Prelates desire, that when they have brought us back to Popish blindnesse we might commit to their dispose the whole managing of our salvation, for they think it was never faire world with them since that time: But he that will mould a modern Bishop into a primitive, must yeeld him to be elected by the popular voyce, undiocest, unrevenu'd, unlorded, and leave him nothing but brotherly equality, matchles temperance, frequent fasting, incessant prayer, and preaching, continual watchings, and labours in his Ministery, which what a rich bootie it would be, what a plump endowment to the many-benefice-gaping mouth of a Prelate, what a relish it would give to his canary-sucking, and swan-eating palat, let old Bishop *Mountain*[31] judge for me.

How little therfore those ancient times make for moderne Bishops hath bin plainly discours'd, but let them make for them as much as they will, yet why we ought not stand to their arbitrement shall now appeare by a threefold corruption [23] which will be found upon them. 1. The best times were spreadingly infected. 2. The best men of those times fouly tainted. 3. The best writings of those men dangerously adulterated. These Positions are to be made good out of those times witnessing of themselves. First, *Ignatius* in his early dayes testifies to the Churches of *Asia,* that even then Heresies were sprung up, and rife every where, as *Eusebius*[32] relates in his 3. Book, 35. chap. after the Greek number. And *Hegesippus*[33] a grave Church writer of prime Antiquity affirms in the same Book of *Euseb.* c. 32. *that while the Apostles were on earth the depravers of doctrine did but lurk, but they once gon, with open forehead they durst preach down the truth with falsities:* yea those that are reckon'd for orthodox began to make sad, and shamefull rents in the Church about the trivial celebration of Feasts, not agreeing when to keep Easter day, which controversie grew so hot, that *Victor* the Bishop of *Rome* Excommunicated all the Churches of *Asia* for no other cause, and was worthily therof reprov'd by

mammock: tear to pieces.

Irenaeus.[34] For can any sound Theologer think that these great Fathers understood what was Gospel, or what was Excommunication? doubtlesse that which led the good men into fraud and error was, that they attended more to the neer tradition of what they heard the Apostles sometimes did, than to what they had left written, not considering that many things which they did, were by the Apostles themselves profest to be done [24] only for the present, and of meer indulgence to some scrupulous converts of the Circumcision, but what they writ was of firm decree to all future ages. Look but a century lower in the 1. *cap.* of *Eusebius* 8. Book. What a universal tetter of impurity had invenom'd every part, order, and degree of the Church, to omit the lay herd which will be little regarded, *those that seem'd to be our Pastors,* saith he, *overturning the Law of Gods worship, burnt in contentions one towards another, and incresing in hatred and bitternes, outragiously sought to uphold Lordship, and command as it were a tyranny.* Stay but a little, magnanimous Bishops, suppresse your aspiring thoughts, for there is nothing wanting but *Constantine* to reigne, and then Tyranny her selfe shall give up all her cittadels into your hands, and count ye thence forward her trustiest agents. Such were these that must be call'd the ancientest, and most virgin times between *Christ* and *Constantine.* Nor was this general contagion in their actions, and not in their writings: who is ignorant of the foul errors, the ridiculous wresting of Scripture, the Heresies, the vanities thick sown through the volums of *Justin Martyr, Clemens, Origen, Tertullian*[35] and others of eldest time? Who would think him fit to write an Apology for Christian Faith to the Roman Senat, that would tell them how of the Angels, which he must needs mean those in *Gen.* call'd the *Sons of God,* mixing with Women were begotten the Devills, as good *Justin Mar-*[25]*tyr* in his Apology told them. But more indignation would it move to any Christian that shall read *Tertullian* terming S. *Paul* a novice and raw in grace, for reproving S. *Peter* at *Antioch,* worthy to be blam'd if we beleeve the Epistle to the *Galatians:* perhaps from this hint the blasphemous Jesuits presum'd in *Italy* to give their judgement of S. *Paul,* as of a hot headed person, as *Sandys* in his Relations[36] tells us.

Now besides all this, who knows not how many surreptitious works are ingraff'd into the legitimate writings of the Fathers, and of those Books that passe for authentick who knows what hath bin tamper'd withall, what hath bin raz'd out, what hath bin inserted, besides the late legerdemain of the Papists, that which *Sulpitius*

tetter: skin disease.

writes concerning *Origens* Books gives us cause vehemently to suspect, there hath bin packing of old. In the third chap. of his 1. Dialogue, we may read what wrangling the Bishops and Monks had about the reading, or not reading of *Origen*, some objecting that he was corrupted by Hereticks, others answering that all such Books had bin so dealt with. How then shall I trust these times to lead me, that testifie so ill of leading themselvs, certainly of their defects their own witnesse may be best receiv'd, but of the rectitude, and sincerity of their life and doctrine to judge rightly, wee must judge by that which was to be their rule.

But it will be objected that this was an unsetl'd state of the Church wanting the temporall Ma-[26]gistrate to suppresse the licence of false Brethren, and the extravagancy of still-new opinions, a time not imitable for Church government, where the temporall and spirituall power did not close in one beleife, as under *Constantine*. I am not of opinion to thinke the Church a *Vine* in this respect, because, as they take it, she cannot subsist without clasping about the Elme of worldly strength, and felicity, as if the heavenly City could not support it selfe without the props and buttresses of secular Authoritie. They extoll *Constantine* because he extol'd them; as our homebred Monks in their Histories blanch the Kings their Benefactors, and brand those that went about to be their Correctors. If he had curb'd the growing Pride, Avarice, and Luxury of the *Clergie*, then every Page of his Story should have swel'd with his Faults, and that which *Zozimus* the Heathen writes of him should have come in to boot: wee should have heard then in every Declamation how hee slew his Nephew *Commodus* a worthy man, his noble and eldest Son *Crispus*, his Wife *Fausta*, besides numbers of his Friends; then his cruell exactions, his unsoundnesse in Religion, favoring the *Arrians* that had been condemn'd in a Counsell, of which himselfe sate as it were President, his hard measure and banishment of the faithfull and invincible *Athanasius*, his living unbaptiz'd almost to his dying day; these blurs are too apparent in his Life. But since hee must needs bee the Load-starre of *Reformation* as some men clat-[27]ter, it will be good to see further his knowledge of *Religion* what it was, and by that we may likewise guesse at the sincerity of his Times in those that were not Hereticall, it being likely that hee would converse with the *famousest Prelates* (for so he had made them) that were to be found for learning.

blanch: whiten, whitewash.

Of his *Arianisme* we heard, and for the rest, a pretty scantling of his Knowledge may be taken by his deferring to be baptiz'd so many yeares, a thing not usuall, and repugnant to the Tenor of *Scripture*, *Philip* knowing nothing that should hinder the *Eunuch* to be *baptiz'd* after *profession* of his *beleife*.[37] Next, by the excessive devotion, that I may not say Superstition both of him and his Mother *Helena*, to find out the Crosse on which *Christ* suffer'd, that had long lien under the rubbish of old ruines, (a thing which the Disciples and Kindred of our Saviour might with more ease have done, if they had thought it a pious duty:) some of the nailes whereof hee put into his Helmet, to beare off blowes in battell, others he fasten'd among the studds of his bridle, to fulfill (as he thought, or his Court *Bishops* perswaded him) the Prophesie of *Zachariah; And it shall be that that which is in the bridle shall be holy to the Lord.*[38] Part of the Crosse, in which he thought such Vertue to reside, as would prove a kind of *Palladium* to save the *Citie* where ever it remain'd, he caus'd to be laid up in a Pillar of Porphyrie by his Statue. How hee or his Teachers could trifle thus with halfe an eye open [28] upon Saint *Pauls* Principles, I know not how to imagine.

How should then the dim Taper of this Emperours age that had such need of snuffing, extend any beame to our Times wherewith wee might hope to be better lighted, than by those Luminaries that God hath set up to shine to us far neerer hand. And what *Reformation* he wrought for his owne time it will not be amisse to consider, hee appointed certaine times for Fasts, and Feasts, built stately Churches, gave large Immunities to the Clergie, great Riches and Promotions to *Bishops*, gave and minister'd occasion to bring in a Deluge of Ceremonies, thereby either to draw in the Heathen by a resemblance of their rites, or to set a glosse upon the simplicity, and plainnesse of Christianity which to the gorgeous solemnities of *Paganisme*, and the sense of the Worlds Children seem'd but a homely and Yeomanly *Religion*, for the beauty of inward Sanctity was not within their prospect.

So that in this manner the *Prelates* both then and ever since comming from a meane, and Plebeyan *Life* on a sudden to be Lords of stately Palaces, rich furniture, delicious fare, and *Princely* attendance, thought the plaine and homespun verity of *Christs* Gospell unfit any longer to hold their Lordships acquaintance, unlesse the poore thred-bare Matron were put into better clothes; her chast and modest vaile surrounded with celestiall beames they over-

scantling: sample.

lai'd with wanton *tresses*, [29] and in a flaring tire bespeccki'd her with all the gaudy allurements of a Whore.

Thus flourish't the Church with *Constantines* wealth, and thereafter were the effects that follow'd; his Son *Constantius* prov'd a flat *Arian*, and his Nephew *Julian* an Apostate, and there his Race ended; the Church that before by insensible degrees welk't and impair'd, now with large steps went downe hill decaying; at this time *Antichrist* began first to put forth his horne, and that saying was common that former times had woodden Chalices and golden *Preists;* but they golden Chalices and woodden *Preists.* Formerly (saith *Sulpitius*) *Martyrdome* by glorious death was sought more greedily, than now Bishopricks by vile Ambition are hunted after (speaking of these Times) and in another place; they gape after possessions, they tend Lands and Livings, they coure over their gold, they buy and sell: and if there be any that neither possesse nor traffique, that which is worse, they sit still, and expect guifts, and prostitute every induement of grace, every holy thing to sale. And in the end of his History thus he concludes, all things went to wrack by the *faction, wilfulnesse,* and *avarice* of the *Bishops,* and by this means *Gods people,* and every *good man* was had in scorn and derision; which S. *Martin* found truly to be said by his friend *Sulpitius;* for being held in admiration of all men, he had onely the *Bishops* his enemies, found God lesse favorable to him after he was *Bishop* than before, and [30] for his last 16. yeares would come at no *Bishops* meeting. Thus you see Sir what *Constantines* doings in the Church brought forth, either in his own or in his Sons Reigne.

Now lest it should bee thought that somthing else might ayle this Author thus to hamper the Bishops of those dayes; I will bring you the opinion of three the famousest men for wit and learning, that *Italy* at this day glories of, whereby it may be concluded for a receiv'd opinion even among men professing the Romish Faith, that *Constantine* marr'd all in the Church. *Dante* in his 19. *Canto* of *Inferno* hath thus, as I will render it you in English blank Verse.

> *Ah* Constantine, *of how much ill was cause*
> *Not thy Conversion, but those rich demaines*
> *That the first wealthy* Pope *receiv'd of thee.*

So in his 20. Canto of *Paradise* hee makes the like complaint, and *Petrarch* seconds him in the same mind in his 108. Sonnet which

tire: attire.
welk't: wilted, declined.
coure: cower, crouch.

is wip't out by the Inquisitor in some Editions; speaking of the Roman *Antichrist* as meerely bred up by *Constantine.*

Founded in chast and humble Povertie,
'Gainst them that rais'd thee dost thou lift thy horn,
Impudent whoore, where hast thou plac'd thy hope?
In thy Adulterers, or thy ill got wealth?
Another Constantine comes not in hast. [31]

Ariosto of *Ferrara* after both these in time, but equall in fame, following the scope of his Poem in a difficult knot how to restore *Orlando* his chiefe Hero to his lost senses, brings *Astolfo* the English Knight up into the moone, where S. *John*, as he feignes, met him. *Cant.* 34.

And to be short, at last his guid him brings
Into a goodly valley, where he sees
A mighty masse of things strangely confus'd,
Things that on earth were lost, or were abus'd.

And amongst these so abused things listen what hee met withall, under the Conduct of the *Evangelist.*

Then past hee to a flowry Mountaine greene,
Which once smelt sweet, now stinks as odiously;
This was that gift (if you the truth will have)
That Constantine *to good* Sylvestro *gave.*

And this was a truth well knowne in *England* before this *Poet* was borne, as our *Chaucers* Plowman shall tell you by and by upon another occasion. By all these circumstances laid together, I do not see how it can be disputed what good this Emperour *Constantine* wrought to the Church, but rather whether ever any, though perhaps not wittingly, set open a dore to more mischiefe in Christendome. There is just cause therefore that when the *Prelates* cry out Let the Church be re-[32]form'd according to *Constantine*, it should sound to a judicious eare no otherwise, than if they should say Make us rich, make us lofty, make us lawlesse, for if any under him were not so, thanks to those ancient remains of integrity, which were not yet quite worne out, and not to his Government.

Thus finally it appears that those purer Times were no such as they are cry'd up, and not to be follow'd without suspicion, doubt and danger. The last point wherein the *Antiquary* is to bee dealt with at his owne weapon, is to make it manifest, that the ancientest, and best of the Fathers have disclaim'd all sufficiency in themselves that men should rely on, and sent all commers to the Scriptures, as all sufficient; that this is true, will not be unduly gather'd by shewing what esteeme they had of Antiquity themselves, and what validity they thought in it to prove Doctrine, or Discipline. I must of necessitie begin from the second ranke of Fathers, because till then Antiquitie could have no Plea. *Cyprian* in his 63. *Epistle*. If any, saith he, of our Auncestors either ignorantly or out of simplicity hath not observ'd that which the Lord taught us by his example (speaking of the Lords Supper) his simplicity *God* may pardon of his mercy, but wee cannot be excus'd for following him, being instructed by the Lord. And have not we the same instructions, and will not this holy man with all the whole Consistorie of Saints and Martyrs that liv'd of old [33] rise up and stop our mouthes in judgement, when wee shall goe about to Father our Errors, and opinions upon their Authority? in the 73. *Epist.* hee adds, in vaine doe they oppose custome to us if they be overcome by reason; as if custome were greater then Truth, or that in spirituall things that were not to be follow'd, which is revel'd for the better by the holy Ghost. In the 74. neither ought Custome to hinder that Truth should not prevaile, for Custome without Truth is but agednesse of Error.

Next *Lactantius*,[39] he that was prefer'd to have the bringing up of *Constantines* children in his second Booke of *Institutions*. Chap. 7. and 8. disputes against the vaine trust in Antiquity, as being the chiefest Argument of the Heathen against the Christians, they doe not consider, saith he, what Religion is, but they are confident it is true, because the Ancients deliver'd it, they count it a trespasse to examine it. And in the eighth, not because they went before us in time, therefore in wisedome, which being given alike to all Ages, cannot be prepossest by the Ancients; wherefore seeing that to seeke the Truth is inbred to all, they bereave themselves of wisedome the gift of God who without judgement follow the Ancients, and are led by others like bruit beasts. St. *Austin* writes to *Fortunatian* that he counts it lawfull in the bookes of whomsoever to reject that which hee finds otherwise than true, and so hee would have others deale by him. He neither ac-[34]counted, as it seems, those Fathers that went before, nor himselfe, nor others of his rank, for men of more than ordinary spirit, that might equally deceive, and be deceiv'd. And[40] oftimes, setting our servile humors aside, yea *God* so ordering, we may find Truth with one man, as soon as in a Counsell, as *Cyprian* agrees 71. Epist. *Many things*, saith he, *are better reveal'd to single persons*. At *Nicaea* in the first, and best reputed Counsell of all the world, there had gon out a Canon to divorce

St. Austin: Augustine.

married Priests, had not one old man *Paphnutius* stood up, and reason'd against it.

Now remains it to shew clearly that the Fathers referre all decision of controversie to the Scriptures, as all-sufficient to direct, to resolve, and to determine. *Ignatius* taking his last leave of the Asian Churches, as he went to martyrdome exhorted them to adhere close to the written doctrine of the Apostles, necessarily written for posterity: so farre was he from unwritten traditions, as may be read in the 36.*c.* of *Eusebius* 3.*b.* In the 74. Epist. Of *Cyprian* against *Stefan* Bish. of *Rome* imposing upon him a tradition, *whence,* quoth he, *is this tradition? is it fetcht from the authority of Christ in the Gospel, or of the Apostles in their Epistles: for God testifies that those things are to be done which are written:* and then thus; *what obstinacie, what presumption is this to preferre humane Tradition before divine ordinance?* And in the same Epist. *If we shall return to the head, and beginning of divine tradition* (which we all know he means the [35] Bible) *humane error ceases, and the reason of heavenly misteries unfolded, whatsoever was obscure, becomes cleare.* And in the 14. Distinct. of the same Epist. directly against our modern fantasies of a still visible Church, he teaches, *that succession of truth may fail, to renew which we must have recourse to the fountaines,* using this excellent similitude, *if a Channel, or Conduit pipe which brought in water plentifully before, suddenly fail, doe we not goe to the fountaine to know the cause, whether the Spring affords no more, or whether the vein be stopt, or turn'd aside in the midcourse: thus ought we to doe, keeping Gods precepts, that if in ought the truth shall be chang'd, we may repaire to the Gospel, and to the Apostles, that thence may arise the reason of our doings, from whence our order, and beginning arose.* In the 75. he inveighs bitterly against Pope *Stefanus,* for that he could boast his Succession from *Peter,* and yet foist in Traditions that were not Apostolicall. And in his Book of the unity of the Church he compares those that neglecting *Gods* Word, follow the doctrines of men, to *Coreh, Dathan,* and *Abiram.*[41] The very first page of Athanasius against the Gentiles, averres the Scriptures to be sufficient of themselves for the declaration of Truth; and that if his friend *Macarius* read other Religious writers, it was but φιλοκάλως *come un virtuoso,* (as the Italians say,) as a lover of elegance: and in his 2*d* Tome the 39. pag, after he hath rekon'd up the Canonicall Books, *In these only,* saith he, *is the doctrine of godlinesse taught, let no man adde to these,* [36] *or take from these;* and in his *Synopsis,* having again set down all the Writers of the old and new Testament, *these,* saith he, *be the anchors, and props of our Faith:* besides these, millions of other Books have bin written by great and wise men according to rule, and agreement with these, of which I will not now speak, as being of infinite number, and meer dependance on the canonical Books. *Basil* in his *2d* Tome writing of true Faith, tells his auditors he is bound to teach them that which he hath learn't out of the Bible: and in the same Treatise, he saith, *That seeing the Commandments of the Lord, are faithfull, and sure for ever; it is a plain falling from the Faith, and a high pride either to make void any thing therin, or to introduce any thing not there to be found:* and he gives the reason, *for Christ saith, My Sheep heare my voyce, they will not follow another, but fly from him, because they know not his voyce.* But not to be endlesse in quotations, it may chance to be objected, that there be many opinions in the Fathers which have no ground in Scripture; so much the lesse, may I say, should we follow them, for their own words shall condemn them, and acquit us, that lean not on them; otherwise these their words shall acquit them, and condemn us. But it will be reply'd, the Scriptures are difficult to be understood, and therfore require the explanation of the Fathers, 'tis true there be some Books, and especially some places in those Books that remain clouded; yet ever that which is most necessary to be known is most [37] easie; and that which is most difficult, so farre expounds it selfe ever, as to tell us how little it imports our *saving knowledge.* Hence to inferre a generall obscurity over all the text, is a meer suggestion of the Devil to disswade men from reading it, and casts an aspersion of dishonour both upon the *mercy, truth,* and *wisdome* of *God:* We count it no gentlenesse, or fair dealing in a man of Power amongst us, to require strict, and punctual obedience, and yet give out all his commands ambiguous and obscure, we should think he had a plot upon us, certainly such commands were no commands, but snares. The very essence of Truth is plainnesse, and brightnes; the darknes and crookednesse is our own. The *wisdome* of *God* created *understanding,* fit and proportionable to Truth the object, and end of it, as the eye to the thing visible. If our *understanding* have a film of *ignorance* over it, or be blear with gazing on other false glisterings, what is that to Truth? If we will but purge with sovrain eyesalve that intellectual ray which *God* hath planted in us, then we would beleeve the Scriptures protesting their own plainnes, and perspicuity, calling to them to be instructed, not only the *wise,* and *learned,* but the *simple,* the *poor,* the *babes,* foretelling an extraordinary effusion of *Gods* Spirit upon every age, and sexe, attributing to all men, and requiring from them the ability of searching, trying, examining all things, and by the Spirit discerning that which is good; and as the

Scriptures [38] themselvs pronounce their own plainnes, so doe the Fathers testifie of them.

I will not run into a paroxysm of citations again in this point, only instance *Athanasius* in his fore-mention'd first page; *the knowledge of Truth,* saith he, *wants no humane lore, as being evident in it selfe, and by the preaching of Christ now opens brighter than the Sun.* If these Doctors who had scarse half the light that we enjoy, who all except 2 or 3 were ignorant of the Hebrew tongue, and many of the Greek, blundring upon the dangerous, and suspectfull translations of the Apostat *Aquila,* the Heretical Theodotion; the Judaïz'd *Symmachus;* the erroneous *Origen;* if these could yet find the Bible so easie, why should we doubt, that have all the helps of Learning, and faithfull industry that man in this life can look for, and the assistance of *God* as neer now to us as ever. But let the Scriptures be hard; are they more hard, more crabbed, more abstruse than the Fathers? He that cannot understand the sober, plain, and unaffected stile of the Scriptures, will be ten times more puzzl'd with the knotty Africanisms, the pamper'd metafors; the intricat, and involv'd sentences of the Fathers; besides the fantastick, and declamatory flashes; the crosse-jingling periods which cannot but disturb, and come thwart a setl'd devotion worse than the din of bells, and rattles.

Now Sir, for the love of holy *Reformation,* what can be said more against these importunat clients of Antiquity, than she her selfe their pa-[39]tronesse hath said. Whether think ye would she approve still to dote upon immeasurable, innumerable, and therfore unnecessary, and unmercifull volumes, choosing rather to erre with the specious name of the Fathers, or to take a sound Truth at the hand of a plain upright man that all his dayes hath bin diligently reading the holy Scriptures, and therto imploring *Gods* grace, while the admirers of Antiquity have bin beating their brains about their *Ambones,* their *Diptychs,* and *Meniaia's?* Now, he that cannot tell of Stations, and Indictions; nor has wasted his pretious howrs in the endles conferring of Councels and Conclaves that demolish one another, although I know many of those that pretend to be great Rabbies in these studies have scarce saluted them from the strings, and the titlepage, or to give 'em more, have bin but the Ferrets and Moushunts of an Index: yet what Pastor, or Minister how learned, religious, or discreet soever does not now bring both his

Ambones: early forms of pulpits. *Diptychs:* wax tablets listing members of a church. *Meniaia:* books of Byzantine rite church offices.

Indictions: churches to be visited after fasts; a period of time used in church documents.

strings: strip holding covers of a book together.

cheeks full blown with Oecumenical, and Synodical, shall be counted a lank, shallow, unsufficient man, yea a dunce, and not worthy to speak about *Reformation* of *Church Discipline*. But I trust they for whom *God* hath reserv'd the honour of Reforming this Church will easily perceive their adversaries drift in thus calling for Antiquity, they feare the plain field of the Scriptures; the chase is too hot; they seek the dark, the bushie, the tangled Forrest, they would imbosk: they feel themselvs strook in the [40] transparent streams of divine Truth, they would plunge, and tumble, and thinke to ly hid in the foul weeds, and muddy waters, where no plummet can reach the bottome. But let them beat themselvs like Whales, and spend their oyl till they be dradg'd ashoar: though wherfore should the Ministers give them so much line for shifts, and delays? Wherfore should they not urge only the Gospel, and hold it ever in their faces like a mirror of Diamond, till it dazle, and pierce their misty ey balls? maintaining it the honour of its absolute sufficiency, and supremacy inviolable: For if the Scripture be for *Reformation,* and Antiquity to boot, 'tis but an advantage to the dozen, 'tis no winning cast; and though Antiquity be against it, while the Scriptures be for it, the Cause is as good as ought to be wisht, Antiquity it selfe sitting Judge.

But to draw to an end; the second sort of those that may be justly number'd among the hinderers of *Reformation,* are Libertines, these suggest that the Discipline sought would be intolerable: for one Bishop now in a Dioces we should then have a Pope in every Parish. It will not be requisit to Answer these men, but only to discover them, for reason they have none, but lust, and licentiousness, and therfore answer can have none. It is not any Discipline that they could live under, it is the corruption, and remisnes of Discipline that they seek. Episcopacy duly executed, yea the Turkish, and Jewish rigor against whor-[41]ing, and drinking, the dear, and tender Discipline of a Father; the sociable, and loving reproof of a Brother; the bosome admonition of a Friend is a *Presbytery,* and a Consistory to them. 'Tis only the merry Frier in *Chaucer* can disple them.

Full sweetly heard he confession
And pleasant was his absolution,
He was an easie man to give pennance.

And so I leave them: and referre the political discourse of Episcopacy to a Second Book.

imbosk: hide.
disple: discipline.

[42] OF REFORMATION, etc.
The Second Book.

Sir,

It is a work good, and prudent to be able to guide one man; of larger extended vertue to order wel one house; but to govern a Nation piously, and justly, which only is to say happily, is for a spirit of the greatest size, and divinest mettle. And certainly of no lesse a mind, nor of lesse excellence in another way, were they who by writing layd the solid, and true foundations of this Science, which being of greatest importance to the life of man, yet there is no art that hath bin more canker'd in her principles, more soyl'd, and slubber'd with aphorisming pedantry than the art of policie; and that most, where a man would thinke should least be, in Christian Common-wealths. They teach not that to govern well is to train up a Nation in true wisdom and vertue, and that [43] which springs from thence magnanimity, (take heed of that) and that which is our beginning, regeneration, and happiest end, likenes to *God,* which in one word we call *godlines,* and that this is the true florishing of a Land, other things follow as the shadow does the substance: to teach thus were meer pulpitry to them. This is the masterpiece of a modern politician, how to qualifie, and mould the sufferance and subjection of the people to the length of that foot that is to tread on their necks, how rapine may serve it selfe with the fair, and honourable pretences of publick good, how the puny Law may be brought under the wardship, and controul of lust, and will; in which attempt if they fall short, then must a superficial colour of reputation by all means direct or indirect be gotten to wash over the unsightly bruse of honor. To make men governable in this manner their precepts mainly tend to break a nationall spirit, and courage by count'nancing upon riot, luxury, and ignorance, till having thus disfigur'd and made men beneath men, as *Juno* in the Fable of *Io,*[42] they deliver up the poor transformed heifer of the Commonwealth to be stung and vext with the breese, and goad of oppression under the custody of some *Argus* with a hundred eyes of jealousie. To be plainer Sir, how to soder, how to stop a leak, how to keep up the floting carcas of a crazie, and diseased Monarchy, or State betwixt wind, and water, swimming still upon her own dead lees, that now is [44] the deepe designe of a politician. Alas Sir! a Com-

slubber'd: stained. *policie:* government.
breese: gadfly.

monwelth ought to be but as one huge Christian personage, one mighty growth, and stature of an honest man, as big, and compact in vertue as in body; for looke what the grounds, and causes are of single happines to one man, the same yee shall find them to a whole state, as *Aristotle* both in his ethicks, and politiks, from the principles of reason layes down; by consequence therfore, that which is good, and agreeable to monarchy, will appeare soonest to be so, by being good, and agreeable to the true wel-fare of every Christian, and that which can be justly prov'd hurtfull, and offensive to every true Christian, wilbe evinc't to be alike hurtful to monarchy: for *God* forbid, that we should separate and distinguish the end, and good of a monarch, from the end and good of the monarchy, or of that, from Christianity. How then this third, and last sort that hinder reformation, will justify that it stands not with reason of state, I much muse? For certain I am, the *Bible* is shut against them, as certaine that neither *Plato,* nor *Aristotle* is for their turnes.[43] What they can bring us now from the Schools of *Loyola* with his Jesuites, or their *Malvezzi*[44] that can cut *Tacitus* into slivers and steaks, we shall presently hear. They alledge 1. That the Church government must be conformable to the civill politie, next, that no forme of Church government is agreeable to monarchy, but that of Bishops. Must Church government that is [45] appointed in the Gospel, and has chief respect to the soul, be conformable, and pliant to civil, that is arbitrary, and chiefly conversant about the visible and external part of man? this is the very maxim that moulded the Calvs of *Bethel* and of *Dan,* this was the quintessence of *Jeroboams* policy, he made Religion conform to his politick interests, and this was the sin that watcht over the Israelites till their final captivity.[45] If this State principle come from the Prelates, as they affect to be counted statists, let them look back to *Elutherius* Bishop of *Rome,* and see what he thought of the policy of *England;* being requir'd by *Lucius* the first Christian King of this Iland to give his counsel for the founding of Religious Laws, little thought he of this sage caution, but bids him betake himselfe to the old, and new Testament, and receive direction from them how to administer both Church, and Common-wealth; that he was *Gods* Vicar, and therfore to rule by *Gods* Laws, that the Edicts of *Cæsar* we may at all times disallow, but the Statutes of *God* for no reason we may reject.[46] Now certaine if Church-government be taught in the Gospel, as the Bishops dare not deny, we may well conclude of what late standing this Position is, newly calculated for the altitude of Bishop elevation, and lettice for their lips. But by what example can they shew

looke what: whatever.

that the form of Church Discipline must be minted, and modell'd out to secular pretences? The ancient Republick of the Jews is evident to [46] have run through the changes of civil estate, if we survey the Story from the giving of the Law to the *Herods*, yet did one manner of Priestly government serve without inconvenience to all these temporal mutations: it serv'd the mild Aristocracy of elective Dukes, and heads of Tribes joyn'd with them; the dictatorship of the Judges, the easie, or hard-handed Monarchy's, the domestick, or forrain tyrannies, Lastly the Roman Senat from without, the Jewish Senat at home with the Galilean Tetrarch, yet the Levites had some right to deal in civil affairs: but seeing the Evangelical precept forbids Churchmen to intermeddle with wordly imployments, what interweavings, or interworkings can knit the Minister, and the Magistrate in their several functions to the regard of any precise correspondency? Seeing that the Churchmans office is only to teach men the Christian Faith, to exhort all, to incourage the good, to admonish the bad, privately the lesse offender, publickly the scandalous and stubborn; to censure, and separate from the communion of *Christs* flock, the contagious, and incorrigible, to receive with joy, and fatherly compassion the penitent, all this must be don, and more than this is beyond any Church autority. What is all this either here, or there to the temporal regiment of Wealpublick, whether it be Popular, Princely, or Monarchical? Where doth it intrench upon the temporal governor, where does it come in his walk? where does it [47] make inrode upon his jurisdiction? Indeed if the Ministers part be rightly discharg'd, it renders him the people more conscionable, quiet, and easie to be govern'd, if otherwise his life and doctrine will declare him. If therfore the Constitution of the Church be already set down by divine prescript, as all sides confesse, then can she not be a handmaid to wait on civil commodities, and respects: and if the nature and limits of Church Discipline be such, as are either helpfull to all political estates indifferently, or have no particular relation to any, then is there no necessity, nor indeed possibility of linking the one with the other in a speciall conformation.

Now for their second conclusion, *That no form of Church government is agreeable to Monarchy, but that of Bishops,* although it fall to pieces of it selfe by that which hath bin sayd: yet to give them play front, and reare, it shall be my task to prove that Episcopacy with that Autority which it challenges in *England* is not only not agreeable, but tending to the destruction of Monarchy. While the Primitive Pastors of the Church of *God* labor'd faithfully in their Ministery, tending only their Sheep, and not seeking, but avoiding all worldly matters as clogs, and indeed derogations, and debase-ments to their high calling, little needed the Princes, and potentates of the earth, which way soever the Gospel was spread, to study ways how to make a coherence between the Churches politie, and theirs: therfore when [48] *Pilate* heard once our Saviour *Christ* professing that *his Kingdome was not of this world,* he thought the man could not stand much in *Cæsars* light, nor much indammage the Roman Empire: for if the life of *Christ* be hid to this world, much more is his Scepter unoperative, but in spirituall things. And thus liv'd, for 2 or 3 ages, the Successors of the Apostles. But when through *Constantines* lavish Superstition they forsook their *first love,* and set themselvs up two Gods instead, *Mammon* and their Belly, then taking advantage of the spiritual power which they had on mens consciences, they began to cast a longing eye to get the body also, and bodily things into their command, upon which their carnal desires, the Spirit dayly quenching and dying in them, they knew no way to keep themselves up from falling to nothing, but by bolstering, and supporting their inward rottenes by a carnal, and outward strength. For a while they rather privily sought opportunity, then hastily disclos'd their project, but when *Constantine* was dead, and 3 or 4 Emperors more, their drift became notorious, and offensive to the whole world: for while *Theodosius* the younger reign'd, thus writes *Socrates* the Historian in his *7th* Book, 11. chap. now began an ill name to stick upon the Bishops of *Rome,* and *Alexandria,* who beyond their Priestly bounds now long agoe had stept into principality; and this was scarse 80. years since their raising from the meanest worldly condition. Of courtesie now let any man tell [49] me, if they draw to themselves a *temporall strength* and *power* out of *Cæsars* Dominion, is not *Cæsars* Empire thereby diminisht? but this was a stolne bit, hitherto hee was but a Caterpiller secretly gnawing at *Monarchy,* the next time you shall see him a Woolfe, a Lyon, lifting his paw against his raiser, as *Petrarch* exprest it, and finally an open enemy, and subverter of the Greeke Empire. *Philippicus* and *Leo,* with divers other Emperours after them, not without the advice of their *Patriarchs,* and at length of a whole Easterne Counsell of 3. hundred thirty eight *Bishops,* threw the Images out of *Churches* as being decreed idolatrous.

Upon this goodly occasion the *Bishop* of *Rome* not only seizes the City, and all the Territory about into his owne hands, and makes himselfe Lord thereof, which till then was govern'd by a Greeke Magistrate, but absolves all *Italy* of their Tribute, and obedience due to the Emperour, because hee obey'd Gods Commandement in abolishing Idolatry.

Mark Sir here how the Pope came by S. *Peters* Patrymony, as he feigns it, not the donation of *Constantine,*[47] but idolatry and rebellion got it him. Yee need but read *Sigonius*[48] one of his owne Sect to know the Story at large. And now to shroud himselfe against a storme from the Greek Continent, and provide a Champion to beare him out in these practises, hee takes upon him by Papall sentence to unthrone *Chilpericus*[49] the rightfull K. of *France,* and gives the Kingdome to *Pepin* for no [50] other cause but that hee seem'd to him the more active man. If he were a freind herein to *Monarchy* I know not, but to the *Monarch* I need not aske what he was.

Having thus made *Pepin* his fast freind, he cals him into *Italy* against *Aistulphus* the *Lombard,* that warr'd upon him for his late Usurpation of *Rome* as belonging to *Ravenna* which he had newly won. *Pepin,* not unobedient to the Popes call, passing into *Italy,* frees him out of danger, and wins for him the whole exarchat of *Ravenna,* which though it had beene almost immediately before, the hereditary possession of that *Monarchy* which was his cheife Patron, and Benefactor, yet he takes, and keepes it to himselfe as lawfull prize, and given to St. *Peter.* What a dangerous fallacie is this, when a spirituall man may snatch to himselfe any temporall Dignity, or Dominion under pretence of receiving it for the Churches use; thus he claimes *Naples, Sicily, England,* and what not? To bee short, under shew of his zeale against the errors of the Greeke Church, hee never ceast baiting, and goring the Successors of his best Lord *Constantine* what by his barking curses, and Excommunications, what by his hindering the Westerne Princes from ayding them against the Sarazens, and Turkes, unlesse when they humour'd him; so that it may be truly affirm'd, he was the subversion, and fall of that *Monarchy,* which was the hoisting of him; this, besides *Petrarch,* whom I have cited, our *Chaucer* also hath [51] observ'd, and gives from hence a caution to *England* to beware of her *Bishops* in time, for that their ends, and aymes are no more freindly to *Monarchy* than the Popes.

Thus hee brings in the Plow-man speaking, 2. *Part. Stanz.* 28.[50]

The Emperour Yafe the Pope sometime
So high Lordship him about
That at last the silly Kime,
The proud Pope put him out,
So of this Realme is no doubt,
But Lords beware, and them defend,
For now these folks be wonders stout
The King and Lords now this amend.

And in the next *Stanza* which begins the third part of the tale he argues that they ought not to bee Lords.

Moses Law forbode it tho
That Preists should no Lordships welde
Christs Gospell biddeth also,
That they should no Lordships held
Ne Christs Apostles were never so bold
No such Lordships to hem embrace
But smeren her Sheep, and keep her Fold.

And so forward. Whether the Bishops of *England* have deserv'd thus to bee fear'd by man so wise as our *Chaucer* is esteem'd, and how agree-[52]able to our *Monarchy*, and *Monarchs* their demeanour ha's been, he that is but meanly read in our *Chronicles* needs not be instructed. Have they not been as the *Canaanites*, and *Philistims* to this Kingdom? what Treasons, what revolts to the Pope, what Rebellions, and those the basest, and most pretenselesse have they not been chiefe in? What could *Monarchy* think when *Becket* durst *challenge* the custody *of Rotchester-Castle,* and the Tower of *London,* as appertaining to his Signory? To omit his other insolencies and affronts to Regall Majestie, till the Lashes inflicted on the anointed body of the King washt off the holy *Unction* with his *blood* drawn by the polluted hands of *Bishops, Abbots,* and *Monks.*

What good upholders of Royalty were the *Bishops,* when by their rebellious opposition against King *John, Normandy* was lost, he himselfe depos'd, and this Kingdom made over to the *Pope?* When the *Bishop* of *Winchester* durst tell the Nobles, the Pillars of the Realme, that there were no Peeres in *England,* as in *France,* but that the King might doe what hee pleas'd. What could Tyranny say more? it would bee petty now if I should insist upon the rendring up of *Tournay*[51] by *Woolseyes* Treason, the Excommunications, Cursings, and Interdicts upon the whole Land. For haply I shall be cut off short by a reply, that these were the faults of the men, and their Popish errors, not of *Episcopacie,* that hath now renounc't the Pope, and is a Protestant. Yes sure; as wise [53] and famous men have suspected, and fear'd the Protestant *Episcopacie* in *England,* as those that have fear'd the Papall.

You know Sir what was the judgement of *Padre Paolo*[52] the great Venetian Antagonist of the *Pope,* for it is extant in the hands of many men, whereby he declares his feare, that when the Hierarchy of *England* shall light into the hands of busie and audacious men, or shall meet with Princes tractable to the Prelacy, then much mischiefe is like to ensue. And can it bee neerer hand, than when *Bish-*

ops shall openly affirme that, No *Bishop,* no *King?*[53] a trimme Paradox, and that yee may know where they have beene a begging for it, I will fetch you the Twin-brother to it out of the Jesuites Cell; they feeling the Axe of Gods reformation hewing at the old and hollow trunk of Papacie, and finding the Spaniard their surest friend, and safest refuge, to sooth him up in his dreame of a fift Monarchy, and withall to uphold the decrepit Papalty have invented this super-politick Aphorisme, as one termes it, One Pope, and one King.

Surely there is not any Prince in *Christendome,* who hearing this rare Sophistry can choose but smile, and if we be not blind at home we may as well perceive that this worthy Motto, No *Bishop,* no *King* is of the same batch, and infanted out of the same feares, a meere ague-cake coagulated of a certaine Fever they have, presaging their time to be but short: and now like those that are sink-[53]ing, they catch round at that which is likeliest to hold them up. And would perswade Regall Power, that if they dive, he must after. But what greater debasement can there be to Royall Dignity, whose towring, and stedfast heighth rests upon the unmovable foundations of Justice, and Heroick vertue, than to chaine it in a dependance of subsisting, or ruining to the painted Battlements, and gaudy rottennesse of Prelatrie, which want but one puffe of the Kings to blow them down like a past-bord House built of *Court-Cards.* Sir the little adoe, which me thinks I find in untacking these pleasant Sophismes, puts mee into the mood to tell you a tale ere I proceed further; and *Menenius Agrippa*[54] speed us.

A Tale.

Upon a time the Body summon'd all the Members to meet in the Guild for the common good (as Aesops Chronicles averre many stranger Accidents) the head by right takes the first seat, and next to it a huge and monstrous Wen little lesse than the Head it selfe, growing to it by a narrower excrescency. The members amaz'd began to aske one another what hee was that took place next their cheif; none could resolve. Whereat the Wen, though unweildy, with much adoe gets up and bespeaks the Assembly to this purpose. That as in place he was second to the head, so by due of merit; that he was to it an ornament, and strength, and of speciall neere relation, and that if the head should faile, none were fitter than himselfe to step into his place; therefore hee [55] thought it for the honour of the Body, that such dignities and rich indowments should be decreed him, as did adorne, and set out the noblest Members. To

ague-cake: an enlargement of the spleen produced by ague.

this was answer'd, that it should bee consulted. Then was a wise and learned Philosopher sent for, that knew all the Charters, Lawes, and Tenures of the Body. On him it is impos'd by all, as cheife Committee to examine, and discusse the claime and Petition of right put in by the Wen; who soone perceiving the matter, and wondring at the boldnesse of such a swolne Tumor, Wilt thou (quoth he) that art but a bottle of vitious and harden'd excrements, contend with the lawfull and free-borne members, whose certaine number is set by ancient, and unrepealable Statute? head thou art none, though thou receive this huge substance from it, what office bearst thou? What good canst thou shew by thee done to the Common-weale? the Wen not easily dash't replies, that his Office was his glory, for so oft as the soule would retire out of the head from over the steaming vapours of the lower parts to Divine Contemplation, with him shee found the purest, and quietest retreat, as being most remote from soile, and disturbance. Lourdan, quoth the Philosopher, thy folly is as great as thy filth; know that all the faculties of the Soule are confin'd of old to their severall vessels, and *ventricles*, from which they cannot part without dissolution of the whole Body; and that thou containst no good thing in thee, but a heape of [56] hard, and loathsome uncleannes, and art to the head a foul disfigurment and burden, when I have cut thee off, and open'd thee, as by the help of these implements I will doe, all men shall see.

But to return, whence was digress't, seeing that the throne of a King, as the wise K. *Salomon* often remembers us, *is establisht in Justice*, which is the universall *Justice* that *Aristotle* so much praises, containing in it all other *vertues*, it may assure us that the fall of Prelacy, whose actions are so farre distant from *Justice*, cannot shake the least fringe that borders the royal canopy: but that their standing doth continually oppose, and lay battery to regal safety, shall by that which follows easily appear. Amongst many secondary, and accessory causes that support Monarchy, these are not of least reckning, though common to all other States: the love of the Subjects, the multitude, and valor of the people, and store of treasure. In all these things hath the Kingdome bin of late sore weak'nd, and chiefly by the Prelates. First let any man consider, that if any Prince shall suffer under him a commission of autority to be exerciz'd, till all the Land grone, and cry out, as against a whippe of Scorpions, whether this be not likely to lessen, and keel the affections of the Subject. Next what numbers of faithfull, and freeborn Englishmen, and good Christians have bin constrain'd to forsake their dearest home, their friends, and kindred, whom nothing but the wide

Lourdan: blockhead.

Ocean, and the savage deserts of *Ame-*[57]*rica* could hide and shelter from the fury of the Bishops. O Sir, if we could but see the shape of our deare Mother *England,* as Poets are wont to give a personal form to what they please, how would she appeare, think ye, but in a mourning weed, with ashes upon her head, and teares abundantly flowing from her eyes, to behold so many of her children expos'd at once, and thrust from things of dearest necessity, because their conscience could not assent to things which the Bishops thought *indifferent.* What more binding than Conscience? what more free than *indifferency?* cruel then must that *indifferency* needs be, that shall violate the strict necessity of Conscience, merciles, and inhumane that free choyse, and liberty that shall break asunder the bonds of Religion. Let the Astrologer be dismay'd at the portentous blaze of comets, and impressions in the aire as foretelling troubles and changes to states: I shall beleeve there cannot be a more ill-boding signe to a Nation (*God* turne the Omen from us) than when the Inhabitants, to avoid insufferable grievances at home, are inforc'd by heaps to forsake their native Country. Now wheras the only remedy, and amends against the depopulation, and thinnesse of a Land within, is the borrow'd strength of firme alliance from without, these Priestly policies of theirs having thus exhausted our domestick forces, have gone the way also to leave us as naked of our firmest, and faithfullest neighbours abroad, by disparaging [58] and alienating from us all Protestant Princes, and Common-wealths, who are not ignorant that our Prelats, and as many as they can infect, account them no better than a sort of sacrilegious, and puritanical Rebels, preferring the *Spaniard* our deadly enemy before them, and set all orthodox writers at nought in comparison of the Jesuits, who are indeed the onely corrupters of youth, and good learning; and I have heard many wise, and learned men in *Italy* say as much. It cannot be that the strongest knot of confederacy should not dayly slak'n, when Religion which is the chiefe ingagement of our league shall be turn'd to their reproach. Hence it is that the prosperous, and prudent states of the united Provinces, whom we ought to love, if not for themselves, yet for our own good work in them, they having bin in a manner planted, and erected by us, and having bin since to us the faithfull watchmen, and discoverers of many a Popish, and Austrian complotted Treason, and with us the partners of many a bloody, and victorious battell, whom the similitude of manners and and language, the commodity of traffick, which founded the old Burgundian league betwixt us, but chiefly Religion should bind to us immortally, even such friends as these, out of some principles instill'd into us by the Prelates, have bin often dismist with distastfull answers, and sometimes unfriendly actions: nor is it to be consider'd to the breach of confederate Nations whose mutual interest is [59] of such high consequence, though their Merchants bicker in the East Indies, neither is it safe, or warie, or indeed Christianly, that the *French* King, of a different Faith, should afford our neerest Allyes as good protection as we. Sir, I perswade my selfe, if our zeale to true Religion, and the brotherly usage of our truest friends were as notorious to the world, as our *Prelatical Schism*, and captivity to *Rotchet Apothegmes*, we had ere this seene our old Conquerours, and afterward Liege-men the *Normans*, together with the *Brittains* our proper Colony, and all the *Gascoins* that are the rightfull *Dowry* of our ancient Kings, come with cap, and knee, desiring the shadow of the *English* Scepter to defend them from the hot persecutions and taxes of the *French*. But when they come hither, and see a Tympany of *Spanioliz'd Bishops* swaggering in the fore-top of the State, and meddling to turne, and dandle the *Royall Ball* with unskilfull and *Pedantick palmes*, no marvell though they think it as unsafe to commit Religion, and liberty to their arbitrating as to a Synagogue of Jesuites.

But what doe I stand reck'ning upon advantages, and gaines lost by the mis-rule, and turbulency of the *Prelats*, what doe I pick up so thriftily their scatterings and diminishings of the meaner Subject, whilst they by their seditious practises have indanger'd to loose the King one third of his main Stock; what have they not done to banish him from his owne Native Countrey? but to [60] speake of this as it ought would ask a Volume by it selfe.

Thus as they have unpeopl'd the Kingdome by expulsion of so many thousands, as they have endeavor'd to lay the skirts of it bare by disheartning and dishonouring our loyallest Confederates abroad, so have they hamstrung the valour of the Subject by seeking to effeminate us all at home. Well knows every wise Nation that their Liberty consists in manly and honest labours, in sobriety and rigorous honour to the Marriage Bed, which in both Sexes should be bred up from chast hopes to loyall Enjoyments; and when the people slacken, and fall to loosenes, and riot, then doe they as much as if they laid downe their necks for some wily Tyrant to get up and ride. Thus learnt *Cyrus* to tame the *Lydians*, whom by Armes he could not, whilst they kept themselves from Luxury; with one easy Proclamation to set up *Stews*, dancing, feasting, and dicing and he made

Rotchet Apothegmes: bishops' expressions.
Tympany: swollen stomach.
Royall Ball: symbol of sovereignty.
Stews: brothels.

them soone his slaves. I know not what drift the *Prelats* had, whose Brokers they were to prepare, and supple us either for a Forreigne Invasion or Domestick oppression; but this I am sure they took the ready way to despoile us both of *manhood* and *grace* at once, and that in the shamefullest and ungodliest manner upon that day which Gods Law, and even our own reason hath consecrated, that we might have one day at least of seven set apart wherein to examin and encrease our knowledge of God, to meditate, and commune of our [61] Faith, our Hope, our eternall City in Heaven, and to quick'n, withall, the study, and exercise of Charity; at such a time that men should bee pluck't from their soberest and saddest thoughts, and by *Bishops* the pretended *Fathers of the Church* instigated by publique Edict,[55] and with earnest indeavour push't forward to gaming, jigging, wassailing, and mixt dancing is a horror to think. Thus did the Reprobate hireling Preist *Balaam* seeke to subdue the Israelites to *Moab,* if not by force, then by this divellish *Pollicy,* to draw them from the Sanctuary of God to the luxurious, and ribald feasts of *Baal-peor.*[56] Thus have they trespas't not onely against the *Monarchy* of *England,* but of Heaven also, as others, I doubt not, can prosecute against them.

I proceed within my own bounds to shew you next what good Agents they are about the Revennues and Riches of the Kingdome, which declares of what moment they are to *Monarchy,* or what availe. Two Leeches they have that still suck, and suck the Kingdome, their Ceremonies, and their Courts. If any man will contend that Ceremonies bee lawfull under the Gospell, hee may bee answer'd otherwhere. This doubtlesse that they ought to bee many and over-costly, no true *Protestant* will affirme. Now I appeale to all wise men, what an excessive wast of Treasury hath beene within these few yeares in this Land not in the expedient, but in the Idolatrous erection of Temples beautified exquisitely to out-vie [62] the Papists, the costly and deare-bought Scandals, and snares of Images, Pictures, rich Coaps, gorgeous Altar-clothes: and by the courses they tooke, and the opinions they held, it was not likely any stay would be, or any end of their madnes, where a pious pretext is so ready at hand to cover their insatiate desires. What can we suppose this will come to? What other materials than these have built up the *spirituall* BABEL to the height of her Abominations? Beleeve it Sir right truly it may be said, that *Antichrist* is *Mammons* Son. The soure levin of humane Traditions mixt in one putrifi'd Masse with the poisonous dregs of hypocrisie in the hearts of *Prelates* that lye basking in the Sunny warmth of Wealth, and Promotion, is the Serpents Egge that will hatch an *Antichrist* wheresoever, and ingender the same Monster as big, or little as the Lump is which breeds him. If the splendor of *Gold* and *Silver* begin to Lord it once againe in the Church of *England,* wee shall see *Antichrist* shortly wallow heere, though his cheife Kennell be at *Rome.* If they had one thought upon *Gods glory* and the advancement of Christian Faith, they would be a meanes that with these expences thus profusely throwne away in trash, rather *Churches* and *Schools* might be built, where they cry out for want, and more added where too few are; a moderate maintenance distributed to every painfull Minister, that now scarse sustaines his Family with Bread, while the *Prelats* revell like [63] *Belshazzar* with their full carouses in *Goblets,* and *vessels* of *gold* snatcht from *Gods Temple.* Which (I hope) the Worthy Men of our Land will consider. Now then for their COURTS, What a Masse of Money is drawne from the Veines into the Ulcers of the Kingdome this way; their Extortions, their open Corruptions, the multitude of hungry and ravenous Harpies that swarme about their Offices declare sufficiently. And what though all this go not oversea? 'twere better it did: better a penurious Kingdom, than where excessive wealth flowes into the *gracelesse* and injurious hands of common sponges to the impoverishing of good and loyall men, and that by such execrable, such irreligious courses.

If the sacred and dreadfull works of holy *Discipline, Censure, Pennance, Excommunication,* and *Absolution,* where no prophane thing ought to have accesse, nothing to be assistant but sage and Christianly *Admonition,* brotherly *Love,* flaming *Charity,* and *Zeale;* and then according to the Effects, Paternall *Sorrow,* or Paternall *Joy,* milde *Severity* melting *Compassion,* if such Divine *Ministeries* as these, wherin the Angel of the *Church* represents the Person of *Christ Jesus,* must lie prostitute to sordid Fees, and not passe to and fro betweene our Saviour that of free grace redeem'd us, and the submissive Penitent, without the truccage of perishing Coine, and the Butcherly execution of Tormentors, Rooks, and Rakeshames sold to lucre, then have the Babilonish [64] Marchants of *Soules* just excuse. Hitherto Sir you have heard how the *Prelates* have weaken'd and withdrawne the externall Accomplishments of Kingly prosperity, the love of the People, their multitude, their valour, their wealth; mining, and sapping the out-works, and redoubts of *Monarchy;* now heare how they strike at the very heart, and vitals.

We know that *Monarchy* is made up of two parts, the Liberty of the subject, and the supremacie of the King. I begin at the root. See what gentle, and benigne Fathers they have beene to our lib-

painfull: painstaking.

erty. Their trade being, by the same Alchymy that the *Pope* uses, to extract heaps of *gold,* and *silver* out of the drossie *Bullion* of the Peoples sinnes, and justly fearing that the quick-sighted *Protestants* eye clear'd in great part from the mist of Superstition, may at one time or other looke with a good judgement into these their deceitfull Pedleries, to gaine as many associats of guiltines as they can, and to infect the temporall Magistrate with the like lawlesse though not sacrilegious extortion, see a while what they doe; they ingage themselves to preach, and perswade an assertion for truth the most false, and to this *Monarchy* the most pernicious and destructive that could bee chosen. What more banefull to *Monarchy* than a Popular Commotion, for the dissolution of *Monarchy* slides aptest into a *Democraty;* and what stirs the Englishmen, as our wisest writers have observ'd, sooner to rebellion, than vio-[65]lent, and heavy hands upon their goods and purses? Yet these devout *Prelates,* spight of our great Charter, and the soules of our Progenitors that wrested their liberties out of the *Norman* gripe with their dearest blood and highest prowesse, for these many years have not ceas't in their Pulpits wrinching, and spraining the *text,* to set at nought and trample under foot all the most sacred, and life blood Lawes, Statutes, and Acts of *Parliament* that are the holy Cov'nant of Union, and Marriage betweene the King and his Realme, by proscribing, and confiscating from us all the right we have to our owne bodies, goods and liberties. What is this, but to blow a trumpet, and proclaime a fire-crosse to a hereditary, and perpetuall civill warre. Thus much against the Subjects Liberty hath been assaulted by them. Now how they have spar'd Supremacie, or likely are hereafter to submit to it, remaines lastly to bee consider'd.

The emulation that under the old Law was in the King toward the *Preist,* is now so come about in the Gospell, that all the danger is to be fear'd from the *Preist* to the *King.* Whilst the *Preists Office* in the Law was set out with an exteriour lustre of Pomp and glory, Kings were ambitious to be *Preists;* now *Priests* not perceiving the heavenly brightnesse, and inward splendor of their more glorious *Evangelick Ministery* with as great ambition affect to be Kings; as in all their courses is easie to be observ'd. Their eyes ever imminent [66] upon worldly matters, their desires ever thirsting after worldly employments, in stead of diligent and fervent studie in the Bible, they covet to be expert in Canons, and Decretals, which may inable them to judge, and interpose in temporall Causes, however pretended *Ecclesiasticall.* Doe they not hord up *Pelfe,* seeke to bee potent in *secular Strength,* in *State Affaires,* in *Lands, Lordships,* and

fire-crosse: sign used to call men together for war.

Demeanes, to *sway* and carry all before them in *high Courts,* and *Privie Counsels,* to bring into their grasp, the *high,* and *principall Offices* of the Kingdom? have they not been bold of late to check the *Common Law,* to slight and brave the indiminishable Majestie of our highest Court the Law-giving and Sacred *Parliament?*[57] Doe they not plainly labour to exempt *Churchmen* from the *Magistrate?* Yea, so presumptuously as to question, and menace *Officers* that represent the *Kings Person* for using their Authority against drunken *Preists?* The cause of protecting *murderous Clergie-men* was the first heart-burning that swel'd up the audacious *Becket* to the pestilent, and odious vexation of *Henry* the second. Nay more, have not some of their devoted Schollers begun, I need not say to nibble, but openly to argue against the Kings *Supremacie?* is not the Cheife of them accus'd out of his owne Booke, and his *late Canons* to affect a certaine unquestionable *Patriarchat,* independent and unsubordinate to the Crowne?[58] From whence having first brought us to a servile *Estate* of *Religion,* [67] and *Manhood,* and having predispos'd his conditions with the *Pope,* that layes claime to this *Land,* or some *Pepin* of his owne creating, it were all as likely for him to aspire to the *Monarchy* among us, as that the *Pope* could finde meanes so on the sudden both to bereave the Emperour of the *Roman Territory* with the favour of *Italy,* and by an unexpected friend out of *France,* while he was in danger to lose his *new-got Purchase,* beyond hope to leap in to the faire *Exarchat* of *Ravenna.*

A good while the *Pope* suttl'y acted the *Lamb,* writing to the Emperour, my Lord *Tiberius,* my Lord *Mauritius,* but no sooner did this his Lord pluck at the Images, and Idols, but hee threw off his Sheepes clothing, and started up a Wolfe, laying his pawes upon the Emperours right, as forfeited to *Peter.* Why may not wee as well, having been forewarn'd at home by our renowned *Chaucer,* and from abroad by the great and learned *Padre Paolo,* from the like beginnings, as we see they are, feare the like events? Certainly a wise, and provident King ought to suspect a *Hierarchy* in his Realme, being ever attended, as it is, with two such greedy Purveyers, Ambition and Usurpation, I say hee ought to suspect a *Hierarchy* to bee as dangerous and derogatory from his Crown as a *Tetrarchy* or a *Heptarchy.* Yet now that the *Prelates* had almost attain'd to what their insolent, and unbrindl'd minds had hurried them; to thrust the Laitie under the despoticall rule of the *Monarch,* that they themselves might con-[68]fine the *Monarch* to a kind of Pupillage under their *Hierarchy,* observe but how their own *Principles* combat one another, and supplant each one his fellow.

Cheife of them: Archbishop Laud.

Having fitted us only for peace, and that a servile peace, by lessening our numbers, dreining our estates, enfeebling our bodies, cowing our free spirits by those wayes as you have heard, their impotent actions cannot sustaine themselves the least moment, unlesse they rouze us up to a *Warre* fit for *Cain* to be the Leader of; an abhorred, a cursed, a Fraternall *Warre*. ENGLAND and SCOTLAND dearest Brothers both in *Nature*, and in CHRIST must be set to wade in one anothers blood; and IRELAND our free Denizon upon the back of us both, as occasion should serve: a piece of Service that the *Pope* and all his Factors have beene compassing to doe ever since the *Reformation*.

But ever-blessed be he, and ever glorifi'd that from his high watch-Tower in the Heav'ns discerning the crooked wayes of perverse, and cruell men, hath hitherto maim'd, and infatuated all their damnable inventions, and deluded their great Wizzards with a delusion fit for fooles and children: had GOD beene so minded hee could have sent a Spirit of *Mutiny* amongst us, as hee did betweene *Abimilech* and the *Sechemites*, to have made our Funerals, and slaine heaps more in number than the miserable surviving remnant, but he, when wee least deserv'd sent out a gentle [69] gale, and message of peace from the wings of those his Cherubins, that fanne his Mercy-seat. Nor shall the *wisdome*, the *moderation*, the *Christian Pietie*, the *Constancy* of our Nobility and Commons of *England* be ever forgotten, whose calme, and temperat connivence could sit still, and smile out the stormy bluster of men more audacious, and precipitant, than of solid and deep reach, till their own fury had run it selfe out of breath, assailing, by rash and heady *approches*, the impregnable situation of our Liberty and safety, that laught such weake enginry to scorne, such poore drifts to make a Nationall Warre of a *Surplice Brabble*, a *Tippet-scuffle*, and ingage the unattainted Honour of *English* Knighthood, to unfurle the streaming *Red Crosse*, or to reare the horrid *Standard* of those fatall *guly* Dragons for so unworthy a purpose, as to force upon their *Fellow-Subjects*, that which themselves are weary of, the *Skeleton* of a *Masse-Booke*. Nor must the *Patience*, the *Fortitude*, the *firme Obedience* of the Nobles and People of *Scotland* striving against manifold Provocations, nor must their sincere and moderate proceedings hitherto, be unremember'd, to the shamefull Conviction of all their Detractors.

Goe on both hand in hand O NATIONS never to be dis-united, be the *Praise* and the *Heroick Song* of all POSTERITY; merit this, but seeke onely *Vertue*, not to extend your Limits; for what

guly: red.

needs? to win a fading triumphant *Lawrell* out of the *teares* of *wretched Men,* but to settle [70] the *pure worship* of *God* in his Church, and *justice* in the State. Then[59] shall the hardest difficulties smooth out themselves before ye; *envie* shall sink to hell, *craft* and *malice* be confounded, whether it be homebred mischeif, or outlandish cunning: yea, other Nations will then covet to serve ye, for Lordship and victory are but the pages of *justice* and *vertue.* Commit securely to true *wisdome* the vanquishing and uncasing of craft and suttletie, which are but her two runnagates: joyn your invincible might to doe worthy, and Godlike deeds, and then he that seeks to break your union, a cleaving curse be his inheritance to all generations.

Sir, you have now at length this question for the time, and as my memory would best serve me in such a copious, and vast theme, fully handl'd, and you your selfe may judge whether Prelacy be the only Church-government agreeable to MONARCHY. Seeing therfore the perillous, and confused estate into which we are faln, and that to the certain knowledge of all men through the irreligious pride and hatefull Tyranny of Prelats (as the innumerable, and grievous complaints of every shire cry out) if we will now resolve to settle affairs either according to pure Religion, or sound Policy, we must first of all begin roundly to cashier, and cut away from the publick body the noysom, and diseased tumor of Prelacie, and come from Schisme to *unity* with our neighbour Reformed sister Churches, [71] which with the blessing of *peace* and *pure doctrine* have now long time flourish'd; and doubtles with all hearty *joy,* and *gratulation,* will meet, and welcome our Christian *union* with them, as they have bin all this while griev'd at our strangenes and little better than separation from them. And for the Discipline propounded, seeing that it hath bin inevitably prov'd that the natural, and fundamental causes of political happines in all governments are the same, and that this Church Discipline is taught in the Word of *God,* and, as we see, agrees according to wish with all such states as have receiv'd it, we may infallibly assure our selvs that it will as wel agree with Monarchy, though all the Tribe of *Aphorismers,* and *Politicasters* would perswade us there be secret, and misterious reasons against it. For upon the setling hereof mark what nourishing and cordial restorements to the State will follow, the Ministers of the Gospel attending only to the work of *salvation* every one within his limited charge, besides the diffusive blessings of *God* upon all our actions, the King shall sit without an old disturber, a dayly incroacher, and intruder; shall ridde his Kingdome of a strong sequester'd, and collateral power; a confronting miter, whose potent wealth, and wakefull ambition he had just cause to hold in jealousie: not to repeat the other present evills which only their removal will remove. And because things simply pure are inconsistent in the masse of nature, nor are the elements [72] or humors in Mans Body exactly *homogeneall*, and hence the best founded Common-wealths, and least barbarous have aym'd at a certaine mixture and temperament, partaking the severall vertues of each other State, that each part drawing to it selfe may keep up a steddy, and eev'n uprightnesse in common.

There is no Civill *Goverment* that hath beene known, no not the *Spartan*, not the *Roman*, though both for this respect so much prais'd by the wise *Polybius*, more divinely and harmoniously tun'd, more equally ballanc'd as it were by the hand and scale of Justice, than is the Common-wealth of *England:* where under a free, and untutor'd *Monarch*, the noblest, worthiest, and most prudent men, with full approbation, and suffrage of the People have in their power the supreame, and finall determination of highest Affaires. Now if Conformity of Church *Discipline* to the Civill be so desir'd, there can be nothing more parallel, more uniform, than when under the Soveraigne Prince *Christs* Vicegerent using the *Scepter* of *David*, according to *Gods Law*, the *godliest*, the *wisest*, the *learnedest* Ministers in their severall charges have the instructing and disciplining of *Gods people* by whose full and free Election they are consecrated to that holy and equall *Aristocracy*. And why should not the Piety, and Conscience of *Englishmen* as members of the Church be trusted in the Election of Pastors to Functions that nothing concerne a *Monarch*, as well as their worldly [73] wisedomes are priviledg'd as *members* of the *State* in suffraging their Knights, and Burgesses to matters that concern him neerely? And if in weighing these severall Offices, their difference in time and qualitie be cast in, I know they will not turn the beame of equall Judgement the moity of a scruple. Wee therfore having already a kind of Apostolicall, and ancient *Church* Election in our State, what a perversnesse would it be in us of all others to retain forcibly a kind of imperious, and stately Election in our *Church*? And what a blindnesse to thinke that what is already Evangelicall as it were by a happy chance in our *Politie*, should be repugnant to that which is the same by divine command in the Ministery? Thus then wee see that our Ecclesiall, and Politicall choyses may consent and sort as well together without any rupture in the STATE, as Christians, and Freeholders. But as for honour, that ought indeed to be different, and distinct as either Office looks a severall way, the Minister whose *Calling* and *end* is

masse of nature: the universe of nature.

spirituall, ought to be honour'd as a Father and Physitian to the Soule (if he be found to be so) with a *Son*-like and *Disciple*-like reverence, which is indeed the dearest, and most affectionate *honour*, most to be desir'd by a wise man, and such as will easily command a free and plentifull provision of outward necessaries, without his furder care of this world.

The Magistrate whose Charge is to see to our Persons, and Estates, is to bee honour'd with [74] a more elaborate and personall *Courtship*, with large Salaries and Stipends, that hee himselfe may abound in those things whereof his legall justice and watchfull care gives us the quiet enjoyment. And this distinction of Honour will bring forth a seemly and gracefull Uniformity over all the Kingdome.

Then shall the Nobles possesse all the Dignities and Offices of temporall honour to themselves, sole Lords without the improper mixture of Scholastick, and pusillanimous upstarts, the *Parliament* shall void her *Upper House* of the same annoyances, the Common, and Civill *Lawes* shall be both set free, the former from the controule, the other from the meere vassalage and *Copy-hold* of the *Clergie*.

And wheras *temporall Lawes* rather punish men when they have transgress't, than form them to be such as should transgresse seldomest, wee may conceive great hopes through the showres of Divine Benediction, watering the unmolested and watchfull paines of the *Ministery*, that the whole Inheritance of God will grow up so straight and blamelesse, that the Civill Magistrate may with farre lesse toyle and difficulty, and far more ease and delight steare the tall and goodly *Vessell* of the Common-wealth through all the gusts and tides of the Worlds mutability.

Here I might have ended, but that some Objections, which I have heard commonly flying about, presse mee to the endevour of an answere. [75] We must not run they say into sudden extreams. This is a fallacious Rule, unlesse understood only of the actions of Vertue about things indifferent, for if it be found that those two extreames be *Vice* and *Vertue, Falshood* and *Truth,* the greater extremity of *Vertue* and superlative *Truth* we run into, the more *vertuous,* and the more *wise* wee become; and hee that flying from degenerate and traditionall corruption, feares to shoot himselfe too far into the meeting imbraces of a Divinely-warranted *Reformation,* had better not have run at all. And for the suddennesse it cannot be fear'd. Who should oppose it? The *Papists?* They dare not. The *Protestants* otherwise affected. They were mad. There is nothing will be remoov'd but what to them is profess'dly indifferent. The long affection which the People have borne to it, what for it selfe, what for the odiousnes of *Prelates,* is evident: from the first yeare of Qu. *Elizabeth,* it hath still beene more and more propounded, desir'd, and beseech't, yea sometimes favourably forwarded by the *Parliaments* themselves. Yet if it were sudden and swift, provided still it be from worse to better, certainly wee ought to hie us from evill like a torrent, and rid our selves of corrupt Discipline, as wee would shake fire out of our bosomes.

Speedy and vehement were the *Reformations* of all the good Kings of *Juda,* though the people had beene nuzzl'd in Idolatry never so long before; they fear'd not the bug-bear danger, nor [76] the Lyon in the way that the sluggish and timorous Politician thinks he sees; no more did our Brethren of the *Reformed Churches* abroad; they ventur'd (God being their guide) out of rigid POPERY, into that which wee in mockery call precise *Puritanisme,* and yet wee see no inconvenience befell them.

Let us not dally with God when he offers us a full blessing, to take as much of it as wee think will serve our ends, and turne him back the rest upon his hands, lest in his anger he snatch all from us again. Next they alledge the *antiquity* of *Episcopacy* through all *Ages.* What it was in the *Apostles* time, that questionlesse it must be still, and therein I trust the Ministers will be able to satisfie the *Parliament.* But if *Episcopacie* be taken for *Prelacie,* all the Ages they can deduce it through, will make it no more venerable than *Papacie.*

Most certaine it is (as all our *Stories* beare witnesse) that ever since their comming to the See of *Canterbury* for neere twelve hundred yeares, to speake of them in generall, they have beene in *England* to our Soules a sad and dolefull succession of illiterate and blind guides: to our purses, and goods a wastfull band of robbers, a perpetuall havock, and rapine: To our state a continuall *Hydra* of mischiefe, and molestation, the forge of discord and Rebellion: This is the Trophey of their Antiquity, and boasted Succession through so many Ages. And for those *Prelat-Martyrs* they glory of, they are to bee judg'd what they [77] were by the *Gospel,* and not the *Gospel* to be tried by them.

And it is to be noted that if they were for Bishopricks and Ceremonies, it was in their prosperitie, and fulnes of bread, but in their persecution, which purifi'd them, and neer their death, which was their garland, they plainely dislik'd and condemn'd the Ceremonies, and threw away those Episcopall ornaments wherein they were instal'd, as foolish and detestable, for so the words of *Ridley* at his degradment, and his letter to *Hooper* expressly shew.[60] Neither doth the Author of our Church History[61] spare to record sadly the fall (for so he termes it) and infirmities of these Martyrs, though we would deify them. And why should their Martyrdom more countenance corrupt doctrine, or discipline, than their subscriptions justify their Treason to the Royall blood of this Relm, by diverting and intaling the right of the Crown from the true heires, to the houses of *Northumberland* and *Suffolk*,[62] which had it tooke effect, this present King had in all likelyhood never sat on this Throne, and the happy union of this Iland had bin frustrated.

Lastly, whereas they adde that some the learnedest of the reformed abroad admire our Episcopacy, it had bin more for the strength of the Argument to tell us that som of the wisest *Statesmen* admire it, for thereby we might guesse them weary of the present discipline, as offensive to their State, which is the bugge we feare; but be-[78]ing they are Church-men, we may rather suspect them for some *Prelatizing-spirits* that admire our *Bishopricks*, not *Episcopacy*. The next objection vanishes of it selfe, propounding a doubt, whether a greater inconvenience would not grow from the corruption of any other discipline, than from that of *Episcopacy*. This seemes an unseasonable foresight, and out of order to deferre, and put off the most needfull constitution of one right *discipline*, while we stand ballancing the discommodity's of two corrupt ones. First constitute that which is right, and of it selfe it will discover, and rectify that which swervs, and easily remedy the pretended feare of having a *Pope* in every Parish, unlesse we call the zealous, and meek censure of the Church, a *Popedom*, which who so does let him advise how he can reject the Pastorly *Rod*, and Sheep-hooke of CHRIST, and those cords of love, and not feare to fall under the iron *Scepter* of his anger that will dash him to peeces like a Potsherd.

At another doubt of theirs I wonder; whether this discipline which we desire, be such as can be put in practise within this Kingdom, they say it cannot stand with the common Law, nor with the Kings safety; the government of Episcopacy, is now so weav'd into the common Law: In *Gods* name let it weave out againe; let not humain quillets keep back divine authority. Tis not the common Law, nor the civil, but piety, and justice, that are our foundresses; they stoop [79] not, neither change colour for *Aristocracy*, *democraty*, or *Monarchy*, nor yet at all interrupt their just courses, but farre above the taking notice of these inferior niceties with perfect sympathy, where ever they meet, kisse each other. Lastly, they are fearfull that the discipline which will succeed cannot stand with the Ks. safety. Wherefore? it is but *Episcopacy* reduc't to what it should be, were it not that the Tyranny of *Prelates* under the name

quillets: quibbles.

of *Bishops* hath made our eares tender, and startling, we might call every good Minister a *Bishop*, as every *Bishop*, yea the *Apostles* themselves are call'd Ministers, and the *Angels ministring Spirits*, and the *Ministers* againe *Angels*. But wherein is this propounded government so shrewd? Because the government of assemblies will succeed. Did not the *Apostles* govern the Church by assemblies, how should it else be Catholik, how should it have Communion? Wee count it Sacrilege to take from the rich *Prelates* their Lands, and revenu's which is Sacrilege in them to keep, using them as they doe, and can we think it safe to defraude the living Church of GOD of that right which GOD has given her in assemblies! O but the consequence: Assemblies draw to them the Supremacy of Ecclesiasticall jurisdiction. No surely, they draw no Supremacy, but that authority which CHRIST, and Saint *Paul* in his name conferrs upon them. The K. may still retain the same Supremacy in the Assemblies, as in the *Parliament*, here he can [80] do nothing alone against the common Law, and there neither alone, nor with consent against the Scriptures. But is this all? No, this Ecclesiasticall Supremacy draws to it the power to excommunicate Kings; and then followes the worst that can be imagin'd. Doe they hope to avoyd this by keeping *Prelates* that have so often don it? Not to exemplifie the malapert insolence of our owne *Bishops* in this kind towards our Kings: I shall turn back to the *Primitive*, and pure times, which the objecters would have the rule of reformation to us.

Not an assembly, but one *Bishop* alone, Saint AMBROSE of *Millan*, held *Theodosius* the most Christian Emperor under excommunication above eight moneths together, drove him from the Church in the presence of his Nobles, which the good Emperor bore with heroick *humility*, and never ceas't by prayers, and teares, till he was absolv'd, for which coming to the Bishop with *Supplication* into the *Salutatory*, some out Porch of the Church, he was charg'd by him of tyrannicall madnes against GOD, for comming into holy ground. At last upon conditions absolv'd, and after great *humiliation* approaching to the Altar to offer (as those thrise pure times than thought meet) he had scarse with-drawne his hand, and stood awhile, when a bold Arch-deacon comes in the Bishops name, and chaces him from within the railes telling him peremptorily that the place wherein he stood, was for none [81] but the *Priests* to enter, or to touch: and this is another peece of pure *Primitive Divinity*. Thinke yee then our Bishops will forgoe the power of excommunication on whomsoever? No certainly, unlesse to compasse sinister ends, and then revoke when they see their time. And yet this most

malapert: saucy.

mild, though withall dredfull, and inviolable Prerogative of *Christs* diadem excommunication servs for nothing with them, but to prog, and pandar for fees, or to display their pride and sharpen their revenge, debarring men the protection of the Law, and I remember not whether in some cases it bereave not men all right to their worldly goods, and Inheritances besides the deniall of Christian buriall. But in the Evangelical, and reformed use of this sacred censure, no such prostitution, no such *Iscariotical* drifts are to be doubted, as that *Spirituall* doom, and sentence, should invade worldly possession, which is the rightfull lot and portion, even of the wickedest men, as frankly bestow'd upon them by the al-dispensing bounty, as *rain*, and *Sun-shine*. No, no, it seekes not to bereave or destroy the body, it seekes to save the Soule by humbling the body, not by Imprisonment, or pecuniary mulct, much lesse by stripes or bonds, or disinheritance, but by Fatherly admonishment, and Christian rebuke, to cast it into godly sorrow, whose end is joy, and ingenuous bashfulnesse to sin: if that can not be wrought, then as a tender Mother takes her Child and holds it over the pit with scarring [82] words, that it may learne to feare, where danger is, so doth excommunication as deerly, and as freely without money, use her wholsome and saving terrors, she is instant, she beseeches, by all the deere, and sweet promises of SALVATION she entices and woos, by all the threatnings, and thunders of the *Law*, and rejected *Gosspel* she charges, and adjures; this is all her Armory, her munition, her Artillery, then she awaites with long-sufferance, and yet ardent zeale. In briefe, there is no act in all the errand of *Gods Ministers* to mankind, wherein passes more loverlike contestation betweene CHRIST and the Soule of a regenerate man lapsing, than before, and in, and after the sentence of Excommunication. As for the fogging proctorage of money, with such an eye as strooke *Gehezi* with Leprosy, and *Simon Magus* with a curse, so does she looke, and so threaten her firy whip against that banking den of theeves that dare thus baffle, and buy and sell the awfull, and majestick wrincles of her brow. He that is rightly and apostolically sped with her invisible arrow, if he can be at peace in his Soule, and not smel within him the brimstone of Hell, may have faire leave to tell all his baggs over undiminish't of the least farding, may eat his dainties, drinke his wine, use his delights, enjoy his Lands, and liberties, not the least skin rais'd, not the least haire misplac't for all that excommunication has done: much more may a King injoy his rights, and Prerogatives un-[83]deflower'd, un-

prog: seek advantage by trickery.
fogging: underhand.

touch'd, and be as absolute, and compleat a King, as all his royalties and revenu's can make him. And therefore little did *Theodosius* fear a plot upon his Empire when he stood excommunicat by Saint *Ambrose,* though it were done either with much hauty pride, or ignorant zeale. But let us rather look upon the reformed Churches beyond the seas, the *Grizons,* the *Suisses,* the *Hollanders,* the *French,* that have a Supremacy to live under as well as we, where do the Churches in all these places strive for Supremacy, where do they clash and justle Supremacies with the Civil *Magistrate?* In *France* a more severe Monarchy than ours, the *Protestants* under this Church government carry the name of the best Subjects the King has; and yet *Presbytery,* if it must be so call'd, does there all that it desires to doe: how easie were it, if there be such great suspicion, to give no more scope to it in *England.* But let us not for feare of a scarre-crow, or else through hatred to be reform'd stand hankering and politizing, when GOD with spread hands testifies to us, and points us out the way to our peace.

Let us not be so overcredulous, unlesse GOD hath blinded us, as to trust our deer Soules into the hands of men that beg so devoutly for the pride, and gluttony of their own backs, and bellies, that sue and sollicite so eagerly, not for the saving of Soules, the consideration of which can have heer no place at all, but for their Bishop-[84]ricks, Deaneries, Prebends, and Chanonies; how can these men not be corrupt, whose very cause is the bribe of their own pleading; whose mouths cannot open without the strong breath, and loud stench of avarice, Simony, and Sacrilege, embezling the treasury of the Church on painted, and guilded walles of Temples wherein GOD hath testified to have no delight, warming their Palace Kitchins, and from thence their unctuous, and epicurean paunches, with the almes of the blind, the lame, and the impotent, the aged, the orfan, the widow, for with these the treasury of CHRIST ought to be, here must be his jewels bestow'd, his rich Cabinet must be emptied heer; as the constant martyr Saint *Laurence* taught the *Roman Prætor.* Sir would you know what the remonstrance of these men would have, what their Petition imply's? They intreate us that we would not be weary of those insupportable greevances that our shoulders have hitherto crackt under, they beseech us that we would think 'em fit to be our Justices of peace, our Lords, our highest officers of State, though they come furnish't with no more experience than they learnt betweene the *Cook,* and the *manciple,* or more profoundly at the Colledge *audit,* or the *regent house,* or to come to their deepest insight, at their *Patrons Table;* they

Chanonies: canons or canonries (?).

would request us to indure still the russling of their Silken Cassocks, and that we would burst our *midriffes* rather than laugh to see them under Sayl in all their Lawn, and Sarce-[85]net, their shrouds, and tackle, with a *geometricall rhomboides* upon their heads: they would bear us in hand that we must of duty still appear before them once a year in *Jerusalem* like good circumcizd *males,* and *Females* to be taxt by the poul, to be scons't our head money, our tuppences in their Chaunlerly Shop-book of *Easter.*[63] They pray us that it would please us to let them still hale us, and worrey us with their band-dogs, and Pursivants; and that it would please the *Parliament* that they may yet have the whipping, fleecing, and fleaing of us in their diabolical Courts to tear the flesh from our bones, and into our wide wounds instead of balm, to power in the oil of Tartar, vitriol, and mercury; Surely a right reasonable, innocent, and soft-hearted Petition. O the relenting bowels of the Fathers. Can this bee granted them unlesse GOD have smitten us with frensie from above, and with a dazling giddinesse at noon day? Should not those men rather be heard that come to plead against their owne preferments, their worldly advantages, their owne abundance; for honour, and obedience to *Gods word,* the conversion of Soules, the *Christian peace* of the Land, and *union* of the reformed *Catholick Church,* the *unappropriating,* and *unmonopolizing* the rewards of *learning* and *industry,* from the greasie clutch of ignorance, and high feeding. We have tri'd already, and miserably felt what *ambition wordly glory and immoderat wealth* can do, what the boisterous and contradictional hand of [86] a temporall, earthly, and corporeall Spiritualty can availe to the edifying of Christs holy *Church;* were it such a desperate hazard to put to the venture the universall Votes of *Christs* Congregation, the fellowly and friendly yoke of a teaching and laborious Ministery, the Pastorlike and Apostolick imitation of meeke and unlordly Discipline, the gentle and benevolent mediocritie of Church-maintenance, without the ignoble Hucsterage of pidling *Tithes?* Were it such an incurable mischiefe to make a little triall, what all this would doe to the flourishing and growing up of *Christs* mysticall body? As rather to use every poore shift, and if that serve not, to threaten uproare and combustion, and shake the brand of Civill Discord?

O Sir, I doe now feele my selfe in wrapt on the sodaine into those mazes and *Labyrinths* of dreadfull and hideous thoughts, that which way to get out, or which way to end I know not, unlesse I turne mine eyes, and with your help lift up my hands to that Eternall and Propitious *Throne,* where nothing is readier than *grace* and

geometricall rhomboides: bishops' miters.

refuge to the distresses of mortall Suppliants: and it were a shame to leave these serious thoughts lesse piously than the Heathen were wont to conclude their graver discourses.

Thou therefore that sits't in light and glory unapprochable, *Parent* of *Angels* and *Men!* next thee I implore Omnipotent King, Redeemer of that lost remnant whose nature thou didst assume, [87] ineffable and everlasting *Love!* And thou the third subsistence of Divine Infinitude, *illumining Spirit,* the joy and solace of created *Things!* one *Tri-personall* GODHEAD! looke upon this thy poore and almost spent, and expiring *Church,* leave her not thus a prey to these importunate *Wolves,* that wait and thinke long till they devoure thy tender *Flock,* these wilde *Boares* that have broke into thy *Vineyard,* and left the print of thir polluting hoofs on the Soules of thy Servants. O let them not bring about their damned *designes* that stand now at the entrance of the bottomlesse pit expecting the *Watch-word to open and let out those dreadfull Locusts* and *Scorpions,* to *re-involve* us in that pitchy *Cloud* of infernall darknes, where we shall never more see the *Sunne* of thy *Truth* againe, never hope for the cheerfull dawne, never more heare the *Bird* of *Morning* sing. Be mov'd with pitty at the afflicted state of this our shaken *Monarchy,* that now lies labouring under her throwes, and struggling against the grudges of more dreaded Calamities.

O thou that after the impetuous rage of five bloody Inundations, and the succeeding Sword of intestine *Warre,* soaking the Land in her owne gore, didst pitty the sad and ceasles revolution of our swift and thick-comming sorrowes when wee were quite breathlesse, of thy *free grace* didst motion *Peace,* and termes of Cov'nant with us, and having first welnigh freed us from *Antichristian* thraldome, didst build up this *Britannick Empire* [88] to a glorious and enviable heighth with all her Daughter Ilands about her, stay us in this felicitie, let not the obstinacy of our halfe Obedience and will-Worship bring forth that *Viper* of *Sedition,* that for these Fourescore Yeares hath been breeding to eat through the entrals of our *Peace;* but let her cast her Abortive Spawne without the danger of this travailling and throbbing *Kingdome.* That we may still remember in our *solemne Thanksgivings,* how for us the *Northren Ocean* even to the frozen *Thule* was scatter'd with the proud Ship-wracks of the *Spanish Armado,* and the very maw of Hell ransack't, and made to give up her conceal'd destruction, ere shee could vent it in that horrible and damned blast.

O how much more glorious will those former Deliverances appeare, when we shall know them not onely to have sav'd us from

five bloody Inundations: the five invasions of Britain.

greatest miseries past, but to have reserv'd us for greatest happinesse to come. Hitherto thou hast but freed us, and that not fully, from the unjust and Tyrannous Claime of thy Foes, now unite us intirely, and appropriate us to thy selfe, tie us everlastingly in willing Homage to the *Prerogative* of thy eternall *Throne.*

And now wee knowe, O thou our most certain hope and defence, that thine enemies have been consulting all the Sorceries of the *great Whore,* and have joyn'd their Plots with that sad Intelligencing Tyrant that mischiefes the World with his Mines of *Ophir,* and lies thirsting to revenge [89] his Navall ruines that have larded our Seas; but let them all take Counsell together, and let it come to nought, let them Decree, and doe thou Cancell it, let them gather themselves, and bee scatter'd, let them embattell themselves and bee broken, let them imbattell, and be broken, for thou art with us.

Then amidst the *Hymns,* and *Halleluiahs* of *Saints* some one may perhaps bee heard offering at high *strains* in new and lofty *Measures* to sing and celebrate thy *divine Mercies,* and *marvelous Judgements* in this Land throughout all AGES; whereby this great and Warlike Nation instructed and inur'd to the fervent and continuall practice of *Truth* and *Righteousnesse,* and casting farre from her the *rags* of her old *vices* may presse on hard to that *high* and *happy* emulation to be found the *soberest, wisest,* and *most Christian People* at that day when thou the Eternall and shortly-expected King shalt open the Clouds to judge the severall Kingdomes of the World, and distributing *Nationall Honours* and *Rewards* to Religious and just *Common-wealths,* shalt put an end to all Earthly *Tyrannies,* proclaiming thy universal and milde *Monarchy* through Heaven and Earth. Where they undoubtedly that by their *Labours, Counsels,* and *Prayers* have been earnest for the *Common good* of *Religion* and their *Countrey,* shall receive, above the inferiour *Orders* of the *Blessed,* the *Regall* addition of *Principalities, Legions,* and *Thrones* into their glorious Titles, and in supereminence [90] of *beatifick Vision* progressing the *datelesse* and *irrevoluble* Circle of *Eternity* shall clasp inseparable Hands with *joy,* and *blisse,* in over measure for ever.

But they contrary that by the impairing and diminution of the true *Faith,* the distresses and servitude of their *Countrey* aspire to high *Dignity, Rule* and *Promotion* here, after a shamefull end in this *Life* (which *God* grant them) shall be thrown downe eternally into the *darkest* and *deepest Gulfe* of HELL, where under the *despightfull controule,* the trample and spurne of all the other *Damned,* that in the anguish of their *Torture* shall have no other

whereby: by means of this singing.

ease than to exercise a *Raving* and *Bestiall Tyranny* over them as their *Slaves* and *Negro's,* they shall remaine in that plight for ever, the *basest,* the *lowermost,* the *most dejected,* most *underfoot* and *downe-trodden Vassals* of *Perdition.*

NOTES

1. Kneeling at Communion, wearing of vestments, and the like, were considered by nearly all Christians to be things indifferent: they were not considered necessary for salvation.
2. By the use of images.
3. Milton suggests that both the Laudian and the Roman Catholic ornaments of worship derive from Jewish practices and the practices of pagan priests.
4. The passage seems to reflect Plato's image in the *Phaedrus* that when perfect the soul soars upward.
5. A difficult sentence, perhaps because the text is defective. If "so that" is supplied after "grace," the meaning may be: "And here [on the road of conformity] doubtless as a result of her false conception of God and holy things, she [the soul] would have stopped atheism if custom and the pangs of conscience had not stopped her consequent unbelief in all the duties of grace revealed by the Gospels; so that instead of the freely chosen and cheerful boldness which the New Testament requires, there came to the soul servile and thrall-like fear."
6. Col. ii 8.
7. John xiii 5–12.
8. Rev. xii 4.
9. See 2 Cor. xii 10, Col. i 13, and Rev. xii 3.
10. Parenthesis supplied by the editor.
11. Milton here follows John Foxe's view that the Reformation began with John Wycliffe in the fourteenth century. Milton used the *Acts and Monuments* of Foxe (1516–78) extensively in preparing this work.
12. This pejorative term for *bishops* is often used instead of *bishops* since the latter term is a translation of the scriptural *episcopus.* In *Of Prelatical Episcopacy* Milton argues that the terms *bishops* and *presbyters* are two names for the same order.
13. Parenthesis supplied by the editor.
14. The Protestant John Dudley, Duke of Northumberland, was the most powerful man in England in the last years of the reign of Edward VI. He had his son's wife, Lady Jane Grey, crowned Queen of England on Edward's death.
15. The influential Bishop Ridley supported Lady Jane.
16. Edward refused to sanction what he considered idolatry.
17. Doctor Shaw was the preacher who urged the claim of his patron, Richard, Duke of Gloucester, to the throne in 1483.
18. 1 Cor. xiii 3.
19. Cyprian was bishop of Carthage from 248 until his death in 258.
20. The *Brazen Serpent* was worshiped in the desert by the Jews, according to 2 Kings xviii 4.
21. The *Ecclesiasticall Constitutions* were drafted by Archbishop Cranmer and others in 1544.
22. Sir John Haywood (ca. 1560–1627), author of *The Life and Reigne of King Edward the Sixt* (1630). Milton also used the *Chronicles* (1587) of Ra-

ɪhael Holinshed (d. ca. 1580) and the *Historie of Great Britaine* (1623) of 'ohn Speed (1552–1629).

23. St. Martin and Sulpitius Severus were fourth-century clergymen, associ- ɪted with Tours.

24. William Camden (1551–1623), author of *Annales* (1615), cited here, ɪnd *Britannia* (1610), Milton's authority used elsewhere in this work.

25. Father Ignatius was bishop of Antioch; he died a martyr's death in 107.

26. Emperor Alexander Severus reigned 222–35.

27. Lampridius was an early fourth-century biographer of Alexander Severus.

28. Cedrenus was an early eleventh-century Greek historian and monk.

29. The learned English writer referred to here was probably Foxe in his book *Acts and Monuments*.

30. Archbishop Laud had ordered the Communion tables to be railed in.

31. George Montaigne (1569–1628), Archbishop of York.

32. Eusebius was the great church historian (ca. 260–ca. 340).

33. Hegesippus, a second-century church historian whose works have not survived.

34. Irenaeus, a Greek church father (ca. 125–202).

35. All church fathers.

36. Sir Edwin Sandys (1561–1629). *Europae Speculum* was published in 1638.

37. Acts viii 26–39.

38. Cf. Zech. xiv 20.

39. Lactantius was a Christian apologist (ca. 260–340).

40. Copies examined read *and*.

41. These were three conspirators against Moses who were swallowed up by the earth (Num. xvi 1–34).

42. For Io, see Aeschylus, *Prometheus Bound*.

43. Copies examined have a comma here.

44. Malvezzi was a seventeenth-century commentator on Tacitus.

45. Copies examined have no punctuation.

46. The story is told in Bede's *Ecclesiastical History*, where it is said to have taken place in the second century.

47. *The donation of Constantine* is a reference to a forged document which purported to give the Bishop of Rome great temporal power in Italy.

48. Sigonius was an Italian historian (ca. 1524–84).

49. Chilpericus was king of France and reigned 561–84.

50. The tale is not Chaucer's but anonymous.

51. Tournai is a Flemish city given up to the French in 1518.

52. Paolo Sarpi (1552–1625) served as counselor of state to the Venetian republic in its conflict with Paul V.

53. "No Bishop, no King" was King James's declaration at the Hampton Court Conference in 1604.

54. Menenius Agrippa was the author of a famous fable, rather similar to Milton's.

55. *The Book of Sports*, promulgated in 1618 and again in 1633.

56. See Num. xxii 1–xxv 3.

57. The Church's High Commission made use of the *ex officio* oath, which required a man to testify against himself.

58. This refers to Laud's *Relation of the Conference* and the Canons of 1640 issued by the Convocations of Canterbury and York.

59. Copies examined read *then*.

60. Foxe reports that Bishop Ridley rejected the surplice. What Ridley wrot to Bishop Hooper seems too general to be very useful to Milton.

61. The author of the church history was Foxe.

62. That is, by their support of Lady Jane.

63. Fined an annual fee according to their shopkeeper's Easter offering recor book.

OF PRELATICAL EPISCOPACY, AND WHETHER IT MAY BE DEDUC'D FROM THE APOSTOLICAL TIMES BY VERTUE OF THOSE TESTIMONIES WHICH ARE ALLEDG'D TO THAT PURPOSE IN SOME LATE TREATISES: ONE WHEREOF GOES UNDER THE NAME OF JAMES ARCH-BISHOP OF ARMAGH.

London, Printed for R. O. and G. D. for Thomas Underhill, and are to be sold at the signe of the Bible, in Wood-Street, 1641.

Of Prelatical Episcopacy, Milton's second attack on the hierarchical system of the Church of England, appeared in June or July 1641. It is a brief work, the shortest of the attacks, but combines two closely related purposes. It is, first, a detailed refutation of Archbishop James Ussher's *The Judgement of Doctor Rainoldes* (May 1641), a tract which sought to prove that bishops constitute an order separate from and superior to that of presbyters. Second, it is an attempt to gain popular support for the concept that, on the contrary, the terms *presbyter* and *bishop* originally were two names for the same office. Both purposes were important to Milton, though the second purpose led to livelier writing. The chief technique he exploited was the use of associations: he identifies his position with all good things, especially purity and the Bible, and associates the position of his opponents with all things unpleasant.[1]

For example, Milton thus describes the desire to look to the Fathers as an important source of authority:

> men began to have itching eares, then not contented with the plentifull and wholsom fountaines of the Gospell, they began after their

[1] Cf. J. Max Patrick's comments in the *Yale Milton*, I, 619–20.

> owne lusts to heap to themselvs teachers, and as if the divine Scripture wanted a supplement, and were to be eek't out, they cannot think any doubt resolv'd, and any doctrine confirm'd, unlesse they run to that indigested heap, and frie of Authors, which they call Antiquity. Whatsoever time, or the heedlesse hand of blind chance, hath drawne down from of old to this present, in her huge dragnet, whether Fish, or Sea-weed, Shells, or Shrubbs, unpickt, unchosen, those are the Fathers. (1641 ed., pp. 2–3.)

The words of a fifth-century bishop, Leontius, cited by his opponents, are in Milton's judgment worthless because of the vested interests of these prelates; they are not reliable witnesses of the primitive nature of episcopacy. Moreover, their judgment on other matters is so ill-informed and unsound as to make their views on the authority of bishops suspect. Reliable sources, such as the church historian Eusebius, are cautious.

> Thus while we leave the Bible to gadde after these traditions of the ancients, we heare the ancients themselvs confessing, that what knowledge they had in this point was such as they had gather'd from the Bible. (P. 6.)

Milton pays special attention to the authority of works associated with the name of Ignatius (ca. 70–ca. 107), for Ignatius was a keystone in his opponents' position.

> Had *God* ever intended that we should have sought any part of usefull instruction from *Ignatius*, doubtles he would not have so ill provided for our knowledge, as to send him to our hands in this broken and disjoynted plight; and if he intended no such thing, we doe injuriously in thinking to tast better the pure Evangelick Manna by seasoning our mouths with the tainted scraps, and fragments of an unknown table; and searching among the verminous, and polluted rags dropt overworn from the toyling shoulders of Time, with these deformedly to quilt, and interlace the intire, the spotlesse, and undecaying robe of Truth, the daughter not of Time, but of Heaven, only bred up heer below in Christian hearts, between two grave and holy nurses the Doctrine, and Discipline of the Gospel. (P. 11.)

On occasion Milton dramatizes the process by which the primitive teachings of the church became corrupted.

> Where ever a man, who had bin any away conversant with the *Apostles*, was to be found, thether flew all the inquisitive eares,

> the exercise of right instructing was chang'd into the curiosity of impertinent fablings: where the mind was to be edified with solid *Doctrine,* there the fancy was sooth'd with solemne stories: with lesse fervency was studied what Saint *Paul,* or Saint *John* had written than was listen'd to one that could say here hee taught, here he stood, this was his stature, and thus he went habited, and O happy this house that harbour'd him, and that cold stone whereon he rested, this Village wherein he wrought such a miracle, and that pavement bedew'd with the warme effusion of his last blood, that sprouted up into eternall Roses to crowne his Martyrdome. Thus while all their thoughts were powr'd out upon circumstances, and the gazing after such men as had sate at table with the *Apostles* (many of which *Christ* hath profest, yea though they had cast out Divells in his name, he will not know at the last day) by this meanes they lost their time, and truanted in the fundamentall grounds of saving knowledge, as was seene shortly by their writings. (P. 14.)

Another authority cited by Milton's opponents was Tertullian. While he admits that Tertullian writes of bishops being appointed by the apostles, Milton denies that the episcopal title is stated to be of a higher order than that of presbyter. But even had Tertullian so declared, Milton notes, his declaration would have been valueless, for he tried to prove that the Son was inferior to the Father. "Beleeve him now for a faithfull relater of tradition, whom you see such an unfaithfull expounder of the Scripture. Besides in his time all allowable tradition was now lost" (p. 17). The position which Milton ascribed to Tertullian is not far removed from the one which Milton himself came to take when he wrote *De Doctrina Christiana.*

The power of Milton's imagery is throughout one of his best weapons. One of his most fully developed is the following:

> Now although, as all men well know, it be the wonted shift of errour, and fond Opinion, when they find themselves outlaw'd by the Bible, and forsaken of sound reason, to betake them with all speed to their old starting hole of tradition, and that wild, and overgrowne Covert of antiquity thinking to farme there at large roome, and find good stabling, yet thus much their owne dëify'de antiquity betrayes them, to informe us that Tradition hath had very seldome or never the gift of perswasion. (P. 19.)

Many Puritans from the early days of Elizabeth's reign had looked to the "best Continental Reformed churches" for a model. Here

Milton recommends their attitude and observes that God has blessed these churches because they have abolished the hierarchy. Continuing to identify his position as *the* Protestant position, Milton persuasively argues that since the Bible is the center of the Protestant religion, not to look to it as to the sole authority is to become susceptible to all manners of corruption.

> He that thinks it the part of a well learned man, to have read diligently the ancient stories of the Church, and to be no stranger in the volumes of the Fathers shall have all judicious men consenting with him; not hereby to controule, and new fangle the Scripture, *God* forbid, but to marke how corruption, and *Apostacy* crept in by degrees, and to gather up, where ever wee find the remaining sparks of Originall truth, wherewith to stop the mouthes of our adversaries, and to bridle them with their own curb, who willingly passe by that which is Orthodoxall in them, and studiously cull out that which is commentitious,[2] and best for their turnes, not weighing the Fathers in the ballance of Scripture, but Scripture in the ballance of the Fathers, if wee therefore making first the Gospell our rule, and Oracle shall take the good which wee light on in the Fathers, and set it to oppose the evill which other men seek from them, in this way of Skirmish wee shall easily master all superstition, and false doctrine; but if we turne this our discreet, and wary usage of them into a blind devotion towards them, and whatsoever we find written by them, wee both forsake our owne grounds, and reasons which led us at first to part from *Rome*, that is to hold to the Scriptures against all antiquity; wee remove our cause into our adversaries owne Court, and take up there those cast[3] principles which will soone cause us to soder up with them againe, in as much as beleeving antiquity for it self in any one point, we bring an ingagement upon our selves of assenting to all that it charges upon us. For suppose we should now neglecting that which is cleare in Scripture, that a Bishop and *Presbyter* is all one both in name, and office . . . then must we bee constrain'd to take upon our selves a thousand superstitions, and falsities which the Papist will prove us downe in from as good authorities, and as ancient, as these that set a Bishop above a *Presbyter*. (Pp. 21–22.)

[2] *commentitious:* fictitious.
[3] *cast:* cast off.

ANIMADVERSIONS UPON THE REMONSTRANTS DEFENCE AGAINST SMECTYMNUUS

London, Printed for Thomas Underhill, and are to be sold at the Signe of the Bible in Woodstreet, 1641.

Almost within a month of the appearance of *Prelatical Episcopacy*, Milton published a third attack; his *Animadversions upon the Remonstrants Defence against Smectymnuus* appeared in July 1641. The five Puritan divines[1] who called themselves Smectymnuus, had with Milton's help attacked Bishop Joseph Hall's defense of episcopacy; in time Hall had answered them. It was at this point that Milton entered the fray again.

Milton answers Hall in *Animadversions* by quoting him, without concern for the context of the quotation, then commenting satirically on it.[2] The satire, though often very effective, can hardly be called fair, and Milton himself was aware that his attack might seem improper to some. In the preface he defends his language.

> *Wee all know that in private and personall injuries, yea in publique sufferings for the cause of Christ, his rule and example teaches us to be so farre from a readinesse to speak evill, as not to answer the reviler in his language though never so much provok't. Yet in the detecting, and convincing of any notorious enimie to truth and his Countries peace, especially that is conceited to have a voluble and smart fluence of tongue, and in the vaine confidence of that, and out of a more tenacious cling to worldly respects, stands up for all the rest to justifie a long usurpation and convicted Pseudepiscopy of Prelates, with all their ceremonies, Liturgies, and tyrannies which*

1 Stephen Marshall, Edward Calamy, Thomas Young, Matthew Newcomen, William Spurstow.

2 See J. Milton French, "Milton as Satirist," *PMLA*, LI (1936), 414–29.

God and man are now ready to explode and hisse out of the land, I suppose and more then suppose, it will be nothing disagreeing from Christian meeknesse to handle such a one in a rougher accent, and to send home his haughtinesse well bespurted with his owne holy-water. . . . And although in the serious uncasing of a grand imposture (for to deale plainly with you Readers, Prelatry is no better) there be mixt here and there such a grim laughter, as may appeare at the same time in an austere visage, it cannot be taxt of levity or insolence: for even this veine of laughing (as I could produce out of grave Authors) hath oft-times a strong and sinewy force in teaching and confuting; nor can there be a more proper object of indignation and scorne together than a false Prophet taken in the greatest dearest and most dangerous cheat, the cheat of soules: in the disclosing whereof if it be harmfull to be angry, and withall to cast a lowring smile, when the properest object calls for both, it will be long enough ere any be able to say why those two most rationall faculties of humane intellect anger and laughter were first seated in the brest of man. (Pp. 1–2, 3–4.)[3]

Though *Animadversions* has no clear plan, the vigor of its language carries the reader along. Some of Milton's wittier comments follow.

Wee know where the shoo wrings you, you fret, and are gall'd at the quick, and O what a death it is to the Prelates to be thus unvisarded, thus unca'sd, to have the Periwigs pluk't off that cover your baldnesse, your inside nakednesse thrown open to publick view. The *Romans* had a time once every year, when their Slaves might freely speake their minds, twere hard if the free borne people of *England*, with whom the voyce of Truth for these many yeares, even against the proverb, hath not bin heard but in corners, after all your Monkish prohibitions, and expurgatorious indexes, your gags and snaffles, your proud *Imprimaturs* not to be obtain'd without the shallow surview,[4] but not shallow hand of some mercenary, narrow Soul'd, and illitterate Chaplain; when liberty of speaking, than which nothing is more sweet to man, was girded, and straight lac't almost to a broken-winded tizzick,[5] if now at a good time, our time of *Parliament*, the very jubily, and resurrection of the State, if now the conceal'd, the aggreev'd, and long persecuted Truth, could not

[3] The biographical context of this passage is set forth by Allan H. Gilbert in "Milton's Defense of Bawdry," *SAMLA Studies in Milton*, ed. J. Max Patrick (Gainesville, Fla., 1953), pp. 54–71.

[4] *surview:* survey.

[5] *tizzick:* lung disease, consumption.

be suffer'd speak, and though she burst out with some efficacy of words, could not be excus'd after such an injurious strangle of silence, nor avoyde the censure of Libelling, twere hard, twere something pinching in a Kingdome of free spirits. (Pp. 7–8.)

Nothing will cure this mans understanding, but some familiar, and Kitchin phisick; which with pardon must for plainnes sake be administer'd to him. Call hither your Cook. The order of Breakfast, Dinner, and Supper, answere me, is it set or no? Set. Is a man therefore bound in the morning to potcht eggs, and vinnegar, or at noon to Brawn, or Beefe, or at night to fresh Sammon, and French Kickshoes?[6] may he not make his meales in order, though he be not bound to this, or that viand? doubtlesse the neat finger'd Artist will answer yes, and help us out of this great controversy without more trouble. Can we not understand an order in Church assemblies of praying, reading, expounding, and administering, unlesse our praiers be still the same Crambe of words? (P. 17.)

At times Milton's idealism is mixed with bitter scorn in a combination which is peculiarly Miltonic, as in his objection to a hireling ministry.

Was morall vertue so lovely, and so alluring, and heathen men so enamour'd of her, as to teach and study her with greatest neglect and contempt of worldly profit and advancement; and is Christian piety so homely and so unpleasant and Christian men so cloy'd with her, as that none will study and teach her, but for lucre and preferment! O Stale-growne piety! O Gospell rated as cheap as thy Master, at thirty pence, and not worth the study, unlesse thou canst buy those that will sell thee! (P. 54.)

The Cave of Mammon (borrowed from Spenser), which hireling ministers enter, is considered by Milton to be a force which prevents Platonic ascent to the contemplation of God.

Certainly never any cleare spirit nurst up from brighter influences with a soule inlarg'd to the dimensions of spacious art and high knowledge ever enter'd there but with scorn, and thought it ever foule disdain to make pelf or ambition the reward of his studies, it being the greatest honor, the greatest fruit and proficiency of learned studies to despise these things. Not liberal science, but illiberal must that needs be that mounts in contemplation meerely for money. And what would it avail us to have a hireling Clergy

6 *French Kickshoes:* fancy dishes.

though never so learned? For such can have neither true wisdom nor grace, and then in vain do men trust in learning, where these be wanting. If in lesse noble and almost mechanik arts according to the difinitions of those Authors, he is not esteem'd to deserve the name of a compleat Architect, an excellent Painter, or the like, that beares not a generous mind above the peasantly regard of wages, and hire; much more must we thinke him a most imperfect, and incompleate Divine, who is so farre from being a contemner of filthy lucre; that his whole divinity is moulded and bred up in the beggarly, and brutish hopes of a fat Prebendary, Deanery, or Bishoprick, which poore and low pitch't desires, if they doe but mixe with those other heavenly intentions that draw a man to this study, it is justly expected that they should bring forth a base born issue of Divinity like that of those imperfect, and putrid creatures that receive a crawling life from two most unlike procreants the Sun, and mudde. (Pp. 54–55.)

Once again Milton identifies his cause with the pure doctrine of Scripture.

Wee shall adhere close to the Scriptures of God which hee hath left us as the just and adequate measure of truth, fitted, and proportion'd to the diligent study, memory, and use of every faithfull man, whose every part consenting and making up the harmonious *Symmetry* of compleat instruction, is able to set out to us a perfect man of God or *Bishop* throughly furnish't to all the good works of his charge: and with this weapon, without stepping a foot further, wee shall not doubt to batter, and throw down your *Nebuchadnezzars* Image and crumble it like the chaffe of the Summer threshing floores, as well the gold of those Apostolick Successors that you boast of, as your *Constantinian* silver, together with the iron, the brasse, and the clay of those muddy and strawy ages that follow. (P. 32.)

The optimism which is so famous in *Areopagitica* is found here too.

But in a *Protestant* Nation that should have throwne off these tatter'd Rudiments long agoe, after the many strivings of Gods Spirit, and our fourscore yeares vexation of him in this our wildernesse since Reformation began, to urge these rotten Principles, and twit us with the present age, which is to us an age of ages wherein God is manifestly come downe among us, to doe some remarkable good to our Church or state, is as if a man should taxe the renovating and re-ingendring Spirit of God with innovation, and that new creature for an upstart noveltie; yea the new Jerusalem, which without your admired linke of succession descends from Heaven, could not scape some such like censure. (P. 35.)

Every one can say that now certainly thou hast visited this land, and hast not forgotten the utmost corners of the earth, in a time when men had thought that thou wast gone up from us to the farthest end of the Heavens, and hadst left to doe marvellously among the sons of these last Ages. O perfect, and accomplish thy glorious acts; for men may leave their works unfinisht, but thou art a God, thy nature is perfection; shouldst thou bring us thus far onward from *Egypt* to destroy us in this Wildernesse though wee deserve; yet thy great name would suffer in the rejoycing of thine enemies, and the deluded hope of all thy servants. When thou hast settl'd peace in the Church, and righteous judgement in the Kingdome, then shall all thy Saints addresse their voyces of joy, and triumph to thee, standing on the shoare of that red Sea into which our enemies had almost driven us. . . . Come forth out of thy Royall Chambers, O Prince of all the Kings of the earth, put on the visible roabes of thy imperiall Majesty, take up that unlimited Scepter which thy Almighty Father hath bequeath'd thee; for now the voice of thy Bride calls thee, and all creatures sigh to bee renew'd. (Pp. 38, 39.)

THE REASON OF CHURCH-GOVERNEMENT URG'D AGAINST PRELATY BY MR. JOHN MILTON.

In two Books.

London, Printed by E. G. for John Rothwell, and are to be sold at the Sunne in Pauls Church-yard. 1641.

The longest of Milton's anti-prelatical treatises is *The Reason of 'hurch-Governement Urg'd against Prelaty.* Written sometime dur-ıg the six months following the publication of *Animadversions,* this vork was published early in 1642 (though dated 1641, Old Style, n its title page). Instead of addressing those who were already ollowing the debate, Milton here speaks to a wider audience. His ppeal is to his audience's ethical sense; perhaps for that reason Ailton appears to commit himself heart, soul, and mind to his cause. *'hurch-Governement* is Milton's first signed pamphlet.

As early as the preface one feels the presence of the man in his vork. It is almost as if Milton sought his readers' approval for him-elf so that they might as a consequence approve his position.

> And if any man incline to thinke I undertake a taske too difficult for my yeares, I trust through the supreme inlightning assistance farre otherwise; for my yeares, be they few or many, what imports it? so they bring reason, let that be lookt on: and for the task, from hence that the question in hand is so needfull to be known at this time chiefly by every meaner capacity, and containes in it the explication of many admirable and heavenly privileges reacht out to us by the Gospell, I conclude the task must be easie. God having to this end ordain'd his Gospell to be the revelation of his power and wisdome in Christ Jesus. And this is one depth of his wisdome, that he could so plainly reveale so great a measure of it to the grosse distorted apprehension of decay'd mankinde. Let others therefore dread and shun the Scriptures for their darknesse, I shall wish I

may deserve to be reckon'd among those who admire and dwel upon them for their clearnesse. (Pp. 2–3.)

In the first chapter Milton offers a particularly revealing portr of the ideal ruler, one who is

> a true knower of himselfe, and himselfe in whom contemplation and practice, wit, prudence, fortitude, and eloquence must be rarely met, both to comprehend the hidden causes of things, and span in his thoughts all the various effects that passion or complexion can worke in mans nature; and hereto must his hand be at defiance with gaine, and his heart in all vertues heroick. (P. 4.)

In *Church-Governement* Milton's argument is that the polity the church is so important that God through the Bible has pr scribed its proper form. It is, then, to the Bible that Milton tur for evidence to support his position. His tone is nearly always di nified, largely because the prelate being addressed is Archbisho James Ussher again, and for him Milton shows a respectful attitu quite different from that shown to Bishop Hall. (*Church-Govern ment* is in part a reply to *Certaine Briefe Treatises*, 1641, whic includes an essay by Ussher.) Milton can nonetheless indulge i harsh irony at times, as when he satirizes the bishops' eagerness t support their position with appeals to antiquity:

> . . . they are so insatiable of antiquity, I should have gladly assented, and confest them yet more ancient. For *Lucifer* before *Adam* was the first prelat Angel, and both he, as is commonly thought, and our forefather *Adam*, as we all know, for aspiring above their orders, were miserably degraded. (P. 11.)

This comparison of the sin of Adam and Lucifer to that of the prel ates pleasantly adumbrates Milton's use of the chain of being i *Paradise Lost*.[1] His belief that acceptance of the ordained order i crucial was perhaps responsible for the vigor of his denunciation o the bishops: they rejected what Milton conceived to be the ordaine order. Thus he sees episcopacy as

> a meere childe of ceremony, or likelier some misbegotten thing, that having pluckt the gay feathers of her obsolet bravery to hide

[1] In "Links between Poetry and Prose in Milton," *English Studies*, XXXVI (1956), 49–62, J. B. Broadbent explores the symbolic, metaphorical, descrip tive, and verbal links; he especially notes connections between the anti-prelatica treatises and *Paradise Lost*.

her own deformed barenesse, now vaunts and glories in her stolne plumes. (P. 12.)

After showing the fallaciousness of grounding episcopacy on Old Testament precedents or contending that it helps prevent schism, Milton considers the contemporary situation. In anticipation of his thesis in *Areopagitica,* he argues that men should be permitted freedom even at the risk of their choosing wrongly; they should be permitted to choose from a variety of religious sects.

As for those many Sects and divisions rumor'd abroad to be amongst us, it is not hard to perceave that they are partly the meere fictions and false alarmes of the Prelates, thereby to cast amazements and panick terrors into the hearts of weaker Christians that they should not venture to change the present deformity of the Church for fear of I know not what worse conveniencies. . . .

It may suffice us to be taught by S. *Paul* that there must be sects for the manifesting of those that are sound hearted. These are but winds and flaws to try the floting vessell of our faith whether it be stanch and sayl well, whether our ballast be just, our anchorage and cable strong. By this is seene who lives by faith and certain knowledge, and who by credulity and the prevailing opinion of the age; whose vertue is of an unchangeable graine, and whose of a slight wash.[2] If God come to trie our constancy we ought not to shrink, or stand the lesse firmly for that, but passe on with more stedfast resolution to establish the truth though it were through a lane of sects and heresies on each side. Other things men do to the glory of God: but sects and errors it seems God suffers to be for the glory of good men, that the world may know and reverence their true fortitude and undaunted constancy in the truth. Let us not therefore make these things an incumbrance, or an excuse of our delay in reforming, which God sends us as an incitement to proceed with more honour and alacrity. For if there were no opposition where were the triall of an unfained goodnesse and magnanimity? Vertue that wavers is not vertue, but vice revolted from it selfe, and after a while returning. (Pp. 28–29.)

The preface to the second of the two books which constitute *The Reason of Church-Governement* is, as E. S. Le Comte puts it, "the most enduring part."[3] Much of this eloquent prose has the further attraction of being autobiographical.

[2] The permanent contrasted with the ephemeral.
[3] *A Milton Dictionary* (New York, 1961), p. 283.

Milton thus writes of his dedication to truth in his prelatical works.

For surely to every good and peaceable man it must in nature needs be a hatefull thing to be the displeaser, and molester of thousands; much better would it like him doubtlesse to be the messenger of gladnes and contentment, which is his chief intended busines, to all mankind, but that they resist and oppose their own true happinesse. But when God commands to take the trumpet and blow a dolorous or a jarring blast, it lies not in mans will what he shall say, or what he shall conceal. (P. 34.)

For me I have determin'd to lay up as the best treasure, and solace of a good old age, if God voutsafe it me, the honest liberty of free speech from my youth, where I shall think it available in so dear a concernment as the Churches good. For if I be either by disposition, or what other cause too inquisitive, or suspitious of my self and mine own doings, who can help it? but this I foresee, that should the Church be brought under heavy oppression, and God have given me ability the while to reason against that man that should be the author of so foul a deed, or should she by blessing from above on the industry and courage of faithfull men change this her distracted estate into better daies without the lest furtherance or contribution of those few talents which God at that present had lent me, I foresee what stories I should heare within my selfe, all my life after, of discourage and reproach. Timorous and ingratefull, the Church of God is now again at the foot of her insulting enemies: and thou bewailst, what matters it for thee or thy bewailing? when time was, thou couldst not find a syllable of all that thou hadst read, or studied, to utter in her behalfe. Yet ease and leasure was given thee for thy retired thoughts out of the sweat of other men. Thou hadst the diligence, the parts, the language of a man, if a vain subject were to be adorn'd or beautifi'd, but when the cause of God and his Church was to be pleaded, for which purpose that tongue was given thee which thou hast, God listen'd if he could heare thy voice among his zealous servants, but thou wert domb as a beast; from hence forward be that which thine own brutish silence hath made thee. Or else I should have heard on the other eare, slothfull, and ever to be set light by, the Church hath now overcom her late distresses after the unwearied labours of many her true servants that stood up in her defence; thou also wouldst take upon thee to share amongst them of their joy: but wherefore thou? where canst thou shew any word or deed of thine which might have hasten'd her peace; what ever thou dost now talke, or write, or look is the almes of other mens active prudence and zeale. Dare not now to say, or doe any thing better than thy former sloth and infancy, or if thou darst, thou dost impudently to make a thrifty purchase of boldnesse to thy selfe out of the painfull merits of other men: what before was thy sin, is now thy duty to be, abject, and worthlesse. These and such like lessons as these, I know would have been my Matins duly, and my Even-song. But now by this litle diligence, mark what a privilege I have gain'd; with good men and Saints to clame my right of lamenting the tribulations of the Church, if she should suffer, when others that have ventur'd nothing for her sake, have not the honour to be admitted mourners. But if she lift up her drooping head and prosper, among those that have something more than wisht her welfare, I have my charter and freehold of rejoycing to me and my heires. (Pp. 35–36.)

Milton then confesses, in a very famous passage, that the cause of truth has kept him from that to which he has dedicated himself: poetry as a *magister vitae*.

. . . if I hunted after praise by the ostentation of wit and learning, I should not write thus out of mine own season, when I have neither yet compleated to my minde the full circle of my private studies, although I complain not of any insufficiency to the matter in hand, or were I ready to my wishes, it were a folly to commit any thing elaborately compos'd to the carelesse and interrupted listening of these tumultuous times. Next if I were wise only to mine own ends, I would certainly take such a subject as of it self might catch applause, whereas this hath all the disadvantages on the contrary, and such a subject as the publishing whereof might be delayd at pleasure, and time enough to pencill it over with all the curious touches of art, even to the perfection of a faultlesse picture, whenas in this argument the not deferring is of great moment to the good speeding, that if solidity have leisure to doe her office, art cannot have much. Lastly, I should not chuse this manner of writing wherin knowing my self inferior to my self, led by the genial power of nature to another task, I have the use, as I may account it, but of my left hand. And though I shall be foolish in saying more to this purpose, yet since it will be such a folly, as wisest men going about to commit, have only confest and so committed, I may trust with more reason, because with more folly to have courteous pardon. For although a Poet soaring in the high region of his fancies with his garland and singing robes about him might without apology speak more of himself than I mean to do, yet for me sitting here below in the cool element of prose, a mortall thing among many readers of no Empyreall[4] conceit, to venture and divulge unusual things of my selfe, I shall petition to the gentler sort, it may not be envy to me. I must say therefore that after I had from my first yeeres by the ceaselesse diligence and care of my father, whom God recompence, bin exercis'd to the tongues, and some sciences, as my age would suffer, by sundry masters and teachers both at home and at the schools, it was found that whether ought was impos'd me by them that had the overlooking, or betak'n to of mine own choise in English, or other tongue, prosing or versing, but chiefly this latter, the stile by certain vital signes it had, was likely to live. But much latelier in the privat Academies of *Italy,* whither I was favor'd to resort, perceiving that some trifles which I had in memory, compos'd at under twenty or thereabout (for the manner is that every one must give some proof of his wit and reading there) met with acceptance above what was lookt for, and other things which I had shifted in scarsity of books and conveniences to patch up amongst them, were receiv'd with written Encomiums, which the Italian is not forward to bestow on men of this side the *Alps,* I began thus farre to assent both to them and divers of my friends here at home, and not lesse to an inward prompting which now grew daily upon me, that by labour and intent study (which I take to be my portion in this life) joyn'd with the strong propensity of nature, I might perhaps leave something so written to aftertimes, as they should not willingly let it die. These thoughts at once possest me, and these other. That if *I* were certain to write as men buy Leases, for three lives and downward,[5] there ought no regard be sooner had, than to Gods glory by the honour and instruction of my country. For which cause, and not only for that I knew it would be hard to arrive at the second rank among the Latines, *I* apply'd my selfe to that resolution which *Ariosto* follow'd against the perswasions of *Bembo,*[6] to fix all the industry and art I could unite to the adorning of my native tongue; not to make verbal curiosities the end, that were a toylsom vanity, but to be an interpreter and relater of the best and sagest things among mine own Citizens throughout this Iland in the mother dialect. That what the greatest and choycest wits of *Athens, Rome,* or modern *Italy,* and those Hebrews of old did for their country, I in my proportion with this over and above of being a Christian, might doe for mine: not caring to be once nam'd abroad, though perhaps I could attaine to that, but content with these Brit-

[4] *Empyreall:* elevated.

[5] A lease remaining in force until each of three specified persons have died.

[6] Ariosto is reported to have told the classically oriented Cardinal Bembo that he would rather be one of the great Italian writers than a lesser Latin writer.

ish Ilands as my world, whose fortune hath hitherto bin, that if the Athenians, as some say, made their small deeds great and renowned by their eloquent writers, *England* hath had her noble atchievments made small by the unskilfull handling of monks and mechanicks.

Time servs not now, and perhaps I might seem too profuse to give any certain account of what the mind at home in the spacious circuits of her musing hath liberty to propose to her self, though of highest hope, and hardest attempting, whether that Epick form whereof the two poems of *Homer*, and those other two of *Virgil* and *Tasso* are a diffuse, and the book of *Job* a brief model: or whether the rules of *Aristotle* herein are strictly to be kept, or nature to be follow'd, which in them that know art, and use judgement is no transgression, but an inriching of art. And lastly what King or Knight before the conquest might be chosen in whom to lay the pattern of a Christian *Heroe*. And as *Tasso* gave to a Prince of *Italy* his chois whether he would command him to write of *Godfreys* expedition against the infidels, or *Belisarius* against the Gothes, or *Charlemain* against the Lombards; if to the instinct of nature and the imboldning of art ought may be trusted, and that there be nothing advers in our climat, or the fate of this age, it haply would be no rashnesse from an equal diligence and inclination to present the like offer in our own ancient stories. Or whether those Dramatick constitutions, wherein *Sophocles* and *Euripides* raigne shall be found more doctrinal and exemplary to a Nation, the Scripture also affords us a divine pastoral Drama in the Song of *Salomon* consisting of two persons and a double *Chorus*, as *Origen* rightly judges. And the Apocalyps of Saint *John* is the majestick image of a high and stately Tragedy, shutting up and intermingling her solemn Scenes and Acts with a sevenfold *Chorus* of halleluja's and harping symphonies: and this my opinion the grave autority of *Pareus* commenting that booke is sufficient to confirm. Or if occasion shall lead to imitat those magnifick Odes and Hymns wherein *Pindarus* and *Callimachus* are in most things worthy, some others in their frame judicious, in their matter most an end faulty: But those frequent songs throughout the law and prophets beyond all these, not in their divine argument alone, but in the very critical art of composition may be easily made appear over all the kinds of Lyrick poesy, to be incomparable. These abilities, wheresoever they be found, are the inspired guift of God rarely bestow'd, but yet to some (though most abuse) in every Nation: and are of power beside the office of a pulpit, to inbreed and cherish in a great people the seeds of vertu, and publick civility, to allay the perturbations of the mind, and set the affections in right tune, to celebrate in glorious and lofty Hymns the throne and equipage of Gods Almightinesse, and what he works, and what he suffers to be wrought with high providence in his Church, to sing the victorious agonies of Martyrs and Saints, the deeds and triumphs of just and pious Nations doing valiantly through faith against the enemies of Christ, to deplore the general relapses of Kingdoms and States from justice and Gods true worship. Lastly, whatsoever in religion is holy and sublime, in vertu amiable, or grave, whatsoever hath passion or admiration in all the changes of that which is call'd fortune from without, or the wily suttleties and refluxes of mans thoughts from within, all these things with a solid and treatable smoothnesse to paint out and describe. Teaching over the whole book of sanctity and vertu through all the instances of example with such delight to those especially of soft and delicious temper who will not so much as look upon Truth herselfe, unlesse they see her elegantly drest, that whereas the paths of honesty and good life appear now rugged and difficult, though they be indeed easy and pleasant, they would then appeare to all men both easy and pleasant though they were rugged and difficult indeed. And what a benefit this would be to our youth and gentry, may be soon guest by what we know of the corruption and bane which they suck in dayly from the writings and interludes of libidinous and ignorant Poetasters, who having scars ever heard of that which is the main consistence of a true poem, the choys of such persons as they ought to introduce, and what is morall and decent to each one, doe for the most part lap up vitious principles in sweet pils to be swallow'd down, and make the tast of vertuous documents harsh and sowr. (Pp. 36–40.)

The thing which I had to say, and those intentions which have liv'd within me ever since I could conceiv my self any thing worth to my Countrie, I return to crave excuse that urgent reason hath pluckt from me by an abortive and foredated discovery. And the accomplishment of them lies not but in a power above mans to promise; but that none hath by more studious ways endeavour'd, and with more unwearied spirit that none shall, that I dare almost averre of my self, as farre as life and free leasure will extend, and that the Land had once infranchis'd her self from this impertinent yoke of prelaty, under whose inquisitorius and tyrannical duncery no free and splendid wit can flourish. Neither doe I think it shame to covnant with any knowing reader, that for some few yeers yet I may go on trust with him toward the payment of what I am now indebted, as being a work not to be rays'd from the heat of youth, or the vapours of wine, like that which flows at wast from the pen of some vulgar Amorist, or the trencher fury of a riming parasite, nor to be obtain'd by the invocation of Dame Memory and her Siren daughters, but by devout prayer to that eternall Spirit who can enrich with all utterance and knowledge, and sends out his Seraphim with the hallow'd fire of his Altar to touch and purify the lips of whom he pleases: to this must be added industrious and select reading, steddy observation, insight into all seemly and generous arts and affaires, till which in some measure be compast, at mine own peril and cost I refuse not to sustain this expectation from as many as are not loath to hazard so much credulity upon the best pledges that I can give them. Although it nothing content me to have disclos'd thus much before hand, but that I trust hereby to make it manifest with what small willingnesse I endure to interrupt the pursuit of no lesse hopes than these, and leave a calme and pleasing solitarynes fed with cherful and confident thoughts, to imbark in a troubl'd sea of noises and hoars disputes, put from beholding the bright countenance of truth in the quiet and still air of delightfull studies to come into the dim reflexion of hollow antiquities sold by the seeming bulk, and there befain to club quotations[7] with men whose learning and beleif lies in marginal stuffings, who when they have like good sumpters[8] laid ye down their hors load of citations and fathers at your dore, with a rapsody of who and who were Bishops here or there, ye may take off their packsaddles, their days work is don, and episcopacy, as they think, stoutly vindicated. Let any gentle apprehension that can distinguish learned pains from unlearned drudgery, imagin what pleasure or profoundnesse can be in this, or what honour to deal against such adversaries. But were it the meanest under-service, if God by his Secretary conscience injoyn it, it were sad for me if I should draw back, for me especially, now when all men offer their aid to help ease and lighten the difficult labours of the Church, to whose service by the intentions of my parents and friends *I* was destin'd of a child, and in mine own resolutions, till comming to some maturity of yeers and perceaving what tyranny had invaded the Church, that he who would take Orders must subscribe slave, and take an oath withall, which unlesse he took with a conscience that would retch, he must either strait perjure, or split his faith, *I* thought it better to preferre a blamelesse silence before the sacred office of speaking bought, and begun with servitude and forswearing. Howsoever thus Church-outed by the Prelats, hence may appear the right I have to meddle in these matters, as before, the necessity and constraint appear'd. (Pp. 40–42.)

[7] *club quotations:* argue by citing authorities.
[8] *sumpters:* pack horses.

In Book II Milton argues against episcopacy that it is opposed to three fundamental Christian principles: the function of the minister is to minister; the "foolishness of the Gospel" condemns worldly wisdom and pride; and the health of the individual Christian's spirit is the concern of God's deputy, the minister of the congregation. His conviction that prelatical episcopacy is altogether contrary to Christianity causes him to wonder how it is that studious men should defend such a bad system. The explanation, Milton discovers, is that good men went

> . . . to the Universities to store themselves with good and solid learning, and there unfortunately fed with nothing else, but the scragged and thorny lectures of monkish and miserable sophistry, were sent home again with such a scholastical burre in their throats, as hath stopt and hinderd all true and generous philosophy from entring, crackt their voices for ever with metaphysical gargarisms,[9] and hath made them admire a sort of formal outside men prelatically addicted, whose unchast'nd and unwrought minds never yet initiated or subdu'd under the true lore of religion or moral vertue, which two are the best and greatest points of learning, but either slightly train'd up in a kind of hypocritical and hackny cours of literature to get their living by, and dazle the ignorant, or els fondly overstudied in uselesse controversies, except those which they use with all the specious and delusive suttlety they are able, to defend their prelatical Sparta, having a Gospel and Church-government set before their eyes, as a fair field wherin they might exercise the greatest vertu's, and the greatest deeds of Christian autority in mean fortunes and little furniture of this world, which even the sage heathen writers and those old *Fabritii,* and *Curii*[10] well knew to be a manner of working, than which nothing could lik'n a mortal man more to God, who delights most to worke from within himself, and not by the heavy luggage of corporeal instrument, they understand it not, and think no such matter, but admire and dote upon worldly riches, and honours, with an easie and intemperat life, to the bane of Christianity: yea they and their Seminaries shame not to professe, to petition and never lin pealing our eares that unlesse we fat them like boores, and cramme them as they list with wealth, with Deaneries, and pluralities, with Baronies and stately preferments, all learning and religion will goe underfoot. Which is such a shamelesse, such a bestial plea, and of that odious impudence in Church-men, who should be to us a pattern of temperance and fru-

[9] *gargarisms:* harsh sounds, made in the throat.
[10] *Fabritii and Curii:* Roman consuls famous for virtue.

gal mediocriry, who should teach us to contemn this world, and the gaudy things thereof, according to the promise which they themselves require from us in baptisme, that should the Scripture stand by and be mute, there is not that sect of Philosophers among the heathen to dissolute, no not *Epicurus,* nor *Aristippus* with all his Cyrenaick rout,[11] but would shut his school dores against such greasy sophisters: not any College of Mountebanks, but would think scorn to discover in themselves with such a brazen forehead the outrageous desire of filthy lucre. (Pp. 62–63.)

Milton ends the work with a challenge to Parliament to find any good thing in prelaty.

[11] Cyrenean philosopher and his followers, who taught that pleasure is the chief end of life.

AN APOLOGY AGAINST A PAMPHLET CALL'D A MODEST CONFUTATION OF THE ANIMADVERSIONS UPON THE REMONSTRANT AGAINST SMECTYMNUUS

London, Printed by E. G. for John Rothwell, and are to be sold at the signe of the Sunne in Pauls Church-yard. 1642.

The last of Milton's five attacks on the bishops, *An Apology against a Pamphlet Call'd A Modest Confutation of the Animadversions upon the Remonstrant against Smectymnuus,* appeared in April 1642. In this work Milton replied to a pamphlet entitled *A Modest Confutation of a Slanderous and Scurrilous Libel, Entitled, Animadversions,* which he supposed to have been written by Bishop Joseph Hall and one of his sons. Just as Milton had attacked the worldliness of the clergy, the *Confutation* had attacked Milton's morals. In his reply Milton wrote some of his most important autobiographical passages, though the *Apology* does not bear his name.[1]

Milton begins by attacking his opponents' title, which he fails to find modest or accurate: his *Animadversions,* he protests, are not slanderous or scurrilous. Hall's previous works, especially *Mundus Alter et Idem,* next come under sharp attack. Then Milton considers the attack on his morals in the *Confutation.* He calls it flinging

> out stray crimes at a venture, which he could never, though he be a Serpent, suck from any thing that I have written; but from his own stufft magazin, and hoard of slanderous inventions, over and above that which he converted to venome in the drawing. (P. 11.)

To the charge that he was "vomited out of the University," Milton replies that he is grateful to be given

> an apt occasion to acknowledge publickly with all gratefull minde, that more than ordinary favour and respect which I found above

[1] The *Apology* has been well edited in the *Yale Milton* and separately by M. C. Jochums in 1950.

> any of my equals at the hands of those curteous and learned men, the Fellowes of that Colledge wherein I spent some yeares: who at my parting, after I had taken two degrees, as the manner is, signifi'd many wayes, how much better it would content them that I would stay; as by many Letters full of kindnesse and loving respect both before that time, and long after I was assur'd of their singular good affection towards me. (P. 12.)

The autobiographical passages which follow reveal as much abou[t] an author's attitude toward himself as any passages in literature[.] His mornings, Milton states, he spent

> up, and stirring, in winter often ere the sound of any bell awake men to labour, or to devotion; in Summer as oft with the Bird that first rouses, or not much tardier, to reade good Authors, or cause them to be read, till the attention bee weary, or memory have his full fraught. Then with usefull and generous labours preserving the bodies health, and hardinesse; to render lightsome, cleare, and not lumpish obedience to the minde, to the cause of religion, and our Countries liberty, when it shall require firme hearts in sound bodies to stand and cover their stations, rather than to see the ruine of our Protestation, and the inforcement of a slavish life. (P. 13.)

> I had my time Readers, as others have, who have good learning bestow'd upon them, to be sent to those places, where the opinion was it might be soonest attain'd: and as the manner is, was not unstudied in those authors which are most commended; whereof some were grave Orators and Historians; whose matter me thought I lov'd indeed, but as my age then was, so I understood them; others were the smooth Elegiack Poets, whereof the Schooles are not scarce. Whom both for the pleasing sound of their numerous writing, which in imitation I found most easie; and most agreeable to natures part in me, and for their matter which what it is, there be few who know not, I was so allur'd to read, that no recreation came to me better welcome. For that it was then those years with me which are excus'd though they be least severe, I may be sav'd the labour to remember ye. Whence having observ'd them to account it the chiefe glory of their wit, in that they were ablest to judge, to praise, and by that could esteeme themselves worthiest to love those high perfections which under one or other name they took to celebrate, I thought with my selfe by every instinct and presage of nature which is not wont to be false, that what imbolded them to this task might with such diligence as they us'd imbolden me, and that what judgement, wit, or elegance was my share, would herein

best appeare, and best value it selfe, by how much more wisely, and with more love of vertue I should choose (let rude eares be absent) the object of not unlike praises. For albeit these thoughts to some will seeme vertuous and commendable, to others only pardonable, to a third sort perhaps idle, yet the mentioning of them now will end in serious. Nor blame it Readers, in those yeares to propose to themselves such a reward, as the noblest dispositions above other things in this life have sometimes preferr'd. Whereof not to be sensible, when good and faire in one person meet, argues both a grosse and shallow judgement, and withall an ungentle, and swainish brest. For by the firme setling of these perswasions I became, to my best memory, so much a proficient, that if I found those authors any where speaking unworthy things of themselves; or unchaste of those names which before they had extoll'd, this effect it wrought with me, from that time forward their art I still applauded, but the men I deplor'd; and above them all preferr'd the two famous renowners of *Beatrice* and *Laura* who never write but honour of them to whom they devote their verse, displaying sublime and pure thoughts, without transgression. And long it was not after, when I was confirm'd in this opinion, that he who would not be frustrate of his hope to write well hereafter in laudable things, ought him selfe to bee a true Poem, that is, a composition, and patterne of the best and honourablest things; not presuming to sing high praises of heroick men, or famous Cities, unlesse he have in himselfe the experience and the practice of all that which is praise-worthy. These reasonings, together with a certaine nicenesse of nature, an honest haughtinesse, and self-esteem either of what I was, or what I might be, (which let envie call pride) and lastly that modesty, whereof though not in the Title page yet here I may be excus'd to make some beseeming profession, all these uniting the supply of their naturall aide together, kept me still above those low descents of minde, beneath which he must deject and plunge himself, that can agree to salable and unlawfull prostitutions. Next, (for heare me out now Readers) that I may tell ye whether my younger feet wander'd; I betook me among those lofty Fables and Romances, which recount in solemne canto's the deeds of Knighthood founded by our victorious Kings; and from hence had in renowne over all Christendome. There I read it in the oath of every Knight, that he should defend to the expence of his best blood, or of his life, if it so befell him, the honour and chastity of Virgin or Matron. From whence even then I learnt what a noble vertue chastity sure must be, to the defence of which so many worthies by such a deare adventure of themselves had sworne. And if I found in the story afterward any of them by word or deed breaking that oath, I judg'd it the same fault of the Poet, as that which is attributed to *Homer;* to have written undecent things of the gods. Only this my minde gave me that every free and gentle spirit without that oath ought to be borne a Knight, nor needed to expect the guilt spurre, or the laying of a sword upon his shoulder to stirre him up both by his counsell, and his arme to secure and protect the weaknesse of any attempted chastity. So that even those books which to many others have bin the fuell of wantonnesse and loose living, I cannot thinke how unlesse by divine indulgence prov'd to me so many incitements as you have heard, to the love and stedfast observation of that vertue which abhorres the society of Bordello's. Thus from the Laureat fraternity of Poets, riper yeares, and the ceaselesse round of study and reading led me to the shady spaces of philosophy, but chiefly to the divine volumes of *Plato,* and his equall *Xenophon.*[2] Where if I should tell ye what I learnt, of chastity and love, I meane that which is truly so, whose charming cup is only vertue which she bears in her hand to those who are worthy. The rest are cheated with a thick intoxicating potion which a certaine Sorceresse the abuser of loves name carries about; and how the first and chiefest office of love, begins and ends in the soule, producing those happy twins of her divine generation knowledge and vertue, with such abstracted sublimities as these, it might be worth your listning, Readers, as I may one day hope to have ye in a still time, when there shall be no chiding; not in these noises, the adversary as ye know, barking at the doore; or searching for me at the Burdello's where it may be he has lost himselfe, and raps up without pitty the sage and rheumatick old *Prelatesse* with all her young *Corinthian Laity* to inquire for such a one. Last of all not in time, but as perfection is last, that care was ever had of me, with my earliest capacity not to be negligently train'd in the precepts of Christian Religion: This that I have hitherto related, hath bin to shew, that though Christianity had bin but slightly taught me, yet a certain reserv'dnesse of naturall disposition, and morall discipline learnt out of the noblest Philosophy was anough to keep me in disdain of farre lesse incontinences than this of the Burdello. But having had the doctrine of holy Scripture unfolding those chaste and high mysteries with timeliest care infus'd, that *the body is for the Lord and the Lord for the body,* thus also I argu'd to my selfe; that if unchastity in a woman whom Saint *Paul* termes the glory of man, be such a scandall and dishonour, then certainly in a man who is both the image and glory of God, it must, though commonly not so thought, be much more deflouring and dis-

[2] Probably the reference is to Xenophon's Socratic dialogue, the *Symposium.*

honourable. In that he sins both against his owne body which is the perfeter sex, and his own glory which is in the woman, and that which is worst, against the image and glory of God which is in himselfe. Nor did I slumber over that place expressing such high rewards of ever accompanying the Lambe, with those celestiall songs to others inapprehensible, but not to those who were not defil'd with women, which doubtlesse meanes fornication: For mariage must not be call'd a defilement. (Pp. 15–18.)

Milton next defends satire and strong language and then proceeds to an analysis of the rest of *A Modest Confutation.* Since the *Confutation* is a reply to both *Animadversions* and the Smectymnuans, this part of the work is complex and at times difficult, though often amusing.

The tenth section of the *Confutation* had charged Milton with seeking a rich widow or a lectureship. To this he replied:

For this I cannot omit without ingratitude to that providence above, who hath ever bred me up in plenty, although my life hath not bin unexpensive in learning, and voyaging about, so long as it shall please him to lend mee what he hath hitherto thought good, which is anough to serve me in all honest and liberall occasions, and something over besides, I were unthankfull to that highest bounty, if I should make my selfe so poore, as to sollicite needily any such kinde of *rich hopes* as this Fortune-teller dreams of. And that he may furder learne how his Astrology is wide all the houses of heav'n in spelling mariages, I care not if I tell him thus much profestly, though it be to the losing of my *rich hopes,* as he calls them, that I think with them who both in prudence and elegance of spirit would choose a virgin of mean fortunes honestly bred, before the wealthiest widow. The feind therefore that told our *Chaldean* the contrary was a lying feind. (P. 42.)

Finally, Milton wearily reaches section twelve.

But now, Readers, we have the Port within sight; his last Section which is no deepe one, remains only to be foarded, and then the wisht shoare. And here first it pleases him much, that he hath discri'd me, as he conceaves, to be unread in the Counsels. Concerning which matter it will not be unnecessary to shape him this answer; That some years I had spent in the stories of those Greek and Roman exploits, wherein I found many things both nobly done, and worthily spoken: when comming in the method of time to that age wherein the Church had obtain'd a Christian Emperor, I so prepar'd my selfe,

> as being now to read examples of wisdome and goodnesse among those who were formost in the Church, not else where to be parallell'd: But to the amazement of what I expected, Readers, I found it all quite contrary; excepting in some very few, nothing but ambition, corruption, contention, combustion: in so much that I could not but love the Historian *Socrates,* who in the proem to his fifth book professes, *He was faine to intermixe affaires of State, for that it would be else an extreame annoyance to heare in a continu'd discourse the endlesse brabbles and counterplottings of the Bishops.* Finding therefore the most of their actions in single to be weak, and yet turbulent, full of strife and yet flat of spirit, and the summe of their best councels there collected, to be most commonly in questions either triviall and vaine, or else of short, and easie decision without that great bustle which they made, I concluded that if their single ambition and ignorance was such, then certainly united in a Councell it would be much more; and if the compendious recitall of what they there did was so tedious and unprofitable, then surely to sit out the whole extent of their tattle in a dozen volumes, would be a losse of time irrecoverable. Besides that which I had read of S. *Martin,* who for his last sixteene yeares could never be perswaded to be at any Councell of the Bishops. And *Gregory Nazianzen* betook him to the same resolution affirming to *Procopius, that of any Councell, or meeting of Bishops he never saw good end; nor any remedy thereby of evill in the Church, but rather an increase. For,* saith he, *their contentions and desire of Lording no tongue is able to expresse.* I have not therefore I confesse read more of the Councels save here and there, I should be sorry to have bin such a prodigall at my time: but that which is better, I can assure this Confuter; I have read into them all. And if I want any thing yet, I shall reply something toward that which in the defence of *Murana* was answer'd by *Cicero to Sulpitius* the Lawyer. If ye provoke me (for at no hand else will I undertake such a frivolous labour) I will in three months be an expert councelist. For be not deceav'd, Readers, by men that would overawe your eares with big names and huge Tomes that contradict and repeal one another, because they can cramme a margent with citations. Do but winnow their chaffe from their wheat, ye shall see their great heape shrink and wax thin past beliefe. (Pp. 52–53.)

Milton ends the work with this prediction: the prelated power

> will soone be dumbe, and the *Divine right of Episcopacy* forthwith expiring, will put us no more to trouble with tedious antiquities and disputes. (P. 59.)

Besides the glories of Milton's prose at its best and the interest the autobiographical passages have for all interested in Milton the poet or Milton the man, the five anti-prelatical works have another interest. Mr. Tillyard notes that

> there was in the nature of Milton's hopes, as revealed in the anti-episcopal pamphlets, something the very reverse of sober. Allowing for the exaltation natural in the years 1640 to 1642, we have to admit that Milton had an unusually sanguine temperament exaggerated by an unusual ignorance of the nature of common humanity.[3]

The banishment of this striking innocence and sanguineness does much to explain why in Milton's great epic he was preoccupied by the Fall and why he colored the regeneration of Adam and Eve with less intensive emotional energy than the events which preceded it.

[3] E. M. W. Tillyard, *Milton* (London, 1956), pp. 120–21.

A NOTE ON THE "POSTSCRIPT" IN SMECTYMNUUS, *AN ANSWER TO A BOOK ENTITULED AN HUMBLE REMONSTRANCE*, 1641[1]

By J. Max Patrick

Don M. Wolfe[2] follows David Masson and Will T. Hale in their contention that Milton may have written the postscript in the Smectymnuan answer to Joseph Hall's *An Humble Remonstrance to the High Court of Parliament* (January 1641) which appeared in March 1641, about two months before *Of Reformation. An Answer* was written by Milton's former tutor, Thomas Young, in co-operation with the four other Smectymnuans. The attribution to Milton is based on some similarities between phrases and facts in *A Postscript* and *Of Reformation*, a reference in *Animadversions* to what "the collector" of the historical citations in the postscript "sayes," evidence that the editions of Holinshed, Speed, and Stow used in *A Postscript* and the *Commonplace Book* are the same, the conjunction of references to Anselm and Cremensis in both of those works, and a notion that words and phrases such as "inhumane butcheries," "vomit," "odious pride," and "bleede afresh" appear to be "authentically Miltonian." Since there is considerable possibility that Milton and his old tutor could have used the same editions, that Yonge was the "collector" referred to, and that the conjoint references to Anselm and Cremensis had a common source, and for other reasons, the contention that Milton wrote *A Postscript* remains only a possibility unconfirmed by impressionistic notions about diction and phrasing. The fact that *A Postscript* refers to a passage in Book II of Bucer's *De Regno Christi* and that Milton, in the address to

1 The complete text of *A Postscript* is printed in the *Yale Milton*, II, 966–75.
2 *Yale Milton*, I, 961–65.

Parliament prefaced to *The Judgement of Martin Bucer*, admits th he did not know of Bucer's opinions about divorce as contained that same second book until 1644 makes it unlikely that he was author.

THE DIVORCE TRACTS, 1643–1645

EDITED BY J. MAX PATRICK AND ARTHUR M. AXELRAD

Foreword

Extracts from:
The Dedicatory Address to Parliament in
Doctrine and Discipline of Divorce, second edition, February 1644

Complete text of the first edition, 1643
The Doctrine and Discipline of Divorce

Summary with extracts of:
The Judgement of Martin Bucer, Concerning Divorce, August 1644
Tetrachordon, March 1645
Colasterion, March 1645

FOREWORD

During his lifetime Milton was probably better known in Eng-nd for his divorce tracts than for any of his other works. The min-ters of Sion College denounced his doctrines as erroneous; Herbert almer thundered against them in a sermon to Parliament; the Com-any of Stationers petitioned against "the Pamphlet . . . concerning ivorce"; and the House of Lords summoned Milton for ques-oning about it.[1] Consequently he gained notoriety as a libertine. n fact, his four pamphlets on the subject seem to have been more enounced than read and understood: hence his citation of Prov. viii 13 on the title page of *The Doctrine and Discipline of Divorce* n its second edition: "He that answereth a matter before he heareth , it is folly and shame unto him."

Before the Protestant Reformation, marriage, like baptism, had the tatus of a sacrament; and as such it fell under ecclesiastical juris-liction as codified in canon law—the rules governing the church aid down by the popes and councils. *Divortium a mensa et thoro* divorce from bed and board) was granted by church courts for adultery, cruelty, and heresy or apostasy; but such a legalized sepa-ation did not annul the marriage: neither partner could remarry during the other's lifetime; and the children of the union were legiti-nate. *Divortium a vinculo matrimonii* (divorce from the bond of natrimony) declared a marriage illegal and therefore null and void: no valid sacrament or true marriage had taken place; children resulting from it were illegitimate; and the parties to it were free to remarry. The courts granted such complete dissolutions on many grounds—mistaken identity, non-consummation, consanguinity, ab-sence of consent, solemn religious vows, murder, and the like. Precontract was a much abused ground: a prior promise to marry made the subsequent marriage of either party illegal as long as the other one desired the promised union. By pretending precontract,

[1] J. Milton French, *The Life Records of John Milton* (New Brunswick, 1949–58), II, 211, 106, 109, 116.

which was difficult to disprove, an unscrupulous person could p vide a church court with a reason for declaring his marriage vc The papal curia showed ingenuity, often at a price, in discover such justifications for full divorce.

As a result of the Reformation, all the Protestant churches (exc the Anglican on some points) followed Luther and Calvin in garding marriage as non-sacramental (therefore a matter for ci jurisdiction), and as dissolvable for adultery or desertion, with rig of remarriage for the innocent party and recognition of the childr as legitimate. Thus in the Protestant countries except England m riage was treated as a civil contract, and this contract was dissolv by the very act of adultery or desertion: the chief function of t civil magistrate was to ensure that divorce proceedings were derly.

Efforts to remove the control of marriage from the Church of Er land and its courts failed in the sixteenth century. In the followi four decades, despite the fact that the Thirty-Nine Articles (1563) had asserted that matrimony was not a divinely ordained sa rament like baptism, church courts kept their power to pronounce divorce *a mensa et thoro* and to nullify an illegal matrimonial bon Unlike other Protestant countries, England made no provision f nullification of a legal marriage because of adultery or desertion: 1613 the Countess of Essex had to prove her virginity in open cou with circumstantial evidence before she obtained an annulme based on non-consummation and thus was enabled to marry h lover: her expenses seem to have been as high as the evidence w implausible. But in general it was usually harder to get a nullificatic than it had been before the Reformation. Her notorious case w evidence of the unsatisfactory nature of the existing system; so w the fact that some priests performed marriage services for the inn cent parties who had been granted divorces *a mensa et thoro* fo adultery or desertion even in the time of Laud; but their doing s was irregular.

This practice was given approval by the Westminster Assemb of Divines. On June 12, 1643, Parliament passed an ordinance fo this body to convene on July 1. It was composed of members of bot houses of Parliament, divines (all of whom had been ordained a priests in the Church of England, though most of them were inter on radically reforming it), and eight Scottish commissioners. It wa to confer on questions referred to it by Parliament concerning th iscipline, government, and liturgy of the Church of England. A ıonth after it convened, the first edition of *Doctrine and Discipline f Divorce* made its appearance anonymously, "Seasonable to be ow thought on in the Reformation intended," as its title page anounced. Obviously Milton intended to influence the suggestions on ıarriage and divorce which the Assembly would make to Parliaıent. It is ironical that because he advocated reforms beyond the onventional Protestant position, which the Assembly took on diorce, conservatives became alarmed, and that he may thus have ontributed to Parliament's failure to liberalize divorce procedures ven to the extent practiced in other Protestant countries. Not until 1670 did divorce *a vinculo* become possible—and then only by speial act of Parliament.

Milton's aim was certainly not to facilitate licentiousness. On the other hand, he was not willing to restrict the just liberties of believing Christians in order to prevent others from committing wickedness which could be punished after the event. His goal was to complete the imperfect reformation of the church in England by ending the codification of prelatical tyranny in what he regarded as unchristian canon laws governing marriage and divorce. More than that, he wanted divorce *a vinculo* recognized as a private matter based on incompatibility. His teachings were revolutionary for his times and would have been regarded as revolutionary by most, probably all, important Christian theologians at least as far back as the time of the apostles. Nevertheless, he contended that he was no innovator but a restorer of the true doctrine and discipline of divorce "from the bondage of Canon Law and other mistakes, to the true meaning of Scripture." Thus in his judgment, what he taught was essentially conservative, a return to, not a departure from, what the Bible taught. It was very much a departure from tradition—but from a tradition which, in his opinion, was false and superstitious. The technique of claiming that an innovation is not new but is a restoration of an original truth is a common and often effective device, one which Milton knowingly used elsewhere. However he seems sincerely to have believed that his intention was to discover and restore what Scripture taught. Such was the aim of the Protestant reformers (though he felt that they had not fully realized it in the matter of divorce), and the goal was consistent with his attacks on prelacy, his pleas for the separation of church and state, and his arguments for toleration. How far his teachings are based on an accurate interpretation of the Bible is for each reader to deci for himself.

In practice he seems to have begun with certain prevalent a sumptions, reasoning as follows. The highest part of man, that whic distinguishes him from animals, is his rational soul. According t the laws of God and Nature, body and matter are inferior to min and spirit and should be subordinated to them. A marriage which merely a physical union is but an animalic coupling; to become truly human marriage, it must involve a union of the participant highest and essential parts: its essence is a harmony and partne ship of rational souls for mutual help, joy, and comfort. Where ther is no union of minds, there is no full human marriage, inasmuch a the essential part is lacking; at best in such a case there is a physica partnership without mental antipathy. But what if there is an in superable antipathy between the man and the woman, rooted i their very natures (for which they are not responsible), and there fore ineradicable? For such a couple to force themselves to con tinue to cohabit, thus denying themselves the achievement of th highest mental-spiritual union with other partners, or (worse still for the church or the state or both to force them to remain yoked t each other for life, this is to turn the natural and divine order o things topsy turvy: it is to rebel against the very nature of thing and the chain of being; it requires enslavement of man's highest par to what is inferior in him; it subordinates marital love, which should be like the love of Christ for his church, to what man has in common with beasts. To give supremacy to the flesh and to force a man and woman to live with each other despite their ingrained antipathy is therefore perverse and unnatural, a denial of their highest faculties; it is also likely to involve either frustration of their legitimate physical needs, or unsatisfactory physical activities between them, or infidelity to their already imperfect union. If divorce for adultery is permitted, with right for the innocent party to remarry, emphasis is being placed on the physical; if frigidity and consequent non-consummation of a marriage is permitted as a basis for a complete dissolution of that marriage, again the emphasis is on the physical. How much more important it is to emphasize the prime and essential requisite of a proper, full, and joyful marriage—the union of those rational souls which gives human beings their distinctive identity! Such marital love complemented by physical union, ever subordinated to the higher union, is the ideal kind of marriage. Not to llow full divorce when such blessed and mutual love is lacking and npossible, and when it is replaced by antipathy, hatred, or aversion -such a denial is manifestly absurd. The mistake made by Adam nd Eve in the Fall, as Milton was to relate it in *Paradise Lost*, vas that they subordinated their higher faculties to their lower ones -a mistake analogous to allowing divorce on physical or legalistic grounds while denying it on higher spiritual ones. To forget the pre-minence of the mental-spiritual virtue which the Lady maintained n *Comus* when exposed to physical temptations and to deny divorce vhen such virtue in marital love is lacking and cannot be achieved s improper, unnatural, and unchristian, particularly if such lower physical grounds are allowed as a basis for divorce.

Accordingly, if through accident, misjudgment, or error a man and a woman find that their union is merely physical (or is so little a union that even physical compatibility is lacking, as well as mental harmony), and if they find that despite their best efforts over a reasonable period of time they are unable to achieve that higher harmony, that distinctively human union which should be a mutual joy and comfort, then they should recognize that they are living in sin, that they have never been truly married to each other, that they should separate forthwith, each partner being free to enter into a true and effective marriage if he or she finds the right person. And both the church and the state should likewise recognize that the imperfect effort at union has failed and never amounted to a true marriage. However, in Milton's view jurisdiction over this nullification was to be exercised neither by the church nor the state: the matter was to be regarded as a private one, to be agreed on by the partners, either of them having the right to take the initiative. Hence, he classified such a right to divorce as part of domestic or household liberty, not as civil or religious liberty.

This interpretation of Milton's doctrines involves some simplification of his positions and is not given in his words. But it will give some idea of his viewpoint subtracted from such scriptural bases as he found for it. Noteworthy is the suggestion that his doctrine of marriage was in some measure a development of his earlier concept of chastity as expounded in the account of his youthful reading in *An Apology Against a Pamphlet* (1642) and in *Comus*. In both he applauded the "noble virtue chastity" as a lofty state of mind and spirit. It was only logical for him, in treating marriage, to emphasize union of mind and spirit as its main aspect.

And similarly in *Areopagitica,* his prime doctrine was that the qui tessence of man, his rational soul and its products, should not subordinated to tyranny and destroyed or frustrated by extern controls. What he was asking for was, in effect, charity toward man highest faculties. So in *Doctrine and Discipline* he linked the pr eminence of mental affinity and marital love with charity: in th first edition the word "charity" appears on the title page; in th second the worthies who effect the reforms he proposes are prom ised that they will be titled "Defenders of Charity"; and in bo editions the last word in the text is "charity."

It was not easy for Milton to derive his theoretical position fro the Bible. The greatest problem was that the Mosaic law in Deute onomy xxiv 1, in allowing a man to divorce a wife "because he hat found some uncleanness in her," was, or seemed to be, more libera than Christ's pronouncements in Matthew xix 3–9, which forbad breaking asunder what God had joined and forbade puttin away a wife "except for fornication," that is, adultery. The Gospe was supposed to liberate believers from the rigidity of the Law but here it seemed to narrow the older provisions and to make then more rigid. Various solutions suggested themselves: according t one, Christ was addressing a particular group, the Pharisees, and th denial of divorce except for adultery was not applicable to others Alternatively it could be argued that "adultery" was to be broadly interpreted: so Milton made a close study of the Scriptures and the commentators to conclude that the word as used there covered many different kinds of activities or intended deeds, including desertion and general mismanagement. In short, Christ's term "adultery" was equivalent to Moses' "uncleanness" and therefore Christians are free to divorce for the same reasons as the Jews. As for Christ's dictum that man should not break what God has joined, the obvious answer was that God cannot be said to have joined two persons who are yoked in antipathy. Another approach, emphasized in the second edition of *Doctrine and Discipline* was to contend that the Law was a key to what Christ meant: "If we examine over all his sayings, we shall find him not so much interpreting the Law with his words, as referring his owne words to be interpreted by the Law."[2]

Doctrine and Discipline was occasioned not only by Milton's desire to advance liberty systematically in its civic, religious, and do-

[2] *Doctrine and Discipline,* 2nd ed., p. 44.

mestic aspects, and by the timeliness of making his ideas available to influence the Westminster Assembly's discussion of marriage and divorce, but also by his personal circumstances. In May or June 1642 Mary Powell became his wife.[3] A few months later she returned to her family's home for a visit. Milton seems to have expected her to stay away only for the rest of the summer, and he was apparently disappointed when she failed to come back—possibly because her family was Royalist and the first civil war began on August 22. At any rate, she did not return until after peace was restored in 1645, "pleading that her mother had bin the inciter of her to that frowardness."[4] Milton accepted her back and she remained with him, bearing his children and, for all we know, living in harmony with him until her death in 1652. Milton's disappointment at her failure to return in 1642, his acceptance of her when she did come in 1645, and his living with her for another seven years all suggest that there was no ineradicable natural antipathy between them. Nor is there any necessity for thinking that he impetuously and mistakenly rushed into marriage with a girl who was a stranger to him. The two families had long been acquainted: as early as June 1627, Mary's father had borrowed £500 from his future son-in-law.[5]

The *Commonplace Book* indicates that Milton probably approved of divorce before he was married. Inevitably when Mary failed to return, he considered it. In the words of the "anonymous" early biographer of Milton (Cyriack Skinner?),

> shee, that was very Yong, and had bin bred in a family of plenty and freedom, beeing not well pleas'd with his reserv'd manner of life . . . went back into the Country with her Mother. Nor though hee sent severall pressing invitations could hee prevayl with her to return . . . till . . . Oxford was surrendr'd (the nighness of her Fathers house to that Garrison having for the most part of the mean time hindred any communication between them) . . . Hee, in this Interval, who had entred into that State for the end design'd by God and Nature, and was then in the full vigor of his Manhood, could ill bear the disappointment hee mett with by her obstinate absent-

[3] The traditional date, 1643, has been rectified by scholars. See B. A. Wright, "Milton's First Marriage," *MLR*, XXVI (1931), 383–400, and XXVII (1932), 6–23.

[4] The "anonymous" life of Milton, p. 22, in *The Early Lives of Milton*, ed. Helen Darbishire (London, 1932)—attributed by her to John Phillips.

[5] French, *Life Records*, I, 135–39.

ing: And therefore thought upon a Divorce, that hee might bee free to marry another; concerning which hee also was in treaty. The lawfulness and expedience of this, duly regulat in order to all those purposes, for which Marriage was at first instituted; had upon full consideration and reading good Authors bin formerly his Opinion: And the necessity of justifying himselfe now concurring with the opportunity, acceptable to him, of instructing others in a point of so great concern to the peace and preservation of Families; and so likely to prevent temptations as well as mischiefs, hee first writt *The Doctrine and Discipline of Divorce*, then *Colasterion*, and after *Tetrachordon:* In these hee taught the right use and design of Marriage; then the Original and practise of Divorces among the Jews, and show'd that our Savior, in those foure places of the Evangelists, meant not the abrogating, but rectifying the abuses of it; rendring to that purpose another Sense of the word Fornication . . . than what is commonly received. Martin Bucers Judgment in this matter hee likewise translated into English. The Assembly of Divines . . . instead of answering, or disproving what those books had asserted, caus'd him to be summon'd for them before the Lords: But that house, whether approving the Doctrin, or not favoring his Accusers, soon dismiss'd him. This was the mending of a decay in the Superstructure, and had for object onely the well beeing of private Persons, or at most of Families.[6]

Attributing the divorce tracts solely or even primarily to Milton's personal circumstances may be a misleading oversimplification, one likely to blind readers to the fact that he was strikingly in advance of his times in emphasizing marital love as a *sine qua non* of true marriage—a view which has increasingly found favor since his day. For example, the Ecumenical Council of the Roman Catholic Church meeting in 1965 gave expression to a concept which began to gather strength when seventeenth-century theologians first timidly rejected the idea that procreation was the only justification for sexual intercourse in marriage. This is the doctrine which places the fostering of conjugal love as a proper function of marriage on the same plane as procreation and education of children. It is perhaps to be regretted that Milton did not proclaim his doctrine of marital love independently of his advocacy of divorce.

[6] *Early Lives*, ed. Darbishire, pp. 22–24. For a masterly and far fuller account of the divorce tracts, one to which this Foreword is indebted, see Ernest Sirluck's Introduction to volume II of the *Yale Milton*.

THE DEDICATORY ADDRESS TO PARLIAMENT IN *THE DOCTRINE AND DISCIPLINE OF DIVORCE,* 1644

The greatly amplified and revised second edition of *Doctrine and Discipline* was in print by February 2, 1643 / 44, the date recorded by George Thomason on his copy (now in the British Museum). It bore Milton's initials on the title page and his full name at the end of the dedicatory address to Parliament and the Westminster Assembly; and the wording of the title page was revised and expanded:

THE Doctrine and Discipline of DIVORCE: Restor'd to the good of both SEXES, *From the bondage of CANON LAW, and other mistakes, to the true meaning of Scripture in the Law and Gospel compar'd. Wherin also are set down the bad consequences of abolishing or condemning of Sin, that which the Law of God allowes, and Christ abolisht not. Now the second time revis'd and much augmented, In Two BOOKS: To the Parlament of* England *with the Assembly. The Author* J. M. *MATTH.* 13.52. Every Scribe instructed to the Kingdome of Heav'n, is like the Maister of a house which bringeth out of his treasury things new and old. *Prov.* 18.13. He that answereth a matter before he heareth it, it is folly and shame unto him. LONDON, *Imprinted in the yeare 1644.*

Like the first edition, this 1644 version was probably printed by Matthew Simmons. Two other editions followed in Milton's lifetime: the third, 1645, shows slight variation; the fourth, issued in the same year, varies considerably in punctuation, spelling, and typography, but there is no reason to believe that Milton was connected with these changes.

The tract, in the revised wording of the 1644 edition, occurs in the main collections of Milton's prose. The apparatus in the *Columbia Milton* enables the 1643 text to be reconstructed. The *Yale Milton,* II, provides the texts of 1643 and 1644 interwoven with a system of arrowheads and brackets which makes it difficult to follow either one. The reprint of the 1643 version in the present volume is the first since the original to be printed as a readily readable unit. Lowell W. Coolidge's annotations in the *Yale Milton*, II, constitute a full and admirable commentary to which the present editors are inevitably indebted.

The chief interests of the 1644 edition are its prefatory address, which is a worthy predecessor to *Areopagitica*, numerous added authorities, which are evidence of Milton's intense study in the interval between the two editions, and developing concepts of Christian liberty, reason, and nature in connection with divorce and marriage.

TO THE PARLAMENT OF ENGLAND, with the ASSEMBLY.

If it were seriously askt, and it would be no untimely question, Renowned Parlament, select Assembly, who of all Teachers and Maisters that have ever taught, hath drawn the most Disciples after him, both in Religion, and in manners, it might bee not untruly answer'd, Custome.[1] Though vertue be commended for the most perswasive in her *Theory;* and Conscience in the plain demonstration of the spirit, finds most evincing, yet whether it be the secret of divine will, or the originall blindnesse we are born in, so it happ'ns for the most part, that Custome still is silently receiv'd for the best instructer. Except it be, because her method is so glib and easie, in some manner like to that vision of *Ezekiel,*[2] rowling up her sudden book of implicit knowledge, for him that will, to take and swallow down at pleasure; which proving but of bad nourishment in the concoction,[3] as it was heedlesse in the devouring, puffs up unhealthily, a certaine big face of pretended learning, mistaken among credulous men, for the wholsome habit of soundnesse and good constitution; but is indeed no other, than that swoln visage of counterfeit knowledge and literature, which not onely in private marrs our education, but also in publick is the common climer into every chaire, where either Religion is preach't, or Law reported: filling each estate of life and profession, with abject and servil principles; depressing the high and Heaven-born spirit of Man, farre beneath the condition wherein either God created him, or sin hath sunke him. To persue

evincing: probably a noun meaning conviction; if adjective or participle, convincing.
originall blindnesse: the spiritual blindness to which Adam's fall reduced man.
concoction: digestion.
habit: appearance.

the Allegory, Custome being but a meer face, as Eccho is a meere voice, rests not in her unaccomplishment, untill by secret inclination, shee accorporat her selfe with error, who being a blind and Serpentine body without a head, willingly accepts what he wants, and supplies what her incompleatnesse went seeking.[4] Hence it is, that Error supports Custome, Custome count'nances Error. And these two betweene them would persecute and chase away all truth and solid wisdome out of humane life, were it not that God, rather than man,[5] once in many ages, cals together the prudent and Religious counsels of Men, deputed to represse the encroachments, and to worke off the inveterate blots and obscurities wrought upon our mindes by the suttle insinuating of Error and Custome: Who with the numerous and vulgar train of their followers, make it their chiefe designe to envie and cry-down the industry of free reasoning, under the terms of humor, and innovation; as if the womb of teeming Truth were to be clos'd up, if shee presume to bring forth ought, that sorts not with their unchew'd notions and suppositions. Against which notorious injury and abuse of mans free soule to testifie and oppose the utmost that study and true labour can attaine, heretofore the incitement of men reputed grave hath led me among others; and now the duty and the right of an instructed Christian cals me through the chance of good or evill report, to be the sole advocate of a discount'nanc't truth: a high enterprise Lords and Commons, a high enterprise and a hard, and such as every seventh Son of a seventh Son does not venture on. Nor have I amidst the clamor of so much envie and impertinence, whether to appeal, but to the concourse of so much piety and wisdome heer assembl'd. Bringing in my hands an ancient and most necessary, most charitable, and yet most injur'd Statute of *Moses:* not repeald ever by him who only had the authority, but thrown aside with much inconsiderat neglect, under the rubbish of Canonicall ignorance; as once the whole law was by some such like conveyance in *Josiahs*[6] time. And hee who shall indeavour the amendment of any old neglected grievance in Church or State, or in the daily course of life, if he be gifted with abilities of mind that may raise him to so high an undertaking, I grant he hath already much whereof not to repent him; yet let me arreed him, not to be the foreman of any mis-judgd opinion, unlesse

humor: mere fancy, whim, or eccentricity.
sorts not with: does not fit in with or suit.
discount'nanc't: disapproved and thrown into disrepute.
whether: whither; anywhere.
conveyance: removal.
arreed: counsel.

his resolutions be firmly seated in a square and constant mind, not conscious to it self of any deserved blame, and regardles of ungrounded suspicions. For this let him be sure he shall be boorded presently by the ruder sort, but not by discreet and well nurtur'd men, with a thousand idle descants[7] and surmises. Who when they cannot confute the least joynt or sinew of any passage in the book; yet God forbid that truth should be truth, because they have a boistrous conceit of some pretences in the Writer.[8] But were they not more busie and inquisitive than the Apostle commends, they would heare him at least, *rejoycing, so the Truth be preacht, whether of envie or other pretence whatsoever:* For Truth is as impossible to be soil'd by any outward touch, as the Sun beam. Though this ill hap wait on her nativity, that shee never comes into the world, but like a Bastard, to the ignominy of him that brought her forth: till Time the Midwife rather than the mother of Truth, have washt and salted the Infant, declar'd her legitimat, and Churcht the father of his young *Minerva,* from the needlesse causes of his purgation.[9] Your selves can best witnesse this, worthy Patriots, and better will, no doubt, hereafter: for who among ye of the formost that have travail'd in her behalfe to the good of Church, or State, hath not been often traduc't to be the agent of his owne byends, under pretext of Reformation. So much the more I shall not be unjust to hope, that however Infamy, or Envy may work in other men to doe her fretfull will against this discourse, yet that the experience of your owne uprightnesse mis-interpreted, will put ye in mind to give it free audience and generous construction. . . . You it concerns chiefly, Worthies in Parlament, on whom, as on our deliverers, all our grievances and cares, by the merit of your eminence and fortitude are devolv'd: Me it concerns next, having with much labour and faithfull diligence first found out, or at least with a fearlesse and communicative candor first publisht to the manifest good of Christendome, that which calling to witnesse every thing mortall and immortall, I beleeve unfainedly to be true. Let not other men thinke their conscience bound to search continually after truth, to pray for enlightning from above, to publish what they think they have so obtaind, and debarr me from conceiving my self ty'd by the same duties. Yee have now, doubtlesse by the favour and appointment of God, yee have now in your hands a great and populous Nation to Reform; from what corruption, what blindnes in Religion yee know well. . . . Mark then, Judges and Lawgivers, and yee

square and constant: well-balanced and just.
regardles of: indifferent to.
boorded: attacked, as by pirates or an enemy in naval warfare.

whose Office is to be our teachers, for I will utter now a doctrine, if ever any other, though neglected or not understood, yet of great and powerfull importance to the governing of mankind. He who wisely would restrain the reasonable Soul of man within due bounds, must first himself know perfectly, how far the territory and dominion extends of just and honest liberty. As little must he offer to bind that which God hath loos'n'd, as to loos'n that which he hath bound. The ignorance and mistake of this high point, hath heapt up one huge half of all the misery that hath bin since *Adam*. In the Gospel we shall read a supercilious crew of masters, whose holinesse, or rather whose evill eye, grieving that God should be so facil to man, was to set straiter limits to obedience, than God had set; to inslave the dignity of man, to put a garrison upon his neck of empty and overdignifi'd precepts: And we shall read our Saviour never more greev'd and troubl'd, than to meet with such a peevish madnesse among men against their own freedome. How can we expect him to be lesse offended with us, when much of the same folly shall be found yet remaining where it lest ought, to the perishing of thousands. . . . For no effect of tyranny can sit more heavy on the Common-wealth, than this houshold unhappines on the family. And farewell all hope of true Reformation in the state, while such an evill as this lies undiscern'd or unregarded in the house. On the redresse wherof depends, not only the spiritfull and orderly life of our grown men, but the willing and carefull education of our children. Let this therefore be new examin'd, this tenure and free-hold of mankind, this native and domestick Charter giv'n us by a greater Lord than that *Saxon* King the Confessor. . . . Doubt not, worthy Senators, to vindicate the sacred honour and judgment of *Moses* your predecessor, from the shallow commenting of Scholasticks and Canonists. Doubt not after him to reach out your steddy hands to the misinform'd and wearied life of man; to restore this his lost heritage into the houshold state; wherwith be sure that peace and love, the best subsistence of a Christian family will return home from whence they are now banisht; places of prostitution wil be lesse haunted, the neighbours bed lesse attempted, the yoke of prudent and manly discipline will be generally submitted to, sober and well order'd living will soon spring up in the Common-wealth. . . . It would not be the first, or second time, since our ancient *Druides*, by whom this Island was the Cathedrall of Philosophy to *France*, left off their pagan rites, that England hath had this honour vouchsaft from

a supercilious crew of masters: a haughtily overbearing set of teachers—the Pharisees.

overdignifi'd: raised to undeserved importance.

Heav'n, to give out reformation to the World. Who was it but our English *Constantine* that baptiz'd the Roman Empire? who but the *Northumbrian Willibrode*, and *Winifride* of *Devon* with their followers, were the first Apostles of *Germany?* who but *Alcuin* and *Wicklef* our Country men open'd the eyes of *Europe,* the one in arts, the other in Religion.[10] Let not England, forget her precedence of teaching nations how to live. . . .

For me, as farre as my part leads me, I have already my greatest gain, assurance and inward satisfaction to have don in this nothing unworthy of an honest life, and studies well employ'd. With what event among the wise and right understanding handfull of men, I am secure. . . .

I seek not to seduce the simple and illiterat; my errand is to find out the choisest and the learnedest, who have this high gift of wisdom to answer solidly, or to be convinc't. I crave it from the piety, the learning and the prudence which is hous'd in this place. It might perhaps more fitly have bin writt'n in another tongue; and I had don so, but that the esteem I have of my Countries judgement, and the love I beare to my native language to serv it first with what I endeavour, made me speak it thus, ere I assay the verdit of outlandish readers. And perhaps also heer I might have ended nameles, but that the addresse of these lines chiefly to the Parlament of *England* might have seem'd ingratefull not to acknowledge by whose Religious care, unwearied watchfulnes, couragious and heroick resolutions, I enjoy the peace and studious leisure to remain,

The Honourer and Attendant of their Noble worth and vertues,

John Milton.[11]

what event: what the outcome will be.

NOTES

1. Milton attacks custom in *Judgement* and *Tetrachordon;* see the *Columbia Milton* Index under "Custom."

2. Ezek. ii 8–10, iii 1–4: God told Ezekiel to eat a scroll and then preach what it said. Milton's personified Custom rolls up her book of easily assimilated knowledge which is to be swallowed or accepted blindly, without understanding. Cf. *Areopagitica,* note 124.

3. On the imagery, see Thomas Kranidas, *The Fierce Equation: A Study of Milton's Decorum* (The Hague, 1965), pp. 73 ff.

4. I.e., Custom accepts from Error what man lacks, and furnishes Error with what Error was looking for to fill out her incompleteness. This description of Custom is closely related to the character genre. Cf. *Areopagitica,* note 393.

5. Such as the Parliament and Westminster Assembly of Divines that Milton is addressing.

6. According to 2 Kings xxii–xxiii and 2 Chron. xxxiv, a book of Mosaic law,

forgotten during a period of Baal worship, was rediscovered in the time of King Josiah.

7. In music, accompaniments or variations; hence, censorious criticisms incidental to the main subject or theme.

8. These ruder men, when they cannot confute any passage in the book, rather than face the truth and accept it, take up an attitude which amounts to saying, *If what this book says is true, God forbid that truth should be truth,* because they have a harsh conception (or crude notion) of claims and pretensions which they attribute to the author and regard as insincere. As Milton's paraphrase of Phil. i 18 in the next sentence suggests, he has in mind the context of that passage, Phil. i 15–18: "Some indeed preach Christ even of envy and strife; and some also of good will: the one preach Christ of contention, not sincerely, supposing to add affliction to my bonds; but the other of love, knowing that I am set for the defence of the gospel. What then? notwithstanding, every way, whether in pretence, or in truth, Christ is preached; and I therein do rejoice, yea, and will rejoice." Milton, then, is saying that if what he states is truth, it should be recognized as such, even if, as his opponents allege, his motivations and pretensions are false. It would seem that he was accused of advocating divorce for incompatibility out of self-interest while professing that he was expounding the true doctrine of the Bible on the subject.

9. I.e., Truth has the misfortune at birth to enter the world like a bastard, to the shame of the man that brought her forth into the world; this misfortune and shame last until Time (who, contrary to the proverb *Time is the mother of Truth,* is the midwife) has cleansed and purified the infant (in a manner comparable to the Old Testament rites of purification and the Anglican service of thanksgiving for women after childbirth), and has declared her legitimate, and has cleansed, from what needlessly caused his purgation, the father who brought forth this new wisdom in a manner like the birth of Minerva, goddess of wisdom, who sprang from Jupiter's forehead. Milton's transferring to a father the rites of purification and thanksgiving ordinarily known as the *churching of women,* and his fusing of pagan myth and Anglican ceremonialism are deliberately grotesque.

10. The first Christian Roman emperor, Constantine, was wrongly assumed to be of British birth. Saints Willibrord and Winfrid (better known as Boniface) were missionaries in Frisia; Charlemagne invited Alcuin to help revive learning at his court; and Wiclif was widely viewed as a forerunner of the Reformation.

11. This is the first appearance of Milton's full name in print.

THE DOCTRINE AND DISCIPLINE OF DIVORCE: RESTOR'D TO THE GOOD OF BOTH SEXES,

FROM THE BONDAGE OF CANON LAW, AND OTHER MISTAKES, TO CHRISTIAN FREEDOM, GUIDED BY THE RULE OF CHARITY. WHEREIN ALSO MANY PLACES OF SCRIPTURE, HAVE RECOVER'D THEIR LONG-LOST MEANING: SEASONABLE TO BE NOW THOUGHT ON IN THE REFORMATION INTENDED.

Matth. 13.52. *Every Scribe instructed to the Kingdome of Heav'n, is like the Maister of a house which bringeth out of his treasurie things old and new.*

London, Printed by T. P. and M. S. In Goldsmiths Alley, 1643.

[1] THE DOCTRINE AND DISCIPLINE OF *DIVORCE;* RESTOR'D TO THE GOOD OF BOTH SEXES.[1]

Many men, whether it be their fate, or fond opinion, easily perswade themselves, if GOD would but be pleas'd a while to withdraw his just punishments from us, and to restraine what power either the devill, or any earthly enemy hath to worke us woe, that then mans nature would find immediate rest and releasement from all evils. But verily they who think so, if they be such as have a minde large anough to take into their thoughts a generall survey of humane things, would soone prove themselves in that opinion farre deceiv'd. For though it were granted us by divine indulgence to be exempt from all that can be harmfull to us from without, yet the perversnesse of our folly is so bent, that we should never lin hammering out of our owne hearts, as it were out of a flint, the

lin: cease from.

seeds and sparkles of new miseries to our selves, till all were in a blaze againe. And no marvell if out of our own hearts, for they are evill; but ev'n out of those things which God meant us, either for a principall good, or a pure contentment, we are still hatching and contriving upon our selves matter of continuall sorrow and perplexitie. What greater good to man than that revealed rule, whereby God vouchsafes to shew us how he would be worshipt?[2] and yet that not rightly understood became [2] the cause that once a famous man in *Israel* could not but oblige his conscience to be the sacrificer, or if not, the jayler of his innocent and only daughter.[3] And was the cause oft-times that Armies of valiant men have given up their throats to a heathenish enemy on the Sabbath day:[4] fondly thinking their defensive resistance to be as then a work unlawfull. What thing more instituted to the solace and delight of man than marriage, and yet the mis-interpreting of some Scripture directed mainly against the abusers of the Law for divorce giv'n them by *Moses*,[5] hath chang'd the blessing of matrimony not seldome into a familiar and co-inhabiting mischiefe; at least into a drooping and disconsolate houshold captivitie, without refuge or redemption. So ungovern'd and so wild a race doth superstition run us from one extreme of abused libertie into the other of unmercifull restraint. For although God in the first ordaining of marriage,[6] taught us to what end he did it, in words expresly implying the apt and cheerfull conversation[7] of man with woman, to comfort and refresh him against the evill of solitary life, not mentioning the purpose of generation till afterwards, as being but a secondary end in dignity, though not in necessitie; yet now, if any two be but once handed in the Church, and have tasted in any sort of the nuptiall bed,[8] let them finde themselves never so mistak'n in their dispositions through any error, concealment, or misadventure, that through their different tempers, thoughts, and constitutions, they can neither be to one another a remedy against lonelines, nor live in any union or contentment all their dayes, yet they shall, so they be but found suitably weapon'd to the lest possibilitie of sensuall enjoyment, be made, spight of *antipathy*[9] to fadge together, and combine as they may to their unspeakable wearisomnes and despaire of all sociable delight in the ordinance which God establisht to that very end. What a calamitie is this, and as the Wise-man,[10] if he were alive, would sigh out in his own phrase, what a *sore evill is this under the Sunne!* All which

familiar: pertaining to a family, intimate.
handed in the Church: married by a priest according to liturgy.
lest: least.
antipathy: incompatibility. *fadge:* fit.

we can referre justly to no other author than the Canon Law and her adherents, not consulting with charitie, the interpreter and guide of our faith, but resting in the meere element of the Text; doubtles by the policy of the devill to make that gracious ordinance become unsupportable, that what with men not daring to venture upon wedlock, and what with men wearied out of it, all inordinate licence might abound. It was for many ages that mariage lay in disgrace with most of the ancient Doctors, as a [3] work of the flesh, almost a defilement, wholly deny'd to Priests, and the second time disswaded to all, as he that reads *Tertullian* or *Jerom* may see at large.[11] Afterwards it was thought so Sacramentall, that no adultery[12] could dissolve it; yet there remains a burden on it as heavy as the other two were disgracefull or superstitious, and of as much iniquitie, crossing a Law not onely writt'n by *Moses*,[13] but character'd in us by nature, of more antiquitie and deeper ground than mariage it selfe; which Law is to force nothing against the faultles proprieties of nature:[14] yet that this may be colourably done, our Saviours words touching divorce, are as it were congeal'd into a stony rigor, inconsistent both with his doctrine and his office, and that which he preacht onely to the conscience, is by canonicall tyranny snatcht into the compulsive censure of a judiciall Court; where Laws are impos'd even against the venerable and secret power of natures impression, to love what ever cause be found to loath. Which is a hainous barbarisme both against the honour of mariage, the dignitie of man and his soule, the goodnes of Christianitie, and all the humane respects of civilitie. Notwithstanding that some the wisest and gravest among the Christian Emperours,[15] who had about them, to consult with, those of the fathers then living, who for their learning and holines of life are still with us in great renown, have made their statutes and edicts concerning this debate, far more easie and relenting in many necessary cases, wherein the Canon is inflexible. And *Hugo Grotius*, a man of these times, one of the best learned, seems not obscurely to adhere in his perswasion to the equitie of those imperiall decrees, in his notes upon the *Evangelists*,[16] much allaying the outward roughnesse of the Text, which hath for the most part been too immoderately expounded; and excites the diligence of others to enquire further into this question, as containing many points which have not yet been explain'd. By which, and by mine owne apprehension of what publick duty each man owes, I conceive my selfe exhorted among the rest to communicate such thoughts as I have, and offer them now in this generall labour of reformation,[17] to the candid view both of Church and

colourably: with the appearance of truth.

Magistrate; especially because I see it the hope of good men, that those irregular and unspirituall Courts have spun their utmost date in this Land; and some better course must now be constituted. He therefore that by adventuring shall be so happy as with successe to ease and set free the minds of ingenuous and apprehensive men from this needlesse [4] thraldome, he that can prove it lawfull and just to claime the performance of a fit and matchable conversation, no lesse essentiall to the prime scope of marriage than the gift of bodily conjunction, or els to have an equall plea of divorce as well as for that corporall deficiency;[18] he that can but lend us the clue that windes out this labyrinth of servitude to such a reasonable and expedient liberty as this, deserves to be reck'n'd among the publick benefactors of civill and humane life; above the inventors of wine and oyle; for this is a far dearer, far nobler, and more desirable cherishing to mans life, unworthily expos'd to sadnes and mistake, which he shall vindicate. Not that licence and levity and unconsented breach of faith should herein be countenanc't, but that some conscionable, and tender pitty might be had of those who have unwarily in a thing they never practiz'd before, made themselves the bondmen of a luckles and helples matrimony. In which Argument he whose courage can serve him to give the first onset, must look for two severall oppositions:[19] the one from those who having sworn themselves to long custom and letter of the Text, will not out of the road: the other from those whose grosse and vulgar apprehensions conceit but low of matrimoniall purposes, and in the work of male and female think they have all. Neverthelesse, it shall be here sought by due wayes to be made appeare, that those words of God in the institution, promising a meet help against lonelines; and those words of Christ, *That his yoke is easie and his burden light,*[20] were not spoken in vaine; for if the knot of marriage may in no case be dissolv'd but for adultery, all the burd'ns and services of the Law are not so intolerable. This onely is desir'd of them who are minded to judge hardly of thus maintaining, that they would be still and heare all out, nor think it equall to answer deliberate reason with sudden heat and noise; remembring this, that many truths now of reverend esteem and credit, had their birth and beginning once from singular and private thoughts; while the most of men

vindicate: rescue.
luckles and helples: lacking the help or means of delivery from servitude.
burd'ns and services of the Law: the prescriptions and proscriptions of the Mosaic law governing conduct, ceremonies, etc., from which the Gospel delivered Christians.
hardly: harshly. *thus maintaining:* such a contention.
equall: fair.

were otherwise possest; and had the fate at first to be generally exploded and exclaim'd on by many violent opposers; yet I may erre perhaps in soothing my selfe that this present truth reviv'd, will deserve to be not ungently receiv'd on all hands; in that it undertakes the cure of an inveterate disease[21] crept into the best part of humane societie: and to doe this with no smarting corrosive, but with a smooth and pleasing lesson, which receiv'd hath the vertue to soften and dispell rooted and knotty sor-[5]rowes; and without enchantment or spel us'd hath regard at once both to serious pitty, and upright honesty; that tends to the redeeming and restoring of none but such as are the object of compassion; having in an ill houre hamper'd themselves to the utter dispatch of all their most beloved comforts and repose for this lives term. But if wee shall obstinately dislike this new overture of unexpected ease and recovery, what remains but to deplore the frowardnes of our hopeles condition, which neither can endure the estate we are in, nor admit of remedy either sharp or sweet. Sharp we our selves distast; and sweet, under whose hands we are, is scrupl'd and suspected as too lushious. In such a posture Christ found the *Jews,* who were neither won with the austerity of *John the Baptist,* and thought it too much licence to follow freely the charming pipe[22] of him who sounded and proclaim'd liberty and reliefe to all distresses: yet Truth in some age or other will find her witnes, and shall be justify'd at last by her own children.

To remove therefore if it be possible, this great and sad oppression which through the strictnes of a literall interpreting hath invaded and disturb'd the dearest and most peaceable estate of houshold society, to the over-burdning, if not the over-whelming of many Christians better worth than to be so deserted of the Churches considerate care, this position shall be laid down; first proving, then answering what may be objected either from Scripture or light of reason.

That indisposition, unfitnes, or contrariety of mind, arising from a cause in nature unchangable, hindring and ever likely to hinder the main benefits of conjugall society, which are solace and peace, is a greater reason of divorce than naturall frigidity, especially if there be no children, and that there be mutuall consent.[23]

For all sense and reason and equity reclaimes that any Law or Cov'nant how solemn or strait soever, either between God and man, or man and man, though of Gods joyning, should bind against a prime and principall scope of its own institution, and of both or either

exploded: scornfully rejected.
reclaimes: cries in protest.
strait: confining.

party cov'nanting: neither can it be of force to ingage a blameles creature to his own perpetuall sorrow, mistak'n for his expected solace, without suffering charity to step in and doe a confest good work of parting those whom nothing holds together, but this of Gods joyning, falsly suppos'd against the expresse end of his own ordinance. And what his chiefe end was of creating woman to be [6] joynd with man, his own instituting words declare, and are infallible to informe us what is mariage, and what is no mariage; unlesse we can think them set there to no purpose: *It is not good,* saith he, *that man should be alone; I will make him a help meet for him.* From which words so plain, lesse cannot be concluded, nor is by any learned Interpreter, than that in Gods intention a meet and happy conversation is the chiefest and the noblest end of mariage; for we find here no expression so necessarily implying carnall knowledg, as this prevention of lonelinesse to the mind and spirit of man. And indeed it is a greater blessing from God, more worthy so excellent a creature as man is, and a higher end to honour and sanctifie the league of mariage, whenas the solace and satisfaction of the minde is regarded and provided for before the sensitive pleasing of the body. And with all generous persons maried thus it is, that where the minde and person pleases aptly, there some unaccomplishment of the bodies delight may be better born with, than when the minde hangs off in an unclosing disproportion, though the body be as it ought; for there all corporall delight will soon become unsavoury and contemptible. And the solitarines of man, which God had namely and principally orderd to prevent by mariage, hath no remedy, but lies under a worse condition than the loneliest single life; for in single life the absence and remotenes of a helper might inure him to expect his own comforts out of himselfe, or to seek with hope; but here the continuall sight of his deluded thoughts without cure, must needs be to him, if especially his complexion incline him to melancholy, a daily trouble and paine of losse in some degree like that which Reprobates feel. Lest therefore so noble a creature as man should be shut up incurably under a worse evill by an easie mistake in that ordinance which God gave him to remedy a lesse evill, reaping to himselfe sorrow while he went to rid away solitarines, it cannot avoyd to be concluded, that if the woman be naturally so of disposition, as will not help to remove, but help to encrease that same God-forbidd'n lonelines which will in time draw on with it a generall discomfort and dejection of minde, not beseeming either

generous persons maried: magnanimous married people.
complexion: natural disposition.
Reprobates: those who have lost God's favor and protection.

Christian profession or morall conversation, unprofitable and dangerous to the Common-wealth, when the houshold estate, out of which must flourish forth the vigor and spirit of all publick enterprizes, is so ill contented and procur'd at home, and cannot be supported; such a mariage can be no mariage whereto [7] the most honest end is wanting: and the agrieved person shall doe more manly, to be extraordinary and singular in claiming the due right whereof he is frustrated, than to piece up his lost contentment by visiting the Stews, or stepping to his neighbours bed, which is the common shift in this mis-fortune, or els by suffering his usefull life to wast away and be lost under a secret affliction of an unconscionable size to humane strength. How vain therefore is it, and how preposterous in the Canon Law to have made such carefull provision against the impediment of carnall performance,[24] and to have had no care about the unconversing inability of minde, so defective to the purest and most sacred end of matrimony: and that the vessell of voluptuous enjoyment must be made good to him that has tak'n it upon trust without any caution, when as the minde from whence must flow the acts of peace and love, a far more precious mixture than the quintessence of an excrement, though it be found never so deficient and unable to performe the best duty of mariage in a cheerfull and agreeable conversation, shall be thought good anough, how ever flat and melancholious it be, and must serve though to the eternall disturbance and languishing of him that complains him. Yet wisdom and charity waighing Gods own institution, would think that the pining of a sad spirit wedded to lonelines should deserve to be free'd, aswell as the impatience of a sensuall desire so providently reliev'd. Tis read to us in the Liturgy, that *wee must not marry to satisfie the fleshly appetite, like brute beasts that have no understanding:*[25] but the Canon so runs, as if it dreamt of no other matter than such an appetite to be satisfy'd; for if it happen that nature hath stopt or extinguisht the veins of sensuality, that mariage is annull'd. But though all the faculties of the understanding and conversing part after triall appeare to be so ill and so aversly met through natures unalterable working, as that neither peace, nor any sociable contentment can follow, tis as nothing, the contract shall stand as firme as ever, betide what will. What is this but secretly to instruct us, that however many grave reasons are pretended to the maried life, yet that nothing indeed is thought worth regard therein, but the prescrib'd satisfaction of an irrationall heat; which cannot be but ignominious to the state of mariage, dishonourable to the

quintessence of an excrement: the essential reproductive fluid as distinct from waste matter supposedly emitted with it. *it:* the mind.

undervalu'd soule of man, and even to Christian doctrine it self. While it seems more mov'd at the disappointing of an impetuous nerve, than at the ingenuous grievance of a minde unreasonably [8] yoakt; and to place more of mariage in the channell of concupiscence, than in the pure influence of peace and love, whereof the souls lawfull contentment is the onely fountain.[26]

But some are ready to object, that the disposition ought seriously to be consider'd before. But let them know again, that for all the warinesse can be us'd, it may yet befall a discreet man to be mistak'n in his choice:[27] the soberest and best govern'd men are lest practiz'd in these affairs; and who knows not that the bashfull mutenes of a virgin may oft-times hide all the unlivelines and naturall sloth which is really unfit for conversation; nor is there that freedom of accesse granted or presum'd, as may suffice to a perfect discerning till too late: and where any indisposition is suspected, what more usuall than the perswasion of friends, that acquaintance, as it encreases, will amend all. And lastly, it is not strange though many who have spent their youth chastly, are in some things not so quicksighted, while they hast too eagerly to light the nuptiall torch; nor is it therfore that for a modest error a man should forfeit so great a happines, and no charitable means to release him. Since they who have liv'd most loosely by reason of their bold accustoming, prove most succesfull in their matches, because their wild affections unsetling at will, have been as so many divorces to teach them experience. When as the sober man honouring the appearance of modestie, and hoping well of every sociall vertue under that veile, may easily chance to meet, if not with a body impenetrable, yet often with a minde to all other due conversation inaccessible, and to all the more estimable and superior purposes of matrimony uselesse and almost liveles: and what a solace, what a fit help such a consort would be through the whole life of a man, is lesse paine to conjecture than to have experience.

And that we may further see what a violent and cruell thing it is to force the continuing of those together, whom God and nature in the gentlest end of mariage never joyn'd, divers evils and extremities that follow upon such a compulsion shall here be set in view. Of evils the first and greatest is that hereby a most absurd and rash imputation is fixt upon God and his holy Laws, of conniving and dispencing with open and common adultery among his chosen people; a thing which the rankest politician would think it shame

ingenuous: without guile; honorable.
influence: flowing in.
fountain: source.

and disworship, that his Laws should countenance; how and in what manner this comes to passe, I shall reserve, till the course of me-[9]thod brings on the unfolding of many Scriptures.[28] Next the Law and Gospel are hereby made liable to more than one contradiction, which I referre also thither. Lastly, the supreme dictate of charitie is hereby many wayes neglected and violated. Which I shall forthwith addresse to prove. First we know St. *Paul* saith, *It is better to marry than to burne.*[29] Mariage therefore was giv'n as a remedy of that trouble: but what might this burning mean? Certainly not the meer motion of carnall lust, not the meer goad of a sensitive desire; God does not principally take care for such cattell.[30] What is it then but that desire which God put into *Adam* in Paradise before he knew the sin of incontinence;[31] that desire which God saw it was not good that man should be left alone to burn in; the desire and longing to put off an unkindly solitarines by uniting another body, but not without a fit soule to his in the cheerfull society of wedlock.[32] Which if it were so needfull before the fall, when man was much more perfect in himself, how much more is it needfull now against all the sorrows and casualties of this life to have an intimate and speaking help, a ready and reviving associate in marriage: whereof who misses by chancing on a mute and spiritles mate, remains more alone than before, and in a burning lesse to be contain'd than that which is fleshly and more to be consider'd; as being more deeply rooted even in the faultles innocence of nature. As for that other burning, which is but as it were the venom of a lusty and over-abounding concoction, strict life and labour with the abatement of a full diet may keep that low and obedient anough: but this pure and more inbred desire of joyning to it self in conjugall fellowship a fit conversing soul (which desire is properly call'd love) *is stronger than death*, as the Spouse of Christ thought, *many waters cannot quench it, neither can the flouds drown it.*[33] This is that rationall burning that mariage is to remedy, not to be allay'd with fasting, nor with any penance to be subdu'd, which how can he asswage who by mis-hap hath met the unmeetest and most unsutable mind? Who hath the power to struggle with an intelligible flame, not in Paradise to be resisted, become now more ardent, by being fail'd of what in reason it lookt for; and even then most unquencht, when the importunity of a provender burning[34] is well anough appeas'd; and yet the soul hath obtain'd nothing of what it justly desires. Certainly such a one forbidd'n to divorce, is in effect forbidd'n to marry, and compell'd to greater difficulties than in a

cattell: animal lusts and desires.
intelligible: reasonable.

single life; for if there be not a more [10] human burning which mariage must satisfy, or els may be dissolv'd, than that of copulation, mariage cannot be honorable for the meer reducing and terminating of lust between two; seeing many beasts in voluntary and chosen couples live together as unadulterously, and are as truly maried in that respect. But all ingenuous men will see that the dignity and blessing of mariage is plac't rather in the mutual enjoyment of that which the wanting soul needfully seeks, than of that which the plenteous body would jollily give away. Hence it is that *Plato* in his festivall discours brings in *Socrates* relating what he fain'd to have learnt from the Prophetesse *Diotima,* how *Love* was the Sonne of *Penury,* begot of *Plenty* in the garden of *Jupiter.* Which divinely sorts with that which in effect *Moses* tells us; that *Love* was the Son of *Lonelines,* begot in Paradise by that sociable and helpfull aptitude which God implanted between man and woman toward each other.[35] The same also is that burning mention'd by St. *Paul,* whereof marriage ought to be the remedy; the flesh hath other naturall and easie curbes which are in the power of any temperate man. When therfore this originall and sinles *Penury* or *Lonelines* of the soul cannot lay it self down by the side of such a meet and acceptable union as God ordain'd in mariage, at least in some proportion, it cannot conceive and bring forth *Love,* but remains utterly unmaried under a formall wedlock, and still burnes in the proper meaning of St. *Paul.* Then enters *Hate,* not that Hate that sins, but that which onely is naturall dissatisfaction and the turning aside from a mistaken object: if that mistake have done injury, it fails not to dismisse with recompence, for to retain still, and not be able to love, is to heap more injury. Thence that wise and pious Law of dismission, *Deut.* 24.1. took beginning; of which anon: He therfore who lacking of his due in the most native and humane end of mariage, thinks it better to part than to live sadly and injuriously to that cherfull covnant (for not to be belov'd and yet retain'd, is the greatest injury to a gentle spirit) he I say who therfore seeks to part, is one who highly honours the maried life, and would not stain it: and the reasons which now move him to divorce, are equall to the best of those that could first warrant him to marry; for, as was plainly shewn, both the hate which now diverts him and the lonelines which leads him still powerfully to seek a fit help, hath not the least grain of a sin in it, if he be worthy to understand himself.

Thirdly, Yet it is next to be feard, if he must be still bound with-[11]out reason by a deafe rigor, that when he perceives the just

festivall discours: Symposium.
sorts: agrees.

expectance of his mind defeated, he will begin even against Law to cast about where he may find his satisfaction more compleat, unlesse he be a thing heroically vertuous, and that are not the common lump of men for whom chiefly the Laws ought to be made, though not to their sins, yet to their unsinning weaknesses, it being above their strength to endure the lonely estate, which while they shun'd, they are fal'n into. And yet there follows upon this a worse temptation; for if he be such as hath spent his youth unblamably, and layd up his chiefest earthly comforts in the enjoyment of a contented mariage, nor did neglect that furderance which was to be obtain'd herein by constant prayers, when he shall find himselfe bound fast to an uncomplying discord of nature, or, as it oft happens, to an image of earth and fleam,[36] with whom he lookt to be the copartner of a sweet and gladsome society, and sees withall that his bondage is now inevitable, though he be almost the strongest Christian, he will be ready to dispair in vertue, and mutin against divine providence: and this doubtles is the reason of those lapses and that melancholy despair which we see in many wedded persons, though they understand it not, or pretend other causes, because they know no remedy, and is of extreme danger; therefore when human frailty surcharg'd, is at such a losse, charity ought to venture much, and use bold physick, lest an over-tost faith endanger to shipwrack.

Fourthly, Mariage is a covnant the very beeing whereof consists, not in a forc't cohabitation, and counterfeit performance of duties, but in unfained love and peace. Thence saith *Salomon* in *Ecclesiastes, Live joyfully with the wife whom thou lovest, all thy dayes, for that is thy portion.*[37] How then, where we find it impossible to rejoyce or to love, can we obay this precept? how miserably doe we defraud our selves of that comfortable portion which God gives us, by striving vainly to glue an error together which God and nature will not joyne, adding but more vexation and violence to that blisfull society by our importunate superstition, that will not heark'n to St. *Paul*, I *Cor.* 7. who speaking of mariage and divorce, determines plain anough in generall that God therein *hath call'd us to peace* and not *to bondage.*[38] Yea God himself commands in his Law more than once, and by his Prophet *Malachy*, as *Calvin* and the best translations read, that *he who hates let him divorce;*[39] that is, he who cannot love, or delight. I cannot therefore be so diffident, as not securely

fleam: phlegm.
mutin: rebel.
surcharg'd: overburdened.

to conclude, that he [12] who can receive nothing of the most important helps in mariage, beeing thereby disinabl'd to return that duty which is his, with a clear and hearty countnance; and thus continues to grieve whom he would not, and is no lesse griev'd, that man ought even for loves sake and peace to move divorce upon good and liberall conditions to the divorc't. And it is a lesse breach of wedlock to part with wise and quiet consent betimes, than still to soile and profane that mystery of joy and union with a polluting sadnes and perpetuall distemper; for it is not the outward continuing of marriage that keeps whole that covnant, but whosoever does most according to peace and love, whether in mariage, or in divorce, he it is that breaks mariage lest; it being so often written, that *Love onely is the fulfilling of every Commandment.*[40]

Fifthly, As those Priests of old were not to be long in sorrow,[41] or if they were, they could not rightly execute their function; so every true Christian in a higher order of Priesthood is a person dedicate to joy and peace, offering himselfe a lively sacrifice[42] of praise and thanksgiving, and there is no Christian duty that is not to be season'd and set off with cherfulnes; which in a thousand outward and intermitting crosses may yet be done well, as in this vale of teares,[43] but in such a bosom affliction as this, which grindes the very foundations of his inmost nature, when he shall be forc't to love against a possibility, and to use dissimulation against his soul in the perpetuall and ceaseles duties of a husband, doubtles his whole duty of serving God must needs be blurr'd and tainted with a sad unpreparednesse and dejection of spirit, wherein God has no delight. Who sees not therfore how much more Christianly it would be to break by divorce that which is more brok'n by undue and forcible keeping, rather than *to cover the Altar of the Lord with continuall teares, so that he regardeth not the offring any more,*[44] rather than that the whole worship of a Christian mans life should languish and fade away beneath the waight of an immeasurable grief and discouragement. And because some think the childer'n of a second matrimony succeeding a divorce would not be a holy seed, why should we not think them more holy than the offspring of a former ill-twisted wedlock, begott'n only out of a bestiall necessitie without any true love or contentment, or joy to their parents, so that in some sense we may call them the *children of wrath*[45] and anguish, which will as little conduce to their sanctifying, as if they had been bastards; for nothing more [13] than disturbance of minde suspends us from approaching to God. Such a disturbance especially as both assaults our faith and trust in Gods providence, and ends, if there be not a miracle of vertue on either side, not onely in bitternes and wrath, the canker of devotion, but in a desperate and vitious carelesnes; when he sees himself without fault of his train'd by a deceitfull bait into a snare of misery, betrai'd by an alluring ordinance, and then made the thrall of heavines and discomfort by an undivorcing Law of God, as he erroneously thinks, but of mans iniquitie, as the truth is; for that God preferres the free and cherfull worship of a Christian, before the grievous and exacted observance of an unhappy mariage, besides that the generall maxims of Religion assure us, will be more manifest by drawing a paralel argument from the ground of divorcing an Idolatresse, which was, lest she should alienate his heart from the true worship of God: and what difference is there whether she pervert him to superstition by enticing sorcery, or disinable him in the whole service of God through the disturbance of her unhelpful and unfit society, and so drive him at last through murmuring and despair to thoughts of Atheism: neither doth it lessen the cause of separating, in that the one willingly allures him from the faith, the other perhaps unwillingly drives him; for in the account of God it comes all to one that the wife looses him a servant; and therefore by all the united force of the *Decalogue* she ought to be disbanded, unlesse we must set mariage above God and charitie, which is a doctrine of devils no lesse than forbidding to marry.

And here by the way to illustrate the whole question of divorce, ere this treatise end, I shall not be loath to spend a few lines in hope to give a full resolv of that which is yet so much controverted, whether an Idolatrous heretick ought to be divorc't. To the resolving whereof we must first know that the *Jews* were commanded to divorce an unbeleeving Gentile for two causes: first, because all other Nations especially the *Canaanites* were to them unclean. Secondly, to avoid seducement. That other Nations were to the *Jews* impure, even to the separating of mariage, will appear out of *Exod.* 34.16. *Deut.* 7.3. 6. compar'd with *Ezra* 9.2. also chap. 10.10, 11. *Nehem.* 13.30. This was the ground of that doubt rais'd among the *Corinthians* by some of the Circumcision;[46] Whether an unbeleever wer not still to be counted an unclean thing, so as that they ought to divorce from such a person. This doubt of theirs St. *Paul* re-[14]moves by an Evangelicall reason, having respect to that vision of St. *Peter*,[47] wherein the distinction of clean and unclean beeing abolisht, all

carelesnes: lack of concern. *train'd:* enticed.
undivorcing: forbidding divorce.
disbanded: let loose; dismissed; probably with word play on relief from the bonds of matrimony and the wedding band.
by some of the Circumcision: by some circumcised Jews who had become Christians.

living creatures were sanctify'd to a pure and christian use, and mankind especially, now invited by a generall call to the covnant of grace. Therefore saith St. *Paul, The unbeleeving wife is sanctify'd by the husband;*[48] that is, made pure and lawfull to his use; so that he need not put her away for fear lest her unbelief should defile him; but that if he found her love stil towards him, he might rather hope to win her. The second reason of that divorce was to avoid seducement, as is prov'd by comparing those places of the Law, to that which *Ezra* and *Nehemiah* did by divine warrant in compelling the *Jews* to forgoe their wives.[49] And this reason is morall and perpetuall in the rule of Christian faith without evasion. Therefore saith the Apostle 2 *Cor.* 6. *Mis-yoke not together with Infidels,* which is interpreted of mariage in the first place. And although the former legall pollution be now don off, yet there is a spirituall contagion in Idolatry as much to be shunn'd; and though seducement were not to be fear'd, yet where there is no hope of converting, there alwayes ought to be a certain religious aversation and abhorring, which can no way sort with mariage. Therefore saith St. *Paul, What fellowship hath righteousnesse with unrighteousnesse? what communion hath light with darknesse? what concord hath Christ with Beliall? what part hath he that beleeveth with an Infidell?* And in the next verse but one, he moralizes and makes us liable to that command of *Isaiah, Wherfore come out from among them, and be ye separate saith the Lord, touch not the unclean thing, and I will receive ye.*[50] And this command thus Gospelliz'd to us, hath the same force with that whereon *Ezra* grounded the pious necessitie of divorcing.

Upon these principles I answer, that a right beleever ought to divorce an idolatrous heretick unlesse upon better hopes: however that it is in the beleevers choice to divorce or not.

The former part will be manifest thus; first, an apostate idolater whether husband or wife seducing was to die by the decree of God, *Deut.* 13.6. 9.[51] that mariage therefore God himself dis-joyns; for others born idolaters the morall reason of their dangerous keeping and the incommunicable antagony that is between Christ and *Belial,* will be sufficient to enforce the commandment of those two inspir'd reformers, *Ezra* and *Nehemiah,* to put an Idolater away as well under the Gospel.[52]

[15] The latter part, that although there be no seducement fear'd, yet if there be no hope giv'n, the divorce is lawfull, will appear by this, that idolatrous mariage is still hatefull to God, therefore still

Gospelliz'd: interpreted in the spirit of the Gospel.
born idolaters: those born into pagan families.
still: always—the usual seventeenth-century meaning.

it may be divorc't by the pattern of that warrant that *Ezra* had; and by the same everlasting reason: neither can any man give an account wherfore, if those whom God joyns, no man may separate, it should not follow, that, whom he joyns not, but hates to joyn, those man ought to separate: but saith the Lawyer, that which ought not have been don, once don availes. I answer, this is but a crochet of the law, but that brought against it, is plain Scripture. As for what Christ spake concerning divorce, tis confest by all knowing men, he meant onely between them of the same faith. But what shall we say then to St. *Paul,* who seems to bid us not divorce an Infidell willing to stay? We may safely say thus; that wrong collections have been hitherto made out of those words by modern Divines. His drift, as was heard before, is plain: not to command our stay in mariage with an Infidel, that had been a flat renouncing of the religious and morall law; but to inform the *Corinthians* that the body of an unbeleever was not defiling, if his desire to live in Christian wedlock shewd any likelihood that his heart was opening to the faith: and therefore advices to forbear departure so long,[53] till nothing have bin neglected to set forward a conversion: this I say he advises, and that with certain cautions; not commands: If we can take up so much credit for him, as to get him beleev'd upon his own word; for what is this els but his counsell in a thing indifferent,[54] *to the rest speak I, not the Lord;* for though it be true that the Lord never spake it, yet from St. *Pauls* mouth wee should have took it as a command, had not himself forewarn'd us, and disclaim'd; which, notwithstanding if we shall still avouch to be a command, he palpably denying it, this is not to expound St. *Paul,* but to out-face him. Neither doth it follow, but that the Apostle may interpose his judgement in a case of Christian libertie without the guilt of adding to Gods word. How doe we know mariage or single life to be of choice, but by such like words as these, *I speak this by permission, not of commandment, I have no command of the Lord, yet I give my judgement.*[55] Why shall not the like words have leave to signifie a freedom in this our present question, though *Beza* deny.[56] Neither is the Scripture hereby lesse inspir'd because St. *Paul* confesses to have writt'n therein what he had not of command; for we grant that the Spirit of God led him to ex-[16]presse himself to christian prudence in a matter which God thought best to leave uncommanded. *Beza* therefore must be warily read when he taxes St.

the Lawyer: the adherent to canon law or its English equivalent.
crochet: quirk.
collections: inferences.
indifferent: not required; to be accepted or rejected at one's own option.
this: this interpreting of advice as a command. *out-face:* defy.

Austin[57] of Blasphemy, for holding that St. *Paul* spake heer as of a thing indifferent: but if it must be a command, I shall yet the more evince it to be a command that we should heerin be left free: and that out of the Greek word[58] us'd in the 12. *v.* which instructs us plainly there must be a joynt assent and good liking on both sides; he that will not deprave the Text, must thus render it; *If a brother have an unbeleeving wife, and she joyn in consent to dwell with him* (which cannot utter lesse to us than a mutuall agreement) let him not put her away for the meer surmise of Judaicall uncleannes: and the reason follows, for the body of an Infidell is not polluted, neither to benevolence, nor to procreation. Moreover, this note of mutuall complacency forbids all offer of seducement; which to a person of zeal cannot be attempted without great offence, if therfore seducement be fear'd, this place hinders not divorce. Another caution was put in this supposed command, of not bringing the beleever into *bondage* heerby, which doubtles might prove extreme, if christian liberty and conscience were left to the humor of a pagan staying at pleasure to play with, or to vexe and wound with a thousand scandals and burdens above strength to bear: if therefore the conceived hope of gaining a soul come to nothing, then charity commands that the beleever be not wearied out with endles waiting under many grievances sore to his spirit; but that respect be had rather to the present suffering of a true Christian, than the uncertain winning of an obdur'd heretick; for this also must appertain to the precept, *Let every man wherein he is call'd therein abide with God, v.* 24. that is, so walking in his inferior calling of mariage, as not by dangerous subjection to that ordinance, to hinder and disturb the higher calling of his christianitie. Last, whether this be a command or an advice, we must look that it be so understood as not to contradict the least point of morall religion that God hath formerly commanded, otherwise what doe we, but set the morall Law and the Gospel at civill war together: and who then shall be able to serve those two masters?[59]

Now whether Idolatry or adultery be the greatest violation of mariage, if any demand, let him thus consider, that among Christian Writers touching matrimony, there be three chief ends therof agreed on; Godly society, next civill, and thirdly, that of the ma-[17]riage-bed.[60] Of these the first in name to be the highest and most excellent, no baptiz'd man can deny; nor that Idolatry smites directly against this prime end, nor that such as the violated end is,

evince: prove.
complacency: contented acquiescence. *seducement:* insidious luring (to idolatry).

such is the violation: but he who affirms adultery to be the highest breach, affirms the bed to be the highest of mariage, which is in truth a grosse and borish opinion, how common soever; as farre from the countnance of Scripture, as from the light of all clean philosophy, or civill nature. And out of question the cherfull help that may be in mariage toward sanctity of life, is the purest and so the noblest end of that contract: but if the particular of each person be consider'd, then of those three ends which God appointed, that to him is greatest which is most necessary: and mariage is then most brok'n to him, when he utterly wants the fruition of that which he most sought therin, whether it were religious, civill, or corporall society.[61] Of which wants to do him right by divorce only for the last and meanest, is a pervers injury, and the pretended reason of it as frigid as frigidity it self, which the *Code* and canon are only sensible of.[62] Thus much of this controversie. I now return to the former argument.[63] And having shewn, that disproportion, contrariety, or numnesse of minde may justly be divorc't, by proving already that the prohibition therof opposes the expresse end of Gods institution, suffers not mariage to satisfie that intellectuall and innocent desire which God himself kindl'd in man to be the bond of wedlock, but only to remedy a sublunary and bestial burning, which frugal diet without mariage would easily chast'n. Next that it drives many to transgresse the conjugall bed, while the soule wanders after that satisfaction which it had hope to find at home, but hath mis't. Or els it sits repining even to Atheism; finding it self hardly dealt with, but misdeeming the cause to be in Gods Law, which is in mans unrighteous ignorance. I have shew'd also how it unties the inward knot of mariage, which is peace and love (if that can be unti'd which was never knit) while it aimes to keep fast the outward formalitie; how it lets perish the Christian man, to compell impossibly the maried man.

The sixt place declares this prohibition to be as respectles of human nature [as it is of religion],[64] and therefore is not of God. He teaches that an unlawfull mariage may be lawfully divorc't. And that those who having throughly discern'd each others disposition which ofttimes cannot be till after matrimony, shall then finde a powerfull relu-[18]ctance and recoile of nature on either side blasting all the

sublunary: beneath the moon and therefore variable, being subject to its influence; composed of or corresponding to the lower, worldly elements and thus gross, subject to decay and change, and lacking in the higher fifth essence and that which distinguishes man from animals, his reason. See *Areopagitica*, note 25.

it: the soul.

respectles of: without consideration or regard for.

content of their mutuall society, that such persons are not lawfully maried (to use the Apostles words) *Say I these things as a man, or saith not the Law also the same? for it is writt'n,*[65] Deut. 22. *Thou shalt not sowe thy vineyard with divers seeds, lest thou defile both. Thou shalt not plow with an Oxe and an Asse together,* and the like. I follow the pattern of St. Pauls reasoning; *Doth God care for Asses and Oxen,* how ill they yoke together, *or is it not said altogether for our sakes? for our sakes no doubt this is writt'n.* Yea the Apostle himself in the forecited 2 *Cor.* 6.14. alludes from that place of *Deut.* to forbid mis-yoking mariage; as by the Greek word is evident, though he instance but in one example of mis-matching with an Infidell:[66] yet next to that, what can be a fouler incongruity, a greater violence to the reverend secret of nature, than to force a mixture of minds that cannot unite, and to sowe the furrow of mans nativity with seed of two incoherent and uncombining dispositions. Surely if any noysomnes of body soon destroys the sympathy of mind to that work, much more will the antipathy of minde infuse it self into all the faculties and acts of the body, to render them invalid, unkindly, and even unholy against the fundamentall law book of nature; which *Moses* never thwarts, but reverences: therfore he commands us to force nothing against sympathy or naturall order, no not upon the most abject creatures; to shew that such an indignity cannot be offer'd to man without an impious crime.[67] And when he forbids all unmatchable and unmingling natures to consort,[68] doubtles by all due consequence, if they chance through misadventure to be miscoupl'd, he bids them part asunder, as persons whom God never joyn'd.[69]

Seventhly, The Canon Law and Divines consent, that if either party be found contriving against the others life, they may be sever'd by divorce;[70] for a sin against the life of mariage is greater than a sin against the bed: the one destroys, the other but defiles: The same may be said touching those persons who beeing of a pensive nature and cours of life, have summ'd up all their solace in that free and lightsom conversation which God and man intends in mariage: wherof when they see themselves depriv'd by meeting an unsociable consort, they ofttimes resent one anothers mistake so deeply, that long it is not ere grief end one of them. When therfore this danger is foreseen that the life is in perill by living together, what matter is it whether helples greef, or wilfull practice be the cause? [19] This is certain that the preservation of life is more worth than the compulsory keeping of mariage; and it is no lesse than cruelty

noysomnes: offensiveness.
unkindly: unlike their proper nature; badly disposed; unsympathetic.

to force a man to remain in that state as the solace of his life, which he and his friends know will be either the undoing or the disheartning of his life. And what is life without the vigor and spiritfull exercise of life? how can it be usefull either to private or publick employment? shall it be therfore quite dejected, though never so valuable, and left to moulder away in heavines for the superstitious and impossible performance of an ill driv'n bargain? nothing more inviolable than vows made to God, yet we read in *Numbers,* that if a wife had made such a vow, the meer will and authority of her husband might break it;[71] how much more may he break the error of his own bonds with an unfit and mistak'n wife, to the saving of his welfare, his life, yea his faith and vertue from the hazard of overstrong temptations; for if man be Lord of the Sabbath, to the curing of a Fevor,[72] can he be lesse than Lord of mariage in such important causes as these?

Eighthly, It is most sure that some ev'n of those who are not plainly defective in body, are yet destitute of all other mariagable gifts; and consequently have not the calling to marry; unlesse nothing be requisite therto but a meer instrumentall body; which to affirm, is to that unanimous Covnant a reproach: yet it is as sure that many such not of their own desire, but by perswasion of friends, or not knowing themselves do often enter into wedlock; where finding the difference at length between the duties of a maried life, and the gifts of a single life; what unfitnes of mind, what wearisomnes, what scruples and doubts to an incredible offence and displeasure are like to follow between, may be soon imagin'd: whom thus to shut up and immure together, the one with a mischosen mate, the other in a mistak'n calling, is not a course[73] that christian wisdome and tendernes ought to use. As for the custom that some parents and guardians have of forcing mariages, it will be better to say nothing of such a savage inhumanity, but only this, that the Law which gives not all freedome of divorce to any creature endu'd with reason so assasinated, is next in crueltie.

Ninthly, I suppose it will be allow'd us that mariage is a human society, and that all human society must proceed from the mind rather than the body, els it would be but a kind of animal or beastish meeting; if the mind therfore cannot have that due company by [20] mariage, that it may reasonably and humanly desire, that mariage can be no human society, but a certain formalitie, or gilding over of little better than a brutish congresse, and so in very wisdome and purenes to be dissolv'd.

But mariage is more than human, *the covnant of God,* Pro. 2. 17.[74] therfore man cannot dissolve it. I answer, if it be more than human so much the more it argues the chief society therof to be in the soul rather than in the body, and the greatest breach therof to be unfitnes of mind rather than defect of body; for the body can have lest affinity in a covnant more than human, so that the reason of dissolving holds good the rather. Again, I answer, that the Sabbath is a higher institution, a command of the first Table,[75] for the breach wherof God hath far more and oftner testify'd his anger than for divorces, which from *Moses* till after the captivity[76] he never took displeasure at, nor then neither, if we mark the Text, and yet as oft as the good of man is concern'd, he not only permits, but commands to break the Sabbath. What covnant more contracted with God, and lesse in mans power than the vow which hath once past his lips? yet if it be found rash, if offensive, if unfruitfull either to Gods glory or the good of man, our doctrin forces not error and unwillingnes irksomly to keep it, but counsels wisdom and better thoughts boldly to break it; therfore to injoyn the indissoluble keeping of a mariage found unfit against the good of man both soul and body, as hath been evidenc't, is to make an Idol of mariage, to advance it above the worship of God and the good of man, to make it a transcendent command, above both the second and the first Table, which is a most prodigious doctrine.

Next, Wheras they cite out of the *Proverbs*, that it is *the covnant of God,* and therfore more than human, that consequence is manifestly false; for so the covnant which *Zedechiah* made with the infidell King of *Babel* is call'd *the covnant of God,* Ezech. 17.19. which would be strange to hear counted more than a human covnant. So every covnant between man and man, bound by oath, may be call'd the covnant of God, because God therin is attested. So of mariage he is the author and the witnes; yet hence will not follow any divine astriction more than what is subordinate to the glory of God and the main good of either party; for as the glory of God and their esteemed fitnes one for the other, was the motive which led them both at first to think without other revelation that God had joyn'd [21] them together: So when it shall be found by their apparent unfitnes, that their continuing to be man and wife is against the glory of God and their mutuall happines, it may assure them that God never joyn'd them; who hath revel'd his gratious will not to set the ordinance above the man for whom it was ordain'd: not to can-

prodigious: monstrous; unnatural.
attested: called to witness.
astriction: obligation.
apparent: plainly seen.
revel'd: revealed.

onize mariage either as a tyrannesse or a goddesse over the enfranchiz'd life and soul of man; for wherin can God delight, wherin be worshipt, wherin be glorify'd by the forcible continuing of an improper and ill-yoking couple; He that lov'd not to see the disparity of severall cattell at the plow, cannot be pleas'd with any vast unmeetnes in mariage. Where can be the peace and love which must invite God to such a house, may it not be fear'd that the not divorcing of such a helples disagreement, will be the divorcing of God finally from such a place? But it is a triall of our patience they say: I grant it: but which of *Jobs* afflictions were sent him with that law, that he might not use means to remove any of them if he could. And what if it subvert our patience and our faith too? Who shall answer for the perishing of all those souls perishing by stubborn expositions of particular and inferior precepts, against the general and supreme rule of charitie? They dare not affirm that mariage is either a Sacrament, or a mystery,[77] though all those sacred things give place to man, and yet they invest it with such an awfull sanctity, and give it such adamantine chains to bind with, as if it were to be worshipt like some *Indian* deity, when it can conferre no blessing upon us, but works more and more to our misery. To such teachers the saying of St. *Peter* at the Councell of *Jerusalem* will do well to be apply'd: *Why tempt ye God to put a yoke upon the necks* of Christian men, which neither the *Jews*, Gods ancient people, *nor we are able to bear:*[78] and nothing but unwary expounding hath brought upon us. To these considerations this also may be added as no improbable conjecture; seeing that sort of men who follow *Anabaptism, Famelism, Antinomianism,*[79] and other *fanatick* dreams, be such most commonly as are by nature addicted to a zeal of Religion, of life also not debausht, and that their opinions having full swinge, do end in satisfaction of the flesh, it may come with reason into the thoughts of a wise man, whether all this proceed not partly, if not cheefly, from the restraint of some lawfull liberty, which ought to be giv'n men, and is deny'd them. As by Physick we learn in menstruous bodies, where natures current hath been stopt, that the suf-[22]focation and upward forcing of some lower part, affects the head and inward sense with dotage and idle fancies. And on the other hand, whether the rest of vulgar men not so religiously professing, doe not give themselves much the more to whordom and adulteries; loving the corrupt and venial discipline of clergy Courts, but hating to hear of perfect reformation: when as they foresee that then fornication shall be austerely censur'd, adultery punisht, and mariage the appointed refuge of nature, though it hap to be never so incongruous and displeasing, must yet of force be worn out, when it can be to no other purpose but of strife and hatred, a thing odious to God. This may be worth the study of skilful men in *Theology,* and the reason of things: and lastly to examin whether some undue and ill grounded strictnes upon the blameles nature of man be not the cause in those places where already reformation is, that the discipline of the Church so often and so unavoidably brok'n, is brought into contempt and derision. And if it be thus, let those who are still bent to hold this obstinate *literality,* so prepare themselves as to share in the account for all these transgressions; when it shall be demanded at the last day by one who will scanne and sift things with more than a literal wisdom of enquiry; for if these reasons be duely ponder'd, and that the Gospel is more jealous of laying on excessive burdens than ever the Law was, lest the soul of a Christian which is inestimable, should be over-tempted and cast away, considering also that many properties of nature, which the power of regeneration it self never alters, may cause dislike of conversing even between the most sanctify'd, which continually grating in harsh tune together may breed some jarre and discord, and that end in rancor and strife, a thing so opposite both to mariage and to Christianitie, it would perhaps be lesse scandal to divorce a natural disparity, than to link violently together an unchristian dissention, committing two ensnared souls inevitably to kindle one another, not with the fire of love, but with a hatred *inconcileable,* who were they disseverd would be straight friends in any other relation. But if an *alphabetical* servility must be still urg'd, it may so fall out, that the true Church may unwittingly use as much cruelty in forbidding to divorce, as the Church of Antichrist doth wilfully in forbidding to marry.[80]

But what are all these reasonings worth, will some reply, when as the words of Christ are plainly against all divorce, except in case of fornication; let such remember as a thing not to be deny'd, that all [23] places of Scripture wherin just reason of doubt arises from the letter, are to be expounded by considering upon what occasion every thing is set down: and by comparing other Texts. The occasion which induc't our Saviour to speak of divorce, was either to convince the extravagance of the Pharises in that point, or to give a sharp and vehement answer to a tempting question. And in such cases that we are not to repose all upon the literall terms of so many words, many instances will teach us: Wherin we may plainly discover how Christ meant not to be tak'n word for word, but like a wise Physician, administring one excesse against another to reduce us to a

alphabetical: literal.
convince: confute.

perfect mean: Where the Pharises were strict, there Christ seems remisse; where they were too remisse, he saw it needfull to seem most severe: in one place he censures an unchast look to be adultery already committed: another time he passes over actuall adultery with lesse reproof than for an unchast look;[81] not so heavily condemning secret weaknes, as open malice: So heer he may be justly thought to have giv'n this rigid sentence against divorce, not to cut off all remedy from a good man who finds himself consuming away in a disconsolate and uninjoy'd matrimony, but to lay a bridle upon the bold abuses of those over-weening Rabbies; which he could not more effectually doe, than by a countersway of restraint, curbing their wild exorbitance almost into the other extreme; as when we bow things the contrary way, to make them come to thir naturall straitnes. And that this was the only intention of Christ is most evident; if we attend but to his own words and protestation made in the same Sermon not many verses before he treats of divorcing, that he came not to abrogate from the Law *one jot or tittle,* and denounces against them that shall so teach.[82] So that the question of divorce following upon this his open profession, must needs confirm us, that what ever els in the politicall Law of more speciall relation to the *Jews,* might cease to us, yet that of those precepts concerning divorce, not one of them was repeal'd by the doctrine of Christ; for if these our Saviours words inveigh against all divorce, and condemn it as adultery, except it be for adultery, and be not rather understood against the abuse of those divorces permitted in the Law, then is that Law of *Moses,* Deut. 24.1. not only repeal'd and wholly anull'd against the promise of Christ and his known profession, not to meddle in matters judicial, but that which is more strange, the very substance and purpose of that Law is contradicted [24] and convinc't both of injustice and impurity, as having authoriz'd and maintain'd legall adultery by statute. *Moses* also cannot scape to be guilty of unequall and unwise decrees, punishing one act of secret adultery by death,[83] and permitting a whole life of open adultery by Law. And albeit Lawyers write that some politicall Edicts, though not approv'd, are yet allow'd to the scum of the people and the necessitie of the times; these excuses have but a weak pulse: for first we read, not that the scoundrel people, but the choicest, the wisest, the holiest of that nation have frequently us'd these laws, or such as these. Secondly, Be it yeelded that in matters not very bad or impure, a human law-giver may slacken somthing of that which is exactly good, to the disposition of the people and the times: but if the perfect, the pure, the righteous law of God, for so are all his statutes and his judgements, be found to have allow'd smoothly without any certain reprehension, that which Christ afterward declares to be adultery, how can wee free this Law from the horrible endightment of beeing both impure, unjust, and fallacious. Neither will it serv to say this was permitted for the hardnes of thir hearts, in that sense, as it is usually explain'd, for the Law were then but a corrupt and erroneous School-master, teaching us to dash against a vital maxim of religion, by dooing foul evil in hope of some uncertain good.[84] This only text not to be match't again throughout the whole Scripture, wherby God in his perfet Law should seem to have granted to the hard hearts of his holy people under his own hand a civil immunity and free charter to live and die in a long successive adultery, under a covnant of works, till the *Messiah*, and then that indulgent permission to be strictly deny'd by a covnant of grace, besides the incoherence of such a doctrin, cannot, must not be thus interpreted, to the raising of a paradox never known till then, only hanging by the twin'd thred of one doubtfull Scripture, against so many other rules and leading principles of religion, of justice, and purity of life. For what could be granted more either to the fear, or to the lust of any tyrant, or politician, than this autority of *Moses* thus expounded; which opens him a way at will to damme up justice, and not only to admit of any *Romish*, or *Austrian* dispences,[85] but to enact a Statute of that which he dares not seem to approve, ev'n to legitimate vice, to make sin it self a free Citizen of the Common-wealth, pretending only these or these plausible reasons. And well he might, all the while that *Moses* shall be alleg'd to have don as much without shewing any reason at all. Yet this could not enter into the heart of *David, Psal.* 94.20. how any such autority as endeavours *to fashion wickednes by law,* should derive it self from God.[86] And *Isaiah* lays *woe upon them that decree unrighteous decrees,* 10.1. Now which of these two is the better Lawgiver, and which deservs most a woe, he that gives out an Edict singly unjust, or he that confirms to generations a fixt and unmolested impunity of that which is not only held to be unjust, but also unclean, and both in a high degree, not only as they themselvs affirm, an injurious expulsion of one wife, but also an unclean freedom by more than a patent to wed another adulterously? How can wee therfore with safety thus dangerously confine the free simplicity of our Saviours meaning to that which meerly amounts from so many letters, whenas it can consist neither with his former and cautionary words, nor with other more pure and holy principles, nor finally with the scope of charity, commanding by his expresse commission in a higher strain. But all rather of necessity must be understood as only against the abuse of that wise and ingenuous liberty which *Moses* gave, and to terrify a roaving conscience from sinning under that pretext.

Others think to evade the matter, by not granting any Law of divorce, but only a dispensation; which is contrary to the words of Christ, who himself calls it a Law *Mark* 10.5. But I answer, admitting it to be a dispensation, yet this is a certain rule, that so long as the cause remains, the dispensation ought: Let it be shewn therfore either in the nature of the Gospel, or of man, why this dispensation should be made void. The Gospel indeed exhorts to highest perfection; but bears with weakest infirmity more than the Law. The nature of man is as weak, and yet as hard: and that weaknes and hardnes as unfit, and as unteachable to be harshly dealt with as [25] ever. I but, say they, there is a greater portion of spirit powr'd upon the Gospel which requires perfecter obedience. But that consequence is deceavable; for it is the Law that is the exacter of our obedience ev'n under the Gospel; how can it then exact concerning divorce, that which it never exacted before? The Gospel is a covnant reveling grace, not commanding a new morality, but assuring justification by faith only, contented if we endeavour to square our moral duty by those wise and equal Mosaick rules, which were as perfect as strict and as unpardonable to the *Jews*, as to us; otherwise the law were unjust, giving grace of pardon without the Gospel, or if it give allowance without pardon, it would be dissolute and deceitfull; saying in general, *do this and live;*[87] and yet deceaving and damning with obscure and hollow permissions. Wee find also by experience that the Spirit of God in the Gospel hath been alwaies more effectual in the illumination of our minds to the gift of faith, than in the moving of our wills to any excellence of vertue, either above the *Jews* or the Heathen.[88] Hence those indulgences in the Gospel; *All cannot receive this saying; Every man hath his proper gift*, with strict charges not to lay on yokes which our Fathers could not bear.[89]

But this that *Moses* suffer'd for the hardnes of thir hearts he suffer'd not by that enacted dispensation, farre be it, but by a meer accidental sufferance of undiscover'd hypocrites, who made ill use of that Law; for that God should enact a dispensation for hard hearts to do that wherby they must live in priviledg'd adultery, however it go for the receav'd opinion, I shall ever disswade my self from so much hardihood as to beleeve: Certainly this is not the

roaving: roving; straying.
Law: the King James Bible translates the Greek word as "precept"; it also means injunction or command.
I: Aye: yes.

manner of God, whose pure eyes cannot behold, much lesse his perfect Laws dispence with such impurity; and if we consider well, we shall finde that all dispensations are either to avoid wors inconveniences, or to support infirm consciences for a time; but that a dispensation should be as long liv'd as a Law to tolerate adultery for hardnes of heart, both sins perhaps of like degree, and yet this obdurate disease cannot be conceav'd how it is the more amended by this unclean remedy, is a notion of that extravagance from the sage principles of piety, that who considers throughly, cannot but admire, how this hath been digested all this while. What may we doe then to salve this seeming inconsistence? I must not dissemble that I am confident it can be don no other way than this.

[26] *Moses, Deut.* 24.1. establisht a grave and prudent Law, full of moral equity, full of due consideration towards nature, that cannot be resisted; a Law consenting with the Laws of wisest men and civilest nations. That when a man hath maried a wife, if it come to passe he cannot love her by reason of some displeasing natural quality or unfitnes in her, let him write her a bill of divorce. The intent of which law undoubtedly was this, that if any good and peaceable man should discover some helples disagreement or dislike either of mind or body, wherby he could not cherfully perform the duty of a husband without the perpetual dissembling of offence and disturbance to his spirit, rather than to live uncomfortably and unhappily both to himself and to his wife, rather than to continue undertaking a duty which he could not possibly discharge, he might dismisse her whom he could not tolerably, and so not conscionably retain. And this Law the Spirit of God by the mouth of *Salomon*, Pro. 30.21. 23. testifies to be a good and a necessary Law; by granting it, that to *dwell with a hated woman* (for *hated* the hebrew word signifies) *is a thing that nature cannot endure.*[90] What follows then but that Law must remedy what nature cannot undergoe. Now that many licentious and hard-hearted men took hold of this Law to cloak thir bad purposes, is nothing strange to beleeve. And these were they, not for whom *Moses* made the Law, God forbid, but whose hardnes of heart taking ill advantage by this Law he held it better to suffer as by accident, where it could not be detected, rather than good men should loose their just and lawfull privilege of remedy: Christ therfore having to answer these tempting Pharises, according as his custom was, not meaning to inform their proud ignorance what *Moses* did in the true intent of the Law, which they had ill cited, suppressing the true cause for which *Moses*

extravagance: deviation.
admire: wonder.

gave it, and extending it to every slight matter, tells them thir own, what *Moses* was forc't to suffer by their abuse of his Law. Which is yet more plain if wee mark that our Saviour in the fifth of *Matth.* cites not the Law of *Moses,* but the Pharisaical tradition falsly grounded upon that law.[91] And in those other places, *Chap.* 19. and *Mark* 10. the Pharises cite the Law, but conceale the wise and human reason there exprest;[92] which our Saviour corrects not in them whose pride deserv'd not his instruction, only returns them what is proper to them; *Moses for the hardnes of your hearts sufferd you,* that is, such as you *to put away your wives;*[93] and *to you he wrote this precept*[94] for that cause, which [27] (*to you*) must be read with an impression, and understood limitedly of such as cover'd ill purposes under that Law; for it was seasonable that they should hear their own unbounded licence rebuk't, but not seasonable for them to hear a good mans requisit liberty explain'd. And to amaze them the more, because the Pharises thought it no hard matter to fulfill the Law, he draws them up to that unseparable institution which God ordaind in the beginning before the fall when man and woman were both perfect, and could have no cause to separate: just as in the same Chap. he stands not to contend with the arrogant young man who boasted his observance of the whole Law, whether he had indeed kept it or not, but skrues him up higher,[95] to a task of that perfection,[96] which no man is bound to imitate. And in like manner that pattern of the first institution he set before the opinionative Pharises to dazle them and not to bind us. For this is a solid rule that every command giv'n with a reason, binds our obedience no otherwise than that reason holds. Of this sort was that command in *Eden; Therfore shall a man cleave to his wife, and they shall be one flesh:*[97] which we see is no absolute command, but with an inference, *Therfore:* the reason then must be first consider'd, that our obedience be not mis-obedience. The first is, for it is not single, because the wife is to the husband *flesh of his flesh,* as in the verse going before. But this reason cannot be sufficient of it self; for why then should he for his wife leave his father and mother, with whom he is farre *more flesh of flesh and bone of bone,* as being made of their substance. And besides it can be but a sorry and ignoble society of life, whose unseparable injunction depends meerly upon flesh and bones. Therfore we must look higher, since Christ himself recalls us to the beginning, and we shall finde that the primitive reason of never divorcing, was that sacred and not vain promise of God to remedy mans lonelines by *making him a help meet for him,* though

impression: emphasis.
skrues him up higher: sets a higher goal for him.

not now in perfection, as at first, yet still in proportion as things now are. And this is repeated *ver.* 20. when all other creatures were fitly associated and brought to *Adam* as if the divine power had bin in some care and deep thought, because *there was not yet found a help meet for man.*[98] And can wee so slightly depresse the all-wise purpose of a deliberating God, as if his consultation had produc't no other good for man, but to joyn him with an accidentall companion of propagation, which his sudden word had already done for every beast? nay a farre lesse good to man it will be found, if she must at all aventures [28] be fastn'd upon him individually. And therefore even plain sense and equity, and, which is above them both, the all-interpreting voice of Charity her self cries loud that this primitive reason, this consulted promise of God *to make a meet help,* is the onely cause that gives authority to this command of not divorcing, to be a command. And it might be further added, that if the true definition of a wife were askt in good earnest, this clause of beeing *a meet help* would shew it self so necessary, and so essential in that demonstrative argument, that it might be logically concluded, therfore shee who naturally and perpetually is no meet help, can be no wife; which cleerly takes away the difficulty of dismissing such a one. Hence is manifest, that so much of the first institution as our Saviour mentions, for he mentions not all, was but to quell and put to nonplus the tempting Pharises; and to lay open their ignorance and shallow understanding of the Scriptures. For, saith he, *have ye not read that he which made them at the beginning, made them male and female, and said, for this cause shall a man cleave to his wife?*[99] which these blind usurpers of *Moses* chair could not gainsay: as if this single respect of male and female were sufficient against a thousand inconveniences and mischiefs to clogge a rational creature to his endles sorrow unrelinquishably. What if they had thus answer'd, Master if thou intend to make wedlock as inseparable as it was from the beginning, let it be made also a fit society, as God intended it, which wee shall soon understand it ought to be, if thou recite the whole reason of the Law. Doubtles[100] our Saviour had applauded their just answer. For then they had expounded this command of Paradise, even as *Moses* himself expounds it by his laws of divorce, that is, with due and wise regard had to the premises and reasons of the first command, according to which, without unclean and temporizing permissions he instructs us in this imperfect state what wee may lawfully doe about divorce.

depresse: disparage.
at all aventures: regardless of all risks. *individually:* indivisibly.
clogge: hamper.

But if it be thought that the Disciples offended at the rigor of Christs answer, could yet obtain no mitigation of the former sentence pronounc't to the Pharises, it may be fully answer'd, that our Saviour continues the same reply to his Disciples, as men leaven'd with the same customary licence, which the Pharises maintain'd; and displeas'd at the removing of a traditional abuse wherto they had so long not unwillingly bin us'd: it was no time then to contend with their slow and prejudicial belief, in a thing wherin an ordinary [29] measure of light in Scripture, with some attention might afterwards inform them well anough. After these considerations to take a law out of Paradise giv'n in time of original perfection, and to take it barely without those just and equal inferences and reasons which mainly establish it, nor so much as admitting those needfull and safe allowances wherwith *Moses* himself interprets it to the faln condition of man, argues nothing in us but rashnes and contempt of those means that God left us in his pure and chast Law, without which it will not be possible for us to perform the strict imposition of this command: or if wc strive beyond our strength, wee shall strive to obay it otherwise than God commands it. And lamented experience daily teaches the bitter and vain fruits of this our presumption, forcing men in a thing wherin wee are not able to judge either of their strength, or their sufferance. Whom neither one vice nor other by naturall addiction, but only mariage ruins, which doubtles is not the fault of that ordinance, for God gave it as a blessing, nor always of mans mis-choosing; it beeing an error above wisdom to prevent, as examples of wisest men so mistaken manifest: it is the fault therfore of a pervers opinion that will have it continu'd in despight of nature and reason, when indeed it was never truly joynd. All those expositers upon the fifth of *Mat.* confesse the Law of *Moses* to be the Law of the Lord, wherin no addition or diminution hath place, yet coming to the point of divorce, as if they fear'd not to be call'd lest in the kingdom of heav'n, any slight evasion will content them to reconcile those contradictions which they make between Christ and *Moses*, between Christ and Christ.

Some will have it no Law, but the granted premises of another Law following, contrary to the words of Christ *Mark* 10.5. and all other translations of gravest authority, who render it in form of a Law; agreeable to *Malach.* 2.16. as it is most anciently and modernly expounded. Besides the bill of divorce declares it to be orderly and legal. And what avails this to make the matter more righteous, if such an adulterous condition shall be mention'd to build a Law upon without either punishment or so much as forbidding, they pretend it is implicitly reprov'd in these words, *Deut.* 24.4. *after she is defil'd;*[101] but who sees not that this defilement is only in respect of returning to her former husband after an intermixt mariage; els why was not the *defiling* condition first forbidden, which [30] would have sav'd the labour of this after law; nor is it seemly or piously attributed to the justice of God and his known hatred of sin, that such a hainous fault as this through all the Law should be only wip't with an implicit and oblique touch[102] (which yet is falsly suppos'd) and that his peculiar people should be let wallow in adulterous mariages almost two thousand yeares for want of a direct Law to prohibit them; tis rather to be confidently assum'd that this was granted to apparent necessities, as being of unquestionable right and reason in the Law of nature, in that it still passes without inhibition, ev'n when greatest cause is giv'n us to expect it should be directly forbidd'n. But it was not approv'd, so much the wors that it was allow'd, as if sin had over masterd the law of God, to conform her steddy and strait rule to sins crookednes,[103] which is impossible. Besides, what needed a positive grant of that which was not approv'd? it restrain'd no liberty to him that could but use a little fraud, it had bin better silenc't, unlesse it were approv'd in some case or other. Can wee conceave without vile thoughts, that the majesty and holines of God could endure so many ages to gratifie a stubborn people in the practice of a foul polluting sin, and could he expect they should abstain, he not signifying his mind in a plain command, at such time especially when he was framing their laws and them to all possible perfection? But they were to look back to the first institution, nay rather why was not that individual institution[104] brought out of Paradise, as was that of the Sabbath, and repeated in the body of the Law, that men might have understood it to be a command? for that any sentence that bears the resemblance of a precept, set there so out of place in another world at such a distance from the whole Law, and not once mention'd there, should be an obliging command to us, is very disputable, and perhaps it might be deny'd to be a command without further dispute: however, it commands not absolutely, as hath bin clear'd, but only with reference to that precedent promise of God, which is the very ground of his institution; if that appeare not in some tolerable sort, how can wee affirm such a matrimony to be the same which God instituted! In such an accident it will best behove our sobernes to follow rather what moral *Sinai* prescribes equal to our strength, than fondly to think within our strength all that lost Paradise[105] relates.

Another while it shall suffice them, that it was not a moral, but a judicial Law, and so was abrogated. Nay rather was not abrogated [31] because judicial; which Law the ministery of Christ came not to deale with. And who put it in mans power to exempt, where Christ speaks in general of not abrogating *the least jot or tittle*, and in special not that of divorce,[106] because it follows among those Laws which he promis'd expresly not to abrogate, but to vindicate from abusive traditions. And if we mark the 31. *ver.* of *Mat.* the 5. he there cites not the Law of *Moses,* but the licencious Glosse which traduc't the Law; that therfore which he cited, that he abrogated, and not only abrogated but disallow'd and flatly condemn'd, which could not be the Law of *Moses;* for that had bin foulely to the rebuke of his great servant. To abrogate a Law made with Gods allowance, had bin to tell us only that such a Law was now to cease, but to refute it with an ignominious note of civilizing adultery, casts the reprooff, which was meant only to the Pharises, ev'n upon him who made the Law. But yet if that be judicial which belongs to a civil Court, this Law is lesse judicial than nine of the ten Commandements; for antiquaries affirm that divorces proceeded among the *Jews* without knowledge of the Magistrate, only with hands and seales under the testimony of some Rabbies to be then present. And it was indeed a pure moral *economical*[107] Law, too hastily imputed of tolerating sin; being rather so clear in nature and reason, that it was left to a mans own arbitrement to be determin'd between God and his own conscience. And that power which Christ never took from the master of family, but rectify'd only to a right and wary use at home, that power the undiscerning Canonist hath improperly usurpt into his Court-leet, and bescribbl'd with a thousand trifling impertinencies, which yet have fil'd the life of man with serious trouble and calamity. Yet grant it were of old a judicial Law, it need not be the lesse moral for that, being conversant, as it is, about vertue or vice. And our Saviour disputes not heer the judicature, for that was not his office, but the morality of divorce, whether it be adultery or no; if therfore he touch the law of *Moses* at all, he touches the moral part therof; which is absurd to imagine that the covnant of grace should reform the exact and perfect law of works, eternal and immutable; or if he touch not the Law at all, then is not the allowance therof disallow'd to us.

Others are so ridiculous as to allege that this licence of divorcing was giv'n them because they were so accustom'd in Egypt. As if an ill custom were to be kept to all posterity; for the dispensation is [32] both universal and of time unlimited, and so indeed no dis-

the licencious Glosse: i.e., the Pharisees' distorted interpretation.
economical: domestic; pertaining to the household.
Court-leet: a local court with limited powers; Milton applies the term in a derogatory sense.

pensation at all; for the over-dated dispensation of a thing unlawfull, serves for nothing but to encrease hardnes of heart, and makes men but wax more incorrigible, which were a great reproach to be said of any Law or allowance that God should give us. In these opinions it would be more Religion to advise well, lest wee make our selves juster than God, by censuring rashly that for sin which his unspotted Law without rebuke allows, and his people without being conscious of displeasing him have us'd. And if we can think so of *Moses,* as that the Jewish obstinacy could compell him to write such impure permissions against the rule of God and his own judgement, doubtles it was his part to have protested publickly what straits he was driv'n to, and to have declar'd his conscience when he gave any Law against his minde; for the Law is the touch-stone of sin and of conscience, must not be intermixt with corrupt indulgences; for then it looses the greatest praise it has, of being certain and infallible, not leading into error, as all the *Jews* were led by this connivence of *Moses,* if it were a connivence. But still they fly back to the primitive institution, and would have us re-enter Paradise against the sword that guards it.[108] Whom I again thus reply to, that the place in *Genesis* contains the description of a fit and perfect mariage, with an interdict of ever divorcing such a union; but where nature is discover'd to have never joyn'd indeed, but vehemently seeks to part, it cannot be there conceav'd that God forbids it; nay he commands it both in the Law and in the Prophet *Malachy,* which is to be our rule. And *Perkins* upon this chap. of *Mat.* deals plainly that our Saviour heer confutes not *Moses* Law, but the false glosses that deprav'd the Law;[109] which being true, *Perkins* must needs grant, that somthing then is left to that law which Christ found no fault with; and what can that be but the conscionable use of such liberty as the plain words import? So that by his own inference, Christ did not absolutely intend to restrain all divorces to the only cause of adultery. This therfore is the true scope of our Saviours will, that he who looks upon the Law concerning divorce, should look also back upon the first institution, that he may endeavour what is perfectest: and he that looks upon the institution should not refuse as sinfull and unlawfull those allowances which God affords him in his following Law; lest he make himself purer than his maker; and presuming above strength, slip into temptations irrecoverably. For this [33] is wonderfull that in all those decrees concerning mariage, God should never once mention the prime institution to disswade them from divorcing; and that he should forbid smaller sins as opposite to the hardnes of their hearts, and let this adulterous matter of divorce

touch-stone: criterion.

passe ever unreprov'd. This is also to be marvell'd at, that seeing Christ did not condemn whatever it was that *Moses* suffer'd, and that therupon the Christian Magistrate permits usury and open stews, and heer with us adultery to be so slightly punisht, which was punisht by death to these hard-hearted *Jews,*[110] why wee should strain thus at the matter of divorce, which may stand so much with charity to permit, and make no scruple to allow usury, esteem'd to be so much against charity. But this it is to embroile our selves against the righteous and all wise judgements and statutes of God; which are not variable and contrarious, as wee would make them, one while permitting and another while forbidding, but are most constant and most harmonious each to other. For how can the uncorrupt and majestick law of God, bearing in her hand the wages of life and death, harbour such a repugnance within her self, as to require an unexempted and impartial obedience to all her decrees, either from us or from our Mediator, and yet debase her self to faulter so many ages with circumcis'd adulteries, by unclean and slubbering permissions.[111]

Yet *Beza's* opinion is that a politick law, but what politick law I know not, unlesse one of *Matchiavel's,* may regulate sin;[112] may bear indeed, I grant, with imperfection for a time, as those Canons of the Apostles did in ceremonial things:[113] but as for sin, the essence of it cannot consist with rule; and if the law fall to regulate sin, and not to take it utterly away, it necessarily confirms and establishes sin. To make a regularity of sin by law, either the law must straiten sin into no sin, or sin must crook the law into no law. The judicial law can serve to no other end than to be the protector and champion of Religion and honest civility, as is set down plainly *Rom.* 13. and is but the arme of moral law, which can no more be separate from Justice than Justice from vertue: their office also in a different manner steares the same cours; the one teaches what is good by precept, the other unteaches what is bad by punishment. But if we give way to politick dispensations of lewd uncleannesse, the first good consequence of such a relaxe will be the justifying of papal stews,[114] joyn'd with a toleration of epidemick whordom. Justice must revolt from [34] the end of her authority, and become the patron of that wherof she was created the punisher. The example of usury, which is commonly alleg'd makes against the allegation which it brings, as I touch'd before. Besides that usury, so much as it is permitted by the Magistrate, and demanded with common equity, is neither against the word of God, nor the rule of charity, as hath been often discus't by men of eminent learning and judge-

suffer'd: allowed.

ment. There must be therfore some other example found out t‹ shew us wherin civil policy may with warrant from God settl‹ wickednes by law, and make that lawfull which is lawlesse. Al‹ though I doubt not but upon deeper consideration, that which i‹ true in Physick, will be found as true in polity: that as of bad pulse‹ those that beat most in order, are much wors than those that kee‹ the most inordinate circuit, so of popular vices those that may be committed legally, will be more pernicious than those which are left to their own cours at peril, not under a stinted priviledge to sin orderly and regularly, which is an implicit contradiction, but under due and fearles execution of punishment. The political law, since it cannot regulate vice, is to restraine it, by using all means to root it out: but if it suffer the weed to grow up to any pleasurable or contented higth upon what pretext soever, it fastens the root, it prunes and dresses vice, as if it were a good plant. Lastly, if divorce were granted, as he sayes, not for men, but to release afflicted wives,[115] certainly it is not only a dispensation, but a most mercifull Law: and why it should not yet be in force, beeing wholly as needfull, I know not what can be in cause but senslesse cruelty. Esteeming therfore to have asserted thus an injur'd law of *Moses* from the unwarranted and guilty name of a dispensation, to be again a most equall and requisite law, wee have the word of Christ himself, that he came not to alter the least tittle of it; and signifies no small displeasure against him that shall teach to doe so. On which relying, I shall not much waver to affirm that those words which are made to intimate, as if they forbad all divorce but for adultery (though *Moses* have constituted otherwise) those words tak'n circumscriptly, without regard to any precedent law of *Moses* or attestation of Christ himself, or without care to preserve those his fundamental and superior laws of nature and charitie, to which all other ordinances give up their seals, are as much against plain equity, and the mercy of religion, as those words of *Take, eat, this is my body,* elementally understood, are against nature and sense.[116]

[35] And surely the restoring of this degraded law, hath well recompenc't the diligence was us'd, by enlightning us further to finde out wherfore Christ took off the Pharises from alleging the law, and referr'd them to the first institution, not condemning, altering, or abolishing this precept of divorce, which is plainly moral, for that were against his truth, his promise, and his prophetick office; but knowing how fallaciously they had cited, and conceal'd the particu-

asserted: set free, vindicated.
circumscriptly: in a limited fashion, without regard to larger fashion.
us'd: i.e., used by Milton.

lar and natural reason of the law, that they might justifie any froward reason of their own, he lets goe that sophistry unconvinc't, for that had bin to teach them els, which his purpose was not. And since they had tak'n a liberty which the law gave not, he amuses[117] and repells their tempting pride with a perfection of paradise, which the law requir'd not; not therby to oblige our performance to that wherto the law never enjoyn'd the fal'n estate of man; for if the first institution must make wedlock, what ever happen, inseparable to us, it must make it also as perfect, as meetly helpfull, and as comfortable as God promis'd it should be, at least in some degree, otherwise it is not equal or proportionable to the strength of man, that he should be reduc't into such indissoluble bonds to his assured misery, if all the other conditions of that covnant be manifestly alter'd.

Next he saith, *they must be one flesh,*[118] which, when all conjecturing is don, wil be found to import no more but only to make legitimate and good the carnal act, which els might seem to have somthing of pollution in it: And inferrs thus much over, that the fit union of their souls be such as may even incorporate them to love and amity; but that can never be where no correspondence is of the minde; nay instead of beeing one flesh, they will be rather two carkasses chain'd unnaturally together; or as it may happ'n, a living soule bound to a dead corps, a punishment too like that inflicted by the tyrant *Mezentius;*[119] so little worthy to be receav'd as that remedy of lonelines which God meant us. Since wee know it is not the joyning of another body will remove lonelines, but the uniting of another compliable mind; and that it is no blessing but a torment, nay a base and brutish condition to be one flesh, unlesse where nature can in some measure fix a unity of disposition.

Lastly, Christ himself tells us who should not be put asunder, namely, those whom God hath joyn'd. A plain solution of this great controversie, if men would but use their eyes; for when is it that God may be said to joyn, when the parties and their friends con-[36]sent? No surely; for that may concurre to leudest ends, or is it when Church-rites are finisht? Neither; for the efficacy of those depends upon the presupposed fitnes of either party. Perhaps after carnal knowledge? lest of all: for that may joyn people whom neither law nor nature dares joyn; tis left, that only then, when the minds are fitly dispos'd, and enabl'd to maintain a cherfull conversation, to the solace and love of each other, according as God intended and promis'd in the very first foundation of matrimony, *I will make him a help meet for him;* for surely what God intended and promis'd, that only can be thought to be of his joyning, and not the contrary. So

amuses: bewilders.

likewise the Apostle witnesseth I *Cor.* 7.15. that in mariage *God hath call'd us to peace.* And doubtles in what respect he hath call'd us to mariage, in that also he hath joyn'd us. The rest whom either disproportion or deadnes of spirit, or somthing distastfull and avers in the immutable bent of nature renders unconjugal, error may have joyn'd; but God never joyn'd against the meaning of his own ordinance. And if he joynd them not, then is there no power above their own consent to hinder them from unjoyning; when they cannot reap the soberest ends of beeing together in any tolerable sort. Neither can it be said properly that such twain were ever divorc't, but onely parted from each other, as two persons unconjunctive, and unmariable together. But if, whom God hath made a fit help, frowardnes or private injuries have made unfit, that beeing the secret of mariage God can better judge than man, neither is man indeed fit or able to decide this matter; however it be, undoubtedly a peaceful divorce is a lesse evil and lesse in scandal than a hatefull hardhearted and destructive continuance of mariage in the judgement of *Moses,* and of Christ, that justifies him in choosing the lesse evil, which if it were an honest and civil prudence in the law, what is there in the Gospel forbidding such a kind of legal wisdom, though wee should admit the common Expositers.

Having thus unfoulded those ambiguous reasons, wherwith Christ, as his wont was, gave to the Pharises that came to sound him, such an answer as they deserv'd, it will not be uneasie to explain the sentence it self that now follows; *Whosoever shall put away his wife, except it be for fornication, and shall marry another, committeth adultery.* First therfore I will set down what is observ'd by *Grotius* upon this point, a man of general learning. Next I produce what mine own thoughts gave me, before I had seen his annotations. *Origen,* saith [37] he, notes that Christ nam'd adultery rather as one example of other like cases, than as one only exception.[120] And that it is frequent not only in human but in divine Laws to expresse one kind of fact, wherby other causes of like nature may have the like plea: as *Exod.* 21.18, 19, 20. 26. *Deut.* 19.5. And from the maxims of civil Law he shews that ev'n in sharpest penal laws, the same reason hath the same right: and in gentler laws, that from like causes to like the Law interprets rightly. But it may be objected, saith he, that nothing destroys the end of wedlock so much as adultery. To which he answers that mariage was not ordain'd only for copulation, but for mutual help and comfort of life; and if we mark

soberest: the most serious; the most important, as being rational.
common Expositers: standard commentaries upon the Bible.
uneasie: difficult.

diligently the nature of our Saviours commands, wee shall finde that both their beginning and their end consists in charity:[121] whose will is that wee should so be good to others, as that wee be not cruel to our selves. And hence it appears why *Mark* and *Luke* and St. *Paul* to the *Cor.* mentioning this precept of Christ, adde no exception;[122] because exceptions that arise from natural equity are included silently under general terms: it would be consider'd therfore whether the same equity may not have place in other cases lesse frequent. Thus farre he. From hence, is what I adde: first, that this saying of Christ, as it is usually expounded, can be no law at all, that man for no cause should separate but for adultery, except it be a supernatural law, not binding us, as wee now are: had it bin the law of nature, either the *Jews,* or some other wise and civil Nation would have pres't it: or let it be so; yet that law *Deut.* 24.1. wherby a man hath leave to part, whenas for just and natural cause discover'd he cannot love, is a law ancienter, and deeper ingrav'n in blameles nature than the other: therfore the inspired Law-giver *Moses* took care that this should be specify'd and allow'd: the other he let vanish in silence, not once repeated in the volume of his law, ev'n as the reason of it vanisht with Paradise. Secondly, this can be no new command, for the Gospel enjoyns no new morality, save only the infinit enlargement of charity, which in this respect is call'd the *new Commandement* by St. *John;*[123] as being the accomplishment of every command. Thirdly, It is no command of perfection further than it partakes of charity, which is *the bond of perfection.*[124] Those commands therfore which compell us to self-cruelty above our strength, so hardly will help forward to perfection, that they hinder and set backward in all the common rudiments of Christianity; as was prov'd. It being thus [38] clear, that the words of Christ can be no kind of command, as they are vulgarly tak'n, wee shall now see in what sense they may be a command, and that an excellent one, the same with that of *Moses,* and no other. *Moses* had granted that only for a natural annoyance, defect, or dislike, whether in body or mind, (for so the Hebrew words plainly note) which a man could not force himself to live with, he might give a bill of divorce; therby forbidding any other cause wherin amendment or reconciliation might have place. This law the Pharises depraving, extended to any slight contentious cause whatsoever. Christ therfore seeing where they halted, urges the negative part of that law, which is necessarily understood (for the determinate permission of *Moses* binds them from further licence) and checking their supercilious drift, declares that no accidental, temporary, or recon-

Thus farre he: Grotius.

ciliable offence, except fornication, can justifie a divorce: he touches not heer those natural and perpetual hindrances of society, which are not to be remov'd: for such, as they are aptest to cause an unchangeable offence, so are they not capable of reconcilement, because not of amendment. Thus is *Moses* law heer solidly confirm'd; and those causes which he permitted, not a jot gainsaid. And that this is the true meaning of this place, I prove also by no lesse an Author than St. *Paul* himself, I *Cor.* 7.10, 11.[125] upon which text Interpreters agree, that the Apostle only repeats the precept of Christ: where while he speaks of *the wives reconcilement to her husband*, he puts it out of controversie, that our Saviour meant only matters of strife and reconcilement; of which sort he would not that any difference should be the occasion of divorce, except fornication.

But because wee know that Christ never gave a judicial law, and that the word *fornication* is variously significant in Scripture, it will be much right don to our Saviours words, to consider diligently, whether it be meant heer, that nothing but actual fornication, prov'd by witnes, can warrant a divorce; for so our Canon Law judges. Neverthelesse, as I find that *Grotius* on this place hath observ'd, the Christian Emperours, *Theodosius* the second, and *Justinian*, men of high wisdom and reputed piety, decree'd it to be a divorsive fornication, if the wife attempted either against the knowledge, or obstinately against the will of her husband, such things as gave open suspicion of adulterizing; as the wilfull haunting of feasts, and invitations with men not of her neer kindred, the lying forth of her hous [39] without probable cause, the frequenting of Theaters against her husbands mind, her endeavour to prevent, or destroy conception.[126] Hence that of *Jerom*, *Where fornication is suspected, the wife may lawfully be divorc't;* not that every motion of a jealous mind should be regarded, but that it should not be exacted to prove all things by the visibility of Law-witnessing, or els to hood-wink the mind: for the Law is not able to judge of these things but by the rule of equity, and by permitting a wise man to walk the middle-way of a prudent circumspection, neither wretchedly jealous, nor stupidly and tamely patient. To this purpose hath *Grotius* in his notes. He shews also that fornication is tak'n in Scripture for such a continual headstrong behaviour, as tends to plain contempt of the husband: and proves it out of *Judges* 19.2. where the Levites wife is said to have playd the whoor against him; which *Josephus* and the *Septuagint*, with the *Chaldaean*, interpret only of stubbornnes and rebellion against her husband: and to this I adde that *Kimchi* and the two other Rabbies who glosse the text, are in the same opinion.[127] *Ben Gersom* reasons that had it bin whoordom, a Jew and a Levite would have disdain'd to fetch her again. And this I shall contribute, that had it bin whoordom she would have chosen any other place to run to, than to her fathers house, it being so infamous for an hebrew woman to play the harlot, and so opprobrious to the parents. Fornication then in this place of the *Judges,* is understood for stubborn disobedience against the husband, and not for adultery. A sin of that sudden activity, as to be already committed, when no more is don, but only lookt unchastly: which yet I should be loath to judge worthy a divorce, though in our Saviours language it bee call'd adultery.[128] Neverthelesse, when palpable and frequent signes are giv'n, the law of God *Num.* 5. so far gave way to the jealousie of a man, as that the woman set before the Sanctuary with her head uncover'd, was adjur'd by the Priest to swear whether she were fals or no; and constrain'd to drink that *bitter water* with an undoubted *curse of rottennesse, and tympany* to follow, unlesse she were innocent.[129] And the jealous man had not bin guiltles before God, as seems by the last *ver.* if having such a suspicion in his head, he should neglect this trial, which, if to this day it be not to be us'd, or be thought as uncertain of effect, as our antiquated law of *Ordalium,*[130] yet all equity will judge that many adulterous demeanors which are of lewd suspicion and example, may be held sufficient to incurre a divorce; though the act [40] it self hath not bin prov'd. And seeing the generosity of our Nation is so, as to account no reproach more abominable, than to be nicknam'd the husband of an adultresse, that our law should not be as ample as the law of God to vindicate a man from that ignoble sufferance, is our barbarous unskilfulnes, not considering that the law should be exasperated according to our estimation of the injury. And if it must be suffer'd till the act be visibly prov'd, *Salomon* himself whose judgement will be granted to surpasse the acutenes of any Canonist, confesses *Prov.* 30.19, 20. that for the act of adultery, it is as difficult to be found as the *track of an Eagle in the air, or the way of a ship in the Sea:*[131] so that a man may be put to unmanly indignities, ere it be found out. This therfore may be anough to inform us that divorsive adultery is not limited by our Saviour to the utmost act, and that to be attested always by eye-witnesse: but may be extended also to divers obvious actions, which either plainly lead to adultery, or give such presumtion wherby sensible men may suspect the deed to be already don. And this the rather may be thought, in that our

Ordalium: trial by ordeal.
generosity: nobility of conduct, particularly in matters of lineage.
exasperated: made more severe.

Saviour chose to use the word *fornication,* which word is found to signify other matrimonial transgressions of main breach to that Covnant besides actual adultery. Thus at length wee see both by this and by other places, that there is scarse any one saying in the Gospel, but must be read with limitations and distinctions, to be rightly understood; for Christ gives no full comments or continu'd discourses, but scatters the heavnly grain of his doctrin like pearle heer and there, which requires a skilfull and laborious gatherer; who must compare the words he finds, with other precepts, with the end of every ordinance, and with the general *analogy* of Evangelick doctrine: otherwise many particular sayings would be but strange repugnant riddles; and the Church would offend in granting divorce for frigidity, which is not heer excepted with adultery, but by them added. And this was it undoubtedly which gave reason to St. *Paul* of his own authority, as he professes, and without command from the Lord, to enlarge the seeming construction of those places in the Gospel, by adding a case wherin a person deserted which is somthing lesse than divorc't, may lawfully marry again. And having declar'd his opinion in one case, he leavs a furder liberty for christian prudence to determin in cases of like importance; using words so plain as are not to be shifted off, *that a brother or a sister is not under bondage in such cases;* adding also, that [41] *God hath call'd us to peace* in mariage. Now if it be plain that a Christian may be brought into unworthy *bondage,* and his religious *peace* not only interrupted now and then, but perpetually and finally hinderd in wedlock by mis-yoking with a diversity of nature as well as of religion, the reasons of St. *Paul* cannot be made special to that one case of infidelity, but are of equal moment to a divorce wherever Christian liberty and peace are without fault equally obstructed. That the ordinance which God gave to our comfort, may not be pinn'd upon us to our undeserved thraldom; to be coop't up as it were in mockery of wedlock, to a perpetual betrothed lonelines and discontent, if nothing wors ensue. There beeing nought els of mariage left between such, but a displeasing and forc't remedy against the sting of a brute desire; which fleshly accustoming without the souls union and commixture of intellectual delight, as it is rather a soiling than a fulfilling of mariage-rites, so is it anough to imbase the mettle of a generous spirit, and sinks him to a low and vulgar pitch of endeavour in all his actions, or, which is wors, leavs him in a dispairing plight of abject and hard'n'd thoughts: which condition, rather than a good man should fall into, a man usefull in the service of God and mankind, Christ himself hath taught us to dispence with the most sacred ordinances of his worship; even for a bodily healing to dispence with that holy and speculative rest of Sabbath;[132] much more then with the erroneous observance of an ill-knotted mariage for the sustaining of an overcharg'd faith and perseverance.

And though bad causes would take licence by this pretext, if that cannot be remedied, upon their conscience be it, who shall so doe. This was that hardnes of heart, and abuse of a good law which *Moses* was content to suffer rather than good men should not have it at all to use needfully. And he who to run after one lost sheep left ninety nine of his own flock at random in the Wildernes,[133] would little perplex his thought for the obduring of nine hunder'd and ninety such as will daily take wors liberties whether they have permission or not. To conclude, as without charity God hath giv'n no commandment to men, so without it, neither can men rightly beleeve any commandment givn. For every act of true faith, as well that wherby we beleeve the law, as that wherby wee endeavour the law is wrought in us by charity: according to that in the divine hymne of St. *Paul,* I Cor. 13. ***Charity beleeveth all things:*** not as if she were [42] so credulous, which is the exposition hitherto current, for that were a trivial praise, but to teach us that charity is the high governesse of our belief, and that wee cannot safely assent to any precept writt'n in the Bible, but as charity commends it to us. Which agrees with that of the same Apostle to the *Ephes.* 4.14, 15. where he tels us that the way to get a sure undoubted knowledge of things, is to hold that for truth, which accords most with charity. Whose unerring guidance and conduct having follow'd as a loadstarre with all diligence and fidelity in this question, I trust, through the help of that illuminating Spirit which hath favor'd me, to have don no every daies work: in asserting after many ages the words of Christ with other Scriptures of great concernment from burdensom and remorsles obscurity, tangl'd with manifold repugnances, to their native lustre and consent between each other: heerby also dissolving tedious and *Gordian* difficulties, which have hitherto molested the Church of God, and are now decided not with the sword of *Alexander,* but with the immaculate hands of charity, to the unspeakable good of Christendom. And let the extrem literalist sit down now and revolve whether this in all necessity be not the due result of our Saviours words: or if he persist to be otherwise opinion'd, let him well advise, lest thinking to gripe fast the Gospel, he be found in

loadstarre: lodestar, guiding star.
Gordian: Gordian knot, baffling to most men except Alexander who untied the knot by cutting it.
revolve: consider.

stead with the canon law in his fist: whose boistrous edicts tyrannizing the blessed ordinance of mariage into the quality of a most unnatural and unchristianly yoke, have giv'n the flesh this advantage to hate it, and turn aside, oft-times unwillingly, to all dissolute uncleannesse, even till punishment it self is weary and overcome by the incredible frequency of trading lust, and uncontroull'd adulteries. Yet men whose Creed is custom, I doubt not but will be still endeavouring to hide the sloth of thir own timorous capacities with this pretext, that for all this tis better to endure with patience and silence this affliction which God hath sent. And I agree, tis true; if this be exhorted and not enjoyn'd; but withall, it will be wisely don to be as sure as may be, that what mans iniquity hath laid on, be not imputed to Gods sending; least under the colour of an affected patience wee detain our selves at the gulphs mouth of many hideous temptations, not to be withstood without proper gifts, which as *Perkins* well notes, God gives not ordinarily, no not to most earnest prayers.[134] Therfore wee pray, *Lead us not into temptation*, a vain prayer, if having led our selves thither, wee love to stay in that perilous [43] condition. God sends remedies, as well as evills; under which he who lies and groans, that may lawfully acquitt himself, is accessory to his own ruin: nor will it excuse him, though he suffer, through a sluggish fearfulnes to search throughly what is lawfull, for feare of disquieting the secure falsity of an old opinion. Who doubts not but that it may be piously said to him who would dismiss frigidity, bear your trial, take it as if God would have you live this life of continence: if he exhort this, I hear him as an Angel, though he speak without warrant: but if he would compell me, I know him for Satan. To him who divorces an adulteresse, Piety might say; Pardon her; you may shew much mercy, you may win a soul: yet the law both of God and man leavs it freely to him. For God loves not to plow out the heart of our endeavours with overhard and sad tasks. God delights not to make a drudge of vertue, whose actions must be all elective and unconstrain'd. Forc't vertue is as a bolt overshot, it goes neither forward nor backward, and does no good as it stands. Seeing therfore that neither Scripture nor reason hath laid this unjust austerity upon divorce, we may resolv that nothing els hath wrought it, but that letter-bound servility of the Canon Doctors, supposing mariage to be a Sacrament, and out of the art they have to lay unnecessary burdens upon all men, to make a fair shew in the fleshly observance of matrimony, though peace and

boistrous: stiffly unyielding, hence lacking in charity.

bolt overshot: a bar (used to fasten a door or gate) jammed because pushed too far.

love with all other conjugal respects fare never so ill. And indeed the Papists who are the strictest forbidders of divorce, are the easiest libertines to admit of grossest uncleannesse; as if they had a designe by making wedlock a supportles yoke, to violate it most, under colour of preserving it most inviolable, and with all delighting, as their mystery is, to make men the day-labourers of their own affliction; as if there were such a scarsity of miseries from abroad, that wee should be made to melt[135] our choisest home-blessings, and coin them into crosses, for want wherby to hold commerce with patience. If any therfore who shall hap to read this discours, hath bin through misadventure ill ingag'd in this contracted[136] evill heer complain'd of, and finds the fits and workings of a high impatience frequently upon him, of all those wild words which men in misery think to ease themselves by uttering, let him not op'n his lips against the providence of heav'n, or tax the waies of God[137] and his divine Truth; for they are equal, easy, and not burdensome; nor do they ever crosse the just and reasonable desires of men, nor involve this our portion [44] of mortall life, into a necessity of sadnes and malecontent, by Laws commanding over the unreducible *antipathies* of nature sooner or later found: but allow us to remedy and shake off those evills into which human error hath led us through the middest of our best intentions; and to support our incident extremities by that authentick precept of sovran charity; whose grand Commission is to doe and to dispose over all the ordinances of God to man; that love and truth may advance each other to everlasting. While we literally superstitious through customary faintnes of heart, not venturing to peirce with our free thoughts into the full latitude of nature and religion, abandon our selvs to serv under the tyranny of usurpt opinions, suffering those ordinances which were allotted to our solace and reviving, to trample over us and hale us into a multitude of sorrows which God never meant us. And where he set us in a fair allowance of way with honest liberty and prudence to our guard, wee never leave subtilizing and casuisting till wee have straitn'd and par'd that liberal path into a razors edge to walk on between a precipice of unnecessary mischief on either side: and starting at every fals alarum, wee doe not know which way to set a foot forward with manly confidence and Christian resolution,

supportles: unbearable.
with all: withal; in addition.
mystery: secret policy; trade or business.
from abroad: from outside—i.e., outside the home.
superstitious: i.e., while we, being irrationally in awe of the letter of the law.
razors edge: a narrow, precarious foothold; the phrase is Greek in origin.

through the confused ringing in our ears, of *panick*[138] scruples and amazements.

Another act of papal encroachment it was, to pluck the power and arbitrement of divorce from the master of family, into whose hands God and the law of all Nations had put it, and Christ so left it, preaching only to the conscience, and not authorizing a judiciall Court to tosse about and divulge the unaccountable and secret reasons of disaffection between man and wife, as a thing most improperly answerable to any such kind of trial. But the Popes of *Rome* perceaving the great revenu and high autority it would give them, ev'n over Princes, to have the judging and deciding of such a main consequence in the life of man as was divorce, wrought so upon the superstition of those ages, as to devest them of that right which God from the beginning had entrusted to the husband: by which means they subjected that ancient and naturally domestick prerogative to an external and unbefitting judicature. For although differences in divorce about dowries, jointures, and the like, besides the punishing of adultery, ought not to passe without referring, if need be, to the Magistrate, yet for him to interpose his jurisdictive power upon the inward and irremediable disposition of man, to command love and [46] *sympathy,* to forbid dislike against the guiltles instinct of nature, is not within the province of any law to reach, and were indeed an uncommodious rudenes, not a just power. For if natures resistles sway in love or hate be once compell'd, it grows careles of itself, vitious, useles to friend, unserviceable and spiritles to the Commonwealth. Which *Moses* rightly foresaw, and all wise Lawgivers that ever knew man, what kind of creature he was. The Parliament also and *Clergy* of *England* were not ignorant of this, when they consented that *Harry the* 8th might put away *his Q. Anne of Cleve,* whom he could not like, after he had bin wedded half a year;[139] unles it were that contrary to the Proverb, they made a necessity of that which might have bin a vertu in them to do. For ev'n the freedom and eminence of mans creation gives him to be a Law in this matter to himself, beeing the head of the other sex[140] which was made for him: whom therfore though he ought not to injure, yet neither should he be forc't to retain in society to his own overthrow, nor to hear any judge therin above himself. It being also an unseemly affront to the sequestr'd and vail'd modesty of that sex, to have her unpleasingnes and other concealements bandied up and down, and aggravated in open Court by those hir'd maisters of

panick: noises heard in mountainous country and the groundless fears aroused by them were attributed to the god Pan.
Proverb: i.e., to make a virtue of necessity.

tongue-fence. Such uncomely exigences it befell no lesse a Majesty than *Henry the* 8th to be reduc't to; who finding just reason in his conscience to forgoe his brothers wife, after many indignities of beeing deluded, and made a boy of by those his two *cardinal* Judges, was constrain'd at last for want of other prooff, that shee had bin carnally known by Prince *Arthur,* ev'n to uncover the nakednes of that vertuous Lady, and to recite openly the obscene evidence of his brothers chamberlain.[141] Yet it pleas'd God to make him see all the tyranny of *Rome,* by discovering this which they exercis'd over divorce; and to make him the beginner of a reformation to this whole Kingdom by first asserting into his *familiary* power the right of just divorce. Tis true, an adultres cannot be sham'd anough by any publick proceeding; but that woman whose honour is not appeach't, is lesse injur'd by a silent dismission, being otherwise not illiberally dealt with, than to endure a clamouring debate of utterles things, in a busines of that civil secrecy and difficult discerning, as not to be over-much question'd by neerest friends. Which drew that answer from the greatest and worthiest *Roman* of his time *Paulus Emilius,* being demanded why hee would put away his wife for no visible reason, *This Shoo,* saith he, and held [46] it out on his foot, *is a neat shoo, a new shoo, and yet none of yee know where it wrings me?*[142] much lesse by the unfamiliar cognisance of a fee'd gamester can such a private difference be examin'd, neither ought it.

Lastly, All law is for some good that may be frequently attain'd without the admixture of a wors inconvenience; but the Law forbidding divorce, never attains to any good end of such prohibition, but rather multiplies evil. If it aim at the establishment of matrimony, wee know that cannot thrive under a loathed and forc't yoke, but is daily violated:[143] if it seek to prevent the sin of divorcing, that lies not in the law to prevent; for he that would divorce and marry again, but for the law, hath in the sight of God don it already. Civil or political sin it never was, neither to Jew nor Gentile, nor by any judicial intendment of Christ, only culpable as it transgresses the allowance of *Moses* in the inward man, which not any law but conscience only can evince. The law can only look whether it be an injury to the divorc't, which in truth it can be none, as a meer separation; for if she consent, wherin has the law to right her? or consent not, then is it either just and so deserv'd, or if unjust, such in all likelihood was the divorcer, and to part from an unjust man is a happines, and no injury to be lamented.[144] But suppose it be an injury, the Law is not able to amend it, unlesse she think it other

familiary: domestic.

than a miserable redresse to return back from whence she was expell'd, or but entreated to be gon, or els to live apart still maried without mariage, a maried widow. Last, if it be to chast'n the divorcer, what Law punishes a deed which is not moral, but natural, a deed which cannot certainly be found to be an injury, or how can it be punisht by prohibiting the divorce, but that the innocent must equally partake? So that wee see the Law can to no rational purpose forbid divorce, it can only take care that the conditions of divorce be not injurious. But what? Shall then the disposal of that power return again to the maister of family? Wherfore not? Since God there put it, and the presumptuous Canon thence bereft it.[145] This only must be provided, that the ancient manner be observ'd in presence of the Minister, and other grave selected Elders; who after they shall have admonisht and prest upon him the words of our Saviour, and he shall have protested in the faith of the eternal Gospel, and the hope he has of happy resurrection, that otherwise than thus he cannot doe, and thinks himself, and this his case not contain'd in that prohibition of divorce [47] which Christ pronounc't, the matter not beeing of malice, but of nature, and so not capable of reconciling, to constrain him furder were to unchristen him, to unman him, to throw the mountain of *Sinai* upon him,[146] with the waight of the whole Law to boot, flat against the liberty and essence of the Gospel, and yet nothing available either to the sanctity of mariage, the good of husband, wife, or childern,[147] nothing profitable either to Church or Common wealth. But this would bring in confusion.[148] Be of good cheer, it would not: it wrought so little disorder among the *Jews*, that from *Moses* till after the captivity not one of the Profets thought it worth rebuking; for that of *Malachy* well lookt into, will appeare to be, not against divorcing, but rather against keeping strange Concubines, to the vexation of their *Hebrew* wives.[149] If therfore wee Christians may be thought as good and tractable as the *Jews* were, and certainly the prohibiters of divorce presume us to be better, then lesse confusion is to be fear'd for this among us than was among them. If wee bee wors, or but as bad, which lamentable examples confirm wee are, then have wee more, or at least as much need of this permitted law, as they to whom God expresly gave it under a harsher covnant. Let not therfore the frailty of man goe on thus inventing needlesse troubles to it self to groan under the fals imagination of a strictnes never impos'd from above, enjoyning that for duty which is an impossible and vain supererogating. *Bee not righteous overmuch,* is the counsel of *Ecclesiastes; why shouldst thou destroy thy self?*[150] Let us not be thus over-curious to strain at *atoms,*[151] and yet to stop every vent and cranny of permissive liberty: lest nature wanting those needful pores, and breathing places which God hath not debarr'd our weaknes, either suddenly break out into some wide rupture of open vice, and frantick heresy, or els inwardly fester with repining and blasphemous thoughts, under an unreasonable and fruitles rigor of unwarranted law. Against which evils nothing can more beseem the religion of the Church or the wisdom of the State, than to consider timely and provide. And in so doing, let them not doubt but they shall vindicate the misreputed honour of God and his great Lawgiver, by suffering him to give his own laws according to the condition of mans nature best known to him, without the unsufferable imputation of dispencing legally with many ages of ratify'd adultery. They shall recover the misattended words of Christ to the sincerity of their true sense from manifold contradictions, and shall [48] open them with the key of charity. Many helples Christians they shall raise from the depth of sadnes and distresse, utterly unfitted, as they are, to serv God or man: many they shall reclaime from obscure and giddy sects, many regain from dissolute and brutish licence, many from desperate hardnes, if ever that were justly pleaded. They shall set free many daughters of *Israel,* not wanting much of her sad plight *whom Satan had bound eighteen years.*[152] Man they shall restore to his just dignity, and prerogative in nature, preferring the souls free peace before the promiscuous draining of a carnal rage. Mariage from a perilous hazard and snare, they shall reduce to be a more certain hav'n and retirement of happy society; when they shall judge according to God and *Moses,* and how not then according to Christ? when they shall judge it more wisdom and goodnes to break that covnant seemingly and keep it really, than by compulsion of law to keep it seemingly, and by compulsion of blameles nature to break it really, at least if it were ever truly joyn'd. The vigor of discipline they may then turn with better successe upon the prostitute loosenes of the times, when men finding in themselvs the infirmities of former ages, shall not be constrain'd above the gift of God in them to unprofitable and impossible observances never requir'd from the civilest, the wisest, the holiest Nations, whose other excellencies in moral vertu they never yet could equal. Last of all, to those whose mind still is to maintain textual restrictions, wherof the bare sound cannot consist somtimes with humanity, much lesse with charity, I would ever answer by putting them in remembrance of a command above all commands, which they seem to have forgot, and who spake it; in comparison wherof this which they so exalt, is but a petty and subordinate precept. *Let them goe* therfore with whom

reduce: lead back, restore. Cf. title of the tract.

I am loath to couple them, yet they will needs run into the same blindnes with the Pharises, *let them goe therfore* and consider well what this lesson means, *I will have mercy and not sacrifice;*[153] for on that *saying all the Law and Profets depend,*[154] much more the Gospel whose end and excellence is mercy and peace: Or if they cannot learn that, how will they hear this, which yet I shall not doubt to leave with them as a conclusion: That God the Son hath put all other things under his own feet; but his Commandments he hath left all under the feet of charity.[155]

The end.

NOTES

1. Milton upheld equity to both sexes in seeking a divorce, but contemporaries accused him of advocating excessive freedom for the wife or tyrannical powers for the husband.

2. Milton may mean the biblical revelation in general, or specifically the Ten Commandments and related revelations such as Exod. xx 24; Deut. xx 1 and xxiii 21; and Lev. xxvi; but he probably has in mind what he later in this tract calls "the generall and supreme rule of charitie" (1643 ed., p. 21) in accordance with which "as oft as the good of man is concern'd," God "not only permits, but commands to break the Sabbath" (ibid., p. 20).

3. Judg. xi 30–39.

4. The army of Mattathias, refusing to fight on the Sabbath, was slain (1 Macc. ii 32–38).

5. Deut. xxiv 1: "When a man hath taken a wife, and married her, and it come to pass that she find no favor in his eyes, because he hath found some uncleanness in her: then let him write her a bill of divorcement, and give it in her hand, and send her out of the house." The abusers of this law were the Pharisees, to whom Jesus stated, Matt. v 31–32: "It hath been said, Whosoever shall put away his wife, let him give her a writing of divorcement: But I say unto you, that whosoever shall put away his wife, saving for the cause of fornication, causeth her to commit adultery: and whosoever shall marry her that is divorced committeth adultery." In Milton's view this passage was misinterpreted in the canon law on divorce as formulated in Gratian's *Decretum,* 1140.

6. Gen. ii 18: "It is not good that the man should be alone; I will make him a help meet for him."

7. Society; consorting together. Cf. Thomas Adams, *Works* (1629), p. 1234: "There is no such fountaine of comfort on earth, as marriage; whether for Societie, or for Posteritie." Aquinas placed the only essential purpose of marriage in reproduction and contended that another man would otherwise have served better as a companion or helpmeet (*Summa Theologica,* English Dominican trans. [21 vols.; 1912–25], I, q. 92, a. 1, c).

8. In canon law a consummated Christian marriage is indissoluble according to Canon 1015. After 1533 its authority in England depended upon Parliament, but its principles continued in large measure to be operative in ecclesiastical courts.

9. The italics are probably intended to emphasize that this is an incompatibility rooted in the contrary natures of the partners, not a mere aversion but an innate incapacity for mutual sympathy and harmony.

10. Solomon, traditionally the author of Ecclesiastes; Eccles. v 13.

11. Milton simplifies what he regards as the corruption of the institution of marriage by reducing it to three phases: (a) "for many ages"—to about 385 when the popes imposed celibacy as "an absolute rule of discipline on the ministers of the altar" (Henry C. Lea, *History of Sacerdotal Celibacy in the Christian Church* [London, 1932], pp. 43–44). In Milton's view the teachings of Tertullian (d. 222) represented this phase; (b) "a second time"—the period of St. Jerome (d. 420) and subsequently, during which, in Milton's view, the refraining from marriage by the monastic orders and priests was urged upon all; (c) "afterwards"—the period in which the doctrine that a valid marriage is sacramental (and therefore binding regardless of adultery or desertion) developed until it was made explicit by the Councils of Florence (1439) and Trent (1545–63).

12. Milton's not mentioning desertion here may be biographically significant: his wife Mary departed from him a few months after their marriage and failed to return "at the time appointed" (E. Phillips' life of Milton). In the second edition (1644), when Mary was still absent, Milton added "or desertion." He thus stated the two grounds for divorce recognized by most Protestants but not admitted by Roman Catholics because of their sacramental view of marriage. Of the Reformed churches, the Anglican was alone in not adopting a more liberal view of divorce for adultery or desertion than the medieval one.

13. See note 5 above.

14. The characteristics of an individual's peculiar nature or constitution; since they belong to his nature they are "faultles" inasmuch as he may not be blamed for them.

15. For more than 500 years, beginning with Constantine (d. 337), the Christian emperors treated marriage and divorce as private and secular. Roman law allowed repudiation for improper conduct or divorce for consenting parties without reasons being stated.

16. *Annotationes in libros Evangeliorum* (Amsterdam, 1641).

17. In July 1643, about a month before this tract was published, the Westminster Assembly of Divines met to discuss reformation of the church.

18. Incapacity to complete a marriage by sexual intercourse was recognized by the Roman Catholic and Anglican churches and by governments as constituting non-fulfillment of a contract, which could be thus made void. In theory English church courts in Milton's lifetime up to the writing of this tract could do no more than pronounce a separation (divorce *a mensa et thoro*, from bed and board) without permission to remarry. In practice the only means to a full divorce was a nullity suit. See A. R. Winnett, *Divorce and Remarriage in Anglicanism* (1958), and L. Dibdin and C. C. Healey, *English Church Law and Divorce* (1912). Milton's argument is that "fit and matchable" mental, spiritual, and social intimacy and harmony between a man and a woman is as essential as physical consummation to the completion of a marriage; and that lack of such harmony should have equal weight with physical incapacity as a basis for divorce (with right to remarry).

19. Two kinds of opposition—from the literalist adherents to canon law tradition and from sensualists who conceive that the only purpose of marriage is sexual gratification.

20. Gen. ii 18; Matt. xi 30.

21. Milton uses medical imagery in this tract to illustrate how "canon-law impediments to divorce have created diseases in human society which result in a distortion of nature" (Kester Svendsen, *Milton and Science* [Cambridge, Mass., 1956], p. 217).

22. Cf. Matt. xi 17: "We have piped unto you, and ye have not danced."

23. Despite Frank Allen Patterson's opinion that Milton here "states exactly what he proposes to prove, defines his conception of marriage, and places careful restrictions" (*The Student's Milton* [1934], p. 111), this thesis modifies the earlier assertions that mental compatibility is *no less essential* to marriage than physical capability and that deficiency in either should have *equal* force in a divorce plea. Moreover the thesis does not accurately summarize what follows. In it Milton asserts that there must be mutual consent for a divorce; but he later reasons that an evil woman should be divorceable without her consent and that a good woman ought to be glad to leave a man who rejects her, even if she does not desire a divorce. Despite the clause about children, there is little mention of them in the tract.

24. Under canon law a marriage could be annulled if physical incapacity preceded it and, after three years, was judged incurable.

25. According to the 1549 and later eds. of *The Booke of the Common Prayer,* marriage "is not to bee enterprised, nor taken in hande unadvisedlye, lightelye, or wantonly, to satisfie mens carnal lustes and appetites, lyke brute beastes that have no understanding." The Anglican marriage service continues that marriage was ordained for the mutual society, help, and comfort that one partner should have of the other both in prosperity and adversity.

26. Milton rhetorically balances the literal physical flowing with figurative equivalents. Cf. *Paradise Lost,* IV, 760.

27. In the second edition Milton added, "and we have plenty of examples," possibly to indicate that he was not necessarily being autobiographical.

28. I.e., in the course of methodically adducing and interpreting many biblical texts, Milton will explain how and why it came about that God became unjustly accused of permitting adultery to the Hebrews in Deut. xxiv 1. The number of scriptural passages cited for this point in the first edition is not large; but in the second, many of the additions treat divorce as a dispensation to the Jews and are supported by ample scriptural authority.

29. 1 Cor. vii 9.

30. Cf. *Paradise Lost,* VIII, 579–82: "But if the sense of touch whereby mankind / Is propagated seem such dear delight / Beyond all other, think the same voutsaf't / To Cattel and each Beast." The OED interpretation that in this passage "Cattel" is used figuratively for "rubbish" seems to be a mere lexicographer's guess; for obviously "such cattell" refers to "carnall lust" and "sensitive desire."

31. This and related references to Adam indicate that Milton was already thinking about the subject of *Paradise Lost.* In that epic before the Fall, the sexual relations of Adam and Eve were "Rites / Mysterious of connubial Love," and "Founded in Reason, Loyal, Just, and Pure" (IV, 742–43, 755); but during or immediately after the Fall, their relationship was entirely sensual and thus incontinent: "Carnal desire enflaming, hee on *Eve* / Began to cast lascivious Eyes, she him / As wantonly repaid; in Lust they burn" (IX, 1013–15).

32. In the *Yale Milton,* II, 251, Coolidge notes that Milton could find but slight support for this explanation in patristic or later commentators and cites Calvin's interpretation as typical: "What Paul here means by the expression 'to burn' is to be inflamed with lust (*libidine aestuare*) so that you cannot resist." Cf. Charles Diodati, *Pious Annotations,* on 1 Cor. vii 9: " 'Than to burn': viz., with a carnall desire: which God doth not give every one the gift to quench without marriage, whereby man is troubled in his minde, and hindered in his spirituall actions, which require a tranquillity of all passions."

33. Song of Sol. viii 6–7: "Love is strong as death. . . . Many waters cannot quench love, neither can the floods drown it." In the allegorical interpretation these words were spoken by Christ's Bride, the church.

34. A desire akin to animals' importunate appetite for provender or fodder.

35. Adam's loneliness led to God's creation of Eve and thus, in a sense, begat their love: Gen. ii 18–24.

36. *An image of earth,* the element corresponding to the humor of black bile (hence: atribilious, melancholy, irascible, sullen), and of phlegm, the element of water or the humor corresponding to it (hence: cold, sluggish, apathetic).

37. Eccles. ix 9 (with omissions).

38. 1 Cor. vii 15: "if the unbelieving depart, let him depart. A brother or a sister [i.e., a believer] is not under bondage in such cases: but God hath called us to peace."

39. Mal. ii 16–a controverted text, corrupted in transmission. The King James Bible gives: "For the Lord, the God of Israel, saith that he hateth putting away"; this agrees with the sense of the Tremellius-Junius Latin in *Testamenti Veteris Biblia Sacra* (Geneva, 1630), *Sibi odio esse dimissionem ait Jehovah Deus Israelis,* and with that of the Revised Standard Version of 1952, "For I hate divorce;" etc. But the King James gives an alternative marginal reading, ". . . if he hate her, put her away," which is the sense of the Vulgate, *Si odio habueris, dimitte,* and agrees with Calvin's rendering in *Praelectiones in Duodecim Prophetas Minores* (Geneva, 1559, p. 772), *Si odio habeas* (quisquis odio habet) *dimittat* (uxorem); however Calvin says that the passage does not give divine sanction for repudiating a wife and interprets Malachi to mean that repudiating a wife is a less serious offense than taking many wives. In *Tetrachordon* (1645 ed., p. 24) Milton translates, "*Let him who hateth put away,*" and comments that "this place also hath bin tamper'd with, as if it were to be thus render'd, *The Lord God saith, that he hateth putting away.*" In *Colasterion* (1645 ed., p. 21), Milton translates ". . . *that he who hateth may put away.*"

40. E.g., Rom. xiii 10: "Love worketh no ill to his neighbor: therefore love is the fulfilling of the law." The anonymous author of *An Answer to a Book Intituled, The Doctrine and Discipline of Divorce* (1644 ed., p. 37) objected to the use of "onely" by Milton in this passage, but he replied in *Colasterion* (1645 ed., p. 21), "I cited no particular Scripture, but spake a general sense, which might bee collected from many places. For seeing love includes Faith, what is ther that can fulfill every commandment but only love?" The reference to "that mystery of joy and union" earlier in this sentence points to another passage which Milton had in mind, Eph. v 25–32. See note 60 below.

41. Lev. xxi 1–4; Ezek. xliv 25.

42. Rom. xii 1: "present your bodies a living sacrifice"; Heb. xiii 15: "let us offer the sacrifice of praise to God continually, that is, the fruit of our lips, giving thanks to his name"; *Boke of Common Prayer* (1552), Communion service: "this our Sacrifice of prayse and thanks geving . . . our selves . . . to be a . . . lively Sacrifice unto thee."

43. The phrase "vale of tears" (*hac lacrymarum valle*) is not biblical but occurs in the prayer *Salve Regina,* "Hail Holy Queen," recited at the end of the Rosary and in the modernized Roman Catholic liturgy at the end of the Mass.

44. Mal. ii 13.

45. Eph. ii 3, referring to all men in an unregenerate condition.

46. 1 Cor. vii 12–16.

47. Acts x 11–28; see below *Areopagitica,* note 124.

48. 1 Cor. vii 14.

49. Ezra x 3; Neh. xiii 25.

50. 2 Cor. vi 14–15, 17; Isa. lii 11.

51. I.e., a convert from Jehovah to paganism who seduced either a wife or husband to idolatry was to be put to death according to God's decree in Deut xiii 6, 9.

52. I.e., two reasons will be sufficient—sufficient in accordance with the Gospel as well as the Mosaic law—to give strength and validity to the command of those two divinely inspired reformers Ezra and Nehemiah, to put away (divorce) an idolater; one of those reasons is the moral one that it is dangerous to keep idolaters as wives or husbands; and the other one is the antagonism between Christ and Belial (or Satan), an antagonism which is so great that it cannot be properly expressed to another. Milton has in mind that the replacement of the Mosaic law by the Christian gospel did not end the force of moral reason, which is eternal, as is God's antipathy to Satan and his idolatrous followers. Therefore, the command given by the Old Testament prophets still has force, being a moral one based on eternal reason and the divine antipathy toward Satan and idolaters.

53. And therefore Paul advises the Corinthians to forbear from separating so long as there is a probability that the unbeliever's heart is opening to faith in Christ.

54. In 1 Cor. vii 10–12, Paul differentiates between God's commands and his own statements—statements which Milton regards as intended as advice to be freely taken or disregarded, not as commands.

55. 1 Cor. vii 6, 25.

56. In *Annotationes Majores in Novum Testamentum* (1594), II, 189, Theodore Beza (Théodore de Bèze, d. 1605) comments on 1 Cor. vii 15 that Paul adds nothing to Christ's naming adultery as the sole cause of divorce.

57. When he accuses St. Augustine. Beza states that Augustine in *De bono conjugali* twists or distorts what Paul intended as permissive.

58. συνευδοκεῖ. The prefix in the first three letters indicates reciprocity of one *with* another. Corresponding to Milton's rendering, "and she joyn in consent" the King James translation of 1 Cor. vii 12 reads "and she be pleased."

59. Milton echoes Matt. vi 24: "No man can serve two masters."

60. This ordering of the ends of Christian marriage and the strong priority given to "godly society," "cherful help . . . toward sanctity of life," and "the inward knot of mariage, which is peace and love" involved a change of emphasis from Christian traditions on marriage, a modification which must have seemed revolutionary to many of Milton's readers. It exemplifies his claim that he was returning to the teachings of Christ and the apostles as he understood them and was clearing away what he regarded as distortions of, and additions to, them. Milton's contemporary, James Ussher, in *A Body of Divinity* (5th ed., 1658, pp. 282–83) stated that the marriage of Christians "is ordained for procreation sake and for their own mutual comfort and preservation, not for fulfilling of lust only"; and that in the holy use of matrimony there must be "holy and Christian conversation together," mutual delight, fidelity, and confidence, and "sober use of the marriage bed." It is noteworthy that, unlike Milton, Ussher does not mention love; nor does he mention the biblical passage which provided the strongest basis for marital love, Eph. v 25–32 (see note 40 above). Indeed, very few earlier theologians did so. Saint John Chrysostom, writing in the fourth century, was one of the few exceptions: he dwelt eloquently on this passage in *Homily XX on Ephesians V*. The Council of Trent, in 1563, was the first ecumenical council to make a statement on the role of love in marriage: the Roman Catechism stated that marital acts could be done "for pleasure or lust," quoted

Jerome, *Against Jovinian,* that "Nothing is more foul than to love one's wife as if she were an adultress," and emphasized the appropriateness of marriage as a symbol of Christ's love for the church inasmuch as "husband and wife are bound by the very greatest mutual charity and benevolence" (II, viii, 35 and 15). On the other hand, *The Holy Sacrament of Matrimony* (1602) by Thomas Sanchez, though it treated the moral and canonical aspects of matrimony more comprehensively than ever before, failed to set a positive value on marital love. Thus Milton was to some extent an innovator in his emphasis on what he regarded as the highest end of marriage, or at least part of a reforming movement of ideas which included some Puritans and some Anglicans. John Donne, preaching in 1621, stated that the institution of marriage had three objects: "it was given for a remedy against burning; And then . . . for propagation, for children; And lastly . . . for mutuall help" (*The Sermons of John Donne,* ed. Simpson and Potter [Berkeley, 1957], Vol. III, p. 244); but he seems to have regarded this ordering as an ascending one; for his emphasis is on the third. Milton himself, in *Christian Doctrine,* I, x, concentrated on the importance of conjugal love and mutual assistance as the prime end and form of marriage.

61. See the Foreword to this section on Milton's plan to write on these three subjects.

62. I.e., to rectify only the last and lowest of these wants by means of divorce is a perverse violation of rights, and the professed reason for this restriction is totally lacking in warmth; and yet this is all that the code of civil law and canon law take into cognizance.

63. The "thesis" of divorce for incompatibility; however Coolidge (*Yale Milton,* II, 269) interprets this as "whether an Idolatrous heretick ought to be divorc't."

64. The bracketed words, supplied in the second edition, seem to have been originally intended and are therefore added here.

65. Up to this point Milton quotes Paul's words in 1 Cor. ix 8–9; but Paul's following words are different: "For it is written in the law of Moses, Thou shalt not muzzle the mouth of the ox that treadeth out the corn. Doth God care for oxen? Or saith he it altogether for our sakes? For our sakes, no doubt this is written: that he that ploweth should plow in hope; and he that treadeth in hope should be a partaker of his hope" (1 Cor. ix 9–10). The passage that Paul thus interprets allegorically is Deut. xxv 4: "Thou shalt not muzzle the ox when he treadeth out the corn." Following the *pattern* of Paul's reasoning, Milton substitutes Deut. xxii 9–10 ff., "Thou shalt not sow thy vineyard," etc., and interprets these injunctions against defiling mixtures as being applicable to human beings (written "for our sakes") when similarly interpreted in an allegorical fashion. The meaning, then, is that inasmuch as God's concern about the misyoking of asses and oxen is a concern for human beings, He must be likewise concerned over the misyoking of a husband and wife; the injunction against such mismatching must be applicable to them too.

66. Paul wrote "Be ye not unequally yoked together [ἑτεροζυγοῦντες] with unbelievers." This sole use of this Greek word in the New Testament corresponds to its use in Deut. xxii 10 in the Greek (Septuagint) version of the Old Testament, thus making it evident for Milton that Paul is alluding to this portion of Deuteronomy, which provides many instances of mismatching, though Paul mentions only marriage with an infidel.

67. The interpretation is extrapolated from Deut. xxii 9–10 and Lev. xix 19.

68. There seems to be no single statement in the Mosaic books forbidding *all* such unions, but Milton draws this inference from Lev. xviii, xix 19, xx 10–21; Deut. xxii 9–12, xxiv 1–2, xxvii 20–23; and related texts.

69. I.e., Moses forbids all unmatchables to consort; if, by chance or ill lu two such beings do consort, it undoubtedly follows in logic that Moses bids the to separate, for God has never joined them.

70. *Decretales Gregorii IX,* IV, xix, and Johann Schneidewein (Joann Oinotomus), *In quattuor Institutionum Imperialum Justiniani Imp. libros cor mentarii* (Venice, 1612), I, iv, 10, are cited by Milton in *Colasterion* (16 ed., p. 24) as his authorities here.

71. According to Num. xxx, if a woman makes such a sacred vow, and h father or husband hears her make it and she disavows it on the same day, it annulled and God will forgive her for making it.

72. Mark ii 27: "The sabbath was made for man, and not man for the sa bath." Having made this statement, Jesus healed the man with the withere hand (Mark iii 5). Cf. Matt. xii 8–13; Luke vi 5–10.

73. *whom thus . . . is not a course:* this wording, headed *Omitted pa. 1 lin. 28,* is taken from a page at the end of the tract (sig. H, unnumbered). seems not to be a correction of printers' faults but Milton's revision after r consideration of the wording printed on page 19: "whom thus to shut up an immure in an unequall and mischosen match, is not a cours"; he refers to suc afterthoughts in *Areopagitica* (1644 ed., p. 21).

74. Prov. ii 10–17; though marriage is not specifically mentioned in this pas sage, "the covenant of her God" was generally interpreted as referring to it.

75. The first of the stone tablets given to Moses by God on which the Te Commandments were written (Exod. xxxi 18). The first bore commands con cerning man's worship of God, including, "Remember the sabbath day, to kee it holy" (Exod. xx 8). The commands of the second deal with man's relation to other men.

76. The period of Jewish exile in Babylon; its end is recorded in Ezra i–ii.

77. Milton probably means that they dare not confirm the Roman Catholi doctrine that marriage is a sacrament and a "mystery" in the sense of a sacra mental rite. The Thirty-Nine Articles of the Church of England denied tha marriage was a sacrament like baptism but called it "an excellent misterie" inas much as the spiritual marriage and unity between Christ and his church is signi fied and represented in it. Milton himself had termed it a "mystery of joy an union" in this tract (1643 ed., p. 12); in *Tetrachordon* (1645 ed., p. 11), h was to refer to "the sacred and misterious bed of marriage" and to add (p. 18) "I dispute not now whether matrimony bee a mystery or no; if it bee of Chris and his Church, certainly it is not meant of every ungodly and miswedde mariage, but then only mysterious, when it is a holy, happy, and peaceful match. But when a Saint is joyn'd with a reprobate, or both alike, wicked wit wicked, fool with fool, a hee drunkard with a she, when the bed hath bin . . but an old haunt of lust and malice mixt together, no love, no goodnes, n loyalty, but counterplotting, and secret wishing one anothers dissolution, this i to me the greatest mystery in the world, if such a mariage as this, can be th mystery of ought, unless it be the mystery of iniquitie."

78. Acts xv 10.

79. These labels were used loosely and pejoratively for extremes of com munism, free love, and immorality attributed to those who believed that only adult baptism was valid, those who adhered to the mysticism taught by Hendrik Niclaes, founder of the Familists or Family of Love, and those who taught that the moral law is not binding upon Christians saved by faith. In the second edition Milton added, "if we understand them not amisse."

80. Protestant extremists identified the Papacy and Roman Catholicism in general with Antichrist; cf. 1 John ii 18, 22, iv 3; 2 John 7; 2 Thess. ii 3–4.

ilton alludes to the Roman Catholic rule against the marriage of priests and o 1 Tim. iv 1–3.

81. Matt. v 28: "whosoever looketh on a woman to lust after her hath committed adultery with her already in his heart." Concerning the woman taken in dultery, Jesus said to the Pharisees, "He that is without sin among you, let him irst cast a stone at her," and when Jesus learned that no man had condemned er, "Neither do I condemn thee: go, and sin no more" (John viii 3–11).

82. Matt. v 17–19.

83. Lev. xx 10; Deut. xxii 22.

84. The next sentence in the body of the text reads: "Wee cannot therfore vith safety thus confine the free simplicity of our Saviours meaning to that which meerly amounts from so many letters; whenas it can consist neither with is former, and cautionary words, nor with the scope of charity, commanding by his expresse commission in a higher strain." This is followed by the last sentence in this paragraph. The alternative wording given above is Milton's revision, provided on sig. H under the heading *Omitted pa. 24. lin. 22.*

85. Any Roman Catholic dispensations to do what is forbidden by ecclesiastical law, or to omit to do what it enjoins, and similar relaxation or suspension of laws for particular cases granted by or to the House of Austria, i.e., the Hapsburg rulers of Austria and Spain.

86. Psalm xciv 20: "Shall the throne of iniquity have fellowship with thee, which frameth mischief by a law?"

87. Gen. xlii 18: "Joseph said . . . This do, and live; for I fear God."

88. This sentence was not retained in the second edition. In *Milton and the Puritan Dilemma* (Toronto, 1942), p. 366, Arthur Barker comments on this passage: "I do not think that Milton ever again expressed this opinion; it contradicted his deepest convictions. But it is perfectly consistent with the demand of the anti-prelatical pamphlets for a divinely authorized discipline; and it is the belief which justified, in the eyes of the Presbyterians, the stern restraining hand of authority." In the second edition Milton made instead "a distinction between sin and natural affection or inclination." The reasons for the deletion are that "Milton was not writing in defence of sin; and the antinomian implications" would have justified Presbyterian attacks; Milton was reacting against the Presbyterian position and his own argument in the anti-prelatical tracts; and he was returning to and developing "the doctrine expressed in *Comus* and *Areopagitica* which involves precisely the belief that the process of regeneration both illuminates the mind and enables the will to progress in the virtue which makes it free."

89. A fusion of Matt. xix 11; 1 Cor. vii 7; and Acts xv 10.

90. Prov. xxx 21–23: "the earth is disquieted, and . . . cannot bear . . . a servant when he reigneth . . . an odious woman when she is married," etc. The meaning of the Hebrew word given by Milton is literally accurate.

91. Matt. v 31 omits the conditions set down in Deut. xxiv 1.

92. Matt. xix 3, 7; Mark x 2, 4.

93. Matt. xix 8: "Moses because of the hardness of your hearts suffered you to put away your wives; but from the beginning it was not so."

94. Mark x 5: "For the hardness of your heart he wrote you this precept."

95. The musical metaphor is that of turning a screw to tune a string to higher pitch.

96. Matt. xix 21: "Jesus said unto him, If thou wilt be perfect, go and sell that thou hast, and give to the poor . . . and follow me."

97. Gen. ii 24.

98. Gen. ii 20.

99. Matt. xix 4–5.

100. The *d* is not capitalized in the 1643 edition.

101. Deut. xxiv 4: "Her former husband, which sent her away, may not tak her again to be his wife, after that she is defiled; for that is abomination befor the Lord: and thou shalt not cause the land to sin."

102. A *hainous fault* should only be rubbed gently (or mildly attacked) wit a slight contact which is not clearly expressed and is indirect.

103. As if sin had gotten the better of the law of God, making that law adjus its undeviating code to sin's crookedness. Also involved is wordplay on "con form" in the sense of "shape" and "rule" meaning a straight line.

104. Refers to that indissoluble institution of marriage, with perhaps word play on "individual" as unique and "single" because first.

105. Probably an indication that Milton was already thinking of his epic. In the Trinity manuscript of his early poems there are plans for plays on Adam and Eve: see Harris Fletcher, ed., *Milton's Poetical Works, Facsimile Edition* II (Cambridge, Mass., 1945), especially p. 17 where the words "Paradise Lost" occur.

106. Matt. v 18.

107. The divorce bill or *get* was written in a very explicit form under the direction of the husband, who handed it to his wife with a formal declaration before witnesses.

108. Cf. *Paradise Lost*, XII, 641–44.

109. William Perkins (1558–1602) wrote numerous theological works, taught at Cambridge, and propounded a systematic though modified Calvinism that was influential in English Puritanism. He is the only English writer on divorce cited by name in this first edition.

110. Lev. xx 10.

111. Milton personifies the law of God as a female figure rather like Justice bearing her scales. This pure and majestic figure bears in her hand men's wages or rewards; according to Rom. vi 23, men may receive either God's gift, "eternal life through Christ," or death, which is "the wages of sin." (Cf. the fourth and fifth sentences in the next paragraph which state that if we give way to politic dispensations of lewd uncleanness, Justice must revolt from the end—i.e., the goal and purpose—of her authority and become the patron of what she was created to punish.) Within herself this personified Divine Law cannot allow anything so incompatible as this: to require unqualified obedience from men or from Christ, their Mediator, and yet to degrade herself by falling short of her own standard of excellence for a long time by granting unclean and slovenly permission for regulated adulteries or for sin according to rule. Cf. the succeeding sentence. Such permissions fail to satisfy the whole law and are the result of cutting, mutilating, or limiting it. Milton probably has in mind Gal. v 1–9, especially verse 3, where Paul says, "I testify again to every man that is circumcised, that he is a debtor to do the whole law." By implication, a man who took advantage of the Pharisaic interpretation of what Moses said about divorce would be committing circumcised or legally regulated adultery, not keeping the whole law of God as is required. (In this interpretation, "faulter" is taken to mean *fall short of a standard;* it could possibly mean "falter" in the sense of *stumble, stagger,* or *give way.*)

112. In *Annotationes,* I, 111, Beza comments on Matt. xix 8 that the moral law unqualifiedly requires good and forbids evil, but that, because of men's wickedness, civil laws cannot completely abolish some things like usury and

erefore permit them by regulation. Machiavelli's account of Renaissance stateaft led to his being credited with advocating ruthless and unethical political pediency.

113. Such things as circumcision, which the apostles tolerated without reiiring it. Cf. 1 Cor. vii 18.

114. Protestant propagandists remarked that brothels existed in Rome and iat they paid taxes to the Pope as a civil ruler.

115. Beza, *Annotationes,* I, 111.

116. Protestants agreed that the italicized words, spoken by Jesus at the Last upper (Matt. xxvi 26–28) were not to be interpreted literally; accordingly iey rejected the doctrine of transubstantiation. That doctrine, as declared by ie Council of Trent, is quoted by Pope Paul VI in *Mysterium Fidei,* his enyclical on the Holy Eucharist: "within the holy sacrament of the Eucharist, fter the consecration of the bread and wine, Our Lord Jesus Christ, true God nd true man, is really, truly, and substantially contained under those outward ppearances."

117. I.e., he reveals the sophistry and fallacious reasoning of what they do nd say, reducing it to nonsense and thus confounding them with what Milton iter (1643 ed., p. 36) refers to as "those ambiguous reasons, wherwith Christ . . . gave to the Pharises . . . such an answer as they deserved."

118. Matt. xix 5; Gen. ii 23–24.

119. According to a myth related by Virgil (*Aeneid,* VIII, 485–88), this Etruscan king had men bound to corpses and left to die.

120. Grotius, *Annotationes* (1641), pp. 98–99.

121. Milton similarly puts "charity" on his title page and as the last word in his tract.

122. Statements made by Christ on adultery are recorded in Mark x 7–12; Luke xvi 18; and 1 Cor. vii 10–11; Grotius cites Mark x 11 and 1 Cor. vii 10, but not Luke. None of these statements include the exception (here italicized) made in Matt. xix 9: "Whosoever shall put away his wife, *except it be for fornication,* and shall marry another, committeth adultery; and whoso marrieth her which is put away doth commit adultery."

123. John xiii 34: "A new commandment . . . as I have loved you, that ye also love one another."

124. Col. iii, especially verse 14: "above all these things put on charity, which is the bond of perfection."

125. "Let not the wife depart from her husband: But and if she depart, let her remain unmarried, or be reconciled to her husband: and let not the husband put away his wife."

126. Milton follows Grotius, *Annotationes,* p. 98, in this and the following sentence, including its citation from Jerome's commentary on Matthew.

127. As Grotius noted but did now "shew" (op. cit., p. 97), some commentators on Judg. xix 2–10 interpreted the Levite's accepting back his concubine after she "played the whore against him and went away unto her father's house," as evidence that she had left his bed and divorced herself from him in mind but had not committed adultery with another man. Hence the Greek word for "fornication" as used in the Bible admitted a broad interpretation. Josephus (*Antiquities,* V, ii), the Greek of the Septuagint, and the Aramaic of the Chaldean paraphrase supported such a view; and, as Milton added to what Grotius supplied, the same opinion was voiced by three rabbinical scholars: Kimchi, Levi ben Gerson (Gersonides), and Rashi.

128. Matt. v 28.

129. Num. v 11 ff.

130. After the Lateran Council of 1215 forbade priests to participate in s trials, Parliament abolished them in England.

131. Prov. xxx 18–20: "There be . . . four [things] which I know not: way of an eagle in the air; the way of a serpent upon a rock; the way of a s in the midst of the sea; and the way of a man with a maid. Such is the way an adulterous woman; she eateth, and wipeth her mouth, and saith, I have d no wickedness."

132. Matt. xii 8–12.

133. Matt. xviii 12.

134. William Perkins, *Christian Oeconomie* (London, 1609), p. 17: "T gifts of God are of two sorts, some are Generall, some are Proper. General g are such as God giveth generally to all. . . . Proper gifts, are those which given only to some certain men; of which sort is the gift of continencie and su like, which though they bee often and earnestly asked, yet they are seldome never granted unto some men."

135. The basic image is that of melting something precious to make coins b cause of a lack of money for commerce. The applied meaning of the image that men should be made to dissolve or squander their finest domestic blessin making them into afflictions for lack of anything else that would allow them exercise patience or endurance. The Hebrew word for gift was sometimes tra lated as "blessing"; cf. 2 Kings v 15; "crosses" is a word applied both to affl tions to be borne and to certain coins which were stamped with a cross mark.

136. Contracted in the commercial sense of the image in the previous se tence—as a laborer is under contract to work for daily wages; Milton also allud to the marriage contract; and he may also be playing on the word's meani *concentrated.*

137. Cf. Milton's attempt in *Paradise Lost,* I, 25–26 to "assert Eternal Prov dence, / And justifie the wayes of God to men."

138. The italicizing of *panick* probably indicates that the scruples are unjus fied and paganly superstitious (in contrast to *Christian* resolution).

139. Henry's marriage to his fourth wife was annulled by Convocation wi ratification by Parliament because his "misliking" her before and after marria made him unable to consummate the marriage, thus qualifying him under canc law for annulment grounded on defective intention.

140. 1 Cor. xi 3: "the head of the woman is the man." Cf. *Paradise Los* IV, 440–43.

141. Catherine of Aragon, widow of Prince Arthur, was allowed by a pap dispensation to marry his brother Henry; Henry asked for an annulment of th union and the case was tried by a legatine court headed by Cardinals Campegg and Wolsey. Henry claimed that the previous marriage had been consummate and that the dispensation was therefore invalid, and a chamberlain testified th after the nuptial night Arthur used words which meant "that he had carnall used her" (Edward Hall, *The Union of the Two Noble and Illustre Famelies* *Lancastre and York* [London, 1550], f. clxxxii).

142. Plutarch's life of Aemilius Paulus (V, 1–2), a third-century Roma consul.

143. For example, "if we disregard entirely the evidence of illegitimate chil dren, in the ninety years between 1570 and 1659 we find forty-nine know cases of notorious marital quarrels, separations *a mensa et thoro,* or annulment among the peerage, which is about 10 per cent. of all marriages. The wors period seems to have been between 1595 and 1620, when something like one third of the older peers were estranged from or actually separated from thei wives" (Lawrence Stone, *The Crisis of the Aristocracy* [Oxford, 1965], p. 661)

144. Despite Milton's explicit reference to "mutual consent" in his stated "thesis," this is the only treatment of it in the tract, and consent by the wife is not found to be essential here.

145. "There is . . . evidence that the ancient practice of private divorce existed . . . especially among the Independents. . . . Milton not only recognizes the practice but even makes the defence of it one of the principal points in his *Doctrine and Discipline of Divorce*" (C. L. Powell, *English Domestic Relations, 1487–1653* [New York, 1917], p. 70). The Westminster Assembly condemned private divorce (ibid., p. 88).

146. *Sinai:* i.e., to impose on him the whole burden of the Mosaic law, which God revealed on Mount Sinai.

147. Despite the qualification concerning children in the "thesis," there are only three references to children in the tract, other than those in phrases like "children of wrath."

148. I.e., this objection will be raised by opponents. Milton's answer follows.

149. Mal. ii 14–16.

150. Eccles. vii 16.

151. Let us not in this manner be oversolicitous to strain at motes, or particles of dust–i.e., to do more than we are supposed to do. Cf. Matt. xxiii 24.

152. Luke xiii 16.

153. With reference to Hos. vi 6, "For I desired mercy, and not sacrifice; and the knowledge of God more than burnt offerings," Christ stated in Matt. ix 13, "go ye and learn what that meaneth, I will have mercy, and not sacrifice: for I am not come to call the righteous, but sinners to repentance."

154. Matt. xxii 40: "On these two commandments [love of God and neighbor] hang all the law and the prophets."

155. 1 Cor. xv 27: "For he hath put all things under his feet. But when he saith all things are put under him, it is manifest that he is excepted, which did put all things under him." 1 Tim. i 5: "the end of the commandment is charity out of a pure heart, and of a good conscience, and of faith unfeigned."

THE JUDGEMENT OF MARTIN BUCER,
CONCERNING DIVORCE, WRITT'N TO
EDWARD THE SIXT, IN HIS SECOND BOOK OF
THE KINGDOM OF CHRIST.
AND NOW ENGLISHT.
WHERIN A LATE BOOK RESTORING
THE *DOCTRINE AND DISCIPLINE OF DIVORCE,*
IS HEER CONFIRM'D AND JUSTIFY'D
BY THE AUTHORITIE OF MARTIN BUCER.
TO THE PARLAMENT OF ENGLAND.

John 3.10. *Art thou a teacher of Israel, and know'st not these things?*

Publisht by Authoritie.
Printed by Matthew Simmons, 1644

About the beginning of May 1644, three months after the second edition of *Doctrine and Discipline* had appeared, Milton heard "that Martin Bucer had writt'n much concerning divorce." About 1550 that renowned leader of German Protestantism, then professor of divinity at Cambridge, had addressed his judgments on the subject to Edward VI in a work which was published as *De Regno Christi* [Of the Kingdom of Christ] in 1551 and which was contained in fuller form in his *Scripta Anglicana* (1557). Milton, delighted to find that his independent ideas on divorce had parallels in the work of this respected theologian, hastened to publish those portions of it which approximated his own statements in *Doctrine and Discipline.* The translation might better be called a redaction or even a digest, for Milton, while not altering Bucer's meaning, boldly avoided the prolixity of the original Latin, recasting it into conc and powerful English. The tract was entered in the Stationers' Re ister on July 15 and was in print in time for George Thomason date his copy August 6. Milton's purpose was not to lean on the a thority of another but to discredit his slanderers by demonstrati that their attacks were applicable to the revered Bucer; also to ga for himself and his own ideas merit by association. He had alrea made similar use of Grotius in the first edition of *Doctrine and D cipline* and of Paulus Fagius in the second. The pamphlet, bas on the 1557 printing of *De Regno Christi,* consists of testimonies approbation of Bucer made by learned men, a prefatory addre to Parliament, twenty-four pages of redacted translations, and brief postscript. The only complete, fully annotated edition is th by Arnold Williams in *Yale Milton,* II. On Bucer, see Hastings Eel *Martin Bucer* (Oxford, 1931) and Constantin Hopf, *Martin Buc and the English Reformation* (Oxford, 1946).

EXTRACTS FROM *THE JUDGEMENT OF MARTIN BUCER*

To the PARLAMENT

. . . the constitution and reformation of a common-wealth . . . is, like a building, to begin orderly from the foundation therof, which is mariage and the family, to set right first what ever is amisse therein. How can there els grow up a race of warrantable men, while the house and home that breeds them, is troubl'd and disquieted under a bondage not of Gods constraining . . . but laid upon us imperiously in the worst and weakest ages of knowledge, by a canonicall tyranny of stupid and malicious Monks. . . . Certainly if it be in mans discerning to sever providence from chance, I could allege many instances, wherein there would appear cause to esteem of me no other than a passive instrument under some power and counsel higher and better than can be human, working to a general good in the whole cours of this matter [of divorce]. For that I ow no light or leading receav'd from any man in the discovery of this truth, what time I first undertook it in *the doctrine and discipline of divorce,* and had only the infallible grounds of Scripture to be my guide, he who tries the inmost heart, and saw with what severe industry and examination of my self, I set down every period, will be my witnes. When I had almost finisht the first edition, I chanc't to read in the notes of *Hugo Grotius* upon the 5. of Matth. whom I strait understood inclining to reasonable terms in this controversie: and somthing he whisper'd rather than disputed about the law of charity, and the true end of wedlock. Glad therfore of such an able assistant, how ever at much distance, I resolv'd at length to put off into this wild and calumnious world. For God, it seems, intended to prove me, whether I durst alone take up a rightful cause against a world of disesteem, and found I durst. My name I did not publish, as not willing it should sway the reader either for me or against me. But when I was told, that the stile, which what it ailes to be so soon distinguishable, I cannot tell, was known by most men, and that some of the Clergie began to inveigh and exclaim on what I was credibly inform'd they had not read, I took it then for my proper season both to shew them a name that could easily contemn such an indiscreet kind of censure, and to reinforce the question with a more accurat diligence: that if any of them would be so good as to leav rayling, and to let us hear so much of his lerning and Christian wisdom, as will be strictly demanded of him in his answering to this probleme, care was had he should not spend his preparations against a nameles pamphlet. By this time I had lernt that *Paulus Fagius*, one of the chief Divines in Germany, sent for by *Frederic* the *Palatine*, to reforme his dominion; and after that invited hither in King *Edwards* dayes to be Professor of Divinity in Cambridge, was of the same opinion touching divorce, which these men so lavishly traduc't in me. What I found, I inserted where fittest place was, thinking sure they would respect so grave an author, at lest to the moderating of their odious inferences. And having now perfected a second edition, I referr'd the judging therof to your high and impartial sentence, honour'd Lords and Commons. . . . for that I knew I had divulg'd a truth linkt inseparably with the most fundamental rules of Christianity, to stand or fall together, and was not un-inform'd that divers lerned and judicious men testify'd their daily approbation of the book. Yet at length it hath pleas'd God, who had already giv'n me satisfaction in my self, to afford me now a means wherby I may be fully justify'd also in the eyes of men. When the book had bin now the second time set forth wel-nigh three months, as I best remember, I then first came to hear that *Martin Bucer* had writt'n much concerning divorce: whom earnestly turning over, I soon perceav'd, but not without amazement, in the same opinion, confirm'd with the same reasons which in that publisht book without the help or imitation of any precedent Writer, I had labour'd out, and laid together. Not but that there is some difference in the handling, in the order, and the number of arguments, but still agreeing in the same conclusion. So as I may justly gratulat mine own mind, with due acknowledgement of assistance from above, which led me, not as a lerner, but as a collateral teacher, to a sympathy of judgment with no lesse a man than *Martin Bucer*. . . . I would ask now the foremost of my profound accusers, whether they dare affirm that to be licentious, new and dangerous, which *Martin Bucer* so often, and so urgently avoucht to be most lawfull, most necessary, and most Christian, without the lest blemish to his good name, among all the worthy men of that age, and since, who testifie so highly of him? . . . This is also another fault which I must tell them; that they have stood now almost this whole year clamouring a farre off, while the book hath bin twice printed, twice bought up, and never once vouchsaft a friendly conference with the author, who would be glad and thankfull to be shewn an error, either by privat dispute, or public answer, and could retract, as well as wise men before him; might also be worth the gaining, as one who heertofore, hath done good service to the Church by their own confession. Or if he be obstinat, their confutation would have render'd him without excuse, and reclam'd others of no mean parts who incline to his opinion. But . . . God, that I may ever magnifie and record this his goodnes, hath unexpectedly rais'd up as it were from the dead, more than one famous light of the first reformation to bear witnes with me, and to doe me honour in that very thing, wherin these men thought to have blotted me: And hath giv'n them the proof of a capacity which they despis'd, running equal, and authentic with some of thir chiefest masters unthought of, and in a point of sagest moment. However, if we know at all, when to ascribe the occurrences of this life to the work of a special providence, as nothing is more usual in the talk of good men, what can be more like to a special providence of God, than in the first reformation of England, that this question of divorce, as a main thing to be restor'd to just freedom, was writt'n, and seriously commended to *Edward* the sixt, by a man call'd from another Countrey to be the instructer of our nation, and now in this present renewing of the Church and Common-wealth, which we pray may be more lasting, that the same question should be again treated and presented to this Parlament, by one enabl'd to use the same reasons without the lest sight or knowledge of what was done before. . . . Ye have a nation that expects now, and from mighty sufferings aspires to be the example of all Christendom to a perfetest reforming. Dare to be as great, as ample, and as eminent in the fair progress of your noble designes, as the full and goodly stature of truth and excellence it self: as unlimited by petty presidents and copies, as your unquestionable calling from heaven givs ye power to be. What are all our public immunities and privileges worth, and how shall it be judg'd that we fight for them with minds worthy to enjoy them, if wee suffer our selvs in the mean while not to understand the most important freedom that God and Nature hath givn us in the family; which no wise Nation ever wanted, till the Popery and superstition of some former ages attempted to remove and alter divine and most prudent Laws for human and most imprudent Canons; wherby good men in the best portion of thir lives, and in that ordinance of God which entitles them from the beginning to most just and requisite contentments, are compell'd to civil indignities, which by the law of *Moses* bad men were not compell'd to. Be not bound about, and straitn'd in the spatious wisdom of your free Spirits, by the scanty and unadequat and inconsistent principles of such as condemn others for adhering to traditions, and are themselves the prostrate worshippers of Custom; and of such a tradition as they can deduce from no antiquitie, but from the rudest, and thickest barbarism of Antichristian times. . . . The autority, the lerning, the godlines of this man consulted with, is able to out-ballance all that the lightnes of a vulgar opposition can bring to counterpoise. I leav him also as my complete suretie and testimonial, if Truth be not the best witnes to it self, that what I formerly presented to your reading on this subject, was good, and just, and honest, not licentious. Not that I have now more confidence by the addition of these great Authors to my party; for what I wrote was not my opinion, but my knowledge; evn then when I could trace no footstep in the way I went: nor that I think to win upon your apprehensions with numbers and with names, rather than with reasons, yet certainly the worst of my detracters will not except against so good a baile of my integritie and judgement, as now appeares for me. They must els put in the fame of *Bucer* and of *Fagius*, as my accomplices and confederats into the same endightment. . . .

JOHN MILTON.

TETRACHORDON:

EXPOSITIONS UPON THE FOURE CHIEF PLACES IN SCRIPTURE, WHICH TREAT OF MARIAGE, OR NULLITIES IN MARIAGE.

ON GEN. 1.27, 28. COMPAR'D AND EXPLAIN'D BY GEN. 2.18, 23, 24. DEUT. 24.1, 2. MATTH. 5.31, 32. WITH MATTH. 19. FROM THE 3D. V. TO THE 11TH. 1 COR. 7 FROM THE 10TH TO THE 16TH. WHERIN THE DOCTRINE AND DISCIPLINE OF DIVORCE, AS WAS LATELY PUBLISH'D, IS CONFIRM'D BY EXPLANATION OF SCRIPTURE, BY TESTIMONY OF ANCIENT FATHERS, OF CIVILL LAWES IN THE PRIMITIVE CHURCH, OF FAMOUSEST REFORMED DIVINES. AND LASTLY, BY AN INTENDED ACT OF PARLAMENT AND CHURCH OF ENGLAND IN THE LAST YEARE OF EDWARD THE SIXTH.

BY THE FORMER AUTHOR J. M.

London: Printed in the yeare 1645

Only one edition of *Tetrachordon*, probably printed by Thomas Paine and Matthew Simmons, appeared in Milton's lifetime. The title, literally "four-stringed," refers to a tetrachord, which Milton's nephew, Edward Phillips, defined in his dictionary as "a Concord, or Interval of three Tones: Among the Ancients, it was an Instrument, or rank of four strings, accounting the *Tetrachord* for one Tone." It would seem that Phillips was thinking of a common chord such as that formed by the notes c'e'g'c", or, more specifically, of the three intervals between those four notes, the essential idea being that when they were sounded together, the effect was pleasing or harmonious to the ear. Whether he and his uncle were aware that the strings on a Greek lyre were tuned to a primitive scale equivalent to that represented on the modern piano by e'f'g'a'—notes, which, struck together, would not be very agreeable—is somewha uncertain; but it is clear that Milton meant by the title that h would demonstrate the agreement or consonance of the teaching on divorce in Genesis, Deuteronomy, Matthew, and First Corinthi ans. (As a rule, when Milton uses a technical term and takes car not to narrow its meaning by precise explanation or the context, i is probably wise not to try to read more into the term than its vague ness conveys.)

Milton's aim was to satisfy those who wished a fuller discussion of scriptural passages on divorce than he had given and, in the address to Parliament, to defend himself against Herbert Palmer's demand (in a sermon to Parliament, August 13, 1644) for suppression of *Doctrine and Discipline.* Milton also wished to vindicate himself against the charge of another minister, Daniel Featley, whose *The Dippers Dipt* (1645) inveighed against the damnable doctrine of "a Tractate of Divorce, in which the bonds of marriage are let loose to inordinate lust," and against other adverse critics. Against them Milton arrayed the results of scholarly research, which rivals the erudition displayed in *Of Prelatical Episcopacy* but excels it in range. As Arnold Williams points out in his preface to the only systematically annotated edition of *Tetrachordon,*[1] in form and method it is a biblical commentary, an example of what is perhaps the prime genre of Renaissance scholarship—scriptural exegesis.

On Milton's reaction to the unfavorable reception of *Tetrachordon,* see his sonnet, "A book was writt of late call'd *Tetrachordon.*"[2]

EXTRACTS FROM *TETRACHORDON*

[1] ". . . nothing now adayes is more degenerately forgott'n, than the true dignity of man. . . ."

[2] Christ has set us "in the free custody of his love . . . to follow that which most edifies, most aides and furders a religious life, makes us holiest and likest to his immortall Image, not that which makes us most conformable and captive to civill and subordinate precepts . . . no ordinance human or from heav'n can binde against the good of man. . . ."

[3] On St. Paul's statements about man and wife in 1 Cor. xi,

[1] *Yale Milton,* II, 572.

[2] *Complete English Poetry of John Milton,* ed. John T. Shawcross (New York, 1963), p. 200.

Col. iii 18, and Eph. v 24: "Neverthelesse man is not to hold her as a servant, but receives her into a part of that empire which God proclaims him to, though not equally, yet largely, as his own image and glory: for it is no small glory to him, that a creature so like him, should be made subject to him. Not but that particular exceptions may have place, if she exceed her husband in prudence and dexterity, and he contentedly yeeld, for then a superior and more naturall law comes in, that the wiser should govern the lesse wise, whether male or female. . . . from her the sin first proceeded, which keeps her justly in the same proportion still beneath."

[4] "God enjoyns not this supposed strictnes of not divorcing either to punish us, or to try our patience."

[9] "We cannot therefore alwayes be contemplative, or pragmaticall abroad, but have need of som delightful intermissions, wherin the enlarg'd soul may leav off a while her severe schooling; and like a glad youth in wandring vacancy, may keep her hollidaies to joy and harmles pastime: which as she cannot well doe without company, so in no company so well as where the different sexe in most resembling unlikenes, and most unlike resemblance cannot but please best and be pleas'd in the aptitude of that variety. Wherof lest we should be too timorous, in the aw that our flat sages would form us and dresse us, wisest *Salomon* among his gravest Proverbs countenances a kinde of ravishment and erring fondnes in the entertainment of wedded leisures; and in the Song of Songs, which is generally beleev'd, even in the jolliest expressions to figure the spousals of the Church with Christ, sings of a thousand raptures between those two lovely ones farre on the hither side of carnall enjoyment."

[10] ". . . we may conclude that such a mariage, wherin the minde is so disgrac't and vilify'd below the bodies interest, and can have no just or tolerable contentment, is not of Gods institution, and therfore no mariage."

[11] "What courts of concupiscence are these, wherein fleshly appetite is heard before right reason, lust before love or devotion? . . . What is this, besides tyranny, but to turn nature upside down, to make both religion, and the minde of man wait upon the slavish errands of the body, and not the body to follow either the sanctity, or the sovranty of the mind unspeakably wrong'd, and with all equity complaining?"

COLASTERION:

A REPLY TO A NAMELES ANSWER AGAINST *THE DOCTRINE AND DISCIPLINE OF DIVORCE.*

WHEREIN THE TRIVIAL AUTHOR OF THAT ANSWER IS DISCOVER'D, THE LICENSER CONFERR'D WITH, AND THE OPINION WHICH THEY TRADUCE DEFENDED.

BY THE FORMER AUTHOR, *J. M.*

Prov. 26.5. *Answer a Fool according to his folly, lest hee bee wise in his own conceit*

Printed in the Year, 1645.

In *Tetrachordon* Milton elaborated and defended his doctrines on divorce with dignity and erudition in a treatise intended primarily for men of good will and sound reason. But if his ideas were to prevail there was need for a more popular, more trivial defense to silence vulgar misrepresentations of his teachings; and his virtuosity was equal to the challenge of answering fools according to their folly. So, as he was finishing *Tetrachordon,* probably in February 1645, he complemented it with a rapidly composed diatribe in which he exposed his shallower calumniators to contempt for their presumption and to correction for their folly. The conventions of seventeenth-century controversy permitted either the dignified decorum of sober defense or the undignified display of a kind of pen-lashing which may well strike the modern reader as offensively base and unworthy of Milton's greatness. In his times, such stooping to a sort of gutter journalism was an accepted convention exercised and read with gusto. *Colasterion* should be viewed in the tradition of such academic exercises as Milton's *Sixth Prolusion,* as a vituperative sally obedient to well-established traditions. For example, in it Milton adopts an Olympian *persona,* assumes that his chief victim is an ignoble varlet, and treats him in an appropriately insulting style and manner.

That opponent, author of *An Answer to a Book, Intituled, The Doctrine and Discipline of Divorce, or, A Plea for Ladies and Gentlewomen, and all other Maried Women against Divorce* (November 1644), has never been identified. (The tract is reproduced in facsimile in William R. Parker, *Milton's Contemporary Reputation,* 1940.) The author was probably a minor clergyman although Milton alleges that he was a serving man turned solicitor, having already deduced from the "low and home-spun expression of his Mother *English*" that he "could for certain bee no other than some mechanic." Milton also asserts that he heard for certain that a divine of note, out of his good will to the tract, had revised it. But all this is obviously a rhetorical invention, a debating stratagem to discredit his critic as a presumptuous upstart. The biblical quotation on the title page, "Answer a Fool according to his folly, lest hee bee wise in his own conceit," and the title itself set the tone of the pamphlet. The Greek word *kolasterion* means a place of punishment—hence a prison or the like—or an instrument, such as a whip, used in punishing—and by extension a punishing or correction.

Colasterion appeared concurrently with *Tetrachordon,* unlicensed, unregistered, with its printer (probably Matthew Simmons) unnamed. The only systematic edition of it is that by Lowell W. Coolidge.[1] As a companion piece to the severity of *Tetrachordon* it affords a sort of comic relief.

Milton begins by stating that he had heard rumors of confutations forthcoming against *Doctrine and Discipline* and reports of attacks on it made by preachers; but he "hop'd as for a blessing to see som peece of diligence, or lerned discretion" attacking him. Instead he found a slanderous summing-up of his teachings as "divorce at pleasure" in William Prynne's *Twelve Considerable Serious Questions Touching Church Government* (1645). With considerable sarcasm Milton disposes of this charge as falsehood joined with rash and heedless calumny. Then the anonymous *Answer* came to his hands:

> Gladly I receiv'd it, and very attentively compos'd my self to read; hoping that now some good man had voutsaft the pains to

[1] *Yale Milton,* II, 710–58.

instruct mee better, than I could yet learn out of all the volumes which for this purpos I had visited. Only this I marvel'd, and other men have since, when as I, in a Subject so new to this age, and so hazardous to please, conceal'd not my name, why this Author defending that part which is so creeded by the people, would conceal his? But ere I could enter three leaves into the Pamflet, (for I deferr the peasantly rudenes, which by the Licencers leav, I met with afterwards) my satisfaction came in abundantly, that it could bee nothing why hee durst not name himself, but the guilt of his own wretchednes. For first, not to speak of his abrupt and bald beginning, his very first page notoriously bewraies him an illiterat, and arrogant presumer in that which hee understands not; bearing us in hand as if hee knew both Greek and Ebrew, and is not able to spell it; which had hee bin, it had bin either writt'n as it ought, or scor'd upon the Printer. . . .

I mean not to dispute Philosophy with this Pork, who never had any, But I appeal to all experience . . . whether any man can with the safety of his life bring a healthy constitution into physic with this designe, to alter his natural temperament, and disposition of minde. How much more vain, and ridiculous would it bee, by altering and rooting up the grounds of nature, which is most likely to produce death or madnes, to hope the reducing of a minde to this or that fitnes, or two disagreeing minds to a mutual sympathy. . . . And if the fault bee in the one, shall the other live all his daies in bondage and misery for anothers perversnes, or immedicable disaffection? . . .

I have now don that, which for many causes I might have thought, could not likely have bin my fortune, to bee put to this under-work of scowring and unrubbishing the low and sordid ignorance of such a presumptuous lozel. Yet *Hercules* had the labour once impos'd upon him to carry dung out of the *Augean* stable. At any hand I would bee rid of him: for I had rather, since the life of man is likn'd to a Scene, that all my entrances and *exits* might mixe with such persons only, whose worth erects them and their actions to a grave and *tragic* deportment, and not have to do with *Clowns and Vices*. But if a man cannot peaceably walk into the world, but must bee infested, somtimes at his face, with dorrs and horsflies, somtimes beneath, with bauling whippets, and shin-barkers, and these to bee set on by plot and consultation with a *Junto* of Clergy men and Licencers, commended also and rejoyc't in by those whose partiality cannot yet forgoe old papisticall principles, have I not cause to bee in such a manner defensive, as may procure mee freedom to pass more unmolested heerafter by these incumbrances, not so much regarded for themselvs, as for those who incite them. And what defence can properly bee us'd in such a despicable encounter as this, but either the flap or the spurn? . . .

[The tract consists of twenty-seven pages; in the portions omitted, Milton answers, point by point, the specific charges which had been made against him.]

THE TRACTATE ON EDUCATION, 1644

EDITED BY THOMAS R. HARTMANN

Foreword

Of Education. To Master Samuel Hartlib (June 1644)

FOREWORD

Of Education was published about June 4 or 5, 1644, anonymously, and with no title page. Thomas Underhill entered it in the Stationers Register on June 4 as "a litle tract touching *Education of Youth*, etc." Thus this eight-page tractate was the first work by Milton to be registered and licensed. George Thomason wrote on his copy, "By mr John Milton 5 June 1644." It was reprinted on pp. 95–117 of the second pagination with *Poems, etc. upon Several Occasions. By Mr. John Milton* and was called "a small Tractate of Education To Mr. Hartlib" on the title page: this second edition was reprinted (Cambridge, 1890) with an introduction and notes by Oscar Browning.

Of Education is one of Milton's most popular and provocative essays. Proposals to reform education frequently call forth wide and varied responses because everyone who has been educated thinks he knows best how it should be done. Milton's tract is no exception; it has been and still is a powerful stimulus of controversies. For instance, Dr. Johnson placed Milton among "the innovators" who, in his opinion, emphasized the natural sciences at the expense of "religious and moral knowledge of right and wrong." Johnson allowed only one part of Milton's method to escape his censure, admitting that he "was careful to instruct his scholars in religion"; and Johnson defended his sharp attack by appealing to the grandest teacher of all: "if I have Milton against me, I have Socrates on my side."[1] David Masson, not without anger, labeled Johnson's criticism "an egregious misrepresentation" and insisted that "Milton included all that Johnson wanted to have included, and more largely and systematically than Johnson would have dared to dream of. . . ."[2] Despite Masson's long defense, some twentieth-century critics have concluded that "*Of Education* is a negligible quantity in the history

[1] Samuel Johnson, *Lives of the English Poets*, ed. G. Birkbeck Hill (3 vols.; Oxford, 1905), I, 99–101. Johnson himself abandoned teaching after an unsuccessful year or so in his own small private school.

[2] Masson, *Life*, III, 251–52.

of pedagogy."[3] And this, in turn, has elicited a heated response i a recent article that describes Milton's detractors as "mediocre" an men with "little minds."[4]

Modern readers often consider Milton's proposals in *Of Educatio* simply preposterous. Compared to our system of education, Milton' plan seems to them impossibly rigorous. How can a twelve-year old boy learn a foreign language (Latin) and begin reading classi cal texts within one year? How can he, in the next three years acquire a working knowledge of several more languages (Greek Hebrew, and—in his spare time—Italian)? How can adolescents bea a fixed plan of studies from morning till evening for six days each week and then study Scripture in Greek on Sundays? How can stu dents of college age endure a curriculum with no elective courses (How could Milton, so great an advocate of freedom, be so dog matic?) On the other hand, how can a teacher be asked to relin quish his favorite anthologies to replace them with such a grea number of complete works by classical authors? The sheer mass o material to be taught and learned seems appalling, and the mere thought of fewer holidays and vacations seems intolerable. Mos modern readers would probably find it easy to agree with Dr. Johnson's criticism of Milton as an educator: ". . . nobody can be taught faster than he can learn. The speed of the horseman must be limited by the power of his horse. Every man that has ever undertaken to instruct others can tell what slow advances he has been able to make, and how much patience it requires to recall vagrant inattention, to stimulate sluggish indifference, and to rectify absurd misapprehension."[5]

Should *Of Education*, then, be cast aside as an unrealistic scheme, an impossible ideal? Milton obviously did not think so. He did not think his plan was a dream. He was also well aware of the difficulties involved, both for students and teachers: ". . . I believe that this is not a bow for every man to shoot [with] that counts himselfe a teacher; but will require sinews almost equall to those which Homer gave Ulysses, yet I am withall perswaded that it may prove much more easie in the assay, than it now seems at distance, and much

[3] J. W. Adamson, *Pioneers of Modern Education* (Cambridge, 1905), p. 127, and D. L. Clark, *John Milton at St. Paul's School* (New York, 1948), p. 108.

[4] W. R. Parker, "Education: Milton's Ideas and Ours," *College English*, XXIV (1962), 1.

[5] Johnson, *Lives*, I, 99.

ıore illustrious. . . ." Readers should also note that Milton had een teaching for more than four years when he composed this amphlet in 1644, and that there is evidence to show that he had een successfully implementing much of his plan in his own school. :dward Phillips, his nephew and one of his first students, testified ıat Milton did follow his scheme for teaching languages and that is students did study many of the books mentioned in *Of Educa-ion.* Noting that "fifty years later, one of the pupils remembered, nd named, twenty-seven of the authors," W. R. Parker chides Mil-on scholars for not realizing that Milton did practice at least the ırst half of what he preached:

> Most of what Milton has thus far advocated is *not theoretical.* He does not say so, but this is almost exactly the curriculum he had followed in teaching his two nephews, John and Edward Phillips, and a few other boys, from early 1640 to June of 1644, when he put his scheme on paper. The proof of this is to be found in Edward Phillips' notes written for John Aubrey, and in Edward's own, more detailed account in 1694, exactly fifty years later. It is not theory, but a fact, that all these subjects were covered in five years' time. It is not theory, but a fact, that Milton was able to give his pupils a working, functional knowledge of a foreign language in a single year's time. It is also a fact that his nephews were able, not many years later, to earn a living as translators. In other words, visionary as this curriculum may have sounded to you, Milton was writing about what, for the most part, he had actually done—and done with boys who by no stretch of the imagination can be called exceptional or "gifted" children.[6]

Besides this information from Milton's biography, readers might control their response to *Of Education* by considering the vast differences between Renaissance education and modern education. Renaissance education was aristocratic and quite rigorous; it was designed for gentlemen's sons to make them virtuous public leaders. In one of the best schools, Milton's own St. Paul's, which was organized by such humanists as John Colet, William Lily, and Erasmus, students were required to do much of what Milton urged in his tract. For example, they mastered Latin and learned Greek and Hebrew; they read widely in the classical authors; and they spent

[6] Parker, pp. 5–7. Cf. Masson, III, 253–54, and the biographies by Aubrey and the Phillips brothers in *The Early Lives of Milton,* ed. H. Darbishire (London, 1932).

five days of the week from early morning until evening in formal study, composed exercises on Saturdays, and worked over the Greek Scriptures on Sundays.[7] After investigating these common Renaissance practices, a reader may be inclined to react to *Of Education* in a different way. He may even take the position of Douglas Bush who seems to prefer Milton's humanist scheme to our modern ones: "American readers, by the way, and perhaps others as well, often recoil from Milton's heavy requirements, but these should be compared with the standards of the age and not with ours; Renaissance humanists did not believe in adjustment to life through the prolongation of infancy."[8]

While those scholars who understand Renaissance education are not troubled by the rigor of Milton's plan, they are sometimes provoked by other aspects of Milton's tract. They have, in fact, raised three important questions about the originality of the work. First, was Milton, like Samuel Hartlib, such a devoted follower of that famous European educator John Amos Comenius that he incorporated the Comenian philosophy in *Of Education*? Secondly, was Milton's proposed academy a new conception or simply St. Paul's School prolonged through the college years? Finally, did Milton offer any new ideas of his own, or was he merely reciting Renaissance commonplaces?

Up until a few years ago, most critics placed Milton in the Comenian camp, although they pointed out certain minor differences between his and Comenius' ideas. In 1953, however, Ernest Sirluck offered an impressive series of arguments showing that these differences are not superficial but fundamental. He admits that both Milton and Comenius taught that the end of education is religious and moral training; that the prevailing curricula were too prolix, difficult, and useless; that foreign languages are mere instruments; and that learning should progress from the sensible to the abstract. But Sirluck demonstrates how common these positions were in the Renaissance and how they are only "insignificant similarities." On the other hand, "the main matters"—Comenius' utilitarian and vocational purposes, his compulsory universal school attendance for both sexes, his use of compilations and no original works other than Scripture, his dislike of literature, and his ideal of pansophy or uni-

[7] See Clark, pp. 109–14, and D. Bush, *English Literature in the Earlier Seventeenth Century: 1600–1660* (rev. ed.; Oxford, 1962), p. 15.

[8] *John Milton: A Sketch of His Life and Writings* (New York, 1964), p. 93.

ersal knowledge—comprised "an educational policy to which Milton was fundamentally opposed."[9]

Milton's originality has also been seen as limited by the influence of his grammar school training. In the final chapter of *John Milton at St. Paul's School,* D. L. Clark says that the "ideal school" described in *Of Education* "was in many respects like St. Paul's school" and "its goals were the traditional goals of the humanistic grammar school."[10] Although many scholars would readily agree with Clark's position and with Sirluck's view that Milton's experience at St. Paul's is the "matrix" out of which the tract grew,[11] they might place more emphasis on the changes Milton imposed on that basic curriculum, especially his postponement of composition and literary exercises until much later when his students were more mature.[12]

There are many accounts of Milton's relationship to his predecessors, especially to the humanists of the sixteenth century. Foster Watson was the first to provide a detailed list of parallels between Milton's tract and a "source." He cited the Spaniard Juan Luis Vives (1492–1540) as the parent of most of Milton's ideas. According to Watson, only Milton's patriotism and his tribute to Hartlib are his own.[13] The solidity of Watson's case was questioned by E. N. S. Thompson, but even Thompson could not deny that Milton borrowed from Vives because of the number of clear parallels and the probability that Milton did read Vives' *De Tradendis Disciplinis* (1531), which was published at Oxford in 1612.[14] O. M. Ainsworth, however, in the only comprehensive book-length study of Milton's tract, added a long list of other authors to show that the ideas of Vives were, by Milton's time, commonplace knowledge.[15] Ainsworth placed Milton squarely in the humanist tradition, and compared *Of Education* to the important English educational writings of the sixteenth century—Elyot's *Governour* (1531), Ascham's *Scholemaster* (1570), and Mulcaster's *Positions* (1581).[16] Finally,

9 Ernest Sirluck, *Yale Milton,* II, 187–205.

10 Clark, p. 250.

11 *Yale Milton,* II, 212.

12 Cf. Parker, p. 6.

13 Foster Watson, "A Suggested Source of Milton's *Tractate of Education,*" *The Nineteenth Century,* LXVI (1909), 607–17.

14 E. N. S. Thompson, "Milton's *Of Education,*" *SP,* XV (1918), 159–75.

15 Oliver M. Ainsworth, *Milton on Education: The Tractate* Of Education *with Supplementary Extracts from Other Writings of Milton* (New Haven, 1928).

16 Ibid., pp. 8–38.

Donald Dorian extended Ainsworth's list even further by addi many lesser-known works published before 1644.[17]

On the basis of these studies of Milton's predecessors, it see clear that *Of Education* offers no new proposals for the reform education, for "the individual elements in Milton's plan are to found," according to Ainsworth and all modern critics, "in earl writers." These same critics, however, follow up this admission claiming a different kind of originality for Milton's tract. They s *Of Education* as a noteworthy synthesis of Renaissance ideas. Dori and Parker follow Ainsworth's judgment: "What is new is the pl itself—the method of combining these elements. By virtue of power to select and organize the methods and materials of schol ship, Milton fully represents for England, as the precedi educational reformers had partially done, the main tendencies humanism at its best. . . ."[18]

Milton's synthesis of the educational ideals of humanism can observed chiefly in the carefully planned structure of his short tre tise. Everything he says flows from two pairs of principles, o regarding the aims of education, the other, the means. The fi aim of education, he says, is to return to a kind of prelapsarian pe fection, to regain the control and order that Adam possessed befo the Fall. This religious aim is then coupled with a secular and polit cal one: to fit a man for the duties of public life. Together, the represent the double vision expressed in the label "Christian h manism." These aims, which are often separated today, were mere distinguished philosophically in the Renaissance when write looked at mankind *sub specie aeternitatis,* as pilgrims searching f absolute values of another world, and, at the same time, *sub spec temporis,* as citizens striving for the common good of their natic in this world. Thus, Milton pointedly states the humanist goals educating the whole man under the stimulus and guidance of on institution. In short, he calls for a totally integrated process growth.

The second pair of principles reveals both what Milton most di liked about the education of his day and what he most desired a substitute. The first of these concerns the order of studies and th time spent on them. Briefly, he held that students should be le

[17] *Yale Milton,* II, 358.

[18] Ainsworth, p. 42; and cf. Clark, p. 108, Dorian, *Yale Milton,* II, 359, an Parker, p. 1. The chief aim of Parker's long essay is to assert Milton's originality

from what is more easily known to what is more difficult. They should move, in other words, from the knowledge of concrete things that can be known by the senses and pictured in the imagination to knowledge that is abstract and invisible. He insisted that this "same method is necessarily to be follow'd in all discreet teaching." Thus, students must study the things God has created so they can learn about God himself. Similarly, they must be exposed to the ideas and the style of great writers in order to learn how to write. They should not study such difficult subjects as logic and metaphysics and literary composition during their early years, but only after they have stocked their minds with the knowledge necessary to understand and utilize these more advanced subjects. Here Milton is reacting to what he considered abuses in his own education; for instance, having young students compose themes in Latin before they have filled their minds with things to say and before they have mastered the Latin language by reading great authors, and having young college students struggle with the difficult problems of logic and metaphysics.

The second principle regarding means of education is Milton's famous view of language study. A language, for him, is merely a tool, not to be studied for its own sake or for a long period of time. The only reason for studying languages at all, according to Milton, is that since no one nation has a monopoly on wisdom, a student must pursue learning in languages other than his own. His key point is this: "Language is but the instrument convaying to us things usefull to be known." Here Milton is objecting to the long and painful study of Latin and Greek in the grammar schools of his day and to the language study handbooks that were becoming more and more popular. As a solution, he proposed a very brief study of Latin grammar—only one year—and an early exposure to increasingly more difficult texts written in Latin. Of course, all the chief subjects in his school would be studied in Latin and Greek, Hebrew being used for Scripture study.

A great many of Milton's ideas on education were first stated in his graduate school speech some twelve years before he published *Of Education*. That speech, the *Seventh Prolusion* (see p. 15), is still one of the best introductions to his tractate. Although many specific comments in the *Seventh Prolusion* reappear in *Of Education*—appeals for longer study hours and less recreation and dissipation; objections to the way grammar, rhetoric, and logic are taught and the time wasted on them; a dislike of metaphysics and the language of lawyers, and a preference for the subjects of history and geography—these works have more important things in common. The first aim of education in the tractate—to regain especially the knowledge of God—is eloquently described in the prolusion when he speaks of seeing God through the study of His creation. The second aim—to qualify men for leadership in public life—is also discussed in the prolusion where it is viewed in a surprisingly realistic way: Milton admits that "a reputation for learning has elevated few men to majestic heights," but those few who have made it, such as Alexander and Augustus, remain as examples of "the kind of man [to whom] the helm or reins of government ought to be entrusted."[19] Again in the tractate, the two chief objections Milton raises against the educational practices of the time concern the order of studies and the time spent on them; likewise in the prolusion, he urges the removal of "the two great impediments to our studies, first our poor way of teaching the Arts, and secondly our own laziness," and then he speaks of a "short cut" in choosing "both the useful arts and what is useful in these arts."[20] In both works, he stresses the education of the whole man: education of the intellect must be joined with moral training; practical and worldly motives must be linked with spiritual and religious motives; the natural goals of men should not be separated from the supernatural. In the *Seventh Prolusion,* Milton sums up his integrated view when he speaks of the spiritual rewards for study and service to men: "Those who lived most moderately in this life and devoted all their time to wholesome studies, and through their studies have helped mankind, will be rewarded in eternity with a wisdom that is unique and the greatest of all."[21]

Milton explains in his first paragraph how *Of Education* came to be written. He was busy with "some other assertions" (presumably the divorce pamphlets, and possibly *Areopagitica*) when "Master Hartlib" asked him to "set down in writing" his views on education. Samuel Hartlib (ca. 1599–ca. 1662), a Prussian who studied at Cambridge and later (1628) settled in England, spent much of his very active life in attempts to reform education. Although he himself wrote a textbook on agriculture, a Latin grammar, and a

[19] See *Seventh Prolusion,* note 17.
[20] Ibid., notes 20 and 23.
[21] Ibid., note 30.

topia, he is better known as the admirer of Comenius, many of whose works he translated, including *A Reformation of Schools* (1642). He also seems to have spent much of his time soliciting and publishing treatises on education. Although Hartlib solicited Milton's manuscript, he probably did not publish it. Ernest Sirluck, who calls Hartlib "that indefatigable bureau of Comenian propaganda," suggests the possibility that Milton's radical departures from the doctrines of Comenius made Hartlib somewhat reluctant to publish the letter Milton sent to him. Sirluck agrees with Masson that Milton, unwilling to see his labor wasted, most probably "published it himself."[22]

The present text is based upon two identical copies of the first edition (1644) of Milton's *Of Education:* New York Public Library, *KC 1644, and Union Theological Seminary Library, 1644 / M65. The second edition (1673) was also used to correct a few typographical errors; it is bound with some minor poems under the title *Poems, Etc. upon Several Occasions . . .* , and three copies are in the New York Public Library, *KC 1673. For a full statement of the few variants in copies of the first and second editions, see Donald C. Dorian, *Yale Milton,* II, 360, 777.

22 Sirluck, *Yale Milton,* II, 206–12, and Masson, III, 233.

[1] OF EDUCATION.

To Master *Samuel Hartlib.*
[June 4 or 5, 1644]

Master Hartlib,

I am long since perswaded, that to say, or doe ought worth memory, and imitation, no purpose or respect should sooner move us, than simply the love of God, and of mankinde. Neverthelesse to write now the reforming of Education, though it be one of the greatest and noblest designes, that can be thought on, and for the want whereof this nation perishes, I had not yet at this time been induc't, but by your earnest entreaties, and serious conjurements; as having my minde for the present halfe diverted in the persuance of some other assertions, the knowledge and the use of which, cannot but be a great furtherance both to the enlargement of truth, and honest living, with much more peace. Nor should the lawes of any private friendship have prevail'd with me to divide thus, or transpose my former thoughts, but that I see those aims, those actions which have won you with me the esteem of a person sent hither by some good providence from a farre country to be the occasion and the incitement of great good to this Iland. And, as I hear, you have obtain'd the same repute with men of most approved wisdom, and some of highest authority among us. Not to mention the learned correspondence which you hold in forreigne parts, and the extraordinary pains and diligence which you have us'd in this matter both heer, and beyond the Seas; either by the definite will of God so ruling, or the peculiar sway of nature, which also is Gods working. Neither can I thinke that so reputed, and so valu'd as you are, you would to the forfeit of your own discerning ability, impose upon me an unfit and over ponderous argument, but that the satisfaction which you professe to have receiv'd from those incidentall discourses which we have wander'd into, hath prest and almost constrain'd you into a perswasion, that what you require from me in this point, I neither ought, nor can in conscience deferre beyond this time both of so much need at once, and so much opportunity to trie what God hath determin'd. I will not resist therefore, what ever it is either of divine, or humane obligement that you lay upon me; but will forthwith set down in writing, as you request me, that voluntary *Idea*,[1] which hath long in silence presented it self to me, of a better Education, in extent and comprehension farre more large, and yet of time farre shorter, and of attainment farre more certain, than hath been yet in practice. Briefe I shall endeavour to be; for that which I have to say, assuredly this nation hath extreame need should be done sooner than spok'n. To tell you therefore what I have benefited herein among old renowned Authors, I shall spare; and to search what many modern *Janua's* and *Didactics*[2] more than ever I shall read, have projected, my inclination leads me not. But if you can accept of these few observations which have flowr'd off, and are as it were the burnishing of many studious and contemplative yeers altogether spent in the search of religious and civil knowledge, and such as pleas'd you so well in the relating, I here give you them to dispose of.

[2] The end then of learning is to repair the ruins of our first parents by regaining to know God aright, and out of that knowledge to love him, to imitate him, to be like him, as we may the neerest by possessing our souls of true vertue, which being united to the heavenly grace of faith makes up the highest perfection. But because our understanding cannot in this body found it selfe but on sensible things, nor arrive so cleerly to the knowledge of God and things invisible, as by orderly conning over the visible and inferior creature, the same method is necessarily to be follow'd in all discreet teaching.[3] And seeing every nation affords not experience and tradition enough for all kinde of learning, therefore we are chiefly taught the languages of those people who have at any time been most industrious after wisdom; So that language is but the instrument convaying to us things usefull to be known. And though a linguist should pride himselfe to have all the tongues that *Babel* cleft the world into, yet, if he have not studied the solid things in them as well as the words and lexicons, he were nothing so much to be esteem'd a learned man, as any yeoman or tradesman competently wise in his mother dialect only. Hence appear the

flowr'd off: reached full development.
burnishing: polishing, i.e., polished results.
conning over: studying.
creature: creation.

many mistakes which have made learning generally so unpleasing and so unsuccessfull; first we do amisse to spend seven or eight yeers meerly in scraping together so much miserable Latin, and Greek, as might be learnt otherwise easily and delightfully in one yeer.[4] And that which casts our proficiency therein so much behinde, is our time lost partly in too oft idle vacancies given both to schools and Universities, partly in a preposterous exaction, forcing the empty wits of children to compose Theams, verses, and Orations, which are the acts of ripest judgement and the finall work of a head fill'd by long reading, and observing, with elegant maxims, and copious invention.[5] These are not matters to be wrung from poor striplings, like blood out of the nose, or the plucking of untimely fruit: besides the ill habit which they get of wretched barbarizing against the Latin and Greek *idiom,* with their untutor'd *Anglicisms,* odious to be read, yet not to be avoided without a well continu'd and judicious conversing among pure Authors digested, which they scarce taste, wheras, if after some preparatory grounds of speech by their certain forms got into memory, they were led to the praxis thereof in some chosen short book lesson'd throughly to them, they might then forthwith proceed to learn the substance of good things, and Arts[6] in due order, which would bring the whole language quickly into their power. This I take to be the most rationall and most profitable way of learning languages, and whereby we may best hope to give account to God to our youth spent herein: And for the usuall method of teaching Arts, I deem it to be an old errour of universities not yet well recover'd from the Scholastick grosnesse of barbarous ages, that in stead of beginning with Arts most easie, and those be such as are most obvious to the sence,[7] they present their young unmatriculated novices at first comming with the most intellective abstractions of Logick and metaphysicks:[8] So that they having but newly left those Grammatick flats and shallows where they stuck unreasonably to learn a few words with lamentable construction, and now on the sudden transported under another climat to be tost and turmoild with their unballasted wits in fadomles and unquiet deeps of controversie,[9] do for the most part grow into hatred and contempt of learning, mockt and deluded all this while with ragged notions and babblements, while they expected worthy and delightfull knowledge; till poverty or youthfull yeers call them importunately their

vacancies: holidays and vacations.
preposterous: reversed (from the Latin *praeposterus,* having the last first).
conversing: living (from the Latin *conversari,* to live with).
praxis: use or application.

severall wayes, and hasten them with the sway [3] of friends either to an ambitious and mercenary, or ignorantly zealous Divinity; Some allur'd to the trade of Law, grounding their purposes not on the prudent, and heavenly contemplation of justice and equity which was never taught them, but on the promising and pleasing thoughts of litigious terms, fat contentions, and flowing fees;[10] others betake them to State affairs, with souls so unprincipl'd in vertue, and true generous breeding, that flattery, and court shifts and tyrannous aphorismes appear to them the highest points of widom; instilling their barren hearts with a conscientious slavery, if, as I rather think, it be not fain'd. Others lastly of a more delicious and airie spirit, retire themselves knowing no better, to the enjoyments of ease and luxury, living out their daies in feast and jollity; which indeed is the wisest and the safest course of all these, unlesse they were with more integrity undertak'n. And these are the errours, and these are the fruits of mispending our prime youth at the Schools and Universities as we do, either in learning meere words or such things chiefly, as were better unlearnt.

I shall detain you now no longer in the demonstration of what we should not doe, but strait conduct ye to a hill side, where I will point ye out the right path of a vertuous and noble Education; laborious indeed at the first ascent, but else so smooth, so green, so full of goodly prospect, and melodious sounds on every side, that the harp of *Orpheus* was not more charming. I doubt not but ye shall have more adoe to drive our dullest and laziest youth, our stocks and stubbs from the infinite desire of such a happy nurture, than we have now to hale and drag our choisest and hopefullest wits to that asinine feast of sowthistles and brambles which is commonly set before them, as all the food and entertainment of their tenderest and most docible age. I call therefore a compleate and generous Education that which fits a man to perform justly, skilfully and magnanimously all the offices both private and publike of peace and war.[11] And how all this may be done between twelve, and one and twenty, lesse time than is now bestow'd in pure trifling at Grammar and *Sophistry*, is to be thus order'd.

First to finde out a spatious house and ground about it fit for an *Academy*, and big enough to lodge a hundred and fifty persons,

hasten them [urge them to enter] . . . *Divinity* [the Anglican priesthood]. Cf. *Areopagitica* (1644 ed., pp. 26–27).
terms: periods when courts are in session.
conscientious slavery: a slavish preoccupation (with pettiness).
delicious and airie spirit: sensuous and superficial spirit.
hopefullest wits: most promising students.
docible: docile, teachable.

whereof twenty of thereabout may be attendants, all under the government of one, who shall be thought of desert sufficient, and ability either to doe all, or wisely to direct, and oversee it done. This place should be at once both School and University, not needing a remove to any other house of Schollership, except it be some peculiar Colledge of Law, or Physick, where they mean to be practitioners; but as for those generall studies which take up all our time from Lilly[12] to the commencing, as they term it, Master of Art, it should be absolute. After this pattern, as many edifices may be converted to this use, as shall be needfull in every City throughout this land, which would tend much to the encrease of learning and civility every where. This number, lesse or more thus collected, to the convenience of a foot company, or interchangeably two troops of cavalry, should divide their daies work into three parts, as it lies orderly. Their studies, their exercise, and their diet.

For their studies, First they should begin with the chief and necessary rules of some good Grammar, either that now us'd,[13] or any better: and while this is doing, their speech is to be fashion'd to a distinct and cleer pronuntiation, as neer as may be to the *Italian,* especially in the vowels. For we Englishmen being farre northerly, doe not open our mouthes in the cold air, wide enough to grace a Southern [4] tongue; but are observ'd by all other nations to speak exceeding close and inward: So that to smatter Latin with an english mouth, is as ill a hearing as law French.[14] Next to make them expert in the usefullest points of grammar, and withall to season them, and win them early to the love of vertue and true labour, ere any flattering seducement, or vain principle seise them wandering, some easie and delightfull book of Education would be read to them; whereof the Greeks have store as *Cebes, Plutarch,* and other Socratic discourses.[15] But in Latin we have none of classic authoritie extant, except the two or three first books of *Quintilian,*[16] and some select peeces elsewhere. But here the main skill and groundwork will be, to temper them such lectures and explanations upon every opportunity, as may lead and draw them in willing obedience, enflam'd with the study of learning, and the admiration of vertue;[17] stirr'd up with high hopes of living to be brave men, and worthy patriots, dear to God, and famous to all ages. That they may despise and scorn all their childish, and ill taught qualities, to delight in manly, and liberall exercises: which he who hath the Art, and proper eloquence to catch them with,

Physick: medicine.
absolute: complete.
enflam'd with: zeal or desire for.

what with mild and effectuall perswasions, and what with the intimation of some fear, if need be, but chiefly by his own example, might in a short space gain them to an incredible diligence and courage: infusing into their young brests such an ingenuous and noble ardor, as would not fail to make many of them renowned and matchlesse men. At the same time, some other hour of the day, might be taught them the rules of Arithmetick, and soon after the elements of Geometry even playing, as the old manner was.[18] After evening repast, till bed time their thoughts will be best taken up in the easie grounds of Religion, and the story of Scripture. The next step would be to the Authors of *Agriculture, Cato, Varro,* and *Columella,*[19] for the matter is most easie, and if the language be difficult, so much the better, it is not a difficultie above their yeers. And here will be an occasion of inciting and inabling them hereafter to improve the tillage of their country, to recover the bad soil, and to remedy the wast that is made of good: for this was one of Hercules praises.[20] Ere halfe these Authors be read, which will soon be with plying hard, and dayly, they cannot choose but be masters of any ordinary prose. So that it will be then seasonable for them to learn in any modern Author, the use of the Globes, and all the maps first with the old names; and then with the new: or they might be then capable to read any compendious method of naturall Philosophy. And at the same time might be entring into the Greek tongue, after the same manner as was before prescrib'd in the Latin; whereby the difficulties of Grammar being soon overcome, all the Historicall Physiology of *Aristotle* and *Theophrastus*[21] are open before them, and as I may say, under contribution. The like accesse will be to Vitruvius, to *Senecas* naturall questions,[22] to *Mela, Celsus, Pliny,* or *Solinus.*[23] And having thus past the principles of *Arithmetic, Geometry, Astronomy* and *Geography* with a generall compact of Physicks, they may descend in *Mathematicks* to the instrumentall science of *Trigonometry,* and from thence to Fortification, *Architecture,* Enginry, or navigation. And in naturall Philosophy they may proceed leisurly from the History of *Meteors,* minerals, plants and living creatures as farre as Anatomy. Then also in course might be read to them out of some not tedious writer the institution of Physick; that they may know the tempers, the humors, the seasons, and how to manage a crudity:[24] which he who can wisely and timely doe, is not onely a great Physician to himselfe, and to his friends, but also may at some [5] time or other,

Enginry: the art of constructing military engines.
institution of Physick: introduction to medicine.
crudity: undigested (or indigestible) matter in the stomach.

save an Army by this frugall, and expencelesse meanes only; and not let the healthy and stout bodies of young men rot away under him for want of this discipline; which is a great pitty, and no lesse a shame to the commander. To set forward all these proceedings in nature and mathematicks, what hinders, but that they may procure, as oft as shall be needfull, the helpfull experiences of Hunters, fowlers, Fishermen, Shepherds, Gardeners, *Apothecaries;* and in the other sciences, *Architects,* Engineers, Mariners, *Anatomists;* who doubtlesse would be ready some for reward, and some to favour such a hopefull Seminary. And this will give them such a reall tincture of naturall knowledge, as they shall never forget, but dayly augment with delight. Then also those Poets which are now counted most hard, will be both facil and pleasant, *Orpheus, Hesiod, Theocritus, Aratus, Nicander, Oppian, Dionysus*[25] and in Latin *Lucretius, Manilius,* and the rurall part of Virgil.[26]

By this time, yeers and good generall precepts will have furnisht them more distinctly with that act of reason which in *Ethics* is call'd *Proairesis:*[27] that they may with some judgement contemplat upon morall good and evill. Then will be requir'd a speciall reinforcement of constant and sound endoctrinating to set them right and firm, instructing them more amply in the knowledge of vertue and the hatred of vice: while their young and pliant affections are led through all the morall works of *Plato, Xenophon, Cicero, Plutarch, Laertius,* and those *Locrian* remnants;[28] but still to be reduc't in their nightward studies wherewith they close the dayes work, under the determinat sentence of *David,* or *Solomon,* or the Evangels and *Apostolic* scriptures. Being perfit in the knowledge of personall duty, they may then begin the study of Economics.[29] And either now, or before this, they may have easily learnt at any odde hour the *Italian* tongue. And soon after, but with warinesse, and good antidote, it would be wholsome enough to let them tast some choise comedies Greek, Latin, or *Italian:* Those tragedies also that treate of houshold matters, as *Trachiniae, Alcestis*[30] and the like. The next remove must be to the study of *Politics;*[31] to know the beginning, end, and reasons of politicall societies; that they may not in a dangerous fit of the common-wealth be such poor, shaken, uncertain reeds, of such a tottering conscience, as many of our great counsellers have lately shewn themselves, but stedfast pillars of the State. After this they are to dive into the grounds of law, and legall justice; deliver'd first, and with best warrant by

determinat sentence: final authoritative judgement.
the Evangels and Apostolic scriptures: the Gospels and the rest of the New Testament.

Moses; and as farre as humane prudence can be trusted, in those extoll'd remains of Grecian Law-givers, *Lycurgus, Solon, Zaleucus, Charondas,*[32] and thence to all the Romane *Edicts* and tables with their *Justinian;*[33] and so down to the *Saxon* and common laws of England, and the Statutes. Sundayes also and every evening may be now understandingly spent in the highest matters of *Theology,* and Church History ancient and modern: and ere this time the Hebrew tongue at a set hour might have been gain'd, that the Scriptures may be now read in their own originall; whereto it would be no impossibility to adde the *Chaldey,* and the *Syrian* dialect. When all these employments are well conquer'd, then will the choise Histories, *heroic poems,* and *Attic* tragedies of statliest, and most regal argument, with all the famous Politicall orations offer themselves; which if they were not only read; but some of them got by memory, and solemnly pronounc't with right accent, and grace, as might be taught, would endue them even with the spirit, and vigor of *Demosthenes* or *Cicero, Euripides,* or *Sophocles.* And now lastly will be the time to read with them those organic[34] arts which inable men to discourse and write perspicuously, elegantly, and according to the fitted stile of lofty, [6] mean, or lowly.[35] Logic therefore so much as is usefull, is to be referr'd to this due place withall her well coucht heads and Topics, untill it be time to open her contracted palm[36] into a gracefull and ornate Rhetorick taught out of the rule of *Plato, Aristotle, Phalereus, Cicero, Hermogenes, Longinus.*[37] To which Poetry would be made subsequent, or indeed rather precedent, as being lesse suttle and fine, but more simple, sensuous and passionate. I mean not here the prosody of a verse, which they could not but have hit on before among the rudiments of grammar; but that sublime art which in *Aristotles poetics,* in *Horace,*[38] and the *Italian* commentaries of *Castelvetro, Tasso, Mazzoni,* and others,[39] teaches what the laws are of a true *Epic* poem, what of a *Dramatic,* what of a *Lyric,* what decorum is, which is the grand master peece to observe.[40] This would make them soon perceive what despicable creatures our common rimers and play-writes be,[41] and shew them, what Religious, what glorious and magnificent use might be made of Poetry both in divine and humane things.[42] From hence and not till now will be the right season of forming them to be able writers and composers in every excellent matter, when they shall be thus frought with an universall insight into things. Or whether they be

Chaldey: Biblical Aramaic, the language of the non-Hebrew parts of the Old Testament (Ezra and Daniel).

Syrian: Syriac, the language of many early Christian versions of the Bible.

to speak in Parliament or counsell, honour and attention would be waiting on their lips. There would then also appear in Pulpits other visages, other gestures, and stuffe otherwise wrought than what we now sit under, oft times to as great a triall of our patience as any other that they preach to us. These are the studies wherein our noble and our gentle youth ought to bestow their time in a disciplinary way from twelve to one and twenty; unlesse they rely more upon their ancestors dead, than upon themselves living. In which methodicall course it is so suppos'd they must proceed by the steddy pace of learning onward, as at convenient times for memories sake to retire back into the middle ward, and sometimes into the rear of what they have been taught, untill they have confirm'd, and solidly united the whole body of their perfected knowledge, like the last embattelling of a Romane legion.[43] Now will be worth the seeing what exercises, and what recreations may best agree, and become these studies.

Their Exercise.

The course of study hitherto briefly describ'd, is, what I can guesse by reading, likest to those ancient and famous schools of *Pythagoras, Plato, Isocrates, Aristotle*[44] and such others, out of which were bred up such a number of renowned Philosophers, orators, Historians, Poets and Princes all over *Greece, Italy,* and *Asia,* besides the flourishing studies of *Cyrene* and *Alexandria.*[45] But herein it shall exceed them, and supply a defect as great as that which *Plato* noted in the common-wealth of Sparta;[46] whereas that City train'd up their youth most for warre, and these in their Academies and *Lycæum,* all for the gown, this institution of breeding which I here delineate, shall be equally good both for Peace and warre. Therefore about an hour and a halfe ere they eat at noon should be allow'd them for exercise and due rest afterwards: But the time for this may be enlarg'd at pleasure, according as their rising in the morning shall be early. The exercise which I commend first, is the exact use of their weapon; to guard and to strike safely with edge, or point; this will keep them healthy, nimble, strong, and well in breath, is also the likeliest meanes to make them grow large, and tall, and to inspire them with a gallant and fearlesse courage, which being temper'd with seasonable lectures and pre-

gown: clothing for academic or contemplative life, in contrast to that for activity and war.
weapon: sword.

cepts [7] to them of true fortitude, and patience, will turn into a native and heroick valour, and make them hate the cowardise of doing wrong. They must be also practiz'd in all the locks and gripes of wrastling, wherein English men were wont to excell, as need may often be in fight to tugge, to grapple, and to close. And this perhaps will be enough, wherein to prove and heat their single strength. The interim of unsweating themselves regularly, and convenient rest before meat may both with profit and delight be taken up in recreating and composing their travail'd spirits with the solemn and divine harmonies of musick heard, or learnt; either while the skilfull *Organist* plies his grave and fancied descant, in lofty fugues, or the whole Symphony with artfull and unimaginable touches adorn and grace the well studied cords of some choise composer; some times the Lute, or soft organ stop waiting on elegant voices either to Religious, martiall, or civill ditties; which if wise men and prophets be not extreamly out, have a great power over dispositions and manners, to smooth and make them gently from rustick harshnesse and distemper'd passions.[47] The like also would not be unexpedient after meat to assist and cherish nature in her first concoction, and send their mindes backe to study in good tune and satisfaction. Where having follow'd it close under vigilant eyes till about two hours before supper, they are by a sudden alarum or watch word, to be call'd out to their military motions, under skie or covert, according to the season, as was the Romane wont; first on foot, then as their age permits, on horse back, to all the art of cavalry; That having in sport, but with much exactnesse, and dayly muster, serv'd out the rudiments of their Souldiership in all the skill of embattailing, marching, encamping, fortifying, beseiging and battering, with all the helps of ancient and modern stratagems, *Tactiks* and warlike maxims, they may as it were out of a long warre come forth renowned and perfect Commanders in the service of their country.[48] They would not then, if they were trusted with fair and hopefull armies, suffer them for want of just and wise discipline to shed away from about them like sick feathers, though they be never so oft suppli'd: they would not suffer their empty and unrecrutible Colonells of twenty men in a company, to quaffe out, or convay into secret hoards, the wages of a delusive list, and a miserable remnant: yet in the mean while to be overmaster'd with a score or two of drunkards, the only souldiery left about them, or else to comply with all rapines and violences. No

descant: variations and elaborations on set themes.
concoction: digestion.
unrecrutible: incapable of getting recruits.

certainly, if they knew ought of that knowledge that belongs to good men or good governours, they would not suffer these things. But to return to our own institute, besides these constant exercises at home, there is another opportunity of gaining experience to be won from pleasure it selfe abroad; In those vernal seasons of the yeer, when the air is calm and pleasant, it were an injury and sullennesse against nature not to go out, and see her riches, and partake in her rejoycing with heaven and earth. I should not therefore be a perswader to them of studying much then, after two or three yeer that they have well laid their grounds, but to ride out in companies with prudent and staid guides, to all the quarters of the land: learning and observing all places of strength, all commodities of building and of soil, for towns and tillage, harbours and Ports for trade. Somtimes taking sea as farre as to our Navy, to learn there also what they can in the practicall knowledge of sailing and of sea fight. These wayes would trie all their peculiar gifts of nature, and if there were any secret excellence among them, would fetch it out, and give it fair opportunities to advance it selfe by,[49] which could not but mightily re-[8]dound to the good of this nation, and bring into fashion again those old admired vertues and excellencies, with farre more advantage now in this puritie of Christian knowledge. Nor shall we then need the *Mounsieurs* of *Paris*[50] to take out hopefull youth into thir slight and prodigall custodies and send them over back again transform'd into mimics, apes and Kicshoes. But if they desire to see other countries at three or four and twenty yeers of age, not to learn principles, but to enlarge experience, and make wise observation, they will by that time be such as shall deserve the regard and honour of all men where they passe, and the society and friendship of those in all places who are best and most eminent. And perhaps then other Nations will be glad to visit us for their breeding, or else to imitate us in their own Country.

Now lastly for their diet there cannot be much to say, save only that it would be best in the same house; for much time else would be lost abroad, and many ill habits got; and that it should be plain, healthfull, and moderat I suppose is out of controversie. Thus Master *Hartlib*, you have a generall view in writing, as your desire was, of that which at severall times I had discourst with you concerning the best and Noblest way of Education; not beginning, as some have done from the cradle, which yet might be worth many considerations, if brevity had not been my scope, many other circumstances also I could have mention'd, but this to such as have the

Kicshoes: frivolous persons.

worth in them to make triall, for light and direction may be enough. Only I believe that this is not a bow for every man to shoot in that counts himselfe a teacher; but will require sinews almost equall to those which Homer gave Ulysses,[51] yet I am withall perswaded that it may prove much more easie in the assay, than it now seems at distance, and much more illustrious: howbeit not more difficult than I imagine, and that imagination presents me with nothing but very happy and very possible according to best wishes; if God have so decreed, and this age have spirit and capacity enough to apprehend.

The end. [8]

shoot in: shoot with.
in the assay: in practice.

NOTES

1. *Idea:* probably in the Platonic sense of an ideal or perfect form.

2. Milton is alluding primarily to two works by Comenius: *Janua linguarum reserata* (1631), translated as *The Gate of Languages Unlocked* (1639), which quickly became popular in England and Europe; and *The Great Didactic,* Comenius' full-blown theory of education, not printed until 1657 but known to Milton through Hartlib.

3. The distinction between sense knowledge and intellectual knowledge (understanding) and the doctrine that all knowledge comes first through the senses were frequently repeated in the Renaissance and can be traced to Aristotle's *On the Soul,* II, 2, and III, 8, especially 432^{a} 6–7.

4. Milton's view of languages as mere "instruments" to be learned quickly echoes the somewhat milder statements of many other humanists and educators, e.g., Erasmus, Elyot, Bacon, Comenius, and Hartlib. Edward Phillips testified that Milton had him and his brother John reading Latin "in a years time" (Darbishire, *Early Lives,* p. 12).

5. Milton would reject the method imposed by most Renaissance grammar schools in which students used anthologies and collections of maxims from classical authors in their composition exercises; he prefers that the students discover their own arguments ("invention") and their own source materials during years of "long reading, and observing." This was his own procedure in his private studies, as evidenced by his *Commonplace Book.*

6. Perhaps a reference to the other tool subjects: logic and rhetoric. With grammar, they formed the trivium of the traditional seven liberal arts. The other four arts (quadrivium) were arithmetic, geometry, astronomy, and music, all of which Milton mentions later.

7. See note 3 above, and *Seventh Prolusion,* p. 18.

8. Cf. *Seventh Prolusion,* p. 23.

9. *Controversie:* a reference to scholastic disputations, e.g., Milton's own *Fourth* and *Fifth Prolusions.*

10. In his *Commonplace Book,* Milton cites the opinion that the study of law be "considered not as a liberal art but as a 'trade and a really mechanical art'" (*Yale Milton,* I, 468). Cf. note 14 below.

11. This definition is similar to those offered by many classical authors: e.g., Plato speaks of "education in virtue from youth upwards, which makes a man eagerly pursue the ideal perfection of citizenship, and teaches him how rightly to rule and how to obey" (*Laws*, I, 644), and Aristotle says that "men must be able to engage in business and go to war, but leisure and peace are better; they must do what is necessary and indeed what is useful, but what is honorable is better. On such principles children and persons of every age which requires education should be trained" (*Politics*, VII, 14, 1333^b 1–5). For the virtue of *magnanimity*, see Aristotle's *Ethics*, IV, 3, especially 1124^a 1–19, which corresponds to Milton's definition in *Christian Doctrine*, II, ix: "Magnanimity is the virtue by which a man is motivated by the complete knowledge of his true worth in taking or not taking, in seeking or fleeing riches, rewards, or honors" (*Columbia Milton*, XVII, 240).

12. William Lily wrote a popular introduction to Latin grammar which Milton used at St. Paul's School.

13. Lily's Latin grammar.

14. Milton's directions for the pronunciation of Latin are drawn from his own experience in Italy. In his *Commonplace Book*, after noting that King Alfred "turn'd the old laws into english," Milton adds: "I would he liv'd now to rid us of this norman gibbrish" (*Yale Milton*, I, 424); and see *Seventh Prolusion*, p. 24, where he complains of lawyers' jargon.

15. The *Pinax* of Cebes is an allegory about the virtues needed for study. Cf. Richard Parsons' edition, *Cebes' Tablet* (Boston, 1887). Besides the famous *Lives*, Plutarch wrote essays, called *Moralia*, on ethical, historical, and educational topics. The "other Socratic discourses" might be selected from the writings of the two great interpreters of Socrates: Plato and Xenophon. E.g., Plato's *Republic* and Xenophon's *Memorabilia* contain some of Socrates' views on education.

16. Quintilian, the famous Roman educator and rhetorician, wrote *De institutione oratoria.*

17. See *Commonplace Book* under the heading "Of the Education of Children" (*Yale Milton*, I, 406).

18. E.g., Plato urged that "calculation and geometry and all other elements of instruction . . . should be presented to the mind in childhood; not, however, under any notion of forcing our system of education. . . . Do not use compulsion, but let early education be a sort of amusement" (*Republic*, VII, 536–37).

19. Cato, Varro and Columella were three Roman authorities on agriculture, whose treatises were titled *De re rustica.*

20. Cf. *Natural History*, XVII, 50, where Pliny mentions the tradition that Hercules introduced the practice of fertilizing land to Italy.

21. Aristotle has been called the father of zoology because of his *History of Animals*, *On the Parts of Animals*, and *On the Generation of Animals;* Theophrastus, the immediate successor of Aristotle as head of the Lyceum, has been called the father of botany for his *History of Plants.*

22. Vitruvius, a first-century Roman, wrote *De architectura;* Seneca's *Questiones naturales* is a general study of physics and astronomy.

23. Mela, etc., were Roman authors of tracts on physics and geography, e.g., the *Natural History* of Pliny the Elder.

24. From ancient times through the Renaissance, the theory of humors was central to medicine; the four humors (yellow bile, blood, phlegm, black bile) were thought to correspond both to the four temperaments (choleric, sanguine, phlegmatic, melancholy) and to the four seasons.

25. The mythical Greek poet Orpheus supposedly wrote the *Lithica*, a poem on precious stones and divination; Hesiod's *Works and Days* is a didactic poem dealing with farm life, morals, mythology, and superstitions; the *Idylls* of Theocritus dramatically present the life of the common people of Sicily; the *Phenomena* of Aratus is a versified "treatise" on astronomy; Nicander wrote two didactic poems, one on snakes and other poisonous creatures (*Theriaca*), and the other on poisons and their antidotes (*Alexipharmaca*); Oppian composed poems on hunting dogs (*Cynegetica*) and on fishing (*Halieutica*); and Dionysius Periegetes wrote *Periegesis*, a geography of the world for schoolboys.

26. Lucretius' *De rerum natura* is a long didactic poem about the composition and laws of the universe; Manilius' *Astronomica* is a poem on astronomy and astrology; Virgil's *Georgics* is a poem on agriculture and animals.

27. A reference to Aristotle's discussion of deliberate choice in *Ethics*, III, 2, especially 1112ª 16–17: "choice involves a rational principle and thought." Cf. *Paradise Lost*, III, 108: "Reason also is choice"; and *Areopagitica* (1644 ed., p. 17): "reason is but choosing." J. F. Huntley notes that Milton chose the less popular and classical term (*proairesis*) in preference to the more popular and scholastic *synteresis* (*PQ*, XLIII [1964], 40–46).

28. Probably refers to Plato's "educational dialogues" (especially *Phaedrus, Phaedo, Symposium, Republic*); Xenophon's *Apology, Memorabilia, Banquet;* Cicero's *De officiis, De finibus;* Plutarch's *Moralia;* Diogenes Laertius' *Lives of the Philosophers;* and *On the Soul of the World*, falsely attributed to Timaeus Locri. For Milton's own readings, see his "Ethical Index" in the *Commonplace Book*.

29. In his *Commonplace Book*, Milton devotes a major section, titled "Economic Index," to opinions on food, conduct, marriage, divorce, education of children, riches, poverty, alms, and usury.

30. Family tragedies by Sophocles and Euripides.

31. By far the longest section in Milton's *Commonplace Book* is the one called "Political"; some of its subsections are "The State," "Love of Country," "Laws," "Customs of Foreign Nations," "King" (two long entries and one short one), "The Tyrant" (two entries), "The King of England," "Liberty," and "Nobility."

32. The "remains" or fragments of these very ancient authors were recorded by later writers such as Aristotle, Plutarch, and Stobaeus; e.g., Plutarch's *Life of Lycurgus* contains a detailed account of Lycurgus' educational ideas.

33. See *Seventh Prolusion*, note 19, for the Twelve Tables of Roman law. In *Commonplace Book*, Milton cites the *Institutes of Justinian* when he considers laws, particularly those concerning liberty and slavery.

34. The *organic arts:* i.e., the instrumental or practical arts used for communication: logic, rhetoric, and poetry.

35. "From Aristotle [Milton] could have learned that style, in prose and verse, should be perspicuous and appropriate to the speaker, to the subject, and to the audience. Not from Aristotle, but from Cicero, he could have learned that style should be elegant, graceful, and ornate and that the plain or lowly style was appropriate to instruction and proof, the middle or mean style for pleasing and conciliation, the grand or lofty style for rousing emotions and urging to action" (D. L. Clark, "John Milton and 'the fitted stile of lofty, mean, or lowly'," *Seventeenth-Century News*, XI [1953], 5).

36. Cicero compared logic to a closed fist and rhetoric to an open hand in *De finibus*, II, 6.

37. Plato's *Phaedrus* and *Gorgias;* Aristotle's *Rhetoric; On Style*, erroneously attributed to Phalereus; Cicero's *De oratore* and *Orator;* Hermogenes' *Ars rhetorica absolutissima* and *De formis orationum;* Longinus' *On the Sublime*.

38. Aristotle's *Poetics* and Horace's *Art of Poetry* were the key texts in Renaissance poetic theory.

39. Ludovico Castelvetro's *Poetica d'Aristotle* (1570); Torquato Tasso's *Discorsi dell'Arte Poetica* (1587) and *Discorsi del Poema Heroico* (1594); and Jacopo Mazzoni's *Defense* of Dante's *Divine Comedy* (1587). See B. Weinberg, *A History of Literary Criticism in the Italian Renaissance* (2 vols.; Chicago, 1961).

40. Many classical and Renaissance critics asserted the primacy of the principle of decorum. For fitness or appropriateness, Aristotle, in his *Rhetoric* and *Poetics*, used the Greek word *prepon*, which Cicero translated into Latin as *decorum*. Horace and Quintilian also made fitness or decorum a fundamental critical principle. Then in the Renaissance, the principle was re-emphasized by Richard Puttenham, Sir Philip Sidney, and Ben Jonson. See "Decorum" and "Fitness" in *Dictionary of World Literature*, ed. J. T. Shipley (New York, 1953).

41. Cf. Milton's contemptuous remarks about his contemporary writers in *Church-Governement* (*Yale Milton*, I, 818).

42. It was common in the Renaissance to stress the didactic and moral benefits of poetry. Cf. Sidney's *Apology for Poetry* and Milton's *Commonplace Book:* "Basil tells us that poetry was taught by God to kindle in the minds of men a zeal for virtue" (*Yale Milton*, I, 382).

43. The analogy is between stages of knowledge and lines (wards) of an army: just as the middle and rear battle lines must be reviewed, so does knowledge previously learned.

44. Pythagoras' famous school, at Crotona in southern Italy, was a religious society devoted to arithmetic and the mystical interpretation of numbers; Plato's Academy in Athens, sometimes called the "first university," was a school of mathematics and philosophy in which ethics and politics were emphasized to develop philosopher-statesmen; also in Athens, Isocrates' school of oratory challenged the Sophists by offering a broader and highly moral education; after about twenty years of study in Plato's Academy, Aristotle founded his own school, the Lyceum, in which logic, philosophy, and almost all the sciences known at the time were discussed in the covered walk called the *peripatos* (hence the name Peripatetic school).

45. The Cyrenaic school was founded by one of Socrates' pupils, Aristippus of Cyrene. A more famous center of learning was at Alexandria; during the last three centuries B.C., its museum was royally endowed for scientific research and its large library held riches for the humanities.

46. Cf. Plato's discussion of Spartan education for war in *Laws*, I, 625–35.

47. Cf. Aristotle, *Politics*, VIII, 5, 1340^b 11–14: "music has a power of forming the character, and should therefore be introduced into the education of the young"; and Plato, *Republic*, III, 401–2.

48. In his *Commonplace Book*, Milton shows his interest in military affairs by citing many authors on the subjects of military discipline, war, civil war, allies, sedition, and besieging of a city (*Yale Milton*, I, 491–506).

49. Cf. Milton's concern for students' individual talents in his *Commonplace Book:* "The nature of each person should be especially observed and not bent in another direction; for God does not intend all people for one thing, but for each one his own work . . ." (*Yale Milton*, I, 405).

50. Cf. *Commonplace Book:* "a dangerous thing, and an ominous thing. to imitate with earnestnesse the fashions of neigbour nations. so the english ran madding after the french in Edward confessors time" (*Yale Milton*, I, 429–30).

51. Book XXI of the *Odyssey* tells the story of the famous bow that no one can string and shoot but Ulysses.

58. Aristotle's [illegible] Horace's Ars Poetica [illegible] the [illegible] [illegible]

[illegible] Ludovico Castelvetro's Poetica d'Aristotele [illegible] Tasso's Discorsi dell'Arte Poetica (1587) and Discorsi del Poema Eroico (1594) [illegible]

[illegible]

[illegible] It was common in the Renaissance to stress the [illegible] Milton's Apology for Smectymnuus [illegible] (Columbia Milton, III, [illegible]).

[illegible]

[illegible] Pythagoras' famous school at Croton [illegible] number. Plato's Academy in Athens [illegible] mathematics and [illegible] philosophers [illegible] Plato's Academy. Aristotle [illegible] school, the Lyceum, in which logic, philosophy, [illegible] [illegible]

[illegible]

[illegible] Plato's dialogues [illegible] [illegible] Republic [illegible]

[illegible] In his Sermon [illegible]

[illegible] Milton [illegible]

[illegible] Book XI of the Odyssey tells [illegible] Ulysses.

THE TRACT FOR LIBERTY OF PUBLICATION, 1644

EDITED BY J. MAX PATRICK

Foreword

The Complete Text of *Areopagitica,* 1644

FOREWORD

Milton's immediate practical purpose in *Areopagitica* was to influence Parliament to revoke a section of the Licensing Order of 1643 which declared that no book, pamphlet, paper, or any part thereof could thenceforth "be printed, bound, stitched or put to sale" by anyone unless it was first approved and licensed by one or more persons appointed for that purpose by Parliament. The Order provided for searching out unlicensed printing presses, seizing their publications, apprehending "all Authors, Printers, and other persons whatsoever imployed in compiling, printing, stitching, binding, publishing and dispersing of said scandalous, unlicensed, and unwarrantable" works, and the punishing and imprisoning of those persons until they gave satisfaction that they would not repeat their offenses.

Milton objected to the arbitrariness of this prepublication censorship by men who could refuse a license for a work until it was revised to suit them, or who could, without appeal, refuse to allow it to be published legally. He did not oppose laws which forbade publication of libel, slander, open superstition, sedition, subversion of law and order, and "that also which is impious or evil absolutely against faith or manners"—moral conduct—but he wanted the responsibility for obeying those laws to belong to the would-be publishers of a work: it was for them to decide what they would publish, not some petty official. And only *after* a work had been made public could action be taken to prove, in a public trial where they would have the right to defend themselves, that they and the publication had broken those known laws.

What chiefly disturbed Milton was that licensers with arbitrary powers might thwart the continuance of the Protestant Reformation in England by preventing the dissemination of publications which could conduce to three main goals: (a) a fuller return than had yet been made in England to the truths Protestants discovered in the Bible; (b) clarification of those truths and purification of men's understanding of them from traditions and from what Protestants regarded as false or incomplete interpretations imposed upon the and (c) continued progress in the understanding and applicati of those Bible-revealed truths. The nature of these goals and so differences among Protestants concerning them must be explain if *Areopagitica* is to be understood properly.

Anglicans, Presbyterians, Congregationalists (Independents), a Baptists all agreed on what the Thirty-Nine Articles of the Chur of England called "the Sufficiency of the Holy Scriptures for S vation." In Article VI, this doctrine was explained: "Holy Scriptu containeth all things necessary to salvation: so that whatsoever not read therein, nor proved thereby, is not to be required of a man, that it should be believed as an article of the Faith, or thought requisite or necessary to salvation." However, there w some disagreement between orthodox Anglicans and Puritans with and without the Church of England concerning traditions and cer monies that had developed during the history of Christianity b were not explicitly stated in Scripture or clearly deducible from The Anglican position, as stated in Article XXXIV, was that the church traditions and ceremonies varied according to the diversiti of countries, times, and manners, and that they were to be respecte if they were edifying and not repugnant to the Word of God, eve though they were ordained "only by man's authority" and had n clear scriptural basis. But the Presbyterians, Congregationalists, an Baptists—and Milton also—refused to accept such additions. In th earlier phase of the Reformation, the Church of England had di carded many of them; and during the revolutionary period of th seventeenth century many more of them—episcopacy, for example were eliminated. The basis for such reforms was to find expressio two years after the publication of *Areopagitica* in the sixth claus of the Westminster Confession of Faith (1646): "The whole cou sel of God, concerning all things necessary for his glory, man's salva tion, faith, and life, is either expressly set down in Scripture, or b good and necessary consequence deduced from Scripture: unt which nothing at any time is to be added, whether by new revela tions of the Spirit, or traditions of men." This denial of the Roma Catholic recognition of the authority of the Tradition of the church and this denial of the Anglican willingness to retain edifying man made traditions that were not repugnant to Scripture had its basi in the Protestant interpretation of such biblical passages as Deut iv 2, Rev. xxii 18–19, Matt. v 18, and 1 Tim. vi 3–5. For convenienc we shall refer to these Presbyterians, Baptists, Congregationalists, and various smaller groups that held the same attitude toward the Bible as Biblicists; in 1644 most of the men so minded, apart from a few Separatists, were members of the Church of England endeavoring to reform it from within.

In *Areopagitica* Milton advocated toleration among these Biblicists and, conscious of their unanimous hostility to the church of Rome, played on that hostility; indeed, he explicitly states in the tract that Roman Catholicism is not to be tolerated and ought to be extirpated. But this intolerance toward Rome is not central in the pamphlet and therefore discussion of it will be deferred until after the main features of the work have been discussed. For *Areopagitica,* though incidentally anti-Catholic, was primarily a Protestant tract written for Protestants, with Protestant ends in view. Milton knew that if he could persuade the Biblicists that something was "Popish"—that is, based on Church Tradition rather than the express or necessarily deductible meaning of Scripture—he would thus convince them that it was wrong and should be eliminated.

Accordingly, he began his main argument by contending that the licensing of publications was a Popish invention. But it is important to remember that such prepublication licensing is only one kind or method of censorship and is not to be equated with that term in its broader sense of social supervision over men's opinions, conduct, and utterances. In that wider sense censorship has existed ever since primitive societies imposed taboos. Nor is licensing to be confused with postpublication censorship. In this sense of judging, disapproving, and suppressing works that had been made public, Milton had to consider a variety of Greek and Roman instances. He was able to show that such censorship of the published word became systematic in the medieval church after the year 800. Later, under the sixteenth-century popes, censorship became strict, comprehensive, and universally applicable, extending to an *Index of Prohibited Books* which were not to be read at all, and an *Index of Expurgations* or passages in books that might otherwise be read. Milton fails to mention that for good and sufficient reasons Roman Catholics could ask their superiors to allow them to read such forbidden works. Then, in Milton's own words, "To fill up the measure of encroachment, their last invention was to order that no Book, pamphlet, or paper should be Printed . . . unlesse it were approv'd and licens't." Thus he contended that licensing was a Roman Catholic invention used for prepublication censorship, which tried to suppress various kinds of works; and he also recognized that licensing was used by the Roman church to sustain its doctrines, especially those Traditions of the Church which Biblicists regarded as man-made impositions upon God's revelations—additions the Biblicists believed were contrary to express biblical commands. All this led to Milton's concluding that this Popish invention of licensing "was snatcht up by our Prelates, and hath caught some of our Presbyters." But he glossed rather lightly over the licensing censorship exercised by Reformed Anglicanism in the sixteenth century; to have done so would have weakened his attack on licensing as "Popish."

Moreover, in 1644 there was less need than there had been to be concerned about Anglican prelates: they had been ousted from power. Milton was now ready to turn his attention to the men responsible for the Licensing Order, to an attack on those whom he guardedly called "some of our Presbyters." His case against them amounted to this—that although, as Biblicists, they accepted the basic Protestant doctrine of scriptural sufficiency and its corollary that God forbade men to add anything to biblical teachings as necessary for true religion, nevertheless those Presbyterians erred in thinking or acting as if they already adequately understood all the main doctrines stated in Scripture; and they deluded themselves that thus, in a sense, they had completed the ideological part of the Reformation. Against them he contended that further progress in man's understanding of God's word was both possible and highly desirable, that continued study and interpretations of the Bible, publication of those interpretations and discussions of them in sermons, meetings, books, and pamphlets, could and would result in fuller, clearer, significantly new and increased understanding of what God had revealed in his Book. But, according to Milton, this growth in scriptural interpretation was being impeded because some of the Presbyterians, wrongly believing that the sufficiency of scriptural truth had been grasped and systematized by Calvin and other theologians, instituted the licensing system. The licensers, who were their agents, were not inclined to allow publication of works that put forth or explored new interpretations of Scripture—works such as Milton's own *Doctrine and Discipline of Divorce Restor'd . . . to the true meaning of Scripture*. In his view, by blocking such works, those Presbyterians were halting the Protestant Reformation, blocking growth in human comprehension and application of the divine revelations. Man was a fallen creature, but by careful use of his inspired reason, aided by God's grace, a believer could regain some of his proper powers and progress with increasing illumination toward richer awareness of what the Word of God revealed. Some men moved faster toward this improved understanding; those who moved more slowly or who stood still in blind stupidity and pride should encourage rather than suppress works conducive to this advance. If pamphlets like *Doctrine and Discipline* were denied publication, dynamic Protestants like Milton would be prevented from helping the progress which God intended men (especially his Englishmen) to make toward an ever fuller comprehension of his Word. It was therefore imperative, according to Milton, to have the Licensing Order revoked so that Christianity in England might continue to advance. Those who supported such restrictive legislation were, at best, like Moses: he came into sight of the Promised Land but never entered it.

Milton's task was a delicate one: in an unlicensed and therefore illegal tract, he was trying to persuade the very men who passed the Licensing Order to revoke it, using as a mainstay of his argument what amounted to alleging that the Order's supporters were guilty of something like Popery (which he knew they hated) and guilty of holding back the Reformation. The challenge to his rhetorical talents could hardly have been greater.

One obvious rhetorical device he employed was none too subtle flattery. He praised the "faithfull guidance and undaunted Wisdome," the "laudable deeds," and "indefatigable vertues," the "milde and equall Government," "magnanimity," and "civil and gentle greatnesse" of the Lords and Commons whom he addressed, passing lightly over the fact that (in his judgment) they had unwisely and tyrannically imposed licensing on the country, and gently assuring them that as prudent and reasonable men they were as willing to repeal an act of their own setting forth as any passed by their predecessors. And he further ingratiated himself by comparing them to the great assemblies of the ancient Greeks, and by paralleling himself to the orators who advised them.

As the title of the tract indicates, Milton had in mind the Court of the Areopagus, or Council of the Areopagites, which, as reformed by Solon about 594 B.C., had "full Power and Authority to enquire how every man lived in the City" of Athens. Solon stipulated that the members of this court should be pure and blameless in thei lives, more grave and serious than other men; Milton's implicatio was that the members of the English Parliament were men of lik quality. The chief object of the ancient tribunal was the mainte nance of laws, and it took particular cognizance of impiety, immora behavior, and public health. (It was before this tribunal that S Paul was arraigned as "a setter forth of strange gods.") Historically their *censorship*—that is, *supervision,* the original broad meanin of the word—over morals became tyrannical, and Pericles narrowe their powers to criminal cases. But Milton seems to have referre to them (and, by application, to the Parliament he addressed) no as the Areopagites became in their degenerated form but as Solo originally intended them. (Privately, being a master of irony, Milto was probably aware of the appropriateness of comparing a legisla tive body which degenerated to the tyranny of the Licensing Ac with an ancient court which declined into arbitrariness.)

Milton's immediate model was the famous Areopagitic Discours which, in the fifth century B.C., the orator Isocrates addressed to th Athenians, urging them to restore the Council of the Areopagites t its original powers and intended functions. The parallel between the two "speeches" lies chiefly in their general form and the fact that each was designed to be read, not orally delivered. Milton probabl regarded the ancient Areopagites as somewhat too conservative and overvigilant in their control of public and private morals; but his implied likening of them to the members of Parliament was good rhetoric: it was calculated to win the good will of the Lords and Commons, to reinforce Milton's contention that he was advocating a return to what prevailed before medieval and modern corruptions crept in, and to strengthen his acknowledgment that it is of the greatest concernment in Church and Commonwealth "to have a vigilant eye on how Bookes demeane themselves, as well as men." Milton took care to point out that the censorship over books exercised by the Areopagus had been confined to those that were "either blasphemous and Atheisticall, or Libellous." Moreover, the books the Areopagites ordered burnt had already been made public. His likening Parliament to this somewhat overmeddling court has disturbed some critics; but he was not entirely idealizing that ancient body; and he was hardly blind to Parliament's similar tendency to meddle.

The plan of *Areopagitica* is a flexible adaptation of the classical oration: after a one-paragraph *exordium* or introduction, Milton combines the *proposition* (setting forth the principal subject or theme) and the *partition* (outline of points or steps in the argument) doing so in less than two paragraphs. Then he interweaves the four-part *confirmation* (adducing of proofs) with short narratives (a *narration* being an account of matters of fact usually given as a comprehensive unit) and with a similarly scattered *reprehension* (a confutation or refutation of the opposing argument). He also includes two *digressions*, the first which Ernest Sirluck appropriately labels "personal" and the second ("national") which leads into the *peroration* or conclusion. Olivier Lutaud classifies the four parts of the *confirmation* as the Historical, Intellectual, Pragmatic, and Moral Arguments, and the *peroration* as the Patriotic Argument. Such classifications are convenient but should not obscure the fact that Milton blends his arguments, allowing different points to rise and then recede, only to recur later, like currents in a mixed stream. He is far from rigid in taking advantage of the classical pattern, and as a result, scholars who have tried to make the tract fit the form of the traditional oration disagree considerably about where to draw lines of demarcation between parts. However, it is helpful to follow the sequence of arguments as set down by Lutaud: Milton begins the *confirmation* by tracing the history of licensing to the invention of the practice by the Roman Catholics and its adoption by Anglican prelates and Presbyterians. The Intellectual Argument discusses the dangers of imposed licensing and censorship in contrast to the benefits of men's using God's gift of reason to choose their own reading matter. This point is backed up by Milton's important contention that in order to know virtue it is essential to learn about vice. The Pragmatic Argument assembles evidence and reasoning to show that the censorship Parliament intended the Licensing Order to effect would be unworkable and self-defeating: in the past all the best states recognized the undesirability and impracticality of such censorship; Plato's relegation of it to the imaginary construct of a utopia illustrates how unsuited it is for reality; if, with similar logical consistency, licensing were imposed upon a real society, censorship would have to extend to every aspect of life and activity until it became so all-embracing an inquisition that it would be both impractical and ridiculous. To attempt to isolate and extirpate all evil is to violate nature, to deny men that growth in virtue which comes from making reasoned choices between good and evil. The fact that the Royalists continue to publish in England despite the Licensing Law shows that it is unworkable; so does the low state of learning in Italy, which is caused by censorship; also the fact that those able to censor properly would be unwilling to undertake such work—with the result that it would fall to incompetents and mercenaries. Such are some of the points made in the Pragmatic Argument. Some of them could obviously be placed in other categories.

The Moral Argument similarly embraces a variety of points. Prepublication licensing discourages learning and learned men, insults the English people by supposing them ignorant and easily deluded, and disgraces ministers by regarding them as incapable of strengthening their flocks against the influence of bad books. By discouraging intelligent ministers who seek better insights into the Word of God, censorship would further mediocrity and glorify stupidity. To submit the population to controls is to prejudge them as unworthy and their pastors as incapable; moreover, it is to disappoint the people's expectations of Parliament and to frustrate the revolutionary struggle by changing the name but keeping essentially the same tyranny that afflicted them previously. To have extolled liberty and then to re-establish a slavery that ruins truth is hypocrisy. What censorship leads to is hypocrisy, indifference, conformism, shallowness, intellectual sloth, and stupidity.

What Sirluck calls the "national" *digression* serves as a transition from the *confirmation* to the *peroration* and with the latter constitutes what Lutaud calls the Patriotic Argument—though patriotic points are, of course, made throughout the discourse. Milton hymns the superiority and blessedness of England, especially as a leader in ideas and reforms, a land and people favored by God, a nation whose heart is in London and in its intellectual ferment—a ferment of productive diversity and discussion. Only by toleration of such free discussion among those who carried the Reformation to its present stage can greater understanding of the truth be achieved. Truth must not be stifled by those who claim a monopoly of it. Not to tolerate unlicensed publication by Biblicists is to betray the Reformation, the Revolution, the Nation, and the advancement of Truth.

The fact that Milton intertwines his arguments and combines the ordinarily separate parts of a classical oration indicates that he intended *Areopagitica* to make a total, cumulative, persuasive effect on his readers. To reduce his case to classified debater's points, ormulated in set oratorical patterns, or to approach the tract as if it were a cold, objective, scrupulously scientific article is to ignore its real nature as a work of rhetorical literature. This, to be sure, involves logic and facts, but it appeals not only to reason, but also makes emotional and ethical appeals and tries to win over the reader with images, associations, connotations, implications, resort to dialogue, hyperbole, denunciation, and all the colors of rhetoric. Moreover, so far, one can hardly see why this Protestant attack on an Order Milton disliked because it threatened the dissemination of his ideas has achieved a worldwide reputation as one of the great documents in the history of liberty.

Behind the immediate political purpose of the tract, transcendent over the particularity of a Protestant pamphlet written to persuade fellow Protestants that they were wrong not to tolerate each other's publications, was Milton's universal appeal based on his adherence to the doctrine that man's higher faculties, notably reason, should be preferred to his lower ones. Central to the pamphlet is the doctrine that responsible freedom necessarily depends on man's having opportunities to use his reason in order to make informed choices and judgments for himself. In order to make the crucial choices between good and evil, between obedience to God and that disobedience which is sin, man must be able to learn about evil and to be exposed to it—an opportunity admirably provided by books. Otherwise, he cannot progress to a positive, dynamic, mature virtue but will remain, at best, in the precariousness of a sheltered innocence, an innocence that is a sort of immature, neutral, ignorant goodness, a goodness so inexperienced, so untried, that it hardly deserves to be classified as virtue. Such innocence is likely to become prey to evil forces if its external protections are removed; the only sure protection is the development of inner strength of character—and that is dependent on having freedom to reject evil and choose good. Such an inner strength is a kind of higher liberty, especially when it becomes a self-chosen capacity for consistent resistance to error, stupidity, and sin, when it develops into an ability to be aloof from the irrationalities of temptation, and when it is realized as the power or virtue to live, think, and develop in a manner that best realizes a man's true self and thus coincides with what God wants him to be.

What a man writes is, properly, a product of his higher faculties, of that reason which distinguishes him from animals and makes him akin to God and the angels. Therefore, Milton argues, to suppress a good book is to suppress what is highest and best in man; it is a denial of his essential humanity, a tyrannical imposition that is contrary to the natural and divine order of things. To choke off what is best in man is not merely to inflict a kind of mental and spiritual death upon him; it is also to deny to other rational men the opportunity to grow in wisdom, virtue, and freedom as a result of being exposed to his ideas. If the power to deny and frustrate what is best and highest in mankind is given to censors who may be too stupid or careless or busy or cautious to risk licensing publication of works they fail to understand and appreciate, then it is clear that this is indeed a subjection of man's highest faculties to lower ones; it is an inexcusable tyranny, a denial of growth toward God and truth.

One of Milton's points is that fully effective censorship is impossible: in time the Truth will prevail. But this process may be delayed. Inasmuch as the English Reformation and Revolution had proceeded in his own lifetime to an extent which seemed to him to be miraculous, the attempt of "some of the Presbyters" to stop it when the Promised Land of full liberty was in sight, by reimposing a "Popish" licensing system, was to be especially condemned. Truth should be given every opportunity to emerge, with open and generous controversy or discussion as its midwife.

Milton's belief that in discussion truth has the advantage was not naïve but had realistic foundations. The point was to be well expressed by Walter Bagehot in the nineteenth century:

> Certain strong and eager minds embrace original opinions, seldom all wrong, never quite true, but of a mixed sort, part truth, part error. These they inculcate on all occasions, and on every side, and gradually bring the cooler sort of men to a hearing of them. These cooler sort of people serve as quasi-judges, while the more eager ones are a sort of advocates; a Court of Inquisition is sitting perpetually, investigating, informally and silently, but not ineffectually, what on great subjects of human interest, is truth and error. There is no sort of infallibility about the court; often it makes great mistakes; most of its decisions are incomplete in thought and imperfect in expression. Still, on the whole, the force of evidence keeps it right. The truth has the best of the proof, and therefore wins most of the judgments. The process is slow. . . . Time in it is reckoned not by days, but by years. . . . Yet on the whole, it creeps along, if you do not stop it. But all is arrested, if persecution begins.

The dialectic of controversy thus gave man's fallen reason the opportunity to find its way to truth.

It may be objected that if reason is man's highest faculty, Milton's appeal in *Areopagitica* should have been directly to it, through logic rather than rhetoric. But Milton was again being realistic. He recognized that communication to be effective must be oriented to the audience, that diction, order, and arrangement must not only be adapted to the subject matter and to what an author wants to achieve but, to be functional, must be accommodated to his audience's knowledge, beliefs, and habits of thought. As Francis Bacon wrote,

> The duty and office of Rhetoric is *to apply Reason to Imagination* for the better moving of the will. . . . Logic handleth reason exact and in truth, and Rhetoric handleth it as it is planted in popular opinions and manners. . . . for the proofs and demonstrations of Logic are toward all men indifferent and the same; but the proofs and persuasions of Rhetoric ought to differ according to the auditors.
>
> Rhetoric is subservient to the imagination, as Logic is to the understanding; and the duty and office of Rhetoric, if it be deeply looked into, is no other than to apply and recommend the dictates of reason to imagination, in order to excite the appetite and will. . . . The end of rhetoric is to fill the imagination with observations and images, to second reason, and not to oppress it.

In accordance with these principles, Milton was using imagination in *Areopagitica* as a sort of messenger between the reason and the affections or passions. His audience had to be moved to action—to repeal the Licensing Order. To this end Milton had to make his argument vivid. He thus resorted to rhetoric, to images, ideas, facts, modes of expression, stylistic devices which would play on his audience's imaginative faculty and thus make the logic of his speech acceptable to them. He tried to win and keep the good will of that audience, to reveal himself to advantage, to present ideas that would incite their emotions, and to express himself in a style that would translate cold, passionless reason into vivid terms. Through reasonable use of man's lower faculties, still keeping those lower faculties in subordination to reason, he would lead men to be more reasonable. Thus rhetoric was a means of securing the dominance of reason.

Milton's immediate audience was intended to be those who were responsible for, or maintainers of, the Licensing Order—Parliamentarians who had carried the Revolution and the Reformation up to a certain point and who tended to want to consolidate them there, working out the implications of the reforms and changes that had been made in the Revolution and were being considered by Parliament and the Westminster Assembly; but those Parliamentarians and most of those divines wished to hold the brake against further, more radical advances. Milton's rhetoric was, accordingly, attuned and accommodated to them. A basic principle of rhetorical persuasion is to be selective—to adduce what is or may be made acceptable to one's auditors, and to avoid or to gloss over what might displease them. Thus in a tract written to advocate revision of a parliamentary order, it is wise to win the support of as many men and groups as possible, but it is usually not wise to elaborate specific alternatives. For some of the men who may be won to abolish X will want it replaced by Y, and others by Z or W; and if a speaker picks on one of these substitutes, the result may be that some of those who would otherwise support the reform will prefer to retain X. Awareness of this accounts in part for Milton's vagueness about the nature, system, and enforcement of postpublication censorship that he envisages. He does commit himself to saying that the state must keep a vigilant eye on how books demean themselves, punishing those who are malefactors with sharpest justice: in other words, those responsible for publishing such works are to be punished; and, when possible, the books themselves will be seized and destroyed. But Milton fails to state all this explicitly. Presumably he envisaged that the laws against such publications would be unambiguous and that trials and punishments would be fair; but again he fails to say so. He can hardly have been unaware that many of his arguments against licensing were valid against postpublication censorship. Yet he is not precise about what kinds of publications would be outlawed.

That in any society there must be some outlawing of publication is obvious. Decent men need some sort of protection against libels and slanders which do them demonstrable harm. Milton is on reasonable ground when he maintains that publication of libelous books is to be a punishable offense. But he more frequently uses the vaguer term "mischievous," by which he seems to mean books dangerous to the preservation of law and order, those that are absolutely evil, outrightly superstitious, and patently impious. However, he does not clarify these limits. He probably intended to allow extreme anti-Romanists to infer that he would not tolerate Roman Catholic books (though his real view was opposed to their suppression), when he wrote, "I mean not tolerated Popery, and open superstition, which, as it extirpats all religions, and civill supremacies, so it self should be extirpat, provided first that all charitable and compassionate means be us'd to win the weak and the misled." This sentence is somewhat involved—perhaps deliberately so—and it changes focus midway from Popery and superstition (which are equated in the singular pronoun "it") to weak and misled persons. What he seems to have in mind was a continuance of the existing laws which made Roman Catholic rites and services and proselytizing illegal; but to them he would add a provision excepting from penalties converts who could be wooed back to Protestantism. Most important, he makes no mention of publication in this context, leaving it open to an anti-Romanist to think that Popish publications would be suppressed, though a careful reader would remember that earlier in the tract Milton explicitly stated that "books of controversie in Religion . . . must be permitted untoucht by the licenser," and that in that context he was writing about "Papisticall" books. The clear implication was that such works would not be outlawed after publication; indeed, he adds that "those books . . . which are likeliest to taint both life and doctrine, cannot be suppresst without the fall of learning, and of all ability in disputation."

A major problem remains: in a tract advocating a fertile interfaith dialogue and toleration of publications as essential for it, how could Milton tolerate Roman Catholic books but otherwise exclude "Popery" from toleration? Two reasons account for this intolerance, one religious and the other political.

Many Anglicans of Milton's times regarded the Roman church as a true but corrupted branch of one Universal Holy Church, which was subdivided into various national bodies. But Milton and the rest of the Anglicans, along with those who inclined to Presbyterian, Congregationalist, Baptist, and other Protestant doctrines—it should be remembered that these groups were only emerging and that most of them were contained within the established church in England as it existed in 1644—regarded Roman Catholicism as heretical, idolatrous, and superstitious, to the extent that it was based on Tradition; therefore in his view it was intolerable. Later, in *Of True Religion* (1673), Milton was to write, "of all known Sects or pretended Religions at this day in Christendom, Popery is the only and greatest Heresie." "Popery, as being Idolatrous, is not to b tolerated either in Public or Private." Concerning native Englishme who are Roman Catholics he asks, "Are we to punish them by cor poral punishment, or fines in their Estates, upon account of thei Religion? I suppose it stands not with the Clemency of the Gospe more than what appertains to the security of the State." However he goes on to assert that "we must remove their Idolatry, and all th furniture thereof, whether Idols or the Mass. . . . If they say tha by removing their Idols we violate their Consciences, we have n warrant to regard Conscience which is not grounded in Scripture." Nevertheless, Milton points out that "We suffer the Idolatrous book of Papists . . . to be sold and read as common as our own" and argues from this fact for the toleration of books by Anabaptists, Arians, Arminians, and Socinians. In short, Milton was willing to allow Roman Catholic books to circulate because they were conducive to the discovery of truth in the dialectic of controversy; but because he and some of his fellow Protestants interpreted the Bible as forbidding certain Roman Catholic practices, he was unable to tolerate them. His position may be likened to that of Christians who interpret the Bible to forbid polygamy and therefore deny to sects who interpret it otherwise their claims for a man to be allowed more than one wife.

The political reason for Milton's not tolerating Roman Catholicism was rooted in seventeenth-century circumstances. (To judge his intolerance of Popery out of the context of those times is rather like denouncing Abraham, Isaac, and Jacob for their polygamy.) Englishmen were aware that throughout the Reformation and Counter-Reformation periods Roman Catholics neglected few opportunities to overthrow other religious and political organizations associated with them. It was common knowledge that the popes encouraged and participated in such efforts to subvert the governments and religions of Protestant states. Protestants were equally intolerant in most countries. In particular, Englishmen remembered the papal bull of February 23, 1570, which declared Queen Elizabeth a deposed, excommunicated heretic and extended the same anathema to those who continued to obey her laws and mandates. Indeed, knowledge of such attempts to extirpate "civill supremacies" and acceptance of the principle that no proper government can tolerate subversion led almost all Protestants of Milton's times to refuse toleration to Roman Catholics. A realist simply could not ignore the overwhelming evidence of the unrelenting threat: the Jesuit mission to England in Elizabethan times, the Pope's blessing the Spanish Armada as a sacred crusade, the papal troops sent to Ireland in 1578, the encouragement given by Gregory XIII's cardinal secretary to English noblemen to commit tyrannicide against Elizabeth I, and the Gunpowder Plot of 1605 to blow up King James and both Houses of Parliament. From an English standpoint all of these were examples of subversive action. In this regard it might accordingly be argued that in willingness to tolerate Roman Catholic books but unwillingness to allow seventeenth-century Roman Catholic practices, Milton was approaching the familiar position of those who distinguish between men's words and their deeds, urging toleration of "mischievous" publications unless they were direct incitements to subversive actions, but advocating that strong steps should be taken against rebellious actions.

In any case, it is important to distinguish between those aspects of *Areopagitica* which were limited by special circumstances of Milton's times and by his Biblicist beliefs and, on the other hand, the strength of the general principles which he propounded and their universal pertinence. It is this broader aspect of his work which has been powerfully conducive to the considerable degree of free speech and publication which now exists in many parts of the world and has been conducive to a tolerance of religious practices which is often broader than Milton himself envisaged.

Areopagitica is not easy to read; its style is often complex, its arguments involved, and its allusions unfamiliar. Nevertheless, a generation that is ready to puzzle over the intricacies of the novels of James Joyce and the compressed difficulties of modern poetry should be willing to devote as much time and labor to unravelling Milton's sentences, following his interwoven image patterns, and attuning themselves to his somewhat unfamiliar modes of expression. The extensive explanatory notes are intended to facilitate understanding, to point to Milton's techniques, and to enable an appreciation of this masterpiece both as a document in the history of ideas and as an outstanding piece of prose literature.

The text of *Areopagitica* printed here is based on a collation of four copies of the 1644 edition, those in the Clark Memorial Library, the University of Illinois Library (M2092), the Newberry Library (A218), and the private library formerly owned by Louis H. Silver.

These have been compared with Ernest Sirluck's edition in the *Yale Milton* and serve only to confirm the excellence of his work except that the following may be added to complement what he records in his textual notes (Vol. II, p. 778). References are to his page numbers:

503 (1644 ed., p. 8, line 21) *Nicolò*] *i* quite clear in A218 and Silver.
515 (1644 ed., p. 12) warfaring] wayfaring *r* corrected to *y* in ink in Silver.
544 (1644 ed., p. 27, line 15) *Jerusalem*] *Ierusalem* So in all four copies examined.
559 (1644 ed., p. 34) Lords] *s* added in ink in Silver.

In addition to regularizing *i* and *j*, *u* and *v* in accordance with modern practice and similarly regularizing *then* and *than*, as well as making certain changes for the sake of clarity which are noticed in the footnotes, I have bracketed additions to the text and have silently corrected the obvious misprints: they are noted by Sirluck (on p. 778 of his edition); however, I have not followed his practice (p. 508) of introducing a comma after "notwithstanding" (1644 ed., p. 10).

Only the one edition of *Areopagitica* appeared in Milton's lifetime; but beginning with the collected editions of 1697 and 1698, it has been frequently reprinted—more so than any other prose work by Milton. Noteworthy are the editions by T. Holt White (1819), J. A. St. John (1848—seriously inaccurate but frequently reprinted in unscholarly editions); Edward Arber (in *English Reprints*, 1868), A. W. Verity (1918, with commentary by Sir Richard Jebb); John W. Hales (1874); Laura E. Lockwood (1911); Merritt Y. Hughes (1947 and 1957); also the facsimile reproductions in *The Noel Douglas Replicas* and *The English Replicas* (1927); the edition in the *Columbia Milton*, IV; and that by Sirluck in the *Yale Milton*, II, which should be consulted for further details about all these editions. There are numerous foreign translations, of which the best is the bilingual one in French and English, with excellent introduction and notes, by Olivier Lutaud (Paris, 1956).

Scholarship on *Areopagitica* is extensive. Recommended are the introductions by Sirluck and Lutaud in their editions and the following:

Wilbur E. Gilman, *Milton's Rhetoric: Studies in his Defense of Liberty* (Columbia, Mo., 1939).

George F. Sensabaugh, *That Grand Whig Milton* (Stanford, 1952)—for influence.

William O. Haller, "Before *Areopagitica*," *PMLA*, XLII (1927), 875–900.

———, *Tracts on Liberty in the Puritan Revolution* (3 vols.; New York, 1934).

———, *Liberty and Reformation in the Puritan Revolution* (New York, 1955).

A. S. P. Woodhouse, *Puritanism and Liberty* (London, 1938).

Arthur Barker, *Milton and the Puritan Dilemma* (Toronto, 1942).

AREOPAGITICA;

A SPEECH OF MR. *JOHN MILTON* FOR THE LIBERTY OF UNLICENC'D PRINTING. TO THE PARLAMENT OF ENGLAND.

[Four lines of Greek verse from Euripides' *The Suppliants.*]

This is true Liberty when free born men
Having to advise the public may speak free,
Which he who can, and will, deserv's high praise,
Who neither can nor will, may hold his peace;
What can be juster in a State than this?

Euripid. Hicetid.

LONDON, Printed in the Yeare, 1644.

FOR THE LIBERTY OF UNLICENC'D PRINTING.

[1] They who to States[1] and Governours of the Commonwealth direct their Speech, High Court of Parlament, or wanting[2] such accesse in a private condition, write that which they foresee may advance the publick good; I suppose them[3] as at the beginning of no meane[4] endeavour, not a little alter'd and mov'd inwardly in their mindes:[5] Some with doubt of what will be the successe,[6] others

1. *States:* governing bodies or men of high standing in a state—in contrast to those "in a private condition."

2. *wanting:* being without—because they are private citizens.

3. *suppose them:* i.e., those who deliver such a speech orally or in writing.

4. *meane:* contemptible or ordinary. Cf. Acts xxi 39: "of no mean city."

5. In keeping with the suggested but rapidly rejected role of a speaker torn by "dispositions" of doubt, fear, hope, and confidence, Milton begins with an anacoluthon—a deliberate change from one syntactical construction to another. The inverted word order, the punctuated pauses or breaks in construction, the obliquity of "not a little alter'd" (i.e., changed or disturbed), and the redun-

with feare of what will be the censure;[7] some with hope, others with confidence of what they have to speake. And me perhaps each of these dispositions, as the subject was whereon I enter'd, may have at other times variously affected;[8] and likely might in these foremost expressions now also disclose which of them sway'd most, but that the very attempt[9] of this addresse thus made, and the thought of whom it hath recourse to, hath got the power within me to a passion, farre more welcome than incidentall to a Preface.[10] Which though I stay not to confesse ere any aske, I shall be blamelesse, if it[11] be no other, then the joy and gratulation which it[12] brings to all who wish and promote their Countries liberty; whereof this whole Discourse propos'd will be a certaine testimony, if not a Trophey.[13] For this is not the liberty which wee can hope, that no grievance ever should arise in the Commonwealth–*that*[14] let no man in this World expect; but when complaints are freely heard, deeply consider'd, and speedily reform'd, then is the utmost bound of civill liberty attain'd, that wise men looke for. To which if I now manifest by the very sound of this which I shall utter, that wee are already in good part arriv'd, and yet from such a steepe disadvantage of tyranny and superstition grounded into our principles as was beyond

---

dancy of "inwardly in their mindes" combine with other features such as the lack of a clear subject for "likely might" to reinforce a sense of distraction and uncertainty.

6. *the successe:* the outcome. Cf. *Paradise Regain'd* IV, 1: "troubl'd at his bad success."

7. *censure:* his auditors' or readers' opinion of the speech.

8. I.e.: As for me–perhaps each of these feelings may have influenced me at other times, varying with the subjects on which I was beginning to speak or write. (Such occasions occurred when he began his prolusions and the tracts on episcopacy, education, and divorce, especially those addressed to Parliament–the 1644 ed. of *Doctrine and Discipline of Divorce* and *The Judgement of Martin Bucer.*)

9. *and likely might . . . very attempt:* and it is likely that in these introductory statements these feelings might now disclose which of them most influenced me were it not that the very attempt, etc.

10. . . . the attempt and the thought have increased the power (the power of utterance and the impelling force to speak) to an intensity of feeling and emotion which is far more welcome in a prefatory statement than it is likely to occur in one. Cf. early in *Second Defense:* "I can hardly refrain from assuming a more lofty and swelling tone than the simplicity of an exordium may seem to justify" (Bohn ed., I, 219).

11. *it:* the passion or emotion.

12. *gratulation which it:* i.e., the expression of such a passion in an attempt of this kind.

13. I.e., this speech in its entirety which I am setting forth will be an undeniable documentary proof, if not a memorial or evidence of victory.

14. *that:* i.e., that freedom from grievances. In the original ed. *that* is preceded by a comma and not italicized.

the manhood of a *Roman* recovery, it will bee attributed first, as is most due, to the strong assistance of God our deliverer, next to your faithfull guidance and undaunted Wisdome, Lords and Commons of *England*.[15] Neither is it in Gods esteeme the diminution of his glory, when honourable things are spoken of good men and worthy Magistrates: which if I now first[16] should begin to [2] doe, after so fair a progresse of your laudable deeds, and such a long obligement upon[17] the whole Realme to your indefatigable vertues, I might be justly reckn'd among the tardiest, and the unwillingest of them that praise yee. Neverthelesse there being three principall things, without which all praising is but Courtship and flattery, First, when that only is prais'd which is solidly worth praise: next when greatest likelihoods are brought that such things are truly and really in those persons to whom they are ascrib'd;[18] the other,[19] when he who praises, by shewing that such his actuall perswasion is of whom he writes, can demonstrate that he flatters not; the former two of these I have heretofore endeavour'd, rescuing the employment from him who went about to impaire your merits with a triviall and malignant *Encomium;*[20] the latter[21] as belonging chiefly to mine owne acquitall,

15. Milton's subtlety in the art of persuasion is noteworthy. He tells the men who required a license for printing that his unlicensed publication manifests the very liberty for which he is arguing. He rhetorically assumes that he will voice the speech, that the Lords and Commons are permitting it, and that they deserve praise for guidance (which they did not provide in this matter) and for wisdom (though in fact they had decreed otherwise). The assertion that the English had already arrived at a large part of this liberty assumes the desirability of moving further. The association of his audience with God is flattering and ingratiating. So is the image of the English surmounting the steep disadvantage of the tyranny (of monarchy) and the superstition (of episcopacy and Popery)—a disadvantage which had been based in, and grounded into, their very origins and fundamentals. In contrast, the ancient Romans after their decline and fall lacked the *virtus*—manliness, valor, and capability—to rise from where they had sunk.

16. *first:* i.e., initially in this discourse. Milton had praised Parliament in *An Apology* and elsewhere.

17. *such a long obligement upon:* after such a long indebtedness laid upon. (The Long Parliament was ending its fourth year.)

18. Comma in the original edition.

19. *the other:* i.e., the third of the "principall things, without which all praising is but Courtship and flattery."

20. I.e., with a commonplace and malevolent eulogy—namely, *A Modest Confutation of a Slanderous and Scurrilous Libell, Entituled, Animadversions . . .* (1642), variously ascribed to Joseph Hall and his sons. In *An Apology* Milton asks how this "private concocter of malecontent," when he is pretending to extol Parliament, can afford to blur over "that publick triumph of their justice" and contends that his meaning is "full of close malignity." *Malignant* was a term applied by anti-Royalists to supporters of monarchy and episcopacy. Milton's

that whom I so extoll'd I did not flatter, hath been reserv'd opportunely to this occasion. For he who freely magnifies what hath been nobly done, and fears not to declare as freely what might be done better, gives ye the best cov'nant of his fidelity; and that[22] his loyalest affection and his hope waits on your proceedings. His highest praising is not flattery, and his plainest advice is a kinde of praising; for though I should affirme and hold by argument, that it would fare better with truth, with learning, and the Commonwealth, if one of your publisht Orders which I should name, were call'd in, yet at the same time it could not but much redound to the lustre of your milde and equall[23] Government, when as private persons are hereby animated to thinke ye better pleas'd with publick advice, than other statists have been delighted heretofore with publicke flattery. And men will then see what difference there is between the magnanimity of a triennial Parlament,[24] and that jealous hautinesse of Prelates and cabin Counsellours that usurpt of late,[25] when as they shall observe yee in the midd'st of your Victories and successes[26] more gently brooking writt'n exceptions against a voted Order, than other Courts which had produc't nothing worth memory but the weake ostentation of wealth, would have endur'd the least signifi'd dislike at any sudden Proclamation. If I should thus farre presume upon the meek demeanour of your civill and gentle greatnesse, Lords and Commons, as what your publisht Order hath directly said, that to gainsay,[27] I might defend my selfe with ease, if any should accuse me of being new[28] or insolent, did they but know how much

---

awareness that his subverting the order against unlicensed printing could b[e] called malignant perhaps accounts for his pointing to his record of praising th[e] Long Parliament and for his contrasting that praise with the false flattery al[-] legedly given by another.

21. *the latter:* the last of the three.

22. *that:* i.e., shows that.

23. *equall:* just.

24. The Triennial Parliaments Act (1641) ensured the automatic summonin[g] of a new parliament if the king failed to call one within three years of the las[t] one's dissolution. Parliaments, being less dependent upon him, could be loftier i[n] purpose and action.

25. Charles I ruled for long periods without Parliament by means of group[s] of favorites, especially a junto called the Cabinet Council, thus appropriatin[g] political power of doubtful legality.

26. Milton refers to victories like Marston Moor in July 1644, taking care no[t] to mention the parliamentary army's later failures.

27. I.e.: If I were to presume so far . . . as to contradict (in speech or ac[-] tion) what your published Licensing Order directly stated. The fact is tha[t] Milton is already contravening that order; his hypothesizing here is a rhetorica[l] device, as is his flattering his auditors for their civility and gentility.

28. *new:* presumptuous.

better I find ye esteem it to imitate the old and elegant humanity of Greece, [3] than the barbarick pride of a *Hunnish* and *Norwegian* statelines.[29] And out of those ages, to whose polite wisdom and letters[30] we ow that we are not yet *Gothes* and Jutlanders,[31] I could name him[32] who from his private house wrote that discourse to the Parlament of Athens, that perswades them to change the forme of *Democraty*[33] which was then establisht. Such honour was done in those days to men who profest the study of wisdome and eloquence, not only in their own Country, but in other Lands, that Cities and Siniories[34] heard them gladly, and with great respect, if they had ought in publick to admonish the State. Thus did *Dion Prusaeus*[35] a stranger and a privat Orator counsell the *Rhodians*

29. Milton's technique is to win his auditors less by reasoning than by flattering rhetorical assumption of their agreement with what he advocates: thus he tells them that he finds that they esteem the *humanitas* (liberal education, good breeding, and refined manners) of the Greeks more than the rude ostentation of Hunnish or Norwegian pomp. Compare Satan's ostentatious barbarism at the beginning of *Paradise Lost,* II. The Huns were major agents in the downfall of Roman civilization; and the Norwegians or Danes (they usually had the same rulers) were notorious for destructive incursions against lands under civilized rulers like King Alfred.

30. *polite wisdom and letters:* polished, refined wisdom and literature.

31. I.e., we owe the fact that we are not still Goths (who overran the Roman Empire) or Jutes (invaders of ancient Britain).

32. Isocrates (d. 338 B.C.), lauded by Cicero for founding the art of systematic oratory in Athens. In the sonnet to Lady Margaret Leigh, Milton called him "that old man eloquent." Being physically incapacitated for public speaking, Isocrates designed his Seventh Oration, *Areopagiticos Logos*—the Areopagitic Discourse—to be read and only supposedly delivered. The harangue was fictively addressed to the Athenian *ecclesia,* an assembly of the people, which Milton loosely termed a "Parlament." In the oration Isocrates advocated that the Court of the Areopagus, then limited to criminal jurisdiction, be restored to its former political dominance, especially as censor of public morals. Its members were former public officials of tried integrity who were elected for life by the people. In contrast to Isocrates' urging restoration of an interfering power, Milton was advocating removal of what he regarded as excessive interference.

33. Isocrates contrasted the degenerate Athenian democracy of his time with a utopianized description of the more primitive democracy ordained by Solon and Cleisthenes.

34. Milton seems to mean free states or republics (Greek *poloi;* Latin *civitates*) and states under the dominion of a king, prince, seignior, or lord. In his times *seigniory* was applied both to the despotism of Turkey and the oligarchic republicanism of Venice. But he is referring to what was "done in those days" of ancient Athens when, for example, Isocrates composed political orations to the Prince of Salamis, Philip of Macedon, and various other states and rulers.

35. Dion of Prusa in Bithynia (d. ca. 117) was a rhetorician and philosopher who opposed tyranny and was surnamed Chrysostom (golden-mouthed) because of his eloquence. He traveled widely and spoke as an outsider with no official position to audiences in Greece and Asia Minor, directing them with

against a former Edict: and I abound with other like examples, which to set heer would be superfluous. But if from the industry of a life wholly dedicated to studious labours, and those naturall endowments haply not the worst for two and fifty degrees of northern latitude,[36] so much must be derogated,[37] as to count me not equall to any of those who had this priviledge, I would obtain to be thought not so inferior, as your selves are superior to the most of them who receiv'd their counsell:[38] and how far you excell them, be assur'd, Lords and Commons, there can no greater testimony appear, than when your prudent spirit acknowledges and obeyes the voice of reason from what quarter soever it be heard speaking; and renders ye as willing to repeal any Act of your own setting forth, as any set forth by your Predecessors.

If ye be thus resolv'd, as it were injury to thinke ye were not, I know not what should withhold me from presenting ye with a fit instance wherein to shew both that love of truth which ye eminently professe, and that uprightnesse of your judgement which is not wont to be partiall to your selves; by judging over again that Order which ye have ordain'd *to regulate Printing. That no Book, pamphlet, or paper shall be henceforth Printed, unlesse the same be first approv'd and licenc't by such,* or at least one of such as shall be thereto appointed. For that part which preserves justly every mans Copy[39] to himselfe, or provides for the poor, I touch not, only wish they be not made pretenses to abuse and persecute honest and painfull[40] Men, who offend not in either of these particulars. But that other clause of Licensing Books, which we thought had dy'd

---

light irony to correct the defects in their states. At Rhodes, in his Thirty-first Discourse, he urged repeal of a law which allowed new names to be put on public statues to replace the ones originally there.

36. Milton refers to the theory which derives from Aristotle's *Politics,* VII, 7, that cold climates make men dull-witted and unsubtle. In *Paradise Lost,* IX, 44–45, Milton fears that cold climate may damp his poetic flights; and in a suppressed passage intended for his *History of Britain,* he acknowledged that "the sunn, which wee want, ripens witts as well as fruits." See Zera S. Fink, "Milton and the Theory of Climatic Influence," *MLQ,* II (1941), 67–80, and his *The Classical Republicans* (Evanston, 1945), pp. 91–94, 191–92. But in the seventh-last paragraph of *Areopagitica,* Milton asserts that the English are "a Nation not slow and dull, but of a quick, ingenious, and piercing spirit," etc.

37. *derogated:* subtracted or regarded as not to be counted in any estimate.

38. I.e., if to count me the equal of such great orators it would be necessary to credit me with much that my devotion to study and natural gifts do not entitle me to claim, nevertheless I wish to obtain this much—to have it recognized that I am not so inferior to them in one respect, which is that you, O Lords and Commons, are superior to most of those who received advice from those orators.

39. *Copy:* copyright.

40. *painfull:* painstaking.

with his brother *quadragesimal* and *matrimonial* when the Prelates expir'd,[41] I shall now attend with such a Homily,[42] as shall lay before ye, first the inventors of it to bee those whom ye will be loath to own; next what is to be thought in [4] generall of reading, what ever sort the Books be; and that this Order avails nothing to the suppressing of scandalous, seditious, and libellous Books, which were mainly intended to be suppresst. Last, that it will be primely to the discouragement of all learning, and the stop of Truth, not only by disexercising and blunting our abilities in what we know already, but by hindring and cropping[43] the discovery that might bee yet further made both in religious and civill Wisdome.

I deny not, but that it is of greatest concernment in the Church and Commonwealth, to have a vigilant eye how Bookes demeane[44] themselves, as well as men; and thereafter to confine, imprison, and do sharpest justice on them as malefactors: For Books are not absolutely dead things, but doe contain a potencie of life in them to be as active as that soule was whose progeny they are: nay they do preserve as in a violl[45] the purest efficacy and extraction of that living intellect that bred them.[46] I know they are as lively, and as vigorously productive, as those fabulous Dragons teeth; and being sown up and down, may chance to spring up armed men.[47] And yet on the other hand unlesse warinesse be us'd, as good almost kill a Man

41. *had dy'd . . . expir'd:* had ended along with the Lenten and matrimonial egulations which were akin to it. Before the Revolution bishops governed the censing of printing, fasting during Lent (including dispensations to individuals eat meat instead of fish), and such matrimonial matters as permission to arry, the publication of banns (including dispensations from this requirement), nd marriage rites. This control of printing, fasting, and marriage by the bishops as thought to have ended with the exclusion of bishops from the House of ords (1642), the establishment of Presbyterianism (1645), and the formal bolition of episcopacy (1646); but the licensing of books (which Milton oposed under any auspices) was revived under civil control; restrictions against ating meat on certain days were partially continued for economic rather than eligious reasons; and marriage was gradually made a civil contract licensed by he civil power—as Milton had advocated in his divorce tracts and was to aplaud in *Considerations Touching the Likeliest Means to Remove Hirelings* 1659).

42. *attend . . . Homily:* direct my mind toward, with such a lecture.

43. *cropping:* cutting off or cutting short.

44. *demeane:* comport or behave.

45. *violl:* vial, small container for liquids.

46. Cf. Francis Bacon, *Of the Advancement of Learning*, I, viii, 6: "But the mages of men's wits and knowledges remain in books, exempted from the vrong of time. . . . They generate still, and cast their seeds in the minds of others."

47. After Cadmus sowed the teeth of a slain dragon, a crop of armed men grew up and fought until only five survived. They helped him build Thebes.

as kill a good Book; who kills a Man kills a reasonable creatur Gods Image; but hee who destroyes a good Booke, kills reason selfe, kills the Image of God, as it were in the eye. Many a ma lives a burden to the Earth; but a good Booke is the pretious lif blood of a master spirit, imbalm'd and treasur'd up on purpose to life beyond life. 'Tis true, no age can restore a life, whereof perhap there is no great losse; and revolutions of ages doe not oft recove the losse of a rejected truth, for the want of which whole Nation fare the worse. We should be wary therefore what persecution w raise against the living labours of publick men, how we spill[48] tha season'd life of man preserv'd and stor'd up in Books; since we se a kinde of homicide may be thus committed, sometimes a martyr dome, and if it extend to the whole impression,[49] a kinde of massa cre, whereof the execution ends not in the slaying of an elemental life, but strikes at that ethereall and fift essence, the breath of reaso it selfe, slaies an immortality rather than a life.[50] But lest I shoul be condemn'd of introducing licence,[51] while I oppose Licencing, refuse not the paines to be so much Historicall, as will serve to shev what hath been done by ancient and famous Commonwealths against this disorder, till the very time that this project of licencin crept out of the *Inquisition*,[52] was catcht up [5] by our Prelates and hath caught some of our Presbyters.

48. *spill:* destroy.

49. *whole impression:* all the copies printed.

50. Milton here expands his earlier statement, "hee who destroyes a g Booke, kills reason it selfe, kills the Image of God." He has in mind that a g book is a product of human reason and that possession of a rational soul tinguishes man from animals and plants: their life is "elementall," based on four terrestrial elements of earth, air, fire, and water, to which they are redu by death. When a man is killed, the elemental natural life which he shares w plants and animals is ended. But when all copies of a book, which is an exp sion of his rational soul, are destroyed, it is not merely the ending of an mental life: rather, such destruction strikes at what is quintessential (high and most essential) in man, at what is heavenly or ethereal in him, at his sential determinant principle—the breath of reason put in him by God. He Milton's concluding paradox that such destruction "slays an immortality." In much as he expresses himself in metaphor and analogue, it is not clear whet by "ethereall and fift essence" he means literally or figuratively that the tional soul, like the stars, is made of the quintessence or fifth essence (as d tinct from the four terrestrial elements). See *Paradise Lost,* III, 713–18. For views about the rational soul follow the references under "Soul" in the Index the *Columbia Milton.*

51. I.e., condemned for introducing irresponsible, unrestrained liberty abuse or disregard of law, propriety, reason, and morality. Cf. the sonnet, "I but prompt the age": "Licence they mean, when they cry liberty, / For w loves that, must first be wise, and good."

52. Christian repression of heresy received aid from civil authorities as ea as the fourth century. In 1231 the Inquisition was set up as a Roman Catho

In *Athens* where Books and Wits were ever busier than in any other part of *Greece*, I finde but only two sorts of writings which the Magistrate car'd to take notice of; those either blasphemous and Atheisticall, or Libellous. Thus the Books of *Protagoras* were by the Judges of *Areopagus* commanded to be burnt, and himselfe banisht the territory for a discourse begun with his confessing not to know *whether there were gods, or whether not:*[53] And against defaming, it was decreed that none should be traduc'd by name, as was the manner of the *Vetus Comoedia*,[54] whereby we may guesse how they censur'd libelling: And this course was quick enough, as *Cicero* writes, to quell both the desperate wits of other Atheists, and the open way of defaming, as the event shew'd.[55] Of other sects and

---

tribunal to combat heresy. It operated more noticeably in other European countries than Spain, but its reinvigoration there in 1478 led to such extensive activity that the term "Inquisition" is widely used to refer only to the Spanish one. Milton often employed it so. In 1908 the Pope changed the title from Inquisition to Holy Office.

Censorship by church officials of books in manuscript was introduced temporarily in England as early as the opening decades of the fifteenth century and was frequently revived. Under the Tudors the licensing of books of all kinds was enforced from 1538 by the Privy Council which, from 1566, involved the Stationers Company in its administration. This system was continued under James I and reached its peak under Charles I with *A Decree of Starre-Chamber, Concerning Printing*, on July 11, 1637. It forbade the importation, printing, or sale of "seditious, scismaticall, or offensive Bookes or Pamphlets," the printing or reprinting of anything without a license and an entry in the Stationers Register; the publication of any printed matter without a signed imprimatur and the names of the author and printer. Further provisions limited the number of master printers and their employees, made it an offense to own, operate, or furnish space for an unlicensed press, gave the Stationers Company a right to search premises to find unlicensed printing, and prohibited import of sale of unlicensed publications.

53. According to Cicero, *Peri Theon* by the Sophist Protagoras (banished from Athens in 411 B.C.) began, "I am unable to know whether the gods exist or not." None of Protagoras' books are now extant.

54. The Old—or earlier—Comedy in Athens, as written by Cratinus, Eupolis, and Aristophanes, lampooned individuals so scurrilously that a decree of 440 B.C. forbade such practices.

55. *And this course . . . event shew'd:* And this procedure (of punishing even doubt about the existence of the gods and of legislating against personal libels in drama) had sufficient vitality to stop the reckless minds of other atheists (from open expression of their blasphemous views), as Cicero points out (in *De natura deorum*, I, 23), and also enough vitality to repress the public practice of libelous scurrilities (in comedy), as the outcome proved. "Quick" involves senses of *vital, brisk, vigorous,* and *acting with speed.* Milton was apparently aware that the decree of 440 B.C. was repealed after three years but that this short enforcement sufficed to clear the Old Comedy of lampoons against named persons; i.e., the decree was vigorous enough to be rapidly effective. In the remaining time of the Old Comedy and in the periods of the Middle and New Comedy, no such legislation seems to have been needed or enacted.

opinions though tending to voluptuousnesse, and the denying of divine providence they tooke no heed. Therefore we do not read that either *Epicurus*, or that libertine school of *Cyrene*, or what the *Cynick* impudence utter'd,[56] was ever question'd by the Laws. Neither is it recorded that the writings of those old Comedians were suppresst, though the acting of them were forbid; and that *Plato* commended the reading of *Aristophanes* the loosest of them all, to his royall scholler *Dionysius*,[57] is commonly known, and may be excus'd, if holy *Chrysostome*,[58] as is reported, nightly studied so much the same Author and had the art to cleanse a scurrilous vehemence into the stile of a rousing Sermon. That other leading City of *Greece*, *Lacedaemon*, considering that *Lycurgus* their Law-giver was so addicted to elegant learning, as to have been the first that brought out of *Ionia* the scatter'd workes of *Homer*, and sent the Poet *Thales* from *Creet* to prepare and mollifie the *Spartan* surlinesse with his smooth songs and odes, the better to plant among

56. Epicurus (d. 270 B.C.) taught that all matter is reducible to atoms whic being eternal, were not made by a divine creator; that gods exist but do n meddle in human affairs; that pleasure (absence of pain) is the only good; an that the highest pleasure involves freedom from painful need and consists in perfect harmony of mind and body based on virtue and plain living. His teach ings were distorted by those who noted only his goal of pleasure and ignore the means to it which he advocated; as a result, epicureanism came to mea devotion to immediate sensual pleasures, ease, and luxury. Milton's reference to Epicurus are unfavorable; e.g., *Paradise Regain'd*, IV, 299.

Aristippus, founder of a school in Cyrene about 370 B.C., was a predecesso of Epicurus and taught that pleasure is the supreme good. His works have no survived, and accounts of him and his doctrines are inconsistent; however, h seems to have distinguished among pleasures according to their intensity, dura tion, and painful consequences. Many anecdotes represent him as a libertine- one who leads a dissolute life without moral restraint. Because of his conduct h was forced to leave Athens.

The Cynic school of philosophy was founded by Antisthenes (d. ca. 370 B.C. who advocated virtue, simple living, and happiness based on freedom from de sires and wants. He was immoderately zealous and sometimes impudent in at tacking the luxury of his age. His disciple, Diogenes of Sinope (d. 323 B.C. indulged in even greater freedom in his remarks, and anecdotes were told abou his impudence. Asked why he carried a lamp in broad daylight, he is said to hav replied, "I am looking for a man, never having seen one; for the Spartans ar children and the Athenians are women." Allegedly when Alexander the Grea found the philosopher sunning himself and asked if he could do him any favor Diogenes replied, "Yes, stand between me and the sun."

57. According to an ancient life of Aristophanes, when Dionysius, ruler o Syracuse, wanted to learn about the Athenian constitution, Plato sent him th writings of Aristophanes.

58. *holy Chrysostome:* St. John Chrysostom (d. 407), a father of the Easter church and patriarch of Constantinople.

them law and civility, it is to be wondered how muselesse and unbookish they were, minding nought but the feats of Warre.[59] There needed no licencing of Books among them for they dislik'd all, but their owne *Laconick Apothegms,*[60] and took a slight occasion to chase *Archilochus* out of their City, perhaps for composing in a higher straine than their owne souldierly ballats and roundels could reach to:[61] Or if it were for his broad verses, they were not therein so cautious, but they were as dissolute in their promiscuous conversing; whence *Euripides* affirmes in *Andromache,*[62] that their women were all unchaste. Thus much may give us light after what sort Bookes were prohibited among the Greeks. The Romans also for many ages train'd up on-[6]ly to a military roughness, resembling most the *Lacedaemonian* guise, knew of learning little but what their twelve Tables,[63] and the *Pontifick* College with their *Augurs* and *Flamins*[64] taught them in Religion and Law, so unacquainted with other learning, that when *Carneades* and *Critolaus,* with the *Stoick Diogenes* comming Embassadours to *Rome,* tooke thereby occasion to give the City a tast of their Philosophy, they were suspected for seducers by no lesse a man than *Cato* the Censor, who mov'd it in the Senat to dismisse them speedily, and to banish all such *Attick* bablers out

59. Milton follows Plutarch's more legendary than factual account of Lycurgus, reputed founder of the constitution of Lacedaemon or Sparta, the capital of Laconia. Thales or Thaletas, a semilegendary Cretan poet, seems to have gone to Sparta in the seventh century B.C. Lycurgus probably lived two centuries earlier. The story of his gathering Homer's works had been used by Milton in *Prolusion VII.*

60. *Laconick Apothegms:* the apothegms or terse maxims favored in Laconia; as a result, *laconic* has become a synonym for *terse.*

61. The ancients ranked Archilochus (seventh century B.C.) as one of the greatest Greek poets and ascribed to him invention of several poetic meters. Plutarch alleges that he was expelled from Sparta for writing that a man did better to throw away his shield than lose his life. Milton conjectures that his poetry was too lofty for the militaristic Spartans who preferred ballads (simple songs) and roundelays. Originally the roundelay was a song which accompanied a round dance. The word became used for songs with refrains and songs sung in a group by individuals taking turns. But Milton presumably refers to camp ditties, marching choruses, and war songs.

62. Lines 590–93.

63. *twelve Tables:* a codification of Roman laws made in 451–50 B.C., which schoolboys had to memorize.

64. The Pontific College or council of high priests supervised the religious life of Rome in ramifications which included management of public engineering projects, the calendar, and similar activities which required technical knowledge. Augurs were priests who determined from omens, such as the singing, flight, and feeding of birds, or the appearance of sacrificial entrails whether the gods were favorable to public undertakings. A flamen was a priest devoted to a particular god for whom he performed sacrifices daily.

of Italy.[65] But *Scipio*[66] and others of the noblest Senators withstood him and his old *Sabin*[67] austerity; honour'd and admir'd the men; and the Censor himself at last in his old age fell to the study of that whereof before he was so scrupulous. And yet at the same time[68] *Naevius* and *Plautus* the first Latine comedians had fill'd the City with all the borrow'd Scenes of *Menander* and *Philemon.*[69] Then began[70] to be consider'd there also what was to be don to libellous books and Authors; for *Naevius* was quickly cast into prison for his unbridl'd pen, and released by the *Tribunes* upon his recantation: We read also that libels were burnt, and the makers punisht by *Augustus.*[71] The like severity no doubt was us'd if ought were

65. In 155 B.C. the Athenians sent to Rome an embassy composed of th three philosophers who headed the Academic, Peripatetic, and Stoic schools Carneades, a moderate Sceptic who taught that various degrees of probabilit could be found and used to guide conduct; Critolaus, a follower of Aristotle and Diogenes the Babylonian whom Milton took care to call a Stoic to dis tinguish him from the Cynic Diogenes of Sinope. Their introduction of Athenia philosophy to the Romans aroused the opposition of Marcus Portius Cato whos office as censor made him responsible for public morals: Carneades illustrate scepticism by maintaining the reality of justice in one lecture and by refutin his case for it in the next one. According to Bacon's *Advancement of Learning* II, i, "when Carneades the philosopher came in embassage to Rome, and . . the young men of Rome began to flock about him, being allured with the sweet ness and majesty of his eloquence and learning," Cato "gave counsel in ope senate that they should give him his dispatch with all speed lest he should infec and enchant the minds and affections of the youth, and at unawares bring in a alteration of the manners and customs of the state."

66. *Scipio:* Scipio the Younger (d. 129 B.C.) great as a commander in war and as a patron of Greek and Latin culture.

67. Throughout his life Cato returned to live frugally on the farm in Sabine territory where he had been reared. Cf. Bacon, *Advancement,* II, v: "Cato . . was well punish'd for his blasphemy against learning . . . for when he was past threescore years old, he was taken with an extreme desire to go to school again and to learn the Greek tongue, to the end to peruse the Greek authors; which doth well demonstrate that his former censure of Grecian learning was rather an affected gravity, than according to the inward sense of his own opinion."

68. *at the same time:* i.e., at the time of the embassy. Comedies by Naevius and Plautus had been acted in Rome as long as seven decades previously.

69. Gnaeus Naevius (d. ca. 199 B.C.) wrote tragedies, an epic, and comedies on the Greek model, in which he satirized Scipio and the patrician family of the Metelli, for which he was thrown into prison. Having made a sort of recantation, he was released but was exiled when he offended again. The adaptations of Athenian comedies made by Plautus (d. 184 B.C.) had a strong influence on English dramatists. Menander (d. 292 B.C.) wrote about a hundred plays but only parts of a few have survived; St. Paul quotes from him in 1 Cor. xv 33. None of the plays of his rival Philemon (d. 263) have survived in Greek except in fragments, but Plautus' *Trinumnius* is based on one of them.

70. *Then began:* actually long before. The Twelve Tables contained provisions against libel.

71. Tacitus, *Annals,* I, 72.

impiously writt'n against their esteemed gods. Except in these two points, how the world went in Books, the Magistrat kept no reckning. And therefore *Lucretius* without impeachment versifies his Epicurism to *Memmius,* and had the honour to be set forth the second time by *Cicero* so great a father of the Commonwealth; although himselfe disputes against that opinion in his own writings.[72] Nor was the Satyricall sharpnesse, or naked plainnes of *Lucilius,* or *Catullus,* or *Flaccus,*[73] by any order prohibited. And for matters of State, the story of *Titus Livius,*[74] though it extoll'd that part which *Pompey* held,[75] was not therefore suppres by Octavius Caesar[76] of the other Faction. But that Naso[77] was by him banisht in his old age, for the wanton Poems of his youth, was but a meer covert of State[78] over

72. Lucretius (d. ca. 55 B.C.) addressed to Memmius, a patron of poets, *De rerum natura* (On the Nature of Things) which presents and defends the theological, moral, and physical system of Epicurus. In particular Lucretius attacked superstitious fear of the gods and argued that the world was formed by a fortuitous concomitance of atoms. St. Jerome in the additions to his translation of an epitome of world history by Eusebius remarks that Lucretius' poem was *Tulli lima dignissimis*—most worthy of Cicero's editing (or revising)—which may mean merely that it was a work so excellent that it deserved to be edited by Cicero. But if the statement means that Cicero did edit it—as some scholars believe—there is no other authority to support it. However, Cicero's letters show that he had read the poem by 54 B.C. Milton apparently means that after it had thus become available for a first time, Cicero set it forth (made it available to the public, presumably in a new edition) for the second time, although Cicero attacks Epicureanism in *The Tusculan Disputations* and in his books on the nature of the gods (*De natura deorum*) and the different conceptions of the chief good (*De finibus*). Some critics have accused him of inconsistency, but opposition to Epicureanism need not prevent appreciation of the artistic and scientific values of Lucretius. Milton himself was similarly hostile to Epicureanism, but in *Of Education* he urged the reading of Lucretius. And he allowed *De rerum natura* to influence *Paradise Lost.*

73. The *Sermones* by Gaius Lucilius (d. 102 B.C.) were informal poems on literary topics, episodes, journeys, banquets, etc. They were marked by outspoken personal criticism of luxury, greed, public men, and writers, and are regarded as the first examples of the genre, satire, in Rome. Catullus (d. 54 B.C.) ranged from the genial to the virulent in his satirical poems. Horace (d. 8 B.C.) modeled his earlier satires on those of Lucilius and perfected the genre; Milton translated his Ode to Pyrrha.

74. *the story of Titus Livius:* Livy's history of Rome. In the *Annals* (IV, 34) of Tacitus, a defender of the right of free speech bolsters his argument by observing that Livy exalted Pompey with such praise that the Emperor Augustus called him "Pompeianus" but continued to be friendly.

75. *part which Pompey held:* Pompey's party or side.

76. *Octavius Caesar:* Julius Caesar's adopted heir, Octavian, who became Emperor Augustus.

77. *Naso:* Ovid. Officially banished because of the immorality of his poetry, traditionally because of his *Ars amatoria* (Art of Love), though his love poems, *Amores,* would qualify better as a work of his youth.

78. *covert of State:* a political disguise or pretext.

some secret cause: and besides, the Books were neither banisht nor call'd in.[79] From hence we shall meet with little else but tyranny in the Roman Empire, that we may not marvell, if not so often bad, as good Books were silenc't.[80] I shall therefore deem to have bin large anough in producing[81] what among the ancients was punishable to write, save only which, all other arguments were free to treat on.

By this time the Emperors were become Christians,[82] whose discipline in this point I doe not finde to have bin more severe than what [7] was formerly in practice. The Books of those whom they took to be grand Hereticks were examin'd, refuted, and condemn'd by the generall Councels;[83] and not till then were prohibited, or burnt by autority of the Emperor. As for the writings of Heathen authors, unlesse they were plaine invectives against Christianity, as those of *Porphyrius* and *Proclus*,[84] they met with no interdict that can be cited, till about the year 400. in a *Carthaginian* Councel,[85] wherein Bishops themselves were forbid to read the Books of Gentiles,[86] but Heresies they might read: while others long before them on the contrary scrupl'd more[87] the Books of Hereticks than of Gentiles. And that the primitive Councels and Bishops were wont only to declare what Books were not commendable, passing no furder, but leaving it to each ones conscience to read or to lay by, till after the yeare 800. is observ'd already by *Padre Paolo*[88] the great unmasker of the *Trentine* Councel. After which time the Popes of *Rome* engrossing what they pleas'd of Politicall rule into their owne

79. But the Books were ordered removed from public libraries.

80. I.e., since we find little else but despotic rule thereafter in the Roman Empire, we should not be surprised if we find that good books were suppressed more often than bad ones.

81. *large . . . producing:* that I have devoted sufficient space to adducing.

82. In 312 the Emperor Constantine is said to have had a vision which converted him to Christianity.

83. *generall Councels:* Councils of the church which were ecumenical—representative of the world—rather than local or regional.

84. *Porphyrius and Proclus:* Neoplatonists hostile to Christianity. Constantine had Porphyry's *Against the Christians* burned in public.

85. The exact date of the Council is uncertain.

86. *Gentiles:* heathens.

87. *scrupl'd more:* had more scruples about.

88. Paolo Servita, the religious name of Pietro Sarpi (d. 1623), "the great Venetian Antagonist of the Pope" as Milton called him in *Of Reformation*. His *History of the Council of Trent* (tr. Nathaniel Brent [London, 1620], pp. 472–73) was Milton's chief source for this paragraph. (See Ernest Sirluck, "Milton's Critical Use of Historical Sources," *MP*, L [1953], 226–31.) Milton refers thirteen times to this *History* in his *Commonplace Book*. He also made considerable use of Sarpi's *History of the Inquisition*, tr. Robert Gentilis (London, 1639).

hands, extended their dominion over mens eyes, as they had before over their judgements, burning and prohibiting to be read, what they fansied not; yet sparing in their censures, and the Books not many which they so dealt with: till *Martin* the 5. by his Bull[89] not only prohibited, but was the first that excommunicated the reading of hereticall Books; for about that time *Wicklef*[90] and *Husse* growing terrible, were they who first drove the Papall Court to a stricter policy of prohibiting. Which cours *Leo* the X,[91] and his successors follow'd, untill the Councell of Trent, and the Spanish Inquisition engendring together brought forth, or perfeted those Catalogues, and expurgating Indexes that rake through the entralls of many an old good Author,[92] with a violation wors than any could be offer'd to his tomb. Nor did they stay in matters Hereticall, but any subject that was not to their palat, they either condemn'd in a prohibition, or had it strait into the new Purgatory of an Index. To fill up the measure of encroachment, their last invention was to ordain that no Book, pamphlet, or paper should be Printed (as if S. *Peter* had bequeath'd them the keys of the Presse also out of Paradise) unlesse it were approv'd and licenc't under the hands of 2 or 3 glutton Friers. For example:

> Let the Chancellor *Cini* be pleas'd to see if in this present work be contain'd ought that may withstand the Printing.
>
> *Vincent Rabatta* Vicar of *Florence*. [8]

> I have seen this present work, and finde nothing athwart the Catholick faith and good manners: In witnesse whereof I have given, etc.
>
> *Nicolò Cini* Chancellor of *Florence*.

89. *Bull:* Martin V in his bull of 1418, *Inter Cunctas*.

90. John Wiclif (d. 1384), whom Milton admired as "that Englishman honor'd of God to be the first preacher of a general reformation to all *Europe*" (*Tetrachordon, Yale Milton,* II, 707), and John Huss (d. 1415), a Bohemian forerunner of Protestantism who was excommunicated in 1411 and burned at the stake as an obstinate heretic in 1415.

91. By a bull of May 3, 1515, Leo X broadened censorship to cover all writings.

92. In 1542 Paul III reorganized the Inquisition, empowered it to oversee books, and forbade publication unless a license had been obtained from it in advance. Three years later the Nineteenth Ecumenical Council began its sessions in Trent. Advised by it, in 1599 Paul IV "perfeted" (perfected—brought to full development) the first *Index of Prohibited Books* applicable to the entire world (previous lists had had regional application), and an *Index of Expurgations,* which indicated prohibited passages in books otherwise allowed to be read. In 1562 and 1563 the Council of Trent added two decrees on the cataloguing of forbidden books. Milton's image of raking through entrails develops from the medical concept of expurgation as a cleaning out of the bowels.

Attending the precedent relation, it is allow'd that this present work of *Davanzati*[93] may be Printed,

Vincent Rabatta, etc.

It may be Printed, *July* 15.

Friar Simon *Mompei d'Amelia* Chancellor of the holy office in *Florence*.

Sure they have a conceit,[94] if he of the bottomlesse pit had not long since broke prison, that this quadruple exorcism would barre him down. I feare their next designe will be to get into their custody the licensing of that which they say[95] *Claudius* intended, but went not through with. Voutsafe to see another of their forms the Roman stamp:[96]

Imprimatur, If it seem good to the revered Master of the holy Palace,

Belcastro Vicegerent.

Imprimatur

Friar *Nicolò Rodolphi* Master of the holy Palace.

Sometimes 5 *Imprimaturs*[97] are seen together dialogue-wise in the Piatza[98] of one Title page, complementing and ducking each to other with their shaven reverences,[99] whether the Author, who stands by in perplexity at the foot of his Epistle, shall to the Presse or to the

93. Bernardo Davanzati Bostiche (d. 1606). The examples are translations of permissions in his *Scisma d'Inghilterra* (Florence, 1638).

94. *conceit:* a mistaken notion.

95. *Quo veniam daret flatum crepitumque ventris in convivio emittendi. Sueton. in Claudio.* (Milton's own note.) In view of Milton's attack, later in this pamphlet, on Talmudists who substitute euphemistic glosses for frank biblical statements, it is interesting to note that no editor of *Areopagitica* known to us provides a translation of this example of Milton's frank and earthy humor. In context it appears as follows in a version of Suetonius doubtfully attributed to Marvell: "being told of a modest person who had like to have kill'd himself with retention, he [the Emperor Tiberius] had thoughts once of publishing an Edict, whereby he would make it lawfull to break wind at the Table, and to ease themselves of any flatulency in any place whatsoever" (*The History of the Twelve Caesars, Emperors of Rome. Written in Latine by Caius Suetonius Tranquillus* [London, 1672], p. 306).

96. I.e., deign to see another of their licensing forms, the certifying imprint as used in Rome.

97. *Imprimatur:* It may be printed.

98. *Piatza:* piazza, a broad open space.

99. *shaven reverences:* with bowing of their shaven heads—a reference to tonsure.

spunge.[100] These are the prety responsories, these are the dear Antiphonies[101] that so bewitcht of late our Prelats, and their Chaplaines with the goodly Eccho they made; and besotted us to the gay imitation of a lordly *Imprimatur*, one from Lambeth house, another from the West end of Pauls;[102] so apishly Romanizing, that the word of command still was set downe in Latine; as if the learned Grammaticall pen that wrote it, would cast no ink without Latine: or perhaps, as they thought, because no vulgar tongue was worthy to expresse the pure conceit[103] of an *Imprimatur;* but rather, as I hope, for that our English, the language of men ever famous, and formost in the atchievements of liberty, will not easily finde servile letters anow to spell such a dictatorie presumption English. And thus ye have the Inventors and the originall of Book-licensing ript up, and drawn as lineally as any pedigree. We have it not, that can be heard of, from any [9] ancient State, or politie, or Church, nor by any Statute left us by our Ancestors elder or later; nor from the moderne custom of any reformed Citty, or Church abroad; but from the most Antichristian Councel, and the most tyrannous Inquisition that ever inquir'd. Till then Books were ever as freely admitted into the World as any other birth; the issue of the brain was no more stifl'd than the issue of the womb: no envious Juno sate cros-leg'd[104] over the nativity of any mans intellectuall off spring; but if it prov'd a Monster, who denies, but that it was justly burnt, or sunk into the Sea. But that a Book in wors condition than a peccant soul, should be to stand before a Jury ere it be borne to the World, and undergo yet in darknesse the judgement of *Radamanth* and his Collegues, ere it can passe the ferry backward into light, was never heard before, till that mysterious iniquity provokt and troubl'd at the first entrance of Reformation, sought out new limbo's and new hells wherein they might include our Books also within the number

100. *spunge:* sponge; i.e., to sponge out or cancel passages not approved by the licensers.

101. Responsories and antiphonies are parts of a church service in which speakers or singers complement each other by alternating. Milton has partly in mind his wordplay on complementing-complimenting in the previous sentence.

102. I.e., the London residences of the Archbishop of Canterbury and the Bishop of London, who were empowered by the 1637 *Decree of Starre-Chamber, Concerning Printing* to control the licensing of "Books, whether of Divinitie, Phisicke, Philosophie, or whatsoever" with the exception of certain kinds of books, chiefly legal, educational, and political, which were assigned to the supervision of other officials.

103. *conceit:* idea.

104. When Jove's son Hercules was about to be born, his jealous wife Juno sent the goddess of childbirth to hinder or prevent the delivery by sitting before the mother's door with legs and fingers crossed.

of their damned.[105] And this was the rare morsell so officiously snatcht up, and so ilfavourdly imitated by our inquisiturient Bishops,[106] and the attendant minorites[107] their Chaplains.[108] That ye like not now these most certain Authors of this licensing order, and that all sinister intention was farre distant from your thoughts, when ye were importun'd the passing it, all men who know the integrity of your actions, and how ye honour Truth, will clear yee readily.

But some will say, What though the Inventors were bad, the thing for all that may be good? It may be so; yet if that thing be no such deep invention, but obvious, and easie for any man to light on, and yet best and wisest Commonwealths through all ages, and occasions have forborne to use it, and falsest seducers, and oppressors of men were the first who tooke it up, and to no other purpose but to obstruct and hinder the first approach of Reformation; I am of those who beleeve, it will be a harder alchymy than *Lullius*[109]

105. Milton makes an image-packed contrast. Human souls are allowed to be born into the world and to live and die there. After death they take Charon's ferry across the river Acheron, thus passing from the daylight of this world to the darkness of Hades. Only then are they tried by a jury composed of its three judges, Rhadamanthus, Minos, and Aeacus. Worse than the condition of such a guilty soul is the condition of a book if, instead of being allowed to emerge into the light of day, it has to stand before a jury in the darkness of Hades and, still unborn, has to submit to judgment as a prerequisite to being ferried in Charon's boat on one of its backward journeys from Hades to the world and its light. All this, Milton asserts, was never heard of in previous history until the Papacy or the Roman Catholic church (which he calls "that mysterious iniquity"), being provoked and troubled at the beginning of the Protestant Reformation, sought out new limbos (infernal regions on the borderlands of Hell) and new hells for those whom they damned—limbos and hells in which they could also include *our* (i.e., Protestant, English) books within the number of *their* damned. Milton's use of "mysterious iniquity" derives from the opinion that the woman identified with Babylon in Rev. xvii 3–5 was a type or biblical prefiguration of Rome and the Papacy.

106. *our inquisiturient Bishops:* our eager-to-be-inquisitorial bishops.

107. *minorites:* persons of minor rank.

108. Bishops frequently delegated censorship and licensing to their chaplains. Milton hints at a similarity between the pride and ostentation of Anglican and Roman Catholic bishops and at a parallel between the Anglican chaplains and the Franciscan Friars Minor who were vowed to strict poverty. The extremer Protestants regarded them as arrogant in specious humility.

109. Raymond Lully (Ramón Lull, d. 1315), the Catalan mystic, logician, philosopher, poet, and martyred missionary. He propounded a method of combining principles or categories common to the sciences and self-evident, as a means of discovering the principles of particular science and aiding the memory. To this end he symbolized principles with letters which he combined in a variety of ways in figures and circles. These were misinterpreted as mystical alchemy, and a whole series of alchemical treatises were attributed to him. Milton uses this alchemy partly as a symbol of something extremely difficult to understand. The aim of alchemy was to transform base metals into gold, and

ever knew, to sublimat any good use out of such an invention. Yet this only is what I request to gain from this reason, that it may be held a dangerous and suspicious fruit, as it certainly deserves, for the tree[110] that bore it, untill I can dissect one by one the properties it has. But I have first to finish, as was propounded, what is to be thought in generall of reading Books, what ever sort they be, and whether be more the benefit, or the harm that thence proceeds?

Not to insist upon the examples of *Moses, Daniel* and *Paul,* who were [10] skilfull in all the learning of the Ægyptians, Caldeans, and Greeks,[111] which could not probably be without their reading their Books of all sorts, in *Paul* especially, who thought it no defilement to insert into holy Scripture the sentences of three Greek Poets, and one of them a Tragedian, the question was, notwithstanding sometimes controverted among the Primitive Doctors, but with great odds on that side which affirm'd it both lawfull and profitable, as was then evidently perceiv'd, when *Julian* the Apostat,[112] and suttlest enemy to our faith, made a decree forbidding Christians the study of heathen learning: for, said he, they wound us with our own weapons, and with our owne arts and sciences they overcome us. And indeed the Christians were put so to their shifts by this crafty means, and so much in danger to decline into all ignorance, that the two *Apollinarii*[113] were fain as a man may say, to coin all the seven

---

part of the process of doing so was sublimation—refinement of the base material by chemical fire. Milton, therefore, means that it will be a harder process than Lully ever knew, to transform such an invention as licensing so as to get any good use out of it. In the following sentence Milton continues to use terms employed by alchemists such as *tree, fruit,* and *properties,* though the parallel to the tree of knowledge in Eden and its dangerous fruit is more obvious.

110. *for the tree:* because of the tree.

111. Acts vii 22: "Moses was learned in all the wisdom of the Egyptians." According to Dan. i 6, 17, 20, God gave Daniel and three others "knowledge and skill in all learning and wisdom" and Nebuchadnezzar found them "ten times better" than all the Chaldean magicians and astronomers in answering his questions. St. Paul cites sentences (*sententiae,* significant sayings) attributed to Aratus (Acts xvii 28), Epimenides (Tit. i 12), and Euripides (1 Cor. xv 33). In 1631 Milton purchased a copy of Aratus, which is extant with his annotations; he recommends him in *Of Education.* Cf. the preface to *Samson Agonistes:* "The Apostle *Paul* himself thought it not unworthy to insert a verse of *Euripides* into the Text of Holy Scripture."

112. Julian the Apostate was emperor, 361–63. His decree forbade Christians to teach and thus indirectly denied learning to them when they refused to be taught by pagans.

113. Apollinaris of Alexandria wrote a grammar for Christians and put books of the Bible into poetic and dramatic form, thus illustrating all kinds of Greek verses. His son, a rhetorician, formulated the gospels and apostolic teachings as Platonic dialogues. Milton's source is the *Ecclesiastical History,* III, xiv, by Socrates Scholasticus—the "Historian" cited in the next sentence.

liberall Sciences[114] out of the Bible, reducing it into divers forms of Orations, Poems, Dialogues, ev'n to the calculating of a new Christian Grammar. But saith the Historian Socrates, The providence of God provided better than the industry of *Apollinarius* and his son, by taking away that illiterat law with the life of him who devis'd it.[115] So great an injury they then held it to be depriv'd of *Hellenick* learning; and thought it a persecution more undermining, and secretly decaying the Church, than the open cruelty of *Decius* or *Dioclesian.*[116] And perhaps it was the same politick drift that the Divell whipt St. *Jerom*[117] in a lenten dream, for reading *Cicero;* or else it was a fantasm bred by the feaver which had then seis'd him. For had an Angel bin his discipliner, unlesse it were for dwelling too much upon Ciceronianisms,[118] and had chastiz'd the reading, not the vanity, it had bin plainly partiall; first to correct him for grave *Cicero,* and not for scurrill Plautus whom he confesses to have bin reading not long before; next to correct him only, and let so many more ancient Fathers wax old in those pleasant and florid studies without the lash of such a tutoring apparition; insomuch that *Basil*[119] teaches how some good use may be made of *Margites*[120] a sportfull Poem, not now extant, writ by *Homer;* and why not then of *Morgante*[121] an Italian Romanze much to the same purpose. But if it be agreed

114. *seven liberall Sciences:* the seven liberal arts consisting of the trivium (grammar, logic, rhetoric) and the quadrivium (arithmetic, geometry, astronomy, music).

115. Julian, killed in war against the Persians.

116. The emperors Decius and Diocletian pursued severely anti-Christian policies in the years 249–51 and 303–5.

117. St. Jerome (d. 420) in Epistle XVIII relates that during Lent he fell into a dreamlike state during a fever and was questioned by God concerning the state of his soul. He answered that he was a Christian but was told, "Thou liest; thou art a Ciceronian, for the works of that author possess thy heart." He was therefore severely lashed by an angel, and when he returned to normal consciousness he found the stripes of the lash on his body. Milton follows Sarpi (*Trent,* p. 472) in attributing the beating to the devil.

118. *Ciceronianisms:* imitations of Cicero's style and diction.

119. Bishop of Caesarea, 370–79. Basil advises Christians to recognize in pagan writers what it is wise to ignore, and to accept what is valuable ("On the Right Use of Greek Literature," *Essays by Plutarch and Basil,* trans. M. Padelford [New York, 1902], p. 4).

120. *Margites* was a satirical, mock-heroic poem about a blockhead. One of the four extant lines states, "For much he knew, but everything knew ill." Aristotle says that this work has the same relation to comedy as the *Iliad* and *Odyssey* have to tragedy (*Poetics,* IV, 10) and ascribes it to Homer.

121. *Il Morgante Maggiore* by Luigi Pulci (d. 1484), a coarse, mock-heroic predecessor of Ariosto's *Orlando Furioso.* See Lord Byron's translation of the first book.

we shall be try'd by visions, there is a vision recorded by *Eusebius*[122] far ancienter than this tale of *Jerom* to the nun *Eustochium*, and besides has nothing of a feavor in it. *Dionysius Alexandrinus* was about the year 240, a person of great name in the Church for piety and learning, who had wont to avail himself much against hereticks by [11] being conversant in their Books; untill a certain Presbyter laid it scrupulously to his conscience, how he durst venture himselfe among those defiling volumes. The worthy man loath to give offence fell into a new debate with himselfe what was to be thought; when suddenly a vision sent from God, it is his own Epistle that so averrs it, confirm'd him in these words: Read any books what ever come to thy hands, for thou art sufficient both to judge aright, and to examine each matter. To this revelation he assented the sooner, as he confesses, because it was answerable to[123] that of the Apostle to the Thessalonians, Prove all things, hold fast that which is good.[124] And he might have added another remarkable saying of the same Author; To the pure all things are pure,[125] not only meats and drinks, but all kinde of knowledge whether of good or evill; the knowledge cannot defile, nor consequently the books, if the will and conscience be not defil'd.[126] For books are as meats and viands are; some of good, some of evill substance; and yet God in that unapocryphall vision,[127] said without exception, Rise *Peter*, kill and eat, leaving the choice to each man's discretion. Wholesome meats to the vitiated stomack differ little or nothing from unwholesome; and best books to a naughty mind are not unappliable to occasions of evill. Bad meats will scarce breed good nourishment in the healthiest concoction;[128] but herein the difference is of bad books, that they to a discreet and judicious Reader serve in many respects to discover, to confute, to forwarn, and to illustrate. Wherof what better witnes can

122. Eusebius, *Ecclesiastical History*, VII, 7, based on Epistle III, "Concerning Baptism," by Dionysius Alexandrinus, bishop of Alexandria, 247–65.

123. *answerable to:* corresponded to; was in harmony with.

124. 1 Thess. v 21; prove = test. Sirluck (*Yale Milton*, II, 512) notes that Milton substituted this canonical verse for a similar but apocryphal one which appeared in Dionysius's epistle.

125. Titus i 15.

126. Cf. *Paradise Lost*, V, 117–19: "Evil into the mind of God or Man / May come and go, so unapprov'd, and leave / No spot or blame behind."

127. I.e., that authentic vision—in contrast to Milton's opinion about Jerome's dream. Acts x 9–28 relates Peter's vision of certain animals which he was ordered to eat. But he said, "Not so, Lord, for I have never eaten any thing that is common or unclean." The voice replied, "What God hath cleansed, that call thou not common." But Peter still refused, though three times commanded to eat. Later, after other events, he stated his interpretation: "God hath shewed me that I should not call any man common or unclean."

128. *concoction:* digestion.

ye expect I should produce, than one of your own now sitting in Parlament, the chief of learned men reputed in this Land, Mr. *Selden*, whose volume of naturall and national laws[129] proves, not only by great autorities brought together, but by exquisite[130] reasons and theorems almost mathematically demonstrative, that all opinions, yea errors, known, read, and collated, are of main service and assistance toward the speedy attainment of what is truest. I conceive therefore, that when God did enlarge the universall diet of mans body, saving ever the rules of temperance,[131] he then also, as before, left arbitrary[132] the dyeting and repasting of our minds; as wherein every mature man might have to exercise his owne leading capacity. How great a vertue is temperance, how much of moment through the whole life of man? yet God committs the managing of so great a trust, without particular Law or prescription, wholly to the demeanour[133] of every grown man. And therefore when he himself tabl'd the Jews from heaven, that Omer which was every mans daily portion of [12] Manna, is computed to have bin more than might have suffic'd the heartiest feeder thrice as many meals. For those actions which enter into a man, rather than issue out of him, and therefore defile not,[134] God uses not to captivat under a perpetuall childhood of prescription, but trusts him with the gift of reason to be his own chooser; there were but little work left for preaching, if law and compulsion should grow so fast upon those things which hertofore were govern'd only by exhortation. *Salomon* informs us that much reading is a wearines to the flesh;[135] but neither he, nor other inspir'd author tells us that such, or such reading is unlawfull; yet certainly had God thought good to limit us herein, it had bin much more expedient to have told us what was unlawfull, than what was wearisome. As for the burning of those Ephesian books by St. *Pauls* converts, tis reply'd the books were magick, the Syriak[136] so renders them. It was a privat act, a voluntary act, and leaves us to voluntary

129. John Selden (d. 1654), *De Jure Naturali et Gentium juxta Disciplinam Ebraeorum* (London, 1640). On p. 2 he advises men to collect not only opinions which support their own ideas but also opinions which oppose them, and thus to have means to clarify those ideas and to make them more precise.

130. *exquisite:* carefully selected.

131. Cf. *Paradise Lost,* XI, 531: "The rule of not too much."

132. *left arbitrary:* as a matter of free choice for the will. Cf. *Paradise Lost,* VIII, 641: "Free in thine own Arbitrement it lies."

133. *demeanour:* management.

134. Cf. Mark vii 15: "There is nothing from without a man, that entering into him can defile him; but the things which come out of him, those are they that defile the man."

135. Eccles. xii 12.

136. *the Syriak:* the Syriac version of Acts xix 19.

imitation: the men in remorse burnt those books which were their own; the Magistrat by this example is not appointed: these men practiz'd[137] the books, another might perhaps have read them in some sort usefully. Good and evill we know in the field of this World grow up together almost inseparably; and the knowledge of good is so involv'd and interwoven with the knowledge of evill, and in so many cunning resemblances hardly to be discern'd, that those confused seeds which were imposed on *Psyche* as an incessant labour to cull out, and sort asunder, were not more intermixt.[138] It was from out the rinde of one apple tasted, that the knowledge of good and evil[139] as two twins cleaving together leapt forth into the World. And perhaps this is that doom which *Adam* fell into of knowing good and evill, that is to say of knowing good by evill. As therefore the state of man now is; what wisdome can there be to choose, what continence to forbeare without the knowledge of evill? He that can apprehend and consider vice with all her baits and seeming pleasures, and yet abstain, and yet distinguish, and yet prefer that which is truly better, he is the true warfaring[140] Christian. I cannot praise a fugitive and cloistered vertue, unexercis'd and unbreath'd, that never sallies out and sees her adversary, but slinks out of the race, where that immortall garland[141] is to be run for, not without dust

137. *practiz'd:* i.e., practiced what was taught in.

138. In *The Golden Ass,* IV–VI, Apuleius relates how Venus, being jealous of Psyche's beauty and the love it inspired in Cupid, poured wheat, oats, lentils, and other seeds into a heap and assigned the girl the seemingly impossible task of sorting them before sundown. Moved by pity, ants accomplished the work. In 1637 Shakerley Marmion retold the story in *Cupid and Psiche.* Milton's going on to juxtapose Psyche and Adam probably reflects Marmion's parallel of them in his explanation of the myth's allegorical significance. See the reprint in George Saintsbury, ed., *Minor Poets of the Caroline Period* (Oxford, 1906), II, 9.

139. Gen. ii 16–17 and iii 5, 22.

140. Printed as *wayfaring,* but corrected by hand in ink to *warfaring* in the four copies which Milton presented to friends for private and college libraries; also so corrected in at least five other copies of the first edition. But see note 257 below.

141. Winners of Olympic races were crowned with wreaths of wild olive. In contrast to these mortal garlands, Milton writes of an immortal garland that, like them, is to be won by trial and endurance in the world, not in retreat from it. Cf. James i 12: "Blessed is the man that endureth temptation: for when he is tried, he shall receive the crown of life, which the Lord hath promised to them that love him"; 2 Tim. iv 7–8: "I have fought a good fight, I have finished my course, I have kept the faith: Henceforth there is laid up for me a crown of righteousness. . . ." But the contrast made by Milton is not the one made by Marvell in "The Garden" between wreaths given for athletic, civic, and poetic achievement on the one hand and the "garlands of repose" on the other: "How vainly men themselves amaze / To win the Palm, the Oke, or Bayes; / And their uncessant Labours see / Crown'd from some single Herb or Tree. . . . / While all Flow'rs and all Trees do close / To weave the Garlands of repose."

and heat. Assuredly we bring not innocence into the world, we bring impurity[142] much rather: that which purifies us is triall, and triall is by what is contrary. That vertue therefore which is but a youngling in the contemplation of evill, and knows not the utmost [13] that vice promises to her followers, and rejects it, is but a blank vertue, not a pure; her whitenesse is but an excrementall[143] whitenesse; Which was the reason why our sage and serious Poet *Spencer*, whom I dare to be known to think a better teacher than *Scotus* or *Aquinas*,[144] describing true temperance under the person of *Guion*, brings him in with his palmer through the cave of Mammon, and the bowr of earthly blisse that he might see and know, and yet abstain.[145] Since therefore the knowledge and survay of vice is in this world so necessary to the constituting of human vertue, and the scanning of error to the confirmation of truth how can we more safely, and with lesse danger scout[146] into the regions of sin and falsity than by reading all manner of tractats, and hearing all manner of reason? And this is the benefit which may be had of books promiscuously read. But of the harm that may result hence three kinds are usually reckn'd. First, is fear'd the infection that may spread; but then all human learning and controversie in religious points must remove out of the world, yea the Bible it selfe; for that oftimes relates blasphemy not nicely,[147] it describes the carnall sense of wicked men not unelegantly, it brings in holiest men passionately murmuring against providence through all the arguments of *Epicurus:* in other great disputes

(Milton's phrase "incessant labour" used with reference to Psyche three sentences earlier is here echoed by Marvell.) Milton's "immortall garland" is neither that of repose nor of mere worldly glory: both of them are corruptible. Cf. Phil. iii 14: "I press toward the mark for the prize of the high calling of God in Jesus Christ." Because Milton, three sentences later, writes about "true temperance," it is probable that he had chiefly in mind the contrast in 1 Cor. ix 24–27 between those who practice temperance in order to win the "corruptible crown" or wreath of olives awarded for athletic victories, and those who, like St. Paul, bring their bodies under subjection in order to win an "incorruptible" one.

142. *impurity:* because of the original sin of Adam and Eve.

143. *excrementall:* not inherent; on the outside—like the athlete's wreaths.

144. In keeping with his later acknowledgment to Dryden that Spenser was his original (Dryden, preface to *Fables*), Milton disparages scholastic philosophy and theology (as he did frequently in other works) by boldly asserting that he had learned less from its two most influential representatives, Duns Scotus and St. Thomas Aquinas, than from the English poet.

145. In *The Faerie Queene*, II, vii–viii and xii, Guyon (temperance) needed the Palmer (reason) to enable him to resist the lures of Acrasia's Bower of Bliss; but Milton's memory erred concerning the earlier episode. On the significance of the error see Ernest Sirluck, "Milton Revises *The Faerie Queene*," *MP*, XLVIII (1950), 90–96, and his note in *Yale Milton*, II, 516.

146. *scout:* spy—a military term.

147. *not nicely:* without squeamishness.

it answers dubiously and darkly to the common reader: And ask a Talmudist what ails the modesty of his marginall Keri, that *Moses* and all the Prophets cannot perswade him to pronounce the textuall Chetiv. 148 for these causes we all know the Bible it self put by the Papist into the first rank of prohibited books. The ancientest Fathers must be next remov'd, as *Clement* of *Alexandria,* and that *Eusebian* book of Evangelick preparation,[149] transmitting our ears through a hoard of heathenish obscenities to receive the Gospel. Who finds not that *Irenaeus, Epiphanius, Jerom,* and others discover more heresies[150] than they well confute, and that oft for heresie which is the truer opinion. Nor boots it to say for these, and all the heathen Writers of greatest infection, if it must be thought to, with whom

148. A Talmudist is one who studies or expounds the Talmud, a body of related law, commentary, and biblical exegesis which was codified in written form about A.D. 200–400 after being orally transmitted for centuries. Soon after its compilation, editors (*Saboraim*) added a *Keri* or marginal gloss which could be read instead of a *Chetiv* or wording in the text if that seemed too coarse or otherwise objectionable to be spoken. In *An Apology* (*Yale Milton,* I, 902), Milton cites examples of frank, immodest language used in Scripture and asks if those who resorted to other wording rather than quoting it directly "were of cleaner language than he that made the tongue." Deploring such substitutions, Milton asserts, "God who is the author both of purity and eloquence, chose this phrase as fittest in that vehement character wherein he spake. Otherwise that plaine word might have easily bin forborne. Which the . . . Rabinicall *Scholiasts* not well attending, have often us'd to blurre the margent with *Keri,* instead of *Ketiv,* and gave us this insuls [stupid, lacking in taste] rule out of their *Talmud, That all words which in the Law are writ obscenely, must be chang'd to more civill words.*" Accordingly Milton denounces them as "Fools who would teach men to read more decently than God thought good to write."

Milton's use of "ails" is puzzling. If the word has its ordinary sense, he may mean: Ask a Talmudist what is ailing or improper in the Chetiv which is cured by the modest wording in the Keri. But this seems more probable: Ask a Talmudist what so exalts the modesty of his marginal gloss that the example set by Moses and all the prophets (of writing frankly) cannot persuade him, etc. Milton may think of *ails* as derived from Latin *ala* or French *aile,* wing. Cf. the address to Parliament in *The Judgement of Martin Bucer* (*Yale Milton,* II, 434) where he states that although he did not sign *Doctrine and Discipline,* his style was recognized: "what ailes it to be so soon distinguishable," he comments, "I cannot tell." This may mean that some flaw or something ailing in it makes it recognizable, but it seems more probable that something in the style lifted it up (as on wings) and thus made it easily distinguishable from other styles. Another possibility is that he is thinking of the *ail* or *awn* or "beard" which grows on barley and distinguishes it from other grains.

149. The Church Fathers, Clement in his *Hortatory Address to the Greeks* and Eusebius in his *Evangelical Preparation,* described lewd pagan rites in order to convince Christians not to participate in them.

150. Irenaeus in *Against Heresies,* Epiphanius in *Panarion,* and Jerome in his attacks on the innovations of Origen, Pelagius, Jovinian, and Vigilantius uncovered or exposed numerous heresies to their readers.

is bound up the life of human learning, that they are writ in an unknown tongue, so long as we are sure those languages are known as well to the worst of men, who are both most able, and most diligent to instill the poison they suck, first into the Courts of Princes, acquainting them with the choisest delights, and criticisms[151] of sin. As perhaps[152] did that *Petronius* whom *Nero* call'd his *Arbiter*, the Master of his revels; and that[153] notorious ribald of *Arezzo*, dreaded, and yet dear to the Italian Courtiers. I name not him for posterities sake, whom [14] Harry the 8. named in merriment his Vicar of hell.[154] By which compendious way all the contagion that foreine books can infuse, will finde a passage to the people farre easier and shorter than an Indian voyage, though it could be sail'd either by the North of *Cataio* Eastward, or of *Canada* Westward,[155] while our Spanish licencing[156] gags the English Presse never so severely. But on the other side that infection which is from books of controversie in Religion, is more doubtfull and dangerous to the learned, than to the ignorant; and yet those books must be permitted untoucht by the licenser.[157] It will be hard to instance where any ignorant man hath bin ever seduc't by Papistical book in English, unlesse it were commended and expounded to him by some of that Clergy: and indeed all such tractats whether false or true are as the Prophesie of *Isaiah*

151. *criticisms:* exquisite refinements.

152. According to Tacitus, the Emperor Nero called his friend Petronius *elegantiae arbiter*—chief judge of taste and etiquette. With scholarly caution Milton's "perhaps" leaves open the question whether "that" Petronius was the one who wrote the *Satyricon.*

153. Here Milton uses "that" to emphasize his contempt. Pietro Aretino, born in 1492 in Arezzo, was notorious for obscene writings, dreaded because of his vituperative satire upon, and blackmail of, individuals, and yet "dear to" or cherished (with perhaps a pun on the expensiveness of the blackmail payments) by Italian courtiers who relished his ridicule of others than themselves.

154. *Vicar of hell:* Anne Boleyn's cousin, the notoriously wicked courtier, Sir Francis Brian.

155. *an Indian voyage . . . Westward:* a voyage to the Orient by some (as yet undiscovered) short passage north of Cathay (China) or through the northmost part of America.

156. *Spanish licencing:* like that imposed by the Spanish Inquisition.

157. I.e., not suppressed in whole or part, but licensed—and thus allowed to be published and available for all to read. Milton here and in what follows presents a basic argument: such books "cannot be suppress without the fall of learning, and of all ability in disputation"; therefore the licensers must permit them to be published and circulated despite the fact that they contain the kind of material the Licensing Order was intended to suppress. Presumably because it might weaken his argument, Milton does not mention that under justifying circumstances Roman Catholics could get permission from ecclesiastical superiors to read prohibited material; nor does he mention the failure of the Licensing Order to set up some similar procedure to allow special access to such writing.

was to the *Eunuch,* not to be *understood without a guide.*[158] But of our Priests and Doctors how many have bin corrupted by studying the comments of Jesuits and *Sorbonnists,*[159] and how fast they could transfuse that corruption into the people, our experience is both late and sad. It is not forgot, since the acute and distinct[160] *Arminius* was perverted meerly by the perusing of a namelesse discours writt'n at *Delf,* which at first he took in hand to confute.[161] Seeing therefore that those books, and those in great abundance which are likeliest to taint both life and doctrine, cannot be suppress without the fall of learning, and of all ability in disputation, and that these books of either sort are most and soonest catching to the learned, from whom to the common people what ever is hereticall or dissolute may quickly be convey'd, and that evill manners are as perfectly learnt without books a thousand other ways which cannot be stopt, and evill doctrine not with books can propagate, except a teacher guide, which he might also doe without writing, and so beyond prohibiting, I am not able to unfold, how this cautelous[162] enterprise of licensing can be exempted from the number of vain and impossible attempts. And he who were pleasantly dispos'd,[163] could not well avoid to lik'n it to the exploit of that gallant man who thought to pound up the crows by shutting his Parkgate. Besides another inconvenience, if learned men be the first receivers out of books, and dispredders[164] both of vice and error, how shall the licencers themselves be confided in, unlesse we can conferr upon them, or they assume to themselves above all others in the Land, the grace of infallibility, and uncorruptednesse? And again if it be true, that a wise man like a

158. Acts viii 27–31. Asked if he understood what he read in Isaiah, the Ethiopian treasurer replied, "How can I, except some man should guide me?"

159. *Sorbonnists:* scholars of the Sorbonne, a center of Roman Catholic theology in Paris.

160. *distinct:* clearheaded, discriminating, discerning.

161. Maurice Kelley, in "Milton and the 'Nameless Discourse Written at Delft'," *MLN,* LXXVI (March 1961), 214–16, identifies the work as *Responsio ad argumenta quaedam Bezae et Calvini ex Tractatu de praedestione in Cap. XI ad Romanos* (1589), by A. Cornelisz and R. Donteclock. It influenced Arminius' rejection of the supralapsarianism of Calvin and Beza (that God did not predestine some to salvation whom as yet He had not proposed to create), and of the sublapsarianism of the two divines at Delft (that God elected some to salvation after decreeing their creation and foreseeing their fall but without an antecedent consideration of Jesus Christ), and his fashioning for himself the synergistic dogma of predestination which Milton later professed in *Christian Doctrine* (that God elected to salvation those fallen and created men who, in time to come, by true obedience of faith would answer God's calling them to salvation).

162. *cautelous:* deceitful.

163. *pleasantly dispos'd:* inclined to be humorous or witty.

164. *dispredders:* circulators.

good refiner can gather gold out of the drossiest volume, and that a fool will be a fool with [15] the best book, yea or without book, there is no reason that we should deprive a wise man of any advantage to his wisdome, while we seek to restrain from a fool, that which being restrain'd will be no hindrance to his folly. For if there should be so much exactnesse always us'd to keep that from him which is unfit for his reading, we should in the judgement of *Aristotle*[165] not only, but of *Salomon*,[166] and of our Saviour,[167] not voutsafe him good precepts, and by consequence not willingly admit him to good books; as being certain that a wise man will make better use of an idle pamphlet, than a fool will do of sacred Scripture. 'Tis next[168] alleg'd we must not expose our selves to temptations without necessity, and next to that, not imploy our time in vain things. To both these objections one answer will serve, out of the grounds already laid, that to all men such books are not temptations, nor vanities; but usefull drugs and materialls wherewith to temper and compose effective and strong med'cins, which mans life cannot want.[169] The rest, as children and childish men, who have not the art to qualifie[170] and prepare these working mineralls, well many be exhorted to forbear, but hinder'd forcibly they cannot be by all the licensing that Sainted[171] Inquisition could ever yet contrive; which is what I promis'd to deliver next, That this order of licencing conduces nothing to the end for which it was fram'd; and hath almost prevented[172] me by being clear already while thus much hath bin explaining. See the ingenuity[173] of Truth, who when she gets a free and willing hand, opens her self faster, than the pace of method and discours[174] can overtake her. It was the task which I begun with, To shew that no Nation, or well instituted State, if they valu'd books at all, did ever

165. In *Ethics,* I, 3, Aristotle says that a knowledge of political science and similar subjects will be useless and unbeneficial to inexperienced young men who are led by their passions; but it is very beneficial to those who regulate their appetites and actions in accordance with reason.

166. Prov. xxiii 9: "Speak not in the ears of a fool; for he will despise the wisdom of thy words."

167. Matt. vii 6: "Give not that which is holy unto the dogs, neither cast ye your pearls before swine."

168. *'Tis next:* i.e., the second harmful effect of "books promiscuously read."

169. *cannot want:* be without—being indispensable in time of illness.

170. *qualifie:* modify or control the strength of.

171. In his dictionary, Milton's nephew, Edward Phillips, notes that the Spanish Inquisition was officially called "The Sacred Council of the Inquisition"; hence Milton's ironic "Sainted."

172. *prevented:* anticipated.

173. *ingenuity:* frankness; openness; freedom from deceit.

174. *discours:* reasoning.

use this way of licencing; and it might be answer'd, that this is a piece of prudence lately discover'd. To which I return, that as it was a thing slight and obvious to think on, so if it had bin difficult to finde out, there wanted not among them long since, who suggested such a cours; which they not following, leave us a pattern of their judgement, that it was not the not knowing, but the not approving, which was the cause of their not using it. *Plato,* a man of high autority indeed, but least of all for his Commonwealth, in the book of his laws,[175] which no City ever yet receiv'd, fed his fancie with making many edicts to his ayrie Burgomasters,[176] which they who otherwise admire him, wish had bin rather buried and excus'd in the *genial* cups of an *Academick* night-sitting.[177] By which laws[178] he seems to tolerat no kind of learning, but by unalterable decree, con-[16]sisting most of practicall traditions, to the attainment whereof a Library of smaller bulk than his own dialogues would be abundant. And there also enacts[179] that no poet should so much as read to any privat man, what he had writt'n, untill the Judges and Law-keepers had seen it, and allow'd it: But that *Plato* meant this Law peculiarly to that Commonwealth which he had imagin'd, and to no other, is evident. Why was he not else a Law-giver to himself, but a transgressor, and to be expell'd by his own Magistrats; both for the wanton epigrams and dialogues which he made,[180] and his perpetuall reading of *Sophron Mimus,*[181] and *Aristophanes,* books of grossest infamy, and also for commending the latter of them though he were the malicious libeller of his chief friends,[182] to be read by the

175. I.e., the imaginary state described in Plato's *Laws,* a work generally less esteemed than his more idealistic *Republic.* Though intended to be applicable to actual societies, the laws were not "receiv'd" or put into practice by any "City," that is, by any *civitas* or state.

176. *Burgomasters:* fictitious civic officials.

177. *Academick night-sitting:* a symposium (in its original meaning of a convivial meeting for drinking and intellectual conversation) held in Plato's Academy. Milton has in mind the Platonic dialogues in such circumstances.

178. *Laws,* VII. There are similar provisions in *Republic,* II and III, but the emphasis on "practicall traditions" points to the *Laws.*

179. *there also enacts:* in *Laws,* VII, 801, Plato also enacts . . . Cf. Milton's "De Idea Platonica," lines 34–38.

180. I.e., presumably those which treat homosexual love; probably *Phaedrus* and *Symposium* and epigrams like the one cited by Diogenes Laertius (III, 23), tr. Thomas Stanley (*History of Philosophy,* 4th ed., p. 187): "My Soul, when I kiss'd Agathon, did start / Up to my Lip, just ready to depart."

181. Sophron (fifth century B.C.), author of mimes—scenes from everyday life written dramatically. Cf. *Apology* (*Yale Milton,* I, 879): "this we know from Laertius [III, 13] that the Mimes of *Sophron* were of such reckning with *Plato,* as to take them nightly to read on."

182. Aristophanes ridiculed Nicias in the *Knights* and Socrates in the *Clouds.*

Tyrant *Dionysius,*[183] who had little need of such trash to spend his time on? But that he knew this licencing of Poems had reference and dependence to many other proviso's there set down in his fancied republic, which in this world could have no place: and so neither he himself, nor any Magistrat, or City ever imitated that cours, which tak'n apart from those other collaterall injunctions must needs be vain and fruitlesse. For if they fell upon[184] one kind of strictnesse, unlesse their care were equall to regulat all other things of like aptnes to corrupt the mind, that single endeavour they knew would be but a fond labour; to shut and fortifie one gate against corruption, and be necessitated to leave others round about wide open. If we think to regulat Printing, thereby to rectifie manners, we must regulat all recreations and pastimes, all that is delightfull to man. No music must be heard, no song be set or sung, but what is grave and *Dorick.*[185] There must be licensing dancers, that no gesture, motion, or deportment be taught our youth but what by their allowance shall be thought honest; for such *Plato* was provided of; It will ask more than the work of twenty licensers to examin all the lutes, the violins, and the ghittars in every house; they must not be suffer'd to prattle, as they doe, but must be licens'd what they may say. And who shall silence all the airs and madrigalls, that whisper softnes in chambers? The Windows also, and the *Balcone's* must be thought on,[186] there are shrewd[187] books, with dangerous Frontispices set to sale;[188] who shall prohibit them, shall

183. See note 57 above. Plato included Aristophanes as a participant in the *Symposium.*

184. *fell upon:* adopted or resorted to.

185. In *Republic,* III, 398–99, Plato suppressed soft, effeminating music but allowed the Dorian mode, which was strong, "masculine," and military. In *Laws,* VII, he made similar provisions for censoring music and dancing.

186. In modern practice a stronger mark of punctuation would be used. Milton's intention may have been to indicate that "on" would be followed by a minute pause broken by a suddenly-intruded, heavily-emphasized "there"—as if the idea thus rapidly introduced occurred suddenly to the speaker. Milton's *reductio ad absurdum* is that if books must be licensed because of their possibly corrupting influence, so must music, dancing, and love songs; and consideration must also be given to licensing windows and balconies because anything displayed on them may also corrupt spectators.

187. *shrewd:* depraved; able to do mischief. For example, the frontispiece of *Les œuvres de Pierre de Ronsard* (Paris, 1609) displays a naked woman; the prudish could take exception to it especially if it were exhibited by a bookseller to lure buyers.

188. Etymologically "Frontispices" is the sounder spelling (from early Latin *specere,* to look). Milton plays on its two meanings—defined in Phillips' dictionary as "the facing, or Fore-front of a building; also an Emblem or Picture set before the Title of a Book, to shew the Design of it." Several possible interpretations seem involved in the punning analogy: (a) there (in windows and

twenty licencers? The villages also must have their visitors[189] to enquire what lectures the bagpipe and the rebbeck[190] reads ev'n to the ballatry, and the gammuth of every *municipal* fidler,[191] for these are the Countrymans *Arcadia's* and his *Monte Mayors*.[192] Next, what more Nationall corruption, for which England hears ill[193] abroad, than household gluttony; [17] who shall be the rectors of our daily rioting?[194] and what shall be done to inhibit the multitudes that frequent those houses where drunk'nes is sold and harbour'd? Our garments also should be referr'd to the licencing of some more sober work-masters to see them cut into a lesse wanton garb. Who shall regulat all the mixt conversation[195] of our youth, male and female together, as is the fashion of this Country, who shall still appoint what shall be discours'd, what presum'd, and no furder? Lastly, who shall forbid and separat all idle resort, all evill company? These things will be, and must be; but how they shall be lest[196] hurtfull, how less enticing, herein consists the grave and governing wisdom of a State. To sequester[197] out of the world into *Atlantick* and *Eutopian* polities,[198] which never can be drawn into use, will not mend our condition; but to ordain wisely as in this world of evill, in the midd'st whereof God hath plac't us unavoidably. Nor is it *Plato's* licensing

---

n balconies) wicked books with dangerous frontispieces (displayed to attract uyers) are set out for sale; (b) there (in windows and on balconies) wicked books" with dangerous forefronts are set to attract buyers—the "books" in this nterpretation being not books but things analogous to them, prostitutes, for xample, with their dangerous façades of painted faces and revealing clothing; c) there, on view in the fronts of buildings you will find something similar to ooks with dangerous frontispieces displayed to attract sales.

189. I.e., inspectors sent to ensure that everything is in order in a district or nstitution. In the 1630s such supervising investigators were sent to report on nglish parishes and universities. They paid particular attention to the sermons r lectures which were read—i.e., delivered—by ordained ministers known as ecturers. Lecturers were not members of the ordinary parish clergy but were pecially employed by individuals or corporations for the sole purpose of reaching.

190. *rebbeck:* a three-stringed fiddle; cf. *L'Allegro*, line 94: "jocond rebecks ound."

191. *ev'n to . . . fidler:* extending their enquiry even to the balladry (comnon street songs and popular dance songs) and the gamut (range of notes) of every town fiddler.

192. I.e., for these are the country fellow's equivalents of the fashionable romances, Sidney's *Arcadia* and Montemayor's *Diana* (ca. 1559).

193. *hears ill:* is ill spoken of.

194. *daily rioting:* debauchery.

195. *conversation:* associating.

196. *lest:* least.

197. *sequester:* withdraw.

198. *Atlantick and Eutopian polities:* imaginary political systems like those of Plato's Atlantis, Bacon's New Atlantis, and More's Utopia.

of books will doe this, which necessarily pulls along with it so many other kinds of licencing, as will make us all both ridiculous and wary, and yet frustrat; but those unwritt'n, or at least unconstraining laws of vertuous education, religious and civill nurture, which Plato there[199] mentions, as the bonds and ligaments of the Commonwealth, the pillars and sustainers of every writt'n Statute; these they be which will bear chief sway in such matters as these, when all licencing will be easily eluded. Impunity and remissenes, for certain are the bane of a Commonwealth, but here the great art lyes to discern in what the law is to bid restraint and punishment, and in what things perswasion only is to work. If every action which is good, or evill in man at ripe years were to be under pittance, and prescription, and compulsion,[200] what were vertue but a name, what praise could be then due to well-doing, what gramercy[201] to be sober, just or continent? many there be that complain of divin Providence for suffering[202] *Adam* to transgresse, foolish tongues! when God gave him reason, he gave him freedom to choose, for reason is but choosing;[203] he had bin else a meer artificiall *Adam*, such an *Adam* as he is in the motions.[204] We our selves esteem not of that obedience, or love, or gift, which is of force: God therefore left him free, set before him a provoking[205] object, ever almost in his eyes[;] herein consisted his merit, herein the right of his reward, the praise of his abstinence. Wherefore did he creat passions within us, pleas-

199. *Laws,* I, 643–44; *Republic,* IV, 424–33.

200. *under . . . compulsion:* subjected to a system involving being allow only a small proportion (i.e., being allowed to print only parts of a work), bei prescribed to (by orders, regulations, and changes imposed by the censors and being compelled (to obedience to licensing, conformity to the judgments the censors, etc., including being compelled not to publish a work).

201. Citing this passage, the *OED* defines "gramercy" as "special merit but this is unlikely. The word originally meant "God reward you greatly," b it lost its force and by Milton's time was used casually like the modern "Thank as a conventional courtesy term to acknowledge small favors. Milton's doctri is that virtue, well-doing, sobriety, justice, and continence are genuine only they rise from a man's inner discipline of reasoned choice or from strength character based on reasoned choice. Mere conformity to externally impose rules and regulations does not deserve to be called virtue or praised as virtue rewarded as virtue. If the actions of a mature man are constricted, prescribe and compelled, virtue will be nothing but a name; what appears to be wel doing will be mere external conformity, and the only praise appropriate for will likewise be merely verbal; and the only thanks proper for such impose sobriety, justice, and continence will be the casual courtesy term, "Gramercy."

202. *suffering:* allowing.

203. Cf. *Paradise Lost,* III, 97–128.

204. *such an Adam . . . motions:* a mere automaton, such an Adam as is th puppet who represents him in puppet shows.

205. *provoking:* arousing desires; enticing.

ures round about us, but that these rightly temper'd are the very ingredients of vertu? They are not skilfull considerers of human things, who [18] imagin to remove sin by removing the matter of sin; for, besides that it is a huge heap increasing under the very act of diminishing, though some part of it may for a time be withdrawn from some persons, it cannot from all, in such a universall thing as books are; and when this is done, yet the sin remains entire. Though ye take from a covetous man all his treasure, he has yet one jewell left, ye cannot bereave him of his covetousnesse. Banish all objects of lust, shut up all youth into the severest discipline that can be exercis'd in any hermitage, ye cannot make them chaste, that came not thither so: such great care and wisdom is requir'd to the right managing of this point. Suppose we could expell sin by this means; look how much we thus expell of sin, so much we expell of vertue: for the matter of them both is the same; remove that, and ye remove them both alike. This justifies the high providence of God, who though he command us temperance, justice, continence, yet powrs[206] out before us ev'n to a profusenes all desirable things, and gives us minds that can wander beyond all limit and satiety. Why should we then affect[207] a rigor contrary to the manner of God and of nature, by abridging or scanting those means, which books freely permitted are, both to the triall of vertue, and the exercise of truth. It would be better done to learn that the law must needs be frivolous which goes to restrain things, uncertainly and yet equally working to good, and to evill. And were I the chooser, a dram of well-doing should be preferr'd before many times as much the forcible hindrance of evill-doing. For God sure esteems the growth and compleating of one vertuous person, more than the restraint of ten vitious. And albeit what ever thing we hear or see, sitting, walking, travelling, or conversing may be fitly call'd our book, and is of the same effect that writings are, yet grant the thing to be prohibited were only books, it appears that this order hitherto is far insufficient to the end which it intends. Do we not see, not once or oftner, but weekly that continu'd Court-libell[208] against the Parlament and City, Printed, as the wet sheets can witnes, and dispers't among us, for all that licencing can doe? yet this is the

206. *powrs:* pours. Cf. *Comus,* lines 710 ff.

207. *affect:* desire.

208. *Mercurius Aulicus* (the Court Mercury), a royalist newspaper. In 1643 its circulation in London was said to be up to 500 (Joseph Frank, *The Beginnings of the English Newspaper* [Cambridge, Mass., 1961], p. 50); it appeared with increasing irregularity until it expired in September 1645. A pro-Cromwellian paper appeared briefly with the same title in 1645 boasting that it needed no license because it bore Cromwell's name (ibid., p. 251).

prime service a man would think, wherein this order should give proof of it self. If it were executed, you'l say. But certain, if execution be remisse or blindfold now, and in this particular, what will it be hereafter, and in other books. If then the order shall not be vain and frustrat, behold a new labour, Lords and Commons, ye must repeal and proscribe all scandalous and unlicenc't books already printed and divulg'd; after ye have [19] drawn them up into a list, that all may know which are condemn'd, and which not; and ordain that no forrein books be deliver'd out of custody, till they have bin read over. This office will require the whole time of not a few overseers, and those no vulgar men. There be also books which are partly usefull and excellent, partly culpable and pernicious; this work will ask as many more officials,[209] to make expurgations, and expunctions, that the Commonwealth of learning be not damnify'd.[210] In fine, when the multitude of books encrease upon their hands, ye must be fain to catalogue all those Printers who are found frequently offending, and forbidd the importation of their whole suspected *typography*. In a word, that this your order may be exact, and not deficient, ye must reform it perfectly according to the model of *Trent*[211] and *Sevil*,[212] which I know ye abhorre to doe. Yet though ye should condiscend[213] to this, which God forbid, the order still would be but fruitlesse and defective to that end whereto ye meant it. If to prevent sects and schisms, who is so unread or so uncatechis'd in story,[214] that hath not heard of many sects refusing books as a hindrance, and preserving their doctrine unmixt for many ages, only by unwritt'n traditions. The Christian faith, for that was once a schism, is not unknown to have spread all over *Asia*, ere any Gospel or Epistle was seen in writing. If the amendment of manners be aym'd at, look into Italy and Spain, whether those places be one scruple the better, the honester, the wiser, the chaster, since all the inquisitionall rigor that hath bin executed upon books.

Another reason, whereby to make it plain that this order will misse the end it seeks, consider[215] by the quality which ought to be in every licencer. It cannot be deny'd but that he who is made judge to sit upon the birth, or death of books whether they may be

209. Before the abolition of episcopacy, Officials were judges in ecclesiastical courts concerned with spiritual offenses. Cf. *Of Reformation* (1641 ed., p. 18): "a band of rooking Officials."
210. *damnify'd:* injured.
211. *Trent:* the Council of Trent.
212. *Sevil:* the Spanish Inquisition's headquarters in Seville.
213. *condiscend:* assent.
214. *story:* history.
215. *consider:* judge.

wafted[216] into this world, or not, had need to be a man above the common measure, both studious, learned, and judicious; there may be else no mean mistakes in the censure of what is passable or not; which is no mean injury. If he be of such worth as behoovs him, there cannot be a more tedious and unpleasing journey-work,[217] a greater losse of time levied upon his head, than to be made the perpetuall reader of unchosen books and pamphlets, oftimes huge volumes. There is no book that is acceptable unlesse at certain seasons; but to be enjoyn'd the reading of that at all times, and in a hand scars legible, whereof three pages would not down[218] at any time in the fairest Print, is an imposition which I cannot beleeve how he that values time, and his own [20] studies, or is but of a sensible[219] nostrill should be able to endure. In this one thing I crave leave of the present licencers to be pardon'd for so thinking: who doubtlesse took this office up, looking on it through their obedience to the Parlament, whose command perhaps made all things seem easie and unlaborious to them; but that this short triall hath wearied them out already, their own expressions and excuses to them who make so many journeys to sollicit their licence, are testimony anough. Seeing therefore those who now possesse the imployment, by all evident signs wish themselves well ridd of it, and that no man of worth, none that is not a plain unthrift of his own hours is ever likely to succeed them, except he mean to put himself to the salary of a Presse-corrector, we may easily foresee what kind of licencers we are to expect hereafter, either ignorant, imperious, and remisse, or basely pecuniary. This is what I had to shew wherein this order cannot conduce to that end, whereof it bears the intention.

I lastly proceed from the no good it can do, to the manifest hurt it causes, in being first the greatest discouragement and affront, that can be offer'd to learning and to learned men. It was the complaint and lamentation of Prelats, upon every least breath of a motion to remove pluralities,[220] and distribute more equally Church revennu's, that then all learning would be for ever dasht and discourag'd.

216. *wafted:* carried, as unborn souls in ancient mythology had to be taken by boat across the river which separated them from the world of the living, in order to be born. Cf. note 105 above.

217. *journey-work:* hack work.

218. *would not down:* could not be endured. The censor would have to keep reading material in scarcely legible handwriting, material which he could not swallow even in the most beautiful print to the extent of three pages at one time.

219. *sensible:* sensitive.

220. *pluralities:* the practice of allowing one person to have more than one income-producing appointment in the church. Cf. Milton's attack on the "whore Plurality" in his sonnet "On the Forcers of Conscience."

But as for that opinion, I never found cause to think that the tenth part[221] of learning stood or fell with the Clergy: nor could I ever but hold it for a sordid and unworthy speech of any Churchman who had a competency[222] left him. If therefore ye be loath to dishearten utterly and discontent, not the mercenary crew of false pretenders to learning, but the free and ingenuous sort of such as evidently were born to study, and love lerning for it self, not for lucre, or any other end, but the service of God and of truth, and perhaps that lasting fame and perpetuity of praise which God and good men have consented shall be the reward of those whose publisht labours advance the good of mankind, then know, that so far to distrust the judgement and the honesty of one who hath but a common repute in learning, and never yet offended, as not to count him fit to print his mind without a tutor and examiner, lest he should drop a scism, or something of corruption, is the greatest displeasure and indignity to a free and knowing spirit that can be put upon him. What advantage is it to be a man over it is to be a boy at school, if we have only scapt the ferular, to come under the fescu of an *Imprimatur?*[223] if serious and elaborat writings, as if they were no [21] more than the theam of a Grammar lad under his Pedagogue must not be utter'd[224] without the cursory eyes of a temporizing and extemporizing licencer.[225] He who is not trusted with his own actions, his drift not being known to be evill, and standing to the hazard of law and penalty,[226] has no great argument to think himself reputed in the Commonwealth wherin he was born, for other than a fool or a foreiner. When a man writes to the world, he summons up all his reason and deliberation to assist him; he searches, meditats, is industrious, and likely consults and conferrs with his judicious friends; after all which done he takes himself to be inform'd in what he

221. In contrast to the claim of supporters of pluralism that *all* learning would be "dasht" (destroyed or frustrated) if the holding of multiple posts were ended, Milton denies that even one tenth of it (corresponding to the tenths paid as tithes) belongs to the clergy.

222. *competency:* sufficient income to live modestly.

223. I.e., what advantage is it to be a man over what it is to be a boy at school if we have merely escaped the ferula (a rod or cane used for beating) in order to come under the fescu (a pointer used in teaching) of having to obtain an *imprimatur* in order to publish?

224. *utter'd:* published.

225. *temporizing and extemporizing licencer:* a complying time-serving licenser who resorts to expedients. Cf. the statements two sentences later about licensers' lack of leisure.

226. I.e., prepared to run the risk of penalties for having published something forbidden by law—such as libel or blasphemy.

writes, as well as any that writ before him; if in this the most consummat act of his fidelity and ripenesse, no years, no industry, no former proof of his abilities can bring him to that state of maturity, as not to be still mistrusted and suspected, unlesse he carry all his considerat[227] diligence, all his midnight watchings, and expence of *Palladian*[228] oyl, to the hasty view of an unleasur'd licencer, perhaps much his younger, perhaps far his inferiour in judgement, perhaps one who never knew the labour of book-writing, and if he be not repulst, or slighted, must appear in Print like a punie[229] with his guardian, and his censors hand on the back of his title to be his bayl and surety, that he is no idiot, or seducer, it cannot be but a dishonor and derogation to the author, to the book, to the priviledge and dignity of Learning. And what if the author shall be one so copious of fancie, as to have many things well worth the adding, come into his mind after licencing, while the book is yet under the Presse, which not seldom happ'ns to the best and diligentest writers; and that perhaps a dozen times in one book. The Printer dares not go behond his licenc't copy; so often then must the author trudge to his leav-giver, that those his new insertions may be viewd; and many a jaunt will be made, ere that licencer, for it must be the same man, can either be found, or found at leisure; mean while either the Presse must stand still, which is no small damage, or the author loose his accuratest thoughts, and send the book forth wors than he had made it, which to a diligent writer is the greatest melancholy and vexation that can befall. And how can a man teach with autority, which is the life of teaching, how can he be a Doctor[230] in his book as he ought to be, or else had better be silent, whenas all he teaches, all he delivers, is but under the tuition, under the correction of his patriarchal[231] licencer to blot or alter[232] what precisely accords not with the hidebound humor which he calls his judge-

227. *considerat:* well-considered; prudent.

228. *Palladian:* scholarly; pertaining to Pallas Athene (Minerva), goddess of wisdom. I.e., of "skilful Knowledge joined with discreet Practice," involving "the Understanding of the noblest Arts, the best Accomplishments of the Mind, together with all Virtues" (William King, *An Historical Account of the Heathen Gods* [Carbondale, 1965], p. 153). Pallas Athene taught men how to extract from olives (which were sacred to her) the oil which burned in the lamps of her scholarly devotees.

229. *punie:* puny: a minor in law; a freshman in schools; hence, one treated like a novice or youngster despite his maturity.

230. *Doctor:* teacher.

231. *patriarchal:* fatherly—used ironically with a jibe at Archbishop Laud whose trial for treason ended a few months before *Areopagitica* was published. One accusation against him was that he tried to reconcile the English and

ment. When every a-[22]cute reader upon the first sight of a pedantick licence, will be ready with these like words to ding the book a coits distance from him,[233] "I hate a pupil teacher, I endure not an instructer that comes to me under the wardship of an overseeing fist. I know nothing of the licencer, but that I have his own hand here for his arrogance; who shall warrant me his judgement?[234] "The State Sir," replies the Stationer,[235] but has a quick return,[236] "The State shall be my governours, but not my criticks; they may be mistak'n in the choice of a licencer, as easily as this licencer may be mistak'n in an author: This[237] is some common stuffe;" and he might [have] added from Sir *Francis Bacon*, That *such authoriz'd books are but the language of the times.*[238] For though a licencer should happ'n to be judicious more than ordnary, which will be a great jeopardy[239] of the next succession, yet his very office, and his commission enjoyns him to let passe nothing but what is vulgarly receiv'd already. Nay, which is more lamentable, if the work of any deceased author, though never so famous in his life time, and even to this day, come to their hands for licence to be Printed, or Reprinted, if there be found in his book one sentence of a ventrous[240] edge, utter'd in the height of zeal, and who knows whether it might

---

Roman churches on condition that the Pope appoint him Patriarch of the Western Church.

232. *alter:* delete or change the wording of. Laud was accused of such changes.

233. I.e., on seeing the imprimatur, a sharp-witted would-be reader, being aware of what censorship involves, will be ready to fling the book the distance traveled by the iron ring used in the game of quoits, uttering words like the following. (The quotation marks do not occur in the original edition but have been added for clarity.)

234. I.e., here I have the imprimatur signed by him, as evidence of his arrogance; but who will guarantee the soundness of his judgment for me?

235. *Stationer:* publisher. The Licensing Act forbade publication of a book without a license from the Master, Wardens, and Assistants of the Company of Stationers.

236. *return:* reply.

237. *This:* this book. In the dialogue with which Milton dramatizes his point the indignant would-be reader apparently points to, or picks up, a book approved by the licenser and comments that its contents are ordinary and unoriginal; i.e., safe, conventional material is unhesitatingly licensed.

238. From *An Advertisement Touching the Controversies of the Church of England,* written in 1589 but not published until it appeared as *A Wise and Moderate Discourse Concerning Church-Affaires,* early in the 1640s: "a book authorized is thought to be but *temporis voces, the language of the time*" (*Letters and Life of Francis Bacon,* ed. James Spedding, I, 78); see note 281 below.

239. *jeopardy:* uncertainty. Chances are that the next successor of this licenser will not be so judicious.

240. *ventrous:* venturous; daring; audacious.

not be the dictat of a divine Spirit, yet not suiting with every low decrepit humor of their own, though it were *Knox*[241] himself, the Reformer of a Kingdom that spake it, they will not pardon him their dash:[242] the sense of that great man shall to all posterity be lost, for the fearfulnesse, or the presumptuous rashnesse of a perfunctory licencer. And to what an author this violence hath bin lately done, and in what book of greatest consequence to be faithfully publisht,[243] I could now instance, but shall forbear till a more convenient season. Yet if these things be not resented seriously and timely by them who have the remedy in their power, but that such iron moulds[244] as these shall have autority to knaw out the choisest periods of exquisitest books, and to commit such a treacherous fraud against the orphan remainders of worthiest men after death, the more sorrow will belong to that haples race of men, whose misfortune it is to have understanding. Henceforth let no man care to learn, or care to be more than worldly wise; for certainly in higher matters to be ignorant and slothfull, to be a common stedfast dunce will be the only pleasant life, and only in request.

And as it[245] is a particular disesteem of every knowing person alive, and most injurious to the writt'n labours and monuments of the dead, so to me it seems an undervaluing and vilifying of the whole Nation. I [23] cannot set so light by[246] all the invention, the art, the wit, the grave and solid judgement which is in England, as that it can be comprehended in any twenty[247] capacities how good soever, much lesse that it should not passe except their superintendence be over it, except it be sifted and strain'd with their strainers, that it should be uncurrant without their manuall stamp. Truth and understanding are not such wares as to be monopoliz'd and traded in by

241. Passages previously printed were omitted from the 1644 edition of John Knox's *History of the Reformation.*

242. *dash:* line drawn to cancel a word or passage.

243. This possibly refers to Part II of Edward Coke's *Institutes of the Laws of England,* which, in 1641, Parliament ordered printed.

244. *such iron moulds:* small yellow moles or spots in paper caused by iron rust, ink stains, or the like; such a spot could obliterate part of the text. In suggesting that the licensers are such "moulds" authorized to gnaw away the finest cadenced statements, Milton may also play on the other sense of "mole"—a small burrowing animal that works in the dark.

245. *it:* licensing.

246. I.e., I cannot so disesteem or so undervalue—probably an ellipsis for "set so light store by." The meaning is clear from the parallelism with "disesteem" and "undervalue" in the previous sentence. Hales suggests that "light" should perhaps be "lite," an old form of "little."

247. The word *twenty* was sometimes used vaguely for a large number. In June 1643, Parliament listed thirty-four licensers.

tickets and statutes and standards.[248] We must not think to make a staple commodity[249] of all knowledge in the Land, to mark and licence it like our broad cloath, and our wooll packs. What is it but a servitude like that impos'd by the Philistims, not to be allow'd the sharpning of our own axes and coulters, but we must repair from all quarters to twenty licencing forges.[250] Had any one writt'n and divulg'd erroneous things and scandalous to honest life, misusing and forfeiting the esteem had of his reason among men, if after conviction this only censure were adjudg'd him, that he should never henceforth write, but what were first examin'd by an appointed officer, whose hand should be annext to passe his credit for him, that now he might be safely read, it could not be apprehended lesse than a disgracefull punishment. Whence to include the whole Nation, and those that never yet thus offended, under such a diffident[251] and suspectfull prohibition, may plainly be understood what a disparagement it is. So much the more, when as dettors and delinquents[252]

248. The nature of truth and understanding is not such that they may be treated as commodities or merchandise whose manufacture and sale is put under the exclusive control of one or more persons. (One of the grievances which conduced to the Puritan Revolution was the granting of such monopolies legally or illegally by the king.) And trade in them cannot be carried on by means of the papers, documents, regulations, and standards involved in ordinary commercial transactions. "Ticket" was a term used for placards, price labels, I.O.U.s, written evidence of special trading rights, trade notices, etc. "Statute" was used for bonds which provided penalties for not paying a debt, for laws regulating or restricting trade, and for legal provisions governing weights and measures. Such weights and measures fixed by law were called "standards."

249. *staple commodity:* a basic commodity such as wool, cloth, or leather. Tudor and Stuart rulers gave to certain staples (merchant corporations or towns or the like) monopolies to trade in staple wares. Thus though Milton's point is that knowledge must not be treated like ordinary merchandise, he also has in mind similarities between restrictions on publication and restrictions on trade.

250. Since the Philistines would not allow smiths and forges to exist in Israel, the Israelites had to go from all parts of their country to their conquerors to have axes and colters (plow blades) sharpened (1 Sam. xiii 19–20). So English authors must go to the licensers. Milton probably also had in mind the feudal regulations under royal rule that prevented men from performing certain tasks for themselves but required them to pay feudal dues to have grain ground at an overlord's mill and plowshares beaten at his forge. For example, in 1641 Sir Bevil Grevile brought pressure on his tenants to grind their grain at his mill: "if they do it not, as they are bound, I will put them in suit" (Mary Coate, *Cornwall in the Great Civil War and Interregnum* [Oxford, 1933], p. 96).

251. *diffident:* distrustful.

252. Men who failed to pay debts were ordinarily jailed in debtors' prisons until they did so, but members of both houses of parliament were protected from lawsuits for debt and were entitled to extend the same privilege to their dependents and servants (a right which Parliament abolished in 1648). However, debtors could not be arrested in certain sanctuaries such as the precincts

may walk abroad without a keeper, but unoffensive books must not stirre forth without a visible jaylor in thir title. Nor is it to the common people lesse than a reproach; for if we be so jealous over them, as that we dare not trust them with an English pamphlet, what doe we but censure them for a giddy, vitious, and ungrounded people; in such a sick and weak estate of faith and discretion, as to be able to take nothing down but through the pipe[253] of a licencer. That this is care or love of them, we cannot pretend, whenas in those Popish places where the Laity are most hated and dispis'd the same strictnes is us'd over them. Wisdom we cannot call it, because it stops but one breach of licence, nor that neither; whenas those corruptions which it seeks to prevent, break in faster at other dores which cannot be shut.

And in conclusion it reflects to the disrepute of our Ministers also, of whose labours we should hope better, and of the proficiencie[254] which thir flock reaps by them, than that after all this light of the Gospel which is, and is to be, and all this continuall preaching, they [24] should be still frequented with[255] such an unprincipl'd, unedify'd, and laick[256] rabble, as that the whiffe of every new pamphlet should stagger them out of thir catechism, and Christian walking.[257] This may have much reason to discourage the Ministers when such a low conceit[258] is had of all their exhortations, and the benefiting of their hearers, as that they are not thought fit to be turn'd loose to three sheets of paper without a licencer, that all the

---

of dissolved monasteries, and they lived and walked abroad in such areas with impunity. Delinquents were those who assisted the king in the civil war. In 1643 their property was confiscated and they were made liable to imprisonment. But in January, 1644, Parliament offered pardon for those who gave themselves up, and they were allowed to compound for their estates (regain them by paying a percentage of their value). Thus instead of being jailed, they were permitted to "walk abroad" or move about "without a keeper."

253. The metaphor is that of an invalid unable to swallow anything other than what can be passed through a tube or straw.

254. *proficiencie:* improvement; advance toward perfection.

255. *frequented with:* associated or congregated with.

256. Milton believed that, in church government and services, the laity should be allowed the active role it was denied under the Laudians; under them, he implies in *Church-Governement* (*Columbia Milton*, III, 261), "we have learnt that scornfull terme of Laick." Cf. H. R. Trevor-Roper, *Archbishop Laud* (London, 1962), p. 155: "To the high churchman it [the Church] was a separate, visible body represented by the clergy, a class quite distinct from the laity whom it guided and directed: but to the Puritan the Church was no such exclusive possession, nor was the minister separated from the congregation by any more mysterious difference than that which separates the plumber from his customers."

257. This term lends some support for "wayfaring"; see note 140 above.

258. *conceit:* opinion.

Sermons, all the Lectures preacht, printed, vented in such numbers, and such volumes, as have now wellnigh made all other books unsalable, should not be armor anough against one single *enchiridion*,[259] without the castle St. *Angelo* of an *imprimatur*.[260]

And lest som should perswade ye, Lords and Commons, that these arguments of lerned mens discouragement at this your order, are meer flourishes, and not reall, I could recount what I have seen and heard in other Countries, where this kind of inquisition tyrannizes; when I have sat among lerned men, for that honor I had, and bin counted happy to be born in such a place of *Philosophic* freedom, as they suppos'd England was, while themselvs did nothing but bemoan the servil condition into which lerning amongst them was brought; that this was it which had dampt the glory of Italian wits;[261] that nothing had bin there writt'n now these many years but flattery and fustian.[262] There it was that I found and visited the famous *Galileo*[263] grown old, a prisner to the Inquisition, for thinking in Astronomy otherwise than the Franciscan and Dominican licencers thought. And though I knew that England then[264] was groaning loudest under the Prelaticall yoak, neverthelesse I took it as a pledge of future happines, that other Nations were so perswaded of her liberty. Yet was it beyond my hope that those Worthies were then breathing in her air, who should be her leaders to such a deliverance, as shall never be forgott'n by any revolution of time that this world hath to finish. When that was once begun, it was as little in my fear, that what words of complaint I heard among lerned men of other parts utter'd against the Inquisition, the same I should hear by as

259. *enchiridion:* something that can be held in the hand; here a pun on a small book or manual and a dagger.

260. I.e., without the prison-fortress of a license. The Castle of St. Angelo, a papal prison in Rome, had been used as a fortress. By such images Milton reinforces his contention that licensing was a Roman Catholic invention.

261. *Italian wits:* creative intelligences; brilliant minds.

262. *fustian:* verbiage.

263. In 1633 Galileo was forced by the Inquisition to renounce heresies found in his *Dialogue on the Two Principal Systems of the World* (which proposed that the earth circles about an immovable sun); and he was imprisoned near Florence. Records show that he was allowed some visitors. The charge that Milton was lying (S. B. Liljegren, *Studies in Milton* [Lund, 1918], pp. 3–36) has been effectively answered. Milton's claim need imply no more than that he found where Galileo was, went to see him, and was allowed to observe him from a distance. If so, it is not surprising that he failed to mention Galileo in the account of the journey given in *Second Defense* and that he did not include him among the great blind men he mentions there: from a distance Galileo's blindness may not have been noticeable.

264. I.e., under Archbishop Laud.

lerned men at home utterd in time of Parlament[265] against an order of licencing; and that so generally, that when I had disclos'd my self a companion of their discontent, I might say, if without envy,[266] that he whom an honest *quaestorship* had indear'd to the *Sicilians*, was not more by them importun'd against *Verres*,[267] than the favourable opinion which I had among many who honour ye, and are known and respected by ye, [25] loaded me with entreaties and perswasions; that I would not despair to lay together that which just reason should bring into my mind, toward the removal of an undeserved thraldom upon lerning. That this is not therefore the disburdning of a particular fancie,[268] but the common grievance of all those who had prepar'd their minds and studies above the vulgar pitch to advance truth in others, and from others to entertain it, thus much may satisfie. And in their name I shall for neither friend nor foe conceal what the generall murmur is; that if we come to inquisitioning again, and licencing, and that we are so timorous of our selvs, and so suspicious of all men, as to fear each book, and the shaking of every leaf, before we know what the contents are, if some who but of late were little better than silenc't from preaching, shall come now to silence us from reading, except what they please, it cannot be guest what is intended by som but a second tyranny over learning: and will soon put it out of controversie that Bishops and Presbyters are the same to us both name and thing.[269] That

265. I.e., in contrast to 1629–40 when Charles I and his ministers ruled without a parliament.

266. I.e., if I may do so without arousing ill will (because of the presumption of comparing himself to Cicero).

267. Verres was an extortionate and cruel governor of Sicily (73–71 B.C.). The Sicilians, remembering that Cicero had administered public funds honestly as their quaestor in 75 B.C., retained him five years later to prosecute Verres, who was forced into exile after Cicero had delivered only a preliminary discourse and the first of the six Verrine Orations which he had intended to deliver.

268. I.e., the unloading or relieving expression of a distinctively personal whim. Milton had tried to depersonalize and universalize his doctrines on divorce, but he was uneasily aware that personal pressures conduced to his writing of the divorce tracts; and in "To the Parlament" prefaced to *The Judgement of Martin Bucer*, he had mentioned "odious inferences" others drew from them. Now, in *Areopagitica*, he tries to guard his case against licensing from being dismissed as personally motivated.

269. Milton ironically turns against the Presbyterians their iterated contention that *presbyter* (minister or priest) and *bishop* are different words for the same ecclesiastical office; and he points to the Episcopalians' counterargument that under presbyterian church government, each minister, whether called presbyter or bishop, would be a tyrant in his own parish. Cf. the ending of the sonnet "On the Forcers of Conscience" (1647?): "New Presbyter is but old Preist writt large."

those evills of Prelaty which before from five or six and twenty Sees were distributivly charg'd upon the whole people,[270] will now light wholly upon learning, is not obscure to us: whenas now the Pastor of a small unlearned Parish, on the sudden shall be exalted Archbishop over a large dioces of books, and yet not remove,[271] but keep his other cure too, a mysticall[272] pluralist. He who but of late cry'd down the sole ordination of every novice Batchelor of Art, and deny'd sole jurisdiction over the simplest Parishioner, shall now at home in his privat chair[273] assume both these over worthiest and excellentest books and ablest authors that write them.[274] This is not, Yee Covnants and Protestations[275] that we have made, this is not to put down Prelaty, this is but to chop[276] an Episcopacy, this is

270. I.e., the evils of episcopal tyranny were previously distributed as burdens imposed upon the entire population from twenty-five or twenty-six bishops' sees. A see or seat is the chair or throne of a bishop in his church; also the position and authority it symbolizes.

271. *remove:* withdraw from his office or cure as pastor.

272. *mysticall:* concealed; hard to define—in contrast to the open pluralism of Laudian churchmen.

273. *privat chair:* corresponding to the bishop's see.

274. In 1633, as part of his effort to curb Lecturers, Laud instructed bishops not to ordain any man to the priesthood unless there was an appointment available for him in the church he committed himself to accept. This order meant that some new university graduates were denied ordination and thus were barred from becoming Lecturers and from preaching. The Presbyterians loudly denounced this restrictive exercise of episcopal power. It was one aspect of the exclusive jurisdiction over spiritual and related matters which each bishop exercised within his diocese. Milton's point is that the Presbyterian who only recently denounced the bishops' monopoly over ordination and jurisdiction now, as a licenser, assumes both jurisdiction over books and authors and the power to ordain whether a book shall be licensed for publication or suppressed.

275. In 1638 the Scots made the National Covenant to resist episcopacy; in 1643 the English Parliament ratified the Solemn League and Covenant with the Scots and in 1644 ordered all Englishmen to subscribe to it. In it the English agreed to abolish episcopacy and to reform the Church of England. In 1641, faced by the King's intention to employ military force against them, the members of Parliament and many citizens subscribed to a Protestation which committed them to defend the true reformed Protestant religion, etc. And in 1641 Parliament presented to the king another protestation, the Grand Remonstrance, accompanied by a petition in which they asked him to "concur with the humble desires" of the people "for depriving the Bishops of their votes in Parliament, and abridging their immoderate power usurped over the Clergy, and other . . . good subjects"; for "taking away such oppressions in religion, Church government and discipline as have been brought in by them," etc.

276. *chop:* "make an Exchange" (Phillips' dictionary); i.e., this is but to exchange one episcopacy for another. As Sirluck observes (*Yale Milton,* II, 541), the *OED* definition "change" in the sense of "alter" (citing this passage as an example) is less appropriate.

but to translate the Palace *Metropolitan*[277] from one kind of dominion into another, this is but an old canonicall slight of *commuting* our penance.[278] To startle thus betimes at a meer unlicenc't pamphlet will after a while be afraid of every conventicle, and a while after will make a conventicle of every Christian meeting.[279] But I am certain that a State govern'd by the rules of justice and fortitude, or a Church built and founded upon the rock of faith and true knowledge, cannot be so pusillanimous. While things are yet not constituted in Religion, that freedom of writing should be restrain'd by a discipline imitated from the Prelats, and learnt by them from the Inquisition to shut us up all again into the brest of a licencer, must needs give cause of doubt and [26] discouragement to all learned and religious men. Who cannot but discern the finenes[280] of this politic drift, and who are the contrivers; that while Bishops were to be baited down, then all Presses might be open; it was the peoples birthright and priviledge in time of Parlament, it was the breaking forth of light. But now the Bishops abrogated and voided out of the Church, as if our Reformation sought no more, but to make room for others into their seats under another name, the Episcopall arts begin to bud again, the cruse of truth must run no more oyle, liberty of Printing must be enthrall'd again under a Prelaticall commission of twenty, the privilege of the people nullify'd, and which is wors, the freedom of learning must groan again, and to her old fetters; all this the Parlament yet sitting. Although their own late arguments and defences against the Prelats might remember them that this obstructing violence meets for the most part with an event utterly opposite to the end which it drives at: instead of suppressing sects and schisms, it raises them and invests them with a reputation: *The punishing of wits enhaunces their autority,* saith the

277. *Palace Metropolitan:* Lambeth Palace, the London home of the Archbishop of Canterbury, Metropolitan and Primate of all England.

278. *canonicall . . . penance:* canon law device of substituting one kind of penitential discipline for another.

279. A conventicle was a private religious meeting of dissenters from the established state church. Such meetings were illegal before the abolition of episcopacy. In 1644, when *Areopagitica* was being written, much of what had been dissent was embraced in the state-supported church. Private meetings outside that rather loose organization were not usually treated as illegal except for Roman Catholics, some persistent Anglicans, and some extreme fanatics. As Milton states two sentences later, "things" were not yet "constituted in Religion": the Westminster Assembly of Divines was still debating what recommendations it would make to Parliament for the settlement of the church. Milton feared that if the Presbyterians imposed their church system rigidly it would mean that any religious meeting outside that system would be treated as an illegal conventicle.

280. *finenes:* subtlety; cunning.

Vicount St. *Albans, and a forbidd'n writing is thought to be a certain spark of truth that flies up in the faces of them who seeke to tread it out.*[281] This order therefore may prove a nursing mother to sects, but I shall easily shew how it will be a step-dame to Truth: and first by disinabling us to the maintenance of what is known already.

Well knows he who uses to consider, that our faith and knowledge thrives by exercise, as well as our limbs and complexion. Truth is compar'd in Scripture to a streaming fountain;[282] if her waters flow not in a perpetuall progression, they sick'n into a muddy pool of conformity and tradition. A man may be a heretick in the truth; and if he beleeve things only because his Pastor sayes so, or the Assembly[283] so determins, without knowing other reason, though his belief be true, yet the very truth he holds, becomes his heresie. There is not any burden that som would gladlier post off[284] to another, than the charge and care of their Religion. There be, who knows not that there be of Protestants and professors[285] who live and dye in as arrant[286] an implicit faith,[287] as any lay Papist of Lo-

281. This is the earlier part of the sentence from Bacon quoted earlier; see note 238 above.

282. Prov. xviii 4: "the wellspring of wisdom as a flowing brook." Psalm lxxxv 11: "Truth shall spring out of the earth." Ecclus. i 5: "the word of God is the fountain of wisdom." Sirluck (*Yale Milton*, II, 543) suggests that Milton may be thinking of Song of Sol. iv 15, "a fountain of gardens, a well of living waters," allegorically interpreted.

283. *Assembly:* the Westminster Assembly of Divines.

284. *post off:* transfer.

285. *professors:* those who declare their adherence to a profession of faith, religion, or sect. At the time of writing the term was often used as an alternative for "Puritan." Cf. Robert Sanderson (*XXXVI Sermons* [London, 1689], pp. 15–16): "appropriating to themselves the Names of Brethren, Professors, Good men" to differentiate themselves from Formalists, would they not have it thought "that they have a Brotherhood and Profession of their own, freer and purer from Superstition and Idolatry, than others have . . . ? And . . . why may they not be called Puritans."

286. *arrant:* unmitigated.

287. I.e., faith grounded on acceptance of the authority claimed by the church, without further inquiry. In contrast, explicit faith is belief in the church's authoritative teachings which involves inquiry into their bases and understanding of their nature. In the medieval church, explicit faith was required of the higher clergy, implicit faith being regarded as sufficient for other clergymen and the laity. According to Milton's last published tract, *Of True Religion, Haeresie, Schism, Toleration, and What Best Means may be us'd against the Growth of Popery* (1673, p. 4), "all Protestant Churches . . . and particularly the Church of England . . . maintain these two points, as the main Principles of true Religion; that the Rule of true Religion is the word of God only; and that *their Faith ought not to be an implicit Faith, that is, to believe, though as the Church believes, against or without express authority of Scripture.*" Cf. *Animadversions* (*Columbia Milton*, III, 171), where Milton accuses Anglican

retto.[288] A wealthy man addicted to his pleasure and to his profits, finds Religion to be a traffick so entangl'd, and of so many piddling accounts, that of all mysteries[289] he cannot skill[290] to keep a stock going upon that trade. What should he doe? fain he would have the name to be religious, fain he would bear up with his neighbours in that. What does he therefore, but resolvs to give over toy-[27]ling,[291] and to find himself out som factor,[292] to whose care and credit he may commit the whole managing of his religious affairs; som Divine of note and estimation that must be. To him he adheres, resigns the whole ware-house of his religion, with all the locks and keyes into his custody; and indeed makes the very person of that man his religion; esteems his associating with him a sufficient evidence and commendatory of his own piety. So that a man may say his religion is now no more within himself, but is becom a dividuall movable,[293] and goes and comes neer him, according as that good man frequents the house. He entertains him, gives him gifts, feasts him, lodges him; his religion comes home at night, praies, is liberally supt, and sumptuously laid to sleep, rises, is saluted, and after the malmsey, or some well spic't bruage,[294] better breakfasted[295] than

---

prelates of trying to cheat English Protestants "into a blind and implicite obedience to whatsoever they shall decree, or think fit." James Ussher attacked Roman Catholic teachers who, he alleged, "perswade the multitude to rest in a blind faith, which they call implicit and folded up, telling them that it is enough for them to believe as the Church believes, though they know not what the Church believes, nor who the Church is . . ." (*A Body of Divinitie,* 5th ed. [London, 1658], p. 198). Cf. Isaac Barrow (*Works,* 5th ed. [London, 1751], III, 224): "The simpler sort of men will in effect be always led not by their own judgment, but by the authority of others; and if they be not fairly guided by those whom God hath constituted and assigned to that end, they will be led by the nose, by those who are concerned to seduce them."

288. I.e., any Roman Catholic layman who made a pilgrimage to Loreto in Italy to the Sanctuary of the Holy House of Nazareth there, with implicit faith that in it the Virgin Mary was born, the Incarnation annunciated, and Jesus conceived, and also faith that angels had miraculously transported it to Dalmatia and then to Recanati near its present site. Faith in the miracle still attracts thousands of pilgrims to the shrine.

289. *all mysteries:* trades, arts, crafts, and occupations.

290. *cannot skill:* lacks the capacity, knowledge, experience, or know-how.

291. *toyling:* working, with perhaps some wordplay on the other sense of getting entangled.

292. *factor:* agent.

293. *dividuall movable:* a commodity which may be divided up and transferred from him.

294. Malmsey is a pleasant fine wine (Phillips' dictionary calls it "luscious"). Bastard malmsey was heavier and sweeter; and tawney bastard was sweeter still. Among spiced brewages, mulled claret and Osey were favorites, the latter being a mixture of bastard malmsey, egg whites, bay salt, and water

he whose morning appetite would have gladly fed on green figs between *Bethany* and *Jerusalem,*[296] his Religion walks abroad at eight, and leavs his kind entertainer in the shop trading all day without his religion.[297]

Another sort there be who when they hear that all things shall be order'd, all things regulated and setl'd; nothing writt'n but what passes through the custom-house of certain Publicans[298] that have the tunaging and poundaging[299] of all free spok'n truth, will straight give themselvs up into your hands, mak'em, and cut'em out what religion ye please; there be delights, there be recreations and jolly pastimes that will fetch the day about from sun to sun, and rock the tedious year as in a delightfull dream. What need they torture their heads with that which others have tak'n so strictly, and so unalterably into their own pourveying.[300] These are the fruits which a dull ease and cessation of our knowledge will bring forth among the people. How goodly, and how to be wisht were such an obedient unanimity as this, what a fine conformity would it starch us all into? doubtles a stanch[301] and solid peece of frame-work, as any January could freeze together.

Nor much better will be the consequence ev'n among the Clergy themselvs; it is no new thing never heard of before, for a *parochiall*[302] Minister, who has his reward, and is at his *Hercules* pil-

---

which were put into a cask into which a bag containing licorice, hot peppers, coriander, and aniseed was inserted.

295. The breakfast probably consisted of foods like dried herring, cheese, oysters, and cold meat. Oliver Cromwell liked sausages and pork liver for breakfast, but his wife preferred marrow pudding. The working classes usually began the day with a hearty meal, but it was fashionable for the leisured to have wine or ale and to postpone the eating of food until later.

296. Matt. xxi 18–21 and Mark xi 12–14 relate that when Jesus was hungry he saw a fig tree; but on reaching it, he "found nothing but leaves," whereupon he caused it to wither, thus demonstrating the power of faith to his disciples.

297. On the relation of this description to the character genre see Benjamin Boyce, *The Polemic Character, 1640–1661* (Lincoln, Neb., 1955), pp. 24, 85–86, 94.

298. *Publicans:* collectors of customs duties.

299. *tunaging and poundaging:* the chief customs revenue derived from a tax on each tun of wine and each £'s worth of other goods. When Charles I came to the throne Parliament refused to grant him tunnage and poundage for life, as was traditional. His attempts to collect this revenue became a major grievance, but in 1641 he signed a bill which made it illegal for a king to collect customs without parliamentary consent. Milton's implication is that exacting fees for licensing books was a similar tyrannical imposition.

300. *pourveying:* purveying or provision.

301. *stanch:* staunch.

302. *parochiall:* narrowly limited in interests as well as being minister of a parish. The italics emphasize the wordplay.

lars[303] in a warm benefice, to be easily inclinable, if he have nothing else that may rouse up his studies,[304] to finish his circuit in an English concordance and a *topic folio,* the gatherings and savings of a sober graduatship, a *Harmony* and a *Catena,*[305] treading the constant round[306] of certain common doctrinall heads, attended with their uses, motives, marks and [28] means,[307] out of which as out of an alphabet or sol fa[308] by forming and transforming, joyning and disjoyning variously a little book-craft, and two hours meditation might furnish him unspeakably to the performance of more than a weekly charge of sermoning:[309] not to reck'n up the infinit helps of interlinearies, breviaries, *synopses,* and other loitering gear.[310] But as for the

303. Hercules was a symbol of heroic physical and moral force. In *Samson Agonistes* the chorus compares Samson with him; and in *Paradise Regained* Milton compares the struggles of Christ and Satan with those of Hercules and Antaeus. (See Eugene M. Waith, *The Herculean Hero* [New York, 1962].) Hercules' heroic wanderings were extensive: their ultimate geographical limit was reached in a place where he erected two pillars (later identified as the mountains beside the Straits of Gibraltar); they became symbols of the limits of ambition and achievement. Milton has in mind the contrast between Hercules and the parochial-minded minister who has *his* reward in the secure, comfortable position of parish pastor—the ultimate that *he* aspired to.

304. This could happen if the books and ideas which would stimulate further study and intellectual growth were denied publication.

305. In contrast to Hercules, who found the limit of his circuitous wanderings and travails in the place where he erected the pillars at the end of the known world, this minister rounds out and comes to the end of his travels and studies with a concordance to the Bible in English; with a commonplace book listing choice passages under appropriate headings—passages which he earnestly gathered and saved before he graduated from college; with a harmony or handbook reconciling seeming discrepancies in Scripture; and with a catena—a "chain" or sequence of extracts from the church fathers, which he could use as a commentary.

306. *treading the constant round:* like a slave continually going round and round on a treadmill.

307. In the handbooks mentioned, especially the topic folio and catena, certain conventional doctrinal headings would be listed, each accompanied with statements of the general uses of the doctrines, the motives or persuasive inducements for accepting them, the marks or characteristics by which they could be recognized and distinguished, and the particular means of applying them. This was a conventional method of organizing sermons, tracts, etc. The marginal headings in Ussher's *A Body of Divinitie,* for example, include "The use of holy Scriptures"; "The motives used in them to perswade"; distinguishing marks such as "Their admirable power," "Their antiquity," and "The hatred of the Devil . . . against them"; and numerous entries about the means for applying them.

308. *sol fa:* musical scale.

309. I.e., rearranging the book-knowledge and two hours' thought are all he needs—and more—to enable him to perform his weekly duty of preaching.

310. *interlinearies . . . gear:* texts in ancient languages with translations on alternate lines, abridgments and digests, synopses or compendia, and similar equipment for being lazy.

multitude of Sermons ready printed and pil'd up, on every text that is not difficult, our London trading St. *Thomas* in his vestry, and adde to boot St. *Martin*, and St. *Hugh*, have not within their hallow'd limits more vendible ware of all sorts ready made:[311] so that penury he never need fear of Pulpit provision, having where so plenteously to refresh his magazin.[312] But if his rear and flanks be not impal'd,[313] if his back dore be not secur'd by the rigid licencer, but that a bold book may now and then issue forth, and give the assault to some of his old collections in their trenches, it will concern him then to keep waking, to stand in watch, to set good guards and sentinells about his receiv'd opinions, to walk the round and counter-round with his fellow inspectors, fearing lest any of his flock be seduc't, who also then would be better instructed, better exercis'd and disciplin'd. And God send that the fear of this diligence which must then be us'd, doe not make us affect the lazines of a licencing Church.

For if we be sure we are in the right, and doe not hold the truth guiltily, which becomes not, if we our selves condemn not our own weak and frivolous teaching, and the people for an untaught and

311. *But as . . . ready made:* But as for the many sermons written on every easily understood biblical text, sermons that are printed and stocked in piles ready for purchasers, there are in the holy limits of St. Thomas's vestry—and in St. Martin's and St. Hugh's also—no ready-made goods which are more vendible. Milton's general meaning is clear: a lazy pastor may easily buy ready-made sermons which he can preach to his congregation. But editors have been puzzled by the allusions. Evelyn's *Diary* (ed. E. S. de Beer [Oxford, 1955], III, 459) gives a clue. Describing the effects of the Great Fire of 1666, Evelyn relates that a roof fell into St. Faith's parish church, "which being filled with the magazines [stocks] of bookes belonging to the Stationers . . . were all consumed." It would appear that publishers and booksellers sometimes used church buildings for storage. Since the Church of St. Thomas Apostle was to the south of St. Paul's Cathedral in the area where bookselling centered, Milton is more probably referring to stocking books in its vestry than in St. Thomas' in Southwark or the Church of St. Thomas Acon (unless "vestry" is a pun on the clothing markets in its district). The Stationers Company probably used St. Martin Ludgate Church for storage because it was next door to their headquarters in Abergavenny House. There is no record of a London church dedicated to St. Hugh. However, he was a sort of unofficial patron saint of shoemakers, and it is not unlikely that the Cordwainers Company (which produced leather bindings for books) had some chapel devoted to St. Hugh. Milton's "to boot" suggests that he had these shoemakers in mind.

312. *magazin:* a repository for merchandise; also a building housing arms, ammunition, and provisions for an army. Milton uses the double-meaning of "magazine" to effect a transition from commercial to military imagery.

313. *impal'd:* fenced about with protective pales or stakes. Milton dramatically speculates that an aggressive book may slip forth to assault the parson's old collections (his catena, topic folio, etc.) which are hiding in their trenches—i.e., on their shelves, etc.

irreligious gadding rout, what can be more fair, than when a man judicious, learned, and of a conscience, for ought we know, as good as theirs that taught us what we know, shall not privily from house to house, which is more dangerous, but openly by writing publish to the world what his opinion is, what his reasons, and wherefore that which is now thought cannot be sound. Christ urg'd it as wherewith to justifie himself, that he preacht in publick;[314] yet writing is more publick than preaching; and more easie to refutation, if need be, there being so many whose businesse and profession meerly it is, to be the champions of Truth; which if they neglect, what can be imputed but their sloth, or unability?

Thus much we are hinder'd[315] and dis-inur'd[316] by this cours[317] of licencing toward the true knowledge of what we seem to know.

314. John xviii 20: "Jesus answered him, I spake openly to the world; I ever taught in the synagogue, and in the temple, whither the Jews always resort; and in secret I have said nothing."

315. The meaning depends on whether "much" goes with "thus" or with the verb: to this extent we are hindered or thus we are greatly hindered. The ambiguity may be deliberate.

316. *dis-inur'd:* retarded from or deprived of or disaccustomed to the use, practice, or operation of something.

317. *cours:* course, procedure, way, practice. This practice of licensing hinders and retards us in our progress or journey toward reaching true knowledge of what we now only seem to know (or know only in appearance but not in depth). The context is a good instance of Milton's providing clues to his meaning and of interrelating allusions. The words "hinder'd and dis-inur'd" are partially paralleled by "hurts and hinders" in the next sentence: "hurt" suggests an element of wordplay between "inur'd" and *injured;* and there is a further parallel, "hinders and retards" in the first sentence of the next paragraph. ". . . the true knowledge of what we seem to know" has its meaning clarified near the end of that paragraph where Milton refers to the mortal glass wherein we contemplate—i.e., to our seeing through, or by means of, a glass darkly, while we are in this life, in contrast to our seeing "face to face" when "we come to the *beatific* vision," when we have finished this journey of life and have reached our true destination. Underlying the passage is an imagery of questing or pilgrimage to the promised land of truth; this is contrastingly anticipated earlier in the account of the parson who, unlike the heroic Hercules, was content to end his travels in his parish and to make his circuit in the round of his handbooks. The questing or pilgrimage imagery is not fully brought out until near the end of the paragraph which follows this one, where there are echoes of the Israelites' pitching their tents, Moses' having his prospect of the Promised Land, and the Israelites' not ending their journey before proceeding into that land. Milton's point is that the procedure of the licensers is a limited and limiting course—one which hinders and stops the course of the reformation, which is itself a course or progress toward a promised land—a land to which an advance may be made along only one route—the path of truth. Englishmen had become inured or accustomed to moving toward true knowledge during the interval of unlicensed publication between the fall of the bishops and the Licensing Act. Now the licensers were trying to dis-inure and hinder them.

For how much it hurts and hinders the licencers themselves in th calling of their Ministry,[318] more than any secular employment, i they will [29] discharge that office as they ought, so that of necessity they must neglect either the one duty or the other, I insist not because it is a particular, but leave it to their own conscience, how they will decide it there.

There is yet behind of what I purpos'd to lay open, the incredible losse, and detriment that this plot of licencing puts us to,[319] more than if som enemy at sea should stop up all our hav'ns and ports, and creeks, it hinders and retards the importation of our richest Marchandize, Truth: nay it was first establisht and put in practice by Antichristian Malice and mystery on set purpose to extinguish, if it were possible, the light of Reformation, and to settle[320] falshood; little differing from that policie wherewith the Turk upholds his *Alcoran,*[321] by the prohibition of Printing. 'Tis not deny'd, but gladly confest, we are to send our thanks and vows to heav'n, louder than most of Nations, for that great measure of truth which we enjoy, especially in those main points between us and the Pope, with his appertinences the Prelats: but he who thinks we are to pitch our tent here, and have attain'd the utmost prospect of reformation,[322] that the mortall glasse wherein we contemplate, can shew us, till we come to *beatific* vision, that man by this very opinion declares, that he is yet farre short of Truth.[323]

Truth indeed came once into the world with her divine Master, and was a perfect shape most glorious to look on:[324] but when he ascended, and his Apostles after him were laid asleep, then strait

318. Milton writes as if the licensers were all clergymen; actually there we thirty-four in all, of whom twenty-two were ministers.

319. Modern punctuation would put a semicolon either here or after "creeks

320. *settle:* establish.

321. *Alcoran:* the Koran.

322. A biblical allusion is involved: after Moses had led the Israelites throu the wilderness, they pitched their tents in Moab near the river Jordan befo entering the Promised Land. Moses died before he could go into it, but first ascended to the top of Pisgah, where he had an ultimate or last "prospect" it; Deut. xxxiv 1: "And the Lord showed him all the land of Gilead," etc.

323. "The mortall glasse wherein we contemplate" alludes to 1 Cor. xiii 1 "For now we see through a glass darkly; but then [when we come to the beati vision of God after death] face to face." Milton's point is that anyone—esp cially the Presbyterian—who thinks that the reformation of the church is to e with the Solemn League and Covenant and Westminster Assembly of Divin is stopping far short of truth—stopping with "what we seem to know," that false knowledge, instead of "true knowledge."

324. John i 17: "For the law was given by Moses, but grace and truth can by Jesus Christ." Cf. in *Paradise Lost,* II, 667, 681, and X, 585 ff., the "execr ble shape" of Death who followed his master and father, Satan, into the worl

arose a wicked race of deceivers, who as that story goes of the *AEgyptian Typhon* with his conspirators, how they dealt with the good *Osiris,* took the virgin Truth, hewd her lovely form into a thousand peeces, and scatter'd them to the four winds.[325] From that time ever since, the sad friends of Truth, such as durst appear, imitating the carefull search that *Isis* made for the mangl'd body of *Osiris,* went up and down gathering up limb by limb still as they could find them.[326] We have not yet found them all, Lords and Commons, nor ever shall doe, till her Masters second comming; he shall bring together every joynt and member, and shall mould them into an immortall feature[327] of lovelines and perfection. Suffer not these licencing prohibitions to stand at every place of opportunity forbidding and disturbing them that continue seeking, that continue to do our obsequies[328] to the torn body of our martyr'd Saint. We boast our light; but if we look not wisely on the Sun it self, it smites us into darknes. Who can discern those planets that are oft *Combust,*[329] and those stars of brightest magnitude that rise

325. Condensed under this allegory and this parallel in Egyptian mythology is Milton's interpretation of early Christian history, an interpretation that is basic for an understanding of many of his ideas. According to it Christ brought into the world a perfect revelation of truth which was preached by the apostles. Then "strait," i.e., immediately after their deaths, there arose deceivers who broke up and distorted this truth. Milton found an anticipatory parallel to this destruction in the story of Osiris who brought civilization to the Egyptians but was murdered by his brother Typhon who cut the body "into fourteen pieces and flung them here and there," according to the account given by Plutarch, "Of Isis and Osiris," in his *Morals* (trans. Philemon Holland, 1657 ed., pp. 1052–53). In Milton's time such pagan myths were not regarded as mere parallels but as valid gropings toward truth by men denied the Judaic-Christian revelation. Thus to the extent that pagan accounts of the war of the Titans and their fall complemented the biblical statement that there was a war in heaven, Milton made use of those accounts as valid history when he wrote *Paradise Lost*.

326. In the Egyptian myth, Isis, wife and sister to Osiris, and Typhon searched out and assembled all the parts of the murdered body but one. So, in Milton's interpretation of Christian history, champions of truth had been searching out and trying to reassemble the perfect shape of truth as revealed in the time of Christ and the Apostles. Censorship could only impede this re-formation which would not be complete until Christ's second coming. Milton's treatment of the myth was probably influenced by Plutarch's allegorical interpretation of it (trans. Holland, p. 1048): Plutarch contrasted Isis, "most wise and full of knowledge," with Typhon, "swollen by ignorance . . . blotting out the Sacred Word . . . which this Goddesse collecteth . . . and delivereth unto those who are initiated," her goal being "the knowledge of that first Prince and Lord, who is apprehended only by intelligence and understanding."

327. *feature:* creation.

328. *obsequies:* acts of veneration and worship.

329. *Combust:* burnt or scorched (their light being overpowered by that of the sun because of their nearness to it).

and set with the Sun, untill the opposite motion of their orbs bring them to such a place in the firmament, where they may be seen evning or morning. The light which we have gain'd, was giv'n us, not to be ever staring on,[330] but by it to discover onward things more remote from our knowledge. It is not the unfrocking of a Priest, the unmitring of a Bishop, and the removing him from off the *Presbyterian* shoulders that will make us a happy Nation, no, if other things as great in the Church, and in the rule of life both economicall[331] and politicall be not lookt into and reform'd, we have lookt so long upon the blaze that *Zuinglius* and *Calvin*[332] hath beacon'd up to us, that we are stark blind. There be who perpetually complain of schisms and sects, and make it such a calamity that any man dissents from their maxims. 'Tis their own pride and ignorance which causes the disturbing, who neither will hear with meeknes, nor can convince, yet all must be supprest which is not found in their *Syntagma*.[333] They are the troublers, they are the dividers of unity, who neglect and permit not others to unite those dissever'd peeces which are yet wanting to the body of Truth. To be still searching what we know not, by what we know, still closing up[334] truth to truth as we find it (for all her body is *homogeneal*[335] and proportionall) this is the golden rule[336] in *Theology* as well as in

330. *staring on:* gazing fixedly. In this standard sense of *staring* the word is of Old English origin; but Milton's fondness for wordplay and the context make it at least possible that he had also in mind the Latin *stare*, to stand still. If so there is a momentary linking in "staring" of two of Milton's recurrent images: those of seeing, discerning, prospects, showing, blinding, eclipsing, and other aspects of vision and those of traveling, proceeding, advancing, questing, going on a pilgrimage, being hindered in progress, and being stopped on a journey—along with related images of going round and round, circling back instead of forward, etc., and, associated with vision, further image-patterns of light and darkness.

331. *economicall:* domestic.

332. Zwingli (d. 1531), who established Protestantism in Zürich, preceded Calvin as a leader of the Reformation. Milton here varies the expression of his now familiar contention that when in prospect of the Promised Land of more fully discovering truth, the Presbyterians wanted not only to end with Calvin's doctrines but, by means of licensing, to prevent others from advancing. Milton here alleges that Zwingli and Calvin set up beacons to guide seekers of truth onward—but that instead of seeing their light as blazing the way forward, Englishmen were blinded by it.

333. *Syntagma:* a collection of doctrines compiled in systematic form. Milton seems to be referring not only to handbooks (see note 310 above) but to be glancing at the Confession of Faith then being drawn up by the Westminster Assembly of Divines.

334. *closing up:* integrating.

335. *homogeneal:* homogeneous; of one nature totally self-consistent.

336. *golden rule:* in arithmetic, the Rule of Proportion, i.e., the process whereby if three quantities are known, a fourth may be found which is to the third as the second is to the first.

Arithmetick, and makes up the best harmony in a Church; not the forc't and outward union of cold, and neutrall, and inwardly divided minds.

Lords and Commons of England, consider what Nation it is whereof ye are, and whereof ye are the governours: a Nation not slow and dull, but of a quick, ingenious, and piercing spirit, acute to invent, suttle and sinewy to discours,[337] not beneath the reach of any point the highest that human capacity can soar to. Therefore the studies of learning in her deepest Sciences have bin to ancient, and so eminent among us, that Writers of good antiquity, and ablest judgement have bin perswaded that ev'n the school of *Pythagoras,*[338] and the *Persian* wisdom[339] took beginning from the old Philosophy of this Iland. And that wise and civill Roman, *Julius Agricola,*[340] who govern'd once here for *Caesar*, preferr'd the naturall wits of Britain, before the labour'd studies of the French. Nor is it for nothing that the grave and frugal *Transilvanian*[341] sends

337. *discours:* reason.

338. Michael Drayton in *Poly-Olbion*, "The First Song," remarks that the ıcient British Druids taught that "When these our souls by death our bodies do rsake, / They instantly again do other bodies take"; and John Selden coments on this doctrine of metempsychosis that Justus Lipsius "doubts whether ythagoras received it from the Druids, or they from him." (Lipsius cited Clemıt of Alexandria as his authority.) Selden in his *Law of Nature and Nations*, ii, further comments that Pythagoras traveled to Britain. Milton reverses his dgment in his *History of Britain* (*Columbia Milton*, X, 51), stating that in e Druids' "opinion of the Soules passing after Death into other Bodies, they ay be thought to have studied *Pythagoras*"; he cites Caesar, *De bello gallico*, 14, as evidence. However, Milton's sweeping statement covers not only ythagorean teaching about souls but also about numerical and musical harıony: he had made oblique reference to this in the mention of the "golden ıle" at the end of the preceding paragraph. For Milton's interest in the Pyıagorean theory of the music of the spheres, see *Prolusion II*. (The "school of ythagoras" was also a name given to Merton Hall, a twelfth-century building, robably so called because of a notion that Pythagoras had lectured there.)

339. *wisdom:* the art of magic. In *The History of Britain* (*Columbia Milton*, , 50), Milton notes that Pliny described the Druids as "skill'd in Magic no less ıan those of *Persia.*" The elder Pliny in *Natural History*, XXX, ii, comments ıat British magical ceremonies were such that it seemed almost possible that the ersians derived the art from that source. But Milton is pushing his contention to n extreme, for Pliny comments on how monstrous the rites of the Druids were; nd in *The History of Britain* (p. 51), Milton admits that they were "Progenitors ot to be glori'd in."

340. Julius Agricola was proconsul in Britain, 78–85, for the Emperors Vesasian, Titus, and Domitian (Tacitus, *Agricola*, 21).

341. Transylvania, on the northeast border of seventeenth-century Hungary, vas a buffer state nominally vassal to the Hungarian Crown, between the Iapsburg dominion and the Turks. Charles I's niece Henrietta Maria was maried to a son of George I of Transylvania. This connection and that country's esolute Protestantism apparently conduced to mature scholars' coming to Eng-

out yearly from as farre as the mountanous borders of *Russia*, a beyond the *Hercynian* wildernes,[342] not their youth, but their stay men, to learn our language, and our *theologic* [31] arts. Yet th which is above all this, the favour and love of heav'n we have gre argument to think in a peculiar manner propitious and propending[3] toward us. Why else was this Nation chos'n before any other, th out of her as out of *Sion* should be proclam'd and sounded forth t first tidings and trumpet of Reformation to all *Europ*. And had it n bin the obstinat perversnes of our Prelats against the divine and a mirable spirit of *Wicklef*, to suppresse him as a schismatic and *i novator*, perhaps neither the *Bohemian Husse* and *Jerom*,[344] nor the name of *Luther*, or of *Calvin* had bin ever known; the glo of reforming all our neighbours had bin compleatly ours. But no as our obdurat Clergy have with violence demean'd the matter, v are become hitherto the latest and backwardest Schollers, of who God offer'd to have made us the teachers.[345] Now once again b all concurrence of signs, and by the generall instinct of holy an devout men, as they daily and solemnly expresse their thought God is decreeing to begin some new and great period in his Churc ev'n to the reforming of Reformation it self: what does he then bu reveal Himself to his servants, and as his manner is, first to h English-men; I say as his manner is, first to us, though we mark n the method of his counsels, and are unworthy. Behold now this va City; a City of refuge,[346] the mansion house of liberty,[347] e compast and surrounded with his protection; the shop of warre hat not there more anvils and hammers waking, to fashion out th plates[348] and instruments of armed Justice in defence of beleaguer'

---

land to study theology, though Milton's statement that they did so has not b corroborated for the 1640s.

342. *Hercynian wildernes:* the wooded mountainous part of middle and sc Germany.

343. *propending:* inclining.

344. Jerome of Prague (d. 1416) was greatly influenced by the teaching Wiclif and Huss.

345. Now as our stubborn clergy have managed or handled the matter, have become, up to the present, the most recent and most backward stud of those whose teachers God offered to make us.

346. The Hebrews had cities of refuge where unintentional killers of r might be protected from avengers (Num. xxxv; Josh. xx 3). The context s gests that Milton thinks of London not only as a refuge from revengeful Ro ists in the civil war but chiefly as a refuge from tyranny and from those v beleaguer truth.

347. Since the residence of a lord of the manor was usually a stronghold, neighbors found refuge in it from attackers; so London is a haven where seek of truth find refuge and liberty from its opponents.

348. *plates:* armor.

Truth, than there be pens and heads there, sitting by their studious lamps, using, searching, revolving new notions and idea's wherewith to present, as with their homage and their fealty the approaching Reformation: others as fast reading, trying all things, assenting to the force of reason and convincement. What could a man require more from a Nation so pliant and so prone to seek after knowledge. What wants there to such a towardly and pregnant soile, but wise and faithfull labourers, to make a knowing people, a Nation of Prophets, of Sages, and of Worthies. We reckon more than five months yet to harvest; there need not be five weeks, had we but eyes to lift up, the fields are white already.[349] Where there is much desire to learn, there of necessity will be much arguing, much writing, many opinions; for opinion in good men is but knowledge in the making. Under these fantastic[350] terrors of [32] sect and schism, we wrong the earnest and zealous thirst after knowledge and understanding which God hath stirr'd up in this City. What some lament of, we rather should rejoyce at, should rather praise this pious forwardnes among men, to reassume the ill deputed care of their Religion into their own hands again. A little generous prudence, a little forbearance of one another,[351] and som grain of charity might win all these diligences to joyn, and unite into one generall and brotherly search after Truth; could we but forgoe this Prelaticall tradition of crowding free consciences and Christian liberties into canons and precepts of men. I doubt not, if some great and worthy stranger should come among us, wise to discern the mould and temper of a people, and how to govern it, observing the high hopes and aims, the diligent alacrity of our extended thoughts and reasonings in the pursuance of truth and freedom, but that he would cry out as *Pirrhus* did, admiring the Roman docility and courage,[352] if such were my *Epirots*, I would not despair the greatest design that could be attempted to make a Church or Kingdom happy. Yet these are the men cry'd out against for schismaticks and sectaries; as if, while the Temple of the Lord was building, some cutting, some squaring the marble, others hewing the cedars, there should be a sort of ir-

349. Cf. John iv 35: "Say not ye, There are yet four months, and then cometh harvest? behold . . . the fields; for they are white already to harvest."

350. *fantastic:* existing only in imagination.

351. Eph. iv 1–3: "walk . . . with all lowliness . . . forbearing one another in love; endeavoring to keep the unity of the Spirit in the bond of peace." Cf. Col. iii 13.

352. Pyrrhus (d. 272 B.C.), king of Epirus, after defeating the Romans at Hereclea, said: "O how easy it would be to conquer the world if I either had the Roman soldiers or were king of Rome" (Florus, *Epitome of Roman History,* I, 18).

rationall men who could not consider there must be many schisms[353] and many dissections made in the quarry and in the timber, ere the house of God can be built. And when every stone is laid artfully together, it cannot be united into a continuity, it can but be contiguous in this world; neither can every peece of the building be of one form; nay rather the perfection consists in this, that out of many moderat varieties and brotherly dissimilitudes that are not vastly disproportionall arises the goodly and gracefull symmetry that commends the whole pile and structure. Let us therefore be more considerat builders, more wise in spirituall architecture, when great reformation is expected. For now the time seems come, wherein *Moses* the great Prophet may sit in heav'n rejoycing to see that memorable and glorious wish of his fulfill'd, when not only our sev'nty Elders, but all the Lords people are become Prophets.[354] No marvell then though some men, and some good men too perhaps, but young in goodnesse, as *Joshua* then was, envy them. They fret, and out of their own weaknes are in agony, lest these divisions and subdivisions will undoe us. [33] The adversarie again applauds, and waits the hour;[355] "when they have branched themselves out," saith he, "small anough into parties and partitions, then will be our time." Fool! he sees not the firm root, out of which we all grow, though into branches:[356] nor will be aware untill he see our small divided maniples[357] cutting through at every angle of his ill united and unweildy brigade.[358] And that we are to hope better

353. *schisms:* literally, cuttings. On the building of Solomon's temple see Kings v–vi.

354. When Moses was told that two men were prophesying, one of his your attendants, Joshua said, "My lord Moses, forbid them." And Moses said un him, "Enviest thou for my sake? would God that all the Lord's people we prophets" (Num. xi 27–29).

355. In the original edition there was a comma here, without quotation mar around what follows.

356. Cf. Rom. xi 16: "if the root be holy, so are the branches."

357. *maniples:* literally, handfulls—as of branches carried by soldiers to serv as a sort of standard; militarily a maniple is a small band of soldiers.

358. In his edition (New York, 1951, p. 46), George Sabine says that th maniples are the divisions of Protestantism compared with the "unweildy" unit of Roman Catholicism. Olivier Lutaud in his edition (Paris, 1956, p. 237 agrees but suggests that Milton is perhaps also hitting at the Anglicans. Bu the application is probably still broader. Almost certainly the "adversarie" in cludes Royalists in general. Moreover, for persuasive purposes Milton has bee rhetorically assuming that London is a city of refuge and liberty in which me of varied viewpoints are reading, thinking new ideas, and writing, all in the pu suit of truth. But actually his tract is an attack on the licensing system as kind of tyranny imposed on that very London and on the nation. A few sen tences earlier, when Milton moves into direct oration with "us" in "lest thes divisions . . . will undoe us," he appears to be differentiating "us" from th

of all these supposed sects and schisms, and that we shall not need that solicitude honest perhaps though over timorous of them that vex in this behalf, but shall laugh in the end, at those malicious applauders of our differences, I have these reasons to perswade me.

First, when a City shall be as it were besieg'd and blockt about, her navigable river infested, inrodes and incursions round, defiance and battell oft rumor'd to be marching up ev'n to her walls, and suburb trenches,[359] that then the people, or the greater part, more than at other times, wholly tak'n up with the study of highest and most important matters to be reform'd, should be disputing, reasoning, reading, inventing, discoursing, ev'n to a rarity, and admiration,[360] things not before discourst or writt'n of, argues first a singular good will, contentednesse and confidence in your prudent foresight, and safe government, Lords and Commons; and from thence derives it self[361] to a gallant bravery and well grounded contempt of their enemies, as if there were no small number of as great spirits among us, as his was, who when Rome was nigh besieg'd by *Hanibal*, being in the City, bought that peece of ground at no cheap rate, whereon *Hanibal* himself encampt his own regiment.[362] Next it is a lively and cherfull presage of our happy successe and victory. For as in a body, when the blood is fresh, the spirits pure and vigorous, not only to vital, but to rationall faculties, and those in the acutest, and the pertest[363] operations of wit and suttlety, it argues in what good plight and constitution the body is, so when the cherfulnesse of the

---

adversarie," but this differentiation is obviously somewhat specious: the ultimate "adversarie" may be Roman Catholicism or prelatical Anglicanism or royalism or all three; but the immediate (though concealed) adversaries attacked by Milton are the imposers of censorship, the very audience to whom he formally addresses his literary oration, and those Presbyterians in general who were increasingly attempting to impose their uniformity on England. It is the "full united and unweildy brigade" of these men and, in particular, of their licensed publications, which will be cut through by the maniples or small bands of truth-seekers and the diversified works written by these seemingly divided "supposed sects and schisms"—Protestant groups which are unified in the root purpose of seeking truth. Milton's cleverness in rhetorically turning against the adversaries their own argument that the sectarians are disunited is noteworthy.

359. Late in 1642 the Royalist army menaced unfortified London from as close as Turnham Green. In the following summer Londoners erected a twelve-mile circle of entrenchments. See Milton's sonnet which begins "Captain or Colonel, or Knight in Arms."

360. *admiration:* even to an extent (or in a manner) highly exceptional and astounding.

361. *derives it self:* proceeds.

362. In 211 B.C. when Hannibal was encamped within Rome itself; see Livy, XXVI, 11.

363. *pertest:* most active, liveliest.

people is so sprightly up, as that it has, not only wherewith to guard well its own freedom and safety, but to spare, and bestow upon the solidest and sublimest points of controversie, and new invention, it betok'ns us not degenerated, nor drooping to a fatall decay, but casting off the old and wrincl'd skin of corruption to outlive these pangs and wax young again, entring the glorious waies of Truth and prosperous vertue destin'd to be [34] come great and honourable in these latter ages. Methinks I see in my mind a noble and puissant Nation rousing herself like a strong man after sleep and shaking her invincible locks:[364] Methinks I see her as an Eagle muing[365] her mighty youth, and kindling her undazl'd eyes at the full midday beam; purging and unscaling her long abused sight at the fountain it self of heav'nly radiance;[366] while the whole noise of timorous and flocking birds, with those also that love the twilight, flutter about, amaz'd at what she means, and in their envious gabble would prognosticat a year of sects and schisms.[367]

364. The reference is to Samson (Judg. xvi 6–20, especially, "I will go ou . . . and shake myself") and his triumph three times over Delilah's effort to learn the secret of his strength. Cf. *Reason of Church-Governement* (*Yale Milton*, I, 858–59) and its account of Samson's "illustrious and sunny locks the laws waving and curling about his god like shoulders." See Watson Kirkconnell, *That Invincible Samson: The Theme of Samson Agonistes in World Literature* (Toronto, 1964).

365. *muing:* mewing, i.e., renewing by moulting. Cf. the image of the snake casting off the skin of corruption two sentences earlier. R. S. Loomis contends that "muing" is a misprint for "newing" (*MLN*, XXXII [1917], 437–38), and G. M. Yule argues for "renuing" (*RES*, XIX [1943], 61–67).

366. I.e., the eagle renews the vigor of its youth and, undazzled by the brilliance of the sun at noon, clarifies its eyes, eliminating impurities from them, removing the scales that encumbered them as a result of long abuse, and taking fire, as it were, from the sun, which is the fountain or source of heavenly radiance. The image of renewal, brightening, and moulting-unscaling derives from the bestiaries. So England revives the vigor of its youth, taking fire or inspiration from a divine source (God, the Son [Sun], the light of the Gospel, Protestantism, the continuing Reformation, and the continuing discovery of truth) eliminating old abuses such as prelatical tyranny and gaining a clearer view of reality. Milton has in mind the parallel in the account of the conversion of Saul, the persecutor of Christians who became the Apostle Paul; Acts ix 3–22: "suddenly there shined round about him a light from heaven. . . . And he was three days without sight. . . . And Ananias . . . said . . . Jesus . . . sent me, that thou mightest receive thy sight, and be filled with the Holy Ghost. And immediately there fell from his eyes as it had been scales; and he received sight forthwith and . . . preached Christ. . . . But all that heard him were amazed, and said; Is not this he that destroyed them which called on this name . . . ? But Saul increased the more in strength."

367. In contrast to the eagle which dares to take independent flight to clear itself of prejudices, corruptions, and falsehoods in order to receive the new light, these other birds join in ineffectual flocks (fearing independence and united

What should ye doe then, should ye suppresse all this flowry crop f knowledge and new light sprung up and yet springing daily in his City, should ye set an *Oligarchy* of twenty ingrossers[368] over :, to bring a famin upon our minds again, when we shall know nothng but what is measur'd to us by their bushel? Beleeve it, Lords and Commons, they who counsell ye to such a suppressing, doe as good s bid ye suppresse your selves; and I will soon shew how. If it be lesir'd to know the immediat cause of all this free writing and free peaking, there cannot be assign'd a truer than your own mild, and ree, and human government; it is the liberty, Lords and Commons, which your own valorous and happy counsels have purchast us, liberty which is the nurse of all great wits; this is that which hath arify'd and enlightn'd our spirits like the influence of heav'n; this is hat which hath enfranchis'd, enlarg'd and lifted up our apprehenions degrees above themselves. Ye cannot make us now lesse capaole, lesse knowing, lesse eagarly pursuing of the truth, unlesse ye irst make your selves, that made us so, lesse the lovers, lesse the ounders of our true liberty. We can grow ignorant again, brutish, 'ormall, and slavish, as ye found us; but you then must first become hat which ye cannot be, oppressive, arbitrary, and tyrannous, as hey were from whom ye have free'd us. That our hearts are now nore capacious, our thoughts more erected to the search and expecation of greatest and exactest[369] things, is the issue of your owne vertu propagated in us; ye cannot suppresse that unlesse ye reinforce an abrogated and mercilesse law, that fathers may dispatch at will their own children.[370] And who shall then stick closest to ye, and excite others? not he who takes up armes for cote and conduct, and his

---

y by their fears and their dislike of truth) and make an ineffectual noise (a erence to the Westminster Assembly?), vainly fluttering about and at a loss understand the significance of what this renewed and reinvigorated nation inds to do, unable to understand the significance of what is happening. With ir envious, idle, unintelligible chatter (a reference to the debates of the stminster Assembly?), they want to prophesy (like the makers of popular nanacs or astrologers or the like) that the meaning of what is going on is t the next year will be full of divisions and dissidence. (There was conerable opposition between Parliament and the Assembly, and Milton is proby playing on this; he goes on to make an apology for the Parliamentarians r rather for a depiction of them acting as he wanted them to act. He uses same propaganda technique of flattering men for allegedly doing, or being out to do, what he wants in his sonnets to Fairfax, Vane, and Cromwell.)

368. *ingrossers:* monopolists. Milton plays on the tensions between Parliant and the Westminster Assembly, particularly the attempts of the latter to gross power to itself and to the Presbyterian ecclesiastical system.

369. *exactest:* clearest; most near truth and perfection.

370. I.e., unless you revive the ancient Roman law (abolished in A.D. 318) nich gave fathers powers of life and death over their children.

four nobles of Danegelt.[371] Although I dispraise not the defence of just immunities, yet love my [35] peace better, if that were all.[372] Give me the liberty to know, to utter, and to argue freely according to conscience, above all liberties.

What would be best advis'd then, if it be found so hurtfull and so unequall to suppresse opinions for the newnes, or the unsutablenes to a customary acceptance, will not be my task to say; I only shall repeat what I have learnt from one of your own honourable number, a right noble and pious Lord, who had he not sacrific'd his life and fortunes to the Church and Commonwealth, we had not now mist and bewayl'd a worthy and undoubted patron of this argument. Ye know him I am sure; yet I for honours sake, and may it be eternall to him, shall name him, the Lord Brook.[373] He writing of Episcopacy, and by the way treating of sects and schisms, left Ye his vote, or rather now the last words of his dying charge, which I know will ever be of dear and honour'd regard with Ye, so full of meeknes and breathing charity, that next to his last testament, who bequeathed love and peace to his Disciples,[374] I cannot call to mind where I have read or heard words more mild and peacefull. He there ex-

371. *not he . . . Danegelt:* not the man who takes up arms to fight becaus of illegal taxation. Coat and conduct money was a county tax for clothing an moving new troops which Charles I tried to get without Parliament's consent his attempts to collect shipmoney or "Danegelt," a tax originally gathered for fleet to repel (or a bribe to placate) the Danes, met the famous resistance o John Hampden. Such attacks on what Milton called "just immunities" in th next sentence were among the causes of the civil war. Four of the coins calle nobles were worth £1 4*s.* 12*d.*, approximately the sum (£1) demanded in th Hampden case. The meaning of the passage is disputed: Who will adhere mos closely to you and stir up others to do so? (a)—not the man whose motivatin concern is in external, material things such as the preservation of his immunit from taxation illegally imposed, even if the sum immediately involved is small (b)—not the man who initially took up arms on principle because of illegal taxa tion, despite the fact that the actual sum involved was slight; for if you suppres liberty such men of principle will not support you.

372. I.e., although I do not disparage or disapprove of the defense of legiti mate rights and privileges [such as freedom from illegal taxes, from trial b others than my peers, and from arbitrary imprisonment], I love my peace an tranquillity better—or would do so if the matter stopped there. Milton goes o to indicate that more is involved—the liberty to know, to speak, and to argu freely, which he cherishes above all other liberties and privileges.

373. Robert Greville, second Lord Brooke (1608–43), a supporter of th parliamentary cause in the House of Lords and a general in the parliamentar army. He was killed in action.

374. John xiv 15–31, especially verse 21, "he that loveth me shall be love of my Father, and I will love him," and verse 27, "Peace I leave with you, m peace I give unto you"; and John xv 10, "If ye keep my commandments, y shall abide in my love; even as I have kept my Father's commandments, an abide in his love."

horts us to hear with patience and humility those, however they may be miscall'd, that desire to live purely, in such use of Gods Ordinances, as the best guidance of their conscience gives them, and to tolerat them, though in some disconformity to our selves.[375] The book it self will tell us more at large being publisht to the world, and dedicated to the Parlament by him who both for his life and for his death deserves, that what advice he left be not laid by without perusall.

And now the time in speciall is,[376] by priviledge to write and speak what may help the furder discussing of matters in agitation. The Temple of *Janus* with his two *controversal* faces might now not unsignificantly be set open.[377] And though all the windes of doctrin were let loose to play upon the earth,[378] so Truth be in the field, we do injuriously by licencing and prohibiting to misdoubt her strength. Let her and Falshood grapple; who ever knew Truth put to the wors, in a free and open encounter. Her confuting is the best and surest suppressing. He who hears what praying there is for light and clearer knowledge to be sent down among us, would think of other matters to be constituted beyond the discipline of *Geneva,*[379] fram'd and fabric'd[380] already to our hands. Yet when the [36] new light which we beg for shines in upon us, there be who envy and oppose, if it come not first in at their casements. What a collusion is this, whenas we are exhorted by the wise man to use diligence, *to seek for wisdom as for hidd'n treasures*[381] early and late, that another order shall enjoyn us to know nothing but by statute. When a man hath

375. Milton refers to the final section of Brooke's *A Discourse Opening the Nature of that Episcopacie, which is Exercised in England* (1641), 2nd ed., 1642 (repr. in William Haller, ed., *Tracts on Liberty in the Puritan Revolution, 1638–1647* [New York, 1934], II, 37 ff.), especially the end (1642 ed., pp. 117–18).

376. Now the time is especially appropriate with Parliament and the Westminster Assembly both sitting in a time of civil war.

377. The Roman god with two faces looking in opposite directions. (A pun on "controversial" is probably also intended.) He had a temple in the Forum whose two doors, likewise facing in opposite directions, were opened in time of war but kept shut in peace. Milton's point is that at a time when Truth and Falsehood are grappling, it would be meaningful to open the doors.

378. Eph. iv 14–15: "That we henceforth be no more children, tossed to and fro, and carried about with every wind of doctrine, by the sleight of men, and cunning craftiness, whereby they lie in wait to deceive; but speaking the truth in love, may grow up into him in all things, which is the head, even Christ."

379. *discipline of Geneva:* Presbyterianism.

380. *fram'd and fabric'd:* composed and constructed.

381. Prov. ii 4–6: "If thou seekest her as silver, and searchest for her as for hid treasures; then shalt thou . . . find the knowledge of God. For the Lord giveth wisdom."

bin labouring the hardest labour in the deep mines of knowledge, hath furnisht out his findings in all their equipage, drawn forth his reasons as it were a battell raung'd,[382] scatter'd and defeated all objections in his way, calls out his adversary into the plain, offers him the advantage of wind and sun, if he please; only that he may try the matter by dint of argument, for his opponents then to sculk, to lay ambushments, to keep a narrow bridge of licencing where the challenger should passe, though it be valour enough in shouldiership, is but weaknes and cowardise in the wars of Truth. For who knows not that Truth is strong next to the Almighty; she needs no policies, nor stratagems, nor licensings to make her victorious;[383] Those are the shifts and the defences that error uses against her power: give her but room, and do not bind her when she sleeps, for then she speaks not true, as the old *Proteus*[384] did, who spake oracles only when he was caught and bound, but then rather she turns herself into all shapes, except her own, and perhaps tunes her voice according to the time, as *Micaiah* did before *Ahab*,[385] untill she be adjur'd to her own likenes.[386] Yet is it not impossible that she may have more shapes than one. What else is all that rank of things indifferent,[387] wherein Truth may be on this side, or on the other, without being unlike her self. What but a vain shadow else is the abolition of *those ordinances, that hand writing nayl'd to the crosse*,[388] what great purchase is this Christian liberty which *Paul* so

382. *battell raung'd:* arranged like an army drawn up for battle.
383. Comma in the original edition.
384. *Proteus:* an elusive sea-god.
385. 1 Kings xxii 1–37, especially verses 13–15. King Ahab's messenger urged Micaiah, prophet of the Lord, to "declare good unto the king" as the other prophets had done. Micaiah agreed and conformed, predicting a victory for Ahab. However, he later recovered his integrity and accurately prophesied defeat.
386. *adjur'd to her own likenes:* bound to an oath under penalty. Cf. 2 Chron. xviii, where Ahab says to Micaiah, "How many times shall I adjure thee that thou say nothing but the truth to me in the name of the Lord?"
387. Cf. Ecclus. xxvii 1: "Many have sinned for a small matter [*margin:* a thing indifferent]."
388. Cf. Col. ii 8–17: "Beware lest any man spoil you through philosophy and vain deceit, after the tradition of men, after the rudiments of the world, and not after Christ. . . . And you . . . hath he quickened . . . having forgiven you all trespasses; blotting out the handwriting of ordinances that was against us, which was contrary to us, and took it out of the way, nailing it to his cross. Let no man therefore judge you in meat, or in drink, or in respect of an holyday, or of the new moon, or of the sabbath days: which are a shadow of things to come. . . ." Milton's point is that truth may have different appearances despite its basic unity and simplicity. The truth may be on either side in matters indifferent. It may take the form of a foreshadowing or type or prefiguring, a truth revealed "according to the time," which later is more fully and more clearly revealed—as the sacrifice of Isaac prefigures the sacrifice of Christ in

often boasts of.[389] His doctrine is, that he who eats or eats not, regards a day, or regards it not, may doe either to the Lord.[390] How many other things might be tolerated in peace, and left to conscience, had we but charity, and were not the chief strong hold of our hypocrisie to be ever judging one another. I fear yet this iron yoke of outward conformity hath left a slavish print upon our necks; the ghost of a linnen decency[391] yet haunts us. We stumble and are impatient at the least dividing of one visible congregation from another, though it be not in fundamentalls; and through our forwardnes to suppresse, and our backwardnes to recover any [37] enthrall'd peece of truth out of the gripe of custom,[392] we care not to keep truth separated from truth, which is the fiercest rent and disunion of all. We doe not see that while we still affect by all means a rigid externall formality, we may as soon fall again into a grosse conforming stupidity, a stark and dead congealment of *wood and hay and stubble*[393] forc't and frozen together, which is more to the sudden degenerating of a Church than many *subdichotomies*[394] of petty schisms. Not that I can think well of every light separation, or that all in a Church is to be expected *gold and silver and pretious stones:*[395] it is

---

hristian teaching. So in the passage quoted from Colossians, Paul treats the gulations of the Mosaic law concerning diet, holy days, and the sabbath as reshadowings of later Christian revelations, as ordinances abolished, and obacles taken out of the way of Christians by means of the crucifixion.

389. E.g., Gal. v 1, "the liberty wherewith Christ hath made us free"; Rom. ii 21, "the glorious liberty of the children of God"; cf. Acts xx 28, "which he th purchased with his own blood" and 2 Pet. ii 1, "the Lord that bought em."

390. Rom. xiv 3–20.

391. *the ghost of a linnen decency:* the external formalism of surplices and stments. Cf. Milton's attack on calling "the Py-bald frippery, and ostentation Ceremony's decency" in *Of Reformation* (1641 ed., p. 4). Cf. *Constitutions d Canons Ecclesiasticall* (1640), Canons VII: ". . . the Administration of ly things is to be performed with all possible decency and reverence"; and III: "the Preaching of Order and Decencie, according to *St. Pauls* rule, doth nduce to edification" (*Yale Milton,* I, 992–93).

392. Cf. the attack on custom at the beginning of *Doctrine and Discipline.*

393. The wood, hay, and stubble represent the labor of some men in contrast that of others who build gold, silver, and precious stones on the Christian undation. Cf. 1 Cor. iii 10–13, where St. Paul says that he has laid the foundaon, which is Christ, "but let every man take heed how he buildeth thereupon. . . Now if any man build upon this foundation gold, silver, precious stones, ood, hay, stubble; every man's work shall be made manifest . . . because it all be revealed by fire; and the fire shall try every man's work of what sort is."

394. *subdichotomies:* minor divisions.

395. See note 393. When tried by fire, the dead congealment of wood, hay, d stubble will prove no solid or worthwhile building, but that built heedfully ill endure.

not possible for man to sever the wheat from the tares,[396] the good fish from the other frie; that must be the Angels Ministry at the end of mortall things.[397] Yet if all cannot be of one mind, as who looks they should be? this doubtles is more wholsome, more prudent, and more Christian that may be tolerated, rather than all compell'd. I mean not tolerated Popery, and open superstition, which as it extirpats all religions and civill supremacies, so it self should be extirpat, provided first that all charitable and compassionat means be us'd to win and regain the weak and the misled: that also which is impious or evil absolutely either against faith or maners[398] no law can possibly permit, that intends not to unlaw it self: but those neighboring differences, or rather indifferences, are what I speak of, whether in some point of doctrine or of discipline, which though they may be many, yet need not interrupt *the unity of Spirit*, if we could but find among us *the bond of peace*.[399] In the mean while if any one would write, and bring his helpfull hand to the slow-moving Reformation which we labour under, if Truth have spok'n to him before others, or seem'd at least to speak, who hath so bejesuited us that we should trouble that man with asking licence to doe so worthy a deed? and consider this, that if it come to prohibiting, there is not ought more likely to be prohibited than truth it self; whose first appearance to our eyes blear'd and dimm'd with prejudice and custom, is more unsightly and unplausible than many errors, even as the person is of many a great man slight and contemptible to see to.[400] And what doe they tell us vainly of new opinions, when this very opinion of theirs, that none must be heard, but whom they like, is the worst and newest opinion of all others; and is the chief cause why sects and schisms doe so much abound, and true knowledge is kept at distance from us; besides yet a greater [38] danger which is in it. For when God shakes a Kingdome with strong and healthfull commotions to a generall reforming,[401] 'tis not untrue that many sectaries and false teachers are then busiest in seducing; but yet more true it is, that God then raises to his own work men of rare abilities, and more than common industry not only to look back and revise

396. Matt. xiii 13–43.

397. Matt. xiii 39: "and the reapers are the angels."

398. *maners:* conduct in its moral aspect. Cf. 1 Cor. xv 33: "evil communications corrupt good manners."

399. Eph. iv 3.

400. E.g., St. Paul who declared himself "weak" in his "bodily presence" (2 Cor. x 10), and Elizabeth I's prime minister, Lord Burleigh.

401. Hag. ii 6–7: "For thus saith the Lord of hosts; Yet once, it is a little while, and I will shake the heavens, and the earth, and the sea, and the dry land; and I will shake all nations, and the desire of all nations shall come; and I will fill this house with glory."

what hath bin taught heretofore, but to gain furder and goe on, some new enlightn'd steps in the discovery of truth. For such is the order of Gods enlightning his Church, to dispense and deal out by degrees his beam,[402] so as our earthly eyes may best sustain it. Neither is God appointed and confin'd, where and out of what place these his chosen shall be first heard to speak; for he sees not as man sees, chooses not as man chooses,[403] lest we should devote ourselves again to set places, and assemblies, and outward callings of men;[404] planting our faith one while in the old Convocation house, and another while in the Chappell at Westminster;[405] when all the faith and religion that shall be there canoniz'd,[406] is not sufficient without plain convincement, and the charity of patient instruction to supple the least bruise of conscience, to edifie the meanest Christian, who desires to walk in the Spirit, and not in the letter of human trust, for all the number of voices that can be there made; no though *Harry* the 7. himself there, with all his leige tombs about him,[407] should lend them voices from the dead, to swell their number. And if the men be erroneous who appear to be the leading schismaticks, what witholds us but our sloth, our self-will, and distrust in the right cause, that we doe not give them gentle meetings and gentle dismissions, that we debate not and examin the matter throughly with liberall and frequent audience; if not for their sakes,

402. Cf. *Paradise Lost,* III, 2, "of th' Eternal Coeternal beam."

403. 1 Cor. i 26–28: "For ye see your calling, brethren, how that not many wise men after the flesh, not many mighty, not many noble, are called: but God hath chosen the foolish things of the world to confound the wise; and God hath chosen the weak things of the world to confound the things which are mighty; and base things of the world, and things which are despised, hath God chosen, yea, and things which are not, to bring to nought things that are."

404. Cf. *Paradise Lost,* XI, 836–38: "God attributes to place / No sanctitie, if none be thither brought / By Men who there frequent, or therein dwell"; "set places" also refers to established offices and those who hold them. Cf. the words of Jesus to the Samaritan woman in John iv 21. Milton is also referring to the Westminster Assembly and, ironically, to the words, "an inward calling of God," with which the Presbyterian ministers justified their claim to divine calling.

405. The clergy of the Church of England assembled for national convocations in the Chapter-house at Westminster until the Long Parliament transferred their powers (adding a few more) to the Assembly of Divines which was meeting, as Milton wrote, in Henry VII's Chapel, also in Westminster.

406. *canoniz'd:* embodied in canons with the intention that they would be imposed on the nation by Parliament. Milton here probably also played ironically on canonized in the sense of consecrated. The Assembly was drawing up a Confession of Faith, the Longer and Shorter Catechisms, a Directory of Worship, and a plan for presbyterian church-government.

407. Henry VII was buried in the Chapel surrounded by tombs which included some who had owed feudal allegiance to him.

yet for our own? seeing no man who hath tasted learning, but will confesse the many waies of profiting by those who not contented with stale receits are able to manage,[408] and set forth new positions to the world. And were they but as the dust and cinders of our feet, so long as in that notion they may yet serve to polish and brighten the armoury of Truth, ev'n for that respect they were not utterly to be cast away. But if they be of those whom God hath fitted for the speciall use of these times with eminent and ample gifts, and those perhaps neither among the Priests, nor among the Pharisees,[409] and we in the hast of a precipitant zeal shall make no distinction, but resolve to stop their mouths, because we fear they [39] come with new and dangerous opinions, as we commonly forejudge them ere we understand them, no lesse than woe to us, while thinking thus to defend the Gospel, we are found the persecutors.

There have bin not a few since the beginning of this Parlament, both of the Presbytery and others who by their unlicenc't books to the contempt of an *Imprimatur* first broke that triple ice clung[410] about our hearts, and taught the people to see day: I hope that none of those were the perswaders to renew upon us this bondage which they themselves have wrought so much good by contemning. But if neither the check that *Moses* gave to young *Joshua,*[411] nor the countermand which our Saviour gave to young *John*, who was so ready to prohibit those whom he thought unlicenc't,[412] be not anough to admonish our Elders[413] how unacceptable to God their testy mood of prohibiting is, if neither their own remembrance what evill hath abounded in the Church by this lett[414] of licencing, and what good they themselves have begun by transgressing it, be not anough, but that they will perswade, and execute the most *Domini-*

408. *manage:* take up; organize and use rationally.

409. I.e., neither among the priests, who had a right to speak by virtue of their office, nor among the Pharisees, who ascribed superior righteousness to themselves and assumed special privileges they denied to others; cf. Matt. xxiii 13: "But woe unto you, scribes and Pharisees, hypocrites! for ye shut up the kingdom of heaven against men."

410. *clung:* stuck fast; congealed. Milton here combines his recurrent imageries of freezing and adhesion and involves them with images of breaking, vision, and light. The interplay of such image patterns is one of the most fascinating features of *Areopagitica.* Another such feature is his allusiveness; for "triple ice" echoes Horace, *Carmina,* i.3.9: *et aes triplex / Circa pectus erat.*

411. See note 354 above.

412. John, traditionally the youngest of the apostles, said (Luke ix 49–50), "Master, we saw one casting out devils in thy name; and we forbade him, because he followed not with us. And Jesus said unto him, Forbid him not: for he that is not against us is for us."

413 *Elders:* The word *presbyterian* derives from Greek *presbuteros,* elderly.

414. *lett:* obstruction.

can[415] part of the Inquisition over us, and are already with one foot in the stirrup so active at suppressing, it would be no unequall distribution in the first place to suppresse the suppressors themselves; whom the change of their condition hath puft up, more than their late experience of harder times hath made wise.

And as for regulating the Presse, let no man think to have the honour of advising ye better than your selves have done in that Order publisht next before this,[416] that no book be Printed, unlesse the Printers and the Authors name, or at least the Printers be register'd. Those which otherwise come forth, if they be found mischievous and libellous, the fire and the executioner will be the timeliest and the most effectuall remedy, that mans prevention can use.[417] For this *authentic* Spanish policy of licencing books, if I have said ought, will prove the most unlicenc't book it self within a short while; and was the immediat image of a Star-chamber decree[418] to that purpose made in those very times when that Court did the rest of those her pious works, for which she is now fall'n from the Starres[419] with *Lucifer*. Whereby ye may guesse what kinde of State prudence, what love of the people, what care of Religion, or good manners there was at the contriving, although with singular hypocrisie it pretended to bind books to their good behaviour. [40] And how it got the upper hand of your precedent Order so well constituted before, if we may beleeve those men whose profession gives them cause to enquire most, it may be doubted[420] there was in it the fraud of some old *patentees* and *monopolizers* in the trade of book-selling; who under pretence of the poor in their Company not to be defrauded, and the just retaining of each man his severall copy,[421] which God forbid should be gainsaid, brought divers glosing colours[422] to the House, which were indeed but colours, and serving to no end except it be to exercise a superiority over their neighbours, men who doe not therefore labour in an honest profession to which learning is in-

415. Most of the inquisitors belonged to the Dominican order.

416. *before this:* the Order of January 29, 1642.

417. Condemned books were ordinarily burned by the executioner, and he also inflicted any physical punishment such as ear-cropping ordered for the printer or author or both.

418. Decree of July 11, 1637. Sirluck (*Yale Milton,* II, 159) describes it as "the fruit of a century of experience" and "the most elaborate instrument in English history for the suppression of undesired publication; nothing was unforeseen except the determination with which it was defied."

419. *fall'n from the Starres:* on July 5, 1641, the Court of Star Chamber was abolished.

420. *doubted:* suspected.

421. *copy:* copyright.

422. *divers glosing colours:* misrepresentations, specious colorings of the truth.

detted, that they should be made other mens vassalls. Another end is thought was aym'd at by some of them in procuring by petition[423] this Order, that having power in their hands, malignant[424] books might the easier escape abroad, as the event shews. But of these *Sophisms* and *Elenchs* of marchandize[425] I skill not: This I know, that errors in a good government and in a bad are equally most incident; for what Magistrate may not be mis-inform'd, and much the sooner, if liberty of Printing be reduc't to the power of a few; but to redresse willingly and speedily what hath bin err'd, and in highest autority to esteem a plain advertisement[426] more than others have done a sumtuous bribe, is a vertue (honour'd Lords and Commons) answerable to Your highest actions, and whereof none can participat but greatest and wiest men.

The End.

423. In April 1643, the Stationers Company petitioned Parliament to restore the control of the press which fell with the Star Chamber: in the public interest there should be a "well-ordered" press; failure to regulate printing would result in poor publishers and an abundance of errors and heresies: "The main care is to appoint severe Examiners for the licensing of things profitable, and suppressing of things harmfull"; and it would be wise to have the Stationers participate in the prosecution of such an order.

424. *malignant:* royalist.

425. *marchandize:* logically fallacious, misleading arguments used to deceive and misrepresent in commerce. Milton denies that he has any expertise in such misrepresentations and sophistical refutations.

426. *advertisement:* a simple warning or notification of the facts.

THE ANTI-MONARCHICAL TRACTS, 1649

EDITED BY JOHN T. SHAWCROSS

Foreword

Complete text of the first edition, February 1649
The Tenure of Kings and Magistrates

Summary with extracts (BY J. MAX PATRICK):
Observations upon the Articles of Peace with the Irish Rebels

Eikonoklastes

FOREWORD

The Tenure of Kings and Magistrates is a tract arguing that kings owe their power to the people, whom they are supposed to represent; when they overstep their power and become tyrannical, it becomes incumbent upon the people to remove them. The trial of Charles I in January 1649 and the protest it raised provoked this philosophic argument from Milton to justify the action against the king and thus expose what he considered false reason on the part of the opposition. The tract, written in the form of an oration, at least brought Milton to the attention of the government being formed under Oliver Cromwell and started another phase of his public career.

The background of *The Tenure* covers a number of years and is quite involved; for this reason, only information essential to understanding the pamphlet, rather than an analysis of the entire religious and political situation, is summarized here.

In the first civil war (1642–46), one point of opposition to Charles I was the abolition of episcopacy. Most of those desiring the removal of the bishops' authority fought on the side of Parliament and were divided into two primary factions: the Presbyterians and the Independents. The former demanded church government through a hierarchy of synods (or classes), and favored a defensive war and a negotiated peace. The latter, seeing in Presbyterianism a polity as potentially tyrannical as prelacy, argued for toleration within specified limits and freedom of conscience and favored a war fought to a decisive conclusion over national, rather than regional, issues. The Independents also found toleration politically expedient in pushing through Parliament the establishment of the New Model Army in 1644 and the Self-Denying Ordinance in April 1645. This ordinance relieved peers of their commissions, opening the way for an army of career men regardless of social status.

The Nineteen Propositions of Newcastle offered to the king by Parliament on July 13, 1646, after his surrender, proposed the establishment of a Presbyterian church as approved by Parliament in March of that year, and insisted upon parliamentary control of the army. But Charles did not accept the Propositions, apparently playing a waiting game and hoping to profit by the dissension among his enemies. During the following months there were abortive attempts at reconciliation between the king and Parliament, with the rise of yet another political force: the army. As a seedbed for Independency, the army refused to disband in 1647 when ordered to do so by Parliament. The army was prompted to refuse not only because they were the main supporters of toleration but also by the arrears of unpaid wages, which were a constant problem throughout the next two years. With revolt incipient, Parliament, in which the Presbyterians were now in the majority, proposed to restore the king's authority to what it was in August 1641 if he would establish a Presbyterian church for three years. To this he conceded on May 12, 1647, in his third answer to the Propositions of Newcastle. But the army prevented this alliance between king and Parliament by capturing the king. Oliver Cromwell finally persuaded the army to offer the king the Heads of Proposals, which would limit the king's power and restrict the state's powers over the liberty of individuals. Religious liberty would be gained, and parliamentary control of the army and offices of state affirmed. These negotiations and the king's refusal of them aided the Levellers, a radical group advocating popular sovereignty with Parliament as the people's representative; they suggested in the Army Council the Agreement of the People, a document to be approved by popular vote, which would establish a government without king or House of Lords, and with a single ruling house to be elected by "the people" (as Article III states but does not define). Some of the aims of Leveller theory included the redistribution of the franchise, legal reform, abolition of a state church, and of the privileges of peers. The debates concentrated on the concept of natural rights and of the role of the people in government, main bases for Milton's argument in *The Tenure*. Cromwell and other army officers persuaded the Levellers and the army to moderate their demands and to present the Agreement to Parliament for action. But in the meantime Charles rejected any further negotiations.

In the Engagement with the Scots commissioners, signed on December 26, 1647, Charles agreed to establish a Presbyterian church in Scotland and England for three years in return for his restoration. Provoked by Charles' indecision, uncertain whether he could be trusted, and annoyed at the rejection of the Four Bills (for the most part, a request for acceptance of the Propositions of Newcastle), Parliament, on January 3, 1648, voted "No More Addresses" with Charles. Under the Duke of Hamilton, the Scots invaded England and the army rose to the threat by unifying its forces and settling its disputes. The second civil war was over, however, by August with Cromwell's defeat of the Scots at the battle of Preston (August 17–20). From September through November 1648, further negotiations for settlement followed with the so-called Treaty of Newport rescinding "No More Addresses." But nothing definite emerged from these talks and, on November 20, the House of Commons passed *A Remonstrance of His Excellency Thomas Lord Fairfax, Lord Generall of the Parliaments Forces, and of the Generall Councell of Officers,* which defended the army's action against the king, demanded reforms in legislation and a republican administration with impartial justice for all, proposed regular payment of soldiers, and called for the immediate dissolution of the Long Parliament. Though this remonstrance was illegal under parliamentary rules, the army protested that it was justified by expediency. Objections, notably set forth in a speech by William Prynne in Parliament on December 4, which dealt with "the Satisfactoriness of the Kings Answers to the Propositions for the Settlement of a Firm and Lasting Peace, and Future Security of the Subjects against All Feared Regal Invasions," deplored the army's "supreme Anarchical Tyranny" and pointed to the king's accession to demands for a limited Presbyterianism. It was the reasoning behind Prynne's argument which Milton felt compelled to attack a month later: that the king was divine, and army action constituted destruction of government and peace. And then on December 6, Colonel Pride purged the Presbyterian members from Parliament, leaving only about ninety members on the rolls. The Rump, the remaining fifty or so members, represented the army.

The most immediate cause of Milton's writing was the presentation to the Commons on January 20, 1649, of *A Serious and Faithfull Representation of the Judgements of Ministers of the Gospel within the Province of London,* which protested the *Remonstrance,* appealing to Royalists and Presbyterians alike against the army, which three days before had approved a modified version of the Agreement of the People. A main recourse in this and the numerous other tracts appearing in the last months of 1648 and January 1649 was to Scripture, interpreted to cast God's disapproval on the action against the king. To counter the effect these biblical references might produce, Milton also cites and explicates Scripture throughout his pamphlet, but he arrives at opposite and more concatenated conclusions. The discussion was primarily concerned with the disposition of the king during his trial, then under way. The Commons' ordinance to create a commission to try Charles, although rejected by the Lords, was passed, accompanied by resolutions that the people hold all judicial power, that the Commons represent the people, and that its decision was therefore law despite disapproval by the king or the House of Lords. The period of the trial began on January 6 and ended on January 25. The king was condemned on January 26–27; sentence of execution was signed on January 29; he was beheaded on January 30. Although it was obvious before the trial that the king would be found guilty despite the speeches to exonerate him of at least part of the accusations, the sentence itself was not certain, and the circumstances of the trial helped pave the way for the picture of Charles as a martyr.

With the execution of Charles, government as formerly known disappeared and the Rump had to establish a new instrument. They abolished kingship and the House of Lords and declared England a Commonwealth, an action foreshadowed by the constitutional proposals previously noted. The Rump was continued, despite some demands for its dissolution, for it provided some civil safeguards against otherwise outright military rule by the army. The new government's Council of State was to be appointed annually by Parliament and used as its executive branch. Toleration was extended to most religious groups, excepting Roman Catholics, Episcopalians, and some extreme sects. But factional agitation continued until 1653, when Cromwell dissolved Parliament by force, primarily because it had neglected certain proposals of the Agreement of the People. It was replaced by a protectorate under the Instrument of Government, a constitution calling for rule by a Lord Protector, with advice from a council of state.

The Tract and Its Results

Milton's support of the new government with *The Tenure of Kings and Magistrates* began in the midst of the discussions of January 1649. In *The Tenure* Milton argues that the power of kings and magistrates has been conferred upon them by the people in covenant for common peace and benefit; when their power is abused, it is the people's right and duty to reassume that power or to alter it in whatever way is most conducive to public good. The people's natural rights as God's creatures predicate this conception of the social contract. Its elements as presented by Milton and its abrogation by tyranny should be read against the background of Aristotle's *Ethics*, particularly Book VIII, and *Politics*, particularly Books III, IV, and V, from which it often derives. Following Calvinist principle, Milton contends that popular resistance to royal or civil authority is lawful when executed by magistrates properly charged with responsibility or when man's divinely free conscience is trespassed by secular action. A major question impeding acceptance of his thesis was the alleged divinity of the king, the "Lord's Anointed." Milton denied royal divinity, reasoning that kings of England were so designated "not of God," but because they "were more bloody then the rest" (1649 ed., p. 25), and "that to say Kings are accountable to none but God, is the overturning of all Law and goverment" (p. 11).

The tract is organized like the prolusion: there are an *exordium* (introduction to capture attention), pages 1–8; a *narration* (statements of "facts" underlying the thesis), pages 8–17, with a kind of division (those matters in contention in the order of discussion), pages 10–17; a *confirmation* (proof of statements), pages 17–25; a *refutation* (denial of opposing arguments), pages 25–28; and a *peroration* (final summing up), pages 29–42. Milton's task was to set down how kings came into being, their responsibilities, the nature of tyranny, and the duty of the people to depose and punish the tyrant legally. He does not concern himself with judging or sentencing Charles. He argues his case by citing authority and by a logic basically Ramist and syllogistic.

The deliberative rhetoric of the tract has not been sufficiently recognized: this branch of rhetoric aimed to persuade (not to accuse or defend, nor to praise or blame); it was concerned with future action; and it vindicated the expedient and exposed the harmful. Milton hoped by his pamphlet to prepare his countrymen to achieve true happiness in a theocracy under the Puritan government. The recent events were preliminary to a permanent settlement leading to the age of Christ in the millennium. An Antichrist was being removed from power, and the factionalism rising from failure to recognize this Antichrist had to be exposed. Milton calls earnestly and calmly all good and faithful Christians "not to fall off from thir first principles; nor to affect rigor and superiority over men not under them; not to compell unforcible things in Religion especially . . . ; nor to assist the clamor and malicious drifts of men whom they themselves have judg'd to be the worst of men . . . ; nor to dart against the actions of thir brethren" (p. 39). And divines are admonished "to attend the office of good Pastors" (p. 41) and to join "the vengeance of God, and the zeale of his people" (p. 42). Milton's aim has been to allay the people's perturbation and to reunite them by disposing of this divisive issue so that the work of the Holy Community can go forward under the Sword of Justice, the two-handed Sword of Michael, for "Heav'n the seat of bliss / Brooks not the works of violence and Warr" (*Paradise Lost* VI, 273–74).

As in the prelatical dispute, Milton did not interrupt his other and personal activities until the political discussion was well advanced. When the second civil war ended with Fairfax's capture of Colchester in August 1648, Milton was apparently at work on various poetic and prose writings, such as *The History of Britain*, having retired from public controversy after the derision which greeted his divorce tracts in 1645. The political events of the last half of 1648 and the frenetic pamphleteering of December and January, however, aroused him to produce *The Tenure of Kings and Magistrates*, with no apparent commission or external pressure. He conceived his action as "a nobler task," freeing "Truth, and Right from Violence" (as he had urged Fairfax to do). The internal compulsion must have been akin to that expressed in his statement in *Reason of Church-Governement* demanding his attention against the prelates: "should the Church be brought under heavy oppression, and God have given me ability the while to reason against that man that should be the author of so foul a deed, or should she by blessing from above on the industry and courage of faithfull men change this her distracted estate into better daies without the lest furtherance or contribution of those few talents which God at that present had lent me, I foresee what stories I should heare within my selfe, all my life after, of discourage and reproach" (1642 ed., p. 35).

The tract called him to the attention of the new government being formed, within which he undoubtedly had many acquaintances, and he was appointed Secretary for Foreign Tongues to the

Council of State on March 15, 1649, a post concerned with writing (mainly in Latin) and translating official letters and documents and drafting governmental replies to its critics.

Milton's *Observations on the Articles of Peace* was printed in May 1649 along with those Articles of Peace "Made and Concluded with the *Irish* Rebels, and Papists, by James Earle of Ormond, For and in behalfe of the late King, and by vertue of his Autoritie" on January 17, plus "A Representation of the *Scotch* Presbytery at *Belfast* in *Ireland*," declared on February 15. The peace treaty, promising independence, was a bid for Irish aid against the Parliamentarians. Cromwell's government felt constrained to expose the treachery of the treaty, since fear of Roman Catholicism loomed large, and to open to public view the alignment of the Ulster Presbyterians with Ormond.

On the day of Charles's burial, February 8, *Eikon Basilike: The Portraiture of His Sacred Majesty in his Solitudes and Sufferings* appeared, written probably by John Gauden, the king's chaplain, with possibly some help from the king, but purporting to be "The King's Book." When Milton undertook to answer this pious vindication is not known, but he seems to have worked on *Eikonoklastes* intermittently from late August through sometime before the beginning of October when it was printed. His chapter by chapter refutation perhaps caused more indignation than support, yet it was republished with slight additions in 1650. A denunciation of the regicides by Claude de Saumaise (Salmasius), *Defensio Regia pro Carolo I*, appeared in England by November 1649, and provoked Milton's next pamphlet, *Pro Populo Anglicano Defensio*, in February 1651. Since January 8, 1650, the date of the Council order, Milton had labored on his noble task in liberty's defense "Of which all *Europe* talks from side to side" (as he liked to hope, in *Sonnet 22*), expanding the concept of natural law central to *The Tenure*. (*Eikonoklastes* and *Pro Populo Anglicano Defensio* were burned at the end of August 1660, shortly before Milton's imprisonment.) In the meantime during the years 1649–51 Milton's studies and personal writings languished.

Date, Editions, and Text of The Tenure of Kings and Magistrates

First printed on or before February 13, 1649, the date inscribed by the bookseller George Thomason in his copy now in the British

Museum, *The Tenure of Kings and Magistrates* seems to have been written during the week or two of January 15 to January 29. The argument is involved because of interpretations suggesting its composition after the king's execution, but see my discussion in *Papers of the Bibliographical Society of America,* listed below.

The first edition is dated 1649; the second, somewhat expanded, both 1649 and 1650. There would seem to be three states of the title page and two of the text of the second edition; these are discussed in the aforementioned article. The main difference between the two editions is that the second adds or alters a few words or lines throughout the text, primarily to clarify a thought or issue, and appends some thirteen and a half pages of testimonies from various divines and further scriptural argument. The title page advertised these changes: "Published now the second time with some additions, and many Testimonies also added out of the best and learnedest among Protestant Divines asserting the position of this book." In 1689 someone cleverly adapted *The Tenure* to apply to the political situation existing as a result of the Bloodless Revolution of 1688, as William R. Parker has shown,[1] in a pamphlet called *Pro Populo Adversus Tyrannus: Or the Sovereign Right and Power of the People Over Tyrants. The Tenure* has been reprinted often in collected or selected prose volumes, the most important editions being those of William Talbot Allison in 1911 (annotated); of William Haller in the *Columbia Milton* in 1932; and of Merritt Y. Hughes in 1947, 1957, and, in the *Yale Milton,* 1962 (all annotated).

The text of *The Tenure of Kings and Magistrates* reproduced here is that of the first edition in the Rare Book Room of the Library of Pennsylvania State University through the kindness of Mr. Charles Mann, director. Corrections have been made of turned letters and misprints; expansions of ampersands and short forms along with modernizations of *than* and *j* for *i* have also silently been made. A textual crux on page 31 has been corrected by the insertion of a comma after "Warr" and the following change:

State. It > State, it

because of the meaning intended. Hughes' nonsyntactical alteration[2] was to insert "they" as subject of "have in plaine tearmes unking'd the King" and a semicolon after "Warr" (a semicolon had been added by Haller). However, the compound subject is "thir

[1] *MLQ,* III (1942), 41–44.
[2] Given in a note in the *Yale Milton.*

Oathes of subjection brok'n, new Supremacy obey'd, new Oaths and Covnants tak'n." The conditional sentence says that, "If these things have unkinged the king, more than has the seven years' war, it must needs be clear that hostility and subjection are two direct and positive contraries, etc."

The present edition[3] reproduces the first edition for three reasons: it represents Milton's full and original argument, it has not been available as an entity since the seventeenth century, and the additions are not integral to the argument. The assumption that Milton intended to print testimonies in the first edition (such as Hughes' calling it a "neglected promise of the first edition"[4]) is a misreading of his words on pages 7–8 where he means only that his arguments will be drawn from and justified by "choicest and most authentic learning." This he supplies in the first edition.

SELECTED BIBLIOGRAPHY

Barker, Arthur. *Milton and the Puritan Dilemma, 1641–1660.* Toronto, 1956.

Fink, Zera S. *The Classical Republicans.* Evanston, Ill., 1962.

Grierson, H. J. C. *Milton and Wordsworth.* Cambridge, 1937.

Haller, William. *Liberty and Reformation in the Puritan Revolution.* New York, 1955.

Hughes, Merritt Y. "Milton's Treatment of Reformation History in *The Tenure of Kings and Magistrates*," *The Seventeenth Century* (Stanford, 1951), pp. 247–63.

Miller, Sonia. "Two References in Milton's *Tenure of Kings*," *JEGP*, L (1951), 320–25.

Parker, William R. *Milton's Contemporary Reputation.* Columbus, 1940.

Sensabaugh, George F. *That Grand Whig, Milton.* Stanford, 1952.

Shawcross, John T. "Milton's 'Tenure of Kings and Magistrates': Date of Composition, Editions, and Issues," *PBSA*, LX (1966), 1–8.

Sirluck, Ernest. "Milton's Political Thought: The First Cycle," *MP*, LXI (1964), 209–24.

Wedgwood, C. V. *A Coffin for King Charles.* New York, 1964.

Wolfe, Don M. *Milton in the Puritan Revolution.* New York, 1941.

Woodhouse, A. S. P. *Puritanism and Liberty.* London, 1938.

[3] The preparation of this edition of *The Tenure* was aided by a grant from the Rutgers University Research Council.

[4] *Yale Milton*, III, 102.

THE TENURE OF KINGS AND MAGISTRATES:

PROVING, THAT IT IS LAWFULL, AND HATH BEEN HELD SO THROUGH ALL AGES, FOR ANY, WHO HAVE THE POWER, TO CALL TO ACCOUNT A TYRANT, OR WICKED KING, AND AFTER DUE CONVICTION, TO DEPOSE, AND PUT HIM TO DEATH; IF THE ORDINARY MAGISTRATE HAVE NEGLECTED, OR DENY'D TO DOE IT. AND THAT THEY, WHO OF LATE, SO MUCH BLAME DEPOSING, ARE THE MEN THAT DID IT THEMSELVES.

THE AUTHOR, J. M.

LONDON, Printed by Matthew Simmons, at the Gilded Lyon in Aldersgate Street, 1649.

If Men within themselves would be govern'd by reason, and not generally give up their understanding to a double tyrannie, of custome from without, and blind affections within, they would discerne better what it is to favour and uphold the Tyrant of a Nation. But being slaves within doores, no wonder that they strive so much to have the public State conformably govern'd to the inward vitious rule, by which they govern themselves. For indeed none can love freedom heartilie, but good men; the rest love not freedom, but licence;[1] which never hath more scope or more indulgence than under Tyrants. Hence is it that Tyrants are not oft offended, nor stand much in doubt of bad men, as being all naturally servile;[2] but in whom vertue and true worth most is eminent, them they feare in earnest, as by right their Masters, against them lies all their hatred and sus-[2]picion. Consequentlie neither doe bad men hate Tirants, but have been alwaies readiest with the falsifi'd names of *Loyalty* and *Obedience*, to colour over their base compliances. And although sometimes for shame, and when it comes to their owne grievances, of purse especially, they would seeme good Patriots, and side with

blind affections: emotional attachments (for kingship); prejudices (against deposition).
offended: struck against.

the better cause, yet when others for the deliverance of their Countrie, endu'd with fortitude and Heroick vertue, to feare nothing but the curse written against those *That doe the worke of the Lord negligently,*[3] would goe on to remove, not onely the calamities and thraldomes of a people, but the roots and causes whence they spring, streight these men, and sure helpers at need, as if they hated onely the miseries but not the mischiefes, after they have juggl'd and palter'd with the World, bandied and borne armes against their King, devested him, disanointed him, nay curs'd him all over in thir Pulpits, and their Pamphlets, to the ingaging of sincere and reall men, beyond what is possible or honest to retreat from, not onely turne revolters from those principles, which onely could at first move them, but lay the staine of disloyaltie, and worse, on those proceedings, which are the necessarie consequences of their owne former actions; nor dislik'd by themselves, were they manag'd to the intire advantages of their owne Faction; not considering the while that he toward whom they boasted their new fidelitie, counted them accessory, and by those Statutes and Laws which they so impotently brandish against others, would have doom'd them to a traytors death for what they have done alreadie.[4] 'Tis true, that most men are apt anough to civill Wars and commotions as a noveltie, and for a flash, hot and active; but [3] through sloth or inconstancie, and weakness of spirit either fainting, ere their owne pretences, though never so just, be halfe attain'd, or through an inbred falshood and wickednesse, betray oft times to destruction with themselves, men of noblest temper join'd with them for causes which they in their rash undertakings were not capable of. If God and a good cause give them Victory, the prosecution whereof for the most part, inevitably drawes after it the alteration of Lawes, change of Government, downfall of Princes with their Families; then comes the task to those Worthies which are the soule of that Enterprize, to bee swett and labour'd out amidst the throng and noises of vulgar and irrationall men. Some contesting for Privileges, customes, formes, and that old intanglement of iniquitie, their gibrish Lawes, though the badge of their ancient slavery.[5] Others who have been fiercest against their Prince, under the notion of a Tyrant, and no meane incendiaries of the Warre against him, when God out of his providence and high disposall[6] hath deliver'd him into the hand of their brethren, on a suddaine and in a new garbe of Allegiance, which their doings have long since cancell'd; they plead for him, pity

fortitude: patience, courage, and strength.
vertue: a capacity to act and achieve.
these men: the Presbyterians.

him, extoll him, protest against those that talke of bringing him to the tryall of Justice, which is the Sword of God, superiour to all mortall things, in whose hand soever by apparent signes his testified wil is to put it. But certainely, if we consider who and what they are, on a suddaine growne so pitifull, wee may conclude, their pity can be no true and Christian commiseration, but either levitie and shallownesse of minde, or else a carnall admiring of that worldly pompe and greatness, from whence they [4] see him fall'n; or rather lastly a dissembl'd and seditious pity, fain'd of industry to beget new commotions. As for mercy, if it bee to a Tyrant, under which name they themselves have cited him so oft in the hearing of God, of Angels, and the holy Church[7] assembl'd, and there charg'd him with the spilling of more innocent blood by farre, than ever *Nero*[8] did, undoubtedly the mercy which they pretend, is the mercy of wicked men; and their mercies, wee read, are cruelties;[9] hazarding the welfare of a whole Nation, to have sav'd one, whom so oft they have tearm'd *Agag,*[10] and villifying the blood of many *Jonathans* that have sav'd *Israel;*[11] insisting with much nicenesse on the unnecessariest clause of their Covnant; wherein the feare of change, and the absurd contradiction of a flattering hostilitie had hamperd them, but not scrupling to give away for complements, to an implacable revenge, the heads of many thousand Christians more.

Another sort there is, who comming in the course of these affaires, to have thir share in great actions above the forme of Law or Custome, at least to give thir voice and approbation, begin to swerve and almost shiver at the majesty and grandeur of som noble deed, as if they were newly enter'd into a great sin; disputing presidents, formes, and circumstances, when the Common wealth nigh perishes for want of deeds in substance, don with just and faithfull expedition. To these I wish better instruction, and vertue equall to their calling; the former of which, that is to say Instruction, I shall indeavour, as my dutie is, to bestow on them; and exhort them not to startle from the just and pious resolution of adhering with all their assistance to the present Parlament and Army, [5] in the glorious way wherein Justice and Victorie hath set them; the onely warrants through all ages, next under immediate Revelation, to exercise supreame power; in those proceedings which hitherto appeare equall to what hath been don in any age or Nation heretofore, justly or magnanimouslie. Nor let them be discourag'd or deterr'd by any new

nicenesse: foolishness, punctiliousness.
unnecessariest clause: to preserve the king's person, crown, and dignity (see p. 366).
startle: swerve.
magnanimouslie: heroic action actuated by a proper regard for dignity.

Apostate Scar crowes,[12] who under show of giving counsell, send out their barking monitories and *mimento's*, emptie of ought else but the spleene of a frustrated Faction. For how can that pretended counsell, bee either sound or faithfull, when they that give it, see not for madnesse and vexation of their ends lost, that those Statutes and Scriptures which both falsly and scandalously, they wrest against their Friends and Associates, would by sentence of the common adversarie, fall first and heaviest upon their owne heads. Neither let milde and tender dispositions be foolishly softn'd from their dutie and perseverance with the unmasculine Rhetorick of any puling Priest or Chaplain,[13] sent as a friendly Letter of advice, for fashion-sake in private, and forthwith publish't by the Sender himselfe, that wee may know how much of friend there was in it, to cast an odious envie upon them, to whom it was pretended to be sent in charitie. Nor let any man bee deluded by either the ignorance or the notorious hypocrisie and selfe-repugnance of our dancing Divines,[14] who have the conscience and the boldnesse, to come with Scripture in their mouthes, gloss'd and fitted for thir turnes with a double contradictory sense, transforming the sacred veritie of God, to an Idol with two faces, looking at once two several ways; and with the same quotations to charge others, which in the [6] same case they made serve to justifie themselves. For while the hope to bee made Classic and Provinciall Lords[15] led them on, while pluralities greas'd them thick and deepe, to the shame and scandall of Religion, more than all the Sects and Heresies they exclaime against,[16] then to fight against the Kings person, and no lesse a party of his Lords and Commons, or to put force upon both the Houses was good, was lawfull, was no resisting of Superiour powers; they onely were powers not to be resisted, who countenanc'd the good and punish't the evill. But now that thir censorious domineering is not suffer'd to be universall, truth and conscience to be freed,[17] Tithes[18] and Pluralities to be no more, though competent allowance provided, and the warme experience of large gifts, and they so good at taking them; yet now to exclude and seize on impeach't Members,[19] to bring Delinquents without exemption to a faire Tribunall by the common Nationall Law against murder, is now to be no lesse than *Corah, Dathan,* and *Abiram.*[20] He who but erewhile in the Pulpits was a cursed Tyrant, an enemie to God and Saints, laden with all the innocent blood spilt in three Kingdomes, and so to bee fought against, is now though nothing penitent or alter'd from his first principles, a lawfull Mag-

pluralities: the holding of multiple posts by a minister, a system supported by the Presbyterians.

Tithes: a church tax equaling a tenth of the annual income.

istrate, a Sovrane Lord, the Lords Annointed,[21] not to bee touch'd,[22] though by themselves imprison'd. As if this onely were obedience, to preserve the meere uselesse bulke of his person, and that onely in prison, not in the field, and to disobey his commands, denie him his dignitie and office, every where to resist his power but where they thinke it onely surviving in thir owne faction.

[7] But who in particular is a Tyrant cannot be determind in a generall discourse, otherwise than by supposition; his particular charge, and the sufficient proofe of it must determine that: which I leave to Magistrates, at least to the uprighter sort of them, and of the people, though in number lesse by many, in whom faction least hath prevaild above the Law of nature and right reason, to judge as they finde cause. But this I dare owne as part of my faith, that if such a one there be,[23] by whose Commission, whole massacres have been committed on his faithfull Subjects, his Provinces offerd to pawne or alienation,[24] as the hire of those whom he had sollicited to come in and destroy whole Cities and Countries; be hee King, or Tyrant, or Emperour, the Sword of Justice is above him; in whose hand soever is found sufficient power to avenge the effusion, and so great a deluge of innocent blood. For if all humane power to execute, not accidentally but intendedly, the wrath of God upon evill doers without exception, be of God; then that power, whether ordinary, or if that faile, extraordinary so executing that intent of God, is lawfull, and not to be resisted.[25] But to unfold more at large this whole Question, though with all expedient brevity, I shall here set downe, from first beginning, the originall of Kings; how and wherefore exalted to that dignitie above their Brethren; and from thence shall prove, that turning to tyranny they may bee as lawfully deposd and punishd, as they were at first elected: This I shall doe by autorities and reasons, not learnt in corners among Schismes and Herisies, as our doubling Divines are ready to calumniate, but fetch't out of the midst of choicest and most authentic learning, and [8] no prohibited Authors, nor many Heathen, but Mosaical, Christian, Orthodoxal, and which must needs be more convincing to our Adversaries, Presbyterial.

No man who knows ought, can be so stupid to deny that all men naturally were borne free, being the image and resemblance of God himselfe, and were by privilege above all the creatures, borne to command[26] and not to obey: and that they livd so, till from the

right reason: justice.
doubling: equivocal.
Mosaical: those containing the laws of Moses.
Presbyterial: those embracing the doctrines of ecclesiastical government derived from Calvin.

root of *Adams* transgression, falling among themselves to doe wrong and violence, and foreseeing that such courses must needs tend to the destruction of them all, they agreed by common league to bind each other from mutual injury, and joyntly to defend themselves against any that gave disturbance or opposition to such agreement. Hence came Citties, Townes and Common-wealths. And because no faith in all was found sufficiently binding, they saw it needfull to ordaine some authoritie, that might restraine by force and punishment what was violated against peace and common right: This autoritie and power of self-defence and preservation being originally and naturally in every one of them, and unitedly in them all, for ease, for order, and least each man should be his owne partial judge, they communicated and deriv'd either to one, whom for the eminence of his wisdom and integritie they chose above the rest, or to more than one whom they thought of equal deserving: the first was calld a King; the other Magistrates. Not to be thir Lords and Maisters (though afterward those names in som places were giv'n voluntarily to such as had bin authors of inestimable good to the people) but, to be thir Deputies and Commissioners, to execute, by [9] vertue of thir intrusted power, that justice which else every man by the bond of nature and of Cov'nant must have executed for himselfe, and for one another. And to him that shall consider well why among free persons, one man by civill right should beare autority and jurisdiction over another, no other end or reason can be imaginable. These for a while governd well, and with much equitie decided all things at thir owne arbitrement: till the temptation of such a power left absolute in thir hands, perverted them at length to injustice and partialitie. Then did they who now by tryall had found the danger and inconveniences of committing arbitrary power to any, invent Lawes either fram'd or consented to by all, that should confine and limit the autority of whom they chose to govern them: that so man of whose failing they had proof, might no more rule over them, but law and reason abstracted as much as might be from personal errors and frailties. When this would not serve, but that the Law was either not executed, or misapply'd, they were constraind from that time, the onely remedy left them, to put conditions and take Oaths from all Kings and Magistrates at their first instalment to doe impartial justice by Law: who upon those termes and no other, receav'd Allegeance from the people, that is to say, bond or Covnant to obey them in execution of those Lawes which they the people had themselves made or assented to. And this oft times with express warning, that if the King or Magistrate prov'd unfaithfull to his trust, the people would be disingag'd. They added also Counselors and Parlaments, not to be onely at his beck, but with him or without him, at set times, or at all times, when any danger threatn'd, to [10] have care of the public safety. Therefore saith *Claudius Sesell*[27] a French Statesman, *The Parlament was set as a bridle to the King;* which I instance rather, because that Monarchy is granted by all to be a farre more absolute than ours. That this and the rest of what hath hitherto been spok'n is most true, might be copiously made appeare throughout all Stories Heathen and Christian; eev'n of those Nations where Kings and Emperours have sought meanes to abolish all ancient memory of the peoples right by their encroachments and usurpations. But I spare long insertions, appealing to the German, French, Italian, Arragonian, English, and not least the Scottish Histories:[28] not forgetting this onely by the way, that *William* the Norman though a Conqueror, and not unsworne at his Coronation, was compelld a second time to take oath at S. *Albanes,* ere the people would be brought to yeild obedience.[29]

It being thus manifest that the power of Kings and Magistrates is nothing else, but what is onely derivative, transferrd and committed to them in trust from the people to the Common good of them all, in whom the power yet remaines fundamentally, and cannot be tak'n from them, without a violation of thir natural birthright, and seeing that from hence *Aristotle*[30] and the best of Political writers have defin'd a King, him who governs to the good and profit of his people, and not for his owne ends, it follows from necessary causes that the titles of Sovran Lord, naturall Lord, and the like, are either arrogancies, or flatteries, not admitted by Emperors and Kings of best note, and dislikt by the Church both of Jews, *Isai.* 26.13.[31] and ancient Christians as appears by *Tertullian*[32] and others. Although generally the [11] people of Asia and with them the Jews also, especially since the time they chose a King,[33] against the advice and counsel of God, are noted by wise authors much inclinable to slavery.[34]

Secondly, that to say, as is usual, the King hath as good right to his crown and dignitie, as any man to his inheritance, is to make the subject no better than the Kings slave, his chattell, or his possession that may be bought and sould. And doubtless if hereditary title were sufficiently inquir'd, the best foundation of it would be found but either in courtesie or convenience. But suppose it to be of right hereditarie, what can be more just and legal, if a subject for certaine crimes be to forfet by Law from himselfe and posterity, all his inheritance to the King, than that a King for crimes proportionall, should forfet all his title and inheritance to the people: unless the people must be thought created all for him, he not for them, and they all in one body inferior to him single, which were a kinde of treason against the dignity of mankind to affirm.

Thirdly it followes, that to say Kings are accountable to none but God, is the overturning of all Law and goverment. For if they may refuse to give account, then all covnants made with them at Coronation; all Oathes are in vaine, and meer mockeries, all Lawes which they sweare to keep, made to no purpose; for if the King feare not God, as how many of them doe not? we hold then our lives and estates, by the tenure of his meer grace and mercy, as from a God, not a mortall Magistrate, a position that none but Court parasites or men besotted would maintain. And no Christian Prince not drunk with high mind, and prouder than those Pagan *Cæsars*, that [12] deifi'd themselves, would arrogate so unreasonably above human condition, or derogate so basely from a whole Nation of men his brethren, as if for him onely subsisting, and to serve his glory, valuing them in comparison of his owne brute will and pleasure no more than so many beasts, or vermine under his feet, not to be reasond with, but to be injurd; among whom there might be found so many thousand men for wisdome, vertue, nobleness of mind and all other respects, but the fortune of his dignity, farr above him. Yet some[35] would perswade us that this absurd opinion was King *Daids;* because in the 51 *Psalm* he cries out to God, *Against thee onely have I sinn'd;* as if *David* had imagind that to murder *Uriah* and adulterate his Wife, had bin no sinne against his neighbor,[36] when as that law of *Moses* was to the King expresly, *Deut.* 17. not to think so highly of himself above his Brethren.[37] *David* therefore by those words could mean no other, than either that the depth of his guiltiness was known to God onely, or to so few as had not the will or power to question him, or that the sin against God was greater beyond compare than against *Uriah.* Whatever his meaning were, any wise man will see that the patheticall words of a Psalme can be no certaine decision to a point that hath abundantly more certaine rules to goe by. How much more rationally spake the Heathen King *Demophoon* in a Tragedy of *Euripides*[38] than these interpreters would put upon King *David, I rule not my people by tyranny, as if they were Barbarians, but am my self liable, if I doe unjustly to suffer justly.* Not unlike was the speech of *Trajan* the worthy Emperor, to one whom he made General of his Prætorian Forces. Take this drawne sword, saith he, to use for me, if I [13] reigne well, if not, to use against me. Thus *Dion* relates.[39] And not *Trajan* onely, but *Theodosius* the younger a Christian Emperor and one of the best, causd it to be enacted as a rule undenyable and fit to be acknowledgd by all Kings and Emperors, that a Prince is bound to the Laws; that on the autority of Law the autority of a Prince depends, and to the Laws ought submit.[40] Which Edict of his remaines yet unrepeald in the *Code* of *Justinian.* 1.1. *tit.* 24. as a sacred constitution to all the succeeding Emperors. How then can any King in Europe maintaine and write himselfe accountable to none but God, when Emperors in thir owne imperiall Statutes have writt'n and decreed themselves accountable to Law. And indeed where such account is not fear'd, he that bids a man reigne over him above Law, may bid as well a savage beast.

It follows lastly, that since the King or Magistrate holds his autoritie of the people, both originally and naturally for their good in the first place, and not his owne, then may the people as oft as they shall judge it for the best, either choose him or reject him, retaine him or depose him though no Tyrant, merely by the libertie and right of free born men to be govern'd as seems to them best. This, though it cannot but stand with plaine reason, shall be made good also by Scripture, *Deut.* 17.14. *When thou art come into the Land which the Lord thy God giveth thee, and shalt say I will set a King over mee, like as all the Nations about mee.*[41] These words confirme us that the right of choosing, yea of changing thir owne goverment is by the grant of God himself in the people. And therefore when they desir'd a King, though then under another forme of goverment, [14] and though thir changing displeasd him, yet he that was himself thir King,[42] and rejected by them, would not be a hindrance to what they intended, furder than by perswasion, but that they might doe therein as they saw good, 1 *Sam.* 8. onely he reserv'd to himself the nomination of who should reigne over them. Neither did that exempt the King as if hee were to God onely accountable, though by his especiall command anointed. Therefore *David first made a Covnant with the Elders of Israel, and so was by them anointed King,* 1 *Chron.* 11. And *Jehoiada* the Priest making *Jehoash* King, made a Cov'nant between him and the people, 2 *Kings* 11.17. Therefore when *Roboam* at his comming to the Crowne, rejected those conditions which the Israelites brought him, heare what they answer him, *what portion have we in David, or inheritance in the son of Jesse. See to thine own house David.*[43] And for the like conditions not perform'd, all Israel before that time deposd *Samuell;* not for his own default, but for the misgovement of his Sons. But som will say to both these examples, it was evilly don. I answer, that not the latter, because it was expressely allow'd them in the Law to set up a King if they pleas'd; and God himself joynd with them in the work; though in some sort it was at that time displeasing to him, in respect of old *Samuell* who had governd them uprightly. As *Livy* praises the Romans who took occasion from *Tarquinius* a wicked Prince to gaine their libertie,[44] which to have extorted, saith hee, from *Numa* or any of the good Kings before, had not bin seasonable. Nor was it in the former example don unlawfully; for when *Roboam* had prepar'd a huge Army to reduce the Israelites, he was forbidd'n by the Profet, 1 *Kings* 12.24. [15] *Thus saith the Lord yee shall not goe up, nor fight against your brethren, for this thing is from me.* He calls them thir brethren, not Rebels, and forbidds to be proceeded against them, owning the thing himselfe, not by single providence, but by approbation, and that not onely of the act, as in the former example, but of the fitt season also; he had not otherwise forbidd to molest them. And those grave and wise Counsellors whom *Rehoboam* first advis'd with,[45] spake no such thing, as our old gray headed Flatterers now are wont, stand upon your birth-right, scorne to capitulate, you hold of God, and not of them; for they knew no such matter, unless conditionally, but gave him politic counsel, as in a civil transaction. Therfore Kingdom and Magistracy, whether supreme or subordinat is calld *a human ordinance,* 1 *Pet.* 2.13, etc. which we are there taught is the will of God wee should submitt to, so farr as for the punishment of evill doers, and the encouragement of them that doe well. *Submitt* saith he, *as free men.*[46] And *there is no power but of God,* saith *Paul, Rom.* 13.[47] as much as to say, God put it into mans heart to find out that way at first for common peace and preservation, approving the exercise therof; els it contradicts *Peter* who calls the same autority an Ordinance of man. It must be also understood of lawfull and just power, els we read of great power in the affaires and Kingdomes of the World permitted to the Devill: for saith he to Christ, *Luke* 4.6. *all this power will I give thee and the glory of them, for it is deliverd to me, and to whomsoever I will, I give it:* neither did hee ly, or Christ gainsay what hee affirm'd:[48] for in the thirteenth of the *Revelation*[49] wee read how the Dragon gave to the beast *his power, his seat, and great autority:* [16] which beast so autoriz'd most expound to be the tyrannical powers and Kingdomes of the earth.[50] Therfore Saint *Paul* in the forecited Chapter tells us that such Magistrates hee meanes, as are, not a terror to the good but to the evill, such as beare not the sword in vaine, but to punish offenders, and to encourage the good.[51] If such onely be mentioned here as powers to be obeyd, and our submission to them onely requird, then doubt-

Tarquinius: a tyrant often considered a type of Rehoboam.

Numa: a legendary king, to whom many books on sacred law were attributed, written through the counsel of Egeria, goddess of fountains.

less those powers that doe the contrary, are no powers ordaind of God, and by consequence no obligation laid upon us to obey or not to resist them. And it may be well observd that both these Apostles, whenever they give this precept, express it in termes not *concret* but *abstract*, as Logicians are wont to speake, that is, they mention the ordinance, the power, the autoritie before the persons that execute it, and what that power is, lest we should be deceavd, they describe exactly. So that if the power be not such, or the person execute not such power, neither the one nor the other is of God, but of the Devill, and by consequence to bee resisted. From this exposition *Chrysostome*[52] also on the same place dissents not; explaining that these words were not writt'n in behalf of a tyrant. And this is verify'd by *David*, himself a King, and likeliest to bee Author of the *Psalm* 94.20. which saith, *Shall the throne of iniquity have fellowship with thee*. And it were worth the knowing, since Kings, and that by Scripture boast the justness of thir title, by holding it immediately of God, yet cannot show the time when God ever set on the throne them or thir forefathers, but onely when the people chose them; why by the same reason, since God ascribes as oft to himself the casting down of Princes from the throne, it should not be [17] thought as lawful, and as much from God when none are seen to do it but the people, and that for just causes. For if it needs must be a sin in them to depose, it may as likely be a sin to have elected. And contrary if the peoples act in election be pleaded by a King, as the act of God, and the most just title to enthrone him, why may not the peoples act of rejection, be as well pleaded by the people as the act of God, and the most just reason to depose him? So that we see the title and just right of reigning or deposing in reference to God, is found in Scripture to be all one; visible onely in the people, and depending meerly upon justice and demerit. Thus farr hath bin considerd briefly the power of Kings and Magistrates; how it was, and is originally the peoples, and by them conferrd in trust onely to bee imployd to the common peace and benefit; with libertie therfore and right remaining in them to reassume it to themselves, if by Kings or Magistrats it be abus'd; or to dispose of it by any alteration, as they shall judge most conducing to the public good.

Wee may from hence with more ease, and force of argument determin what a Tyrant is, and what the people may doe against him. A Tyrant whether by wrong or by right comming to the Crowne, is he who regarding neither Law nor the common good, reigns onely for himself and his faction: Thus St. *Basil*[53] among others de-

demerit: merit, deserving.

fines him. And because his power is great, his will boundless and exorbitant, the fulfilling whereof is for the most part accompanied with innumerable wrongs and oppressions of the people, murders, massacres, rapes, adulteries, desolation, and subversion of Citties and whole provinces; look how great a good and happiness a just [18] King is, so great a mischeife is a Tyrant; as hee the public Father of his Countrie, so this the common enemie. Against whom what the people lawfully may doe, as against a common pest, and destroyer of mankinde, I suppose no man of cleare judgement need goe furder to be guided than by the very principles of nature in him. But because it is the vulgar folly of men to desert thir owne reason, and shutting thir eyes to think they see best with other mens, I shall shew by such examples as ought to have most waight with us, what hath bin don in this case heretofore. The *Greeks* and *Romans* as thir prime Authors witness held it not onely lawfull, but a glorious and Heroic deed, rewarded publicly with Statues and Garlands, to kill an infamous Tyrant at any time without tryal;[54] and but reason, that he who trod down all Law, should not bee voutsaf'd the benefit of Law. Insomuch that *Seneca* the Tragedian brings in *Hercules* the grand suppressor of Tyrants, thus speaking,[55]

> . . . . *Victima haud ulla amplior*
> *Potest, magisque opima mactari Jovi*
> *Quam Rex iniquus* . . . .
>
> . . . . *There can be slaine*
> *No sacrifice to God more acceptable*
> *Than an unjust and wicked King* . . . .

But of these I name no more, lest it bee objected they were Heathen; and come to produce another sort of men that had the knowledge of true Religion. Among the Jews this custome of tyrant-killing was not unusual. First *Ehud*, a man whom God had raysd to deliver Israel from *Eglon* King of *Moab*, who had conquerd and rul'd over them eighteene yeares, being sent to him as an Ambassador with a [19] present slew him in his owne house.[56] But hee was a forren Prince, an enemie, and *Ehud* besides had special warrant from God. To the first I answer, it imports not whether forren or native: For no Prince so native but professes to hold by Law; which when he himselfe overturnes, breaking all the Covnants and Oaths that gave him title to his dignity, and were the bond and alliance between him and his people, what differs he from an outlandish King or from an enemie? For looke how much right the King

outlandish: foreign.

of *Spaine*[57] hath to govern us at all, so much right hath the King of *England* to govern us tyrannically. If he, though not bound to us by any league, comming from *Spaine* in person to subdue us or to destroy us, might lawfully by the people of *England* either bee slaine in fight, or put to death in captivity, what hath a native King to plead, bound by so many Covnants, benefits and honours to the welfare of his people, why he through the contempt of all Laws and Parlaments, the onely tie of our obedience to him, for his owne wills sake, and a boasted prærogative unaccountable, after sev'n years warring and destroying of his best subjects, overcom, and yeilded prisoner, should think to scape unquestionable, as a thing divine, in respect of whom so many thousand Christians destroy'd should lye unaccounted for, polluting with thir slaughterd carcasses all the Land over, and crying for vengeance against the living that should have righted them. Who knows not that there is a mutual bond of amity and brotherhood between man and man over all the World, neither is it the English Sea that can sever us from that duty and relation: a straiter bond yet there is between fellow-subjects, neighbours, and friends; But [20] when any of these doe one to another so as hostility could doe no worse, what doth the Law decree less against them, than open enemies and invaders? or if the Law be not present, or too weake, what doth it warrant us to less than single defence or civil warre? and from that time forward the Law of civill defensive Warr differs nothing from the Law of forren hostility. Nor is it distance of place that makes enmitie, but enmity that makes distance. He therefore that keeps peace with me neer or remote of whatsoever Nation, is to mee as farr as all civil and human offices an Englishman and a nighbour: but if an Englishman forgetting all Laws, human, civil and religious offend against life and libertie, to him offended and to the Law in his behalf, though born in the same womb, he is no better than a Turk, a Sarasin, a Heathen. This is Gospel,[58] and this was ever Law among equals; how much rather than in force against any King whatsoever, who in respect of the people is confessd inferior and not equal: to distinguish therfore of a Tyrant by outlandish, or domestic is a weak evasion. To the second that he was an enemie, I answer, what Tyrant is not? yet *Eglon* by the Jewes had bin acknowledgd as thir Sovran, they had servd him eighteen yeares, as long almost as wee our *William* the Conqueror,[59] in all which time he could not be so unwise a Statesman but to have tak'n of them Oaths of Fealty and Allegeance by which they made themselves his proper subjects, as thir homage and present sent by *Ehud* testifyd. To the

unaccountable: indefensible and used irresponsibly.

third, that he had special warrant to kill *Eglon* in that manner, it cannot bee granted, because not expressd; tis plain that he was raysd by God to be a Deliverer, and went on just principles, such as were then and ever held [21] allowable, to deale so by a Tyrant that could no otherwise be dealt with. Neither did *Samuell* though a Profet, with his owne hand abstain from *Agag;* a forren enemie no doubt; but mark the reason, *As thy Sword hath made women childless;*[60] a cause that by the sentence of Law it selfe nullifies all relations. And as the Law is between Brother and Brother, Father and Son, Maister and Servant, wherfore not between King or rather Tyrant and People? And whereas *Jehu* had special command to slay *Jehoram*[61] a successive and hereditarie Tyrant, it seemes not the less imitable for that; for where a thing grounded so much on naturall reason hath the addition of a command from God, what does it but establish the lawfulness of such an act. Nor is it likely that God who had so many wayes of punishing the house of *Ahab* would have sent a subject against his Prince, if the fact in it selfe as don to a Tyrant had bin of bad example. And if *David* refus'd to lift his hand against the Lords anointed,[62] the matter between them was not tyranny, but private enmity, and *David* as a private person had bin his own revenger, not so much the peoples; but when any tyrant at this day can shew to be the Lords anointed, the onely mention'd reason why *David* withheld his hand, he may then but not till then presume on the same privilege.[63]

We may pass therfore hence to Christian times. And first our Saviour himself, how much he favourd tyrants and how much intended they should be found or honourd among Christians, declares his minde not obscurely; accounting thir absolute autoritie no better than Gentilisme, yea though they flourishd it over with the splendid name of Benefactors;[64] charging those that would be his Disciples to usurp no [22] such dominion; but that they who were to bee of most autoritie among them, should esteem themselves Ministers and Servants to the public.[65] *Matt.* 20.25. *The Princes of the Gentiles exercise Lordship over them,* and *Mark* 10.42. *They that seem to rule,* saith he, either slighting or accounting them no lawful rulers, *but yee shall not be so, but the greatest among you shall be your servant.*[66] And although hee himself were the meekest, and came on earth to be so, yet to a tyrant we hear him not voutsafe an humble word: but *Tell that Fox, Luc.* 13.[67] And wherfore did his mother the Virgin *Mary* give such praise to God in her profetic song,[68] that he had now by the comming of Christ *Cutt down Dynasta's or proud Monarchs from the throne,*[69] if the Church, when God manifests his power in them to doe so, should rather choose all miserie and vassalage to serve them, and let them still sit on thir potent seats to bee ador'd for doing mischiefe. Surely it is not for nothing that tyrants by a kind of natural instinct both hate and feare none more than the true Church and Saints of God, as the most dangerous enemies and subverters of Monarchy, though indeed of tyranny; hath not this bin the perpetual cry of Courtiers, and Court Prelates? whereof no likelier cause can be alleg'd, but that they well discern'd the mind and principles of most devout and zealous men, and indeed the very discipline of Church, tending to the dissolution of all tyranny. No marvel then if since the faith of Christ receav'd, in purer or impurer times, to depose a King and put him to death for tyranny hath bin accounted so just and requisit, that neighbour Kings have both upheld and tak'n part with subjects in the action. And *Ludovicus Pius,* himself an Emperor, and sonne of [23] *Charles* the great, being made Judge, *Du Haillan*[70] is my author, between *Milegast* King of the *Vultzes* and his subjects who had depos'd him, gave his verdit for the subjects, and for him whom they had chos'n in his room. Note here that the right of electing whom they please is by the impartial testimony of an Emperor in the people. For, said he, *A just Prince ought to be prefer'd before an unjust, and the end of goverment before the prerogative.*[71] And *Constantinus Leo,* another Emperor in the *Byzantine* Laws saith, *that the end of a King is for the general good, which he not performing is but the counterfet of a King.*[72] And to prove that some of our owne Monarchs have acknowledg'd that thir high office exempted them not from punishment, they had the Sword of St. *Edward*[73] born before them by an Officer who was calld Earle of the palace eev'n at the times of thir highest pomp and solemnitie, to mind them, saith *Matthew Paris,*[74] the best of our Historians, that if they errd, the Sword had power to restraine them. And what restraint the Sword comes to at length, having both edge and point, if any *Sceptic* will needs doubt, let him feel. It is also affirm'd from diligent search made in our ancient books of Law,[75] that the Peers and Barons of England had a legall right to judge the King: which was the cause most likely, for it could be no slight cause, that they were call'd his Peers, or equals. This however may stand immovable, so long as man hath to deale with no better than man; that if our Law judge all men to the lowest by thir Peers, it should in all equity ascend also, and judge the highest.

indeed: in truth.
Ludovicus Pius: Louis the Pious, Holy Roman Emperor (818–40).
Du Haillan: Bernard de Girard, Sieur du Haillan (ca. 1535–1610).
Constantinus Leo: Leo III of the Byzantine Empire.
St. Edward: Edward the Confessor.

And so much I find both in our own and forren Storie, that Dukes, Earles, and Marqueses were at first not hereditary,[76] not empty and vain titles, but names of trust [24] and office, and with the office ceasing, as induces me to be of opinion, that every worthy man in Parlament, for the word Baron imports no more, might for the public good be thought a fit Peer and judge of the King; without regard had to petty caveats, and circumstances, the chief impediment in high affaires, and ever stood upon most by circumstantial men. Whence doubtless our Ancestors who were not ignorant with what rights either Nature or ancient Constitution had endowd them, when Oaths both at Coronation, and renewd in Parlament would not serve, thought it no way illegal to depose and put to death thir tyrannous Kings. Insomuch that the Parlament drew up a charge against *Richard the second*,[77] and the Commons requested to have judgement decree'd against him, that the realme might not bee endangerd. And *Peter Martyr*[78] a Divine of formost rank, on the third of *Judges* approves thir doings. Sir *Thomas Smith*[79] also a Protestant and a Statesman in his Commonwealth of *England* putting the question whether it be lawful to rise against a Tyrant, answers that the vulgar judge of it according to the event, and the learned according to the purpose of them that do it. But far before those days *Gildas*[80] the most ancient of all our Historians, speaking of those times wherein the Roman Empire decaying quitted and relinquishd what right they had by Conquest to this Iland, and resign'd it all into the peoples hands, testifies that the people thus re-invested with thir own original right, about the year 446, both elected them Kings, whom they thought best (the first Christian Brittish Kings that ever raign'd heer since the Romans) and by the same right, when they apprehended cause, usually depos'd and put them to [25] death. This is the most fundamental and ancient tenure that any King of *England* can produce or pretend to; in comparison of which, all other titles and pleas are but of yesterday. If any object that *Gildas* condemns the Britanes for so doing, the answer is as ready; that he condemns them no more for so doing, than hee did before for choosing such, for saith he, *They anointed them Kings, not of God, but such as were more bloody than the rest.*[81] Next hee condemns them not at all for deposing or putting them to death, but for doing it over hastily, without tryal or well examining the cause, and for electing others worse in thir room. Thus we have here both Domestic and most ancient examples that the people of Britain have deposd and put to death thir Kings in those primitive Christian times. And to couple

Baron: a tenant holding immediately from the king or other feudal superior.

reason with example, if the Church in all ages, Primitive, Romish, or Protestant held it ever no less thir duty than the power of thir Keyes,[82] though without express warrant of Scripture, to bring indifferently both King and Peasant under the utmost rigor of thir Canons and Censures Ecclesiastical, eev'n to the smiting him with a final excommunion,[83] if he persist impenitent, what hinders but that the temporal Law both may and ought, though without a special Text or president, extend with like indifference the civil Sword,[84] to the cutting off without exemption him that capitally[85] offends. Seeing that justice and Religion are from the same God, and works of justice ofttimes more acceptable. Yet because that some[86] lately with the tongues and arguments of Malignant backsliders have writt'n that the proceedings now in Parlament against the King, are without president from any Protestant State or Kingdom, the [26] examples which follow shall be all Protestant and chiefly Presbyterian.

In the yeare 1546. The *Duke of Saxonie, Lantgrave of Hessen,* and the whole Protestant league raysd open Warr against *Charles the fifth* thir Emperor, sent him a defiance, renounc'd all faith and allegeance toward him, and debated long in Counsell whether they should give him so much as the title of *Cæsar. Sleidan. l.* 17.[87] Let all men judge what this wanted of deposing or of killing, but the power to doe it.

In the yeare 1559. the Scotch Protestants claiming promise of thir Queen Regent for libertie of conscience, she answering that promises were not to be claim'd of Princes beyond what was commodious for them to grant, told her to her face in the Parlament then at *Sterling,* that if it were so, they renounc'd thir obedience; and soone after betooke them to Armes. *Buchanan Hist. l.* 16.[88] certainely when allegeance is renounc'd, that very hour the King or Queen is in effect depos'd.

In the yeare 1564. *John Knox*[89] a most famous Divine and the reformer of *Scotland* to the Presbyterian discipline, at a generall Assembly maintaind op'nly in a dispute against *Lethington*[90] the Secretary of State, that Subjects might and ought execute Gods judgements upon thir King; that the fact of *Jehu* and others against thir King having the ground of Gods ordinary command to put such and such offenders to death[91] was not extraordinary, but to bee imitated of all that prefer'd the honour of God to the affection of flesh and wicked Princes, that Kings, if they offend, have no privilege to be exempted from the punishments of Law more than any

Queen Regent: Mary of Guise, widow of James V and mother of Mary, Queen of Scots.

[27] other subject; so that if the King be a Murderer, Adulterer, or Idolater, he should suffer not as a King, but as an offender; and this position hee repeates againe and againe before them. Answerable was the opinion of *John Craig* another learned Divine, and that Lawes made by the tyranny of Princes, or the negligence of people, thir posterity might abrogate, and reform all things according to the original institution of Common-welths. And *Knox* being commanded by the Nobilitie to write to *Calvin* and other learned men for thir judgements in that question refus'd; alleging that both himselfe was fully resolv'd in conscience, and had heard thir judgements, and had the same opinion under hand-writing of many the most godly and most learned that he knew in Europe; that if he should move the question to them againe, what should he doe but shew his owne forgetfulness or inconstancy. All this is farr more largely in the Ecclesiastic History of *Scotland l.* 4.[92] with many other passages to this effect all the book over; set out with diligence by Scotchmen of best repute among them at the beginning of these troubles, as if they labourd to inform us what wee were to doe and what they intended upon the like occasion.

And to let the world know that the whole Church and Protestant State of *Scotland* in those purest times of reformation were of the same beleif, three years after, they met in the feild *Mary* thir lawful and hereditary Queen, took her prisoner yeilding before fight, kept her in prison and the same yeare deposd her.[93] *Buchan. Hist. l.* 18.

And four years after that, the Scots in justification of thir deposing Queen *Mary*, sent Embassadors [28] to Queen *Elizabeth*,[94] and in a writt'n Declaration alleag'd that they had us'd towards her more lenity than shee deservd; that thir Ancestors had heretofore punishd thir Kings by death or banishment; that the Scots were a free Nation, made King whom they freely chose,[95] and with the same freedome un-Kingd him if they saw cause, by right of ancient laws and Ceremonies yet remaining, and old customes yet among the High-landers in choosing the head of thir Clanns, or Families; all which with many other arguments bore witness that regal power was nothing else but a mutuall Covnant or stipulation between King and people. *Buch. Hist. l.* 20. These were Scotchmen and Presbyterians; but what measure then have they lately offerd, to think such liberty less beseeming us than themselves, presuming to put him upon us for a Maister whom thir Law scarce allows to be thir own equall? If now then we heare them in another straine than heretofore in the purest times of thir Church, we may be confident

John Craig: (1512–1600), an advocate of Knox's reforms.

it is the voice of Faction speaking in them, not of truth and Reformation.

In the yeare 1581. the States of *Holland* in a general Assembly at the *Hague*, abjur'd all obedience and subjection to *Philip* King of *Spaine;* and in a Declaration justifie thir so doing; for that by his tyrannous goverment against faith so oft'n giv'n and brok'n he had lost his right to all the Belgic Provinces; that therfore they deposd him and declar'd it lawful to choose another in his stead. *Thuan. l.* 74.[96] From that time, to this no State or Kingdom in the World hath equally prosperd: But let them remember not to look with an evil and prejudicial eye upon thir neighbours walking by the same rule.[97]

[29] But what need these examples to Presbyterians, I meane to those who now of late would seem so much to abhorr deposing, whenas they to all Christendom have giv'n the latest and the liveliest example of doing it themselves. I question not the lawfulness of raising Warr against a Tyrant in defence of Religion, or civil libertie; for no Protestant Church from the first *Waldenses*[98] of *Lyons,* and *Languedoc* to this day but have don it round, and maintaind it lawfull. But this I doubt not to affirme, that the Presbyterians, who now so much condemn deposing, were the men themselves that deposd the King, and cannot with all thir shifting and relapsing, wash off the guiltiness from thir owne hands. For they themselves, by these thir late doings have made it guiltiness, and turnd thir owne warrantable actions into Rebellion.

There is nothing that so actually makes a King of *England,* as rightful possession and Supremacy *in all causes both civil and Ecclesiastical:* and nothing that so actually makes a Subject of *England,* as those two Oaths of Allegeance and Supremacy observd *without equivocating, or any mental reservation.* Out of doubt then when the King shall command things already constituted in Church, or State, obedience is the true essence of a subject, either to doe, if it be lawful, or if he hold the thing unlawful, to submit to that penaltie which the Law imposes, so long as he intends to remaine a subject. Therefore when the people or any part of them shall rise against the King and his autority executing the Law in any thing establishd civil or Ecclesiastical, I doe not say it is rebellion, if the thing commanded though establishd be unlawfull, and that they sought first all due means [30] of redress (and no man is furder bound to Law) but I say it is an absolute renouncing both of Supremacy and Allegeance, which in one word is an actual and total deposing of the King, and the setting up of another supreme autority over them. And whether the Presbyterians have not don all this and much more, they will not put mee, I suppose, to reck'n up a seven yeares story fresh in the memory of all men.[99] Have they not utterly broke the Oath of Allegeance, rejecting the Kings command and autority sent them from any part of the Kingdom whether in things lawful or unlawful? Have they not abjur'd the Oath of Supremacy by setting up the Parlament without the King, supreme to all thir obedience, and though thir Vow and Covnant bound them in general to the Parlament, yet somtimes adhering to the lesser part of Lords and Commons that remaind faithful as they terme it, and eev'n of them, one while to the Commons without the Lords, another while to the Lords without the Commons?[100] Have they not still declar'd thir meaning, whatever their Oath were, to hold them onely for supreme whom they found at any time most yeilding to what they petitiond? Both these Oaths which were the straitest bond of an English subject in reference to the King, being thus broke and made voide, it follows undeniably that the King from that time was by them in fact absolutely deposd, and they no longer in reality to be thought his subjects, notwithstanding thir fine clause in the Covnant to preserve his person, Crown, and dignitie,[101] set there by som dodging Casuist with more craft than sinceritie to mitigate the matter in case of ill success, and not tak'n I suppose by any honest man, but as a condition sub-[31]ordinate to every the least particle that might more concern Religion, liberty, or the public peace. To prove it yet more plainly that they are the men who have deposd the King, I thus argue. We know that King and Subject are relatives, and relatives have no longer being than in the relation; the relation between King and Subject can be no other than regal autority and subjection. Hence I inferr past their defending, that if the Subject who is one relative, takes away the relation, of force he takes away also the other relative; but the Presbyterians who were one relative, that is to say Subjects, have for this sev'n years tak'n away the relation, that is to say the Kings autoritie, and thir subjection to it, therefore the Presbyterians for these sev'n yeares have removd and extinguishd the other relative, that is to say the King, or to speake more in brief have depos'd him; not onely by depriving him the execution of his autoritie, but by conferring it upon others. If then thir Oathes of subjection brok'n, new Supremacy obey'd, new Oaths and Covnants tak'n, notwithstanding frivolous evasions, have in plaine tearmes unking'd the King, much more than hath thir sev'n yeares Warr, not depos'd him onely, but outlawd him, and defi'd him as an alien, a rebell to Law, and enemie to the State, it must needs be cleare to any man not averse from reason, that hostilitie and subjection are two direct and positive contraries; and can no more in one subject stand together in respect of the same King, than one person at the same time can be in two remote places. Against whom therfore the Subject is in act of hostility we may be confident that to him he is in no subjection: and in whom hostility takes place of subjection, for they can by no meanes consist to-[32]gether, to him the King can bee not onely no King, but an enemie. So that from hence wee shall not need dispute whether they have depos'd him, or what they have defaulted towards him as no King, but shew manifestly how much they have don toward the killing him. Have they not levied all these Warrs against him whether offensive or defensive (for defence in Warr equally offends, and most prudently before hand) and giv'n Commission to slay where they knew his person could not bee exempt from danger? And if chance or flight had not sav'd him, how oft'n had they killd him, directing thir Artillery without blame or prohibition to the very place where they saw him stand? Have they not converted his revenue to other uses, and detain'd from him all meanes of livelyhood, so that for them long since he might have perisht, or have starv'd? Have they not hunted and pursu'd him round about the Kingdom with sword and fire? Have they not formerly deny'd to Treat with him,[102] and thir now recanting Ministers preach'd against him, as a reprobate incurable, an enemy to God and his Church markt for destruction, and therfore not to bee treated with? Have they not beseig'd him and to thir power forbid him Water and Fire, save what they shot against him to the hazard of his life? Yet while they thus assaulted and endangerd it with hostile deeds, they swore in words to defend it with his Crown and dignity; not in order, as it seems now, to a firm and lasting peace, or to his repentance after all this blood; but simply, without regard, without remorse or any comparable value of all the miseries and calamities sufferd by the poore people, or to suffer hereafter through his obstinacy or impenitence. No under-[33]standing man can bee ignorant that Covnants are ever made according to the present state of persons and of things; and have ever the more general laws of nature and of reason included in them, though not express'd. If I make a voluntary Covnant as with a man to doe him good, and hee prove afterward a monster to me, I should conceave a disobligement. If I covnant, not to hurt an enemie, in favor of him and forbearance, and hope of his amendment, and he, after that, shall doe me tenfould injury and mischief to what hee had don when I so Covnanted, and stil be plotting what may tend to my destruction, I question not but that his after actions release me; nor know I Covnant so sacred that withholds mee from demanding

Justice on him. Howbeit, had not thir distrust in a good cause, and the fast and loos of our prevaricating Divines oversway'd, it had bin doubtless better, not to have inserted in a Covnant unnecessary obligations, and words not works of a supererogating Allegeance to thir enemy; no way advantageous to themselves, had the King prevail'd, as to thir cost many would have felt; but full of snare and distraction to our friends, usefull onely, as we now find, to our adversaries, who under such a latitude and shelter of ambiguous interpretation have ever since been plotting and contriving new opportunities to trouble all againe. How much better had it bin, and more becomming an undaunted vertue to have declard op'nly and boldly whom and what power the people were to hold Supreme, as on the like occasion Protestants have don before, and many conscientious men now in these times have more than once besought the Parlament to doe, that they might go on upon a sure foundation, and [34] not with a ridling Covnant in thir mouthes, seeming to sweare counter almost in the same breath Allegeance and no Allegeance; which doubtless had drawn off all the minds of sincere men from siding with them, had they not discern'd thir actions farr more deposing him than thir words upholding him; which words made now the subject of cavillous interpretations, stood ever in the Covnant by judgement of the more discerning sort an evidence of thir feare not of thir fidelity. What should I return to speak on, of those attempts for which the King himself hath oft'n charg'd the Presbyterians of seeking his life, whenas in the due estimation of things they might without a fallacy be sayd to have don the deed outright. Who knows not that the King is a name of dignity and office, not of person: Who therfore kils a King, must kill him while he is a King. Then they certainly who by deposing him have long since tak'n from him the life of a King, his office and his dignity, they in the truest sence may bee said to have killd the King: nor onely by thir deposing and waging Warr against him, which besides the danger to his personal life, set him in the fardest opposite point from any vital function of a King, but by thir holding him in prison vanquishd and yeilded into thir absolute and *despotic* power, which brought him to the lowest degradement and incapacity of the regal name. I say not by whose matchless valour next under God, lest the story of thir ingratitude thereupon carry me from the purpose in hand, which is to convince them that they, which I repeat

supererogating Allegeance: deeds of allegiance done by sainted persons or those who act above and beyond what is necessary for salvation.
Protestants: the Dutch.
by whose: Cromwell's.

againe, were the men who in the truest sense killd the King, not onely as is provd before, but by depressing him thir King farr below the rank of a subject to the con-[35]dition of a Captive, without intention to restore him, as the Chancellour of *Scotland*[103] in a speech told him plainly at *Newcastle*, unless hee granted fully all thir demands, which they knew he never meant. Nor did they Treat or think of Treating with him, till thir hatred to the Army that deliverd them, not thir love or duty to the King, joyn'd them secretly with men sentencd so oft for Reprobates in thir owne mouthes, by whose suttle inspiring they grew madd upon a most tardy and improper Treaty. Whereas if the whole bent of thir actions had not bin against the King himselfe, but against his evill Councel, as they faind, and publishd, wherefore did they not restore him all that while to the true life of a King, his Office, Crown, and Dignity, when he was in thir power, and they themselves his neerest Counselers. The truth therefore is, both that they would not, and that indeed they could not without thir own certaine destruction, having reduc'd him to such a final pass, as was the very death and burial of all in him that was regal, and from whence never King of *England* yet revivd, but by the new re-inforcement of his own party, which was a kind of resurrection to him. Thus having quite extinguisht all that could be in him of a King, and from a total privation clad him over like another specifical thing with formes and habitudes destructive to the former, they left in his person dead as to Law and all the civil right either of King or Subject the life onely of a Prisner, a Captive and a Malefactor. Whom the equal and impartial hand of justice finding, was no more to spare than another ordnary man; not onely made obnoxious to the doome of Law by a charge more than once drawn up against him, and his owne con-[36]fession to the first Article at *Newport*,[104] but summond and arraignd in the sight of God and his people, curst and devoted to perdition worse than any *Ahab*, or *Antiochus*,[105] with exhortation to curse all those in the name of God that made not Warr against him, as bitterly as *Meroz*[106] was to be curs'd, that went not out against a Canaanitish King, almost in all the Sermons, Prayers, and Fulminations that have bin utterd this sev'n yeares by those clov'n tongues of falshood and dissention, who now, to the stirring up of new discord, acquitt him; and against thir owne discipline, which they boast to be the throne and scepter of Christ, absolve him, unconfound him, though unconverted, unrepentant, unsensible of all thir pretious

Treaty: the Treaty of Newport, negotiated during September to November 1648, well after the passage of "No More Addresses."
specifical: species of.

Saints and Martyrs whose blood[107] they have so oft layd upon his head: and now againe with a new sovran anointment can wash it all off, as if it were as vile, and no more to be reckn'd for than the blood of so many Dogs in a time of Pestilence: giving the most opprobrious lye to all the acted zeale that for these many yeares hath filld thir bellies, and fed them fatt upon the foolish people. Ministers of sedition, not of the Gospell, who while they saw it manifestly tend to civil Warr and bloodshed, never ceasd exasperating the people against him; and now that they see it likely to breed new commotion, cease not to incite others against the people that have savd them from him, as if sedition were thir onely aime whether against him or for him. But God as we have cause to trust, wil put other thoughts into the people, and turn them from looking after these firebrands, of whose fury, and fals prophecies we have anough experience; and from the murmurs of new discord will incline them to heark'n rather [37] with erected minds to the voice of our supreme Magistracy, calling us to liberty and the flourishing deeds of a reformed Common-wealth;[108] with this hope that as God was heretofore angry with the Jews who rejected him and his forme of Goverment to choose a King, so that he will bless us, and be propitious to us who reject a King to make him onely our leader, and supreme governour in the conformity as neer as may be of his own ancient goverment; if we have at least but so much worth in us to entertaine the sense of our future happiness, and the courage to receave what God voutsafes us: wherin we have the honour to precede other Nations who are now labouring to be our followers. For as to this question in hand what the people by thir just right may doe in change of goverment, or of governour, we see it cleerd sufficiently; besides other ample autority eev'n from the mouths of Princes themselves. And surely they that shall boast, as we doe, to be a free Nation, and not have in themselves the power to remove, or to abolish any governour supreme, or subordinate with the goverment it self upon urgent causes, may please thir fancy with a ridiculous and painted freedom, fit to coz'n babies; but are indeed under tyranny and servitude; as wanting that power, which is the root and sourse of all liberty, to dispose and *œconomize* in the Land which God hath giv'n them, as Maisters of Family in thir own house and free inheritance. Without which natural and essential power of a free Nation, though bearing high thir heads, they can in due esteem be thought no better than slaves and vassals born, in

ancient goverment: both through observance of the golden rule and through communal action (the commonweal).

œconomize: to manage the household affairs.

the tenure and occupation of another inheriting Lord. Whose goverment, thought not illegal, or intolerable, hangs over them as a Lordly [38] scourge, not as a free goverment; and therfore to be abrogated. How much more justly then may they fling off tyranny, or tyrants? who being once depos'd can be no more than privat men, as subject to the reach of Justice and arraignment as any other transgressors. And certainly if men, not to speak of Heathen, both wise and Religious have don justice upon Tyrants what way they could soonest, how much more mild and human then is it to give them faire and op'n tryall? To teach lawless Kings and all that so much adore them, that not mortal man, or his imperious will, but Justice is the onely true sovran and supreme Majesty upon earth. Let men cease therfore out of faction and hypocrisie to make outcrys and horrid things of things so just and honorable. And if the Parlament and Military Councel do what they doe without president, if it appeare thir duty, it argues the more wisdom, vertue, and magnanimity, that they know themselves able to be a president to others. Who perhaps in future ages, if they prove not too degenerat, will look up with honour and aspire toward these exemplary, and matchless deeds of thir Ancestors, as to the highest top of thir civil glory and emulation. Which heretofore in the persuance of fame and forren dominion spent it self vain-gloriously abroad; but henceforth may learn a better fortitude to dare execute highest Justice on them that shall by force of Armes endeavour the oppressing and bereaving of Religion and thir liberty at home: that no unbridl'd Potentate or Tyrant, but to his sorrow for the future, may presume such high and irresponsible licence over mankind to havock and turn upside-down whole Kingdoms of men as though they were no more in respect of his perverse [39] will than a Nation of Pismires. As for the party calld Presbyterian, of whom I beleive very many to be good and faithful Christians, though misled by som of turbulent spirit, I wish them earnestly and calmly not to fall off from thir first principles; nor to affect rigor and superiority over men not under them; not to compell unforcible things in Religion especially, which if not voluntary, becomes a sin; nor to assist the clamor and malicious drifts of men whom they themselves have judg'd to be the worst of men, the obdurat enemies of God and his Church: nor to dart against the actions of thir brethren, for want of other argument those wrested Lawes and Scriptures thrown by Prelats and Malignants against thir own sides, which though

president: precedent.
unforcible things: such as the forcing of conscience, urged earlier in the Westminster Assembly; see Milton's *On the Forcers of Conscience.*

they hurt not otherwise, yet tak'n up by them to the condemnation of thir owne doings give scandal to all men and discover in themselves either extreame passion or apostacy. Let them not oppose thir best friends and associats who molest them not at all, infringe not the least of thir liberties; unless they call it thir liberty to bind other mens consciences, but are still seeking to live at peace with them and brotherly accord. Let them beware an old and perfet enemy,[109] who though he hope by sowing discord to make them his instruments, yet cannot forbeare a minute the op'n threatning of his destind revenge upon them when they have servd his purposes. Let them feare therefore, if they bee wise, rather what they have don already, than what remaines to doe, and be warn'd in time they put no confidence in Princes[110] whom they have provokd, lest they be added to the examples of those that miserably have tasted the event. Stories can inform them how *Christiern* the second, King of *Denmark* not [40] much above a hundred yeares past, driv'n out by his Subjects, and receavd againe upon new Oaths and conditions, broke through them all to his most bloody revenge; slaying his cheif opposers when he saw his time, both them and thir children invited to a feast for that purpose.[111] How *Maximilian* dealt with those of *Bruges*, though by mediation of the *German* Princes reconcil'd to them by solem and public writings drawn and seald. How the massacre at *Paris* was the effect of that credulous peace which the French Protestants made with *Charles* the ninth thir King:[112] and that the main visible cause which to this day hath sav'd the *Netherlands* from utter ruine, was thir finall not beleiving the perfidious cruelty which as a constant maxim of State hath bin us'd by the Spanish Kings on thir Subjects that have tak'n armes and after trusted them; as no later age but can testifie, heretofore in *Belgia* it self, and this very yeare in *Naples*. And to conclude with one past exception, though farr more ancient, *David* after once hee had tak'n armes, never after that trusted *Saul*, though with tears and much relenting he twise promis'd not to hurt him.[113] These instances, few of many, might admonish them both English and Scotch not to let thir owne ends, and the driving on of a faction betray them blindly into the snare of those enemies whose revenge looks on them as the men who first begun, fomented and carri'd on beyond the cure of any sound or safe accommodation all the evil which hath since unavoidably befall'n them and thir King.

discover: uncover, expose.
an old and perfet enemy: Charles I.
Stories: histories.
Maximilian I: Holy Roman Emperor, in 1490.
yeare: 1648.

I have something also to the Divines, though brief to what were needfull; not to be disturbers of the civil affairs, being in hands better able and more belonging to manage them; but to study harder and [41] to attend the office of good Pastors, knowing that he whose flock is least among them hath a dreadfull charge, not performd by mounting twise into the chair with a formal preachment huddl'd up at the od hours of a whole lazy week, but by incessant pains and watching *in season and out of season,*[114] *from house to house* over the soules of whom they have to feed. Which if they ever well considerd, how little leasure would they find to be the most pragmatical Sidesmen of every popular tumult and Sedition? And all this while are to learne what the true end and reason is of the Gospel which they teach; and what a world it differs from the censorious and supercilious lording over conscience. It would be good also they liv'd so as might perswade the people they hated covetousness, which worse than heresie, is idolatry; hated pluralities[115] and all kind of Simony; left rambling from Benefice to Benefice, like ravnous Wolves seeking where they may devour the biggest. Of which if som, well and warmely seated from the beginning, be not guilty, twere good they held not conversation with such as are: let them be sorry that being call'd to assemble about reforming the Church, they fell to progging and solliciting the Parlament, though they had renouncd the name of Priests,[116] for a new setling of thir Tithes and Oblations; and double lin'd themselves with spiritual places of commoditie beyond the possible discharge of thir duty. Let them assemble in Consistory with thir Elders and Deacons, according to ancient Ecclesiastical rule, to the preserving of Church discipline, each in his several charge, and not a pack of Clergie men by themselves to belly cheare in thir presumptuous Sion, or to promote designes, abuse and gull the sim-[42]ple Laity, and stirr up tumult, as the Prelats did, for the maintenance of thir pride and avarice. These things if they observe and waite with patience, no doubt but all things will goe well without their importunities or exclamations: and the Printed letters which they send subscrib'd with the ostentation of great Charac-

chair: pulpit.
pragmatical Sidesmen: those not actually in the discussion but who intrude themselves officiously.
idolatry: as worship of the Calf of Gold (Exod. xxxii).
progging: urging annoyingly.
Consistory: a low diocesan court, composed of ministers, elders, and deacons of a congregation; it dealt with spiritual and ecclesiastical matters.
belly cheare: drink excessively.
Sion: Sion College, seat of the Presbyterian London assembly from 1647.

ters[117] and little moment, would be more considerable than now they are. But if they be the Ministers of Mammon[118] instead of Christ, and scandalize his Church with the filthy love of gaine, aspiring also to sit the closest and the heaviest of all Tyrants, upon the conscience, and fall notoriously into the same sins, whereof so lately and so loud they accus'd the Prelates, as God rooted out those immediately before, so will he root out them thir imitators: and to vindicate his own glory and Religion, will uncover thir hypocrisie to the open world; and visit upon thir own heads that *curse ye Meroz,*[119] the very *Motto* of thir Pulpits, wherwith so frequently, not as *Meroz,* but more like Atheists they have mock'd the vengeance of God, and the zeale of his people.

NOTES

1. Compare Milton's *Sonnet 11,* autumn 1645 (?).

2. Compare Aristotle, *Politics,* V, 11: "Hence tyrants are always fond of ba men, because they love to be flattered, but no man who has the spirit of a fre man in him will lower himself by flattery" (*Works,* ed. Benjamin Jowett [O ford, 1921], Vol. X).

3. Jer. xlviii 10 (Milton's note). The remainder of the verse is significant justification of the regicide: "and cursed be he that keepeth back his swo from blood."

4. Milton refers in these lines to the Presbyterians' conspiring with the kir against Parliament and to Charles's plea of expediency for his promises to ther The Engagement (December 26, 1647) guaranteed the establishment of Pre byterianism for three years and the suppression of Independency in return f aid against Parliamentarian forces.

This long sentence, beginning, "And although sometimes for shame," says effect that although some (the Presbyterians) seem good patriots, yet they revc against the principle of others (the Parliamentarians) who would remove bot the troubles of the people and the causes from which those troubles arise. The have themselves opposed the king in various ways, yet they accuse the othe of disloyalty; they do not realize that the king has used them for his advantag and would have doomed them for their prior action.

5. *their gibrish Lawes:* the various rules of conduct and action, written Anglo-Norman, accrued since the coming of the Normans.

6. Refers to the transference of the Sword of Justice from God's superic agent (Michael) to whose hand He wills (Parliament's). The "apparent signes below lie in God's having provided victory for the Parliamentarians; see als the beginning of p. 5.

7. The Church-Covenant was an earthly example of God's divine mercy (c grace); that the Presbyterians had cited Charles's tyranny therein without th temperance of mercy indicates the speciousness of their recent appeal.

8. A parallel is suggested between the pagan Nero's killing the early Chris tians and Charles's war with the Puritans, the true servants of God.

9. Prov. xii 10 (Milton's note): "A righteous man regardeth the life of hi beast: but the tender mercies of the wicked are cruel."

10. King of the Amalekites, spared by Saul, who thus turned back from following God and his commandments (1 Sam. xv 9, 11). The Presbyterians are paralleled with Saul, who is rejected by God from being king over the Israelites, and the Parliamentarians with Samuel, who slew Agag, the spiller of innocent blood.

11. Jonathan, son of Saul, delivered Israel from the oppressor, only to be sentenced to death by his father for having tasted of honey against his command. However, with the tasting came enlightenment, and had others tasted, says Jonathan, more Philistines would have been destroyed (1 Sam. xiv 26–45). Like Saul, the Presbyterians were dishonoring the many sons who have freed England from Charles's yoke, some dying in the battle. And thus behind Milton's brief reference may be the admonition that if more opponents of Charles had taken advantage of God's providence against the perverse decrees of the Presbyterians, victory would have been more resounding.

12. For example, William Prynne in *A Vindication of the Imprisoned and Secluded Members of the House of Commons* (January 23, 1649) and *A Briefe Memento to the Present Unparliamentary Junto Touching their Present Intentions and Proceedings to Depose and Execute Charles Stewart, their Lawfull King* (January 4, 1649).

13. John Gauden, whose *The Religious and Loyal Protestation . . . Sent to a Colonell, to Bee Presented to the Lord Fairfax and His Councell of Warre* (January 15, 1649) concludes with praise of Parliament, should it not proceed with "trying and destroying our Soveraign Lord the King," for its "*masculine*, Heroick, truly Christian and Divine" action, rather than "foolish and *feminine*."

14. Probably Charles's chaplain, Henry Hammond, is among those ministers referred to here as having appealed to Lord Fairfax in January 1649 to save Charles. *Dancing* indicates their ability to "turn" nimbly from one scriptural argument to another; see the next line.

15. Presbyterian administrators working through the classis (or synod), which included all ministers or elders in a district, and the province, which had jurisdiction over various classes. The Westminster Assembly had hoped to establish such provinces throughout England.

16. Refers to demands in the Westminster Assembly in 1646 for legislation to repress heresy and "error."

17. For Milton a minister of God had only God to account to for his beliefs, not the Presbyterians who would force conformity with their beliefs. Compare Milton's *On the Forcers of Conscience* for the whole passage.

18. Milton argues that the clergy should be supported by the parishioners through "competent allowance" and "large gifts." By 1652, however, there were proposals for state support, which he rejects in *Sonnet 16*.

19. Eleven members of Parliament charged on July 6, 1647, for correspondence with the queen.

20. Rebels against Moses and Aaron, and thus against the Lord (Num. xvi 1–35). *A Serious and Faithfull Representation of the Judgements of Ministers of the Gospel within the Province of London* (January 18, 1649) had related the English rebels to them (p. 9).

21. David had spared Saul, saying: "Behold, this day thine eyes have seen how that the Lord had delivered thee to day into mine hand in the cave: and some bade me kill thee: but mine eye spared thee; and I said, I will not put forth mine hand against my lord; for he is the Lord's anointed" (1 Sam. xxiv 10). The claims of divine origin for the Stuart kings lie in the background.

22. Psalm cv 15: "Touch not mine anointed."

23. Charles, whom Milton indicts as "*Author or Instigator*" of the massacre of English Protestants in Ulster in 1641 (*Eikonoklastes,* p. 116).

24. Charles bribed the rebels by relinquishing rights to "more then five Irish Counties" (*Eikonoklastes,* p. 114).

25. Rom. xiii 1–2: "Let every soul be subject unto the higher powers. For there is no power but of God: the powers that be are ordained of God. Whosoever therefore resisteth the power, resisteth the ordinance of God." Further on the verse warns against dereliction of duty such as that adjured upon the Parliamentarians: "they that resist shall receive to themselves damnation."

26. Gen. i 26: "and let them have dominion over the fish of the sea, and over the fowl of the air, and over the cattle, and over all the earth, and over every creeping thing that creepeth upon the earth."

27. Claude de Seissel, from whose *La Grande Monarchie de France* (1519) Milton quotes in his *Commonplace Book* in 1642–44 (?): "The King of France considers it necessary to submit to the decrees of his general parliament . . . the 'bridle' of the King." All *Commonplace Book* (hereafter *CPB*) quotations are from Miss Ruth Mohl's edition in the *Yale Milton,* Vol. I.

28. Among the various historians recorded in the *CPB* are: Sleidan (German history); Girard, De Thou, Commines, Gilles, Seissel (French history); Sigonius, Jovius, Sarpi, Guicciardini, Villani (Italian history); Guicciardini (Spanish history); Malmesbury, Stow, Holinshed, Speed, Smith, Lambard, Du Chesne, Camden, Gildas (English history); and Buchanan (Scottish history).

29. Milton's point is that William the Conqueror was unacceptable to the people until he had sworn to uphold their laws and customs at St. Albans; see his notes in the *CPB,* p. 181: "the crowning of Ks in England not admitted till thire oath receav'd of justice to be administerd, according to the laws. Stow & Holinsh. William conqueror. and other Ks." Royalists contended that he had acquired office through conquest.

30. In the *Nicomachean Ethics,* VIII, x: "he will not look to his own interests but to those of his subjects" (*Works,* ed. W. D. Ross [Oxford, 1925], Vol. IX). In his only reference to Aristotle in the *CPB,* on p. 182 under "King," Milton cites the previous statement: "the tyrant looks to his own advantage, the king to that of his subjects"; his note in English, giving Book IX, ch. 10, and quotation in Greek, entered ca. 1639–41, is in the margin.

31. "O Lord our God, other lords besides thee have had dominion over us: but by thee only will we make mention of thy name."

32. From *Apologeticus* (p. 31) Milton quotes: "Augustus, the founder of the Empire, was unwilling even to be called 'Lord,' for this also is a name of God. I will certainly call the Emperor 'Lord,' but at a time when I am not compelled to say 'Lord' instead of 'God'. . . . In what way is the father of his country Lord?" (*CPB,* p. 181).

33. 1 Sam. viii 4–5: "Then all the elders of Israel gathered themselves together, and came to Samuel unto Ramah, And said unto him, Behold, thou art old, and thy sons walk not in thy ways: now make us a king to judge us like all the nation." Despite warnings of what life under a king would be and of the turning of the Lord against them, the elders still demanded a king to "judge us, and go out before us, and fight our battles" (20).

34. For example, Aristotle (*Politics,* VII, 7: "whereas the natives of Asia are intelligent and inventive, but they are wanting in spirit, and therefore they are always in a state of subjection and slavery"), Jean Bodin (*De republica libri sex,* V, i), and Calvin (*Institutes,* IV, xx 8).

35. For example, David Jenkins in *God and the King* (1649). Part of Psalm 4 is quoted.

36. David committed adultery with Bathsheba, wife of Uriah the Hittite; to ırry her and thus hide her illegitimate pregnancy, David had Uriah placed the forefront of battle, where he was killed (2 Sam. xi 2–17).

37. "That his heart be not lifted up above his brethren, and that he turn not ide from the commandment, to the right hand, or to the left" (Deut. xvii 20). ıe Mosaic law is promulgated in chs. xii ff.

38. *Heraclidae,* lines 418–21.

39. Dio Cassius, *Roman History,* LXVIII, xvi.

40. George Buchanan links Trajan and Theodosius II, and relates this idea *Rerum Scoticarum Historia,* Book XX.

41. The quotation omits "and shalt possess it, and shalt dwell therein" after ;iveth thee." The civil wars were in effect the means of determining who ›ssessed England.

42. The Lord, who unsuccessfully tried to dissuade the people from their ›sire by showing them the nature of the king they would have. Still they de›sed Samuel.

43. 1 Kings xii 16. Rehoboam, son of Solomon, had been beseeched by the raelites: "Thy father made our yoke grievous: now therefore make thou the :ievous service of thy father, and his heavy yoke which he put upon us, lighter, ıd we will serve thee" (verse 4), but instead he promised to chastise them ith scorpions.

44. Livy, *Roman History,* II.

45. 1 Kings xii 6–7; these were "the old men, that stood before Solomon his ıther while he yet lived." Their advice was to grant the Israelites' wish. He ext spoke to "the young men that were grown up with him, and which stood efore him"; their advice was to threaten the people with worse oppression.

46. "Submit yourselves to every ordinance of man for the Lord's sake: hether it be to the king, as supreme; Or unto governors, as unto them that are ›nt by him for the punishment of evildoers, and for the praise of them that do vell. For so is the will of God, that with well doing ye may put to silence the ;norance of foolish men: As free, and not using your liberty for a cloke of ıaliciousness, but as the servants of God" (verses 13–16).

47. Rom. xiii 1; "Whosoever therefore resisteth the ordinance of God" (verse).

48. "Jesus answered and said unto him, Get thee behind me, Satan: for it is vritten, Thou shalt worship the Lord thy God, and him only shalt thou serve" Luke iv 8).

49. Rev. xiii 2.

50. The beast was identified with the Papacy, which had acquired the alle;iance of the world's kings. Charles's defeat was interpreted as making England eady for the millennium, the fifth monarchy under the reign of Christ. See Aichael Fixler's *Milton and the Kingdoms of God* (Evanston, Ill., 1964), pp. .46–51, for a discussion of *The Tenure* as a moderate statement of the coming ›ermanent settlement. Millennial thought is also seen in the *Nativity Ode, Paralise Lost,* and *Paradise Regain'd.*

51. Rom. xiii 3, 4.

52. St. John Chrysostom (345–407), whose works were employed by the Royalists to defend monarchy; reference is to his *Homily XXIII on the Book of Genesis.* Milton records notes from other homilies in the *CPB,* pp. 5 and 151, ›ntered ca. 1639–41.

53. "In this respect a tyrant differs from a king; the one considers at ever point his own advantage, the other provides what is helpful to his subjects (*CPB*, p. 185), from St. Basil the Great, *Works,* I, 456. He is also quoted o pp. 55 and 57 of the *CPB*.

54. Remarks in Xenophon and Livy, among others, would give rise to thi statement.

55. *Hercules Furens,* lines 922–24. He had just killed the tyrant Lycus.

56. Judg. iii 14–15: "So the children of Israel served Eglon the king of Moa eighteen years. But when the children of Israel cried unto the Lord, the Lor raised them up a deliverer, Ehud the son of Gera, a Benjamite, a man left handed: and by him the children of Israel sent a present [a dagger] unto Eglo the king of Moab."

57. As a Roman Catholic, with the memory of Philip II's marriage to Mar Tudor and wooing of Elizabeth not long past, a Spanish king would create horrific reaction in Milton's English audience.

58. The Golden Rule: "Therefore all things whatsoever ye would that me should do to you, do ye even so to them: for this is the law and the prophets" (Matt. vii 12).

59. He reigned just over twenty years (1066–87).

60. 1 Sam. xv 33.

61. "And thou shalt smite the house of Ahab thy master" (2 Kings ix 7); Jehoram was the son of Ahab.

62. Saul; see 1 Sam. xxiv 6, xxvi 9.

63. This was a major point of disagreement, for the Royalists argued fo Charles's divinity. Thus Milton has stressed the privateness of enmity in Davic and Saul's contention as opposed to the tyranny of Charles.

64. "And he said unto them, The Kings of the Gentiles exercise lordship ove them, and they that exercise authority upon them are called benefactors" (Luke xxii 25).

65. "Whoever will be great among you, let him be your minister; And whosoever will be chief among you, let him be your servant" (Matt. xx 26–27).

66. The entire sentence is drawn from Mark x 42–44.

67. "The same day there came certain of the Pharisees, saying unto him, Get thee out, and depart hence: for Herod will kill thee. And he said unto them, Go ye, and tell that fox" (Luke xiii 31–32).

68. Luke i 46–55.

69. "He hath put down the mighty from their seats" (Luke i 52).

70. Girard, *L'Histoire de France,* IV, 248, is quoted in the *CPB,* p. 185: "Ludovicus pius beeing made judge of a certain German tyrant, approves the people who had depos'd him, & sets his younger brother [Celeadrage] up in his stead." Additional citations appear on pp. 53, 61, 109, 110, 112, 182, 183, 186, and 191.

71. Girard, IV, 248.

72. Johann Leunclavius, *Juris Graeco-Romani* (Frankfurt, 1596), II, 178, which Milton also quotes in the *CPB*, p. 182: "from the book of law of Basilius, Constantine, and Leo, where he says: 'The duty of an emperor is to do good, and when he is lacking in beneficence, he seems to counterfeit the recognized role of emperor.'" The book of law was *Eclogue,* or *Delectus Legum Compendiarus, Factus ab Leone, et Constantino* . . . (703). Milton cites Leunclavius further in the *CPB* (pp. 109, 112).

73. In the *CPB*, p. 183, Milton refers to use of St. Edward's sword by Henry III: "the Earle of Chester bare the sword of St Edward before the K. in token

that he was Earle of ye palace, and had autority to correct the K. if he should see him swerve from the limits of Justice" (Holinshed, *Chronicles,* III, 219). Speed (*Historie,* p. 203) names the sword Curtana. This same evidence is used in *Pro Populo Anglicano Defensio,* ch. VIII.

74. Matthew the Monk (d. 1259), whose *Chronica maiora* and *Historia Anglorum* were frequently sources for later historians.

75. Perhaps William Hughes' *The Booke Called the Mirrour of Justice* (1646), a translation of an early work in French.

76. "Dukes, counts, Marquises &c. were not hereditary at first, but only places of goverment, & office in ye time of Charles ye great" (Girard, III, 163), cited in the *CPB,* p. 191.

77. "Richard the 2d was not only depos'd by parliament, but sute made by the commons that 'he might have judgement decreed against him' to avoid farder mischeif in the realm" was Milton's notation in the *CPB,* p. 185, from Holinshed, III, 512. Richard II figured large in the month before Charles's trial as example of deposition that brought happiness to the nation, as an anonymous pamphlet of December 28, 1648 (*The People Informed of Their Oppressors and Oppressions*), argued.

78. The next entry in the *CPB,* p. 185, after the above, quotes Peter Martyr (Pietro Martire Vermigli, 1500–62) from *In librum Iudicum* (1571), ch. 3: "To those who select an officer of higher rank according to certain laws of the commonwealth which authorize them to place him in command, . . . it is permitted, if the officer should not adhere to his agreements and promises, to reduce him in rank and even compel him by force to satisfy that conditions and agreements which he had promised, and they may do so by arms if it cannot be done otherwise." The biblical text was Judg. iii 30: "So Moab was subdued that day under the hand of Israel. And the land had rest fourscore years"; it is discussed under "Whether It Is Permissible for Subjects to Rise Against Their Rulers."

79. Smith's *Commonwealth of England* (1621), V, 4, supplied the following answer to Milton's "whether it be lawfull to rise against a tyrant?": "the common people judge of that act according to the event, and successe. and the learned according to the purpose of the doers" (*CPB,* p. 185).

80. Milton read Gildas' *De excidio et conquestu Britanniae* in Jerome Commelin's collection *Rerum britannicarum* (Heidelberg, 1587).

81. Gildas wrote, "Kings were anointed, not by God, but as those who stood out as more fierce; and a little later they were slain by the anointers, not according to trial of the truth, and others more fierce were chosen" (*Epistle,* p. 119). Milton recorded the idea in the *CPB,* p. 195.

82. The keys of the kingdom given to Peter (Matt. xvi 18–19), which will open the Golden Gates of Heaven or the Iron Gates of Hell.

83. To excommunicate; to remove from communion, both with God through the rite of Communion and with the Church-Covenant. Compare 1 Sam. xxvi 8–9: "Then said Abishai to David, God hath delivered thine enemy into thine hand this day: now therefore let me smite him, I pray thee, with the spear even to the earth at once, and I will not smite him the second time. And David said to Abishai, Destroy him not: for who can stretch forth his hand against the Lord's anointed, and be guiltless?" The seemingly analogous situation of the king and the people does not extend to David's injunction, for Milton has argued by ancient example that "they anointed them Kings, not of God."

84. Milton was to praise Sir Henry Vane for knowing "Both spirituall power and civill, what each means, / What severs each thou hast learnt . . . / The bounds of either sword to thee we ow" (*Sonnet 17,* lines 10–12).

85. Puns on the meanings of *capitally:* (a) with momentous results; (b) with results in death; (c) by reason and will (derived from the head); and (d) with the obligatory result of "cutting off" his head.

86. Such as *Katadynastes* by John Geree (January 18), *The Apologeticall Declaration* (January 24), and *A Vindication of the Ministers of the Gospel* (January 27).

87. "The German princes renounce their loyalty and their duty to the Emperor because of their religion, which he has tried to destroy" (Sleidan, XVII, 296), quoted in *CPB,* p. 244, and referred to also in *Eikonoklastes,* ch. IX, p. 85.

88. George Buchanan (1506–82), *Rerum Scoticarum Historia* (1582), XVI, 193. Milton cites this work in a different context in the *CPB,* p. 198 (in an amanuensis' hand). Similar matter is implied in a note from Thuanus, *Historia Sui Temporis* (1620), XXI, 647, in the *CPB,* p. 244: "Also the Scottish reformers of the church."

89. Knox (1505–72) was well known for his opposition to Mary, Queen of Scots.

90. William Maitland of Lethington (1528?–1573), who frequently championed the queen against Knox's demands.

91. See note 61 above.

92. Knox's *The History of the Reformation of the Church of Scotland* (1644), Book IV.

93. Mary, Queen of Scots, was forced to abdicate in 1567.

94. From Thuanus (II, 769) Milton records in the *CPB,* p. 185, that "The Scottish nobles, through deputies sent to Elizabeth after Mary had been driven from the kingdom, contend by many examples that this was done legally."

95. "Scotland was at first an elective kingdom for a long time" is noted in the *CPB,* p. 186, from "Hist. Scot.," which may refer to Buchanan as here. Thuanus had also remarked that the Scots had freely chosen and deposed their kings.

96. The *CPB,* p. 183, reads: "The Estates General of Holland take away Philip's power, in a treatise, moreover, published at The Hague, and the provinces are commanded to disclaim obedience to him" (Thuanus, III, 513). "Belgic Provinces" included those to the south (Spanish Netherlands) and to the north (Holland).

97. The Dutch States General had protested the trial of King Charles through ambassadors.

98. The Waldenses were the followers of Peter Waldo, who broke with the Papacy ca. 1179 over post-Apostolic dogma and practice. See *Sonnet 18* on their massacre in April 1655 by the House of Savoy.

99. *The Grand Remonstrance* was passed by Parliament on November 22, 1641, and published on December 1; it shifted power from the king to Parliament and from the House of Lords to the House of Commons.

100. The Presbyterians generally sided with the Independent minority during 1648; in the vote over Charles's proposal for Episcopal settlement they sided with the Lords on October 26, 1648, to accept it, and with the Commons on October 27 to reject it.

101. See note 4 and Milton's remarks on p. 348.

102. Parliament voted on January 3, 1648, not to permit further negotiations with Charles in the bill called "No More Addresses"; the vote was justified in the *Declaration of Parliament* (January 17) and published in *The Votes of the Lords & Commons Assembled in Parliament, Touching No Farther Addresses to the King* (February 18).

103. The Chancellor of Scotland was John Campbell, Earl of Loudon. Charles was taken prisoner at Newcastle-on-Tyne in May 1646.

104. It stated that the war was just and lawful.

105. Antiochus IV (175–164 B.C.), persecutor of the Jews, was overthrown by Judas Maccabeus in 166 (1 Macc. i); see also *Paradise Regain'd*, III, 159–65. For Ahab, see p. 359 and note 61.

106. "Curse ye Meroz, said the angel of the Lord, curse ye bitterly the inhabitants thereof; because they came not to the help of the Lord, to the help of the Lord against the mighty" (Judg. v 23). Jabin, the Canaanite king, was not subdued until his captain Sisera lay dead at the hand of Jael, for the people would not join Barak in his pursuit.

107. Milton must have ironically thought of his conviction that the "Blood of martyrs is the seed of the Church" (Tertullian, *Apologeticus*, p. 50).

108. *The Joynt Resolution and Declaration of the Parliament* (January 11, 1649) declared that the House of Commons now had the supreme power of the land. "Reformed" puns on "re-formed"; compare "his forme of goverment" two lines later.

109. Refers to Charles, but the obvious allusion to "that old serpent, called the Devil, and Satan, which deceiveth the whole world" (Rev. xii 9) charges the king with being Antichrist.

110. "Put not your trust in princes" (Psalm cxlvi 3).

111. Buchanan, XX, 243.

112. Milton refers to the massacre (on St. Bartholomew's Day, August 24, 1572) in a citation from Thuanus in the *CPB*, p. 188.

113. In 1 Sam. xix 6 and xxvi 21.

114. "Preach the word; be instant in season, out of season . . . For the time will come when they will not endure sound doctrine" (2 Tim. iv 2–3).

115. See p. 349 and gloss.

116. Compare *On the Forces of Conscience*, lines 1–4, 20, for the remainder of the tract: "you have thrown off your Prelate Lord / And with stiff vows renounc'd his Liturgie / To seise the widow'd whore Plurality / From them whose sin ye envi'd, not abhorr'd . . . / New Presbyter is but old Preist writt large."

117. Refers to *A SERIOUS AND FAITHFUL REPRESENTATION OF MINISTERS OF THE GOSPEL within the province of London* (January 18, 1649).

118. "The least erected Spirit that fell from heav'n" (*Paradise Lost*, I, 679–80); the name literally means "wealth."

119. See note 106.

OBSERVATIONS UPON
THE ARTICLES OF PEACE WITH THE IRISH REBELS,
ON THE LETTER OF ORMOND TO COL. JONES,
AND THE REPRESENTATION OF THE PRESBYTERY AT BELFAST

published on pages 45–65 of a tract entitled, ARTICLES OF PEACE, MADE AND CONCLUDED WITH THE IRISH REBELS AND PAPISTS, BY JAMES EARLE OF ORMOND, FOR AND IN BEHALFE OF THE LATE KING, AND BY VERTUE OF HIS AUTORITIE. ALSO A LETTER SENT BY ORMOND TO COL. JONES, GOVERNOUR OF DUBLIN, WITH HIS ANSWER THEREUNTO. AND A REPRESENTATION OF THE SCOTCH PRESBYTERY AT BELFAST IN IRELAND. UPON ALL WHICH ARE ADDED OBSERVATIONS. *Publisht by Autority.*

London; Printed by *Matthew Simmons* in *Aldergate-streete.* 1649.

On March 28, 1649, the Council of State ordered Milton to prepare observations on "Articles of Peace, made and concluded with the Irish Rebels and Papists" in the previous January "by James Earle of Ormond, for and in behalfe of the late King," along with some related documents. The result was a piece of wartime propaganda published by authority of the new and extremely precarious republican government. It did not bear Milton's name, and there is no certainty that he was totally or finally responsible for its contents and phrasing. Not infrequently the letters of state which he prepared or Latinized for the Council were only partially his; its members had the final decision and doubtless they made the initial suggestions for what went forth in the name of Parliament. For example, in composing the earliest extant letters from the Commonwealth to Hamburg, Milton wrote under the guidance of Henry

Marten. At least some of the points made in *Observations* probably originated with shrewd, experienced politicians like Marten and Henry Bradshaw: Milton may have been responsible only for phrasing, developing, and integrating ideas into what should be regarded as a group publication. He may have composed a draft which the Council radically revised before he finally polished it. That he was a significant contributor is evident both from the Council's order and from internal evidence, not only in style but in echoes from the *Commonplace Book*.

Ormonde's peace of 1649 faced the Commonwealth with an alliance of Royalists, Roman Catholics, and Ulster Presbyterians in an Ireland which might be used by foreigners as a base from which to invade England—a country exhausted by two civil wars, unrecognized by foreign powers, and internally disunited. In such circumstances government-sponsored propaganda usually resorts to any means to arouse supporters, win over the hesitant, and unite as many citizens as possible against any foe. Such propaganda may be likened to a modern party speech in an election campaign, a speech in which the evils of the opposing party, its record, and its program are misrepresented and exaggerated. The opposition leaders are accused of menacing national security, of being allied with hostile forces, of unfairness, inhumanity, ignorance, hypocrisy, ruthlessness, and immorality. Such a speech plays on prejudices, oversimplifies issues, and is often intended to deceive its hearers. Those responsible for it offer as an excuse political expediency or the retaliation required because the other side stoops to such tactics. Men of high standards deplore such methods but in time of national emergency are usually willing to employ them. The *Observations* should be read as such a partisan piece of propaganda. As such it obeys a kind of decorum—the decorum of adjustment to, and exploitation of, the weaknesses of its enemies and the prejudices of the British, Protestant audience for which it was intended. That audience, and Milton himself, had been strongly indoctrinated with anti-Roman Catholic opinions as expressed in John Foxe's *Actes and Monuments* and preached from Protestant pulpits. And this propaganda drew strength from the Popes' alliance with England's Spanish enemy, the Gunpowder Plot, denunciations of Roman Catholicism by John Donne and other converts from it, and credulous acceptance of the exaggerated number of Protestants believed killed by the Irish Catholic rebels. In an age which witnessed the St. Bartholomew massacre, the slaughter of the Waldensians, and the horrors of the Thirty Years War, such figures seemed valid. More incredible was the fact that Ormonde and the Ulster Presbyterians made extravagant concessions to the Irish rebels, concessions which threatened English sovereignty in Ireland and thus seemed to be outright treason.

Accordingly the Articles of Peace are denounced as the means whereby the Ulster Presbyterians became "accomplices and assistants to . . . those inhumane Rebels and Papists." After "the mercilesse and barbarous Massacre of so many thousand English," it was unthinkable "that those bloudy Rebels . . . should be now grac'd and rewarded with such freedomes and enlargements as none of their Ancestors could ever merit," though "their endlesse treasons and revolts" made them fit only to be "govern'd by Edicts and Garrisons." The treaty made by Ormonde not only threatened English Protestantism but extended to the ridiculous by repealing acts like the one which prohibited having plows drawn by horses' tails. Such practices proved that the Irish were "not only sottish but indocible and averse from all Civility and amendment." Other conquered nations had the ingenuity to benefit from "a civilizing Conquest," but the Irish preferred their "savage Customes." Yet to "such as these" the treaty entrusted the Militia; and it committed the managing of peace and war to Papists! The king's releasing Ireland from obedience to England, without the consent of Parliament, was a crime which might "strongly conduce to the disthrowning him." Charles I sat "like a demigod in lawlesse and unbounded *anarchy*"; exalting himself above law, he became inhuman and sold the justice due for the more than two hundred thousand who were "cut to pieces by those Irish Barbarians." (Milton later echoed this passage at the beginning of the second book of *Paradise Lost*).

The *Observations* next attacked Ormonde's letter to the Governor of Dublin. To the charge that the Parliamentarians were subverters of religion the reply was that the greatest subverter of true religion is Antichrist, "whom they generally believe to be the Pope and Church of *Rome*," and it is this Antichrist that Ormonde and his master have strengthened. But Parliament has broken the Papists' temporal power and their "public Superstitions," and has encouraged "true Ministers of the Gospel," taking care not "to imploy the Civill sword further than the edge of it could reach."

To the charge that Parliament murdered the king, the *Observa-*

tions replied that his trial and punishment was an "impartiall and noble peece of Justice, wherein the hand of God appear'd so evidently on our side." Far from bringing anarchy or Turkish tyranny, the Parliamentarians have set up government by a national council "chos'n and assembld for the public good," this being the original form of English government, not rule by three estates. Nor is England ruled by the "*Scum of the House of Commons.*" It is the Irish who have a Parliament consisting of dregs carrying on "in the *Irish* Dialect." Ormonde as "head of a mixt Rabble, part Papists, part Fugitives, and part Savages" is guilty of the crimes of blasphemy, reviling and murdering magistrates, and oppression which he alleges against his opponents.

As for the Presbytery of Belfast, it is claiming powers outside its jurisdiction, meddling in state affairs, breeding continual disturbance, and preparing the way to assert for themselves absolute jurisdiction like that claimed by popes. Far from properly acknowledging the dependence of Ireland upon England, they have despised the proper dominion of Parliament and have manifestly broken the Covenant. They are guilty of hypocrisy, deceit, and sowing sedition. "And wheras they affirm that the tolerating of all Religions in the manner that we tolerat them, is an innovation, we must acquaint them that we are able to make it good if need be, both by Scripture and the Primitive Fathers, and the frequent assertion of whole Churches and Protestant States." And it is not true that "*we oppose the Presbyteriall government*"; it has been established "with all freedom, wherever it hath been desir'd. Nevertheless as we perceave it aspiring to be a compulsive power upon all . . . or to require the fleshly arm of Magistracy in the execution of a spirituall Discipline . . . we hold it no more to be *the hedg and bulwark of Religion,* than the Popish and Prelaticall Courts, or the *Spanish Inquisition.*" And it is a calumny to say that we tolerate paganism and Judaism: we detest the latter but know ourselves commanded by St. Paul in *Rom.* xi 18 to respect Jews and endeavor their conversion.

Milton then treats various charges connected with Parliament's treatment of Charles I, particularly the Presbyterians' "grand accusation" that it was without rule or example: in answer he stresses the fact that John Knox "taught professedly the doctrine of deposing, and of killing Kings." In conclusion Milton wonders "if the Earth can bear this unsufferable insolency of upstarts; who from a ground which is not thir own dare send such defiance to the sovran

Magistracy of *England,* by whose autoritie and in whose right they inhabit there." Let them take heed lest their treasonous attempts and practices have not made them more guilty of rebelling than the Irish rebels whom they now assist.

It is easy for modern readers to sympathize with the unfortunate Irish, to be indignant about the pamphlet's attacks on their savagery, to point out that English misgovernment was at least partially responsible for that savagery, and to denounce this tyranny over a conquered people. Such features were characteristic of the ruthlessness and immorality (or amorality) of international politics in the seventeenth century. Milton shared many of the faults of his times. Because in some respects he was superior to them, because he used words like *toleration, charity, liberty,* and *right reason* and preached somewhat limited concepts of them, and because he had unusual talents and intelligence, some readers are shocked that he would participate in wartime propaganda of this sort, particularly because he did so with such zest and effectiveness. It is but little mitigation to point out that Spenser who, unlike Milton, lived in Ireland, was quite as unsympathetic toward its people; that had they or the Spaniards been dominant in England there would have been similar ruthlessness; that unfairness, brutality, ignorance, prejudice, and duplicity prevailed then in international politics and are not unknown today; and that it is realistic to judge men in the light of their times.

EIKONOKLASTES.
IN ANSWER TO A BOOK INTITUL'D
EIKON BASILIKE,
THE PORTRATURE OF HIS SACRED MAJESTY IN HIS SOLITUDES AND SUFFERINGS.
The Author *J. M.*
[Quotations of Prov. xxviii 15–17 and passages from Sallust follow]
Publish'd now the second time, and much enlarg'd.
London, Printed by *T.N.* and are to be sold by *Tho. Brewster* and *G. Moule* at the three Bibles in *Pauls* Church-Yard near the West-end, 1650.
[*Second edition*]

February 8, 1649, saw the burial of Charles I and the publication of *Eikon Basilike* (the King's Image), an apology and defense professedly written by that monarch in his final months but largely composed by his chaplain, John Gauden. It was followed within a year by some sixty editions in Britain and abroad. This pious vindication evoked sympathy and sentiment and, in the popular mind, created the executed king into a sort of myth of martyr and saint. Such effective propaganda obviously had to be countered by a powerful reply. Milton furnished it in *Eikonoklastes* (the Image-Breaker), a title based on the Greek word from which "iconoclast" is derived, one who attacks cherished beliefs as shams. It was published about October 6, 1649.

In his image-shattering, Milton was too good a rhetorician to admit that, apart from one reason, the king's book deserved a reply. He accordingly alleges that the book's contents are too slight to require an answer written for staid men of sound principles; however, one is called for because it was attributed to the king; and his name "among the blockish vulgar" was enough "to make it wise, and excellent, and admir'd, nay to set it next the Bible," though otherwise it contained "little els but the common grounds of tyranny and popery, drest up, the better to deceiv, in a new Protestant guise, and trimmly garnish'd over." For this reason, Milton states, and not because sound men need to have it answered, "I take it on me as a work assign'd rather, than by me chos'n or affected. Which was the cause both of beginning it so late, and finishing it so leasurely, in the midst of other imployments and diversions." In other words, not because he chose the task for himself or because he desired it, but because the attribution of the book to the king enabled it to deceive the "blockish vulgar," Milton took it upon himself "as a work assigned," that is marked out for him, designated for him, or allotted to him to answer; inasmuch as there was nothing of moment in the book itself which required a reply other than the attribution to the king which misled the masses to exalt it, he did not rush to do the job but began it late—probably as late as August—and completed it at his leisure, giving priority to other employments and diversions. The nonchalance with which Milton thus dismisses the royal vindication as trivial and the replying to it as incidental and casual is an obvious rhetorical device, an example of what the Italians called *sprezzatura*, the gentlemanly pretense of careless ease and facility and amateur status, except that Milton resorts to it less to ingratiate the reader by deprecating his own work than in order to belittle the royal *apologia*. His statement about the writing of *Eikonoklastes* is clearly not to be accepted literally in all respects.

One fact seems certain: Milton was busy from February 1649, with his duties as Secretary for Foreign Tongues and with the composition of *The Tenure of Kings* and *Observations upon the Articles.* The late publication of *Eikonoklastes,* eight months after the *Eikon* appeared must have been due, at least in part, to delays in its composition caused by the pressure of his other work. There is a possibility that Milton's "I take it on me as a work assigned" means that he was officially ordered to write it; but no entry to that effect was made in the Order Book of the Council of State. Moreover, the Council probably knew that another reply, *Eikon Alethine* was being written: it was published anonymously about August 26. It may be conjectured that satisfaction with Milton's work on *Observations upon the Articles* led to a suggestion in a Council meeting that Milton compose a reply to the king's book, that no formal order for him to do so was passed because he was already rather fully occupied, that he nevertheless began to plan such a work as early as May, after he had finished the *Observations*, and that dissatisfaction with *Eikon Alethine* led him to more intense work on it in September. Later, on page 94 of the original edition of *Defensio Secunda*, Milton mentions the king's book and states, "Ordered [or bidden] to reply, I opposed my *Eikonoklastes* to his *Eikon* . . . judging that Queen Truth should come before King Charles." But it is noteworthy that even here, though he obviously wants to give the impression that the work was officially requested, he fails to state who or what assigned it.

Milton's purpose was to debunk the myth of Charles, the idolized royal martyr-saint, to take tactical advantage of the book's attribution to him, to identify those who admired the book or its professed author with the credulous, the vulgar, the irrational, and the superstitious, and to do all this by answering the *Eikon* chapter by chapter —a method unconducive to golden prose. The attack appeared in a second edition no earlier than late June 1650 with some verbal additions and deletions and numerous changes in punctuation, spelling, and phrasing. The best modern edition is that by Merritt Y. Hughes in the *Yale Milton*, III.

"To descant on the misfortunes of a person fall'n from so high a dignity, who hath payd his final debt both to Nature and his Faults, is neither of it self a thing commendable, nor the intention of this discours." So Milton begins his Preface, going on to disclaim that it was ambition or desire for a name which motivated him: "I never was so thirsty after Fame, nor so destitute of other hopes and means . . . to attaine it." Indeed, kings are commonly weak at arguments and prove but puny adversaries. Milton makes no scruple, however, "to take up this Gauntlet, though a Kings, in the behalf of Libertie, and the Common-wealth." Moreover, it is manifestly the cunning drift of the factious and defeated party to take advantage of *Eikon Basilike* to promote their designs, "now the third time to corrupt and disorder the mindes of weaker men . . . to the dishonour of this present Government, and the retarding of a generall peace. . . ." Milton's readers may perhaps be few, "but those few such of value and substantial worth, as truth and wisdom, not respecting numbers and bigg names, have bin ever wont in all ages to be contented with."

So adored a book obviously needs to be answered. Milton's purpose is to refute its errors, not to rip up and relate the misdoings of Charles's whole life. The populace, "exorbitant and excessive in all their motions, are prone ofttimes not to a religious onely, but to a civil kinde of Idolatry in idolizing thir Kings," and now all but a few of them, "imbastardiz'd from the ancient nobleness of thir Ancestors, are ready to fall flatt and give adoration to the Image and Memory of this Man, who hath offer'd at more cunning fetches to undermine our Liberties, and putt Tyranny into an Art, than any British King before him." This debasement is unnatural for Englishmen but is attributable to the prelates and their fellow preachers of another name and sect and to the factiousness of men who are divided from the public by their own ends and inclinations. At first the king was generally beloved, but he broke parliaments at home and betrayed Protestants abroad until all men except court vassals opposed his tyrannical proceedings. Then some ambitious men found that they could make use of him, and so a party in his support grew up and he was emboldened to set up his standard against Parliament. The chief of his adherents never loved him; they used him to set a good face on their own malignant designs.

Allegations, not reasons, are the main content of Charles's book. His fair words will be paralleled to his far differing deeds by Milton. And readers should note that instead of repenting his misdeeds, the king attempts to justify the most apparent of his evil-doings: he washes over his foulest actions, disables Parliament, dishonors all Protestant churches which are not prelatical, and utters opprobrious things.

Milton inveighs particularly against the turncoat Presbyterians who turned from fighting the king to supporting him, and from alliance with the other Parliamentarians to spitting at them as sectarians. "I never knew that time in *England*," Milton declares, "when men of truest Religion were not called Sectaries." And he goes on to assert that those who remain Parliamentarians are specially honored by God, selected by Him to stand steadfast in His cause, dignified with the defense of truth and public liberty.

Milton begins the work proper, as he does in several other tracts, with a historical survey—in this case, of Charles's relations with his parliaments. The first he ended to protect the Duke of Buckingham against accusations of crimes which included poisoning James I. The dissolution of the second [to prevent the impeachment of Buckingham] was an even greater affront to the House of Commons. In his fifth year Charles issued a proclamation forbidding it as a presumption to prescribe him any time for Parliament either by persuasion or petition; so that the people began to despair of parliaments. Then he resorted to illegal actions such as monopolies and ship money, giving evident proof that he never meant to recall parliaments. After eight or nine years of these enormities, his necessities forced him to call a Parliament in England, and his first demand was for subsidies to maintain a war against Scotland, a war abominated by the whole kingdom. When Parliament delayed, he broke off their sitting. Indeed, he never called Parliament except in greedy hope of subsidies, never for their true purpose, redress of grievances. It is therefore untrue that he called this last Parliament of his own choice; and this shows how little truth may be expected from the rest of this book.

Milton then proceeds to point-by-point arguments against statements in the King's Book, noting, amongst other things the superstitious rigor of his Sunday's chapel, the licentious remissness of his Sunday's theater, and his failure to disclaim his oppressive acts and impositions until this last Parliament hung over him. Despite his promises, the only reformation of religion we could expect from him would be either "som politic form of an impos'd Religion, or els perpetual vexation, and persecution of all those that comply'd not with such a form." As for his political promises, his resolve was always the same, "to set up an arbitrary Government of his own" to tie all Britain "to the conscience, judgement, and reason of one Man." For Parliament or the nation to have reason, judgment, or conscience was vain if it thwarted the king's will. And as for the devotional portion of this opening section of the book, it is an ordinary compilation quilted out of scriptural phrases, the sort of outward devotion in which the worst of kings indulged. But this king attributes to his own making whole prayers stolen from other men and even borrows for Christian use prayer offered to a heathen God, a vain amatorious poem from Sidney's *Arcadia:* such a heathen fiction is hardly to be used as a Christian's prayerbook in a time of affliction. (Milton here refers to the famous Pamela prayer which occurs on page 248 of the early editions of *Arcadia,* in the Third Book. Some scholars have contended that Milton conspired with John Bradshaw, president of the Council of State, to interpolate this poem into some editions of *Eikon Basilike* in order to discredit it and the king. The accusation originated with a charge of forgery made against Milton by Thomas Wagstaff in 1693, and it was repeated by Samuel Johnson in his notoriously prejudiced *Life of Milton.* It was made untenable by Francis Madan in his book[1] and, recently revived again by William Empson,[2] who was then ignorant of Madan's work, but it remains untenable.[3] Milton expatiates on how this adapted borrowing reveals the idolatry of the king and his book and asks, "What greater argument of disgrace and ignominy could have bin thrown with cunning upon the whole Clergy, than that the King among all his Preistery, and all those numberles volumes of thir theological distillations . . . was forc'd to robb Sr. *Philip* and his Captive Shepherdess of thir Heathen orisons, to supply in any fashion his miserable indigence, not of bread, but of a single prayer to God"? Thus the man accounted a saint and martyr by the people resorted to ignoble shifts to seem holy!

In subsequent chapters Milton treats what *Eikon Basilike* says on such matters as the execution of Stafford, the attempt to arrest five members of Parliament, the Irish Rebellion, the calling in of the Scots, the Covenant, differences over church government, the events of the civil war, the reformation of the times, the king's penitential meditations, and his meditations upon death. Throughout the pamphlet, the method followed is that of commenting on and criticizing given quotations from the royal book. The attack hits both style and content, with emphasis on disparities between the king's words and his deeds, on the unreasonableness of claims to divine right, and on popular credulity manifested in the idolizing of Charles.

A few brief quotations will reveal some of Milton's attitudes. On court ladies he comments (ch. II): "not the best of women; who when they grow to that insolence as to appeare active in State affaires, are the certain sign of a dissolute, degenerat, and pusillanimous Common-wealth." In chapter III, on Charles's entering the House of Commons to arrest five members: "heer like a rott'n building newly trimm'd over he represents it speciously and fraudulently to impose upon the simple Reader; and seeks by smooth and supple words not heer only, but through his whole Book, to make som beneficial use or other ev'n of his worst miscarriages." On the king's

[1] *A New Bibliography of the Eikon Basilike of Charles the First* (London, 1950).

[2] *Milton's God* (London, 1961).

[3] See also Merritt Y. Hughes' admirable summary of the controversy in the *Yale Milton,* III, 152–61, especially note 13.

calling his attendants gentlemen (ch. III): "Gentlemen indeed; the ragged infantrie of Stewes and Brothels; the spawn and shipwrack of Taverns and Dicing Houses"! In reference to Charles's actions (ch. IV): "who knows not that one great Hogg may doe as much mischief in a Garden, as many little Swine"?

Concerning the king's claim that "His letting some men goe up to the Pinnacle of the Temple was a temptation to them to cast him down headlong," Milton remarks (ch. V): "In this *Simily* we have himself compar'd to *Christ,* the Parlament to the *Devill,* and his giving them that Act of settling, to his letting them goe up to the *Pinnacle of the Temple.* A tottring and giddy Act rather than a settling. This was goodly use of Scripture [Matt. iv 5–6] in his Solitudes. But it was no Pinnacle of the Temple, it was a Pinnacle of *Nebuchadnezzars* Palace, from whence hee and Monarchy fell headlong together."[4]

In chapter VI, treating the king's claim that Parliament's advice was not binding on him, Milton concludes

> that the Kings negative voice was never any Law, but an absurd and reasonless Custom, begott'n and grown up either from the flattery of basest times, or the usurpation of immoderate Princes. . . . What an abusive thing were it then to summon Parlaments, that by the Major part of voices greatest matters may be there debated and resolv'd, when as one single voice after that, shall dash all thir Resolutions? . . . To know the will of God better than his whole Kingdom, whence should he have it? Certainly Court-breeding and his perpetual conversation with Flatterers, was but a bad Schoole. . . . He confesses a rational sovrantie of soule, and freedom of will in every man, and yet with an implicit repugnancy would have his reason the sovran of that sovranty, and would captivate and make useless that natural freedom of will in all other men but himself.

On the queen's departure for Europe in 1642, Milton remarks in chapter VII that he and his readers are not concerned to "hear a Husband divulge his Household privacies, extolling to others the vertues of his Wife; an infirmity not seldom incident to those who have least cause": what is undisputed is that she was a bad subject. The book

> ascribes *Rudeness and barbarity worse than Indian* to the English Parlament, and *all vertue* to his Wife, in straines that come almost to

[4] Cf. the beginning of *Paradise Lost,* II, and the end of *Paradise Regain'd.*

Sonnetting. How fit to govern men, undervaluing and aspersing the great Counsel of his Kingdom, in comparison of one Woman. Examples are not farr to seek, how great mischeif and dishonour hath befall'n to Nations under the Government of effeminate and Uxorious Magistrates. Who being themselves govern'd and overswaid at home under a Feminine usurpation, cannot be but farr short of spirit and autority without dores, to govern a whole nation.

The king's claim to have ruled seventeen years with Justice, Peace, Plenty, and Religion, Milton counters by drawing attention in chapter IX to the courts of Star Chamber and High Commission, the abolition of parliaments, the displacing of honest judges, and the sale of offices. "Who can number the extortions, the oppressions, the public robberies, and rapines, committed on the Subject both by Sea and Land, under various pretences?" "For our Religion, where was there a more ignorant, profane, and vitious Clergy, learned in nothing but the antiquitie of thir pride, thir covetousnes and superstition; whose insincere and levenous Doctrine corrupting the people first taught them loosness, then bondage; loosning them from all sound knowledge and strictness of life, the more to fit them for the bondage of Tyranny and superstition." And as for Wealth and Plenty, their presence "in a land where Justice raignes not, is no argument of a flourishing State, but of a neerness rather to ruin or commotion."

In chapter X Milton argues that Charles began the civil war. "No King had ever at his first comming to the Crown, more love and acclamation from a people; never any people found wors requital of thir Loyaltie and good affection: First by his extraordinary feare and mistrust that thir Liberties and Rights, were the impairing and diminishing of his regal power, the true Original of Tyranny: Next by his hatred to all those who were esteem'd Religious; doubting that thir principles too much asserted libertie." Concerning Charles's contention that petitioners should have accepted any answer which he chose to give them as their superior, Milton asks:

what law in any trial or dispute enjoynes a free man to rest quieted, though not satisfi'd, with the will and reason of his Superior? It were a mad law that would subject reason to superioritie of place. And if our highest consultations and purpos'd lawes must be terminated by the Kings will, then is the will of one man our Law, and no suttletie of dispute can redeem the Parlament, and Nation from being Slaves, neither can any Tyrant require more than that his will or reason, though not satisfying, should yet be rested in, and determin all things. . . . neither God nor the Lawes have subjected us to his will, nor sett his reason to be our sovran above Law. . . . The Parlament therefore without any usurpation hath had it alwaies in thir power to limit and confine the exorbitancie of Kings, whether they call it thir will, thir reason, or thir conscience.

Milton's attacks against the king grow more intense in the later apters. He begins chapter XIII by noting "that Kings . . . as all her Officers of the Public, were at first chos'n and install'd onely consent and suffrage of the People, to govern them as Freemen Laws of thir own framing, and to be, in consideration of that gnity and riches bestow'd upon them, the entrusted Servants of e Common-wealth. . . ." That we should yield kings subjection to ır own ruin and hold our safety and natural freedom by their mere ft "was never the intent of God, whose ways are just and equal; ever the intent of Nature, whose works are also regular; never of ıy People not wholly barbarous. . . ." To Charles's denouncing cts, schisms, and heresies, Milton answers that nothing has "more arks of Scism and Sectarism than English Episcopacy; whether we ok at Apostolic times, or at reformed Churches." Nothing can be Catholic or universal in Religion, but what the Scripture teaches; hatsoever without Scripture pleads to be universal in the Church, being universal is but the more Scismatical. . . . Christian liber- e purchas'd with the death of our Redeemer, and establish'd by e sending of his free Spirit to inhabit in us, is not now to depend pon the doubtful consent of any earthly Monarch."

In chapter XVI Milton defends the ordinance against the Book of Common Prayer, asserting that the sense of Scripture and Apostoli- al practice would have taught Charles better concerning liturgies ian his human reasonings and conjectures. Milton admits no need or set forms of prayer: if good desires are "rightly conceav'd in the eart, wholesom words will follow of themselves": liturgies were either prescribed nor used by the founders of the church. God left ur affections to be guided by his sanctifying spirit, and likewise our vords to be put into us without premeditation: to lay them aside for ther outward dictates of men "were to injure him and his perfet Gift, who is the spirit, and the giver of our abilitie to pray. . . . Cannot unpremeditated babling be rebuk'd, and restraind in whom ve find they are, but the spirit of God must be forbidd'n in all nen? But it is the custom of bad men and Hypocrits to take advantage of the least abuse of good things, that under that covert the may remove the goodness of those things rather than the abuse."

In chapter XVII, on differences in church government, Milto repeats many of his old arguments against prelacy and his conter tion that the interests of tyranny and episcopacy were incorporate into each other. Later chapters deal with the events of the war, th divulging of Charles's captured letters, the king's going to the Scot the Scots delivering him to the English, and the denial to Charle of attendance by his chaplains. ("A chaplain is a thing so diminu tive, and inconsiderable, that how he should come heer among mat ters of so great concernment, to take such room up in the Discourse of a Prince, if it be not wonderd, is to be smil'd at.") Milton con cludes by commenting that the royal prayers for forgiveness of hi enemies

> may happly catch the People . . . but how they please God, is to be much doubted. . . . Which perhaps may gain him after death a short, contemptible, and soon fading reward; not what he aims at, to stirr the constancie and solid firmness of any wise Man, or to unsettle the conscience of any knowing Christian . . . but to catch the worthles approbation of an inconstant, irrational, and Image-doting rabble. . . . The rest, whom perhaps ignorance without malice, or some error, less than fatal, hath for the time misledd, on this side Sorcery or obduration, may find the grace and good guidance to bethink themselves, and recover.

THE DEFENSES, 1651–1655

EDITED AND TRANSLATED BY JOHN R. MULDER

Foreword

Selections from:

Pro Populo Anglicano Defensio
The Defense of the People of England: "The First Defense"
February 1651

Pro Populo Anglicano Defensio Secunda
The Second Defense of the People of England
May 1654

Pro se Defensio
The Defense of Himself: "The Third Defense"
August 1655

FOREWORD

The three pamphlets known as the *Latin Defenses* were written during the years of Milton's public office. As Secretary for Foreign Tongues he was commissioned for the first; the other two he wrote spontaneously, partly out of a zeal for causes, partly out of an appetite for controversy. Milton would have been grieved at the slender representation of the *Defenses* in these pages, for he thought highly of his international performance on behalf of the Commonwealth. Posterity, however, has been less enthusiastic. The language barrier in part accounts for it—relatively few people now read the *Defenses* in the original Latin—but there are other reasons. The political theory of these tracts announces nothing new in Milton's way of thinking. The concepts he opposes—the divine right of kings, the analogy between family and civil government, hereditary succession—as well as those he advances—the theory of compact, the supreme power of Parliament, government by law—he had already expounded elsewhere, particularly in the *Tenure*. Moreover, many readers have felt that the invective and sarcasm, often scurrilous, of the *Defenses* is unworthy of the "sublime" Milton. It should be remembered however that the tone of the *Defenses* follows that of "conventional" pamphleteering, and that the scurrility is neither more nor less than was expected either of Milton or of his opponents.

The *Defenses* and their background remain of considerable value for the study of Milton's life. It was therefore thought best, within the scope of this volume, to provide the reader with a background to their historical context, to translate primarily the passages of biographical interest, and to guide those who want to know more of the *Defenses* to the available sources.

The translation follows the principle used in the selection of passages. Therefore, to turn Miltonic Latin into Miltonic English seemed plainly a work of supererogation. Lucidity without loss of accuracy has been the aim. Consequently, Milton's stately and involuted Latin periods have frequently been broken up into manageable English sentences. Also, the translation has modified the use of those stylistic features which, although indispensable to Latin oratory, make for rather stilted English prose. This is particularly true of Milton's consistent recourse to the Latin superlative. The division into paragraphs throughout is the translator's own.

JOANNIS MILTONI ANGLI PRO POPULO ANGLICANO DEFENSIO CONTRA *CLAUDII ANONYMI*, ALIAS *SALMASII*, DEFENSIONEM REGIAM.

Londini, Typis *Du Gardianis*. Anno Domini 1651.

THE DEFENSE OF THE PEOPLE OF ENGLAND AGAINST CLAUDIUS ANONYMOUS, ALIAS SALMASIUS, BY JOHN MILTON, ENGLISHMAN. London, 1651.

"The First Defense"

The anonymous Claudius of the title is Claude de Saumaise or Salmasius (1588–1653), a French scholar of international reputation. He had been for almost twenty years a professor at Leyden when, in November 1649, he published his *Defensio Regia* or *Defense of King Charles I*. This book increased the already vehement opposition of the continental monarchies against the English regicides, and the Council of State therefore asked its Latin Secretary to answer the charges made by Salmasius. Milton was eager to enter the lists against an opponent of renown before an international audience. Although he no longer had the use of his left eye and his right eye was causing him severe pain after an hour's reading, he finished his *Defense* within a year, and entered it in the Stationers Register on December 31, 1650. Within two years it was reprinted eleven times abroad and twice in England.[1] It was widely read in France, Germany, Holland, and Sweden, and publicly burned in Paris and Toulouse.

The *Defense of King Charles I* was a threat to the Commonwealth because of Salmasius' reputation as a scholar. Milton's intention, therefore, was to prove him ignorant. Accordingly, he closely followed the structure of the *Defense of King Charles I,* making his *Defense of the People* a point-by-point refutation of the arguments of Salmasius. His usual method is that of quoting Salmasius and then answering him. First, the errors of fact in the opponent's account of Charles's death are corrected (ch. I). That the king is not above the people is then proved from: the law of the Old Testament (ch. II), the law of the New Testament (ch. III), the practice of both Hebrews and Christians (ch. IV), and the law of Nature (ch. V). The power of the people surpasses that of the king (chs. VI and VII). In England the sovereign power of the people is vested in the Commons (ch. VIII), and English history furnishes many a precedent of the Commons' passing judgment on the king (ch. IX). Charles was executed after due process of law (chs. X and XI), for the crimes of tyranny and high treason (ch. XII).

The title *Defense of the People* is of course misleading if "people" is understood in its modern sense. The opinion of the majority had opposed the regicide, and Milton is throughout defending a forcibly truncated parliament—the Rump—and the army. Salmasius had called Pride's purge an instance of military despotism. Milton's answer to that charge, in chapter VI, illustrates his definition of "people": "Since the better, that is, the sounder, party in the House expressed the true power of the people, why may we not say that its actions were the actions of the people? If the majority of the legislators prefer to live as slaves or to sell out the government, should the minority not take hold of every opportunity to prevent this and to maintain freedom?" Milton is not alone in restricting "people" to mean something like "the reasonable part of the populace." In the seventeenth century only some of the Levellers seem to have used "people" to mean "the total male population"—and even they tended to except servants. Aside from vitriolic taunts on the bad Latin and the domineering wife of Salmasius, this *Defense* contains little that is not expressed in earlier works of Milton. Its main argument, that ruler and people enter into a Covenant, the Constitution, based on the law of God and of nature, was already developed in the *Tenure,* in which Milton first applied his theory of church polity to civil government. The *First Defense* does however contain new material in the two lucid and forceful paragraphs on Christian liberty, found early in chapter III. Milton is there engaged in answering Salmasius' argument that Christ preached subjection to temporal authority when he urged the payment of taxes. Milton argues that Christ paid taxes not because he thought them just, but because he wished to avoid trouble with the authorities, knowing that he still needed his freedom to fulfill his destiny. Christ was deliberately ambiguous on the question of taxation, argues Milton, because his questioners were trying to trap him. His ambiguity is therefore proof of his opposition to the tax burden. If read according to the spirit instead of according to the letter, says Milton, the New Testament everywhere endorses Christian liberty. The two paragraphs quoted here are an example of Milton's spiritual reading:

> Let us see whether the gospel, that heavenly hymn of liberty, assigns us as slaves to kings and tyrants, from whose limitless power the old law, even though it taught a form of slavery, did deliver the people of God.[2]
>
> Your first argument is taken from the person of Christ who, everyone knows, took on the likeness not only of a subject but even of a slave,[3] for the very reason that we might be free not only inwardly, but also politically. How incongruous are the words sung by Mary, mother of Christ, announcing his coming—"he hath scattered the proud in the imagination of their hearts; he hath put down the mighty from their seats, and exalted them of low degree"[4]—if his coming rather strengthened the thrones of tyrants, and forced all Christians to accept the harshness of their rule. By his birth, his servitude and his suffering under tyrants, he has bought for us all true liberty. As he has not withheld the means to bear slavery with patience, if necessary, so has he not withheld the means to strive nobly for liberty, but has given them in fuller measure. Therefore Paul drew this conclusion not only on evangelical but also on civil liberty: "Art thou called, being a servant? care not for it; but if thou mayest be made free, use it rather. Ye are bought with a price; be not ye the servants of men."[5] In vain then do you urge slavery upon us from the example of Christ, who paid with his servitude for the foundation of our liberty, even our civil liberty. On our behalf he indeed took on the likeness of a slave, but he never took off the soul of a deliverer. Thus on the subject of the right of kings he taught something altogether different from what you teach. . . .
>
> Please make an effort to understand that on the rights of kings he did not hold the kind of opinion that kings find pleasing. One gathers this quite clearly from the answer with which he apparently preferred to send away his interrogators instead of teaching them. He asks to see the tribute money. "Whose image is that?" "Caesar's,"

they answer. "Then return to Caesar the things that are Caesar's and to God the things that are God's."[6] And is there anyone at all who does not know that one should return to the people the things that belong to the people? "Return to all men what you owe them," declares Paul.[7] Not everything therefore belongs to Caesar. Our liberty does not belong to Caesar but is truly a gift from God himself, given to us at birth. To hand over to any sort of Caesar this liberty, which we did not receive from him, would be most foul and unworthy the origin of man. If someone, looking upon the features of the human face, were to ask of whom it was a likeness, would not any one at once answer that it was a likeness of God? Since therefore we belong to God, which means that we are truly free and are to be returned to God only, we certainly cannot, without the gravest sin of sacrilege, surrender ourselves as slaves to Caesar, a mere man and moreover an unjust, a dishonest man, and a tyrant.

NOTES

1. *Joannis Miltoni Angli Pro Populo Anglicano Defensio, contra Claudii anonymi, alias Salmasii, Defensionem Regiam.* Londoni, Typis Du Gardianis. 1651. Fourteen editions appeared between 1651 and 1695. They were listed by F. F. Madan in "Milton, Salmasius, and Dugard," *The Library,* 4th Series, IV (1923–24), 119–45. To Madan's notes on variations among copies of these editions Maurice Kelley added a list of variations in copies in the Princeton Library: "A Note on Milton's *Pro Populo Anglicano Defensio,*" *The Library,* 4th Series, XVII (1937), 466–67. Variations among the more than forty copies in the University of Illinois Library are described by Clarissa O. Lewis in "A Further Note on Milton's *Pro Populo Anglicano Defensio,*" *The Library,* 4th Series, XXIII (1943), 45–47. For a note on existing manuscript copies and for a list of presentation copies, see French, *Life Records,* II, 354–57. The Columbia editors reprinted the text of the 1658 edition, revised by Milton and listed by Madan as No. 14. C. W. Keyes' excellent critical notes enable one to study the numerous differences between the 1651 and 1658 editions (*Columbia Milton,* VII, 563–87). W. R. Parker has itemized these differences in *Milton's Contemporary Reputation* (Columbus, 1940), pp. 40–41. The present translation was made from the Princeton University Library copy, Ex 3859/37/15, of the third issue of the first edition (Madan 1), which was checked against the *Columbia Milton* reprint of the 1658 edition. J. M. French has settled the issue of the date in "The Date of Milton's *First Defense,*" *The Library,* 5th Series, III (1948), 56–58. See also, by the same author, "The Burning of Milton's *Defensio* in France," *MLN,* LVI (1941), 275–77. For a more detailed account of Salmasius' *Defensio Regia* than is provided in the introduction, see the *Yale Milton,* IV, 962–1035.

2. The *Commonplace Book* quotes from the Latin of the German jurist Schickardt (1592–1635): "Nor was the King of the Hebrews above the Laws" (*Columbia Milton,* XVIII, 186).

3. Phil. ii 7: "But made himself of no reputation, and took upon him the form of a servant, and was made in the likeness of men."

4. Luke i 51. In the original text Milton consistently uses his favorite Latin version of the Bible, the Tremellius-Junius version.

5. 1 Cor. vii 21.

6. Matt. xxii 19–21.

7. Rom. xiii.

JOANNIS MILTONI ANGLI PRO POPULO ANGLICANO DEFENSIO SECUNDA. CONTRA INFAMEM LIBELLUM ANONYMUM CUI TITULUS, *REGII SANGUINIS CLAMOR AD COELUM ADVERSUS PARRICIDAS ANGLICANOS.*

Londoni, Typis Neucomianis, 1654.

THE SECOND DEFENSE OF THE PEOPLE OF ENGLAND, BY JOHN MILTON, ENGLISHMAN, AGAINST THE INFAMOUS ANONYMOUS LIBEL ENTITLED THE CRY OF THE KING'S BLOOD TO HEAVEN, AGAINST THE ENGLISH PARRICIDES. London, 1654.

Milton was still expecting a published answer from his opponent, when Salmasius died in 1653. For want of an illustrious enemy Milton now decided to answer a lesser attack on his first *Defense of the People,* namely, the anonymous *Regii Sanguinis Clamor,* or *The Cry of the King's Blood* (The Hague, 1652). The author of the *Cry* was Pierre du Moulin, an Anglican clergyman and a Royalist, living in London, who for obvious reasons preferred not to sign his name. He sent his manuscript to Salmasius, who gave it to his protégé Alexander More. More saw it through the press and even added a preface which he asked the printer, Vlack, to sign. In spite of More's precautions to avoid being associated with the *Cry,* there was a strong rumor in Holland that he was the author. Milton took the rumor as fact: his *Second Defense* is aimed at More. It was published in May, 1654.[1] A few weeks earlier Milton had learned from the Dutch ambassador that More was not the author, but "that was all one; he having writ it, it should go to the world; one of them was as bad as the other" (Aubrey). The conclusion is not quite true: More was a little worse than Du Moulin. Milton had investigated More's background and discovered the kind of dirt that is gold to the pamphleteer. Milton's attacks on the conduct of his enemy were not just the lurid fabrications that were then part of the conventions of pamphlet warfare; Kester Svendsen has recently shown that Milton's charges are substantiated by the records still available in Holland and Geneva.[2]

Alexander More was born in southern France, in 1616, of a Scottish father and a French mother. At the age of twenty, he was professor of Greek in Geneva but was asked to leave the city in 1649 because his affair with a servant girl had caused a scandal. Salmasius thereupon secured More a position as professor of theology in Middleburg, but again a servant girl proved More's downfall. He was accused by the wife of Salmasius of having got with child her maid Pontia, the pseudonym for Elizabeth Guerret. More publicly prosecuted the Salmasiuses for slander. Although he cleared himself in court, his reputation was by now somewhat soiled, and Milton, throughout the *Second Defense,* delights in holding More up to ridicule.

The structure of the *Second Defense* is again largely determined by the structure of the pamphlet to which it is an answer. In the proem Milton glories in the results of his *First Defense,* hailing the victory over Salmasius as a triumph for liberty, and declaring himself the champion not only of England but of all free men everywhere. He then selects from the *Cry* five points for lengthy rebuttal: the attack on his appearance, the "greatness" of Salmasius, "patron of kings," the attack on his own character, the unlawfulness of the judgment passed upon the king, and the attack on Cromwell. The *Cry,* borrowing a line from Virgil's description of the Cyclops Polyphemus, had described Milton as "a monster horrid, ugly, huge, of light bereft." This one reference to his blindness stung Milton into a long defense of blindness as the sign of greatness and special destiny. His answer to the supposed greatness of Salmasius includes a eulogy of Queen Christina of Sweden for her refusal to be "patronized" by Salmasius. The attack on his character he cancels out with an autobiographical account. As to the unlawfulness of the royal execution, he defends it as the will of the people, and he expresses his admiration for the judges, particularly in his portrait of John Bradshaw, who had presided over the trial. The attack on Cromwell is answered in the famous Cromwell portrait. The *Second Defense* then ends with an address to the people of England.

The invective interspersed throughout the *Second Defense* is its least interesting feature. More intriguing is the difference in tone between this and the previous *Defense*. Foreign opinion of the Commonwealth had changed for the better. Believing that his *First Defense* and the state letters for which he had been responsible had significantly contributed to the improvement of England's reputation abroad, Milton now confidently addresses his international audience with many grand oratorical flourishes. This is particularly evident in the following passage on his blindness, which is partly a Latin prose parallel to the invocation of Book III of *Paradise Lost*.

> And now for my opponent's charges against me. Is there anything in my career or conduct for which he can blame me? Manifestly nothing. Then what does he do? He does what only a crude barbarian would do—he speaks with scorn of my appearance and my blindness and calls me
>
> A monster horrid, ugly, huge, of light bereft.
>
> I never dreamt I would have to vie for beauty with the Cyclops. Yet he suddenly changes his mind: "Although he is not huge, there is nothing more bony, bloodless, and shrivelled." Though it is pointless for a male to speak of his beauty, I will spend a few words on mine, because I have reason to be thankful to God for my looks and because I can thus confound liars. Otherwise, someone might happen to think of me as a monster with the head of a dog, or as a rhinoceros, the way the Spanish populace, on the authority of their priests, think of heretics.
>
> As far as I know, no one who has seen me has ever found me ugly. I refuse to decide whether or not that makes me handsome. I admit that I am not very tall, but my height is average rather than short. And what if, like so many men of excellence in peace and war, I were small? If one's stature amply allows one to be virtuous, why should it be called slight? What is said about my being so weak is a lie. On the contrary, I am a man of courage and strength, and in earlier years I learned, through daily practice, how to handle my sword with skill. Commonly armed with this weapon, I used to think myself a match for any man, even one far stronger than myself, and I had no fear of any harm that men can do to one another. I have today the same courage and equal strength—only my eyes are not the same. However, they appear as sound, as bright and sparkling as those of men with perfect sight. My eyes are the only dissembling part of me, but they dissemble against my will. As to my complexion, which he calls "entirely bloodless," it has remained the opposite of the pale and colorless cast. So much so that, even though

I am past forty, almost anyone takes me for nearly ten years younger. That my flesh or skin is shrivelled is equally untrue.

If I should lie on any of these points I would deserve the ridicule of many thousands of my countrymen and not a few foreigners who know me personally. Therefore, since on so superfluous a topic this man tells so many shameless and unfounded lies, one can hope little better from his other arguments.

So far I have been forced to speak of *my* appearance. I hear that *your* appearance, More, is really contemptible, and the living image of the wickedness and malice within you. Yet I care not to elaborate on it, as I prefer that it remain hidden from others.

Oh, that I could with equal ease refute this beastly opponent on the subject of my blindness, but I cannot. Let me then bear it. To be blind is not miserable; to be unable to bear blindness, that is miserable. Why should I not bear that which should be borne with equanimity by everyone to whom it may befall?

Why should I not bear what I know may happen to any mortal and has happened to some of the finest and most outstanding figures of all times? Or shall I rehearse the names of those oldest and wisest poets of antiquity whose calamity the gods are said to have recompensed with gifts far preferable to eyesight; whose fellow men revered them so much that they preferred to accuse the gods themselves rather than to blame these poets for a crime. . . . Moreover, it is well-known that the Patriarch Isaac,[3] who of all mortals was then to God most dear, lived many a year in blindness, as did perhaps for some time his son Jacob,[4] no less dear to God. Finally, we are fully sure, upon the divine testimony of Christ our Saviour, that the blind man who was healed by him had been blind even from the womb, for no sin of his own or of his parents.[5]

As for me, after frequent and profoundly serious examination of my innermost self, I call Thee, my God, to witness, searcher of the inmost spirit and of all thoughts, that I am unaware of any old or recent offense so heinous that I above others should deserve to be burdened with this calamity. Since the royalists now exult in their belief that I am atoning for my writings, I call the same God to witness that I have never at any time written anything without the firm conviction, then and now, that my writing was honest, true, and pleasing to God. I was never moved by ambition, by hope of gain or fame, but only by the desire to do my duty to my country, rightly and with devotion. I wrote first of all to deliver not only my country but also the Church.

I was publicly given the task to oppose the *Defense of the King* at a time when I was not only in poor health, but had also nearly lost the sight of my other eye. My physicians warned that, should I undertake the task, I would certainly soon lose both. I was not deterred by this warning, thinking that I heard not a physician's voice—not that of Aesculapius[6] from the shrine of Epidaurus—but the inward voice of a diviner guardian. Since my fate proposed to me two destinies, on the one hand blindness, on the other, duty, I was forced either to lose my sight or to desert the highest duty. I thought then of the double destiny which [Achilles] the son of Thetis tells us his mother brought back for him from the Delphic oracle:

> A two-fold fate leads to my final end:
> If I remain to scale the walls of Troy,
> I shall not leave from here, but gain great fame;
> If I return to my sweet native land,
> I shall have length of days—without renown.
>
> *Iliad* IX, 411–16

Then I pondered that many purchased a lesser good with a greater evil, for instance, glory with death. I however intended to exchange a lesser evil, blindness, for the greater good of fulfilling one of the highest tasks. Since this is in itself more substantial than glory, it should also be more desired and revered. I concluded therefore that I should use my short span of light for the greatest possible benefit of the commonwealth. This was the motive for my choice and the cause of my loss.

Let the wicked slanderers of the judgments of God cease their libellous fictions about me. They must know that my lot causes me neither grief nor shame and that my conviction remains unshaken. I have no reason to believe that God is angered. On the contrary, in all the things that matter, I feel and recognize his mercy and paternal goodness towards me. Above all, I acquiesce in this burden, because I derive from him my solace and the strength to do his will, more mindful of his largesse than of any denial. Moreover, I would not exchange the knowledge of what I have accomplished for even the most expert of their performances. I would not care to lose the always calm and pleasant recollection of my course of action.

As to blindness, I would rather have mine than theirs or yours, More. Yours is an intellectual blindness, because you are so immersed in the lowest senses that you see nothing sound or substantial. The blindness you vilify in me obscures the colour and surface of things, but allows the mind to ponder on their true and abiding qualities. Besides, there is much I had rather not see and much I can easily leave unseen, while there is little left that I would desire to see. I do not think it miserable, as you do, to be numbered among the blind, the sick, the grieving, and the weak, since I may hope that this brings me closer to the mercy and protection of God, my father. Upon the witness of the Apostle,[7] one may gain great strength through weakness. May I be one of the weakest of men so long as my weakness be the cause of the effective flowering of that immortal and better strength, and so long as my darkness remain the more brightly illumined by the light of the divine countenance. Then I shall be both weak and strong, simultaneously blind and most perceptive. Thus my infirmity shall become my perfection and crowning glory, and thus my darkness will clothe me in radiance.

Surely, we, the blind, are not the last objects of God's care. The less we are able to discern anything but Him, the more merciful is his regard for us. Woe to the man who mocks us; woe to him who injures us—he ought to be exposed to public execration.[8] The divine law and favor not only protect us from the injuries of men but also render us almost sacrosanct. The cause of our darkness appears to be not so much the weakness of our eyes but rather the shadow of heavenly wings over us, and often we are again illumined by a far surpassing inner light. Hence the extraordinary kindness and regard of my friends on their frequent visits. With some of them I may indeed imitate the dialogue of the true friends Pylades and Orestes:

> Orest. Go before me and guide my step.
> Py. That task is dear to me.
>
> Euripides, *Orestes*, 795

And elsewhere:

> Reach out for your friend and helper.
> Lean on my shoulder, for I will guide you through life.
>
> Euripides, *Heracles*, 1398, 1402

They do not think that my misfortune has reduced me to nothingness, or that all of a man's worth and wisdom lies in his eyes.

Besides, I am not languishing in indolence but am still fighting in the first ranks of the great battle for liberty. Therefore, although my eyes have deserted me, the leaders of the state have not deserted me. With due regard for man's condition they grant me the favors and privileges of one who has honorably discharged his duty; they readily offer me leisure and rest, without loss of dignity or of public office. They do not minimize the benefit of my service, and, although I am now less useful, they think that I ought to receive no less consideration. Indeed they have given me such honor that I am like those ancient Athenians whose maintenance in the public hall was officially decreed.

Let no one mourn the honorable loss of my eyes so long as God and men give me solace in my blindness. Far be it from me to mourn it. Far be it from me to be so weak that I cannot easily despise the slanderers of my blindness, or to be so implacable that I cannot more easily forgive them.

The author of the *Cry* had pictured Milton as debauched and profligate, expelled from Cambridge, and forced to flee to Italy in disgrace. Milton's divorce pamphlets were attributed to his licentiousness. The political pamphlets were said to have been written to sway a wavering tribunal to the murder of the king. Milton's answer is the famous autobiographical passage of the *Second Defense*, which follows here. Pride in his accomplishments is plainly evident, yet this autobiography is more than an expression of exuberant confidence. Formal rhetoric distinguished between three kinds of proof: logical, ethical, and pathetic. Logical proof persuades the reason, ethical proof engages the moral sense, and pathetic proof sways the emotions. The autobiographical passage is intended as ethical proof: the speaker attempts to gain the assent of his audience by showing that he has always been on the side of honesty and justice, thus implying that his present cause too must be honest and just. Therefore one should not blame Milton for omitting significant autobiographical detail. Private problems and personal sorrows are not touched upon, because they are not to the purpose. Milton's aim is to convey an impression of general, rather impersonal integrity.

I was born at London from upright parents, my father a man of spotless reputation, my mother a very chaste woman and particularly known throughout the neighborhood for her charity. My father destined me while still a child for the study of humane letters, which I took up so eagerly that from the age of twelve on I hardly ever took to bed from my intense studies before midnight. Thus was the first harm done to my eyes, whose natural weakness was aggravated by frequent headaches. Because all this did not slow down my zeal for learning, my father saw to it that I received daily instruction both at a grammar school and at home by other masters.

After I had thus been taught several languages and had tasted the sweetness of philosophy, my father sent me to Cambridge, one of the two universities of the nation. There I studied for seven years the curriculum in arts and sciences, far from every vice, approved by all good men, till having been admitted, and with distinction, to what is called the degree of Master, I did not flee to Italy, as this scandalous liar rumors, but freely returned home, and even left behind me a longing for my person among most of the fellows of the college, who had very much courted my friendship.

At my father's country home, to which he had retired to pass his old age,[9] I spent most of my time, entirely at ease, in the perusal of Greek and Latin writers; sometimes however I would exchange the country for the town, either to buy books or to add something new to my knowledge of mathematics or music, in both of which I then delighted. Having thus passed five years, being desirous, after my mother's death, to see foreign countries, particularly Italy, I gained my father's permission and started out with my manservant.[10]

On my departure the illustrious Sir Henry Wotton, who had long been ambassador of King James to Venice, treated me in the friendliest manner, not only wishing me well but also giving me an elegant letter filled with the most useful instructions for the traveler abroad.[11] On the recommendation of others, the very noble Sir Thomas Scudamore,[12] Viscount of Sligo and ambassador of King Charles, received me most courteously in Paris and of his own accord introduced me, accompanied by several of his household, to the very learned Hugo Grotius,[13] then ambassador from the Queen of Sweden to the King of France, whom I very much wished to meet. Upon my departure for Italy some days later, he gave me letters to the English merchants along my route, that they might render me every assistance in their power.

I boarded a ship at Nice and traveled to Genoa, soon after to Leghorn and Pisa, and from there to Florence. In this city, which I have always revered above the rest for the rare grace both of its language and of its genius, I lived for about two months.[14] There I soon became intimate with many aristocratic and learned men. I also regularly attended the meetings of their private academies, an institution highly commendable for its promotion both of humane letters and of friendly intercourse;[15] for time will never efface the ever pleasant and delightful memories I have of you, Jacopo Gaddi, and also of you—Carlo Dati, Frescobaldi, Coltellini, Bonmattei, Chimentelli, Francini, and many others.[16]

From Florence I went on to Siena and from there to Rome, the city whose long history and early renown detained me for about two months, during which I was most courteously treated by Luc Holste[17] and other men of scholarship and insight. After that I reached Naples, and there a certain monk, with whom I had traveled from Rome, introduced me to Giovanni Baptista Manso, Marquis of Villa, an aristocrat of great wisdom, to whom the distinguished Italian poet Torquato Tasso dedicated his book on friendship.[18] During my stay there he treated me in the most amiable manner indeed, for he himself showed me the sights of the city and the palace of the viceroy, and more than once came to see me in person at my lodgings. When I left he gravely begged my pardon, saying that he had very much desired to be of far greater service, but had found that impossible in that city because of my refusal to be secretive on the point of religion.

The sad tidings from England of the civil war made me renounce my plan to cross over to Sicily and Greece,[19] for I held it base that I should be leisurely making the scholar's tour abroad while my countrymen were fighting for liberty at home. As I was about to go back to Rome, merchants warned me that they had been informed by letters of a plot being laid for me by the English Jesuits in case I should return to Rome, because I had been too outspoken about religion; for I had made it my rule never to introduce the subject of religion in these parts, but not to feign anything, whatever the consequence, should I be asked a question about my faith. I therefore returned to Rome notwithstanding the plot. When questioned, I hid from no one what I was; when attacked, I was for almost two more months[20] as outspoken a defender of the orthodox faith as before, in the very city of the Pontiff himself.

God willing, I reached Florence again unharmed, no less busy paying calls on those who longed to see me, than if I had returned to my native land. Except for a trip of a few days to Lucca,[21] I gladly stayed there as many months as before, when I crossed the Appenine and, by way of Bononia and Ferrara, made for Venice. After I had let slip by one month of sightseeing in this city, and had taken care of the shipping of the books which I had gathered throughout Italy, I traveled, by way of Verona, Milan and the Appennine, and finally along Lake Leman, to Geneva.

Since the mention of this city brings to my mind the slanderer More, I am moved again to call God to witness that in all these places, where so much is allowed, I led a blameless life, untouched by any vice or scandal,[22] always thinking to myself that, if I could hide from the eyes of men, I certainly could not hide from those of God. In Geneva I daily conversed with Giovanni Diodati, the very learned professor of theology.[23] Then, taking the same route as before, I returned through France to my own country, after an absence of a year and about three months, arriving at almost the same time that Charles broke the peace with the Scots and opened again another war, called the Bishops' War.[24] Upon the defeat of the royal troops in the first encounter, and seeing all the English filled with a well-deserved hatred for him, Charles not long thereafter called a parliament, not willingly, but because dire circumstances forced him to it. As for myself, I looked about in hope of finding a fixed abode in these troubled and changeable times, and rented a house in the city sufficiently large for me and my books.[25] There I gladly took refuge in my interrupted studies, finding it not difficult to leave the outcome of events first of all to God and then to those elected by the people for that duty.

Meanwhile parliament acted vigorously, and the pride of the bishops began to wane.[26] From the very moment that freedom of speech was first granted, every mouth was open against the bishops; some bemoaned their individual vices, others the vice of the very institution itself, arguing against their being the single exception among all the reformed churches, and agreeing that the church was to be governed by the example of the brethren, though most of all by the word of God.[27]

I now became fully aware of the importance of these issues. Because I saw that men were on the true road to liberty and that, after those earliest steps, they were moving straight towards the delivery of all mortal life from slavery, if only the discipline sprung from religion would flow out to include the morals and institutions of the commonwealth—moreover, because I had thus trained myself from my youth that I could not possibly be unaware of the difference between divine and human law—also because I had asked myself the question if I could ever be useful to anyone should I now fail my country, the church itself, and so many brethren facing danger for the gospel's sake—I resolved, notwithstanding my preoccupation with other matters,[28] to apply myself to these issues with all my heart and every power of concentration. Accordingly, I first dedicated to a certain friend the two volumes *Of Reformation Touching Church Discipline in England*. Then, because two bishops, of renown above the rest, argued their cause against certain ministers of the highest rank, and because I was convinced that, on matters which I had studied only out of love of truth and a sense of Christian duty, I would hardly speak worse than those who strove only for their own gain and their unlawful tyranny, I gave answer to the one bishop in two books, *Of Prelatical Episcopacy* and *Of the Reason of Church Government*, and to the other in some *Animadversions* which I had jotted down, and in an *Apology* written soon thereafter. Thus I lent support to the ministers who were said to be but barely holding up under the eloquence of those men, and from that time on I was ready to engage in any further reply they might make.

When the bishops had finally fallen under the general attack and we were freed from them, my thoughts turned elsewhere to see how I could further the cause of that true and substantial liberty which we must seek not without but within, and which must first of all be gained not through strife but through the right ordering and right governing of life. Therefore, reflecting that there are in all three kinds of liberty—ecclesiastical, domestic or private, and civil—without which any one can hardly live out his days in comfort, and having already written on the first and seeing the Magistrate carefully dealing with the other, I undertook for myself the second which was still left, namely domestic liberty. As this also appeared to consist of three questions, the right conduct of married life, the proper upbringing of children, and finally the right freedom of thought, I set out my feelings on the just way not only of binding the marriage tie, but also, if necessary, of loosening it. And I argued from the divine law, which Christ never lifted; much less did he bestow on any other civil law an authority greater than the entire law of Moses. Moreover, the right interpretation of the single exception of fornication, as it was first set out in my rehearsal of mine own and others' opinions, was more fully illumined by our famous Selden in his *Hebrew Wife*, published about two years later.[29] In vain does he proclaim liberty in parliament and the courts who at home is bound in a bondage most unworthy a man, and that to an inferior; I therefore wrote some books on this subject, at that particular time when husband and wife were often the bitterest enemies, he staying at home with the children, she tarrying in the enemy camp and threatening her husband with slaughter and destruction.

Thereupon I dealt in a small book with the education of children, indeed briefly, but I deemed it sufficient for those who would undertake that matter with the zeal it requires, for nothing can be of greater moment for imbuing the minds of men with virtue, the source of true and inward liberty, and nothing can exceed its influence on the good government and the perpetual protection of a commonwealth.

Finally I wrote, in the form of an oration, my *Areopagitica* on the liberty of printing, in order that the decision as to truth and falsehood, on publication and suppression, might not rest with a few men in charge of the examination of books, men often without learning and of slow wit, whose caprice will suffer no one to bring to light anything that might be above vulgar understanding.

I did not touch upon civil liberty, the last remaining kind, as I saw that the Magistrate was satisfactorily looking after it; nor did I write anything on the rights of kings until the King, declared an enemy by Parliament, vanquished in war, and now a prisoner, pleaded his cause before the Judges and was sentenced to death. Then however certain Presbyterian Ministers, at first the direst foes of Charles, angered by the preference for the Independent party over theirs, and by its greater power in the Council, cried out at the sentence pronounced upon the King, not because they were angry at the deed, but because it had not been done by their party; they even dared to affirm that the doctrine of Protestants and of all reformed churches shrank from so fiercely sentencing against kings. At that point I thought that so open a falsehood should be openly opposed; yet even then I neither wrote nor advised anything concerning Charles, but merely showed in general what action may be taken against tyrants, and I supported my argument with the evidence of not a few of the most learned Theologians, almost like a zealous preacher making war on the rare ignorance or the singular shamelessness of the men who were promising better things. This book[30] was published after the death of the king, as it was written rather to calm the minds of men than to make any declaration about Charles, which was not a concern of mine but of the Magistrates; moreover, such a declaration had already been made.

In the privacy of my home I thus labored alternately for the church and the commonwealth, without recompense, neither the one nor the other giving me anything more in return than security; I did indeed gain a good conscience, good men thought well of me, and the very events proved how just had been this freedom of speech. Some men gratuitously acquired material goods, others won honors, but no one ever saw me currying favor, no one ever saw me use my friends in pursuit of any thing, none saw me fixed at the doors of parliament with beggarly expression, or clinging to the entrance of lesser assemblies. I usually kept myself at home, and sustained myself, albeit frugally, from my own income, even though during this civil strife a large portion of it was often held back and a rather heavy tax was imposed on me.[31]

After completing these tasks, thinking that I would now have abundant leisure, I turned to writing a national history, rehearsed from the very beginning and to be brought down, if I could manage it, in one unbroken thread up to this age. I had already unwound four books, when, after the change of the kingdom of Charles into a commonwealth, lo and behold! I, who never thought of such a thing, was called upon by what is known as the Council of State,

> then first established by Act of Parliament, and was asked to aid them, particularly in foreign affairs.[32]
>
> Not long afterwards, there appeared the book attributed to the King, certainly written with the greatest hatred towards Parliament. Ordered to reply, I opposed my *Eikonoklastes* to the *Eikon*, not intending, as it is painted, "an offense against the King's departed soul," but judging that Queen Truth should come before King Charles. Because I well foresaw that this slander would come readily from some evil tongue, I have, in the very introduction and often in other parts, wherever proper, protected myself against such an attack. Then Salmasius ventured forth. . . .

The title of the *Second Defense* is even less accurate than that f the first. Of the original one hundred and seventy-three pages ot even half amount to a defense of the regicide. The larger part f the *Second Defense* concerns the political situation in the coun- y in 1654. That situation was not without danger. Cromwell had ispelled the Rump in April 1653. The hundred and forty "Saints" f Barebone's Parliament withdrew in November of that year. A nonth later the Council of Officers made Cromwell the head of tate, for life, with the title of Protector. He would be assisted by a ermanent council of state. He was to convene a parliament, nomi- ated for three years. However, it would be September 1654, before he parliamentary elections could be concluded. In the meantime Cromwell was for all intents and purposes absolute king of England. n the middle of his reign, May 1654, the *Second Defense* appeared.

In the *First Defense* Milton had argued for the Rump as the ex- ression of the will of the people. Now he sees that it is clearly mpossible to do the same for the Protectorate. He prefers to say hat the nation is without will power, and that the Protectorate is he only recourse of a people without moral fiber. The conclusion of he *Second Defense* is in fact a lengthy exhortation to the people o make themselves worthy of liberty through the practice of virtue. Meanwhile Milton praises the virtue of the Protector in his famous portrait of Cromwell.

Ostensibly, the portrait of Cromwell was prompted by the attack made on the character of the Protector by the author of the *Cry*. Like the autobiographical passage, the account of Cromwell's career appears at first intended as ethical proof. Yet it is soon interrupted by the praise given to General Falkland, a moderate and no longer a supporter of Cromwell, and a few paragraphs later the portrait changes into a direct address to the Protector, filled with grave warning and sage counsel. The whole passage leaves no doubt that although Milton saw no alternative to defending the Protectorate his hope of its success was not unqualified.

The portrait is clearly not just a short biography. It is more than that. The defense of Cromwell's career furnishes Milton with the occasion to sketch an ideal leader, and the portrait has justifiably been linked with the popular seventeenth-century literary genre, the *character*. Yet the portrait also derives from epideictic or panegyric oratory, one of the kinds of classical rhetoric. Epideictic oratory became especially important under the Roman emperors, and the praise of the leader grew into a separate genre. Not only does the Cromwell portrait include a number of the required *topoi* or commonplaces, it also clearly follows the threefold formula that had become tradition: praise of the subject's ancestors, of his rise to greatness, and of the deeds of his maturity.[33]

> Oliver Cromwell descends from a noble and illustrious house.[34] The name was famous under the Kings of old for distinguished public service and grew more famous through its early support of the restoration and strengthening of the orthodox religion amongst us. He grew up in the privacy of his family and when he had attained, in similar seclusion, the age of ripe and settled judgment, he was known most of all for his tender care of the purer Reformed religion and for his spotless conduct. For the longest time a trust in God and a greatness of soul were cultivated within his silent breast.
>
> When parliament was last called by the king,[35] the votes of his town gained him a seat in the house where he presently became known for the honesty of his judgment and the strength of his counsel. When a call to arms was heard, he postponed his own tasks and was given command of a troop of horse.[36] Because good men came flocking to his standard from everywhere and thus increased his forces, he soon surpassed almost the highest generals in the scope and swift execution of his feats. Nor is this a wonder. He was a soldier well trained in self-knowledge, who had first routed or forced into submission every inward enemy such as vain hopes, fears, and desires; a commander first over himself, a conqueror of himself, he had learnt to be first over himself triumphant. Hence, the very first day that he entered the field against an external enemy, he was already a veteran, and he entered the camp with full knowledge of fighting in the field.
>
> This discourse imprisons me so that I cannot with fitting worth set

out how many cities he captured, how many and how great were the battles in which he was never conquered, never routed, how he traversed the whole realm of Britain, gaining victory after victory. All this is a great work of history and demands as it were another field of discourse and a narrative proportioned to the deeds. This one mark of his rare and almost divine virtue suffices. There bloomed in him such strength of will or intellect, or such control of discipline, applied not only to strategy but even more to Christian conduct and holiness, that from everywhere he drew to his camp, as to the finest training ground of military science as well as religion and piety, all the good and brave men—or he made them good and brave, most of all by his example. In the face of opposition he kept them —as he still does—at their posts throughout the war, even during the occasional armistice, through many a change of heart and many a turn of events; he kept them, not with plenty of booty and by relaxing discipline, but only with authority and token payment. No greater praise is normally bestowed upon Cyrus, or Epaminondas, or the most outstanding General among the ancients. Hence no man ever took less time to raise for himself an army larger or better trained, obedient to every command, welcomed and beloved by the citizens, to the enemy in battle indeed frightening, but after their subjection arousing admiration; camped in enemy field or quartered in their houses, this army was so far from causing grief and damage that the enemy, at the thought of the violence, the drunkenness, the impiety, and the lust of their own royalist troops, were delighted with the turn of events and believed that not their foes but their friends had arrived. This army protected the good, terrified the wicked and urged every virtue and piety.

Nor should you, Fairfax,[37] be passed over, in whom both nature and divine favors have wedded the highest courage to the rarest modesty and saintliest way of life. By your just deserts you are called to receive part of this praise, although you have now cut yourself off, like Scipio Africanus of old at Liternum, and remain as much as you can in hiding. You did not vanquish merely the enemy; you have also vanquished ambition and that victor over the highest of mortals, glory. In a most pleasant and glorious retirement you are reaping the fruits of your virtues and famous deeds, which is the end of all effort and of even the greatest of human undertakings. Your retirement is like that enjoyed by the heroes of antiquity after battles and exploits no more famous than yours; the poets, in their attempts to praise them, had no hope of being able to render it in any more fitting manner than by fabling that they were received in heaven to sup with the gods. Yet whether your health, as I mainly believe, or some other cause has made you withdraw, I am fully convinced that nothing could have severed you from the public service, unless you had seen how great a protector of liberty, how strong and loyal a pillar and rampart of England's welfare, you were to leave in your successor. For, as long as you, Cromwell, are safe, any one who fears for the safety of England has no sufficient faith in God, because he must see how God favors you, how openly He everywhere brings you aid. Then however you were left to fight alone on other battlefields.

But why a long account? I will rehearse, if I can, your most important deeds with a brevity equal to the speed of your usual performance. When all Ireland, except for one city, was lost, you dispatched an army and in one battle broke the power of the Irish. You were from day to day achieving the remainder of your task, when you were suddenly recalled to the war in Scotland. Hence you marched unwearied upon the Scots, who with their king were preparing a forced entry into England. That same kingdom, which all our kings during eight hundred years had not been able to conquer, was by you subdued in about one year and added to the dominion of the English. Their remaining troops, well-trained indeed and well-equipped, made a last desperate effort and suddenly forced their way into England, which was then almost stripped of garrisons, but when they had reached as far as Worcester, you overtook them with forced marches and brought them down in a single battle, in which almost all the nobles of that nation were taken prisoners.[38]

From now on peace reigned at home. Then we felt, although not for the first time, that you were no less strong in counsel than in the arts of war. In the parliament you took daily care that the peace treaty with the enemy should be faithfully observed, or that matters of possible interest to the commonwealth should be promptly decided upon. Seeing that delays were contrived, that everyone was more interested in his own than in the general advancement, that the people complained of being disappointed in their hopes and of being circumvented by the power of a few men, you did what they, in spite of so many warnings, would not do, and put an end to their wilful rule.[39] Another parliament is called, with the power to vote now granted only to those fit to vote.[40] The delegates meet, do nothing; after exhausting one another with continued dissent and altercation, most of them grow aware of their ineptitude and lack of talent for handling matters of such importance, and they dissolve themselves.

Cromwell, we are deserted; you alone remain; to you is returned all power over our affairs; in you alone does it reside. We all make way for your invincible virtue, none opposing except the type of man who, without equal merit, seeks equal honors for himself, or who hates to see them bestowed upon someone more worthy, or who does not understand that nothing in human society is more pleasing to God or more agreeable to reason, nothing in the state more just or more useful than that the power should belong to the worthiest man. All recognize that you, Cromwell, are that man, that those deeds have been performed by you, the greatest and most glorious of citizens, the guide in public counsel, the General of the bravest troops, the father of the country. By the latter title do the voices of all good men spontaneously and wholeheartedly hail you. Your actions know no other worthy titles, endure none other, and those proud titles which the vulgar mind thinks so great, they justly spurn.

For what is a title but a kind of definition of one's worth? As your deeds surpass every degree of admiration so do they surely surpass every title, and, like the tops of pyramids, hide themselves in the heavens, outstripping the atmosphere of popular titles. Although the summing up and definition of the highest virtues, under that mortal crown called honor, adds nothing to one's worth but is nevertheless useful, you assumed a certain title most like that of *pater patriae*, that of 'father of the country.' Yet you wished not to be carried aloft, but insisted on coming down so many steps from on high and on being pressed, as it were, into a special rank for the benefit of the state, spurning the title of king in favor of a far greater majesty. And rightly so. For if you, in your newly acquired greatness, should be captivated by the very name which you as a citizen had been able to overthrow and virtually reduce to nothing, you would almost act as if, after conquering an idolatrous nation with the aid of the true God, you were to worship the gods you had vanquished. Therefore, Cromwell, follow the greatness of your soul, for it becomes you. As deliverer of the country, as the founder and also the guardian and defender of liberty, you can take on no character more worthy or more exalted, for your deeds have surpassed not only the exploits of kings but also the fabled feats of our heroes.

Think moreover how dear a thing, and by how dear a parent given in your care, is that liberty, which the country gave to you for protection and safekeeping. What it once expected from the choicest men of the whole nation, it now expects from you alone and through you alone hopes to pursue. Be awed that so much is expected of you and that you are the country's only hope. Stand in awe of the scarred faces of all the brave men who under your leadership so mightily struggled for liberty, and of the souls of those who fell in the battle. Hold in awe also our regard and repute among foreign nations, the great hopes for their future expected from our liberty, so bravely won, and from our commonwealth, so gloriously sprung up; no like dishonor or shame could befall this nation than that the commonwealth so soon should vanish, as if nipped in the bud. Finally stand in awe of yourself so that, after gaining the liberty for which you have borne so many hardships and faced so many dangers, you will not suffer her violation by you, or her slightest impairment by others.

Indeed, if we cannot be free, you yourself have no freedom, for nature is so ordered that whoever seizes the liberty of others is the very first to surrender his own and discovers that he is the first in bondage, and deservedly so.[41] Truly, if the protector of liberty and as it were her tutelary deity, deemed the most just, the holiest and best of men, should afterwards assail her whom he himself defended, then this would of necessity be the virtually killing blow to the entire cause of all virtue and piety; honesty and virtue themselves will have manifestly waned, there will thereafter be but slender trust in religion, and reputation will be a frail thing indeed—no deeper wound, after that first,[42] could be inflicted upon the human race.

You have undertaken the heaviest task by far; it will profoundly tax you; it will scrutinize your entire and inmost self and declare your character, your resources, and your wisdom; it will show whether there lives indeed in you that piety, faith, justice, and self-discipline that led us to believe that the will of God carried you above others to this highest office. To rule by your counsel three powerful nations, to lead the people away from an evil establishment to a better and more fruitful order than heretofore, to direct your concern and attention to the remotest regions, to guard, to foresee, to shun no effort, to despise every enticing delight, to flee the display of wealth and power, these are the strenuous efforts next to which war is but a game; these will toss and shake you, these demand a man maintained by divine help, counseled and illumined by intercourse with divinity itself.

I have no doubt that you very often rehearse these and other matters for yourself and keep turning them over in your mind, as also by what means you may best accomplish these great ends while rendering to us our liberty safe and strong. To accomplish this, there is in my judgment no more direct means than by admitting, as you do, among the first of your counselors the same men who first stood by you in times of toil and crisis, men indeed of the highest modesty, integrity and bravery. . . . To these most gifted and outstanding citizens you may, without hesitation, justly entrust our liberty; no one could easily say to whom it might more safely be given in trust.

After this, I wish you would leave the church to the church and would prudently relieve yourself and the magistrates from that burden which now constitutes one half of your power and is most incompatible with it. Nor should you allow the two so remote powers of civil and ecclesiastical government to sport foully together, seeming each to strengthen the other by mingling their false riches, whereas in fact each shakes and finally topples the other. I wish you would take away all power from the church; yet power will never leave so long as money, the poison of the church, the quinsy of truth, shall be the wages for preaching the gospel, even violently forced from the unwilling. Would that you would drive out of the church those money-lenders who do not barter doves but the dove, the holy spirit itself!

I wish moreover that you would enact fewer new laws than you repeal old ones, for a commonwealth often has men who itch with a sort of rash to execute many laws, as poetasters itch to pour out many verses.[43] But the more laws there are, the worse they usually are, no longer acting as guide-lines but as stumbling-blocks. Would you might keep only those that are still necessary. The others you enact should not force the good under the same yoke with the bad, nor should they, while preventing the deceit of the dishonest, prohibit the normal freedom of good men; rather, they should apply to real vices and should not, because of the fault of abusers, forbid those things in themselves allowed. For laws have only been framed to keep the reins on evil motives; liberty best fashions and promotes virtue.

Next I wish that you would look more carefully than was done till now to the education and morals of our youth; I hope that you feel it unjust that the clever and the slow, the diligent and the idle, are brought up at the state's expense. May you rather put aside the scholar's rewards for those already learned and well deserving of them.

Moreover, I wish you would allow those desirous of liberty in the pursuit of wisdom to bring to light whatever they have found, at their own risk, without the private censorship of some civil servant, for in this way shall truth come to full bloom. The censure of the half-educated, their envy, their narrow-mindedness, or their fictions about the superstitions of others, should not always dole out all of science according to their little measure and bestow it upon us at their caprice.

Finally, I wish that you would fear neither truth nor falsehood, but that you would give ear least of all to those who never believe themselves free unless they prevent the freedom of others; who work never more diligently or vehemently than when shackling not only the bodies but also the minds of their brethren, thus introducing into both state and church the worst of all tyrannies, that of their own depraved habits and opinions. May you always be on the side of those who believe that not only their following or party but all the citizens alike have an equal right to freedom. In my judgment any man who holds that this liberty, which is to be administered by the magistrates, will not suffice, gives a closer ear to his ambition and to the crowds than to real liberty; particularly now that the people themselves, tossed by so many factions, like waves still heaving after the storm, refuse to admit this desirable and perfect state of things.

NOTES

1. *Joannis Miltoni Angli pro Populo Anglicano Defensio secunda. Contra infamem libellum anonymum cui titulus, Regii sanguinis clamor ad coelum adversus parricidas Anglicanos. Londoni, Types Neucomianis. 1654.* It appeared once in England and twice in Holland. The Hague printer Vlack made a reprint of the London copy in July 1654. The second reprint, also by Vlack, was bound with More's *Fides Publica* and appeared in October of the same year. The editors of the *Columbia Milton* reprinted the London edition in VIII, 1–255. The present translation is made from the Princeton University Library copy, Ex 3859/371, of the London edition.

For the dates of both the London edition and the Hague reprints, see French, *Life Records,* III, 376, 407, 411–12, and 421–22. In the same volume (pp. 380–81), French lists the presentation copies extant.

For a more extensive account of *Regii Sanguinis Clamor* than is provided in the introduction, see the *Yale Milton,* IV, 1036–81.

2. "Milton's *Pro se Defensio* and Alexander More," *University of Texas Studies in Literature and Language,* I (1959), 11–29, and "Milton and Alexander More: New Documents," *JEGP,* LX (1961), 796–807.

3. Gen. xxvii 1: "When Isaac was old, and his eyes were dim, so that he could not see."

4. Gen. xlviii 10: "Now the eyes of Israel were dim for age, so that he could not see."

5. John ix 3: "Neither hath this man sinned, nor his parents: but that the works of God should be made manifest in him."

6. The god of physicians.

7. Heb. xi 34: "Out of weakness we were made strong."

8. Deut. xxvii 18: "Cursed be he that maketh the blind to wander out of the way."

9. About 1625 the elder Milton gradually began to withdraw from his business. From this time on, the family seems to have used a house in suburban Hammersmith as a pleasant escape from the city weather and the threats of the plague. The city dwelling in Bread Street was retained for some years after

the family began to spend the larger part of the year in Hammersmith, but by September 1632 the elder Milton gave Hammersmith as his official place of residence. Then, after January 1635, he acquired a country home in Horton. For a detailed discussion of the historical evidence see Harris F. Fletcher, *The Intellectual Development of John Milton* (Urbana, 1956), I, 405–14.

10. In May 1638. The dates in the notes are those of French's *Life Records.*

11. Sir Henry Wotton (1568–1639), formerly in the service of Robert Devereaux, second earl of Essex. After his patron's downfall he left England and traveled in France and Italy. Sent by the Duke of Tuscany to warn James VI of Scotland of a plot on his life, he was knighted upon James's succession to the English throne and received the post of ambassador to Venice. Installed as Provost of Eton College in 1624, he entertained a close friendship with Izaak Walton. In 1651 appeared the *Reliquiae Wottonianae,* with Walton's *Life.* In the 1645 edition of the Poems, Sir Henry's letter precedes *Comus.* It can be found in French, *Life Records,* I, 361–63.

12. "Sir Thomas" is actually Sir John Scudamore (1600–71), ambassador to France from 1635 to 1639, a friend and correspondent of Archbishop Laud. A zealous Royalist, he took part in the civil war, was captured in 1643 and imprisoned for three years.

13. Hugo Grotius (1583–1645), Dutch humanist, was the author of *De jure belli ac pacis* (1625), a standard authority on international law. Grotius and Scudamore were on intimate terms. Grotius was planning for a union of all Protestants except followers of Calvin, and he addressed Laud through Scudamore.

14. August and September 1638.

15. The Italian academies were literary clubs. Membership in an academy was fashionable and every respectable town counted at least three or four such societies; in 1638 there were fifteen of them in Rome alone. Occasionally an academy was devoted to the study of the sciences, such as that of the Roman *Lincei* or "Lynxes," of which Galileo had been a member.

16. Jacopo Gaddi (1602–68), a patrician and a well-known Latinist, was a member of the earliest and most illustrious of all academies, the Florentine, and founder of one of his own, that of the *Svogliati* or "Disgusted." Carlo Dati (1619–76), then nineteen years old, appears to have been Milton's favorite Florentine friend. Exceptionally gifted, he had at one time been a pupil of Galileo; he became a mathematician, antiquarian, and philologist, and received in his later years a pension from Louis XIV. Dati's encomium to Milton precedes the Latin poems in the 1645 edition. For two letters from Dati to Milton, see French, *Life Records,* II, 201–9 and 221–23. Agostino Coltellini (1613–93), a lawyer by training, was four times elected president of the Florentine Academy, and was also the founder of the *Apatisti* or "Indifferents." This academy eventually counted among its members several cardinals and princes, a pope, and many foreign scholars. Benedetto Bonmattei (1581–1647), a priest and distinguished teacher, was the author of a commentary on Dante and of a Tuscan grammar. The latter was still in preparation in 1638, and Milton sent Bonmattei a letter listing a number of points which the foreign student of Italian would like to see included (French, *Life Records,* I, 382–89). Little is known of the three other men. Chimentelli, a priest, later became professor of Greek at Pisa. Frescobaldi and Francini were both young aristocrats and members of several academies. Francini's "Ode to Milton" was prefixed to the Latin poems of the 1645 edition. Milton omits mention of Antonio Malatesti, a witty poet, intimate friend of Dati and Coltellini, and a favorite of Galileo. Among the books Milton took back to England was a manuscript copy of *La Tina,* a collection of fifty

ribald Italian sonnets, written by Malatesti and dedicated by him to John Milton, apparently to tease the virtuous Englishman on his temperance. The manuscript was not discovered till some eighty years after Milton's death. The visit to Galileo's villa, to which Milton refers in the *Areopagitica,* may have taken place during these months.

17. Luc Holste (1596–1661) was a German humanist and a convert from Lutheranism to Catholicism. As Vatican librarian, Holste showed Milton the collection of rare books and manuscripts, and made him a present of two volumes. A letter from Milton to Holste is extant (cf. French, *Life Records,* I, 390–92). Among the "other men of scholarship" are the two minor poets Salvaggi and Salzelli whose tributes to Milton precede the Latin poems of the 1645 edition. During an illness, Salzelli received from Milton the Latin poem in *scazons* or "limping measure," included in the 1645 edition. Milton does not mention his visit to the English Jesuit College in Rome. The visitors' book of the college records that, on October 30, 1638, Milton and three other Englishmen had dinner with the Fathers.

18. Manso's Latin testimonial, prefixed to the Latin poems in the 1645 edition, reads: "If only your creed were equal to your mind, figure, grace, face and morals, then would you no longer be an Angle but an angel." See also Milton's Latin poem "Mansus," written before his leaving Naples.

19. The plan was unusual: Englishmen rarely traveled to Greece.

20. January and February 1639. On February 27 Milton attended a comic opera at the Casa Barberini, residence of Cardinal Francesco Barberini, the Papal Secretary. The following day he had a private audience with the Cardinal and was much impressed. See again Milton's letter to Holste, note 17 above. It was probably at the Cardinal's musical entertainment that Milton heard the famous singer Leonora Baroni, whom he commemorated in three Latin epigrams.

21. The ancestral home of his friends the Diodatis.

22. "That Englishman [Milton] was hated by the Italians, among whom he lived a long time, on account of his overstrict morals." Letter from Heinsius to Vossius, dated Venice, February 19, 1653 (French, *Life Records,* III, 322).

23. June 1639. Giovanni Diodati (1576–1649) was an uncle of Milton's friend Charles Diodati. He translated the Bible into Italian, taught Hebrew in Geneva, and tutored a few select young men in his villa; among them was Charles Gustav, crown prince of Sweden.

24. Milton returned to England early in August 1939; the second expedition against Scotland was not to take place for another year.

25. On Aldersgate Street.

26. Parliament was recalled on November 3, 1640. Strafford, the king's right hand, was imprisoned on November 11. In the next month Laud was taken into protective custody. In May 1641 Strafford was beheaded.

27. This is a reference to the Solemn League and Covenant, which promised to endeavor "The Reformation of Religion . . . according to the word of God and the example of the best reformed Churches." For the complete text of the Covenant, see Masson, III, 13 ff.

28. *other matters:* the teaching of pupils; probably also the preparation of an edition of his minor poems, and plans for an English epic; cf. the ending of *Epitaphium Damonis.*

29. John Selden (1584–1654) was a jurist, an antiquary, a student of the Orient, and a minor statesman. He was elected to the House of Commons in 1623, and re-elected in 1626, 1628, and 1640. His most controversial work was the *History of Tythes* (1618), in which he argued that tithing was not divinely

commanded. He later was a lay member in the Westminster Assembly of Divines. The work to which Milton here refers is Selden's *Uxor Ebraica* (1646).

30. *The Tenure.*

31. In September 1645 Milton moved to a larger house in the Barbican so that he might increase his income by taking in more pupils. In 1647 he received his father's legacy, stopped teaching, and moved to a small house in High Holborn.

32. The Council, appointed on February 14, 1649, approached Milton on March 13. A week later Milton took the oath as Secretary for Foreign Tongues.

33. For more information on epideictic oratory and its commonplaces, see E. R. Curtius, *European Literature and the Latin Middle Ages* (New York, 1953), pp. 68–71 and 154–82. The portrait of Cromwell may be compared with Milton's *Sonnet 16*, addressed to Cromwell. See also Marvell's poems, "An Horation Ode upon Cromwel's Return from Ireland" and "The First Anniversary of the Government under O.C.," in H. Margoliouth's edition (Oxford, 1951), I, 87–90 and 103–13. An interesting contrast is furnished by Clarendon's portrait of Cromwell in his *History of the Rebellion*, ed. W. Dunn Macray (Oxford, 1888), VI, 91–97. For an evaluation of Milton's attitude toward Cromwell, see Donald M. Wolfe's *Milton in the Puritan Revolution* (New York, 1941), pp. 242–48.

34. The Cromwells of Huntingdon descended from Morgan Williams, a Welshman who had married the sister of Cromwell, Henry VIII's minister. The son of this marriage had adopted his uncle's name.

35. In Charles's last parliament, convened in 1640, Cromwell was a member for Cambridge. He had represented his own town, Huntingdon, in the parliament of 1628.

36. In the summer of 1642 Cromwell was in Cambridgeshire, raising a troop of volunteer horse for Parliament. Milton here probably refers to Cromwell's appointment as captain of horse in Essex's parliamentarian army of 1646.

37. General Fairfax had opposed the execution of the king; he resigned his commission when the Council of State resolved on the expedition against Scotland in 1650. Milton addressed to him his *Sonnet 15*.

38. The victory of Worcester, September 1651.

39. Cromwell's *coup d'état:* the abolition of the Rump in April 1653.

40. The Short or "Barebone's" Parliament, July–December 1653.

41. The *Commonplace Book* quotes from St. Augustine's *City of God:* "If a form of government includes slavery, it is the ruler who is the slave, rather than the subject" (*Columbia Milton,* XVIII, 196).

42. The fall of Adam.

43. The *Commonplace Book* quotes from the Italian of the satirist Boccalini (1556–1613): "The kings of Spain will not allow lawyers and solicitors to go to the Indies, regarding the study of laws, by a famous edict, not as a liberal art but as an essentially mechanical trade, brought into the world for the affliction of mankind" (*Columbia Milton,* XVIII, 191).

JOANNIS MILTONI ANGLI
PRO SE DEFENSIO
CONTRA *ALEXANDRUM MORUM* ECCLESIASTEN, LIBELLI FAMOSI, CUI TITULUS, *REGII SANGUINIS CLAMOR AD COELUM ADVERSUS PARRICIDAS ANGLICANOS,* AUTHOREM RECTE DICTUM.
Londini, Typis Neucomianis. 1655.

THE DEFENSE OF HIMSELF BY JOHN MILTON, ENGLISHMAN, AGAINST ALEXANDER MORE, WHO IS RIGHTLY CALLED THE AUTHOR OF AN INFAMOUS LIBEL ENTITLED THE CRY OF THE KING'S BLOOD TO HEAVEN, AGAINST THE ENGLISH PARRICIDES. London, 1655.

"The Third Defense"

The *Second Defense* was not nearly so widely read as the first. Yet More, now a professor at Amsterdam, felt sufficiently threatened by Milton's attack on his character to answer with his *Fides Publica* (1654), and a *Supplementum* (1655). He argues, of course, that Milton's charges are mere slander and that he, More, is not the author of the *Cry*. Milton saw fit to reply with another *Defense*. Since he realized that the original great debate had become a private quarrel, his *Third Defense* bears the modest title of *Defense of Himself*.[1] This pamphlet, more than any other, reveals Milton's gift for venomous satire. It repeats the earlier attacks on More's morals. As to the authorship of the anonymous *Cry,* Milton argues that, even if More were not the author, he was certainly its editor, and thus according to Justinian's *Civil Law* responsible for it. Milton here ingeniously avoids having to admit that he erroneously ascribed the *Cry* to More. The *Defense of Himself* is largely *argumentum ad hominem,* an attack on the character of the opponent. The following passage is representative of the tone and level of discourse.

> Pay attention now, I beseech you, and look at an utter and complete hypocrite if ever there was one. He sees that he must say something for himself; much to his dislike he examines himself and discovers that a foul man can find none but a foul answer. He looks about for some place of refuge near him, for some little pillar to lean on, for some cover to hide under, for some companions with whom he may band together in a partnership of crime, for some kind or other of men to involve in his private quarrel, so that he may, with the approval of others, defend his own cause as a common cause, threatening a community. He can find nothing more fit upon which to transfer his shame, nothing closer at hand on which to unburden his rottenness than the church of God itself.
>
> He says: "If only my case had been properly handled, I could have put a buckle on my mouth and been silent, after the example of my Lord; but one seeks to wound our whole order and the Church of God through my side." You high priest of brothels and stews! who should have a buckle not just on your mouth but also on your groin. It would have been so much better had you remained silent "after the example of your Lord," as one upon whom Christ the Lord imposed silence with a muzzle, than to have brought such shame upon God's Church.
>
> You say that "I stigmatize, though not directly, your entire Order." I do so? Tell me where? Show the place if you can; unless perhaps you think that my words against mercenaries also apply to the Ministers of the Gospel. You are mistaken, More. But something else, not unlike it, you might more reasonably have complained about. It is not I who have stigmatized your order indirectly, but Pontia, your high priestess, put the stigma on you, quite out of order, indirectly, and directly, and crosswise.
>
> You say: "The Church of God, to which I have devoted all my time, is wounded through my side." Through your side, you foulest of men? It is said that you are so far from having devoted all your time to the Church that you have sometimes neglected your duty to preach in the morning and have more than once devoted the very hours of religious service to the secret satisfaction of your lusts. I will not even mention the time which you, a Minister of the Church, have devoted to infamous libel. Through your side? There is nothing at all that wounds the Church more deeply than that your defiled side should lie so corruptingly close to the Church. If with "by your side" you intend us to understand that through your baseness and your crimes the Church is scorned by the wicked, spotted

with stains and infested with scandal, I will certainly agree that this is true.

Therefore your entire order, particularly the French Ministers, who know you best, are doing their utmost to remove and shed from themselves your infesting sickness, that they may no longer suffer the peril of that pestilent side of yours; they refuse to hear of any cause or explanation, that they may not become partners in your crimes and scandals; they wish you thrown out of their ranks and expelled according to your deserts, and they are attempting to fasten that "buckle" you spoke of over your shameless mouth.

NOTES

1. *Joannis Miltoni pro se Defensio contra Alexandrum Morum Ecclesiasten Libelli famosi, cui titulus, Regii sanguinis clamor ad coelum adversus Parricidas Anglicanos, authorem recte dictum.* Londini, Typis Neucomianis. 1655. The title page of the Thomason copy in the British Museum is dated, in manuscript, Aug. 8. Vlack made a reprint of the London edition in The Hague later that year. See French, *Life Records*, IV, 44. The Columbia editors reprinted the Thomason copy in IX, 1–297. The present translation is made from the Princeton University Library copy, Ex 3859/373, of the London edition. For detailed accounts of More's *Fides Publica* and *Supplementum*, see *Yale Milton*, IV, 1082–1128.

Milton's satire is evaluated by J. M. French in "Milton as Satirist," *PMLA*, LI (1936), 414–29. Kester Svendsen analyzes the style of the *Third Defense* in "Milton's *Pro se Defensio* and Alexander More," *University of Texas Studies in Literature and Language*, I (1959), 11–29.

THE POLITICAL AND RELIGIOUS TRACTS OF 1659–1660

EDITED BY BARBARA KIEFER LEWALSKI

Foreword

A Treatise of Civil Power, February 1659

Considerations Touching the Likeliest Means to Remove Hirelings, August 1659. EDITED WITH A FOREWORD BY WILLIAM B. HUNTER, JR.

Foreword with accounts of:

Letter to a Friend, October 1659

Proposalls of Certaine Expedients, October–December 1659

The Present Means, March 1660

Brief Notes upon a Late Sermon, April 1660

The complete text of

The Readie and Easie Way, April 1660

FOREWORD

Trying to cope with the English political crisis of 1659–60 was for the Puritans like trying to tame a whirlwind. The coalition, united in 1642 against the king and the Anglican establishment, had long since disintegrated as a result of internecine conflict over new models for reformation in church and state. Oliver Cromwell's Protectorate had imposed an uneasy peace upon this chaos and a policy of broad religious toleration; with his death the storms of controversy raged with ever-increasing violence. In the twenty months from Oliver's death on September 3, 1658, to the restoration of Charles II in May 1660, the government changed hands six times, economic conditions steadily worsened, the populace manifested overwhelming dissatisfaction with Puritan rule, and the Royalists gained strength daily. These months also saw a torrent of pamphlets unleashed, in which the conflicting factions proposed and argued for their respective principles and plans. To this polemic maelstrom Milton contributed eight tracts, beginning with *A Treatise of Civil Power in Ecclesiastical Causes* (February 1659), a calm, closely reasoned discourse on religious toleration, and ending with the second edition of *The Readie and Easie Way to Establish a Free Commonwealth*, an impassioned and despairing plea to his countrymen to retain commonwealth government.

These conditions go far to account for the puzzling features of Milton's eight tracts—the rapidly changing political alignments, the several different proposals for settling the government, the use of contradictory arguments which locate political power at various times in the people themselves, in the worthy few, and in the regenerate saints. Such inconsistencies, characteristic of Milton's polemic writing in general but intensified in the tracts of 1659–60, have been variously explained[1] and I have argued elsewhere[2] that

[1] S. B. Liljegren, *Studies in Milton* (Lund, 1918); Arthur Barker, *Milton and the Puritan Dilemma* (Toronto, 1942); E. M. Clark, ed., *Ready and Easy Way* (New Haven, 1915); Don M. Wolfe, *Milton in the Puritan Revolution*

these tracts especially repay rhetorical rather than logical or philosophical analysis—a rhetorical analysis in keeping with Aristotle's broad definition of rhetoric as "the faculty of observing in any given case the available means of persuasion." The tracts cannot be approached simply in their own terms and in terms of the development of Milton's thought, but must be seen also in terms of the specific audience addressed and in relation to other contemporary proposals, which reveal the limits of the possible. As practical politician and skilled rhetorician Milton was always ready to adapt his program and argument to the pressure of changing circumstances, albeit at some cost to logical consistency. But his changes and adaptations were dictated by certain guiding principles.

In the tracts of 1659–60 the relative importance of these various principles in Milton's thought is clearly revealed, for at this point Milton was forced by circumstances to retrench his earlier, grander political vision in order to try to preserve those values which he took to be indispensable. Like most Puritans, Milton constantly invoked the old formula naming religious and civil liberty as the prime ends of government, the great goals of the Good Old Cause. But for Milton the absolute value was religious liberty. From the time of writing *Areopagitica* he had identified religious liberty as the chief good which governments could promote, and in *A Treatise of Civil Power* he defended religious liberty for all Protestants as a corollary of Christian liberty—that freedom from the bondage of the Law which Christ won for his own in order that they might serve God freely, out of love. Milton's most profound political conviction is that only in an environment of freedom and religious toleration can good men serve God properly and develop in virtue. His certainty that the Stuarts would deny this religious liberty to the Puritan sects is the primary reason for his relentless opposition to the Restoration.

Civil liberty, the second of Milton's basic political principles, was modified considerably in 1659–60 in the interests of the prior claims of religious liberty. In *The Readie and Easie Way* Milton defined civil liberty as the enjoyment of civil rights, the due administration of justice, and the "advanc'ments of every person according to his merit." Significantly omitted in this definition is the right of all

(New York, 1941); Ernest Sirluck, ed., *Complete Prose Works of John Milton*, Vol. II (New Haven, 1959), Introduction.

[2] "Milton: Political Beliefs and Polemical Methods, 1659–1660," *PMLA*, LXXIV (1959), 191–202.

en, or at least of the worthy, to choose and change and participate their government, which Milton had defined in *The Tenure of ings and Magistrates* (1649) as an essential aspect of civil liberty. ut this aspect of civil liberty was left out only under duress, as is dicated by Milton's provision in *The Readie and Easie Way* for road suffrage and general participation in governmental affairs at e local level.

A third guiding principle of Milton's political thought, at least om the time of writing *Eikonoklastes* (1650), is that the exercise suffrage and the right to participate in government should be stricted to the worthy, the good. One suspects that even Milton's nqualified argument for popular sovereignty in *Tenure* is predi-ated upon his belief that a majority of the people will prove to be orthy and good in Milton's special sense. That sense involves omething more than Aristotle's aristocracy of the best and most irtuous, and something less than the millenarian ideal of rule by egenerate saints. Milton's political worthies are likely to come from ne ranks of the regenerate since, according to *De Doctrina,* the enewal of intellect and will caused by regeneration qualifies the aints more adequately than other men to discharge the duties and ffices of the natural as well as the supernatural order. But Milton's rminian theology and the corollaries deriving from it qualify this osition. Milton's belief that original sin does not totally deprave, is admiration of the natural and political virtue of the Greeks, his elief that the general call to salvation vouchsafed to all mankind roduces in all a partial renewal of intellect and will, and his belief hat even the regenerate may fall from grace, prevent him from dis-inguishing from society at large some special group of saints worthy o rule on the basis of their sainthood. Milton's test of political vorthiness is always love of, and support for, liberty, especially re-igious liberty: the regenerate, because of their restored powers, are nore likely to display this quality, but in *The Readie and Easie Vay* Milton proposes to promote it through education and other urely natural means. During the last years of the Interregnum, he ontinued to assert the precept that the worthy should rule, but at he practical level he was forced to make serious compromises. In he eight tracts under consideration here he accepted or proposed s governors many whom he did not at this time consider virtuous r liberty-loving, let alone regenerate saints—the Long Parliament, he Wallingford-House Army officers—because the primary good, religious liberty, was yet safer with them than it would be under the Stuarts.

Most flexible of all Milton's political principles is the concept underlying most of his models of government since 1649, that the ideal form of government for a virtuous people is an aristocratic commonwealth with a supreme council representative of and responsible to the citizens. Even Milton's praise of Cromwell's Protectorate in the *Second Defense* (1654) was joined with a plea to the people to make themselves worthy to elect parliaments and with an instruction to Cromwell to share power with a council of able men—provisions which seem to envisage the Protectorate turning into an aristocratic commonwealth with unicameral legislature and council of state. *The Readie and Easie Way* unequivocally affirms the superiority of such a commonwealth and defends it on biblical and classical grounds; Milton's departures from this model and temporary acquiescence in some others during the final months of the Interregnum obviously stem from the imminence of the Stuart restoration, which was seen to threaten Puritan religious liberty. Milton readily justified such changes in his government model by appealing to Aristotle's dictum that an aristocratic commonwealth is suited only to a virtuous people. Accordingly, Milton read the English people's repudiation of a commonwealth and their desire for restoration of the monarchy as clear evidence of their degeneracy and debasement.

Shorn of its particular theological basis and special political applications, Milton's fundamental political insight is that only those persons who have attained to a personal experience of freedom and who continually exercise a mature, morally responsible independence of thought and action can properly value or long maintain political or other external freedoms. It is an insight not without relevance to mankind's continuing experience with many kinds of threats to human freedom.

A TREATISE OF CIVIL POWER IN ECCLESIASTICAL CAUSES:

SHEWING THAT IT IS NOT LAWFULL FOR ANY POWER ON EARTH TO COMPELL IN MATTERS OF RELIGION.

The author J. M.

London, Printed by *Tho. Newcomb, Anno* 1659

Of Civil Power (February 1659) is Milton's most thorough exposition and defense of religious liberty, which he takes to be the primary end of government. This tract and its companion discourse on church disestablishment (*Hirelings,* August 1659) together present Milton's final view of the nature and organization of the Christian church, but in *Of Civil Power* the major issue is political rather than ecclesiastical—the role and duty of the Christian magistrate regarding religion. The tract is unusual among Milton's pamphlets for its brevity and succinctness, its emotional restraint, its plain and unadorned diction, and its comparatively straightforward syntax—features which are in keeping with Milton's description of it as a statement of general truth "to all Christian magistrates equally belonging." Yet the tract has also an explicit polemical function: it is addressed to the English parliament then in session, it is offered as a means of saving them "much labor and interruption," and its every argument is deployed with consummate rhetorical skill to persuade a specific audience.

Significantly, the pamphlet makes no mention whatsoever of Oliver's son Richard Cromwell, who had succeeded to the Protectorate in September 1658. That omission is yet more surprising since ministers, county magistrates, and important persons from all over the country were deluging Richard in the autumn and winter of 1658–59 with congratulatory messages, many of which included petitions to settle the church along presbyterian lines and to stamp out the "blasphemous and heretical" sects that had proliferated so amazingly during the past decade. Milton's apparently deliberate snub no doubt indicates his dissatisfaction with the Protectorean government, which had failed to disestablish the church as he had advised in 1654, had grown more conservative in religious matters and more monarchical in structure by the end of Oliver's reign, and was confidently expected to adopt restrictive religious policies under Richard. In any case, at this time Milton addresses the Parliament alone as the magistrate of England, singling out as his particular audience for this tract those members who need to be reminded that "any law against conscience is alike in force against any conscience, and so may . . . justly redound upon your selves."

The large Presbyterian element in Richard's parliament can hardly constitute the particular audience Milton hopes to persuade, for his tract identifies the Presbyterians as the chief present threat to English religious liberty. In their Westminster Confession of 1647 the Presbyterians had defined a strong anti-tolerationist position. Designating the magistrate as keeper of both tables of the Decalogue—the four commandments defining sins against God as well as the six defining sins against men—and appealing to the example of state enforcement of religious duties in ancient Israel, the Presbyterians called upon the magistrate to repress blasphemy, impiety, idolatry, and heresy. They also urged him to establish and maintain Presbyterian worship and discipline throughout the nation, enforcing at least outward conformity to them, though, to be sure, many Presbyterians in the Parliament had opposed and indeed prevented settlement of a rigid presbyterian system as threatening to subject civil magistrates to clerical domination. In 1659 the stricter Presbyterians were demanding with increasing vehemence that the magistrate settle presbyterian government and suppress all other religious expression, especially the radical sects—Baptists, Quakers, Millenarians, Fifth Monarchists, Seekers, Antinomians, and the like. The rigid Presbyterians, therefore, hardly constitute a receptive audience for Milton's plea. On the other hand, he need not address lengthy arguments to those liberals "alreadie perfet and resolvd" about separation of church and state, though he expresses his delight to discover some of them in the Parliament. Rather, his specific audience consists of some moderate Presbyterians in the Parliament and especially the Congregationalists, whose theory of the magistrate's role relation to the church has some points of contact with both the ɜsbyterian and the more liberal positions.

Like the Presbyterians, the Congregationalists traditionally iden- ɩed the magistrate as the keeper of both tables of the Law. Such ıssic Congregationalist statements as *The Apologeticall Narration* 644) and *The Ancient Bounds* (1645) maintained that the magis- ıte was charged with the defense of true religion against blas- ıemy, idolatry, and heresy; since the Congregationalists had no pe that Parliament would establish their discipline, they did not clude the establishment and enforcement of church government ıong his functions. In 1659 the Congregationalists, enticed by me overtures from moderate Presbyterians seeking to accommo- ıte them in an orthodox establishment, and scandalized by the ectacle of the rapidly proliferating sects, were actively demand- g the magistrate's support of some kind of orthodox national re- ;ious establishment and his suppression of the sects.

On the other hand, in the process of defending themselves against ıreatened Presbyterian oppression at the time of the Westminster ssembly, the Congregationalists had developed an argument for leration based upon Christian liberty which linked them, all un- illingly, with the Independents and the radical sects. Essentially ıe concept of Christian liberty is based upon the Pauline opposi- on of the Law and the Gospel, the rigid stipulations of the Hebraic ɜremonial and judicial law against the freedom enjoyed by Chris- ans under the new dispensation of grace. In the Congregationalist efinition Christian liberty is the gospel privilege of true—that is, octrinally orthodox—believers and it involves freedom from coer- ıon in matters of religion that are indifferent or of little importance; s basis is the wholly spiritual nature of the Christian faith and hrist's sole magistracy over the Christian conscience. The Inde- endents and most sectaries, arguing usually for disestablishment nd full Protestant religious toleration, characteristically extended ıe Christian liberty concept, applying the benefits of Christian berty to all Protestants who met a simple doctrinal test such as rofessing faith in God by Jesus Christ. In this more liberal version f the Christian liberty theory, the magistrate could repress only lasphemy, idolatry, popery, and the most fundamental heresies uch as Socinianism, but not sectarian belief or practice.

Milton's rhetorical tactic in this tract is to seem to accept the Congregationalist premise—Christian liberty for the practitioners of true religion—but then to redefine the key terms in such a way th this premise leads directly to radical conclusions. The implication that the Congregationalists' natural sympathy and alignment shoul be with the sectaries rather than with the Presbyterians. Milton radical definition of Christian liberty is built up in the four basi arguments of his tract, each of them substantiated from Scripture that the magistrate is not able to judge in matters of religion sinc religion is wholly dependent upon the Spirit's illumination; that h has no right to judge or act in religious matters since Christ has re served these to his own jurisdiction; that force in religion wrongfull violates Christian liberty which sets the believer free from cere monies and circumstances in the worship of God; that force ca accomplish no good, promoting neither the glory of God nor tru piety but only hypocrisy. Milton's definition of true religion is eve more radical than that of most sectaries, for he identifies as its sig not a fundamental doctrine but simply a method. Citing the univer sally accepted Protestant premise that the only source of true re ligion is Scripture interpreted by the private conscience accordin to the Spirit's illumination, he avoids the conservative deductio that the Spirit's illumination guarantees the agreement of the re generate on religious fundamentals and instead concludes that th Spirit's mysterious action makes any human judgment of another' religion wholly impossible. The only external mark of true religio is therefore the conscientious reading of Scripture; and any belief o practice based upon such reading—that is, any Protestant religio of any kind, even Socinianism—must be true religion, not heresy All the Congregationalist bases for the magistrate's repression ar similarly redefined: blasphemy is only evil speaking against Go and man; idolatry among Christians is only Roman Catholic wor ship; heresy can only be Roman Catholic doctrine which is base upon church tradition and teaching as well as Scripture; the defens of true religion can only be the defense of every Christian's right t his own conscientious belief and practice.

Occasionally in this tract Milton undertook to strengthen his po- sition by moving beyond his radical Christian liberty argument t the other notable contemporary tolerationist theory advanced b the Levellers, some Baptists, and a few radicals such as Roger Wil- liams—the complete segregation of the orders of nature and grace Strictly applied, this theory gave the magistrate authority only ove things perceptible by the light of nature—civil affairs and matter of the second table—and placed all matters of religion, which can be apprehended only by God's freely given grace, wholly beyond the magistrate's competence. But Milton did not press this argument to its logical consequence of total religious freedom: for him, as for most seventeenth-century liberals, the limiting case was Roman Catholicism. Nevertheless, though Milton argued that Roman Catholicism as the only real heresy could not claim toleration as true religion, he yet insisted that it could not be repressed on those religious grounds but only as a Roman civil power or as idolatry. Behind the latter basis for the magistrate's repression is the understanding that Milton shared with the Independents Henry Stubbe and Thomas Collier as well as with some Quakers, that the magistrate retained some power in matters of the first table, specifically to repress blasphemy and idolatry, not from a religious ground but because these evils were evident by the light of nature itself. In Milton's theory the wilder Antinomian sects might also be available to magisterial repression as blasphemers but not as heretics, for they were the chief objects of the Blasphemy Act of 1650, which Milton cites as providing a reasonable definition of what blasphemy is.

In arguing for nearly complete toleration of all Protestant Christians, in developing his radical definition of true religion, and in appealing occasionally (if somewhat confusingly) to the doctrine of complete segregation of the orders of nature and grace, Milton's tract has considerable interest as a document advancing religious and intellectual liberty for mankind. But in this as in *Areopagitica*, in some ways its nearest analogue among Milton's works, Milton's primary concern is the need to preserve for good men that freedom which is not only a privilege but is the very condition of true religious service of God. He desires above all else to promote "our *free*, *elective*, and *rational* worship."

The copy text of the tract is a photostat of the copy in the Thomason collection at the British Museum; it has been collated with the copy at the Widener Library. Milton's characteristic *then* has been changed to *than* where the sense demands it, a few abbreviations have been expanded, and a few printing errors silently corrected. The punctuation of the original has been respected even in those instances where a period or question mark is followed by a small letter rather than a capital; in some cases at least this appears to be a deliberate device of style signaling a break which is less than complete, a new sentence element which is not a wholly new departure.

A TREATISE OF CIVIL POWER

TO THE *PARLAMENT* OF THE Commonwealth of *ENGLAND* with the dominions therof.

I Have prepar'd, supream Councel, against the much expected time of your sitting,[1] *this treatise; which, though to all Christian magistrates equally belonging, and therfore to have bin written in the common language of Christendom, natural dutie and affection hath confin'd, and dedicated first to my own nation: and in a season wherin the timely reading therof, to the easier accomplishment of your great work, may save you much labor and interruption: of two parts usually propos'd, civil and ecclesiastical, recommending civil only to your proper care, ecclesiastical to them only from whom it takes both that name and nature. Yet not for this cause only do I require or trust to finde acceptance, but in a twofold respect besides: first as bringing cleer evidence of scripture and protestant maxims to the Parlament of* England, *who in all thir late acts, upon occasion, have professd to assert only the true protestant Christian religion, as it is containd in the holy scriptures: next, in regard that your power being but for a time, and having in your selves a Christian libertie of your own, which at one time or other may be oppressd, therof truly sensible, it will concern you while you are in power, so to regard other mens consciences, as you would your own should be regarded in the power of others; and to consider that any law against conscience is alike in force against any conscience, and so may one way or other justly redound upon your selves. One advantage I make no doubt of, that I shall write to many eminent persons of your number, alreadie perfet and resolvd in this important article of Christianitie. Some of whom I remember to have heard often for several years, at a councel next in autoritie to your own, so well joining religion with civil prudence, and yet so well distinguishing the different power of either,*[2] *and this not only voting, but frequently reasoning why it should be so, that if any there present had bin before of an opinion contrary, he might doubtless have departed thence a convert in that point, and have confessd, that then both commonwealth and religion will at length, if ever, flourish in Christendom, when either they who govern discern between civil and*

common language: Latin (which Milton used for his *Defensio* and *Defensio Secunda*).

religious, or they only who so discern shall be admitted to govern. Till then nothing but troubles, persecutions, commotions can be expected; the inward decay of true religion among our selves, and the utter overthrow at last by a common enemy. Of civil libertie I have written heretofore by the appointment, and not without the approbation of civil power:[3] *of Christian liberty I write now, which others long since having don with all freedom under heathen emperors, I should do wrong to suspect, that I now shall with less under Christian governors, and such especially as profess openly thir defence of Christian libertie; although I write this not otherwise appointed or induc'd than by an inward perswasion of the Christian dutie which I may usefully discharge herin to the common Lord and Master of us all, and the certain hope of his approbation, first and chiefest to be sought: In the hand of whose providence I remain, praying all success and good event on your publick councels to the defence of true religion and our civil rights.*

John Milton

A Treatise of Civil power in Ecclesiastical causes.

Two things there be which have bin ever found working much mischief to the church of God, and the advancement of truth; force on the one side restraining, and hire on the other side corrupting the teachers thereof. Few ages have bin since the ascension of our Saviour, wherin the one of these two, or both together have not prevaild. It can be at no time therfore unseasonable to speak of these things; since by them the church is either in continual detriment and oppression, or in continual danger. The former shall be at this time my argument; the latter as I shall finde God disposing me, and opportunity inviting. What I argue, shall be drawn from the scripture only; and therin from true fundamental principles of the gospel; to all knowing Christians undeniable. And if the governors of this commonwealth since the rooting out of prelats have made least use of force in religion, and most have favord Christian liberty of any in this Iland before them since the first preaching of the gospel, for which we are not to forget our thanks to God, and their due praise, they may, I doubt not, in this treatise finde that which not only will confirm them to defend still the Christian liberty which we enjoy, but will incite them also to enlarge it, if in aught they yet straiten it.[4] To them who perhaps herafter, less experienc'd in religion, may come to govern or give us laws, this or other such, if

the latter: The Likeliest Means, published in August 1659.

they please, may be a timely instruction: however to the truth it will be at all times no unneedfull testimonie; at least some discharge of that general dutie which no Christian but according to what he hath receivd, knows is requir'd of him if he have aught more conducing to the advancement of religion than what is usually endeavourd, freely to impart it.

It will require no great labor of exposition to unfold what is here meant by matters of religion; being as soon apprehended as defin'd, such things as belong chiefly to the knowledge and service of God: and are either above the reach and light of nature without revelation from above, and therfore liable to be variously understood by humane reason, or such things as are enjoind or forbidden by divine precept, which els by the light of reason would seem indifferent to be don or not don; and so likewise must needs appeer to everie man as the precept is understood. Whence I here mean by conscience or religion, that full perswasion whereby we are assur'd that our beleef and practise, as far as we are able to apprehend and probably make appeer, is according to the will of God and his Holy Spirit within us, which we ought to follow much rather than any law of man, as not only his word every where bids us, but the very dictate of reason tells us: *Acts* 4.19. *whether it be right in the sight of God, to hearken to you more than to God, judge ye.* That for beleef or practise in religion according to this conscientious perswasion no man ought to be punishd or molested by any outward force on earth whatsoever, I distrust not, through Gods implor'd assistance, to make plane by these following arguments.

First it cannot be deni'd, being the main foundation of our protestant religion, that we of these ages, having no other divine rule or autoritie from without us warrantable to one another as a common ground but the holy scripture, and no other within us but the illumination of the Holy Spirit so interpreting that scripture as warrantable only to our selves and to such whose consciences we can so perswade, can have no other ground in matters of religion but only from the scriptures. And these being not possible to be understood without this divine illumination, which no man can know at all times to be in himself, much less to be at any time for certain in any other, it follows cleerly, that no man or body of men in these times can be the infallible judges or determiners in matters of religion to any other mens consciences but thir own. And therfore those Beroeans are commended, *Acts* 17.11, who after the preaching even of S. *Paul, searchd the scriptures daily, whether those things were so.* Nor did they more than what God himself in many places commands us by the same apostle, to search, to try, to judge of these things our selves: And gives us reason also, *Gal.* 6.4, 5. *let every man prove his own work, and then shall he have rejoicing in himself alone, and not in another: for every man shall bear his own burden.* If then we count it so ignorant and irreligious in the papist to think himself dischargd in Gods account, beleeving only as the church beleevs, how much greater condemnation will it be to the protestant his condemner, to think himself justified, beleeving only as the state beleevs. With good cause therfore it is the general consent of all sound protestant writers, that neither traditions, councels nor canons of any visible church, much less edicts of any magistrate or civil session, but the scripture only can be the final judge or rule in matters of religion, and that only in the conscience of every Christian to himself. Which protestation[5] made by the first publick reformers of our religion against the imperial edicts of *Charls* the fifth, imposing church-traditions without scripture, gave first beginning to the name of *Protestant;* and with that name hath ever bin receivd this doctrine; which preferrs the scripture before the church, and acknowledges none but the Scripture sole interpreter of it self to the conscience. For if the church be not sufficient to be implicitly beleevd, as we hold it is not, what can there els be nam'd of more autoritie than the church but the conscience; than which God only is greater, 1 *John* 3.20? But if any man shall pretend, that the scripture judges to his conscience for other men, he makes himself greater not only than the church, but also than the scripture, than the consciences of other men; a presumption too high for any mortal; since every true Christian able to give a reason of his faith, hath the word of God before him, the promisd Holy Spirit, and the minde of Christ within him, 1 *Cor.* 2.16; a much better and safer guide of conscience, which as far as concerns himself he may far more certainly know than any outward rule impos'd upon him by others whom he inwardly neither knows nor can know; at least knows nothing of them more sure than this one thing, that they cannot be his judges in religion. 1 *Cor.* 2.15. *the spiritual man judgeth all things, but he himself is judgd of no man.* Chiefly for this cause do all true protestants account the pope antichrist, for that he assumes to himself this infallibilitie over both the conscience and the scripture; *sitting in the temple of God,* as it were opposite to God, *and exalting himself above all that is called god, or is worshipd,* 2 Thess. 2.4. That is to say not only above all judges and magistrates, who though they be calld gods, are far beneath infallible, but also above God himself, by giving law both to the scripture, to the conscience, and to the spirit it self of God within us. Whenas we finde, *James* 4.12, *there is one lawgiver, who is able to save and to destroy:*

who art thou that judgest another? That Christ is the only lawgiver of his church and that it is here meant in religious matters, no well grounded Christian will deny. Thus also *S. Paul*, Rom. 14.4. *who art thou that judgest the servant of another? to his own Lord he standeth or falleth: but he shall stand; for God is able to make him stand.* As therfore of one beyond expression bold and presumptuous, both these apostles demand, *who art thou* that presum'st to impose other law or judgment in religion than the only lawgiver and judge Christ, who only can save and can destroy, gives to the conscience? And the forecited place to the *Thessalonians* by compar'd effects resolvs us, that be he or they who or wherever they be or can be, they are of far less autoritie than the church, whom in these things as protestants they receive not, and yet no less antichrist in this main point of antichristianism, no less a pope or popedom than he at *Rome*, if not much more; by setting up supream interpreters of scripture either those doctors whom they follow, or, which is far worse, themselves as a civil papacie assuming unaccountable supremacie to themselves not in civil only but ecclesiastical causes. Seeing then that in matters of religion, as hath been prov'd, none can judge or determin here on earth, no not church-governors themselves against the consciences of other beleevers, my inference is, or rather not mine but our Saviours own, that in those matters they neither can command nor use constraint; lest they run rashly on a pernicious consequence, forewarnd in that parable *Mat.* 13. from the 26 to the 31 verse: *least while ye gather up the tares, ye root up also the wheat with them. Let both grow together until the harvest: and in the time of harvest I will say to the reapers, Gather ye together first the tares etc.* whereby he declares that this work neither his own ministers nor any els can discerningly anough or judgingly perform without his own immediat direction, in his own fit season; and that they ought till then not to attempt it. Which is further confirmd 2 *Cor.* 1.24. *not that we have dominion over your faith, but are helpers of your joy.* If apostles had no dominion or constraining power over faith or conscience, much less have ordinary ministers. 1 *Pet.* 5.2, 3. *feed the flock of God not by constraint* etc. *neither as being lords over Gods heritage.* But some will object, that this overthrows all church-discipline, all censure of errors, if no man can determin. My answer is, that what they hear is plane scripture; which forbids not church-sentence or determining, but as it ends in violence upon the conscience unconvinc'd. Let who so will interpret or determin, so it be according to true church-discipline; which is exercis'd on them only who have willingly joind themselves in that covnant of union, and proceeds only to a separation from the rest, proceeds never to any corporal inforcement or forfeture of monie; which in spiritual things are the two arms of Antichrist, not of the true church; the one being an inquisition, the other no better than a temporal indulgence of sin for monie, whether by the church exacted or by the magistrate; both the one and the other a temporal satisfaction for what Christ hath satisfied eternally; a popish commuting of penaltie, corporal for spiritual; a satisfaction to man especially to the magistrate, for what and to whom we owe none: these and more are the injustices of force and fining in religion, besides what I most insist on, the violation of Gods express commandment in the gospel, as hath bin shewn. Thus then if church-governors cannot use force in religion, though but for this reason, because they cannot infallibly determin to the conscience without convincement, much less have civil magistrates autoritie to use force where they can much less judge; unless they mean only to be the civil executioners[6] of them who have no civil power to give them such commission, no nor yet ecclesiastical to any force or violence in religion. To summe up all in brief, if we must beleeve as the magistrate appoints, why not rather as the church? if not as either without convincement, how can force be lawfull? But some are ready to cry out, what shall then be don to blasphemie? Them I would first exhort not thus to terrifie and pose the people with a Greek word: but to teach them better what it is; being a most usual and common word in that language to signifie any slander, any malitious or evil speaking, whether against God or man or any thing to good belonging: blasphemie or evil speaking against God malitiously, is far from conscience in religion; according to that of *Mark*[7] 9.39. *there is none who doth a powerfull work in my name, and can likely speak evil of me.* If this suffice not, I referre them to that prudent and well deliberated act *August* 9.1650;[8] where the Parlament defines blasphemie against God, as far as it is a crime belonging to civil judicature, *pleniùs ac meliùs Chrysippo & Crantore;*[9] in plane English more warily, more judiciously, more orthodoxally than twice thir number of divines have don in many a prolix volume: although in all likelihood they whose whole studie and profession these things are, should be most intelligent and authentic therin, as they are for the most part, yet neither they nor these unnerring always or infallible. But we shall not carrie it thus; another Greek apparition stands in our way, *heresie* and *heretic;* in like manner also rail'd at to the people as in a tongue unknown. They should first interpret to them, that heresie, by what it signifies in that language, is no word of evil note; meaning only the choise or following of any opinion good or bad in religion or any other learning: and thus not only in heathen authors, but in the New testament it self without censure or blame.[10] *Acts* 15.5. *certain of the heresie of the Pharises which beleevd.* and 26.5. *after the exactest heresie of our religion I livd a Pharise.* In which sense Presbyterian or Independent may without reproach be calld a heresie. Where it is mentiond with blame, it seems to differ little from schism 1 *Cor.* 11.18, 19. *I hear that there be schisms among you* etc. *for there must also heresies be among you* etc; though some who write of heresie after their own heads, would make it far worse than schism; whenas on the contrarie, schism signifies division, and in the worst sense; heresie, choise only of one opinion before another, which may bee without discord. In apostolic times therfore ere the scripture was written, heresie was a doctrin maintaind against the doctrin by them deliverd:[11] which in these times can be no otherwise defin'd than a doctrin maintaind against the light, which we now only have, of the scripture. Seeing therfore that no man, no synod, no session of men, though calld the church, can judge definitively the sense of scripture to another mans conscience, which is well known to be a general maxim of the Protestant religion, it follows planely, that he who holds in religion that beleef or those opinions which to his conscience and utmost understanding appeer with most evidence or probabilitie in the scripture, though to others he seem erroneous, can no more be justly censur'd for a heretic than his censurers; who do but the same thing themselves while they censure him for so doing. For ask them, or any Protestant, which hath most autoritie, the church or the scripture? they will answer, doubtless, that the scripture: and what hath most autoritie, that no doubt but they will confess is to be followd. He then who to his best apprehension follows the scripture, though against any point of doctrine by the whole church receivd, is not the heretic; but he who follows the church against his conscience and perswasion grounded on the scripture. To make this yet more undeniable, I shall only borrow a plane similie, the same which our own writers, when they would demonstrate planest that we rightly preferre the scripture before the church, use frequently against the Papist in this manner. As the Samaritans beleevd Christ, first for the womans word, but next and much rather for his own,[12] so we the scripture; first on the churches word, but afterwards and much more for its own, as the word of God; yea the church it self we beleeve then for the scripture. The inference of it self follows: if by the Protestant doctrine we beleeve the scripture not for the churches saying, but for its own as the word of God, then ought we to beleeve what in our conscience we apprehend the scripture to say, though the visible church with all her doctors gainsay; and being taught to beleeve them only for the scripture, they who so do are not heretics, but the best protestants: and by their opinions, whatever they be, can hurt no protestant, whose rule is not to receive them but from the scripture: which to interpret convincingly to his own conscience none is able but himself guided by the Holy Spirit; and not so guided, none than he to himself can be a worse deceiver. To protestants therfore whose common rule and touchstone is the scripture, nothing can with more conscience, more equitie, nothing more protestantly can be permitted than a free and lawful debate at all times by writing, conference or disputation of what opinion soever, disputable by scripture: concluding, that no man in religion is properly a heretic at this day, but he who maintains traditions or opinions not probable by scripture; who, for aught I know, is the papist only; he the only heretic, who counts all heretics but himself. Such as these, indeed, were capitally punishd by the law of *Moses,* as the only true heretics, idolaters, plane and open deserters of God and his known law:[13] but in the gospel such are punishd by excommunion only. *Titus* 3.10. *an heretic, after the first and second admonition, reject.* But they who think not this heavie anough and understand not that dreadfull aw and spiritual efficacie which the apostle hath expressd so highly to be in church-discipline, 2 *Cor.* 10. of which anon, and think weakly that the church of God cannot long subsist but in a bodilie fear, for want of other prooff will needs wrest that place of S. *Paul Rom.* 13. to set up civil inquisition, and give power to the magistrate both of civil judgment and punishment in causes ecclesiastical. But let us see with what strength of argument. *Let every soul be subject to the higher powers.*[14] First, how prove they that the apostle means other powers than such as they to whom he writes were then under; who medld not at all in ecclesiastical causes, unless as tyrants and persecuters; and from them, I hope, they will not derive either the right of magistrates to judge in spiritual things, or the dutie of such our obedience. How prove they next, that he intitles them here to spiritual causes, from whom he witheld, as much as in him lay, the judging of civil; 1 *Cor.* 6.1, etc. If he himself appeald to *Cesar,* it was to judge his innocence, not his religion. *For rulers are not a terror to good works, but to the evil.* then are they not a terror to conscience, which is the rule or judge of good works grounded on the scripture. But heresie, they say, is reck'nd among evil works *Gal.* 5.20: as if all evil works were to be punishd by the magistrate; wherof this place, thir own citation, reck'ns up besides heresie a sufficient number to confute them; *un-*

probable: capable of being proved, demonstrable.

cleanness, wantonness, enmitie, strife, emulations, animosities, contentions, envyings; all which are far more *manifest* to be judgd by him than heresie, as they define it; and yet I suppose they will not subject these evil works nor many more such like to his cognisance and punishment. *Wilt thou then not be affraid of the power? do that which is good and thou shalt have praise of the same.* This shews that religious matters are not here meant; wherin from the power here spoken of they could have no praise. *For he is the minister of God to thee for good.* true; but in that office and to that end and by those means which in this place must be cleerly found, if from this place they intend to argue. And how for thy good by forcing, oppressing and insnaring thy conscience? Many are the ministers of God, and thir offices no less different than many; none more different than state and church-government. Who seeks to govern both must needs be worse than any lord prelat or church-pluralist: for he in his own facultie and profession, the other not in his own and for the most part not throughly understood makes himself supream lord or pope of the church as far as his civil jurisdiction stretches, and all the ministers of God therin, his ministers, or his curates rather in the function onely, not in the government: while he himself assumes to rule by civil power things to be rul'd only by spiritual: when as this very chapter v.6 appointing him his peculiar office, which requires utmost attendance, forbids him this worse than church-plurality from that full and waightie charge, wherin alone he is *the minister of God, attending continually on this very thing.* To little purpose will they here instance *Moses,* who did all by immediate divine direction, no nor yet *Asa, Jehosaphat,* or *Josia,*[15] who both might when they pleasd receive answer from God, and had a commonwealth by him deliverd them, incorporated with a national church exercis'd more in bodily than in spiritual worship, so as that the church might be calld a commonwealth and the whole commonwealth a church: nothing of which can be said of Christianitie, deliverd without the help of magistrates, yea in the midst of thir opposition; how little then with any reference to them or mention of them, save onely of our obedience to thir civil laws, as they countnance good and deterr evil: which is the proper work of the magistrate, following in the same verse, and shews distinctly wherin he is the minister of God, *a revenger to execute wrath on him that doth evil.* But we must first know who it is that doth evil: the heretic they say among the first. Let it be known then certainly who is a heretic: and that he who holds opinions in religion professdly from tradition or his own inventions and not from Scripture but rather against it, is the only heretic; and yet though such, not alwaies punishable by the magistrate, unless he do evil against a civil Law, properly so calld, hath been already prov'd without need of repetition. *But if thou do that which is evil, be affraid.* To do by scripture and the gospel according to conscience is not to do evil; if we therof ought not to be affraid, he ought not by his judging to give cause. causes therfore of Religion are not here meant. *For he beareth not the sword in vain.* Yes altogether in vain, if it smite he knows not what; if that for heresie which not the church it self, much less he, can determine absolutely to be so; if truth for error, being himself so often fallible, he bears the sword not in vain only, but unjustly and to evil. *Be subject not only for wrath, but for conscience sake:* how for conscience sake against conscience? By all these reasons it appeers planely that the apostle in this place gives no judgment or coercive power to magistrates, neither to those then nor these now in matters of religion; and exhorts us no otherwise than he exhorted those *Romans.* It hath now twice befaln me to assert, through Gods assistance, this most wrested and vexd place of scripture; heretofore against *Salmasius* and regal tyranie over the state;[16] now against *Erastus*[17] and state-tyranie over the church. If from such uncertain or rather such improbable grounds as these they endue magistracie with spiritual judgment, they may as well invest him in the same spiritual kinde with power of utmost punishment, excommunication; and then turn spiritual into corporal, as no worse authors did than *Chrysostom, Jerom* and *Austin,* whom *Erasmus* and others in thir notes on the New Testament have cited to interpret that *cutting off* which S. *Paul* wishd to them who had brought back the Galatians to circumcision, no less than the amercement of thir whole virilitie; and *Grotius* addes that this concising punishment of circumcisers became a penal law therupon among the *Visigothes:*[18] a dangerous example of beginning in the spirit to end so in the flesh: wheras that cutting off much likelier seems meant a cutting off from the church, not unusually so termd in scripture, and a zealous imprecation, not a command. But I have mentiond this passage to shew how absurd they often prove who have not learnd to distinguish rightly between civil power and ecclesiastical. How many persecutions then, imprisonments, banishments, penalties and stripes; how much bloodshed have the forcers of conscience to answer for, and protestants rather than papists! For the papist, judging by his principles, punishes them who beleeve not as the church beleevs though against the scripture: but the protestant, teaching every one to beleeve the scripture though against the church, counts heretical and persecutes, against his own principles, them who in any particular so beleeve as he in general teaches them; them who most honor and beleeve divine scripture, but not against it any humane interpretation though universal; them who interpret scripture only to themselves, which by his own position none but they to themselves can interpret; them who use the scripture no otherwise by his own doctrine to thir edification, than he himself uses it to thir punishing: and so whom his doctrine acknowledges a true beleever, his discipline persecutes as a heretic. The papist exacts our beleef as to the church due above scripture; and by the church, which is the whole people of God, understands the pope, the general councels prelatical only and the surnam'd fathers: but the forcing protestant though he deny such beleef to any church whatsoever, yet takes it to himself and his teachers, of far less autoritie than to be calld the church and above scripture beleevd: which renders his practise both contrarie to his beleef, and far worse than that beleef which he condemns in the papist. By all which well considerd, the more he professes to be a true protestant, the more he hath to answer for his persecuting than a papist. No protestant therfore of what sect soever following scripture only, which is the common sect wherin they all agree, and the granted rule of everie mans conscience to himself, ought, by the common doctrine of protestants, to be forc'd or molested for religion. But as for poperie and idolatrie, why they also may not hence plead to be tolerated, I have much less to say. Their religion the more considerd, the less can be acknowledgd a religion; but a Roman principalitie rather, endevouring to keep up her old universal dominion under a new name and meer shaddow of a catholic religion; being indeed more rightly nam'd a catholic heresie against the scripture; supported mainly by a civil, and, except in *Rome*, by a forein power: justly therfore to be suspected, not tolerated by the magistrate of another countrey. Besides, of an implicit faith, which they profess, the conscience also becoms implicit; and so by voluntarie servitude to mans law, forfets her Christian libertie. Who then can plead for such a conscience, as being implicitly enthrald to man instead of God, almost becoms no conscience, as the will not free, becoms no will. Nevertheless if they ought not to be tolerated, it is for just reason of state more than of religion; which they who force, though professing to be protestants, deserve as little to be tolerated themselves, being no less guiltie of poperie in the most popish point. Lastly, for idolatrie, who knows it not to be evidently against all scripture both of the Old and New Testament, and therfore a true heresie, or rather an impietie; wherin a right conscience can have naught to do; and the works therof so manifest, that a magistrate can hardly err in prohibiting and quite removing at least the publick and scandalous use therof.

From the riddance of these objections I proceed yet to another reason why it is unlawfull for the civil magistrate to use force in matters of religion; which is, because to judge in those things, though we should grant him able, which is prov'd he is not, yet as a civil magistrate he hath no right. Christ hath a government of his own, sufficient of it self to all his ends and purposes in governing his church; but much different from that of the civil magistrate; and the difference in this verie thing principally consists, that it governs not by outward force, and that for two reasons. First because it deals only with the inward man and his actions, which are all spiritual and to outward force not lyable: secondly to shew us the divine excellence of his spiritual kingdom, able without worldly force to subdue all the powers and kingdoms of this world, which are upheld by outward force only. That the inward man is nothing els but the inward part of man, his understanding and his will, and that his actions thence proceeding, yet not simply thence but from the work of divine grace upon them, are the whole matter of religion under the gospel, will appeer planely by considering what that religion is; whence we shall perceive yet more planely that it cannot be forc'd. What evangelic religion is, is told in two words, faith and charitie; or beleef and practise. That both these flow either the one from the understanding, the other from the will, or both jointly from both, once indeed naturally free, but now only as they are regenerat and wrought on by divine grace, is in part evident to common sense and principles unquestiond, the rest by scripture: concerning our beleef, *Mat.* 16.17. *flesh and blood hath not reveald it unto thee, but my father which is in heaven:* concerning our practise, as it is religious and not meerly civil, *Gal.* 5.22, 23 and other places declare it to be the fruit of the spirit only. Nay our whole practical dutie in religion is containd in charitie, or the love of God and our neighbour, no way to be forc'd, yet the fulfilling of the whole law;[19] that is to say, our whole practise in religion. If then both our beleef and practise, which comprehend our whole religion, flow from faculties of the inward man, free and unconstrainable of themselves by nature, and our practise not only from faculties endu'd with freedom, but from love and charitie besides, incapable of force, and all these things by transgression lost, but renewd and regenerated in us by the power and gift of God alone, how can such religion as this admit of force from man, or force be any way appli'd to such religion, especially under the free offer of grace in the gospel, but it must forthwith frustrate and make of no effect both the religion and the gospel?

And that to compell outward profession, which they will say perhaps ought to be compelld though inward religion cannot, is to compell hypocrisie not to advance religion, shall yet, though of it self cleer anough, be ere the conclusion further manifest. The other reason why Christ rejects outward force in the goverment of his church, is, as I said before, to shew us the divine excellence of his spiritual kingdom, able without worldly force to subdue all the powers and kingdoms of this world, which are upheld by outward force only: by which to uphold religion otherwise than to defend the religious from outward violence, is no service to Christ or his kingdom, but rather a disparagement, and degrades it from a divine and spiritual kingdom to a kingdom of this world: which he denies it to be, because it needs not force to confirm it: *John.* 18.36. *if my kingdom were of this world, then would my servants fight, that I should not be deliverd to the Jewes.* This proves the kingdom of Christ not governd by outward force; as being none of this world, whose kingdoms are maintaind all by force onely: and yet disproves not that a Christian commonwealth may defend it self against outward force in the cause of religion as well as in any other;[20] though Christ himself, coming purposely to dye for us, would not be so defended. 1 *Cor.* 1.27. *God hath chosen the weak things of the world to confound the things which are mighty.* Then surely he hath not chosen the force of this world to subdue conscience and conscientious men, who in this world are counted weakest; but rather conscience, as being weakest, to subdue and regulate force, his adversarie, not his aide or instrument in governing the church. 2 *Cor.* 10.3, 4, 5, 6. *for though we walk in the flesh, we do not warre after the flesh: for the weapons of our warfare are not carnal; but mightie through God to the pulling down of strong holds; casting down imaginations and everie high thing that exalts it self against the knowledge of God; and bringing into captivitie everie thought to the obedience of Christ: and having in a readiness to aveng all disobedience.* It is evident by the first and second verses of this chapter, that the apostle here speaks of that spiritual power by which Christ governs his church, how allsufficient it is, how powerful to reach the conscience and the inward man with whom it chiefly deals and whom no power els can deal with. In comparison of which as it is here thus magnificently describ'd, how uneffectual and weak is outward force with all her boistrous tooles, to the shame of those Christians and especially those churchmen, who to the exercising of church discipline never cease calling on the civil magistrate to interpose his fleshlie force;[21] an argument that all true ministerial and spiritual power is dead within them: who think the gospel, which both began and spread over the whole world for above three hundred years under heathen and persecuting emperors, cannot stand or continue, supported by the same divine presence and protection to the worlds end, much easier under the defensive favor onely of a Christian magistrate, unless it be enacted and settled, as they call it, by the state, a statute or a state-religion: and understand not that the church it self cannot, much less the state, settle or impose one tittle of religion upon our obedience implicit, but can only recommend or propound it to our free and conscientious examination: unless they mean to set the state higher than the church in religion, and with a grosse contradiction give to the state in thir settling petition that command of our implicit beleef, which they deny in thir setled confession[22] both to the state and to the church. Let them cease then to importune and interrupt the magistrate from attending to his own charge in civil and moral things, the settling of things just, things honest, the defence of things religious settled by the churches within themselves; and the repressing of thir contraries determinable by the common light of nature; which is not to constrain or to repress religion, probable by scripture, but the violaters and persecuters therof: of all which things he hath anough and more than anough to do, left yet undon; for which the land groans and justice goes to wrack the while: let him also forbear force where he hath no right to judge; for the conscience is not his province: least a worse *woe* arrive him, for worse offending, than was denounc'd by our Saviour *Matt.* 23.23. against the Pharises: ye have forc'd the conscience, which was not to be forc'd; but judgment and mercy ye have not executed: this ye should have don, and the other let alone. And since it is the councel and set purpose of God in the gospel by spiritual means which are counted weak, to overcom all power which resists him; let them not go about to do that by worldly strength which he hath decreed to do by those means which the world counts weakness, least they be again obnoxious to that saying which in another place is also written of the Pharises, *Luke* 7.30. *that they frustrated the councel of God.* The main plea is, and urgd with much vehemence to thir imitation, that the kings of *Juda,* as I touchd before, and especially *Josia* both judgd and us'd force in religion. 2 *Chron.* 34.33. *he made all that were present in Israel to serve the Lord thir God:* an argument, if it be well weighed, worse than that us'd by the false prophet *Shemaia* to the high priest, that in imitation of *Jehoiada* he ought to put *Jeremie* in the stocks, *Jer.* 29.24, 26, etc. for which he receivd his due denouncement from God. But to this besides I return a threefold answer: first, that the state of religion under the gospel is far differing from what it was under the law: then was the state of rigor, childhood, bondage and works, to all which force was not unbefitting; now is the state of grace, manhood, freedom and faith; to all which belongs willingness and reason, not force: the law was then written on tables of stone, and to be performd according to the letter, willingly or unwillingly; the gospel, our new covnant, upon the heart of every beleever, to be interpreted only by the sense of charitie and inward perswasion: the law had no distinct government or governors of church and commonwealth, but the Priests and Levites judg'd in all causes not ecclesiastical only but civil, *Deut.* 17.8, etc. which under the gospel is forbidden to all church-ministers, as a thing which Christ thir master in his ministerie disclam'd *Luke* 12.14; as a thing beneathe them 1 *Cor.* 6.4; and by many of our statutes, as to them who have a peculiar and far differing government of thir own. If not, why different the governors? why not church-ministers in state-affairs, as well as state-ministers in church-affairs? If church and state shall be made one flesh again as under the law, let it be withall considerd, that God who then joind them hath now severd them; that which, he so ordaining, was then a lawfull conjunction, to such on either side as join again what he hath severd, would be nothing now but thir own presumptuous fornication.[23] Secondly, the kings of *Juda* and those magistrates under the law might have recours, as I said before, to divine inspiration; which our magistrates under the gospel have not, more than to the same spirit, which those whom they force have oft times in greater measure than themselves: and so, instead of forcing the Christian, they force the Holy Ghost; and, against that wise forewarning of *Gamaliel,*[24] fight against God. Thirdly, those kings and magistrates us'd force in such things only as were undoubtedly known and forbidden in the law of *Moses,* idolatrie and direct apostacie from that national and strict enjoind worship of God; wherof the corporal punishment was by himself expressly set down: but magistrates under the gospel, our free, elective and rational worship, are most commonly busiest to force those things which in the gospel are either left free, nay somtimes abolishd when by them compelld, or els controverted equally by writers on both sides, and somtimes with odds on that side which is against them. By which means they either punish that which they ought to favor and protect, or that with corporal punishment and of thir own inventing, which not they but the church hath receivd command to chastise with a spiritual rod only. Yet some are so eager in thir zeal of forcing, that they refuse not to descend at length to the utmost shift of that parabolical prooff *Luke* 14.16, etc.

compell them to come in. therfore magistrates may compell in religion. As if a parable were to be straind through every word or phrase, and not expounded by the general scope therof: which is no other here than the earnest expression of Gods displeasure on those recusant Jewes, and his purpose to preferre the gentiles on any terms before them; expressd here by the word *compell.* But how compells he? doubtless no otherwise than he draws, without which no man can come to him, *John* 6.44: and that is by the inward perswasive motions of his spirit and by his ministers; not by the outward compulsions of a magistrate or his officers. The true people of Christ, as is foretold *Psal.* 110.3, *are a willing people in the day of his power.* then much more now when he rules all things by outward weakness, that both his inward power and their sinceritie may the more appeer. *God loveth a chearfull giver:* then certainly is not pleasd with an unchearfull worshiper; as the verie words declare of his evangelical invitations. *Isa.* 55.1. *ho, everie one that thirsteth, come. John* 7.37. *if any man thirst. Rev.* 3.18. *I counsel thee.* and 22.17. *whosoever will, let him take the water of life freely.* And in that grand commission of preaching to invite all nations *Mark* 16.16, as the reward of them who come, so the penaltie of them who come not is only spiritual. But they bring now some reason with thir force, which must not pass unanswerd; that the church of *Thyatira* was blam'd *Rev.* 2.20. for suffering the false *prophetess to teach and to seduce.* I answer, that seducement is to be hinderd by fit and proper means ordaind in church-discipline; by instant and powerfull demonstration to the contrarie; by opposing truth to error, no unequal match; truth the strong to error the weak though slie and shifting. Force is no honest confutation; but uneffectual, and for the most part unsuccessfull, oft times fatal to them who use it: sound doctrine diligently and duely taught, is of herself both sufficient, and of herself (if some secret judgment of God hinder not) alwaies prevalent against seducers. This the *Thyatirians* had neglected, suffering, against Church-discipline, that woman to teach and seduce among them: civil force they had not then in thir power; being the Christian part only of that citie, and then especially under one of those ten great persecutions, wherof this the second was raisd by *Domitian:* force therfore in these matters could not be requir'd of them, who were then under force themselves.

I have shewn that the civil power hath neither right nor can do right by forcing religious things: I will now shew the wrong it doth; by violating the fundamental privilege of the gospel, the new-

Domitian: Roman emperor, A.D. 81–96.

birthright of everie true beleever, Christian libertie. 2 *Cor.* 3.17. *where the spirit of the Lord is, there is libertie. Gal.* 4.26. *Jerusalem which is above, is free; which is the mother of us all.* and 31. *we are not children of the bondwoman but of the free.* It will be sufficient in this place to say no more of Christian libertie, than that it sets us free not only from the bondage of those ceremonies, but also from the forcible imposition of those circumstances, place and time in the worship of God:[25] which though by him commanded in the old law, yet in respect of that veritie and freedom which is evangelical, S. *Paul* comprehends both kindes alike, that is to say, both ceremonie and circumstance, under one and the same contemtuous name of *weak and beggarly rudiments, Gal.* 4.3, 9, 10. *Col.* 2.8. with 16: conformable to what our Saviour himself taught *John* 4.21, 23. *neither in this mountain nor yet at Jerusalem. In spirit and in truth: for the father seeketh such to worship him.* that is to say, not only sincere of heart, for such he sought ever, but also, as the words here chiefly import, not compelld to place, and by the same reason, not to any set time; as his apostle by the same spirit hath taught us *Rom.* 14.6, etc. *one man esteemeth one day above another, another* etc. *Gal.* 4.10. *Ye observe dayes, and moonths* etc. *Col.* 2.16. These and other such places of scripture the best and learnedest reformed writers have thought evident anough to instruct us in our freedom not only from ceremonies but from those circumstances also, though impos'd with a confident perswasion of moralitie in them, which they hold impossible to be in place or time.[26] By what warrant then our opinions and practises herin are of late turnd quite against all other Protestants, and that which is to them orthodoxal, to us become scandalous and punishable by statute, I wish were once again better considerd; if we mean not to proclame a schism in this point from the best and most reformed churches abroad. They who would seem more knowing, confess that these things are indifferent, but for that very cause by the magistrate may be commanded. As if God of his special grace in the gospel had to this end freed us from his own commandments in these things, that our freedom should subject us to a more greevous yoke, the commandments of men. As well may the magistrate call that common or unclean which God hath cleansd, forbidden to S. *Peter Acts* 10.15; as well may he loos'n that which God hath strait'nd, or strait'n that which God hath loos'nd,[27] as he may injoin those things in religion which God hath left free, and lay on that yoke which God hath taken off. For he hath not only given us this gift as a special privilege and excellence of the free gospel above the servile law, but strictly also hath commanded us to keep it and enjoy it. *Gal.* 5.13. *you are calld to libertie.* 1 *Cor.* 7.23. *be not made the servants of men. Gal.* 5.14. *stand fast therfore in the libertie wherwith Christ hath made us free; and be not intangl'd again with the yoke of bondage.* Neither is this a meer command, but for the most part in these forecited places accompanied with the verie waightiest and inmost reasons of Christian religion: *Rom.* 14.9, 10. *for to this end Christ both dy'd and rose and reviv'd, that he might be Lord both of the dead and living. But why dost thou judge thy brother? etc.* how presum'st thou to be his lord, to be whose only Lord, at least in these things, Christ both dy'd and rose and livd again? *We shall all stand before the judgment seat of Christ.* why then dost thou not only judge, but persecute in these things for which we are to be accountable to the tribunal of Christ only, our Lord and lawgiver? 1 *Cor.* 7.23. *ye are bought with a price; be not made the servants of men.* some trivial price belike, and for some frivolous pretences paid in their opinion, if bought and by him redeemd who is God from what was once the service of God, we shall be enthrald again and forc'd by men to what now is but the service of men. *Gal.* 4.31, with 5.1. *we are not children of the bondwoman* etc. *stand fast therfore* etc. *Col.* 2.8. *beware least any man spoil you,* etc. *after the rudiments of the world, and not after Christ.* Solid reasons wherof are continu'd through the whole chapter. *v.*10. *ye are complete in him, which is the head of all principalitie and power.* not completed therfore or made the more religious by those ordinances of civil power, from which Christ thir head hath dischargd us; *blotting out the handwriting of ordinances, that was against us, which was contrarie to us; and took it out of the way, nailing it to his cross, v.*14: blotting out ordinances written by God himself, much more those so boldly written over again by men. ordinances which were against us, that is, against our frailtie, much more those which are against our conscience. *Let no man therfore judge you in respect of* etc. *v.*16. *Gal.* 4.3, etc. *even so we, when we were children, were in bondage under the rudiments of the world: but when the fullness of time was come, God sent forth his son* etc. *to redeem them that were under the law, that we might receive the adoption of sons* etc. *Wherfore thou art no more a servant, but a son* etc. *But now* etc. *how turn ye again to the weak and beggarly rudiments, wherunto ye desire again to be in bondage? ye observe dayes* etc. Hence it planely appeers, that if we be not free we are not sons, but still servants unadopted; and if we turn again to those weak and beggarly rudiments, we are not free; yea though willingly and with a misguided conscience we desire to be in bondage to them; how much more than if unwillingly and against our conscience? Ill was our condition chang'd from legal to evangelical, and small advantage gotten by the gospel, if for the spirit of adoption to freedom, promisd us, we receive again the spirit of bondage to fear; if our fear which was then servile towards God only, must be now servile in religion towards men: strange also and preposterous fear, if when and wherin it hath attaind by the redemption of our Saviour to be filial only towards God, it must be now servile towards the magistrate. Who by subjecting us to his punishment in these things, brings back into religion that law of terror and satisfaction, belonging now only to civil crimes; and thereby in effect abolishes the gospel by establishing again the law to a far worse yoke of servitude upon us than before. It will therfore not misbecome the meanest Christian to put in minde Christian magistrates, and so much the more freely by how much the more they desire to be thought Christian (for they will be thereby, as they ought to be in these things, the more our brethren and the less our lords) that they meddle not rashly with Christian libertie, the birthright and outward testimonie of our adoption: least while they little think it, nay think they do God service, they themselves like the sons of that bondwoman be found persecuting them who are freeborne of the spirit; and by a sacrilege of not the least aggravation bereaving them of that sacred libertie which our Saviour with his own blood purchas'd for them.

A fourth reason why the magistrate ought not to use force in religion, I bring from the consideration of all those ends which he can likely pretend to the interposing of his force therin: and those hardly can be other than first the glorie of God; next either the spiritual good of them whom he forces, or the temporal punishment of their scandal to others. As for the promoting of Gods glory, none, I think, will say that his glorie ought to be promoted in religious things by unwarrantable means, much less by means contrarie to what he hath commanded. That outward force is such, and that Gods glory in the whole administration of the gospel according to his own will and councel ought to be fulfilld by weakness, at least so refuted, not by force; or if by force, inward and spiritual, not outward and corporeal, is already prov'd at large. That outward force cannot tend to the good of him who is forc'd in religion, is unquestionable. For in religion whatever we do under the gospel, we ought to be therof perswaded without scruple; and are justified by the faith we have, not by the work we do. *Rom.* 14.5. *Let every man be fully perswaded in his own mind.* The other reason which follows necessarily, is obvious *Gal.* 2.16, and in many other places of St. *Paul,* as the groundwork and foundation of the whole gospel, that we are *justified by the faith of Christ, and not by the works of the law.* if not by the works of Gods law, how then by the injunctions of mans law? Surely force cannot work perswasion, which is faith; cannot therfore justifie nor pacifie the conscience; and that which justifies not in the gospel, condemns; is not only not good, but sinfull to do. *Rom.* 14.23. *Whatsoever is not of faith, is sin.* It concerns the magistrate then to take heed how he forces in religion conscientious men: least by compelling them to do that wherof they cannot be perswaded, that wherin they cannot finde themselves justified, but by thir own consciences condemnd, instead of aiming at thir spiritual good, he force them to do evil; and while he thinks himself *Asa, Josia, Nehemia,* he be found *Jeroboam,* who causd Israel to sin;[28] and thereby draw upon his own head all those sins and shipwracks of implicit faith and conformitie, which he hath forc'd, and all the wounds given to those *little ones,* whom to offend he will finde worse one day than that violent drowning mentioned *Matt.* 18.6. Lastly as a preface to force, it is the usual pretence, That although tender consciences shall be tolerated, yet scandals thereby given shall not be unpunishd, prophane and licentious men shall not be encourag'd to neglect the performance of religious and holy duties by color of any law giving libertie to tender consciences.[29] By which contrivance the way lies ready open to them heerafter who may be so minded, to take away by little and little, that liberty which Christ and his gospel, not any magistrate, hath right to give: though this kinde of his giving be but to give with one hand and take away with the other, which is a deluding not a giving. As for scandals, if any man be offended at the conscientious liberty of another, it is a taken scandal not a given. To heal one conscience we must not wound another: and men must be exhorted to beware of scandals in Christian libertie, not forc'd by the magistrate; least while he goes about to take away the scandal, which is uncertain whether given or taken, he take away our liberty, which is the certain and the sacred gift of God, neither to be touchd by him, nor to be parted with by us. None more cautious of giving scandal than St. *Paul.* Yet while he made himself *servant to all,* that he *might gain the more,* he made himself so of his own accord, was not made so by outward force, testifying at the same time that he *was free from all men,* 1 *Cor.* 9.19: and therafter exhorts us also *Gal.* 5.13. *ye were calld to libertie* etc. *but by love serve one another:* then not by force. As for that fear least prophane and licentious men should be encourag'd to omit the performance of religious and holy duties, how can that care belong to the civil magistrate, especially to his force? For if prophane and licentious persons must not neglect the performance of religious and holy duties, it implies, that such duties they can perform; which no Protestant will affirm. They who mean the outward performance, may so explane it; and it will then appeer yet more planely, that such performance of religious and holy duties especialy by prophane and licentious persons, is a dishonoring rather than a worshiping of God; and not only by him not requir'd but detested: *Prov.* 21.27. *the sacrifice of the wicked is an abomination: how much more when he bringeth it with a wicked minde?* To compell therfore the prophane to things holy in his prophaneness, is all one under the gospel, as to have compelld the unclean to sacrifise in his uncleanness under the law. And I adde withall, that to compell the licentious in his licentiousness, and the conscientious against his conscience, coms all to one; tends not to the honor of God, but to the multiplying and the aggravating of sin to them both. We read not that Christ ever exercis'd force but once; and that was to drive prophane ones out of his temple, not to force them in:[30] and if thir beeing there was an offence, we finde by many other scriptures that thir praying there was an abomination: and yet to the Jewish law that nation, as a servant, was oblig'd; but to the gospel each person is left voluntarie, calld only, as a son, by the preaching of the word; not to be driven in by edicts and force of arms. For if by the apostle, *Rom.* 12.1, we are *beseechd* as *brethren by the mercies of God* to *present* our *bodies a living sacrifice, holy, acceptable to God, which is* our *reasonable service* or worship, then is no man to be forc'd by the compulsive laws of men to present his body a dead sacrifice, and so under the gospel most unholy and unacceptable, because it is his unreasonable service, that is to say, not only unwilling but unconscionable. But if prophane and licentious persons may not omit the performance of holy duties, why may they not partake of holy things? why are they prohibited the Lords supper; since both the one and the other action may be outward; and outward performance of dutie may attain at least an outward participation of benefit? The church denying them that communion of grace and thanksgiving, as it justly doth, why doth the magistrate compell them to the union of performing that which they neither truly can, being themselves unholy, and to do seemingly is both hatefull to God, and perhaps no less dangerous to perform holie duties irreligiously than to receive holy signes or sacraments unworthily. All prophane and licentious men, so known, can be considerd but either so without the church as never yet within it, or departed thence of thir own accord, or excommunicate: if never yet within the church, whom the apostle, and so consequently the church have naught to do to judge, as he professes 1 *Cor.* 5.12, them by what autoritie doth the magistrate judge, or, which is worse, compell in relation to the church? if departed of his own accord, like that lost sheep *Luke* 15.4, etc. the true church either with her own or any borrowd force worries him not in again, but rather in all charitable manner sends after him; and if she finde him, layes him gently on her shoulders; bears him, yea bears his burdens; his errors, his infirmities any way tolerable, *so fulfilling the law of Christ, Gal.* 6.2: if excommunicate, whom the church hath bid go out, in whose name doth the magistrate compell to go in? The church indeed hinders none from hearing in her publick congregation, for the doors are open to all: nor excommunicates to destruction, but, as much as in her lies, to a final saving. Her meaning therfore must needs bee, that as her driving out brings on no outward penaltie, so no outward force or penaltie of an improper and only a destructive power should drive in again her infectious sheep; therfore sent out because infectious, and not driven in but with the danger not only of the whole and sound, but also of his own utter perishing. Since force neither instructs in religion nor begets repentance or amendment of life, but, on the contrarie, hardness of heart, formalitie, hypocrisie, and, as I said before, everie way increase of sin; more and more alienates the minde from a violent religion expelling out and compelling in, and reduces it to a condition like that which the *Britains* complain of in our storie, driven to and fro between the *Picts* and the sea.[31] If after excommunion he be found intractable, incurable, and will not hear the church, he becoms as one never yet within her pale, *a heathen or a publican, Mat.* 18.17; not further to be judgd, no not by the magistrate, unless for civil causes; but left to the final sentence of that judge, whose coming shall be in flames of fire; that *Maran athà* 1 *Cor.* 16.22; than which to him so left nothing can be more dreadful and ofttimes to him particularly nothing more speedie, that is to say, the Lord cometh: In the mean while deliverd up to Satan, 1 *Cor.* 5.5. 1 *Tim.* 1.20 that is, from the fould of Christ and kingdom of grace to the world again which is the kingdom of Satan; and as he was receivd *from darkness to light, and from the power of Satan to God Acts* 26.18, so now deliverd up again from light to darkness, and from God to the power of Satan; yet so as is in both places manifested, to the intent of saving him, brought sooner to contrition by spiritual than by any corporal severitie. But grant it belonging any way to the magistrate, that prophane and licentious persons omit not the performance of holy

Maran athà: Aramaic expression meaning, "Our Lord, come."

duties, which in them were odious to God even under the law, much more now under the gospel, yet ought his care both as a magistrate and a Christian, to be much more that conscience be not inwardly violated, than that licence in these things be made outwardly conformable: since his part is undoubtedly as a Christian, which puts him upon this office much more than as a magistrate, in all respects to have more care of the conscientious than of the prophane; and not for their sakes to take away (while they pretend to give) or to diminish the rightfull libertie of religious consciences.

On these four scriptural reasons as on a firm square this truth, the right of Christian and evangelic liberty, will stand immoveable against all those pretended consequences of license and confusion, which for the most part men most licentious and confus'd themselves, or such as whose severitie would be wiser than divine wisdom, are ever aptest to object against the waies of God: as if God without them when he gave us this libertie, knew not of the worst which these men in thir arrogance pretend will follow: yet knowing all their worst, he gave us this liberty as by him judgd best. As to those magistrates who think it their work to settle religion, and those ministers or others, who so oft call upon them to do so, I trust, that having well considerd what hath bin here argu'd, neither they will continue in that intention, nor these in that expectation from them: when they shall finde that the settlement of religion belongs only to each particular church by perswasive and spiritual means within it self, and that the defence only of the church belongs to the magistrate. Had he once learnt not further to concern himself with church affairs, half his labor might be spar'd, and the commonwealth better tended. To which end, that which I premis'd in the beginning, and in due place treated of more at large, I desire now concluding, that they would consider seriously what religion is: and they will find it to be in summe, both our beleef and our practise depending upon God only. That there can be no place then left for the magistrate or his force in the settlement of religion, by appointing either what we shall beleeve in divine things or practise in religious (neither of which things are in the power of man either to perform himself or to enable others) I perswade me in the Christian ingenuitie of all religious men, the more they examin seriously, the more they will finde cleerly to be true: and finde how false and deceivable that common saying is, which is so much reli'd upon, that the Christian Magistrate is *custos utriusque tabulae*, keeper of both tables; unless is meant by keeper the defender only: neither can that maxim be maintaind by any prooff or argument which hath not in this discours first or last bin refuted. For the two tables, or ten commandements, teach our dutie to God and our neighbour from the love of both; give magistrates no autoritie to force either: they seek that from the judicial law; though on false grounds, especially in the first table, as I have shewn; and both in first and second execute that autoritie for the most part not according to Gods judicial laws but thir own. As for civil crimes and of the outward man which all are not, no not of those against the second table, as that of coveting; in them what power they have, they had from the beginning, long before *Moses* or the two tables were in being. And whether they be not now as little in being to be kept by any Christian as they are two legal tables, remanes yet as undecided,[32] as it is sure they never were yet deliverd to the keeping of any Christian magistrate. But of these things perhaps more some other time; what may serve the present hath bin above discourst sufficiently out of the scriptures: and to those produc'd might be added testimonies, examples, experiences of all succeeding ages to these times asserting this doctrine: but having herin the scripture so copious and so plane, we have all that can be properly calld true strength and nerve; the rest would be but pomp and incumbrance. Pomp and ostentation of reading is admir'd among the vulgar: but doubtless in matters of religion he is learnedest who is planest. The brevitie I use, not exceeding a small manual, will not therfore, I suppose, be thought the less considerable, unless with them perhaps who think that great books only can determin great matters. I rather chose the common rule, not to make much ado where less may serve. Which in controversies and those especially of religion, would make them less tedious, and by consequence read ofter, by many more, and with more benefit.

NOTES

1. Richard's parliament assembled on January 27, 1659. Milton's pamphlet was evidently published almost immediately thereafter, for it was advertised in the newsbook *The Publick Intelligencer* of February 7–14, 1659.

2. Former members of Commonwealth Councils of State who were members of Richard's parliament include Thomas Harrison, Henry Neville, Edmund Ludlow, Thomas Scott, Sir Charles Fleetwood, and Sir Henry Vane. In 1652 Milton had addressed a sonnet to Vane, eulogizing him as one who knew "Both spirituall power and civill, what each means, / What severs each."

3. Milton's *Eikonoklastes* (probably) and *Defensio* (certainly) were commissioned by the Commonwealth government.

4. The religious regulations of the last Protectorate constitution, *The Humble Petition and Advice,* were still in effect, calling for maintenance of a godly ministry; promulgation of an orthodox confession of faith; suppression of all

who revile the ministry or this confession; belief in the Trinity and the Scriptures as conditions of toleration; and repression of popery, prelacy, horrible blasphemies, licentiousness, and profaneness.

5. Johann Phillippson (1506–56), known as Sleidan, described in his *Commentaries* (trans. John Daus [London, 1560], fol. cxlviii) the protest of the princes of the League of Schmalkald to the ambassador of Emperor Charles V in February 1537, asserting that the authority of Scripture takes precedence over that of the church, and denying any basis for religious determinations other than the Scripture.

6. An appeal to the traditionally strong Erastian sentiment in the Parliament, which in the 1640s kept it from establishing strict Presbyterianism in England on the ground that Presbyterian discipline tended to make the civil magistrate merely the executioner of clerical judgments. See note 17.

7. *Marc:* 1659.

8. This act provides for punishment by imprisonment or banishment of those who declare themselves God, or equal to Him, or possessed of His attributes, or who state that God desires or condones moral evils, or that He does not punish sin. It was directed against extreme Sectaries of an Antinomian complexion, especially the Ranters, Adamites, Familists, and some Quakers. This act was much less severe than the Presbyterian *Ordinance for the Suppression of Blasphemies and Heresies* of May 2, 1648, which set forth a long list of errors (concerning the nature of God, Christ, Scripture, and predestination) punishable by death if not recanted, and a much longer list of minor religious errors (such as belief in purgatory, rejection of infant baptism, and use of religious images) punishable by imprisonment. See David Masson, *Life of John Milton,* 7 vols. (London, 1859–94), III, 600–1.

9. Horace, *Epistles,* I.ii.4, cites the Homeric poems as "better and more complete" guides to wisdom than either Chrysippus the Stoic philosopher or Crantor the Academic philosopher.

10. As Barker notes (*Dilemma,* 241–42), this is essentially the definition of heresy propounded by the radicals, e.g., Roger Williams, *The Bloudy Tenent* (London, 1644), p. 59. Milton invokes it here to oppose the conservative position stated, for example, by the Congregationalist William Ames, *Conscience with the Power and Cases Thereof* (London, 1643), IV, 9–10; Ames defines heresy as error that is "contrary to that doctrine which belongs to the summe and substance of faith and manners" and that is held with stubbornness, that is, the heretic "opposeth himselfe to the plaine Scripture, and will not through the naughtinesse of his mind perceive the sense of it."

11. See Rom. xvi 17; 2 John i 10.

12. See John iv 7–42.

13. See for example, Exod. xxxii 22–28; Lev. xx 1–6, 27.

14. In the passage which follows many of the phrases of Rom. xiii 1–5 are explicated in an attempted demonstration that this famous definition of the magistrate's function cannot be used to argue his responsibilities in religious affairs.

15. The Mosaic ordinances for worship and sacrifice, for punishment of idolatry, and for destruction of idols are alluded to here. Asa (1 Kings xv 9–22; 2 Chron. xiv 1–5), Jehosaphat (2 Chron. xix), and Josiah (2 Chron. xxxiv 1–7) were noteworthy for destroying idols and groves and restoring worship according to the Mosaic law.

16. See *First Defense, Columbia Milton,* VII, 165 ff.; *Yale Milton,* IV, 381 ff. Both in *Tenure* and in the *Defensio* Milton undertook to discredit Rom. xiii 1–5 as a proof text for Royalist denunciation of rebellion.

17. The German-Swiss theologian Thomas Erastus (1524–83) held that the ns of professing Christians are to be punished by civil authority rather than by cclesiastical sanctions such as withholding sacraments or excommunication; in 659 Erastus' theses were translated and published in England under the title, *he Nullity of Church Censures*. "Erastianism" denotes the doctrine of the ate's supremacy in ecclesiastical causes. By a somewhat disingenuous argu- ıent Milton here associates the Presbyterian doctrine of the magistrate's re- ponsibility to establish and defend religion with Erastianism since it gives the ıagistrate some authority in religious matters, though in fact rigid Presbyterian- m tended rather to subordinate the magistrate to the clergy.

18. See Gal. v 12: "I would that they were even cut off which trouble you." rasmus in his *Annotationes ad Novum Testamentum* (*Opera* VI [London, 705], p. 823) cites two interpretations of the "cutting off" which Paul wished ɔ the new circumcisers among the Galatians—amputation of the genitals and xcommunication from the church. Erasmus cites Ambrose, Theophylactus, and hrysostom as explaining the passage in the former sense, but indicates his own elief that the latter meaning is more in keeping with the dignity of the Apostle. Ie cites Augustine [Austin] for still a third meaning which Milton seems to ave remembered wrongly, to the effect that the apostle here begs the false eachers to make themselves eunuchs for the Kingdom of Heaven, that is, to ease disturbing the church by their preaching of circumcision. Milton's pas- age owes more to Grotius, however, than to Erasmus. Grotius in *Annotationes n Epistolam ad Galatas* (*Opera omnia theologica*, II, Tom 2 [Amsterdam, 679], p. 877) quotes from Chrysostom and Jerome in support of the corporal neaning of *cut off*, and cites the Law of the Visigoths, xiii. 4, as providing for uch amputation for circumcisers.

19. See Mark xii 32.

20. This qualification justifies the Puritan revolt against Charles, as well as ırmed resistance to the Restoration.

21. An allusion to the barrage of Presbyterian petitions to Richard to estab- ish and maintain a Presbyterian national church.

22. The Presbyterians' Westminster Confession of Faith declared for liberty of conscience in terms which seem quite liberal: "God alone is Lord of the con- science, and hath left it free from the doctrines and commandments of men which are in any thing contrary to his word, or beside it, in matters of faith and worship." But all possible tolerationist implications are removed from this pre- cept by a further proviso: "The civil magistrate may not assume to himself the administration of the Word and Sacraments, or the power of the keys of the kingdom of heaven; yet he hath authority, and it is his duty to take order, that unity and peace be preserved in the church, that the truth of God be kept pure and entire, and all blasphemies and heresies be suppressed, all corruptions and abuses in worship and discipline prevented or reformed, and all the ordinances of God duly settled, administered, and observed." In this passage Milton in- sinuates again that despite the disclaimer about the separation of powers the fact that the Presbyterians give the magistrate power in religion is tantamount to Erastianism.

23. See Matt. xix 1–6 for the description of the marriage relation, which provides the basis for Milton's church-state analogy.

24. See Acts v 38–39. Gamaliel advised the Council of the High Priest not to imprison or otherwise restrain Peter and the apostles, "for if this counsel or this work be of men, it will come to nought: But if it be of God, ye cannot over- throw it; lest haply ye be found even to fight against God."

25. This limited definition of Christian liberty argues the Christian's freedom from the Jewish ceremonial law and from Sabbatarian ordinances. In *De Doctrina,* Book I, ch. 27, Milton gives a much more radical definition of Christian liberty, a definition which he also suggests tentatively in the concluding paragraph of this tract—the abrogation of the Decalogue itself as a legal code binding upon Christians, though not of its essence, which is part of the eternal moral law. Milton no doubt refrains from pressing his radical understanding of Christian liberty here in order to avoid giving offense to his Congregationalist audience.

26. In *De Doctrina,* Book II, ch. 7, "On the Time for Divine Worship," Milton cites Bucer, Calvin, Peter Martyr, Musculus, Ursinus, and Gomarus as authorities supporting his conception of the Christian's freedom from imposed ceremonies and circumstances of time and place in divine worship.

27. Perhaps an allusion to Job xii 23: "he enlargeth the nations, and straiteneth them again," or to Matt. xix 6: "what therefore God hath joined together, let not man put asunder."

28. See note 13. Nehemiah viii–xiii records Nehemiah's restoration of ceremonies of worship and reformation of abuses after the Jews returned from the Babylonian captivity. Jeroboam, king of the ten Israelite tribes who rebelled against the House of David (1 Kings xii 26–33), instituted idol worship among the Israelites and was severely punished (1 Kings xiv 10–20).

29. This statement seems to be directed against the Congregationalist position on toleration set forth at their Savoy Conference, October 12, 1658: that tender consciences should be respected but that the fundamentals of Christian doctrine should be promulgated and that the magistrate should take care "that men of corrupt minds and conversations do not licentiously publish and divulge blasphemy and error." (*A Declaration of the Faith and Order Owned and Practised in the Congregational Churches in England,* London [February] 1659, Preface.)

30. See John ii 14–16, recording Christ's driving the money-changers out of the Temple with a whip of small cords.

31. See Milton, *History of Britain,* Book III. Complaining to Ætius, consul of Rome, of the maurading of the Picts and the Scots, the Britons declared, "The barbarians drive us to the Sea, the Sea drives us back to the barbarians; thus bandied up and down between two deaths we perish, either by the Sword or by the Sea."

32. See note 25.

CONSIDERATIONS TOUCHING THE LIKELIEST MEANS TO REMOVE HIRELINGS OUT OF THE CHURCH

WHEREIN IS ALSO DISCOURSED OF TITHES, CHURCH FEES, AND CHURCH-REVENUES: AND WHETHER ANY MAINTENANCE OF MINISTERS CAN BE SETTLED BY LAW.

In the opening sentence of his *Treatise of Civil Power in Ecclesiastical Causes,* addressed in February 1659 to Richard Cromwell's parliament, Milton urged that there were two primary weaknesses in the English church. The first was the power civil government exercised over it, for there was yet no clear legal division between church and state. The purpose of the *Treatise* was to correct this "mischief" by restricting civil and religious power each to its own domain. The second weakness he judged to be the practice of forced tithing by which Englishmen had to contribute to the support of their churches. Milton promised to argue this second point in a later tract. *Considerations Touching the Likeliest Means to Remove Hirelings out of the Church* accordingly appeared the following August, addressed to the reconstituted Rump, which was at that time the ostensible governmental authority.

The issue of *Hirelings* was one of long standing, having been argued for years by Puritans of various shades without the achievement of any general agreement. On April 29, 1652, the abolition of forced tithing was moved in the Rump Parliament. This motion was referred to a committee; within a few days Milton remarked on the issue in his sonnet to Cromwell which decried the "hireling wolves whose Gospell is their maw." The committee, however, took no action and had to be prodded the following October—still, however, without result. Indeed, there was no report upon the tithing issue before Cromwell dissolved the Rump on April 20, 1653.

But the issue was by no means dead. The following July the "Little" or "Barebones" Parliament began its sessions. One of its first appointments was a committee to consider the issue of tithing. This committee reported on December 2 in favor of retaining the practice, declaring that the incumbents had a "legal propriety" in the tithe. The issue was bitterly debated from December 6 to 10, when the committee recommendation was defeated by a very close vote. Failure to agree on such a major issue before the House helped to bring about the dissolution of the Parliament on December 12. Earlier in the fall the Presbyterian William Prynne had published a vigorous and extended support of the practice of tithing, *A Gospel Plea . . . for the Lawfulnes and Continuance of the Ancient Setled Maintenance and Tenthes of the Ministers of the Gospel,* which seems to be the main object of Milton's arguments in *Hirelings.* Possibly he collected much of his material for the pamphlet in 1653 or even earlier in notes he could have taken from *Tithes Too Hot to Be Touched,* which appeared in 1646 or 1647 and was connected with the name of Sir Henry Spelman.

Although the issue of the relationship of state and church lay at the core of the dispute, the actual argument was carried on by various interpretations of certain biblical passages found in the Old Testament books of the Law and interpretations of them in the New Testament. After a short introductory statement which places the issue of tithing in what he thought was the correct Protestant perspective, Milton turns to the argument proper, which he distributes into four subdivisions, each discussed in the remaining "paragraphs" of the treatise. First, he defines what hire is: "Hire of it self is neither a thing unlawful, nor a word of any evil note," but it receives its evil connotation from being excessive or from being given or taken in the wrong way.

From this definition Milton moves to the question of "what recompence ought be given to church-ministers"—that is, how much they should receive for their services to the church—and concludes that unlike the Old Testament Levites, who were supported by the other tribes, the Christian minister should not depend upon a large income from his Christian activities but should earn his own livelihood as St. Paul did. Any further maintenance, he argues in the next section, should come from "them who receive thir teaching," not from the community as a whole. Finally, he argues that such contributions should be made not by law but by "the benevolence and free gratitude of such as receive them." A procedure of this sort, Milton observes, will extirpate hirelings from the church: ministers who remain active under such conditions will clearly be motivated by love of God rather than by love of money. This is the "means to remove hirelings."

The pamphlet is distinguished by the vigor of Milton's argument. From this standpoint the organization and punctuation of many sentences is unusual and sometimes difficult when they are read silently. Spoken aloud, however, they are powerful. For instance, when inveighing against the (paid) activity of the minister at a funeral, he argues, "At burials thir attendance they alleage on the corps; all the guests do as much unhir'd: But thir praiers at the grave; superstitiously requir'd: yet if requir'd, thir last performance to the deceasd of thir own flock. But the funeral sermon: at thir choise: or if not, an occasion offerd them to preach out of season, which is one part of thir office. But somthing must be spoken in praise: if due, thir duty; if undue, thir corruption. . . ." This might be paraphrased as a dialogue, the respondent perhaps *sotto voce:*

Minister: "At burials we must attend the corpse."
Respondent: "All the other mourners do this without pay."
Min.: "We must also be at the grave to pray for the dead."
Res.: "Pure superstition, at best performed at the wish of the deceased."
Min.: "We must also compose a funeral sermon."
Res.: "Purely optional with the minister, just another chance to perform."
Min.: "And somebody must say some good words about the deceased."
Res.: "Uh huh, if the words deserve to be said. If they don't it is mere bribery to say them."

Basic to Milton's thought in *Hirelings* as elsewhere is his emphasis upon freedom, both for the communicant and for the minister, and especially his plea for free study and interpretation of the Bible as opposed to interpretation in the light of formal theology. The result of this attitude is that Milton decries the need for a highly educated ministry, a point which he especially emphasized because one of the major arguments for tithing was that it would repay the considerable expenses which a candidate for the ministry had spent on his education. This phase of the tract, indeed, has been of greatest interest in recent scholarship, which has emphasized its connection with Christ's disclaimer of classical learning in *Paradise Regain'd.* But like *Of Civil Power, Hirelings* was evidently too radical for the majority in its own day, for both tracts appear to have been received with complete indifference.

The text which follows is based on collation of copies of the 1659 first edition in the Huntington Library, Newberry Library, and Harvard Library, all of which appear to be identical. Ampersands have been expanded and a few changes of punctuation have been made, the originals being given in the footnotes. The 1698 edition of the collected prose works exhibits no significant variations except typographical ones, although several of the changes made here in the punctuation coincide with it.

SELECTED BIBLIOGRAPHY

Barker, Arthur. *Milton and the Puritan Dilemma, 1641–1660.* Toronto, 1956.

Davies, Godfrey. *Restoration of Charles II.* San Marino, Cal., 1955.

Hause, E. M. "The Nomination of Richard Cromwell," *Historian,* XXVII (1965), 185–209.

Hunter, William B., Jr. "Milton and Richard Cromwell," *ELN,* III (1966), 252–59.

Lewalski, Barbara K. "Milton on Learning and the Learned-Ministry Controversy," *HLQ,* XXIV (1961), 267–81.

—— "Milton: Political Beliefs and Polemical Methods, 1659–60," *PMLA,* LXXIV (1959), 191–202.

Schultz, Howard. *Milton and Forbidden Knowledge.* New York, 1955.

Wolfe, Don M. *Milton in the Puritan Revolution.* New York, 1941.

TO THE PARLAMENT
of the Commonwealth of England with the dominions therof.

Owing to your protection, supream Senat, this libertie of writing which I have us'd these 18 years[1] *on all occasions to assert the just rights and freedoms both of church and state, and so far approv'd, as to have bin trusted with the representment and defence of your actions to all Christendom against an adversarie of no mean repute, to whom should I address what I still publish on the same argument, but to you whose magnanimous councels first opend and unbound the age from a double bondage under prelatical and regal tyrannie; above our own hopes heartning us to look up at last like men and Christians from the slavish dejection, wherin from father to son we were bred up and taught; and thereby deserving of these nations, if they be not barbarously ingrateful, to be acknowledgd, next under God, the authors and best patrons of religious and civil libertie, that ever these Ilands brought forth. The care and tuition of whose peace and safety, after a short but scandalous night of interruption,*[2] *is now again by a new dawning of Gods miraculous providence among us, revolvd upon your shoulders. And to whom more appertain these considerations which I propound, than to your selves and the debate before you, though I trust of no difficultie yet at present of great expectation, not whether ye will gratifie, were it no more than so, but whether ye will hearken to the just petition of many thousands best affected both to religion and to this your returne, or whether ye will satisfie, which you never can, the covetous pretences and demands of insatiable hirelings, whose disaffection ye well know both to your selves and your resolutions. That I, though among many others in this common concernment, interpose to your deliberations what my thoughts also are, your own judgment and the success therof hath given me the confidence: which requests but this, that if I have prosperously, God so favoring me, defended the publick cause of this commonwealth to foreiners, ye would not think the reason and abilitie, wheron ye trusted once, and repent not, your whole reputation to the world, either grown less by more maturitie and longer studie, or less available in* English *than in another tongue: but that if it suffic'd som years past to convince and satisfie the uningag'd of other nations in the justice of your doings, though then held paradoxal, it may as well suffice now against weaker opposition in matters, except here in* England *with a spiritualtie of men devoted to thir temporal gain, of no controversie els among Protestants. Neither do I doubt, seeing daily the acceptance which they finde who in thir petitions venture to bring advice also and new modells of a commonwealth, but that you will interpret it much more the dutie of a Christian to offer what his conscience perswades him may be of moment to the freedom and better constituting of the church: since it is a deed of highest charitie to help undeceive the people, and a work worthiest your autoritie, in all things els authors, assertors and now recoverers of our libertie, to deliver us, the only people of all Protestants left still undeliverd, from the oppressions of a Simonious decimating clergie; who shame not against the judgment and practice of all*

revolvd upon: restored to.
uningag'd: unbiased.
decimating: collecting a tenth or tithe.

other churches reformd, to maintain, though very weakly, thir Popish and oft refuted positions, not in a point of conscience, wherin they might be blameles, but in a point of covetousnes and unjust claim to other mens goods; a contention foul and odious in any man, but most of all in ministers of the gospel, in whom contention, though for thir own right, scarce is allowable. Till which greevances be remov'd and religion set free from the monopolie of hirelings, I dare affirme, that no modell whatsoever of a commonwealth will prove succesful or undisturbd; and so perswaded, implore divine assistance on your pious councels and proceedings to unanimitie in this and all other truth.

JOHN MILTON.

CONSIDERATIONS TOUCHING THE LIKELIEST MEANS TO REMOVE HIRELINGS OUT OF THE CHURCH

The former treatise, which leads in this, begann with two things ever found working much mischief to the church of God, and the advancement of truth; force on the one side restraining, and hire on the other side corrupting the teachers therof. The latter of these is by much the more dangerous: for under force, though no thank to the forcers, true religion oft-times best thrives and flourishes: but the corruption of teachers, most commonly the effect of hire, is the very bane of truth in them who are so corrupted. Of force not to be us'd in matters of religion, I have already spoken; and so stated matters of conscience and religion in faith and divine worship, and so severd them from blasphemie and heresie, the one being such properly as is despiteful, the other such as stands not to the rule of Scripture, and so both of them not matters of religion, but rather against it, that to them who will yet use force, this only choise can be left, whether they will force them to beleeve, to whom it is not given from above, being not forc'd thereto by any principle of the gospel, which is now the only dispensation of God to all men, or whether being Protestants, they will punish in those things wherin the Protestant religion denies them to be judges, either in themselves infallible or to the consciences of other men, or whether, lastly, they think fit to punish error, supposing they can be infallible that it is so, being not wilful, but conscientious, and, according to the best light of him who errs, grounded on scripture: which kinde of error all men religious, or but only reasonable, have thought worthier of pardon; and the growth therof to be prevented by

treatise: A Treatise of Civil Power (February 1659).

spiritual means and church-discipline, not by civil laws and outward force; since it is God only who gives as well to beleeve aright, as to beleeve at all; and by those means which he ordaind sufficiently in his church to the full execution of his divine purpose in the gospel. It remanes now to speak of hire; the other evil so mischeevous in religion: wherof I promisd then to speak further, when I should finde God disposing me, and opportunity inviting. Opportunity I finde now inviting; and apprehend therin the concurrence of God disposing; since the maintenance of church-ministers, a thing not properly belonging to the magistrate, and yet with such importunity call'd for, and expected from him, is at present under publick debate. Wherin least any thing may happen to be determind and establishd prejudicial to the right and freedom of church, or advantageous to such as may be found hirelings therin, it will be now most seasonable, and in these matters wherin every Christian hath his free suffrage, no way misbecoming Christian meeknes to offer freely, without disparagement to the wisest, such advice as God shall incline him and inable him to propound. Since heretofore in commonwealths of most fame for government, civil laws were not establishd till they had been first for certain dayes publishd to the view of all men, that who so pleasd might speak freely his opinion therof, and give in his exceptions, ere the law could pass to a full establishment. And where ought this equity to have more place, then in the libertie which is unseparable from Christian religion? This, I am not ignorant, will be a work unpleasing to some: but what truth is not hateful to some or other, as this, in likelihood, will be to none but hirelings. And if there be among them who hold it thir duty to speak impartial truth, as the work of thir ministry, though not performd without monie, let them not envie others who think the same no less their duty by the general office of Christianity, to speak truth, as in all reason may be thought, more impartially and unsuspectedly without monie.

Hire of it self is neither a thing unlawful, nor a word of any evil note, signifying no more then a due recompence or reward; as when our Saviour saith, *the laborer is worthy of his hire.*[3] That which makes it so dangerous in the church, and properly makes the *hireling*, a word always of evil signification, is either the excess thereof, or the undue manner of giving and taking it. What harme the excess therof brought to the church, perhaps was not found by experience till the days of *Constantine:* who out of his zeal thinking he could be never too liberally a nursing father of the church, might be not unfitly said to have either overlaid it or choakd it in the

least: lest.

nursing.[4] Which was foretold, as is recorded in ecclesiastical traditions, by a voice heard from heaven on the very day that those great donations and church-revenues were given, crying aloud, *This day is poison pourd into the church.*[5] Which the event soon after verifi'd; as appeers by another no less ancient observation, *That religion brought forth wealth, and the daughter devourd the mother.* But long ere wealth came into the church, so soone as any gain appeerd in religion, hirelings were apparent; drawn in long before by the very sent thereof. *Judas* therefor, the first hireling, for want of present hire answerable to his coveting, from the small number or the meanness of such as then were the religious, sold the religion it self with the founder therof, his master. *Simon Magus* the next, in hope only that preaching and the gifts of the holy ghost would prove gainful, offerd beforehand a sum of monie to obtain them.[6] Not long after, as the apostle foretold, hirelings like wolves came in by herds, *Acts* 20.29. *For, I know this, that after my departing shall greevous wolves enter in among you, not sparing the flock.* Tit. 1.11. *Teaching things which they ought not, for filthy lucres sake.* 2 Pet. 2.3. *And through covetousnes shall they with feigned words make merchandise of you.* Yet they taught not fals doctrin only, but seeming piety: 1 *Tim.* 6.5. *supposing that gain is Godlines.* Neither came they in of themselves only, but invited oft-times by a corrupt audience: 2 *Tim.* 4.3. *For the time will come, when they will not endure sound doctrin, but after thir own lusts they will heap*[7] *to themselves teachers, having itching ears:* and they on the other side, as fast heaping to themselves disciples, *Acts* 20. 30, doubtles had as itching palmes. 2 *Pet.* 2.15. *Following the way of* Balaam, *the son of* Bosor, *who lovd the wages of unrighteousnes.* Jude 11. *They ran greedily after the error of* Balaam *for reward.* Thus we see that not only the excess of hire in wealthiest times, but also the undue and vitious taking or giving it, though but small or mean, as in the primitive times, gave to hirelings occasion, though not intended, yet sufficient, to creep at first into the church. Which argues also the difficulty, or rather the impossibility, to remove them quite; unless every minister were, as St. *Paul,* contented to teach *gratis:*[8] but few such are to be found. As therefor we cannot justly take away all hire in the church, because we cannot otherwise quite remove all hirelings, so are we not for the impossibility of removing them all, to use therefor no endevor that fewest may come in: but rather, in regard the evil, do what we can, will alwayes be incumbent and unavoidable, to use

sent: scent.
in regard: because.

our utmost diligence, how it may be least dangerous. Which will be likeliest effected, if we consider, first, what recompence God hath ordaind should be given to ministers of the church; (for that a recompence ought to be given them, and may by them justly be received, our Saviour himself from the very light of reason and of equity hath declar'd: *Luke* 10.7. *The laborer is worthy of his hire*) next by whom; and lastly, in what manner.

What recompence ought be given to church-ministers, God hath answerably ordaind according to that difference which he hath manifestly put between those his two great dispensations, the law and the gospel. Under the law he gave them tithes; under the gospel, having left all things in his church to charity and Christian freedom, he hath given them only what is justly given them. That, as well under the gospel as under the law, say our English divines, and they only of all Protestants, is tithes; and they say true, if any man be so minded to give them of his own the tenth or twentith: but that the law therefor of tithes is in force under the gospel, all other Protestant divines, though equally concernd, yet constantly deny. For although hire to the laborer be of moral and perpetual right, yet that special kinde of hire, the tenth, can be of no right or necessity, but to that special labor for which God ordaind it. That special labor was the Levitical and ceremonial service of the tabernacle, *Numb.* 18.21, 31.[9] which is now abolishd: the right therefor of that special hire must needs be withall abolishd, as being also ceremonial. That tithes were ceremonial, is plane; not being given to the Levites till they had bin first offerd a heave-offering to the Lord, *Vers.* 24, 28. He then who by that law brings tithes into the gospel, of necessity brings in withall a sacrifice, and an altar;[10] without which tithes by that law were unsanctifi'd and polluted, *Vers.* 32. and therefor never thought on in the first Christian times, till ceremonies, altars, and oblations, by an ancienter corruption were brought back long before. And yet the *Jewes* ever since thir temple was destroid, though they have Rabbies and teachers of thir law, yet pay no tithes, as having no Levites to whom, no temple where to pay them, no altar wheron to hallow them; which argues that the *Jewes* themselves never thought tithes moral, but ceremonial only.[11] That Christians therefor should take them up, when *Jewes* have laid them down, must needs be very absurd and preposterous. Next, it is as cleer in the same chapter, that the priests and Levites had not tithes for their labor only in the tabernacle, but in regard they were to have no

abolishd: abolished by the New Testament gospel.
heave-offering: an offering ceremonially elevated by the priest at the altar.

other part nor inheritance in the land, *Vers.* 20, 24. and by that means for a tenth lost a twelfth. But our levites undergoing no such law of deprivement, can have no right to any such compensation: nay, if by this law they will have tithes, can have no inheritance of land, but forfeit what they have. Besides this, tithes were of two sorts, those of every year, and those of every third year: of the former, every one that brought his tithes, was to eat his share. *Deut.* 14. 23. *Thou shalt eat before the Lord thy God, in the place which he shall chuse to place his name there, the tithe of thy corn, of thy wine, and of thine oyle, etc.* Nay, though he could not bring his tithe in kinde, by reason of his distant dwelling from the tabernacle or temple, but was thereby forc'd to turn it into monie, he was to bestow that monie on whatsoever pleasd him; oxen, sheep, wine, or strong drink; and to eat and drink therof there before the Lord both he and his houshold, *Ver.* 24, 25, 26. As for the tithes of every third year, they were not given only to the Levite, but to the stranger, the fatherles, and the widdow, *Vers.* 28, 29. and *Chap.* 26. 12, 13. So that ours, if they will have tithes, must admitt of these sharers with them. Nay, these tithes were not paid in at all to the Levite, but the Levite himself was to come with those his fellow guests and eat his share of them only at his house who provided them; and this not in regard of his ministerial office, but because he had no part nor inheritance in the land. Lastly, the priests and Levites, a tribe, were of a far different constitution from this of our ministers under the gospel: in them were orders and degrees both by family, dignity and office, mainly distinguishd; the high priest, his brethren and his sons, to whom the Levites themselves paid tithes, and of the best, were eminently superior, *Num.* 18. 28, 29. No Protestant, I suppose, will liken one of our ministers to a high priest, but rather to a common Levite. Unless then, to keep their tithes, they mean to bring back again bishops, archbishops and the whole gang of prelatry, to whom will they themselves pay tythes, as by that law it was a sin to them, if they did not, *v.* 32. Certainly this must needs put them to a deep demurr, while the desire of holding fast thir tithes without sin, may tempt them to bring back again bishops as the likenes of that hierarchy that should receive tithes from them, and the desire to pay none, may advise them to keep out of the church all orders above them. But if we have to do at present, as I suppose we have, with true reformed Protestants, not with Papists or prelates, it will not be deni'd that in the gospel there

a twelfth: the tribe of Levi, one of the twelve Hebrew tribes, gave up that twelfth of its inheritance (of the Hebrew race) so as to receive the tithe (tenth) from the other tribes.

be but two ministerial degrees, presbyters and deacons: which if they contend to have any succession, reference or conformity with those two degrees under the law, priests and Levites, it must needs be such whereby our presbyters or ministers may be answerable to priests, and our deacons to Levites[12]: by which rule of proportion it will follow, that we must pay our tithes to the deacons only, and they only to the ministers. But if it be truer yet that the priesthood of Aaron typifi'd a better reality, 1 Pet. 2. 5. signifying the Christian true and *holy priesthood, to offer up spiritual sacrifice;* it follows hence, that we are now justly exempt from paying tithes, to any who claim from *Aaron,* since that priesthood is in us now real, which in him was but a shaddow. Seeing then by all this which hath bin shewn that the law of tithes is partly ceremonial, as the work was for which they were given, partly judicial, not of common, but of particular right to the tribe of *Levi,* nor to them alone, but to the owner also and his houshold, at the time of thir offering, and every three year to the stranger, the fatherles, and the widdow, thir appointed sharers, and that they were a tribe of priests and deacons improperly compar'd to the constitution of our ministery, and the tithes given by that people to those deacons only, it follows that our ministers at this day, being neither priests nor Levites, nor fitly answering to either of them, can have no just title or pretence to tithes, by any consequence drawn from the law of *Moses.* But they think they have yet a better plea in the example of *Melchisedec,* who took tithes of *Abram* ere the law was given:[13] whence they would inferr tithes to be of moral right. But they ought to know, or to remember, that not examples, but express commands oblige our obedience to God or man: next, that whatsoever was don in religion before the law written, is not presently to be counted moral, when as so many things were then don both ceremonial and Judaically judicial, that we need not doubt to conclude all times before Christ, more or less under the ceremonial law. To what end servd els those altars and sacrifices, that distinction of clean and unclean entring into the ark, circumcision and the raising up of seed to the elder brother, *Gen.* 38. 8? If these things be not moral, though before the law, how are tithes, though in the example of *Abram* and *Melchisedec*? But this instance is so far from being the just ground of a law, that after all circumstances duly

presbyter: The Greek derivation is usually translated *elder* in the King James version. Elders and deacons are the basis of church rule among Presbyterians and several other Protestant groups.
Aaron: brother of Moses and chief priest.
shaddow: a synonym for *type.*
ceremonial law: law of Moses.

waighd both from *Gen.* 14. and *Heb.* 7, it will not be allowd them so much as an example. *Melchisedec,* besides his priestly benediction, brought with him bread and wine sufficient to refresh *Abram* and his whole armie; incited to do so, first, by the secret providence of God, intending him for a type of Christ and his priesthood; next by his due thankfulnes and honor to *Abram,* who had freed his borders of *Salem* from a potent enemie: *Abram* on the other side honors him with the tenth of all, that is to say, (for he took not sure his whole estate with him to that warr) of the spoiles, *Heb.* 7. 4. Incited he also by the same secret providence, to signifie as grandfather of *Levi,* that the Levitical priesthood was excelld by the priesthood of Christ. For the giving of a tenth declar'd, it seems in those countreys and times, him the greater who receivd it. That which next incited him, was partly his gratitude to requite the present, partly his reverence to the person and his benediction: to his person, as a king and priest; greater therefor than *Abram;* who was a priest also, but not a king. And who unhir'd will be so hardy as to say, that *Abram* at any other time ever paid him tithes, either before or after; or had then, but for this accidental meeting and obligement; or that els *Melchisedec* had demanded or exacted them, or took them otherwise, than as the voluntarie gift of *Abram*? But our ministers, though neither priests nor kings more than any other Christian, greater in thir own esteem than *Abraham* and all his seed, for the verbal labor of a seventh dayes preachment, not bringing, like *Melchisedec,* bread or wine at thir own cost, would not take only at the willing hand of liberality or gratitude, but require and exact as due the tenth, not of spoiles, but of our whole estates and labors; nor once, but yearly. We then it seems by the example of *Abram* must pay tithes to these *melchisedecs:* but what if the person of *Abram* can either no way represent us, or will oblige the ministers to pay tithes no less than other men? *Abram* had not only a priest in his loines, but was himself a priest; and gave tithes to *Melchisedec* either as grandfather of *Levi,* or as father of the faithful. If as grandfather (though he understood it not) of *Levi,* he oblig'd not us but *Levi* only, the inferior priest, by that homage (as the apostle to the *Hebrewes* cleerly anough explanes) to acknowledge the greater. And they who by *Melchisedec* claim from *Abram* as *Levi's* grandfather, have none to seek thir tithes of but the Levites, where they can finde them. If *Abram* as father of the faithful paid tithes to *Melchisedec,* then certainly the ministers also,

grandfather of Levi: Abraham was Levi's great-grandfather.

in his loines: as great-grandfather of the yet-unconceived Levi, from whom the Levitical priesthood was descended.

if they be of that number, paid in him equally with the rest. Which may induce us to beleeve, that as both *Abram* and *Melchisedec*, so tithes also in that action typical and ceremonial, signifi'd nothing els but that subjection, which all the faithful, both ministers and people owe to Christ, our high priest and king. In any literal sense from this example they never will be able to extort that the people in those dayes paid tithes to priests; but this only, that one priest once in his life, of spoiles only, and in requital partly of a liberal present, partly of a benediction, gave voluntary tithes, not to a greater priest than himself as far as *Abram* could then understand, but rather to a priest and king joind in one person. They will reply, perhaps, that if one priest paid tithes to another, it must needs be understood that the people did no less to the priest. But I shall easily remove that necessitie by remembring them that in those dayes was no priest, but the father, or the first born of each familie; and by consequence no people to pay him tithes, but his own children and servants, who had not wherewithall to pay him, but of his own. Yet grant that the people then paid tithes, there will not yet be the like reason to enjoin us: they being then under ceremonies, a meer laitie, we now under Christ, a royal priesthood, 1 *Pet.* 2. 9, as we are coheirs, kings and priests with him, a priest for ever after the order or manner of *Melchisedec*. As therefor *Abram* paid tithes to *Melchisedec* because *Levi* was in him, so we ought to pay none because the true *Melchisedec* is in us, and we in him who can pay to none greater, and hath freed us by our union with himself, from all compulsive tributes and taxes in his church. Neither doth the collateral place, *Heb.* 7, make other use of this story, than to prove Christ, personated by *Melchisedec*, a greater priest than *Aaron: Vers.* 4. *Now consider how great this man was, etc.* and proves not in the least manner that tithes be of any right to ministers, but the contrary: first the Levites had *a commandment to take tithes of the people according to the law, that is of thir brethren, though they com out of the loines of Abraham, Vers.* 5. The commandment then was, it seems, to take tithes of the *Jewes* only, and according to the law. That law changing of necessity with the priesthood, no other sort of ministers, as they must needs be another sort, under another priesthood, can receive that tribute of tithes which fell with that law, unless renu'd by another express command and according to another law: no such law is extant. Next, *Melchisedec* not as a minister, but as Christ himself in person blessd *Abraham*, who *had the promises, Vers.* 6; and in him blessd all both ministers and people, both of the law and gospel: that blessing declar'd him greater and better than whom he blessd, *Vers.*

7; receiving tithes from them all not as a maintenance, which *Melchisedec* needed not, but as a signe of homage and subjection to thir king and priest: wheras ministers bear not the person of Christ in his priesthood or kingship, bless not as he blesses, are not by their blessing greater than *Abraham,* and all the faithful with themselves included in him, cannot both give and take tithes in *Abram,* cannot claim to themselves that signe of our allegiance due only to our eternal king and priest, cannot therefor derive tithes from *Melchisedec.* Lastly, the eighth verse hath thus: *Here men that die receive tithes: There he received them, of whom it is witnesd that he liveth.* Which words intimate that as he offerd himself once for us, so he received once of us in *Abraham,* and in that place the typical acknowledgment of our redemption: which had it bin a perpetual annuitie to Christ, by him claimd as his due, *Levi* must have paid it yearly, as well as then, *Vers.* 9. and our ministers ought still to som *Melchisedec* or other, as well now as they did in *Abraham.* But that Christ never claimd any such tenth as his annual due, much less resign'd it to the ministers, his so officious receivers without express commission or assignement, will be yet cleerer as we proceed. Thus much may at length assure us, that this example of *Abram* and *Melchisedec,* though I see of late they build most upon it, can so little be the ground of any law to us, that it will not so much avail them as to the autoritie of an example. Of like impertinence is that example of *Jacob, Gen.* 28. 22,[14] who of his free choise, not enjoind by any law, vowd the tenth of all that God should give him: which, for aught appeers to the contrarie, he vowd as a thing no less indifferent before his vow, then the foregoing part thereof; That the stone which he had set there for a pillar, should be God's house. And to whom vowd he this tenth, but to God; not to any priest; for we read of none to him greater than himself? and to God, no doubt, but he paid what he vowd; both in the building of that *Bethel* with other altars els where, and the expence of his continual sacrifices, which none but he had right to offer. However therefor he paid his tenth, it could in no likelihood, unless by such an occasion as befell his grandfather, be to any priest. But, say they, *All the tithe of the land, whether of the seed of the land, or of the fruit of the tree, is the Lords, holy unto the Lord, Levit.* 27. 30. And this before it was given to the Levites; therefor since they ceasd. No question; *For the whole*[15] *earth is the Lords, and the fulnes therof, Psal.* 24. 1; and the light of nature shews us no less: but that the tenth is his more than the rest, how know I, but as he so declares it?

typical: in the sense of *type* as defined above.
grandfather: Abraham.

He declares it so here of the land of *Canaan* only, as by all circumstance appeers; and passes by deed of gift this tenth to the Levite; yet so as offerd to him first a heave-offring, and consecrated on his altar, *Numb.* 18. all which I had as little known, but by that evidence. The Levites are ceasd, the gift returns to the giver. How then can we know that he hath given it to any other, or how can these men presume to take it unofferd first to God, unconsecrated, without an other cleer and express donation, wherof they shew no evidence or writing? Besides, he hath now alienated that holy land: who can warrantably affirme, that he hath since hallowd the tenth of this land; which none but God hath power to do or can warrant? Thir last prooff they cite out of the gospel, which makes as little for them; *Matth.* 23. 23;[16] where our Saviour denouncing woe to the Scribes and Pharises, who paid tithe so exactly, and omitted waightier matters, tels them, that these they ought to have don, that is, to have paid tithes. For our Saviour spake then to those who observd the law of *Moses,* which was yet not fully abrogated, till the destruction of the temple. And by the way here we may observe out of thir own prooff, that the Scribes and Pharises, though then chief teachers of the people, such at least as were not Levites, did not take tithes, but paid them: So much less covetous were the Scribes and Pharises in those worst times than ours at this day. This is so apparent to the reformed divines of other countreys, that when any one of ours hath attempted in Latine to maintain this argument of tithes, though a man would think they might suffer him without opposition in a point equally tending to the advantage of all ministers, yet they forbear not to oppose him, as in a doctrin not fit to pass unoppos'd under the gospel. Which shews the modestie, the contentednes of those forein pastors with the maintenance given them, thir sinceritie also in the truth, though less gainful, and the avarice of ours: who through the love of their old Papistical tithes, consider not the weak arguments, or rather conjectures and surmises which they bring to defend them. On the other side, although it be sufficient to have prov'd in general the abolishing of tithes, as part of the Judaical or ceremonial law, which is abolishd all, as well that before as that after *Moses,* yet I shall further prove them abrogated by an express ordinance of the gospel, founded not on any type, or that municipal law of *Moses,* but on moral, and general equitie, given us instead: 1 *Cor.* 9. 13, 14. *Know ye not, that they who minister about holy things, live of the things of the temple; and they which wait at the altar, are partakers with the altar? so also the Lord hath ordaind, that they who preach*

alienated: disavowed.
municipal: limited to Israel.

the gospel, should live of the gospel. He saith not, Should live on things which were of the temple or of the altar, of which were tithes, for that had given them a cleer title: but abrogating that former law of *Moses,* which determind what and how much, by a later ordinance of Christ, which leaves the what and how much indefinit and free, so it be sufficient to live on, he saith, *The Lord hath so ordaind, that they who preach the gospel, should live of the gospel;* which hath neither temple, altar nor sacrifice: *Heb.* 7. 13. *For he of whom these things are spoken, pertaineth to another tribe, of which no man gave attendance at the altar:* his ministers therefor cannot thence have tithes. And where the Lord hath so ordaind, we may finde easily in more than one evangelist: *Luke* 10. 7, 8. *In the same house remane, eating and drinking such things as they give: For the laborer is worthy of his hire, etc. And into whatsoever citie you enter, and they receive you, eat such things as are set before you.* To which ordinance of Christ it may seem likeliest, that the apostle referrs us both here and 1 *Tim.* 5. 18, where he cites this as the saying of our Saviour, *That the laborer is worthy of his hire:* and both by this place of *Luke,* and that of *Matth.* 10. 9, 10, 11, it evidently appeers that our Saviour ordaind no certain maintenance for his apostles or ministers publickly or privatly in house or citie receivd, but that, what ever it were, which might suffice to live on: and this not commanded or proportiond by *Abram* or by *Moses,* whom he might easily have here cited, as his manner was, but declar'd only by a rule of common equitie which proportions the hire as well to the abilitie of him who gives as to the labor of him who receives, and recommends him only as worthy, not invests him with a legal right. And mark wheron he grounds this his ordinance; not on a perpetual right of tithes from *Melchisedec,* as hirelings pretend, which he never claimd either for himself, or for his ministers, but on the plane and common equitie of rewarding the laborer; worthy somtimes of single, somtimes of double honor, not proportionable by tithes. And the apostle in this forecited chapter to the *Corinthians, Vers.* 11, affirms it to be no great recompence, if carnal things be reapd for spiritual sown; but to mention tithes, neglects here the fittest occasion that could be offerd him, and leaves the rest free and undetermind. Certainly if Christ or his apostles had approv'd of tithes, they would have either by writing or tradition recommended them to the church: and that soone would have appeerd in the practise of those primitive and the next ages. But for the first three hundred years and more, in all the ecclesiastical storie, I finde no such doctrin or example:[17] though error by that time had brought back again priests, altars and oblations; and in many other points of religion had miserably Judaiz'd the church. So that the defenders of tithes, after a long pomp and tedious preparation out of Heathen authors, telling us that tithes were paid to *Hercules* and *Apollo,* which perhaps was imitated from the *Jewes,*[18] and as it were bespeaking our expectation, that they will abound much more with autorities out of Christian storie, have nothing of general approbation to beginn with from the first three or four ages, but that which abundantly serves to the confutation of thir tithes; while they confess that churchmen in those ages livd meerly upon freewill offerings. Neither can they say, that tithes were not then paid for want of a civil magistrate to ordain them, for Christians had then also lands, and might give out of them what they pleasd; and yet of tithes then given we finde no mention. And the first Christian emperors, who did all things as bishops advis'd them, suppli'd what was wanting to the clergy not out of tithes, which were never motiond, but out of thir own imperial revenues; as is manifest in *Eusebius, Theodorit* and *Sozomen,*[19] from *Constantine* to *Arcadius.* Hence those ancientest reformed churches of the *Waldenses,*[20] if they rather continu'd not pure since the apostles, deni'd that tithes were to be given, or that they were ever given in the primitive church; as appeers by an ancient tractate inserted in the *Bohemian* historie. Thus far hath the church bin alwaies, whether in her prime, or in her ancientest reformation, from the approving of tithes: nor without reason; for they might easily perceive that tithes were fitted to the *Jewes* only, a national church of many incomplete synagogues, uniting the accomplishment of divine worship in one temple; and the Levites there had thir tithes paid where they did thir bodilie work; to which a particular tribe was set apart by divine appointment, not by the peoples election: but the Christian church is universal; not ti'd to nation, dioces or parish, but consisting of many particular churches complete in themselves; gatherd, not by compulsion or the accident of dwelling nigh together, but by free consent chusing both thir particular church and thir church-officers. Wheras if tithes be set up, all these Christian privileges will be disturbd and soone lost, and with them Christian libertie. The first autoritie which our adversaries bring, after those fabulous apostolic canons,[21] which they dare not insist upon, is a provincial councel held at *Cullen,*[22] where they voted tithes to be *Gods rent,* in the year three hundred fifty six; at the same time perhaps when the three kings reignd there, and of like autoritie. For to what purpose

ages: centuries.
motiond: proposed.
Cullen: Cologne.

do they bring these trivial testimonies, by which they might as well prove altars, candles at noone,[23] and the greatest part of those superstitions, fetchd from Paganism or Jewism, which the Papist, inveigl'd by this fond argument of antiquitie, retains to this day? to what purpose those decrees of I know not what bishops, to a Parlament and people who have thrown out both bishops and altars, and promisd all reformation by the word of God? And that altars brought tithes hither, as one corruption begott another, is evident by one of those questions which the monk *Austin* propounded to the Pope, *Concerning those things, which by offerings of the faithful came to the altar;* as *Beda* writes, *l.* 1. *c.* 27.[24] If then by these testimonies we must have tithes continu'd, we must again have altars. Of fathers, by custom so calld, they quote *Ambrose, Augustin,*[25] and som other ceremonial doctors of the same leaven: whose assertion without pertinent scripture, no reformed church can admitt; and what they vouch, is founded on the law of *Moses,* with which, every where pitifully mistaken, they again incorporate the gospel; as did the rest also of those titular fathers, perhaps an age or two before them, by many rights and ceremonies, both Jewish and Heathenish introduc'd; whereby thinking to gain all, they lost all: and instead of winning Jewes and Pagans to be Christians, by too much condescending they turnd Christians into Jewes and Pagans. To heap[26] such unconvincing citations as these in religion, wherof the scripture only is our rule, argues not much learning nor judgment, but the lost labor of much unprofitable reading. And yet a late hot Quærist for tithes, whom ye may know by his wits lying ever beside him in the margent,[27] to be ever beside his wits in the text, a fierce reformer once, now ranckl'd with a contrary heat, would send us back, very reformedly indeed, to learn reformation from *Tyndarus* and *Rebuffus,* two canonical Promooters. They[28] produce next the ancient constitutions of this land, *Saxon* laws, edicts of kings, and thir counsels, from *Athelstan,* in the year nine hundred twenty eight, that tithes by statute were paid: and might produce from *Ina,* above two hundred years before,[29] that *Romescot,* or *Peters* penny, was by as good statute law paid to the Pope, from seven hundred twenty five, and almost as long continu'd. And who knows not that this law of tithes was enacted by those kings and barons upon the opinion they had of thir divine right, as the very words import of *Edward* the Confessor, in the close of that law: *For so blessed* Austin *preachd and taught;* meaning the monk, who first brought the *Romish* religion into *England* from *Gregory* the Pope.[30] And by the

Romescot: an obligation owed to Rome. *Scot* exists today only in the phrase "scot free."

way I add, that by these laws, imitating the law of *Moses,* the third part of tithes only was the priests due; the other two were appointed for the poor, and to adorne or repare churches; as the canons of *Ecbert* and *Elfric* witnes: *Concil. Brit.*[31] If then these laws were founded upon the opinion of divine autoritie, and that autoritie be found mistaken and erroneous, as hath bin fully manifested, it follows, that these laws fall of themselves with thir fals foundation. But with what face or conscience can they alleage *Moses,* or these laws for tithes, as they now enjoy or exact them; wherof *Moses* ordains the owner, as we heard before, the stranger, the fatherles and the widdow partakers with the Levite;[32] and these fathers which they cite, and these though Romish rather than English laws, allotted both to priest and bishop the third part only. But these our Protestant, these our new reformed English presbyterian divines, against thir own cited authors, and to the shame of thir pretended reformation, would engross to themselves all tithes by statute; and supported more by thir wilful obstinacie and desire of filthie lucre than by these both insufficient and impertinent autorities, would perswade a Christian magistracie and parlament, whom we trust God hath restor'd for a happier reformation, to impose upon us a Judaical ceremonial law, and yet from that law to be more irregular and unwarrantable, more complying with a covetous clergie, than any of those Popish kings and parlaments alleagd. Another shift they have to plead, that tithes may be moral as well as the sabbath, a tenth of fruits as well as a seaventh of dayes.[33] I answer, that the prelats who urge this argument, have least reason to use it; denying morality in the sabbath, and therin better agreeing with reformed churches abroad than the rest of our divines: As therefor the seaventh day is not moral, but a convenient recourse of worship in fit season, whether seaventh or other number, so neither is the tenth of our goods, but only a convenient subsistence morally due to ministers. The last and lowest sort of thir arguments, that men purchas'd not thir tithe with thir land and such like pettifoggerie, I omitt; as refuted sufficiently by others: I omitt also thir violent and irreligious exactions, related no less credibly: thir seising of pots and pans from the poor, who have as good right to tithes as they; from som, the very beds; thir sueing and imprisoning;[34] worse than when the canon law was in force; worse than when those wicked sons of *Eli*[35] were priests, whose manner was thus to seise thir pretended priestly due by force, 1 *Sam.* 2. 12, *etc. Whereby men abhorrd the offering of the Lord;* and it may be feard that many will as much abhorr the gospel, if such violence as this be sufferd in her ministers, and in that which they also pretend to be the offering of the Lord. For those sons of *belial* within som limits made seisure of what they knew was thir own by an undoubted law; but these, from whom there is no sanctuarie, seise out of mens grounds, out of mens houses thir other goods of double, somtimes of treble value, for that, which did not covetousnes and rapine blinde them, they know to be not thir own by the gospel which they preach. Of som more tolerable than these, thus severely God hath spoken: *Esa.* 46. 10,[36] *etc. They are greedy dogs; they all look to thir own way, every one for his gain, from his quarter.* With what anger then will he judge them who stand not looking, but under colour of a divine right, fetch by force that which is not thir own, taking his name not in vain, but in violence? Nor content as *Gehazi*[37] was to make a cunning, but a constraind advantage of what thir master bids them give freely, how can they but returne smitten, worse than that sharking minister, with a spiritual leprosie? And yet they cry out sacrilege, that men will not be gulld and baffl'd the tenth of thir estates by giving credit to frivolous pretences of divine right. Where did God ever cleerly declare to all nations, or in all lands (and none but fooles part with thir estates, without cleerest evidence, on bare supposals and presumptions of them who are the gainers thereby) that he requir'd the tenth as due to him or his son perpetually and in all places? Where did he demand it, that we might certainly know, as in all claimes of temporal right is just and reasonable? or if demanded, where did he assigne it, or by what evident conveyance to ministers? unless they can demonstrate this by more than conjectures, thir title can be no better to tithes than the title of *Gehazi* was to those things which by abusing his masters name he rookd from *Naaman.* Much less where did he command that tithes should be fetchd by force, where left not under the gospel whatever his right was, to the freewill-offrings of men? Which is the greater sacrilege, to bely divine autoritie, to make the name of Christ accessory to violence, and, robbing him of the very honor which he aimd at in bestowing freely the gospel, to committ Simonie and rapin, both secular and ecclesiastical, or on the other side, not to give up the tenth of civil right and proprietie to the tricks and impostures of clergie men, contriv'd with all the art and argument that thir bellies can invent or suggest; yet so ridiculous and presuming on the peoples dulnes or superstition, as to think they prove the divine right of thir maintenance by *Abram* paying tithes to *Melchisedec,* when as *Milchisedec* in that passage rather gave maintenance to *Abram;* in whom all both priests and ministers, as well as lay-men paid tithes, not receivd them. And because I affirmd above, beginning this first part of my discourse, that God hath given to ministers of the gospel that maintenance only which is justly given them, let us see a little what hath bin thought of that other maintenance besides tithes, which of all Protestants, our English divines either only or most apparently both require and take. Those are, fees for christnings, marriages, and burials: which, though whoso will may give freely, yet being not of right, but of free gift, if they be exacted or establishd, they become unjust to them who are otherwise maintaind; and of such evil note, that even the councel of *Trent, l.* 2. *p.* 240, makes them lyable to the laws against Simonie, who take or demand fees for the administring of any sacrament: *Che la sinodo volendo levare gli abusi introdotti, etc.*[38] And in the next page, with like severity condemns the giving or taking for a benefice, and the celebrating of marriages, christnings, and burials, for fees exacted or demanded: nor counts it less Simonie to sell the ground or place of burial. And in a state assembly at *Orleans,* 1561, it was decreed, *Che non si potesse essiger cosa alcuna, etc., p.* 429. *That nothing should be exacted for the administring of sacraments, burials, or any other spiritual function.*[39] Thus much that councel, of all others the most Popish, and this assembly of Papists, though, by thir own principles, in bondage to the clergie, were induc'd, either by thir own reason and shame, or by the light of reformation then shining in upon them, or rather by the known canons of many councels and synods long before, to condemne of Simonie spiritual fees demanded. For if the minister be maintaind for his whole ministry, why should he be twice paid for any part therof? why should he, like a servant, seek vailes over and above his wages? As for christnings, either they themselves call men to baptism, or men of themselves com: if ministers invite, how ill had it becomd *John* the Baptist to demand fees for his baptising, or Christ for his christnings? Far less becoms it these now, with a greedines lower than that of tradesmen calling passengers to thir shop, and yet paid beforehand, to ask again, for doing that which those thir founders did freely. If men of themselves com to be baptiz'd, they are either brought by such as already pay the minister, or com to be one of his disciples and maintainers: of whom to ask a fee as it were for entrance, is a piece of paultry craft or caution, befitting none but beggarly artists. Burials and marriages are so little to be any part of thir gain, that they who consider well, may finde them to be no part of thir function. At burials thir attendance they alleage on the corps; all the guests do as much unhir'd: But thir praiers at the grave; superstitiously requir'd: yet if requir'd, thir

vailes . . . wages: pay beyond one's salary.
passengers: passers-by.
artists: artisans.

last performance to the deceasd of thir own flock. But the funeral sermon: at thir choise: or if not, an occasion offerd them to preach out of season, which is one part of thir office. But somthing must be spoken in praise: if due, thir duty; if undue, thir corruption: a peculiar Simonie of our divines in *England* only. But the ground is broken, and especially thir unrighteous possession, the chancel. To sell that will not only raise up in judgment the Councel of *Trent* against them, but will lose them the best champion of tithes, thir zealous antiquary, Sir *Hen: Spelman;* who in a book written to that purpose, by many cited canons, and som even of times corruptest in the church, proves that fees exacted or demanded for sacraments, marriages, burials, and especially for interring, are wicked, accursed, Simoniacal and abominable.[40] Yet thus is the church, for all this noise of reformation, left still unreformd, by the censure of thir own synods, thir own favorers, a den of theeves and robbers. As for marriages, that[41] ministers should meddle with them, as not sanctifi'd or legitimat without their celebration, I finde no ground in scripture either of precept or example. Likeliest it is (which our *Selden* hath well observd, *l.* 2, *c.* 28, *ux. Eb.*) that in imitation of heathen priests who were wont at nuptials to use many rites and ceremonies, and especially, judging it would be profitable, and the increase of thir autoritie, not to be spectators only in busines of such concernment to the life of man, they insinuated that marriage was not holy without their benediction, and for the better colour, made it a sacrament; being of it self a civil ordinance,[42] a houshold contract, a thing indifferent and free to the whole race of mankinde, not as religious, but as men: best, indeed, undertaken to religious ends, and, as the apostle saith, 1 *Cor.* 7, *in the Lord.*[43] Yet not therefor invalid or unholy without a minister and his pretended necessary hallowing, more than any other act, enterprise or contract of civil life, which ought all to be don also in the Lord and to his glorie. All which, no less than marriage, were by the cunning of priests heretofore, as material to thir profit, transacted at the altar. Our divines denie it to be a sacrament; yet retaind the celebration, till prudently a late parlament recoverd the civil liberty of marriage from thir incroachment; and transferrd the ratifying and registring therof from the canonical shop to the proper cognisance of civil magistrates.[44] Seeing then, that God hath given to ministers under the gospel, that only which is justly given them, that is to say, a due and moderat livelihood, the hire of thir labor, and that the heave-offering of tithes is abolishd with the altar, yea though not abolishd, yet lawles, as they enjoy them, thir Melchisedecian right also trivial

ux. Eb.: John Selden, *Uxor Ebraica* (1646).

and groundles, and both tithes and fees, if exacted or establishd, unjust and scandalous, we may hope, with them remov'd, to remove hirelings in som good measure, whom these tempting baits, by law especially to be recoverd, allure into the church.

The next thing to be considerd in the maintenance of ministers, is by whom it should be given. Wherin though the light of reason might sufficiently informe us, it will be best to consult the scripture: *Gal.* 6. 6. *let him that is taught in the word, communicate, to him that teacheth, in all good things:* that is to say, in all manner of gratitude, to his abilitie. 1 *Cor.* 9. 11. *if we have sown unto you spiritual things, is it a great matter if we reap your carnal things?* to whom therefor hath not bin sown, from him wherefor should be reapd? 1 *Tim.* 5. 17. *let the elders that rule well, be counted worthie of double honor; especially they who labor in the word and doctrin.* By these places we see, that recompence was given either by every one in particular who had bin instructed, or by them all in common, brought into the church-treasurie, and distributed to the ministers according to thir several labors: and that was judgd either by som extraordinarie person, as *Timothie*, who by the apostle was then left evangelist at *Ephesus,* 2 *Tim.* 4. 5, or by som to whom the church deputed that care. This is so agreeable to reason and so cleer, that any one may perceive what iniquitie and violence hath pre-vaild since in the church, whereby it hath bin so orderd, that they also shall be compelld to recompence the parochial minister, who neither chose him for thir teacher, nor have receivd instruction from him, as being either insufficient, or not resident, or inferior to whom they follow; wherin to barr them thir choise, is to violate Christian liberty. Our law-books testifie, that before the councel of *Lateran,* in the year 1179,[45] and the fifth of our *Henry* 2, or rather before a decretal epistle of Pope *Innocent* the third, about 1200, and the first of king *John, any man might have given his tithes to what spiritual person he would:*[46] and, as the L. *Coke* notes on that place, *instit. part* 2, that *this decretal bound not the subjects of this realm; but, as it seemd just and reasonable.* The Pope took his reason rightly from the above cited place, 1 *Cor.* 9. 11: but falsly suppos'd every one to be instructed by his parish-priest. Whether this were then first so decreed or rather long before, as may seem by the laws of *Edgar* and *Canute,* that tithes were to be paid, not to whom he would that paid them, but to the cathedral church or the parish-

Coke . . . part 2: Part 2 of Sir Edward Coke's *The Institutes of the Laws of England.*

whether this: that English subjects did not have to support their parish ministers.

priest, it imports not; since the reason which they themselves bring, built on fals supposition, becoms alike infirme and absurd, that he should reap from me, who sows not to me; bee the cause either his defect, or my free choise. But here it will be readily objected, What if they who are to be instructed be not able to maintain a minister, as in many villages? I answer, that the scripture shews in many places what ought to be don herin. First I offer it to the reason of any man, whether he think the knowledge of Christian religion harder than any other art or science to attain. I suppose he will grant that it is far easier; both of it self, and in regard of Gods assisting spirit, not particularly[47] promisd us to the attainment of any other knowledge, but of this only: since it was preachd as well to the shepherds of *Bethleem* by angels, as to the eastern Wisemen by that starr: and our Saviour declares himself anointed to preach the gospel to the poore, *Luke* 4. 18. then surely to thir capacitie. They who after him first taught it, were otherwise unlearned men: they who before *Hus*[48] and *Luther* first reformd it, were for the meanenes of thir condition calld, *the poore men of Lions:* and in *Flanders* at this day, *les gueus,* which is to say, beggars. Therefor are the scriptures translated into every vulgar tongue, as being held in main matters of belief and salvation, plane and easie to the poorest: and such no less than thir teachers have the spirit to guide them in all truth, *Joh.* 14. 26, and 16. 13. Hence we may conclude, if men be not all thir life time under a teacher to learn Logic, natural Philosophie, Ethics or Mathematics, which are more difficult, that certainly it is not necessarie to the attainment of Christian knowledge that men should sit all thir life long at the feet of a pulpited divine;[49] while he, a lollard indeed over his elbow-cushion, in almost the seaventh part of 40. or 50. years teaches them scarce half the principles of religion; and his sheep oft-times sit the while to as little purpose of benifiting as the sheep in thir pues at *Smithfield;* and for the most part by som Simonie or other, bought and sold like them: or, if this comparison be too low, like those woemen, 1 *Tim.* 3. 7.[50] *ever learning and never attaining;* yet not so much through thir own fault, as through the unskilful and immethodical teaching of thir pastor, teaching here and there at random out of this or that text as his ease or fansie, and oft-times as his stealth guides him. Seeing

les gueus: a name given in contempt to the Protestant nobles who opposed Margaret of Parma, regent of the Netherlands, and afterward adopted by various bodies of Dutch and Flemish partisans in the wars with Spaniards in the sixteenth century (*OED*).

lollard: a follower of Wycliffe and hence any reformer; with pun on the meaning *loafer*.

seaventh: i.e., on Sundays.

Smithfield: London meat market.

then that Christian religion may be so easily attaind, and by meanest capacities, it cannot be much difficult to finde waies, both how the poore, yea all men may be soone taught what is to be known of Christianitie, and they who teach them, recompenc'd. First, if ministers of thir own accord, who pretend that they are calld and sent to preach the gospel, those especially who have no particular flock, would imitate our Saviour and his disciples who went preaching through the villages, not only through the cities, *Matth.* 9. 35, *Mark* 6. 6, *Luke* 13. 22, *Acts* 8. 25. and there preachd to the poore as well as to the rich, looking for no recompence but in heaven: *John* 4. 35, 36. *Looke on the fields; for they are white alreadie to harvest: and he that reapeth, receiveth wages, and gathereth fruit unto life eternal.* This was their wages. But they will soone reply, we our selves have not wherewithall; who shall bear the charges of our journey? To whom it may as soone be answerd, that in likelihood they are not poorer than they who did thus; and if they have not the same faith which those disciples had to trust in God and the promise of Christ for thir maintenance as they did, and yet intrude into the ministerie without any livelihood of thir own, they cast themselves into a miserable hazzard or temptation, and oft-times into a more miserable necessitie, either to starve, or to please thir paymasters rather than God: and give men just cause to suspect, that they came neither calld nor sent from above to preach the word, but from below, by the instinct of thir own hunger, to feed upon the church. Yet grant it needful to allow them both the charges of thir jorney and the hire of thir labor, it will belong next to the charitie of richer congregations, where most commonly they abound with teachers, to send som of thir number to the villages round, as the apostles from *Jerusalem* sent *Peter* and *John* to the citie and villages of *Samaria, Acts* 8, 14, 25; or as the church at *Jerusalem* sent *Barnabas* to *Antioch, chap.* 11. 22; and other churches joining sent *Luke* to travail with *Paul,* 2 *Cor.* 8. 19: though whether they had thir charges born by the church or no, it be not recorded. If it be objected that this itinerarie preaching will not serve to plant the gospel in those places, unless they who are sent, abide there som competent time, I answer, that if they stay there a year or two, which was the longest time usually staid by the apostles in one place, it may suffice to teach them, who will attend and learn, all the points of religion necessary to salvation; then sorting them into several congregations of a moderat number, out of the ablest and zealousest among them to create elders, who, exercising and requiring from themselves what they have learnd (for no learning is retaind without constant exercise and methodical repetition) may teach and govern the rest: and so exhorted to continue faithful and stedfast, they may securely be committed to the providence of God and the guidance of his holy spirit, till God may offer som opportunitie to visit them again and to confirme them: which when they have don, they have don as much as the apostles were wont to do in propagating the gospel, *Acts* 14. 23. *And when they had ordaind them elders in every church, and had praied with fasting, they commended them to the Lord, on whom they beleevd.* And in the same chapter, *Vers.* 21, 22, *When they had preachd the gospel to that citie, and had taught many, they returned again to* Lystra *and to* Iconium *and* Antioch, *confirming the soules of the disciples,* and *exhorting them to continue in the faith.* And *Chap.* 15. 36. *Let us go again and visit our brethren.* And *Vers.* 41. *He went thorow* Syria *and* Cilicia, *confirming the churches.* To these I might add other helps, which we enjoy now, to make more easie the attainment of Christian religion by the meanest: the entire scripture translated into English with plenty of notes; and som where or other, I trust, may be found som wholsom bodie of divinitie, as they call it, without schoole terms and metaphysical notions,[51] which have obscur'd rather than explan'd our religion, and made it seem difficult without cause. Thus taught once for all, and thus now and then visited and confirmd, in the most destitute and poorest places of the land, under the government of thir own elders performing all ministerial offices among them, they may be trusted to meet and edifie one another whether in church or chappel, or, to save them the trudging of many miles thether, neerer home, though in a house or barn. For notwithstanding the gaudy superstition of som devoted still ignorantly to temples, we may be well assur'd that he who disdaind not to be laid in a manger, disdains not to be preachd in a barn; and that by such meetings as these, being, indeed, most apostolical and primitive, they will in a short time advance more in Christian knowledge and reformation of life, than by the many years preaching of such an incumbent, I may say, such an incubus oft times, as will be meanly hir'd to abide long in those places. They have this left perhaps to object further, that to send thus and to maintaine, though but for a year or two, ministers and teachers in several places, would prove chargeable to the churches, though in towns and cities round about. To whom again I answer, that it was not thought so by them who first thus propagated the gospel, though but few in number to us, and much less able to sustain the expence. Yet this expence would be much less, than to hire incumbents or rather incumbrances, for life-time; and a great means (which is the subject of this discourse) to diminish hirelings. But be the expence less or more, if it be found burdensom to the churches, they have in this land an easie remedie in thir recourse to the civil magistrate; who hath in his hands the disposal of no small revenues; left, perhaps, anciently to superstitious, but meant undoubtedly to good and best uses; and therefor, once made publick, appliable by the present magistrate to such uses as the church or solid reason from whomsoever shall convince him to think best. And those uses may be, no doubt, much rather than as glebes and augmentations are now bestowd, to grant such requests as these of the churches; or to erect in greater number all over the land schooles and competent libraries to those schooles, where languages and arts may be taught free together, without the needles, unprofitable and inconvenient removing to another place. So all the land would be soone better civiliz'd, and they who are taught freely at the publick cost, might have thir education given them on this condition, that therewith content, they should not gadd for preferment out of thir own countrey, but continue there thankful for what they receivd freely, bestowing it as freely on thir countrey, without soaring above the meannes wherin they were born. But how they shall live when they are thus bred and dismissd, will be still the sluggish objection. To which is answerd, that those publick foundations may be so instituted, as the youth therin may be at once brought up to a competence of learning and to an honest trade; and the hours of teaching so orderd, as thir studie may be no hindrance to thir labor or other calling. This was the breeding of S. *Paul*, though born of no mean parents, a free citizen of the Roman empire: so little did his trade debase him, that it rather enabld him to use that magnanimitie of preaching the gospel through *Asia* and *Europe* at his own charges: thus those preachers among the poor *Waldenses*, the ancient stock of our reformation, without these helps which I speak of, bred up themselves in trades, and especially in physic and surgery as well as in the studie of scripture (which is the only true theologie) that they might be no burden to the church; and by the example of Christ, might cure both soul and bodie; through industry joining that to their ministerie, which he joind to his by gift of the spirit. Thus relates *Peter Gilles* in his historie of the *Waldenses* in *Piemont*.[52] But our ministers think scorn to use a trade, and count it the reproach of this age, that tradesmen preach the gospel. It were to be wishd they were all tradesmen; they would not then

glebes and augmentations: lands given a clergyman as part of his benefice and increases of clerical pay by an action in a court.
needles: needless.
countrey: district, region.

so many of them, for want of another trade, make a trade of thir preaching: and yet they clamor that tradesmen preach; and yet they preach, while they themselves are the worst tradesmen of all. As for church-endowments and possessions, I meet with none considerable before *Constantine,* but the houses and gardens where they met, and thir places of burial: and I perswade me, that from them the ancient *Waldenses,* whom deservedly I cite so often,[53] held, *that to endow churches is an evil thing;* and, that the church then fell off and turnd whore[54] sitting on that beast in the *Revelation,* when under Pope *Sylvester* she receivd those temporal donations. So the forecited tractate of thir doctrin testifies. This also thir own traditions of that heavenly voice witnesd, and som of the ancient fathers then living, foresaw and deplor'd. And indeed, how could these endowments thrive better with the church, being unjustly taken by those emperors, without suffrage of the people, out of the tributes and publick lands of each citie, whereby the people became liable to be oppressd with other taxes. Being therefor given for the most part by kings and other publick persons, and so likeliest out of the publick, and if without the peoples consent, unjustly, however to publick ends of much concernment to the good or evil of a commonwealth, and in that regard made publick though given by privat persons, or which is worse, given, as the clergie then perswaded men, for thir soul's health, a pious gift, but as the truth was, ofttimes a bribe to God or to Christ for absolution, as they were then taught, from murders, adulteries, and other hainous crimes, what shall be found heretofore given by kings or princes out of the publick, may justly by the magistrate be recalld and reappropriated to the civil revenue: what by privat or publick persons out of thir own, the price of blood or lust, or to som such purgatorious and superstitious uses, not only may but ought to be taken off from Christ, as a foul dishonor laid upon him, or not impiously given, nor in particular to any one, but in general to the churches good, may be converted to that use, which shall be judgd tending more directly to that general end. Thus did the princes and cities of *Germany* in the first reformation; and defended thir so doing by many reasons, which are set down at large in *Sleidan, l.* 6, *an.* 1526, and *l.* 11, *an.* 1537, and *l.* 13, *an.* 1540. But that the magistrate either out of that church revenue which remanes yet in his hand, or establishing any

Pope Sylvester: Sylvester I (314–35) was pope during much of the reign of Constantine, when, as Milton has observed, the church received a great many benefactions.

thir: Waldensian.

Sleidan: John Sleidan (1506–56), chronicler of the Reformation in *De statu religionis et reipublicae* (1555).

other maintenance instead of tithe, should take into his own power the stipendiarie maintenance of church-ministers, or compell it by law, can stand neither with the peoples right nor with Christian liberty, but would suspend the church wholly upon the state, and turn her ministers into state-pensioners. And for the magistrate in person of a nursing father to make the church his meer ward, as alwaies in minoritie, the church, to whom he ought as a magistrate, *Esa.* 49, 23, *To bow down with his face toward the earth, and lick up the dust of her feet,* her to subject to his political drifts or conceivd opinions by mastring her revenue, and so by his examinant committies to circumscribe her free election of ministers, is neither just nor pious; no honor don to[55] the church, but a plane dishonor: and upon her, whose only head is in heaven, yea upon him, who is her only head, sets another in effect, and, which is most monstrous, a human on a heavenly, a carnal on a spiritual, a political head on an ecclesiastical bodie; which at length by such heterogeneal, such incestuous conjunction, transformes her oft-times into a beast of many heads and many horns. For if the church be of all societies the holiest on earth, and so to be reverenc'd by the magistrate, not to trust her with her own belief and integritie, and therefor not with the keeping, at least with the disposing of what revenue shall be found justly and lawfully her own, is to count the church not a holy congregation, but a pack of giddy or dishonest persons, to be rul'd by civil power in sacred affairs. But to proceed further in the truth yet more freely, seeing the Christian church is not national, but consisting of many particular congregations, subject to many changes, as well through civil accidents as through schism and various opinions, not to be decided by any outward judge, being matters of conscience, whereby these pretended church-revenues, as they have bin ever, so are like to continue endles matter of dissention both between the church and magistrate, and the churches among themselves, there will be found no better remedie to these evils, otherwise incurable, than by the incorruptest councel of those *Waldenses*, our first reformers, to remove them as a pest, an apple of discord in the church, (for what els can be the effect of riches and the snare of monie in religion?) and to convert them to those more profitable uses above expressd or other such as shall be judgd most necessarie; considering that the church of Christ was founded in poverty rather than in revenues, stood purest and prosperd best without them, receivd them unlawfully from them who both erroneously and un-

yea upon him: Christ, the head of the church.
beast . . . horns: the beast upon which the whore of Babylon rode: Rev. xvii 3.

justly, somtimes impiously, gave them, and so justly was ensnar'd and corrupted by them. And least it be thought that these revenues withdrawne and better imploid, the magistrate ought in stead to settle by statute som maintenance of ministers, let this be considerd first, that it concerns every mans conscience to what religion he contributes; and that the civil magistrate is intrusted with civil rights only, not with conscience, which can have no deputy or representer of it self, but one of the same minde: next, that what each man gives to the minister, he gives either as to God, or as to his teacher; if as to God, no civil power can justly consecrate to religious uses any part either of civil revenue, which is the peoples, and must save them from other taxes, or of any mans proprietie, but God by special command, as he did by *Moses,* or the owner himself by voluntarie intention and the perswasion of his giving it to God; forc'd consecrations out of another mans estate are no better than forc'd vowes; hateful to God, who *loves a chearful giver;* but much more hateful, wrung out of mens purses to maintaine a disapprov'd ministerie against thir conscience; however unholy,[56] infamous and dishonorable to his ministers, and the free gospel[57] maintaind in such unworthy manner as by violence and extortion: If he give it as to his teacher, what justice or equitie compells him to pay for learning that religion which leaves freely to his choise whether he will learn it or no, whether of this teacher or another, and especially to pay for what he never learnd, or approves not; whereby, besides the wound of his conscience, he becoms the less able to recompence his true teacher? Thus far hath bin enquir'd by whom church-ministers ought to be maintaind; and hath bin prov'd most natural, most equal and agreeable with scripture, to be by them who receive thir teaching; and by whom, if they be unable. Which waies well observd, can discourage none but hirelings, and will much lessen thir number in the church.

It remanes lastly to consider in what manner God hath ordaind that recompence be given to ministers of the gospel: and by all scripture it will appeer that he hath given it them not by civil law and freehold, as they claim, but by the benevolence and free gratitude of such as receive them: *Luke* 10. 7, 8. *Eating and drinking such things as they give you. If they receive you, eate such things as are set before you. Matth.* 10. 7, 8. *As ye go, preach, saying, The kingdome of God is at hand, etc. Freely ye have receivd, freely give.* If God have ordaind ministers to preach freely, whether they receive

proprietie: property. *but God by:* unless God permits it by.
Moses: who permitted the Levites to take tithes.
freehold: tenure for life.

recompence or not, then certainly he hath forbidd both them to compell it, and others to compell it for them. But freely given, he accounts it as given to himself: *Phillip.* 4. 16, 17, 18. *Ye sent once and again to my necessitie. Not because I desire a gift; but I desire fruit that may abound to your account. Having receivd of* Epaphroditus *the things which were sent from you, an odour of sweet smell, a sacrifice acceptable, well pleasing to God.* Which cannot be from force or unwillingnes. The same is said of almes, *Heb.* 13. 16. *To do good and to communicate, forgett not: for with such sacrifices God is well pleasd.* Whence the primitive church thought it no shame to receive all thir maintenance as the almes of thir auditors. Which they who defend tithes, as if it made for thir cause, when as it utterly confutes them, omitt not to set down at large; proving to our hands out of *Origen, Tertullian, Cyprian,* and others, that the clergie livd at first upon the meer benevolence of thir hearers:[58] who gave what they gave, not to the clergie, but to the church; out of which the clergie had thir portions given them in baskets; and were thence calld *sportularii, basket-clerks:*[59] that thir portion was a very mean allowance, only for a bare livelihood; according to those precepts of our Saviour, *Matth.* 10, 7, *etc;* the rest was distributed to the poore. They cite also out of *Prosper,*[60] the disciple of St. *Austin,* that such of the clergie as had means of thir own, might not without sin partake of church-maintenance; not receiving thereby food which they abound with, but feeding on the sins of other men: that the holy ghost saith of such clergie men, they eat the sins of my people: and that a councel at *Antioch,* in the year 340, sufferd not either priest or bishop to live on church-maintenance without necessitie. Thus far tithers themselves have contributed to thir own confutation, by confessing that the church livd primitively on almes. And I add, that about the year 359, *Constantius* the emperor having summond a general councel of bishops to *Ariminum* in *Italie,* and provided for thir subsistence there, the *British* and *French* bishops judging it not decent to live on the publick, chose rather to be at thir own charges.[61] Three only out of *Britain* constraind through want, yet refusing offerd assistance from the rest, accepted the emperor's provision; judging it more convenient to subsist by publick than by privat sustenance. Whence we may conclude, that *bishops* then in this Iland had thir livelihood only from benevolence: in which regard this relater *Sulpitius Severus,* a good author of the same time, highly praises them. And the *Waldenses,* our first reformers, both from the scripture and these primitive examples, maintaind those among them who bore the of-

made for: supported.

fice of ministers, by almes only. Take thir very words from the historie written of them in *French,*[62] *Part.* 3. *l.* 2. *c.* 2. *La nourriture et ce de quoy nous sommes couverts etc. Our food and cloathing is sufficiently administerd and given to us by way of gratuitie and almes, by the good people whom we teach.* If then by almes and benevolence, not by legal force, not by tenure of freehold or copyhold: for almes, though just, cannot be compelld; and benevolence forc'd, is malevolence rather, violent and inconsistent with the gospel; and declares him no true minister therof, but a rapacious hireling rather, who by force receiving it, eats the bread of violence and exaction, no holy or just livelihood, no not civilly counted honest; much less beseeming such a spiritual ministry. But, say they, our maintenance is our due, tithes the right of Christ, unseparable from the priest, no where repeald; if then, not otherwise to be had, by law to be recoverd: for though *Paul* were pleasd to forgoe his due, and not to use his power, 1 *Cor.* 9. 12,[63] yet he had a power, *v.* 4,[64] and bound not others. I answer first, because I see them still so loath to unlearn thir decimal arithmetic, and still grasp thir tithes as inseparable from a priest, that ministers of the gospel are not priests; and therefor separated from tithes by thir own exclusion; being neither calld priests in the new testament, nor of any order known in scripture: not of *Melchisedec,* proper to Christ only; not of *Aaron,* as they themselves will confess; and the third priesthood,[65] only remaining, is common to all the faithful. But they are ministers of our high priest. True; but not of his priesthood, as the Levites were to *Aaron:* for he performs that whole office himself incommunicably. Yet tithes remane, say they, still unreleasd, the due of Christ; and to whom payable, but to his ministers? I say again, that no man can so understand them, unless Christ in som place or other so claim them. That example of *Abram*[66] argues nothing but his voluntarie act; honor once only don, but on what consideration, whether to a priest or to a king, whether due the honor, arbitrarie that kinde of honor or not, will after all contending be left still in meer conjecture: which must not be permitted in the claim of such a needy and suttle spiritual corporation pretending by divine right to the tenth of all other mens estates; nor can it be allowd by wise men or the verdit of common law. And the tenth part, though once declar'd holy, is declar'd now to be no holier than the other nine, by that command to *Peter Act.* 10. 15. 28: whereby all distinction of holy and unholy is remov'd from all things.[67] Tithes therefor though claimd, and holy under the law, yet are now releasd and quitted both by that command to *Peter,*

not by tenure of freehold or copyhold: not by custom or usage.

and by this to all ministers, above-cited *Luke* 10; *eating and drinking such things as they give you:* made holy now by thir free gift only. And therefor S. *Paul*, 1 *Cor*. 9. 4, asserts his power, indeed; but of what? not of tithes, but, *to eat and drink such things as are given* in reference to this command: which he calls not holy things or things of the gospel, as if the gospel had any consecrated things in answer to things of the temple, *v*. 13, but he calls them *your carnal things, v*. 11. without changing thir property. And what power had he? not the power of force but of conscience only, whereby he might lawfully and without scruple live on the gospel; receiving what was given him, as the recompence of his labor. For if Christ the master hath professd his kingdom to be not of this world,[68] it suits not with that profession either in him or his ministers to claim temporal right from spiritual respects. He who refus'd to be the divider of an inheritance between two brethren,[69] cannot approve his ministers by pretended right from him to be dividers of tenths and freeholds out of other mens possessions, making thereby the gospel but a cloak of carnal interest, and, to the contradiction of thir master, turning his heavenly kingdom into a kingdom of this world, a kingdom of force and rapin. To whom it will be one day thunderd more terribly than to *Gehazi*,[70] for thus dishonoring a far greater master and his gospel, *is this a time to receive monie and to receive garments and olive-yards and vinyards and sheep and oxen?* The leprosie of *Naaman* linkd with that apostolic curse of *perishing* imprecated on *Simon Magus*,[71] may be feard will *cleave to* such *and to* thir *seed for ever*. So that when all is don, and bellie hath us'd in vain all her cunning shifts, I doubt not but all true ministers, considering the demonstration of what hath bin here prov'd, will be wise, and think it much more tolerable to hear, that no maintenance of ministers, whether tithes or any other, can be settl'd by statute; but must be given by them who receive instruction; and freely given, as God hath ordaind. And indeed what can be a more honorable maintenance to them than such, whether almes or willing oblations, as these[72] which being accounted both alike as given to God, the only acceptable sacrifices now remaining, must needs represent him who receives them much in the care of God and neerly related to him, when not by worldly force and constraint, but with religious awe and reverence;[73] what is given to God, is given to him, and what to him, accounted as given to God. This would be well anough, say they; but how many will so give? I answer, as many, doubtles, as shall be well taught; as many as God shall so move. Why are ye so distrustful both of your own doctrin and of Gods promises, fulfilld in the experience of those disciples first sent:

Luke 22. 35. *When I sent you without purse and scrip and shooes, lackd ye anything? And they said, Nothing.* How then came ours, or who sent them thus destitute, thus poor and empty both of purse and faith? Who stile themselves embassadors of Jesus Christ, and seem to be his tithe-gatherers, though an office of thir own setting up to his dishonor, his exacters, his publicans rather, not trusting that he will maintain them in thir embassy, unless they binde him to his promise by a statute law that we shall maintain them. Lay down for shame that magnific title, while ye seek maintenance from the people: it is not the manner of embassadors to ask maintenance of them to whom they are sent. But he who is Lord of all things, hath so ordaind: trust him then; he doubtles will command the people to make good his promises of maintenance more honorably unaskd, unrak'd for. This they know, this they preach, yet beleeve not: but think it as impossible without a statute law to live of the gospel, as if by those words they were bid go eat thir bibles, as *Ezechiel* and *John* did thir books;[74] and such doctrins as these are as bitter to thir bellies: but will serve so much the better to discover hirelings, who can have nothing, though but in appearance, just and solid to answer for themselves against what hath bin here spoken, unless perhaps this one remaning pretence, which we shall quickly see to be either fals or uningenuous. They pretend that thir education either at schoole or universitie hath bin very chargeable;[75] and therefor ought to be repar'd in future by a plentiful maintenance: whenas it is well known that the better half of them, and oft times poor and pittiful boyes of no merit or promising hopes that might intitle them to the publick provision but thir povertie and the unjust favor of friends, have had the most of thir breeding both at schoole and universitie by schollarships, exhibitions and fellowships at the publick cost; which might ingage them the rather to give freely, as they have freely receivd. Or if they have missd of these helps at the latter place, they have after two or three years left the cours of thir studies there, if they ever well began them, and undertaken, though furnishd with little els but ignorance, boldnes and ambition, if with no worse vices, a chaplainship in som gentlemans house, to the frequent imbasing of his sons with illiterate and narrow principles. Or if they have livd there upon thir own, who knows not that seaven years charge of living there, to them who fly not from the government of thir parents to the license of a universitie,

unrak'd for: unsought.
chargeable: expensive.
exhibitions: gifts from an endowment.
livd there upon thir own: at a university.

but com seriously to studie, is no more than may be well defraid and reimbours'd by one years revenue of an ord'nary good benifice? If they had then means of breeding from thir parents, 'tis likely they have more now; and if they have, it needs must be mechanique and uningenuous in them to bring a bill of charges for the learning of those liberal arts and sciences, which they have learnd (if they have indeed learnd them, as they seldom have) to thir own benefit and accomplishment. But they will say, we had betaken us to som other trade or profession, had we not expected to finde a better livelihood by the ministerie. This is that which I lookd for, to discover them openly neither true lovers of learning, and so very seldom guilty of it, nor true ministers of the gospel. So long agoe out of date is that old *true saying,* 1 *Tim.* 3. 1. *if a man desire a bishoprick, he desires a good work:* for now commonly he who desires to be a minister, looks not at the work but at the wages; and by that lure or loubel may be toald from parish to parish all the town over. But what can be planer Simonie, than thus to be at charges beforehand to no other end than to make thir ministry doubly or trebly beneficial? to whom it might be said as justly as to that *Simon, thy monie perish with thee, because thou hast thought that the gift of God may be purchas'd with monie: thou hast neither part nor lot in this matter.*[76] Next, it is a fond error, though too much beleevd among us, to think that the universitie makes a minister of the gospel; what it may conduce to other arts and sciences, I dispute not now: but that which makes fit a minister, the scripture can best informe us to be only from above; whence also we are bid to seek them; *Matth.* 9. 38. *Pray ye therefor to the Lord of the harvest, that he will send forth laborers into his harvest.* Acts 20. 28. *The flock, over which the holy ghost hath made you over-seers.* Rom. 10. 15. *How shall they preach, unless they be sent?* by whom sent? by the universitie, or the magistrate, or thir belly? no surely: but sent from God only, and that God who is not thir belly. And whether he be sent from God or from *Simon Magus,* the inward sense of his calling and spiritual abilitie will sufficiently tell him; and that strong obligation felt within him, which was felt by the apostle, will often express from him the same words: 1 *Cor.* 9. 16. *Necessity is laid upon me, yea, woe is me, if I preach not the gospel.* Not a beggarly necessity, and the woe feard otherwise of perpetual want, but such a necessitie as made him willing to preach the gospel *gratis,* and to embrace

breeding: education.
mechanique: base.
loubel: low-bell: a bell used to frighten birds at night so that they might be caught.

povertie rather than as a woe to fear it. 1 *Cor.* 12. 28. *God hath set som in the church, first apostles, etc.* Eph. 4. 11, *etc. He gave som apostles, etc. For the perfeting of the saints, for the work of the ministerie, for the edifying of the body of Christ, till we all come to the unitie of the faith.*[77] Whereby we may know that as he made them at the first, so he makes them still, and to the worlds end. 2 *Cor.* 3. 6. *Who hath also made us fit or able ministers of the new testament.* 1 Tim. 4. 14. *The gift that is in thee, which was given thee by prophesie and*[78] *the laying on of the hands of the presbyterie.* These are all the means which we read of requir'd in scripture to the making of a minister. All this is granted you will say: but yet that it is also requisite he should be traind in other learning; which can be no where better had than at universities. I answer, that what learning either human or divine can be necessary to a minister, may as easily and less chargeably be had in any private house. How deficient els and to how little purpose are all those piles of sermons, notes, and comments on all parts of the bible, bodies and marrows of divinitie, besides all other sciences, in our English tongue; many of the same books which in Latine they read at the universitie? And the small necessitie of going thether to learn divinitie, I prove first from the most part of themselves, who seldom continue there till they have well got through Logic, thir first rudiments; though, to say truth, Logic also may much better be wanting in disputes of divinitie, than in the suttle debates of lawyers and statesmen, who yet seldom or never deal with syllogisms. And those theological disputations there held by Professors and graduates are such as tend least of all to the edification or capacitie of the people, but rather perplex and leaven pure doctrin with scholastical trash than enable any minister to the better preaching of the gospel. Whence we may also compute, since they com to recknings, the charges of his needful library: which, though som shame not to value at 600 l,[79] may be competently furnishd for 60 l. If any man for his own curiositie or delight be in books further expensive, that is not to be recknd as necessarie to his ministerial either breeding or function. But Papists and other adversaries cannot be confuted without fathers and councels, immense volumes and of vast charges. I will shew them therefor a shorter and a better way of confutation: *Tit.* 1. 9. *Holding fast the faithful word, as he hath bin taught, that he may be able by sound doctrin, both to exhort and to con-*

chargeably: expensively.
marrows: summaries.
Logic: a basic course for freshmen.
leaven: corrupt by admixture.

vince gain-sayers: who are confuted as soon as heard, bringing that which is either not in scripture or against it. To persue them further through the obscure and intangld wood of antiquitie, fathers and councels fighting one against another, is needles, endles, not requisite in a minister, and refus'd by the first reformers of our religion. And yet we may be confident, if these things be thought needful, let the state but erect in publick good store of libraries, and there will not want men in the church, who of thir own inclinations will become able in this kinde against Papist or any other adversarie. I have thus at large examind the usual pretences of hirelings, colourd over most commonly with the cause of learning and universities: as if with divines learning stood and fell; wherin for the most part thir pittance is so small: and, to speak freely, it were much better, there were not one divine in the universitie; no schoole-divinitie known, the idle sophistrie of monks, the canker of religion; and that they who intended to be ministers, were traind up in the church only by the scripture,[80] and in the original languages therof at schoole; without fetching the compas of other arts and sciences, more than what they can well learn at secondary leasure and at home. Neither speak I this in contempt of learning or the ministry, but hating the common cheats of both; hating that they who have preachd out bishops, prelats and canonists, should, in what serves thir own ends, retain thir fals opinions, thir Pharisaical leaven, thir avarice and closely thir ambition, thir pluralities, thir nonresidences, thir odious fees, and use thir legal and Popish arguments for tithes: that Independents should take that name, as they may justly from the true freedom of Christian doctrin and church-discipline subject to no superior judge but God only, and seek to be Dependents on the magistrate for thir maintenance; which two things, independence and state-hire in religion, can never consist long or certainly together. For magistrates at one time or other, not like these at present our patrons of Christian libertie, will pay none but such whom by thir committies of examination, they find conformable to their interest and opinions: and hirelings will soone frame themselves to that interest and those opinions which they see best pleasing to thir paymasters; and to seem right themselves, will force others as to the truth. But most of all they are to be revil'd and sham'd, who cry out with the distinct voice of notorious hirelings, that if ye settle not our maintenance by law, farwell the gospel: than which nothing can be utterd more fals, more ignominious, and, I may say, more blasphe-

preachd out: rid the country of, by preaching against.
closely: secretly. *pluralities:* holding appointments in more than one congregation.

mous against our Saviour; who hath promisd, without this condition, both his holy spirit and his own presence with his church to the worlds end: nothing more fals (unless with thir own mouths they condemne themselves for the unworthiest and most mercenary of all other ministers) by the experience of 300. years after Christ, and the churches at this day in *France, Austria, Polonia,* and other places witnessing the contrary under an advers magistrate not a favorable: nothing more ignominious, levelling or rather undervaluing Christ beneath *Mahomet.* For if it must be thus, how can any Christian object it to a Turk, that his religion stands by force only; and not justly fear from him this reply, yours both by force and monie in the judgment of your own preachers. This is that which makes atheists in the land, whom they so much complain of: not the want of maintenance or preachers, as they alleage, but the many hirelings and cheaters that have the gospel in thir hands; hands that still crave, and are never satisfi'd. Likely ministers, indeed, to proclaim the faith or to exhort our trust in God, when they themselves will not trust him to provide for them in the message wheron, they say, he sent them; but threaten for want of temporal means to desert it; calling that want of means, which is nothing els but the want of thir own faith; and would force us to pay the hire of building our faith to their covetous incredulitie. Doubtles, if God only be he who gives ministers to his church till the worlds end; and through the whole gospel never sent us for ministers to the schools of Philosophie, but rather bids us beware of such *vain deceit, Col.* 2. 8. (which the primitive church, after two or three ages[81] not remembring, brought herself quickly to confusion) if all the faithful be now *a holy and a royal priesthood,* 1 *Pet.* 2. 5. 9, not excluded from the dispensation of things holiest, after free election of the church and imposition of hands, there will not want ministers, elected out of all sorts and orders of men, for the Gospel makes no difference from the magistrate himself to the meanest artificer, if God evidently favor him with spiritual gifts, as he can easily and oft hath don, while those batchelor divines and doctors of the tippet have bin passd by. Heretofore in the first evangelic times (and it were happy for Christendom if it were so again) ministers of the gospel were by nothing els distinguishd from other Christians but by thir spiritual knowledge and

Polonia: Poland. Protestant clergy received no state support in such countries.
ages: centuries.
free election of the church: that is, Congregationalism, a system of church government used by several Protestant groups whereby the rule of a congregation rests in its own members.
imposition of hands: ordination of a new minister.
tippet: a black scarf worn about the neck of the minister.

sanctitie of life, for which the church elected them to be her teachers and overseers, though not thereby to separate them from whatever calling she then found them following besides, as the example of S. *Paul* declares, and the first times of Christianitie. When once they affected to be calld a clergie, and became as it were a peculiar tribe of levites, a partie, a distinct order in the commonwealth, bred up for divines in babling schooles and fed at the publick cost, good for nothing els but what was good for nothing, they soone grew idle: that idlenes with fulnes of bread begat pride and perpetual contention with thir feeders the despis'd laitie, through all ages ever since; to the perverting of religion, and the disturbance of all Christendom. And we may confidently conclude, it never will be otherwise while they are thus upheld undepending on the church, on which alone they anciently depended, and are by the magistrate publickly maintaind a numerous faction of indigent persons, crept for the most part out of extream want and bad nurture, claiming by divine right and freehold the tenth of our estates, to monopolize the ministry as their peculiar, which is free and open to all able Christians, elected by any church. Under this pretence exempt from all other imployment, and inriching themselves on the publick, they last of all prove common incendiaries, and exalt thir horns[82] against the magistrate himself that maintains them, as the priest of *Rome* did soone after against his benefactor the emperor,[83] and the presbyters of late in *Scotland*.[84] Of which hireling crew together with all the mischiefs, dissentions, troubles, warrs meerly of their kindling, Christendom might soone rid herself and be happie, if Christians would but know thir own dignitie, thir libertie, thir adoption, and let it not be wonderd if I say, thir spiritual priesthood, whereby they have all equally access to any ministerial function whenever calld by thir own abilities and the church, though they never came neer commencement or universitie. But while Protestants, to avoid the due labor of understanding thir own religion, are[85] content to lodge it in the breast or rather in the books of a clergie man, and to take it thence by scraps and mammocks as he dispences it in his sundays dole, they will be alwaies learning and never knowing, alwaies infants, alwaies either his vassals, as lay-papists are to their priests, or at odds with him, as reformed principles give them som light to be not wholly conformable, whence infinit disturbances in the state, as they do, must needs follow. Thus much I had to say; and, I suppose, what may be anough to them who are not

as their peculiar: as their own.
thir adoption: by God into the priesthood of believers.
mammocks: pieces.

avariciously bent otherwise, touching the likeliest means to remove hirelings out of the church; than which nothing can more conduce to truth, to peace and all happines both in church and state. If I be not heard nor beleevd, the event will bear me witnes to have spoken truth: and I in the mean while have borne my witnes not out of season to the church and to my countrey.

The end.

event: outcome.

NOTES

1. The eighteen years beginning with the *First Defence of the English People* (1651), which Parliament had commissioned Milton to write against Salmasius' *Defensio Regia* (1649).

2. The "short but scandalous night of interruption" may refer to the period from the dissolution of the Rump in 1653 to its restoration in May 1659, to the few days between the dissolution of Richard Cromwell's parliament and the restoration of the Rump, or to the whole of Richard's rule. See William B. Hunter, Jr., "Milton and Richard Cromwell," *ELN*, III (1966), 252 ff.

3. Luke x 7. William Prynne's first argument in *A Gospel Plea* (1653), pp. 3 ff., is based on this text.

4. Early church historians emphasize Constantine's bounty. Especially in his *Life of Constantine* Eusebius testifies to such support. See Christopher B. Coleman, *Constantine the Great and Christianity,* Columbia University Studies in History, Economics, and Public Law, No. 146 (New York, 1914). Milton had used the same argument in *Of Reformation* (1641 ed., pp. 27 ff.).

5. As early as his *Apology Against a Pamphlet* (1642), Milton had made this same argument (*Yale Milton,* I, 946–47), tracing there the quotation to John Gower's *Confessio Amantis.* See also M. C. Jochums, "As Ancient as Constantine," *SEL,* IV (1964), 101–7. But the quotation appeared in an authority which Milton thought to be very old: John Dubrau's *Rerum bohemicarum antiqui scriptores,* which was attached to his *Historia bohemica ab origine* (Hanover, 1602). In a section outlining the heresies of the Waldensians, it reports that the church "defecerit a Sylvestro, cum venenum temporalium in Ecclesiam infusum est" (p. 233). Milton twice later in *Hirelings* specifically refers to the Dubrau history. The source of the quotation in the next sentence has not been identified.

6. This story, as reported in Acts viii 9–25, is the source of the word *simony.*

7. The King James version has "shall they heap." With only very slight changes such as this, the texts throughout are drawn from this translation.

8. Paul had supported himself by making tents: Acts xviii 4.

9. The argument which follows derives from Num. xviii 21–31, which is one basis for the laws of tithing.

10. Here and often in the subsequent argument, Milton holds that the Communion table is not an altar. In one of his early acts as Archbishop, Laud in 1634 ordered uniformity in the position of Communion tables at the east end of the church, separated from the congregation by a railing. Puritans bitterly resented the action because they thought that it suggested that the table was an altar. When it came to power in 1641, the Long Parliament had the table placed in the nave and the railing removed.

11. From the same passage in Numbers, Sir Henry Spelman in his *Larger Vorke of Tithes,* included in the collection of pamphlets *Tithes Too Hot to Be 'ouched* (London, ca. 1646), pp. 140–41, had argued that tithes were moral obligatory upon everyone) rather than ceremonial (merely symbolic).

12. The Old Testament was thus regularly interpreted as foreshadowing the Jew. Often the Old Testament equivalent of the New Testament was said to e a *type* of the latter. See, e.g., the discussion of Aaron in the next sentence.

13. Gen. xiv 18–20. In *A Gospel Plea,* pp. 57 ff., William Prynne had argued t some length from this passage as a support of tithing, as did Spelman, *Larger Vorke,* pp. 104 ff. The point is that Abram (or Abraham) in his action antedates the revelation of Old Testament law to Moses and hence it is a universal noral obligation; Melchizedek is Christ himself or the type of Christ. John Selden begins his *History of Tithes* (1618) with a discussion of the same pasage. The author of Hebrews, vii 1–10, interprets Christ as a priest after the order of Melchizedek.

14. At a place which he named Bethel, Jacob vowed that "this stone, which I have set for a pillar, shall be God's house: and of all that thou shalt give me I will surely give the tenth unto thee" (Gen. xxviii 22). Selden, pp. 4 ff., had argued that the verses do not authorize the practice of tithing since Jacob was himself a priest, but Spelman, *Larger Worke,* p. 109, says they do.

15. *whole:* not in the King James version.

16. "Woe unto you, scribes and Pharisees, hypocrites! for ye pay tithe of mint and anise and cummin, and have omitted the weightier matters of the law, judgment, mercy, and faith: these ought ye to have done, and not to leave the other undone."

17. A fact admitted by Prynne, *A Gospel Plea,* p. 146, and answered on the following pages. Spelman, *Larger Worke,* has a similar argument in Chapter VI, showing that the clergy then lived on free-will offerings, as Milton goes on to observe.

18. In *A Gospel Plea,* p. 73, Prynne so translated (in capitals for emphasis) from pagan authors cited by Hugo Grotius, *De jure belli ac pacis.* Spelman's list of pagan examples (*Larger Worke*) runs from pp. 114–28. Selden had made the same point, *History of Tithes,* chapter III. A widespread theory was that all Hellenic civilization, including mythology, was descended from Hebrew originals.

19. Eusebius, Theodorit and Sozomen were three ancient writers of church history who together cover the Christian era to the death of the Emperor Arcadius (408). They are conveniently available in *A Select Library of Nicene and Post-Nicene Fathers,* 2nd Series, II and III.

20. The Waldenses (see Milton's "Sonnet on the Late Massacre in Piedmont") were a religious group in the Italian Alps who were considered either to have preserved the pristine purity of apostolic Christianity or to have been the original Protestants. At the end of the sentence Milton refers to Dubrau's *Rerum bohemicarum antiqui scriptores,* p. 223.

21. The "Apostolic Canons" are the last book of the so-called *Apostolic Constitutions,* an apocryphal work supposedly drawn up by the apostles and transmitted to the church by Clement of Rome. Selden questions their authority in his *History of Tithes,* p. 42, but Spelman, *Larger Worke,* cites their authority as he begins one phase of his argument for tithing, pp. 88 f.

22. The Council of Agrippinense, that is, of Cologne, which Spelman, *Larger Worke,* p. 89, says decreed that tithes were to be called "Gods rent." According to John F. Benton, Milton's slighting reference to the council may be traced to one of the Capitula of Bishop Heiton of Basle (cap. XV; Migne, *Patrologia*

Latina, CV, 765). Early in the eleventh century Bishop Burchard of Worm included this decree in his *Decretorum libri XX* (Liber III, cap. 135) under the heading "Ex concilio Agrippinense." Burchard appears to have made the false identification along with other texts as being canons of a council of Cologne. Ivo of Chartres included the text in his *Decretum,* III, 201. Benton observes that the authority of Burchard and Ivo spread the misinformation. Milton's point here is that the authority of the council, urged by Spelman, is poorly grounded. He goes on to class such authority with that of the medieval romance, the *Three Kings of Cologne* (EETS, Original Series, No. 85).

23. From the time of Tertullian (*Apol.* 46) and Lactantius (*Inst.* VI, 2) some early church leaders had objected to burning candles in churches during the daytime. The practice nevertheless developed in the medieval church and was continued by the Anglican. Puritan groups forbade it.

24. See the *Ecclesiastical History* (Loeb ed.), I, 117.

25. Prynne, *A Gospel Plea,* p. 143, cited a multitude of Church Fathers, beginning with Ambrose, Jerome, and Augustine.

26. "*Prynn*" added in the margin of the reprint in Milton's *Works* (1698). Prynne is the "Quærist" in the next sentence, who in his *A Gospel Plea,* p. 144, cited as authorities the Roman Catholic writers Alphanus Tyndarus, *Tractatus . . . in Materia Compensationum* (1549) and Pierre Rebuffus, *De Decimis* (1584) in support of tithing. These are again quoted in his *Ten Considerable Queries Concerning Tithes* (London, 1659), p. 3.

27. Milton makes another ironic reference to Prynne's "margins" in the sonnet "On the New Forcers of Conscience": "Clip ye as close as marginal P——'s ears." The line was canceled before publication.

28. Prynne, *A Gospel Plea,* p. 145. His authority is Sir Henry Spelman, *Concilia, Decreta, Leges, Constitutiones, in re Ecclesiarum Orbis Britanniae* (London, 1639), a collection of ancient laws. Athelstan's laws concerning tithes appear on pp. 398 and 402. Spelman begins his argument that tithes "are due by the Law of the Land," *Larger Worke,* p. 129, by citing Athelstan (but with the date 924).

29. In his *History of Britain* Milton observed that Ina's laws are "the first of Saxon that remain extant today" (*Columbia Milton,* X, 178). He could have found this law of Romescot or Denarius S. Petri in Spelman, *Concilia,* p. 230 (dated 725).

30. *Romescot* is confirmed in the *Leges ecclesiasticae* of Edward the Confessor, No. 11 (Spelman, *Concilia,* p. 621). The ninth law, concerned with tithes, says that they are to be offered on the authority of Augustine, the first monk sent (by Pope Gregory) as missionary to England: "Haec enim beatus Augustinus predicavit et docuit, et haec concessa sunt a Rege, et Baronibus, et populo," translated here in part by Milton. Selden, p. 225, quotes the same words. Milton is probably following the latter source, for Selden ends the statement here; Spelman continues for several more lines.

31. Milton is now quoting from Spelman, *Concilia,* the Canons of Egbert (ca. 750), #5 (p. 259), repeated in the Canons of Aelfric, #24 (p. 578). Both state that church offerings are to be divided among the priests, the poor, and church repair and upkeep.

32. Deut. xiv 29, referred to above.

33. This is Prynne's argument, *A Gospel Plea,* pp. 87–88, and Spelman's, *Larger Worke,* p. 148.

34. Prynne, *A Gospel Plea,* p. 29: "in cases of necessity, when the wants of the Apostles, Ministers and Saints of God require it, Christians are not bound to

y them the Tithes of their Lands and other setled Dues, but even to sell their ry Lands, Houses, Estates, and lay them down at the Apostles and Ministers t."

35. "Now the sons of Eli were sons of Belial" (1 Sam. ii 12). Cf. *Paradise st,* I, 490 ff.

36. The reference should be lvi 11.

37. The prophet Elisha refused any reward for healing Naaman, who suffered m leprosy. Later Elisha's servant Gehazi asked for the reward. When the ophet discovered this, he gave the leprosy to Gehazi instead. 2 Kings v.

38. ". . . for the Council, wishing to correct the abuses which have been ought in, etc.," quoted from Paulo Sarpi, *Historia del Concilio Tridentino* ondon, 1619). Milton also based some of the argument in *Areopagitica* upon is book. See E. Sirluck's notes in the *Yale Milton,* II, 500 ff.

39. *funstion:* 1659.

40. Spelman, *Concilia,* p. 259.

41. *marriages that:* 1659.

42. Masson notes (*Life,* V, 281) that Milton's second marriage was per-rmed "not by a clergyman, but by a justice of the peace."

43. 1 Cor. vii 22. The chapter is concerned with marriage.

44. *magistrates Seeing:* 1659. The Marriage Act of 1653 made these pro-sions.

45. This is the Third Lateran Council. Among other actions it condemned e Waldenses and (in its Canon vii) forbade the exaction of payment for rials, marriages, or administration of sacraments in general.

46. Selden makes this same point, p. 138.

47. *paricularly:* 1659.

48. John Huss, fifteenth-century follower of the reformer Wycliffe. Even be-re his time were the Waldenses, the "poore men of Lions" or Lyons.

49. In *A Gospel Plea,* p. 31, Prynne had argued that ministers should be hooled for "sixteen or twenty years . . . double the years, study, industry, that ost other Artists (except Lawyers and Physicians) spend."

50. This should be 2 Tim. iii 7: "Ever learning and never able to come to e knowledge of the truth."

51. Milton may be referring to his own *Christian Doctrine,* which fits this efinition.

52. *Histoire ecclésiastique des Eglises Réformées, recueillies en quelques lées de Piedmont . . . commençant dès l'an 1160* (Geneva, 1644), pp. 15–16.

53. Translating from Dubrau's *Rerum bohemicarum antiqui scriptores,* p. 223.

54. Rev. xvii 4 ff. The whore of Babylon, often interpreted by Protestants as e Roman Catholic Church and in particular by the Waldensians, Dubrau, . 223.

55. *to to:* 1659.

56. *however, unholy:* 1659.

57. *ministers and the free gospel:* 1659.

58. Paraphrased from Spelman, *Larger Worke,* p. 16. In *A Gospel Plea,* p. 46, Prynne recognizes that there was no tithing in the primitive church but n the following pages answers arguments based on this fact.

59. Spelman discusses the practice of presenting gifts in baskets to the early hurch in *Larger Worke,* pp. 17 ff.

60. St. Prosper of Aquitaine, active with Augustine in the Pelagian contro-ersy. The reference again is to Spelman, *Larger Worke,* p. 27, who cites the uthority of the Council of Antioch in the preceding and the following para-raphs.

61. This information is found in Spelman, *Concilia,* p. 24, but Milton h gone to his source and is loosely translating from Sulpicius Severus, *Histo sacra,* II, 41. See *Nicene and Post-Nicene Fathers,* 2nd Series, XI, 116.

62. Milton is referring to Jean Paul Perrin, *Histoire des Vaudois* (Genev 1619), pp. 228–29 in Part 3, translated into English as *Luther's Forerunne* (London, 1624), p. 57. Samuel Morland, *The History of the Evangelic Churches of the Valleys of Piemont* (London, 1658), p. 74, quotes the stateme in its original Waldensian language and adds an English translation (which not identical with Milton's).

63. "If others be partakers of this power over you, are not we rather? Neve theless we have not used this power; but suffer all things, lest we should hind the gospel of Christ."

64. "Have we not power to eat and to drink?" In *A Gospel Plea,* pp. 41–4 Prynne had used the passage to prove the power of the church to require tithe

65. I.e., of all Christian believers. See 1 Peter ii 5 and 9.

66. I.e., Abram and Melchizedec, discussed earlier.

67. In Acts x 9 ff., St. Peter becomes very hungry. During a dream he told that he may eat anything, including the unclean food of the Old Test ment: "what God hath cleansed, that call not thou common."

68. John xviii 36.

69. Luke xii 13–14: "And one of the company said unto him, Master, spea to my brother, that he divide the inheritance with me. And he said unto hir Man, who made me a judge or a divider over you?"

70. See note 37 above. The quotation which follows is from 2 Kings v 26.

71. Refers again to Acts viii 18–23.

72. *them, then such whether almes or willing oblations as these:* 1659.

73. *reverence:* 1659.

74. Ezek. iii 1 and Rev. x 10.

75. This is Prynne's argument, *A Gospel Plea,* p. 32, but Milton is more prob ably answering *A Resolution of a Doubt Touching the Alienation of Tithe* pp. 10–11, included in *Tithes Too Hot to Be Touched.*

76. Acts viii 20–21.

77. The point of the quotations is that God calls certain people to th ministry.

78. *with:* in the King James version.

79. Prynne, *A Gospel Plea,* p. 32, had urged the cost of a library as one rea son for public support of the ministry, though he did not name any specifi sum. *A Resolution of a Doubt* also argues its necessity for a minister and place its value at £600.

80. *only, by the scripture and . . . :* 1659.

81. Milton generally is hostile to any church developments after the Counc of Nicaea (325).

82. A phrase used several times in 1 Samuel and Psalms, generally meanin to rise in power.

83. The power of the church grew steadily after the benefactions of Con stantine, permitting it increasing dominance.

84. Hostile relations with Scotland reached their climax at the Battle o Worcester (September 3, 1651), when Charles II, supported by the Scottis Presbyterians, was decisively beaten by Cromwell. But minor royalist insurrec tions continued in Scotland, especially in the summer of 1653, when the meet ing of the Presbyterian General Assembly in Edinburgh was forcibly dispersed

85. *religion are:* 1659.

THE READIE AND EASIE WAY TO ESTABLISH A FREE COMMONWEALTH; AND THE EXCELLENCE THEROF COMPAR'D WITH THE INCONVENIENCIES AND DANGERS OF READMITTING KINGSHIP IN THIS NATION.

The second edition revis'd and augmented.

FOREWORD

With accounts of: Milton's *Letter to a Friend, Concerning the Ruptures of the Commonwealth* (October 20, 1659); "*Proposalls of Certaine Expedients for the Preventing of a Civill War Now Feard, and the Settling of a Firme Government by J. M.*" (Columbia Manuscript, written Oct.–Dec. 1659); *The Present Means, and Brief Delineation of a Free Commonwealth, Easy to Be Put into Practice, and Without Delay. In a Letter to General Monk* (March 1660, first published by Toland in 1698); and *Brief Notes upon a Late Sermon* (April 1660).

Milton's changing political proposals and allegiances in his eight tracts of 1659–60 reveal his readiness to support the institutions and the men in power at the time each tract was written, on the apparent assumption that some commonwealth government, however imperfect, must be firmly settled if a Stuart restoration were to be averted. In *A Treatise of Civil Power* (February 1659), Milton's dissatisfaction with the Protectorean government may be inferred from the absence of any allusion to the Protector Richard Cromwell, especially if this omission is viewed in the light of Milton's warm endorsement of Oliver Cromwell as Protector in the *Second Defense*

(1654; see the translation by John R. Mulder pp. 409–28), and in the light of his harsh denunciation in *Considerations Touching the Likeliest Means to Remove Hirelings* (August 1659) of all or part of the Protectorate period as a "short but scandalous night of interruption" in the nation's "peace and safety." However, Richard Cromwell seemed firmly entrenched at the time when *A Treatise of Civil Power* was written, and Milton silently acquiesced to that apparently stable government.

Considerations Touching the Likeliest Means appeared three months after an army coup had overthrown the Protectorate and restored the Rump Parliament (the part of the Long Parliament which was left sitting after Pride's Purge of 1648 and which had itself been dismissed from power by Oliver Cromwell in 1653); in May 1659 the restored Rump was barely fifty members strong. In his *Second Defense* Milton had denounced the Rump Commonwealthsmen as sinful, self-seeking, and arbitrary, and had applauded Oliver's turning them out; now, affected by and lending his support to the upsurge of republican sentiment in mid-1659, he hailed the restored Rump as the "*authors, assertors and now recoverers of our libertie.*"

Milton's *Letter to a Friend, Concerning the Ruptures of the Commonwealth* (October 20, 1659) was addressed to a new political crisis, the new deposition of the Rump on October 12 by the Wallingford-House Army faction led by Generals Lambert and Desborough. Milton vigorously denounced the "ambition" of the officers and declared that the best settlement would be the return of the Rump with Parliament and army swearing oaths of mutual protection to each other; however, he also recognized some justification for the army's action in the Rump's failure to guarantee religious liberty, and he argued realistically that acceptance of the *fait accompli* was necessary to the very survival of the Puritan cause, since the army "only now have the Power." Accordingly, he proposed the formation and perpetuation of a single-chamber legislature composed of army officers and as many members of the Rump as the army would admit: this was exactly the composition of the army interim government, the Committee of Safety, installed two days after the tract's assigned date, and the resemblance seems to argue Milton's intimate knowledge of the army's intentions. He also proposed formation of local community committees to guard against oligarchy.

The next, perhaps unpublished, tract, *Proposalls of Certaine Expedients for the Preventing of a Civill War Now Feard* (*Columbia Milton,* XVIII, 3–7) must have been written between October 22, when the Committee of Safety was instituted, and December 26, when the Rump was restored for the third time; in it Milton completely withdrew his support for the army government and called unequivocally for the return and perpetuation of the Rump. This tract shows Milton adding his voice to the vehement clamor for restoration of the Rump coming forth from all sides during November and December 1659—from the city of London, from countless popular petitions, and especially from General George Monk, commander in chief of the army in Scotland, who was marching to London with his army to support the Rump's claims.

The first edition of Milton's *Readie and Easie Way to Establish a Free Commonwealth* is dated by Thomason March 3, 1660, though as J. Milton French points out[1] there is some evidence for publication in February. The tract contains two specific proposals. One of them, presented in the body of the pamphlet, was evidently formulated between February 4, 1660, when the Rump sent out writs providing for carefully controlled elections to fill up its numbers, and February 21, when the members of the Long Parliament secluded in Pride's Purge were brought back to sit in parliament by General Monk. This basic plan called for augmentation of the Rump through elections strictly limited to the well-affected, and then for perpetuating that legislature as a Supreme Council; certain judiciary and educational functions were to be reserved to local committees of the "nobilitie and chief gentry," providing thereby some scope for local self-government. But the introduction to the tract, added after the restoration of the secluded members, contained a second proposal. The suggestion that the Parliament "now sitting more full and frequent" might make an even better perpetual Senate than the Rump, and the studied omission of any reference to the already voted resolution for calling a new parliament, serve as an invitation to the Long Parliament then sitting to perpetuate itself; interestingly enough Milton made this proposal despite the fact that he had probably already composed his scathing "Character of the Long Parliament," later added to his *History of Britain.*

Milton's open letter to Monk, *The Present Means, and Brief De-*

[1] *Life Records of John Milton,* 5 vols. (New Brunswick, 1949–58), IV, 300.

lineation of a Free Commonwealth, was probably written at the en of March. On March 16, Monk forced the retirement of the Lon Parliament, thus putting an end to its abortive efforts to impos conditions for the king's return and setting the election machiner in motion for the new "full and free" parliament which the populac was demanding with increasing vehemence; it was the general con sensus that the laws excluding Royalists from voting for or sitting i the new parliament would not be enforced. In these circumstances Milton's *Letter* proposed that the coming new parliament be made perpetual council, and, echoing the addresses which several othe republican polemicists were making to Monk at this time, it im plored Monk to save the Commonwealth by enforcing the royalis exclusion provisions.

Brief Notes upon a Late Sermon was Milton's answer to Dr. Mat thew Griffith's vehemently royalist sermon of March 25, *The Fea of God and the King;* in it Milton reluctantly conceded that th people's debased state might require a temporary king or pro tector, chosen from among their own deserving statesmen for "th space of a raign or two," and intimated that Monk, "the General wh hath so eminently born his part in the whole action," might cas himself in this role. Milton's suggestions resemble the proposals fo a Monk Protectorate urged by Thomas Scot, Arthur Haslerigg, and other republican leaders in supposedly secret meetings with Monk during March;[2] these parallel appeals to Monk's personal ambition and this common readiness to sacrifice republican principles in a last desperate move to save the Puritan cause further exhibit Milton's closeness to the sources of power and strategy in republican-radical circles in 1659–60.

The second edition of the *Readie and Easie Way* was probably published after April 20, only a few days before the return of Charles on May 1. It was virtually the last piece of Puritan polemic published during the Interregnum and evidently at that moment no printer or bookseller wished to associate himself with such a work, so it came forth with the simple designation, "Printed for the author." In late April there was widespread suspicion, though no certain proof, that Monk was in negotiation with Charles; the new elections were leaning, as expected, to the Cavalier interest; the pamphlet writers were heaping ridicule upon all the Puritan parlia-

[2] See Sir Richard Baker, *Chronicle of the Kings of England* (London, 1684), p. 639.

mentary and army leaders, often placing Milton prominently among them; and the Royalists were effectively winning Presbyterian cooperation in their restoration plans by extending to them rather hollow promises of forgiveness and of a liberal settlement of religious differences.[3] The now desperate republican-radical coalition endeavored to provoke an army uprising by publishing inflammatory tracts warning the soldiers to expect loss of pay, severe punishment, and repression of free religious expression if Charles returned, but soon the republican leaders abandoned this effort and began to campaign for seats in the parliament that was to convene on April 25. The last blow for the Good Old Cause was Lambert's short-lived revolt (April 10–22) supported in large part by the self-styled "Saints" of the Fifth Monarchy. Milton's revised and enlarged tract again supported the only conceivable prospects for maintaining Puritan control in the given circumstances. On the one hand, he proposed to perpetuate the parliament now being elected, undertaking to win support for this expedient from the parliamentary Presbyterians and the army by painting for them a grim picture of the vicious retaliation, thwarted self-interest, religious persecution, and moral degeneracy which would accompany restoration of the monarchy; he also sought support from other republicans, notably the Harringtonian faction, by indicating, albeit reluctantly, his willingness to accommodate some of their proposals. On the other hand, he supported Lambert's uprising by adding to his tract passages justifying and encouraging the use of force by a minority to impose its will upon a degenerate majority when the issue is the preservation of liberty for all.

Milton's prospectus for a free commonwealth in the much enlarged second edition of the *Readie and Easie Way* has often been regarded as a utopian plan, an "exotic model," not unlike those gently ridiculed in the tract itself. And indeed some of the details of the plan, and some of the arguments supporting it, are derived from a wide spectrum of ancient and modern political theories and models of government. But the major provisos, the fundamental terms, of Milton's plan are geared directly to the immediate political situation in England in March and April 1660 and constitute, as the title precisely states, a ready and easy way to deal with pres-

[3] See R. S. Bosher, *The Making of the Restoration Settlement* (London, 1951), pp. 130–38.

ent emergencies. The tract's substance and tone are therefore at the farthest possible remove from utopianism.

Various ancient and modern commonwealth constitutions are cited in Milton's tract as sources for some details of his plan. However, Milton did not treat these authorities as models for his proposed commonwealth, but rather found precedents in them for something like the perpetual aristocratic supreme council which he saw as the best recourse in the given national emergency. As notable ancient examples of perpetual councils Milton mentioned the Jewish Sanhedrin, the Athenian Areopagus, the Spartan Ephori, and the Roman Senate. On the contemporary scene he examined at some length the functions of such an institution in the constitutions of Venice and the United Provinces of the Netherlands.

The constitution of Venice had supposedly remained unchanged for thirteen centuries and it was often designated in the seventeenth century as the supreme example of a mixed polity in which an aristocracy of wisdom and virtue held predominant power.[4] Milton repudiated in his commonwealth plan even a chief magistrate as constitutionally controlled as the Venetian Doge, and he could find no useful precedent in the rotating Venetian Senate which held the fundamental legislative powers such as the determination of war and peace and the control of taxation. But he did cite as a precedent for his senate the Venetian Grand Council, a permanent body comprised of all the male citizens whose functions were to ratify the laws passed by the Senate, and to elect the doge, the senators, and other magistrates by an elaborate balloting procedure which progressively screened electors and candidates.

The United Provinces were generally regarded as a spectacularly successful example of commonwealth government: after throwing off Spanish domination the Dutch had developed the finest army and fleet in Europe and had amassed great wealth through commerce and manufacturing. Milton regarded their republican constitution as one source of their greatness, but again he repudiated the "monarchical" element in it—the almost dictatorial power which William of Orange and his descendants were given or assumed in times of national emergency by being elected statholders (chief magistrates) of several provinces at once and also captains general of the armed forces of the Union. The States-General, a rotating

[4] See Zera S. Fink, *The Classical Republicans* (Evanston, 1945), pp. 28–51.

council comprised of delegates from the provinces whose duties were to determine matters of finance, defense, foreign affairs and other common concerns, also offered little to Milton's purpose beyond a negative illustration of the need to settle the sovereign power firmly in the national council; in the United Provinces the policies voted by the States-General were subject to the referendum of the provincial legislatures (the States), any one of which could repudiate or withdraw from the action voted. However, the provincial States were an important source for Milton's proposal of strong local government organizations with important judicial and educational functions and perhaps a right of referendum on legislation. He found another such source in the self-perpetuating, permanent municipal corporations of the United Provinces, which were composed of the chief families of the cities and which had considerable local powers and the right to choose the delegates to the provincial States and the States-General.

Milton's plan also owes something to Harrington's model commonwealth proposed initially in his *Oceana* (London, 1656) and reiterated in 1659–60 in various tracts set forth by his followers in the Rota Club. Harrington provided for a dual magistracy imitating the Roman consular system, and for a popularly elected bicameral parliament in which a specially qualified Senate of 300 would propose and debate matters and a "Prerogative Tribe" of 1050, representing the people, would vote upon them without debate. Because Harrington firmly believed that the right institutions would obviate all trouble and dissension, he did not seek to limit suffrage to the well-affected, but planned rather to establish certain mechanical safeguards which would promote stability by preventing the causes of disunity—the disproportionate acquisition and use of wealth and power by some one class or group or individual in society. The safeguards were an agrarian law abolishing primogeniture and setting limits on land accumulation, a scheme of rotation in which one third of the parliament would change annually, and an elaborate Venetian system of ballots for refining the choice of electors and candidates. Milton viewed Harrington's plan as a rival to his own and earnestly argued the greater simplicity and safety of his own proposal. He demured especially to Harrington's principle of rotation but nevertheless indicated his willingness to see it used if this were judged desirable by others, for he evidently felt that, at this juncture of affairs, republicans of all sorts ought to make common cause.

What has been said regarding Milton's proposals, at various times, to perpetuate legislatures with which he was quite disenchanted, and what has been shown regarding the very considerable difference between the local, or advisory, or otherwise restricted perpetual councils which Milton cites as precedents and his own sovereign national senate, suggest that Milton was not really devoted in principle to a perpetual legislature. Rather, in calling for a perpetual council at this time he probably meant little more than the continuation of the government in power until settlement could be assured and the threat of the king's return could be dispelled. The earnest argument and citation of authority supporting the transformation of an existing "well-affected" parliament into a perpetual council is no doubt simply Milton's expedient to quell the constant agitation for a "full and free" (i.e., unrestricted) parliament which would be certain to restore the king. If the settlement which Milton advocated had been brought to pass, and if the danger of restoration had been eliminated, Milton would almost certainly have been among the first to present proposals for a liberalized constitution. Even in this tract he provided that the popular militia or army might overthrow the "perpetual" senate should they prove tyrannical or recalcitrant.

Milton's tract, then, deserves its title: it proposes no new institutions or complicated machinery, only the stabilization of the status quo as a ready and easy way to settle the government. However, he does not deceive himself that he can convince his countrymen on this issue. His clear-sighted despair, coupled with a forlorn hope that God might yet produce a miracle, is evident in his forthright support of Lambert's effort to thwart majority will by minority force, in his violent denunciations of those degenerates who would turn their faces from the Promised Land to return again to Egyptian slavery, in the poignant pleas of the opening passage calling for a little "Shroving-time" before the long "Lent of Servitude" in which to take leave of liberty, and in the emotion-fraught images of the peroration in which Milton imagines himself, like Jeremiah, speaking to the stones and trees what his degenerate countrymen will not hear—the "last words of our expiring liberty."

The copy text is a photostat of the Widener Library copy of the second edition of *Readie and Easie Way*. E. M. Clark (*Ready and Easy Way,* New Haven, 1915) and also editors who have included this tract in collections of Milton's works have taken the Widener copy of *REW* to be the only surviving copy of the second edition. I have, however, discovered another in the Bibliothèque Nationale [Nc 8° 1132], and have collated the two; there are no differences. In the present text, Milton's characteristic *then* has been changed to *than* where appropriate, abbreviations have been expanded, and a few printer's errors have been silently corrected. A full record of the numerous variants between the first and second editions is included in the *Columbia Milton,* VI, 359–67, and also in Clark's scholarly edition of this tract.

The readie and easie way to establish a free COMMONWEALTH; *and the excellence therof compar'd with the inconveniencies and dangers of readmitting Kingship in this Nation.* The second edition revis'd and augmented.

. . . . *et nos*
consilium dedimus Syllae, *demus populo nunc.*[1]

Although since the writing of this treatise, the face of things hath had som change, writs for new elections have bin recall'd, and the members at first chosen, readmitted from exclusion, yet not a little rejoicing to hear declar'd the resolution of those who are in power, tending to the establishment of a free Commonwealth,[2] and to remove, if it be possible, this [4] noxious humor of returning to bondage, instilld of late by som deceivers,[3] and nourishd from bad principles and fals apprehensions among too many of the people, I thought best not to suppress what I had written, hoping that it may now be of much more use and concernment to be freely publishd, in the midst of our Elections to a free Parlament, or their sitting to consider freely of the Government; whom it behoves to have all things represented to them that may direct thir judgment therin; and I never read of any State, scarce of any tyrant grown so incurable, as to refuse counsel from [5] any in a time of public deliberation; much less to be offended. If thir absolute determination be to enthrall us, before so long a Lent of Servitude, they may permitt us a little Shroving-time first,[4] wherin to speak freely, and take our leaves of Libertie. And because in the former edition through haste, many faults escap'd, and many books were suddenly dispersd, ere the note to mend them could be sent, I took the opportunitie from this occasion to revise and somwhat to enlarge the whole discourse, especially that part which argues for a perpetual Senat. The treatise thus revis'd and enlarg'd, is as follows. [6]

The Parliament of *England,* assisted by a great number of the people[5] who appeerd and stuck to them faithfullest in defence of religion and thir civil liberties, judging kingship by long experience a government unnecessarie, burdensom and dangerous,[6] justly and magnanimously abolishd it; turning regal bondage into a free Commonwealth, to the admiration and terrour of our emulous neighbours. They took themselves not bound by the light of nature or religion, to any former covnant,[7] from which the King himself by many forfeitures of a latter date or discoverie, and our [7] own longer consideration theron had more and more unbound us, both to himself and his posteritie; as hath bin ever the justice and the prudence of all wise nations that have ejected tyrannie. They covnanted *to preserve the Kings person and autoritie in the preservation of the true religion and our liberties;* not in his endeavoring to bring in upon our consciences a Popish religion, upon our liberties thraldom, upon our lives destruction, by his occasioning, if not complotting, as was after discoverd, the *Irish* massacre,[8] his fomenting and arming the rebellion, his covert leaguing with the rebels against us, his refusing more [8] than seaven times, propositions most just and necessarie to the true religion and our liberties, tenderd him by the Parlament both of *England* and *Scotland.*[9] They made not thir covnant concerning him with no difference between a king and a god, or promisd him as *Job* did to the Almightie, *to trust in him, though he slay us:*[10] they understood that the solemn ingagement,[11] wherin we all forswore kingship, was no more a breach of the covnant, than the covnant was of the protestation[12] before, but a faithful and prudent going on both in the words, well weighd, and in the true sense of the covnant, *without respect* [9] *of persons,*[13] when we could not serve two contrary maisters, God and the king, or the king and that more supreme law, sworn in the first place to maintain, our safetie and our libertie. They knew the people of *England* to be a free people, themselves the representers of that freedom; and although many were excluded, and as many fled (so they pretended) from tumults to *Oxford,* yet they were left a sufficient number to act in Parlament;[14] therefor not bound by any statute of preceding Parlaments, but by the law of nature only, which is the only law of laws truly and properly to all mankinde fundamental; the beginning and [10] the end of all Government;[15] to which no Parlament or people that will throughly reforme, but

Popish religion: episcopacy.

may and must have recourse; as they had and must yet have in church reformation (if they throughly intend it) to evangelic rules; not to ecclesiastical canons, though never so ancient, so ratifi'd and establishd in the land by Statutes, which for the most part are meer positive laws, neither natural nor moral, and so by any Parlament for just and serious considerations, without scruple to be at any time repeal'd. If others of thir number, in these things were under force,[16] they were not, but under free conscience; if others were [11] excluded by a power which they could not resist, they were not therefore to leave the helm of government in no hands, to discontinue thir care of the public peace and safetie, to desert the people in anarchie and confusion; no more than when so many of thir members left them, as made up in outward formalitie a more legal Parlament of three estates against them.[17] The best affected also and best principl'd of the people, stood not numbring or computing on which side were most voices in Parlament, but on which side appeerd to them most reason, most safetie, when the house divided upon [12] main matters: what was well motiond and advis'd, they examind not whether fear or perswasion carried it in the vote; neither did they measure votes and counsels by the intentions of them that voted; knowing that intentions either are but guessd at, or not soon anough known; and although good, can neither make the deed such, nor prevent the consequence from being bad: suppose bad intentions in things otherwise welldon; what was welldon, was by them who so thought, not the less obey'd or followd in the state; since in the church, who had not rather follow *Iscariot* or *Simon* the magician, [13] though to covetous ends, preaching, than *Saul*, though in the uprightness of his heart persecuting the gospell?[18] Safer they therefor judgd what they thought the better counsels, though carried on by some perhaps to bad ends, than the wors, by others, though endevord with best intentions: and yet they were not to learn that a greater number might be corrupt within the walls of a Parlament as well as of a citie;[19] wherof in matters of neerest concernment all men will be judges; nor easily permitt, that the odds of voices in thir greatest councel, shall more endanger them by corrupt or credulous votes, than [14] the odds of enemies by open assaults; judging that most voices ought not alwaies to prevail where main matters are in question; if others hence will pretend to disturb all counsels, what is that to them who pretend not, but are in real danger; not they only so judging, but a great though not the greatest, number of thir chosen Patriots, who might

best affected: republican term for the adherents of Parliament against the king.

be more in waight, than the others in number; there being in number little vertue, but by weight and measure wisdom working all things: and the dangers on either side they seriously thus waighd: from the treatie,[20] short fruits of long labours and seaven [15] years warr; securitie for twenty years, if we can hold it; reformation in the church for three years: then put to shift again with our vanquishd maister. His justice, his honour, his conscience declar'd quite contrarie to ours; which would have furnishd him with many such evasions, as in a book entitl'd *an inquisition for blood,*[21] soon after were not conceald: bishops not totally remov'd, but left as it were in ambush, a reserve, with ordination in thir sole power; thir lands alreadie sold, not to be alienated, but rented, and the sale of them call'd *sacrilege;*[22] delinquents few of many brought to condigne punish-[16]ment; accessories punishd;[23] the chief author, above pardon, though after utmost resistance, vanquish'd; not to give, but to receive laws; yet besought, treated with, and to be thankd for his gratious concessions, to be honourd, worshipd, glorifi'd. If this we swore to do, with what righteousness in the sight of God, with what assurance that we bring not by such an oath the whole sea of bloodguiltiness upon our own heads?[24] If on the other side we preferr a free government, though for the present not obtaind, yet all those suggested fears and difficulties, as the event will prove, easily [17] overcome, we remain finally secure from the exasperated regal power, and out of snares; shall retain the best part of our libertie, which is our religion, and the civil part will be from these who deferr us, much more easily recoverd, being neither so suttle nor so awefull as a King reinthron'd. Nor were thir actions less both at home and abroad than might become the hopes of a glorious rising Commonwealth:[25] nor were the expressions both of armie and people, whether in thir publick declarations or several writings other than such as testifi'd a spirit in this nation no less noble and well fitted to the liberty of a Com-[18]monwealth, than in the ancient *Greeks* or *Romans*. Nor was the heroic cause unsuccessfully defended to all Christendom against the tongue of a famous and thought invincible adversarie; nor the constancie and fortitude that so nobly vindicated our liberty, our victory at once against two the most prevailing usurpers over mankinde, superstition and tyrannie unpraisd or uncelebrated in a written monument,[26] likely to outlive detraction, as it hath hitherto convinc'd or silenc'd not a few of our detractors, especially in parts abroad. After our liberty and religion thus prosperously fought for, gaind [19] and many years possessd, except in those unhappie interruptions,[27] which God hath remov'd, now that nothing remains, but in all reason the certain hopes of a speedie and immediat settlement for ever in a firm and free Commonwealth, for this extolld and magnifi'd nation, regardless both of honour wonn or deliverances voutsaf't from heaven, to fall back or rather to creep back so poorly as it seems the multitude would to thir once abjur'd and detested thraldom of Kingship, to be our selves the slanderers of our own just and religious deeds, though don by som to covetous and ambitious ends, [20] yet not therefor to be staind with their infamie, or they to asperse the integritie of others, and yet these now by revolting from the conscience of deeds welldon both in church and state, to throw away and forsake, or rather to betray a just and noble cause for the mixture of bad men who have ill manag'd and abus'd it (which had our fathers don heretofore, and on the same pretence deserted true religion, what had long ere this become of our gospel and all protestant reformation so much intermixt with the avarice and ambition of som reformers?) and by thus relapsing, to verifie all the [21] bitter predictions of our triumphing enemies, who will now think they wisely discernd and justly censur'd both us and all our actions as rash, rebellious, hypocritical and impious, not only argues a strange degenerate contagion suddenly spread among us fitted and prepar'd for new slaverie, but will render us a scorn and derision to all our neighbours. And what will they at best say of us and of the whole *English* name, but scoffingly as of that foolish builder, mentiond by our Saviour,[28] who began to build a tower, and was not able to finish it. Where is this goodly tower of a Commonwealth, which the English boasted [22] they would build to overshadow kings, and be another *Rome* in the west?[29] The foundation indeed they laid gallantly; but fell into a wors confusion, not of tongues, but of factions, than those at the tower of *Babel;* and have left no memorial of thir work behinde them remaining, but in the common laughter of *Europ*. Which must needs redound the more to our shame, if we but look on our neighbours the United Provinces, to us inferior in all outward advantages; who notwithstanding, in the midst of greater difficulties, courageously, wisely, constantly went through with the same work, [23] and are setl'd in all the happie enjoiments of a potent and flourishing Republic to this day.

Besides this, if we returne to Kingship, and soon repent, as undoubtedly we shall, when we begin to finde the old encroachments coming on by little and little upon our consciences, which must necessarily proceed from king and bishop united inseparably in one interest, we may be forc'd perhaps to fight over again all that we have fought, and spend over again all that we have spent, but are never like to attain thus far as we are now advanc'd to the recoverie of our freedom, never to have [24] it in possession as we now have it, never to be voutsaf't heerafter the like mercies and signal assistances from heaven in our cause, if by our ingratefull backsliding we make these fruitless; flying now to regal concessions from his divine condescensions and gratious answers to our once importuning praiers against the tyrannie which we then groand under: making vain and viler than dirt the blood of so many thousand faithfull and valiant *English* men, who left us in this libertie, bought with thir lives; losing by a strange after game of folly, all the battels we have wonn, together with all *Scotland* as to our conquest, [25] hereby lost, which never any of our kings could conquer,[30] all the treasure we have spent, not that corruptible treasure only, but that far more precious of all our late miraculous deliverances; treading back again with lost labour all our happie steps in the progress of reformation; and most pittifully depriving our selves the instant fruition of that free government which we have so dearly purchasd, a free Commonwealth, not only held by wisest men in all ages[31] the noblest, the manliest, the equallest, the justest government, the most agreeable to all due libertie and proportiond equalitie, both human, civil, and [26] Christian, most cherishing to vertue and true religion, but also (I may say it with greatest probabilitie) planely commended, or rather enjoind by our Saviour himself, to all Christians, not without remarkable disallowance, and the brand of *gentilism* upon kingship. God in much displeasure gave a king to the *Israelites*, and imputed it a sin to them that they sought one:[32] but *Christ* apparently forbids his disciples to admitt of any such heathenish government: *the kings of the gentiles,* saith he, *exercise lordship over them;* and they that *exercise authoritie upon them, are call'd benefactors: but ye shall not be so; but he that* [27] *is greatest among you, let him be as the younger; and he that is chief, as he that serveth.*[33] The occasion of these his words was the ambitious desire of *Zebede's* two sons, to be exalted above thir brethren in his kingdom, which they thought was to be ere long upon earth. That he speaks of civil government, is manifest by the former part of the comparison, which inferrs the other part to be alwaies in the same kinde. And what government coms neerer to this precept of Christ, than a free Commonwealth; wherin they who are greatest, are perpetual servants and drudges to the public at thir own cost and [28] charges, neglect thir own affairs; yet are not elevated above thir brethren; live soberly in thir families, walk the streets as other men, may be spoken to freely, familiarly, friendly, without adoration. Wheras a king must be ador'd like a Demigod, with a dissolute and haughtie court about him, of vast expence and luxurie, masks and revels, to the debaushing of our prime gentry both male and female; not in thir passetimes only, but in earnest, by the loos imploiments of court service, which will be then thought honorable. There will be a queen also of no less charge; in most likelihood outlandish [29] and a Papist; besides a queen mother such alreadie;[34] together with both thir courts and numerous train: then a royal issue, and ere long severally thir sumptuous courts; to the multiplying of a servile crew, not of servants only, but of nobility and gentry, bred up then to the hopes not of public, but of court offices; to be stewards, chamberlains, ushers, grooms, even of the close-stool;[35] and the lower thir mindes debas'd with court opinions, contrarie to all vertue and reformation, the haughtier will be thir pride and profuseness: we may well remember this not long since at home; or need but [30] look at present into the *French* court, where enticements and preferments daily draw away and pervert the Protestant Nobilitie. As to the burden of expence, to our cost we shall soon know it; for any good to us, deserving to be termd no better than the vast and lavish price of our subjection and their debausherie; which we are now so greedily cheapning, and would so fain be paying most inconsideratly to a single person; who for any thing wherin the public really needs him, will have little els to do, but to bestow the eating and drinking of excessive dainties, to set a pompous [31] face upon the superficial actings of State, to pageant himself up and down in progress among the perpetual bowings and cringings of an abject people, on either side deifying and adoring him for nothing don that can deserve it. For what can hee more than another man? who even in the expression of a late court-poet, sits only like a great cypher set to no purpose before a long row of other significant figures.[36] Nay it is well and happy for the people if thir King be but a cypher, being oft times a mischief, a pest, a scourge of the nation, and which is wors, not to be remov'd, not [32] to be controul'd, much less accus'd or brought to punishment, without the danger of a common ruin, without the shaking and almost subversion of the whole land. Wheras in a free Commonwealth, any governor or chief counselor offending, may be remov'd and punishd without the least commotion. Certainly then that people must needs be madd or strangely infatuated, that build the chief hope of thir common happiness or safetie on a single person: who if he happen to be good, can do no more than another man, if to be bad, hath in his hands to do more evil without check, than millions of other [33] men. The happiness of a nation

cheapning: bargaining about.
single person: republican term for a king or a protector.

must needs be firmest and certainest in a full and free Councel of thir own electing, where no single person, but reason only swaies. And what madness is it, for them who might manage nobly thir own affairs themselves, sluggishly and weakly to devolve all on a single person; and more like boyes under age than men, to committ all to his patronage and disposal, who neither can performe what he undertakes, and yet for undertaking it, though royally paid, will not be thir servant, but thir lord? how unmanly must it needs be, to count such [34] a one the breath of our nostrils, to hang all our felicity on him, all our safetie, our well-being, for which if we were aught els but sluggards or babies, we need depend on none but God and our own counsels, our own active vertue and industrie; *Go to the Ant, thou sluggard,* saith *Solomon; consider her waies, and be wise; which having no prince, ruler, or lord, provides her meat in the summer, and gathers her food in the harvest.*[37] which evidently shews us, that they who think the nation undon without a king, though they look grave or haughtie, have not so much true spirit and understanding in them [35] as a pismire: neither are these diligent creatures hence concluded to live in lawless anarchie, or that commended, but are set the examples to imprudent and ungovernd men, of a frugal and self-governing democratie or Commonwealth; safer and more thriving in the joint providence and counsel of many industrious equals, than under the single domination of one imperious Lord. It may be well wonderd that any Nation styling themselves free, can suffer any man to pretend hereditarie right over them as thir lord; when as by acknowledging that right, they conclude themselves his [36] servants and his vassals, and so renounce thir own freedom. Which how a people and thir leaders especially can do, who have fought so gloriously for liberty, how they can change thir noble words and actions, heretofore so becoming the majesty of a free people, into the base necessitie of court flatteries and prostrations, is not only strange and admirable, but lamentable to think on. That a nation should be so valorous and courageous to winn thir liberty in the field, and when they have wonn it, should be so heartless and unwise in thir counsels, as not to know how to use it, value it, what to do with it [37] or with themselves; but after ten or twelve years prosperous warr and contestation with tyrannie, basely and besottedly to run their necks again into the yoke which they have broken, and prostrate all the fruits of thir victorie for naught at the feet of the vanquishd, besides our loss of glorie, and such an example as kings or tyrants

admirable: astonishing.
heartless: lacking in courage.

never yet had the like to boast of, will be an ignomine if it befall us, that never yet befell any nation possessd of thir libertie; worthie indeed themselves, whatsoever they be, to be for ever slaves: but that part of the nation which consents not with them, as I perswade me [38] of a great number, far worthier than by their means to be brought into the same bondage. Considering these things so plane, so rational, I cannot but yet furder admire on the other side, how any man who hath the true principles of justice and religion in him, can presume or take upon him to be a king and lord over his brethren, whom he cannot but know whether as men or Christians, to be for the most part every way equal or superior to himself: how he can display with such vanitie and ostentation his regal splendor so supereminently above other mortal men; or being a Christian, can as-[39]sume such extraordinarie honour and worship to himself, while the kingdom of Christ our common King and Lord, is hid to this world, and such *gentilish* imitation forbid in express words by himself to all his disciples. All Protestants hold that Christ in his church hath left no vicegerent of his power, but himself without deputie, is the only head therof, governing it from heaven: how then can any Christian-man derive his kingship from Christ, but with wors usurpation than the Pope his headship over the church, since Christ not only hath not left the least shaddow of a command for any such vice-[40]gerence from him in the State, as the Pope pretends for his in the Church, but hath expressly declar'd, that such regal dominion is from the gentiles, not from him, and hath strictly charg'd us, not to imitate them therin.[38]

I doubt not but all ingenuous and knowing men will easily agree with me, that a free Commonwealth without single person or house of lords,[39] is by far the best government, if it can be had; but we have all this while say they bin expecting it, and cannot yet attain it. Tis true indeed, when monarchie was dissolvd, the form of a Commonwealth should have forthwith bin fram'd; and the [41] practice therof immediatly begun; that the people might have soon bin satisfi'd and delighted with the decent order, ease and benefit therof: we had bin then by this time firmly rooted past fear of commotions or mutations, and now flourishing: this care of timely setling a new government instead of ye old, too much neglected, hath bin our mischief. Yet the cause therof may be ascrib'd with most reason to the frequent disturbances, interruptions and dissolutions which the Parlament hath had partly from the impatient or disaffected people, partly from som ambitious leaders in the Armie;[40] much contrarie, I beleeve, to the mind and [42] approba-

expecting: waiting for.

tion of the Armie it self and thir other Commanders, once undeceivd, or in thir own power. Now is the opportunitie, now the very season wherein we may obtain a free Commonwealth and establish it for ever in the land, without difficulty or much delay. Writs are sent out for elections, and which is worth observing in the name, not of any king, but of the keepers of our libertie,[41] to summon a free Parlament: which then only will indeed be free, and deserve the true honor of that supreme title, if they preserve us a free people. Which never Parlament was more free to do; being now call'd, not as here-[43]tofore, by the summons of a king, but by the voice of libertie: and if the people, laying aside prejudice and impatience, will seriously and calmly now consider thir own good both religious and civil, thir own libertie and the only means thereof, as shall be heer laid before them, and will elect thir Knights and Burgesses[42] able men, and according to the just and necessarie qualifications (which for aught I hear, remain yet in force unrepeald, as they were formerly decreed in Parlament)[43] men not addicted to a single person or house of lords, the work is don; at least the foundation firmly laid of a free Common-[44]wealth, and good part also erected of the main structure. For the ground and basis of every just and free government (since men have smarted so oft for commiting all to one person) is a general councel of ablest men, chosen by the people to consult of public affairs from time to time for the common good. In this Grand Councel must the sovrantie, not transferrd, but delegated only, and as it were deposited, reside;[44] with this caution they must have the forces by sea and land committed to them for preservation of the common peace and libertie; must raise and manage the public revenue, at least with som in-[45]spectors deputed for satisfaction of the people, how it is imploid; must make or propose, as more expressly shall be said anon, civil laws; treat of commerce, peace, or warr with foreign nations, and for the carrying on som particular affairs with more secrecie and expedition, must elect, as they have alreadie out of thir own number and others, a Councel of State.[45]

And although it may seem strange at first hearing, by reason that mens mindes are prepossessd[46] with the notion of successive Parlaments, I affirme that the Grand or General Councel being well chosen, should be perpetual: for so [46] thir business is or may be, and oft times urgent; the opportunitie of affairs gaind or lost in a moment. The day of counsel cannot be set as the day of a festival; but must be readie alwaies to prevent or answer all occasions. By this continuance they will become everie way skilfullest, best provided of intelligence from abroad, best acquainted with the people at home, and the people with them. The ship of the Commonwealth is alwaies under sail; they sit at the stern; and if they stear well, what need is ther to change them; it being rather dangerous? Add to this, that the Grand Councel is both [47] foundation and main pillar of the whole State; and to move pillars and foundations, not faultie, cannot be safe for the building. I see not therefor, how we can be advantag'd by successive and transitorie Parlaments; but that they are much likelier continually to unsettle rather than to settle a free government;[47] to breed commotions, changes, novelties and uncertainties; to bring neglect upon present affairs and opportunities, while all mindes are suspense with expectation of a new assemblie, and the assemblie for a good space taken up with the new setling of it self. After which, if they finde no great work to do, [48] they will make it, by altering or repealing former acts, or making and multiplying new; that they may seem to see what thir predecessors saw not, and not to have assembld for nothing: till all law be lost in the multitude of clashing statutes. But if the ambition of such as think themselves injur'd that they also partake not of the government, and are impatient till they be chosen, cannot brook the perpetuitie of others chosen before them,[48] or if it be feard that long continuance of power may corrupt sincerest men, the known expedient is, and by som lately propounded,[49] that annually (or if the space be lon-[49]ger, so much perhaps the better) the third part of Senators may go out according to the precedence of thir election, and the like number be chosen in thir places, to prevent the setling of too absolute a power, if it should be perpetual: and this they call *partial rotation.* But I could wish that this wheel or partial wheel in State, if it be possible, might be avoided; as having too much affinitie with the wheel of fortune.[50] For it appeers not how this can be don, without danger and mischance of putting out a great number of the best and ablest: in whose stead new elections may bring in [50] as many raw, unexperienc'd and otherwise affected, to the weakning and much altering for the wors of public transactions. Neither do I think a perpetual Senat, especially chosen and entrusted by the people, much in this land to be feard, where the well-affected either in a standing armie, or in a setled militia have thir arms in thir own hands. Safest therefor to me it seems and of least hazard or interruption to affairs, that none of the Grand Councel be mov'd, unless by death or just conviction of som crime: for what can be expected firm or stedfast from a floating foundation? however, I forejudge [51] not any probable expedient, any temperament that can be found in things of this nature so disputable

suspense: suspended, in suspense.

on either side. Yet least this which I affirme, be thought my single opinion, I shall add sufficient testimonie. Kingship it self is therefor counted the more safe and durable,[51] because the king and, for the most part, his councel, is not chang'd during life: but a Commonwealth is held immortal; and therin firmest, safest and most above fortune: for the death of a king, causeth ofttimes many dangerous alterations; but the death now and then of a Senator is not felt; the main bodie of them still continuing perma-[52]nent in greatest and noblest Commonwealths, and as it were eternal. Therefor among the *Jews,* the supreme councel of seaventie, call'd the *Sanhedrim,* founded by *Moses,*[52] in *Athens,* that of *Areopagus,*[53] in *Sparta,* that of the Ancients,[54] in *Rome,* the Senat,[55] consisted of members chosen for term of life; and by that means remaind as it were still the same to generations. In *Venice* they change indeed ofter than every year som particular councels of State, as that of six, or such other; but the true Senat, which upholds and sustains the government, is the whole aristocracie immovable.[56] So in the United Provinces,[57] the [53] States General, which are indeed but a councel of state deputed by the whole union, are not usually the same persons for above three or six years; but the States of every citie, in whom the sovrantie hath bin plac'd time out of minde, are a standing Senat, without succession, and accounted chiefly in that regard the main prop of thir liberty. And why they should be so in every well orderd Commonwealth, they who write of policie, give these reasons; "That to make the Senat successive, not only impairs the dignitie and lustre of the Senat, but weakens the whole Commonwealth, and [54] brings it into manifest danger; while by this means the secrets of State are frequently divulgd, and matters of greatest consequence committed to inexpert and novice counselors, utterly to seek in the full and intimate knowledge of affairs past."[58] I know not therefor what should be peculiar in *England* to make successive Parlaments thought safest, or convenient here more than in other nations, unless it be the fickl'ness which is attributed to us as we are Ilanders:[59] but good education and acquisit wisdom ought to correct the fluxible fault, if any such be, of our watry situation. It [55] will be objected, that in those places where they had perpetual Senats, they had also popular remedies against thir growing too imperious: as in *Athens,* besides *Areopagus,* another Senat of four or five hunderd; in *Sparta,* the *Ephori;* in *Rome,* the Tribunes of the people.[60] But the event tels us, that these remedies either little availd the people, or brought them to such a licentious and unbridl'd democratie, as in fine ruind themselves with thir own excessive power. So that the main reason

acquisit: acquired.

urg'd why popular assemblies are to be trusted with the peoples libertie, rather than a Senat of principal men, because [56] great men will be still endeavoring to inlarge thir power, but the common sort will be contented to maintain thir own libertie, is by experience found false; none being more immoderat and ambitious to amplifie thir power, than such popularities; which was seen in the people of *Rome;* who at first contented to have thir Tribunes, at length contended with the Senat that one Consul, then both; soon after, that the Censors and Praetors also should be created Plebeian, and the whole empire put into their hands; adoring lastly those, who most were advers to the Senat, till *Marius* by fulfilling thir inor-[57]dinat desires, quite lost them all the power for which they had so long bin striving, and left them under the tyrannie of *Sylla:*[61] the ballance therefor must be exactly so set, as to preserve and keep up due autoritie on either side, as well in the Senat as in the people. And this annual rotation of a Senat to consist of three hunderd, as is lately propounded,[62] requires also another popular assembly upward of a thousand, with an answerable rotation. Which besides that it will be liable to all those inconveniencies found in the foresaid remedies, cannot but be troublesom and chargeable, both in thir motion and thir session, to the whole land; unweildie with [58] thir own bulk, unable in so great a number to mature thir consultations as they ought, if any be allotted them, and that they meet not from so many parts remote to sit a whole year lieger in one place, only now and then to hold up a forrest of fingers, or to convey each man his bean or ballot into the box, without reason shewn or common deliberation;[63] incontinent of secrets, if any be imparted to them, emulous and always jarring with the other Senat. The much better way doubtless will be in this wavering condition of our affairs, to deferr the changing or circumscribing of our Senat, more than may be done with ease, [59] till the Commonwealth be throughly setl'd in peace and safetie, and they themselves give us the occasion. Militarie men hold it dangerous to change the form of battel in view of an enemie: neither did the people of *Rome* bandie with thir Senat while any of the *Tarquins* livd,[64] the enemies of thir libertie, nor sought by creating Tribunes to defend themselves against the fear of thir Patricians, till sixteen years after the expulsion of thir kings, and in full securitie of thir state, they had or thought they had just cause given them by the Senat. Another way will be, to welqualifie and refine elections: [60] not committing all to the noise and shouting of a rude multitude, but permitting only those of them who

thir motion: their journeying.
lieger: resident, stationary (obs. form of *ledger*).

are rightly qualifi'd, to nominat as many as they will; and out of that number others of a better breeding, to chuse a less number more judiciously, till after a third or fourth sifting and refining of exactest choice, they only be left chosen who are the due number, and seem by most voices the worthiest.[65] To make the people fittest to chuse, and the chosen fittest to govern, will be to mend our corrupt and faulty education, to teach the people faith not without vertue, temperance, modestie, sobrietie, parsi-[61]monie, justice; not to admire wealth or honour; to hate turbulence and ambition; to place every one his privat welfare and happiness in the public peace, libertie and safetie. They shall not then need to be much mistrustfull of thir chosen Patriots in the Grand Councel; who will be then rightly call'd the true keepers of our libertie, though the most of thir business will be in forein affairs. But to prevent all mistrust, the people then will have thir several ordinarie assemblies (which will henceforth quite annihilate the odious power and name of Committies)[66] in the chief towns of every countie, without the [62] trouble, charge, or time lost of summoning and assembling from far in so great a number, and so long residing from thir own houses, or removing of thir families, to do as much at home in thir several shires, entire or subdivided, toward the securing of thir libertie, as a numerous assembly of them all formd and conven'd on purpose with the wariest rotation. Wherof I shall speak more ere the end of this discourse: for it may be referrd to time, so we be still going on by degrees to perfection. The people well weighing and performing these things, I suppose would have no cause to fear, though the *Parlament*, [63] abolishing that name, as originally signifying but the *parlie* of our Lords and Commons with thir *Norman* king when he pleasd to call them,[67] should, with certain limitations of thir power, sit perpetual, if thir ends be faithfull and for a free Commonwealth, under the name of a Grand or General Councel. Till this be don, I am in doubt whether our State will be ever certainly and throughly setl'd; never likely till then to see an end of our troubles and continual changes or at least never the true settlement and assurance of our libertie. The Grand Councel being thus firmly constituted to perpetuitie, and still, upon [64] the death or default of any member, suppli'd and kept in full number, ther can be no cause alleag'd why peace, justice, plentifull trade and all prosperitie should not thereupon ensue throughout the whole land; with as much assurance as can be of human things, that they shall so continue (if God favour us, and our wilfull sins provoke him not) even to the coming of our true and rightfull and only to be expected King,[68] only worthie as he is our only Saviour, the Messiah, the Christ, the only heir of his eternal father, the only by him anointed and ordaind since the work of our redemption finishd, [65] Universal Lord of all mankinde. The way propounded is plane, easie and open before us; without intricacies, without the introducement of new or obsolete forms, or terms, or exotic models; idea's that would effect nothing, but with a number of new injunctions to manacle the native liberty of mankinde; turning all vertue into prescription, servitude, and necessitie, to the great impairing and frustrating of Christian libertie: I say again, this way lies free and smooth before us; is not tangl'd with inconveniencies; invents no new incumbrances; requires no perilous, no injurious alteration or circum-[66]scription of mens lands and proprieties; secure, that in this Commonwealth, temporal and spiritual lords remov'd,[69] no man or number of men can attain to such wealth or vast possession, as will need the hedge of an Agrarian law[70] (never successful, but the cause rather of sedition, save only where it began seasonably with first possession) to confine them from endangering our public libertie; to conclude, it can have no considerable objection made against it, that it is not practicable: least it be said hereafter, that we gave up our libertie for want of a readie way or distinct form propos'd of a free [67] Commonwealth. And this facilitie we shall have above our next neighbouring Commonwealth (if we can keep us from the fond conceit of somthing like a duke of *Venice*, put lately into many mens heads, by som one or other sutly driving on under that notion his own ambitious ends to lurch a crown)[71] that our liberty shall not be hamperd or hoverd over by any ingagement to such a potent familie as the house of *Nassaw*[72] of whom to stand in perpetual doubt and suspicion, but we shall live the cleerest and absolutest free nation in the world.

On the contrarie, if ther be a king, which the incon-[68]siderate multitude are now so madd upon, mark how far short we are like to com of all those happinesses, which in a free state we shall immediatly be possessd of. First, the Grand Councel, which, as I shewd before, should sit perpetually (unless thir leisure give them now and then some intermissions or vacations, easilie manageable by the Councel of State left sitting) shall be call'd, by the kings good will and utmost endeavor, as seldom as may be. For it is only the king's right, he will say, to call a parlament; and this he will do most commonly about his own affairs rather than the kingdom's, as will [69] appeer planely so soon as they are call'd. For what will thir business then be and the chief expence of thir time, but an endless tugging between petition of right and royal prerogative, especially about the negative voice, militia, or subsidies,[73] demanded and oft times extorted without reasonable cause appeering to the Commons, who are the only true representatives of the people, and thir libertie, but will be then mingl'd with a court-faction; besides which within thir own walls, the sincere part of them who stand faithfull to the people, will again have to deal with two troublesom counter-working [70] adversaries from without, meer creatures of the king, spiritual, and the greater part, as is likeliest, of temporal lords, nothing concernd with the peoples libertie. If these prevail not in what they please, though never so much against the peoples interest, the Parlament shall be soon dissolvd, or sit and do nothing; not sufferd to remedie the least greevance, or enact aught advantageous to the people. Next, the Councel of State shall not be chosen by the Parlament, but by the king, still his own creatures, courtiers and favorites; who will be sure in all thir counsels to set thir maister's grandure and absolute [71] power, in what they are able, far above the peoples libertie. I denie not but that ther may be such a king, who may regard the common good before his own, may have no vitious favorite, may hearken only to the wisest and incorruptest of his Parlament: but this rarely happens in a monarchie not elective; and it behoves not a wise nation to committ the summ of thir welbeing, the whole state of thir safetie to fortune. What need they; and how absurd would it be, when as they themselves to whom his chief vertue will be but to hearken, may with much better management and dispatch, with much more [72] commendation of thir own worth and magnanimitie govern without a maister. Can the folly be paralleld, to adore and be the slaves of a single person for doing that which it is ten thousand to one whether he can or will do, and we without him might do more easily, more effectually, more laudably our selves? Shall we never grow old anough to be wise to make seasonable use of gravest autorities, experiences, examples? Is it such an unspeakable joy to serve, such felicitie to weare a yoke? to clink our shackles, lockt on by pretended law of subjection more intolerable and hopeless to be ever shaken off, than [73] those which are knockt on by illegal injurie and violence? *Aristotle,* our chief instructor in the Universities, least this doctrine be thought *Sectarian,* as the royalist would have it thought, tels us in the third of his Politics,[74] that certain men at first, for the matchless excellence of thir vertue above others, or som great public benifit, were created kings by the people; in small cities and territories, and in the scarcitie of others to be found like them: but when they abus'd thir power and governments grew larger, and the number of prudent men increasd, that then the people soon deposing thir tyrants, betook them, in [74] all civilest places, to the form of a free Commonwealth. And why should we thus disparage and prejudicate our own nation, as to fear a scarcitie of able and worthie men united in counsel to govern us, if we will but use diligence and impartiality to finde them out and chuse them, rather yoking our selves to a single person, the natural adversarie and oppressor of libertie, though good, yet far easier corruptible by the excess of his singular power and exaltation, or at best, not comparably sufficient to bear the weight of government, nor equally dispos'd to make us happie in the enjoyment of our libertie under him. [75]

But admitt, that monarchie of it self may be convenient to som nations;[75] yet to us who have thrown it out, receivd back again, it cannot but prove pernicious. For kings to com, never forgetting thir former ejection, will be sure to fortifie and arm themselves sufficiently for the future against all such attempts hereafter from the people: who shall be then so narrowly watchd and kept so low, that though they would never so fain and at the same rate of thir blood and treasure, they never shall be able to regain what they now have purchasd and may enjoy, or to free themselves from any yoke impos'd [76] upon them: nor will they dare to go about it; utterly disheartn'd for the future, if these thir highest attempts prove unsuccesfull; which will be the triumph of all tyrants heerafter over any people that shall resist oppression; and thir song will then be, to others, how sped the rebellious *English*? to our posteritie, how sped the rebells your fathers? This is not my conjecture, but drawn from God's known denouncement against the gentilizing *Israelites;* who though they were governd in a Commonwealth of God's own ordaining, he only thir king, they his peculiar people, yet affecting rather to [77] resemble heathen, but pretending the misgovernment of *Samuel's* sons,[76] no more a reason to dislike thir Commonwealth, than the violence of *Eli's* sons[77] was imputable to that priesthood or religion, clamourd for a king. They had thir longing; but with this testimonie of God's wrath; *ye shall cry out in that day because of your king whom ye shall have chosen, and the Lord will not hear you in that day.*[78] Us if he shall hear now, how much less will he hear when we cry heerafter, who once deliverd by him from a king, and not without wondrous acts of his providence, insensible and unworthie of those high mercies, [78] are returning precipitantly, if he withold us not, back to the captivitie from whence he freed us. Yet neither shall we obtain or buy at an easie rate this new guilded yoke which thus transports us: a new royal-revenue must be found, a new episcopal; for those are individual: both which being wholy dissipated or bought by privat persons or assign'd for service don, and especially to the Armie, cannot be recoverd without a general detriment and confusion to mens estates,[79] or a heavie imposition on all mens purses; benifit to none, but to the worst and ignoblest sort of men, whose hope is to be either the mini-[79]sters of court riot and excess, or the gainers by it: But not to speak more of losses and extraordinarie levies on our estates, what will then be the revenges and offences rememberd and returnd, not only by the chief person, but by all his adherents; accounts and reparations that will be requir'd, suites, inditements, inquiries, discoveries, complaints, informations, who knows against whom or how many, though perhaps neuters, if not to utmost infliction, yet to imprisonment, fines, banishment, or molestation; if not these, yet disfavor, discountnance, disregard and contempt on all but [80] the known royalist or whom he favors, will be plenteous: nor let the new royaliz'd presbyterians perswade themselves that thir old doings, though now recanted, will be forgotten; what ever conditions be contriv'd or trusted on. Will they not beleeve this; nor remember the pacification, how it was kept to the *Scots;*[80] how other solemn promises many a time to us? Let them but now read the diabolical forerunning libells, the faces, the gestures that now appeer foremost and briskest in all public places; as the harbingers of those that are in expectation to raign over us; let them but hear the insolencies, the mena-[81]ces, the insultings of our newly animated common enemies crept lately out of thir holes, thir hell, I might say, by the language of thir infernal pamphlets,[81] the spue of every drunkard, every ribald; nameless, yet not for want of licence, but for very shame of thir own vile persons, not daring to name themselves, while they traduce others by name; and give us to foresee that they intend to second thir wicked words, if ever they have power, with more wicked deeds. Let our zealous backsliders forethink now with themselves, how thir necks yok'd with these tigers of Bacchus,[82] these new [82] fanatics of not the preaching but the sweating-tub,[83] inspir'd with nothing holier than the Venereal pox, can draw one way under monarchie to the establishing of church discipline with these new-disgorg'd atheismes: yet shall they not have the honor to yoke with these, but shall be yok'd under them; these shall plow on their backs. And do they among them who are so forward to bring in the single person, think to be by him trusted or long regarded? So trusted they shall be and so regarded, as by kings are wont reconcil'd enemies; neglected and soon after discarded, if not prosecuted for [83] old traytors; the first inciters, beginners, and more than to the third part actors of all that followd;[84] it will be found also, that there must be then as necessarily as now (for the contrarie part will be still feard) a standing armie; which for certain shall not be this, but of the fiercest

neuters: neutral persons in the war.

Cavaliers, of no less expence, and perhaps again under *Rupert:*[85] but let this armie be sure they shall be soon disbanded, and likeliest without arrear or pay; and being disbanded, not be sure but they may as soon be questiond for being in arms against thir king: the same let them fear, who have contributed monie; [84] which will amount to no small number that must then take thir turn to be made delinquents and compounders.[86] They who past reason and recoverie are devoted to kingship, perhaps will answer, that a greater part by far of the Nation will have it so; the rest therefor must yield. Not so much to convince these, which I little hope, as to confirm them who yield not,[87] I reply; that this greatest part[88] have both in reason and the trial of just battel, lost the right of their election what the government shall be: of them who have not lost that right, whether they for kingship be the greater number, [85] who can certainly determin?[89] Suppose they be; yet of freedom they partake all alike, one main end of government: which if the greater part value not, but will degeneratly forgoe, is it just or reasonable, that most voices against the main end of government should enslave the less number that would be free? More just it is doubtless, if it com to force, that a less number compell a greater to retain, which can be no wrong to them, thir libertie, than that a greater number for the pleasure of thir baseness, compell a less most injuriously to be thir fellow slaves. They who seek nothing but thir own just libertie, have [86] alwaies right to winn it and to keep it, when ever they have power, be the voices never so numerous that oppose it. And how much we above others are concernd to defend it from kingship, and from them who in pursuance therof so perniciously would betray us and themselves to most certain miserie and thraldom, will be needless to repeat.

Having thus far shewn with what ease we may now obtain a free Commonwealth, and by it with as much ease all the freedom, peace, justice, plentie that we can desire, on the other side the difficulties, troubles, uncertainties, nay rather impossibilities to enjoy these [87] things constantly under a monarch, I will now proceed to shew more particularly wherin our freedom and flourishing condition will be more ample and secure to us under a free Commonwealth than under kingship.

The whole freedom of man consists either in spiritual or civil libertie. As for spiritual, who can be at rest, who can enjoy any thing in this world with contentment, who hath not libertie to serve God and to save his own soul, according to the best light which God hath planted in him to that purpose, by the reading of his reveal'd will and the guidance of his [88] holy spirit? That this is best pleasing to God, and that the whole Protestant Church allows no supream judge or rule in matters of religion, but the scriptures, and these to be interpreted by the scriptures themselves, which necessarily inferrs liberty of conscience, I have heretofore prov'd at large in another treatise, and might yet furder by the public declarations, confessions, and admonitions of whole churches and states, obvious in all historie since the Reformation.

This liberty of conscience which above all other things ought to be to all men dearest and most precious, no government more inclinable not to favor only but to protect, than a free Commonwealth; as being most magnanimous, most fearless and confident of its own fair proceedings. Wheras kingship, though looking big, yet indeed most pusillanimous, full of fears, full of jealousies, startl'd at every ombrage, as it hath bin observd of old to have ever suspected most and mistrusted them who were in most esteem for vertue and generositie of minde, so it is now known to have most in doubt and suspicion them who are most reputed to be religious. Queen *Elizabeth* though her self accounted so good a Protestant, so moderate, so [90] confident of her Subjects love would never give way so much as to Presbyterian reformation in this land, though once and again besought, as *Camden* relates,[90] but imprisond and persecuted the very proposers therof; alleaging it as her minde and maxim unalterable, that such reformation would diminish regal autoritie. What liberty of conscience can we then expect of others, far wors principl'd from the cradle, traind up and governd by *Popish* and *Spanish* counsels, and on such depending hitherto for subsistence?[91] Especially what can this last Parlament expect, who having reviv'd lately and [91] publishd the covnant,[92] have reingag'd themselves, never to readmitt Episcopacie: which no son of *Charls* returning, but will most certainly bring back with him, if he regard the last and strictest charge of his father, *to persevere in not the doctrin only, but government of the church of* England; *not to neglect the speedie and effectual suppressing of errors and schisms;*[93] among which he accounted Presbyterie one of the chief: or if notwithstanding that charge of his father, he submitt to the covnant, how will he keep faith to us with disobedience to him; or regard that faith given, which must [92] be founded on the breach of that last and solemnest paternal charge, and the reluctance, I may say the antipathie which is in all kings against Presbyterian and Independent discipline? for they hear the gospel speaking much of libertie; a word which monarchie and her bishops both fear and hate, but a free

another treatise: Of Civil Power.
ombrage: shadow.

Commonwealth both favors and promotes; and not the word only, but the thing it self. But let our governors beware in time, least thir hard measure to libertie of conscience be found the rock wheron they shipwrack themselves as others have now don before them in the cours wherin God was di-[93]recting thir stearage to a free Commonwealth, and the abandoning of all those whom they call *sectaries,* for the detected falshood and ambition of som, be a wilfull rejection of thir own chief strength and interest in the freedom of all Protestant religion, under what abusive name soever calumniated.

The other part of our freedom consists in the civil rights and advancements of every person according to his merit: the enjoyment of those never more certain, and the access to these never more open, than in a free Commonwealth. Both which in my opinion may be best and soonest obtaind, if [94] every countie in the land were made a kinde of subordinate Commonaltie or Commonwealth, and one chief town or more, according as the shire is in circuit, made cities, if they be not so call'd alreadie; where the nobilitie and chief gentry from a proportionable compas of territorie annexd to each citie, may build, houses or palaces, befitting thir qualitie, may bear part in the government, make thir own judicial laws, or use these that are, and execute them by thir own elected judicatures and judges without appeal, in all things of civil government between man and man. so they shall have justice in thir own [95] hands, law executed fully and finally in thir own counties and precincts, long wishd, and spoken of, but never yet obtaind; they shall have none then to blame but themselves, if it be not well administerd; and fewer laws to expect or fear from the supreme autoritie; or to those that shall be made, of any great concernment to public libertie, they may without much trouble in these commonalties or in more general assemblies call'd to thir cities from the whole territorie on such occasion, declare and publish thir assent or dissent by deputies within a time limited sent to the Grand Council: yet so as this thir [96] judgment declar'd shal submitt to the greater number of other counties or commonalties, and not avail them to any exemption of themselves, or refusal of agreement with the rest, as it may in any of the United Provinces, being sovran within it self, oft times to the great disadvantage of that union.[94] In these imploiments they may much better than they do now, exercise and fit themselves, till thir lot fall to be chosen into the Grand Councel, according as thir worth and merit shall be taken notice of by the people. As for controversies that shall happen between men of several counties, they may repair, [97] as they do now, to the capital citie, or any other more commodious, indifferent place and equal judges. And this I finde to have bin practisd in the old *Athenian* Commonwealth, reputed the first and ancientest place of civilitie in all *Greece;* that they had in thir several cities, a peculiar; in *Athens,* a common government; and thir right, as it befell them, to the administration of both.[95] They should have heer also schools and academies at thir own choice, wherin thir children may be bred up in thir own sight to all learning and noble education not in grammar only, but in all liberal arts and exerci-[98]ses. This would soon spread much more knowledge and civilitie, yea religion through all parts of the land, by communicating the natural heat of government and culture more distributively to all extreme parts, which now lie numm and neglected, would soon make the whole nation more industrious, more ingenuous at home, more potent, more honorable abroad. To this a free Commonwealth will easily assent; (nay the Parlament hath had alreadie som such thing in designe) for of all governments a Commonwealth aims most to make the people flourishing, vertuous, noble and high spi-[99]rited. Monarchs will never permitt: whose aim is to make the people, wealthie indeed perhaps and well fleec't, for thir own shearing and the supplie of regal prodigalitie; but otherwise softest, basest, vitiousest, servilest, easiest to be kept under; and not only in fleece, but in minde also sheepishest; and will have all the benches of judicature annexd to the throne, as a gift of royal grace that we have justice don us; whenas nothing can be more essential to the freedom of a people, than to have the administration of justice and all public ornaments in thir own election and within thir own bounds, with-[100]out long travelling or depending on remote places to obtain thir right or any civil accomplishment; so it be not supreme, but subordinate to the general power and union of the whole Republic. In which happy firmness as in the particular above mentiond, we shall also far exceed the United Provinces, by having, not as they (to the retarding and distracting oft times of thir counsels or urgentest occasions) many Sovranties united in one Commonwealth, but many Commonwealths under one united and entrusted Sovrantie. And when we have our forces by sea and land, either of a faithful Armie [101] or a setl'd Militia, in our own hands to the firm establishing of a free Commonwealth, publick accounts under our own inspection, general laws and taxes with thir causes in our own domestic suffrages, judicial laws, offices and ornaments at home in our own ordering and administration, all distinction of lords and commoners, that may any way divide or sever the publick interest, remov'd, what can a perpetual senat have then wherin to grow corrupt, wherin to encroach upon us or usurp; or if they do, wherin to be formidable? Yet if all this avail not to remove the fear or envie of a perpetual [102] sitting, it may be easilie provided, to change a third part of them yearly or every two or three years, as was above mentiond; or that it be at those times in the peoples choice, whether they will change them, or renew thir power, as they shall finde cause.

I have no more to say at present: few words will save us, well considerd; few and easie things, now seasonably don. But if the people be so affected, as to prostitute religion and libertie to the vain and groundless apprehension, that nothing but kingship can restore trade, not remembring the frequent plagues and pesti-[103]lences that then wasted this citie, such as through God's mercie we never have felt since,[96] and that trade flourishes no where more than in the free Commonwealths of *Italie, Germanie,* and the Low-Countries before thir eyes at this day, yet if trade be grown so craving and importunate through the profuse living of tradesmen, that nothing can support it, but the luxurious expences of a nation upon trifles or superfluities, so as if the people generally should betake themselves to frugalitie, it might prove a dangerous matter, least tradesmen should mutinie for want of trading, and that therefor we must forgoe and set [104] to sale religion, libertie, honor, safetie, all concernments Divine or human to keep up trading, if lastly, after all this light among us, the same reason shall pass for current to put our necks again under kingship, as was made use of by the *Jews* to returne back to *Egypt* and to the worship of thir idol queen,[97] because they falsly imagind that they then livd in more plentie and prosperitie, our condition is not sound but rotten, both in religion and all civil prudence; and will bring us soon, the way we are marching, to those calamities which attend alwaies and unavoidably on luxurie, all national judgments [105] under forein or domestic slaverie: so far we shall be from mending our condition by monarchizing our government, whatever new conceit now possesses us. However with all hazard I have ventur'd what I thought my duty to speak in season, and to forewarne my countrey in time: wherin I doubt not but ther be many wise men in all places and degrees, but am sorrie the effects of wisdom are so little seen among us. Many circumstances and particulars I could have added in those things wherof I have spoken; but a few main matters now put speedily in execution, will suffice to recover us, and set all right: and ther [106] will want at no time who are good at circumstances; but men who set thir mindes on main matters and sufficiently urge them, in these most difficult times I finde not many. What I have spoken, is the language of that which is not call'd amiss *the good Old Cause:*[98] if it seem strange to any, it will not seem more strange, I hope, than convincing to backsliders. Thus much I should perhaps have said though I were sure I should have spoken only to trees and stones; and had none to cry to, but with the Prophet, *O earth, earth, earth!* to tell the very soil it self, what her perverse inhabitants are deaf [107] to.[99] Nay though what I have spoke, should happ'n (which Thou suffer not, who didst create mankinde free; nor Thou next, who didst redeem us from being servants of men!) to be the last words of our expiring libertie. But I trust I shall have spoken perswasion to abundance of sensible and ingenuous men: to som perhaps whom God may raise of these stones to become children of reviving libertie;[100] and may reclaim, though they seem now chusing them a captain back for *Egypt,*[101] to bethink themselves a little and consider whether they are rushing; to exhort this torrent also of the people, not to be [108] so impetuos, but to keep thir due channell; and at length recovering and uniting thir better resolutions, now that they see alreadie how open and unbounded the insolence and rage is of our common enemies, to stay these ruinous proceedings; justly and timely fearing to what a precipice of destruction the deluge of this epidemic madness would hurrie us through the general defection of a misguided and abus'd multitude.

NOTES

1. ". . . And we, We who have given counsel to Sulla, let us now give it to the people," an adaptation of Juvenal's *First Satire,* lines 15–17. By this quotation, added in the second edition, Milton presents himself as one who has tried unsuccessfully to remonstrate with the tyrant Sulla (General Monk whom he advised in *The Present Means* on ways to establish a Commonwealth) and who now turns to the people. See note 61 below.

2. In his speech to the secluded members when he restored them to the House on February 21, 1660, Monk declared "that I have nothing before my eyes but God's glory, and the Settlement of these nations upon Commonwealth foundations" (William Cobbett, *Parliamentary History of England,* 12 vols. [London, 1806–12], III, 1580). Before disbanding, the Long Parliament attempted to ensure Presbyterian domination in the new parliament by barring from election all Papists, all who had assisted the Irish rebellion, all who had been in arms against Parliament or whose fathers had been, unless they had subsequently manifested their good affection.

3. In *Brief Notes* Milton identified Matthew Griffith as one of these deceivers. In March and April 1660, the press was flooded with royalist pamphlets bearing such titles as, *Englands Monarchy Asserted and Proved to Be . . . the Best Commonwealth* (March 8, 1660); Roger L'Estrange, *A Plea for Limited Monarchy* (April 1660), and *England's Genius Pleading for King Charles* (April 30, 1660).

4. Shrove Tuesday, the day before the long Lenten discipline began, was traditionally a day of carnival, feasting, and amusement.

5. By April 1660, only a scattered and dwindling number of republicans, the rank and file of the army, the Fifth Monarchists, and some few other radical sectaries remained ardent anti-Royalists. Since Pride's Purge and the regicide, Milton was unable to claim majority support for the rebellion even from the Puritan faction, to say nothing of the nation as a whole, but he continued to claim the adherence of a large number of the worthiest.

6. Cf. the House of Commons resolution, "that the Office of a King in this Nation, and to have the Power thereof in any Single Person, is unnecessary, burdensome, and dangerous to the Liberty, Safety, and publick Interest of the People of this Nation; and therefore ought to be abolished;" proposed February 7, 1649, enacted March 17. *Journals of the House of Commons [1547–1847]* (London, n.d.), VI, 133, 166.

7. In the Solemn League and Covenant taken on September 25, 1643, the House of Commons vowed to "preserve the rights and privileges of the Parliaments, and the liberties of the kingdoms, and to preserve and defend the King's Majesty's person and authority, in the preservation and defense of the true religion and liberties of the kingdoms, that the world may bear witness . . . that we have no thoughts or intentions to diminish His Majesty's just power and greatness" (Samuel Gardiner, *Constitutional Documents of the Puritan Revolution, 1625–60* [Oxford, 1906], p. 269). The Presbyterians, though they began the revolution, opposed the regicide and the commonwealth government as flagrant violations of this Covenant and Milton here summarizes the answers to their objections which he worked out at length in *Tenure* and the *Defensio*. The Covenant was restored March 5, 1660, by the reconstituted Long Parliament.

8. Charles did not instigate the Irish rebellion (which began with the massacre of October 23, 1641), but in 1643 he authorized Lord Ormonde to offer the Irish a free parliament as a means of securing their military support, and he encouraged negotiations with them until 1648.

9. Seven important sets of propositions offered as bases for settlement to Charles were: the Nineteen Propositions (June 2, 1642), the Treaty of Oxford (February 1643), the Treaty of Uxbridge (February 1645), the Proposals of the Scots (February and March 1646), the Propositions (April 21, 1647), and the Treaty of Newport (October 1648).

10. Job xiii 15.

11. *ingagement:* the Engagement, the oath required under the Commonwealth of all members of the House of Commons, "I do declare and promise, That I will be true and faithful to the Commonwealth of *England*, as the same is now established, without a King or House of Lords," enacted October 11, 1649. *Commons Journal*, VI, 306.

12. The formal protest set forth in May 1641, in which Parliament complained of Popish efforts to subvert the fundamental laws of England and Ireland, of the levying of a Popish army in Ireland, of the bringing of two armies into England, and of illegal taxes during the long intermission of Parliament; the document then declared a resolution to defend "the true, reformed, Protestant Religion, expressed in the Doctrine of the Church of *England*, against all Popery and Popish Innovations, and . . . His Majesty's Royal Person, Honour, and Estate." *Commons Journal*, II, 132.

13. The Solemn League and Covenant used this phrase in the pledge to extirpate Popery.

14. On December 6, 1648, Colonel Pride expelled about 140 members of the House of Commons, and at the beginning of the civil war about 175 mem-

bers of Parliament, most of them Lords, withdrew from Westminster to set up a royalist parliament at Oxford. The Rump Parliament comprised some 50 or 60 members, but even fewer than this were present in the restored Rump of 1659.

15. See Milton's explanation in *Tenure* of the dictates of the natural law regarding the establishment and alteration of a government; also Sirluck's study of Milton's conception and use of the Law of Nature, "Introduction," *Complete Prose,* II, 1–158.

16. Milton here attempts to answer Roger L'Estrange's charge in *Reply to "Plain English,"* that the Parliament was acting under army pressure in their vote of January 3, 1648, of "No Further Addresses," which brought negotiations with King Charles to an end.

17. The counter-parliament at Oxford had the three estates, king, lords, and commons.

18. Judas complained when Mary Magdalen anointed Christ's feet with costly spikenard that it ought rather to have been sold for the poor, "not that he cared for the poor, but because he was a thief, and had the bag [i.e., held the purse of the apostles] and bare what was put therein" (John xii 3–6). Simon Magus, impressed by Philip's miracles, sought to buy the apostles' power of conferring the Holy Ghost (Acts viii 9–24). Milton's point is that such men gave testimony to Christ despite their inner wickedness, and so did more good than the upright persecutor of the Gospel, Saul (Acts xxii 1–21); by the same token the Rump and the army, though accused on all sides of self-seeking and corruption, may serve the good end of a commonwealth.

19. *they were not to learn . . . citie:* they already knew that the majority in Parliament (the Presbyterians seeking to restore the king and to bring in the Scotch army to repress Independency) might be as corrupt as the rabble of London which had often attempted to coerce parliaments.

20. The Treaty of Newport, a series of negotiations in the Isle of Wight in the fall of 1648, was the final effort at accord between the Parliament and Charles; it was rejected by Parliament because Charles would grant it only ten of the twenty years' control of the army that it wanted, and because he refused to abolish episcopacy absolutely, to alienate bishops' lands permanently, to bind himself to maintain a Presbyterian establishment for more than three years, or to drop the demand for an act of oblivion for his supporters, which would free them from the stigma of delinquency and thus enable them to reclaim their sequestered estates (John Rushworth, *Historical Collections,* 7 vols. [London, 1659–1701], VII, 1281–1338).

21. James Howell, *An Inquisition after Blood, to the Parliament and the Army* (July 1649), asserted that, in the Treaty of Newport, Charles acted "in his politic capacity" and so was not really bound by his pledge.

22. In the negotiations at Newport, Charles declared that he could not consent to the total abolition of bishops or to the total alienation of their lands, "because he is yet perswaded in his Judgment that the former is of Apostolical Institution, and that to take away the latter is Sacrilege" (Rushworth, VII, 1334). See also *Eikon Basilike* (London, 1649), ch. xi, and *Eikonoklastes,* ch. xi.

23. Notably, the Earl of Strafford, executed in 1641, and Archbishop Laud in 1644.

24. If Charles was responsible for all the bloodshed of the civil war, as Milton argues, leniency to him would be tantamount to participation in his guilt.

25. Such actions included the conquest of Ireland and Scotland, the wresting of naval supremacy from the Dutch, and the destruction of the Spanish fleet at Santa Cruz in 1657.

26. Milton here refers with pride to his (first) *Defense of the English People*. See the account of the *Defenses* p. 403. Milton added this passage in the second edition of *Readie and Easie Way* (hereafter, *REW*) partly to answer critics' attacks, but at this late date few other Puritans who had played significant roles in the rebellion cared to call attention to that fact.

27. Perhaps an allusion to the Protectorate period, and certainly to the disruptions of the past few months in which the army forced the overthrow of Richard's parliament, restored and then again turned out the Rump Parliament, substituting its own Committee of Safety, and then restored the Rump again.

28. Luke xiv 28–30.

29. After expelling the Tarquin kings, Rome enjoyed a republic for five hundred years.

30. After subduing the rebellious Irish, Cromwell defeated the Scots at the battles of Dunbar and Worcester, and subjected them to England under the governorship of General Monk; George Buchanan in *De Jure Regni apud Scotos* (Edinburgh, 1579) asserted with pride that Scotland had been free from foreign dominion for two thousand years.

31. Milton may be thinking, among others, of Plato, Solon, Aristotle, Polybius, Cicero, Machiavelli, Sir Thomas More, Guicciardini, Contarini, Bodin.

32. See 1 Sam. viii 11–18. In his first *Defense* (ch. 2) Milton had also cited this passage, which enumerates the exactions the Hebrews would suffer under kings, as evidence that God disapproved of their change from a "commonwealth" to a kingship.

33. Luke xxii 25–26; also Mark x 32–45. In *Tenure* and the first *Defense*, Milton also interpreted these passages as applying to civil government. The Royalist satire on the first edition of *REW*, masking as a Harringtonian tract by its title, *The Censure of the Rota upon Mr. Milton's Book* (March 26, 1660), commented wittily upon this interpretation: "for . . . you wrest Scripture most unmercifully, to prove, that though Christ said, 'His kingdom was not of this world'; yet his commonwealth is. For if the text which you quote . . . be to be understood of civil government, (and to infer commonwealth . . .) you must prove that he erected a republick of his Apostles, and that, notwithstanding the Scripture everywhere calls his government, The Kingdom of Heaven, it ought to be corrected, and rendered, The Commonwealth of Heaven, or rather, The Commonwealth of this world."

34. Charles' mother, Queen Henrietta Maria, was of French origin and a zealous Roman Catholic; as here prophesied, Charles II also married a Catholic, Catherine of Portugal, on May 21, 1662.

35. Appointments of a "groom of the king's stool" in the fifteenth and sixteenth centuries are recorded in *A Collection of Ordinances and Regulations for the Government of the Royal Household . . . from King Edward III to King William and Queen Mary* (London, 1790), pp. 18, 156.

36. This reference has not been identified, and the parallels sometimes suggested are not very apt: Shakespeare's *Winter's Tale* I.ii.6–9; "Prologue" to *Henry V*, lines 15–18; *The True and Honourable Historie of Sir John Oldcastle* IV.i.20; Chapman's *Bussy d'Ambois* I.i.34–36.

37. Prov. vi 6. The commonwealth of the ants was often cited as a precedent in nature for a republic, while the Royalists appealed to the opposite example of the "royal" government of the bees.

38. See note 33. The Royalists' claims for the king as vicegerent of God were usually grounded upon Paul, Rom. xiii 1, "Let every soul be subject unto the higher powers. For there is no power but of God: and the powers that be are ordained of God."

39. Parliament on May 19, 1649, declared England to be "a Commonwealth and Free State . . . and that without any King or House of Lords" (Gardiner, *Constitutional Documents,* p. 388). The statement was reaffirmed by the Rump on May 7, 1659 (*Commons Journal,* VII, 645).

40. The restored Rump and then the reconstituted Long Parliament were under constant pressure from the disaffected people of London and elsewhere to dissolve and make way for a full and free parliament; the army leaders had been involved in the dissolution of Richard's parliament and then of the restored Rump.

41. The writs for election to the new parliament went out in the name of the "Keepers of the Liberties of England."

42. Representatives to Commons from counties and shires were called knights, those from towns, boroughs, and universities were burgesses.

43. The various disabling provisions passed in January and February 1660 by the restored Rump barred from parliament all who refused to abjure the king and his family, all Papists and abettors of the Irish rebellion, all who had engaged in any plot or design in behalf of Charles or any of his line or any single person, all who had married Papists or allowed their children to do so, all sons of sequestered Royalists except those who had borne arms for the Parliament and were faithful to it.

44. This phraseology is consistent with the argument for popular sovereignty developed in *Tenure.*

45. A council of state of thirty-one, ten of whom were not members of the House, had been set up in May 1659; another was established after the Rump was restored in December; and yet another after the secluded members were returned to parliament in February 1660.

46. *prepossessd:* from first edition; second edition: *prepossed.*

47. As E. M. Clark points out (*REW* ed., p. 111), this passage is reminiscent of Jean Bodin, *The Six Bookes of a Commonweale,* trans. Richard Knolles (London, 1606), p. 233: "The Genowaies use every yeare to change their great Counsell of fower hundred, and Senat of three score. . . . Whereas the great Counsell of Geneva, the Senat, and privie counsell are once chosen for ever . . . whereby it commeth to passe, that the Commonweal of Geneva is more firme, and lesse subject unto alteration or seditious innovation than is that of Genua." But the primary source is no doubt the unsettlement in England due to changes in government during the preceding months.

48. Clark notes the close resemblance of this to Bodin, *Commonweale,* p. 277: "But if the desire of honour bee so great, as that the citisens cannot otherwise be satisfied, except they all by turnes may have place in the Senat, we must then imitat that which *Solon* did; who in the Popular estate of the Athenians by him framed, appointed a mutable Senat of foure hundred citisens every yeare to be changed."

49. I.e., by Harrington and the Rota Club.

50. Milton likens the Harringtonian rotation machinery (*rota,* a wheel) to the wheel as the emblem of the goddess Fortuna.

51. I.e., by Bodin, *Commonweale,* p. 413.

52. *Sanhedrim:* supreme legislative and judicial assembly of Israel, composed of seventy-one members chosen for life, from different classes of society; it derived from the seventy elders appointed by Moses (Num. xi 16–17).

53. *Areopagus:* see Notes to *Areopagitica.*

54. *Ancients:* under Lycurgus' constitution, as Plutarch describes it in the Life of Lycurgus, the council of thirty ancients, all over sixty years of age and

elected for life by the people, was the supreme authority of the state and also held wide-ranging judicial powers.

55. The Roman Senate attained supremacy in the state by the third century B.C.; it was composed of ex-magistrates and its members were appointed by the consuls for life.

56. The doge was assisted in his executive function by the Council of Six, chosen for terms ranging from a few months to one year, but the Great Council was a permanent, self-perpetuating assembly of all the aristocracy of Venice.

57. See the foreword to this tract.

58. Clark (p. lxii) has demonstrated that this is a close translation of a passage in Bodin, using the Latin version (Frankfurt, 1641) rather than the English translation of 1606. But whereas Milton casts the Senate as itself the bearer of the (delegated) sovereignty, Bodin understands the function of the Senate to be simply to "give advise and councell to them which have the soveraigntie in everie Commonweale."

59. The idea that island or sea-shore dwellers are fickle or deceitful may be found in Plato's *Laws* (*Dialogues,* ed. Jowett, 5 vols. [New York, 1892], IV, 704), and in Bodin's *Commonweale* (p. 564).

60. Aristotle in the *Constitution of Athens* describes a council of four hundred under Solon and of five hundred under Cleisthenes, comprised of the various tribes; the five ephors of Sparta, annually and popularly elected, were originally created as a curb on the ancients, but soon became corrupt and tyrannical; the Roman tribunes, originally two officers (later ten) representing the plebeians, could veto acts of the Senate and soon became more powerful even than the consuls.

61. Gaius Marius (155–86 B.C.), a famous Roman general of plebeian origin who held the consulship seven times, collaborated with the Roman demagogues, and at the end of his career participated in a slaughter of senators and nobles. Cornelius Sulla [Sylla] (138–78 B.C.), was also a great Roman general, the rival of Marius and leader of the patricians. He returned to Rome in the year of Marius' death, established himself as dictator, and carried on a reign of terror, publishing long lists of his enemies who were to be killed by anyone, wherever found.

62. The Harrington plan is again considered and criticized.

63. In Harrington's scheme the larger council did not deliberate or discuss but merely voted by dropping balls into a box upon the propositions laid before it by the Senate.

64. *Tarquins:* legendary kings of Rome. The last of them, Tarquinus Superbus, was banished in 510 B.C., and a republic was established.

65. The "refining" procedure here described owes something to Plato's *Laws,* something to Venetian practice, and something to Harrington's proposals.

66. The local committees under the Protectorate, presided over by Cromwell's notorious eleven major generals, were in very bad odor.

67. Milton, in the first *Defense* (*Columbia Milton,* VII, 437–39) and elsewhere, often depicted England as having had commonwealth institutions before the Norman conquest, and ascribed royalist perversions to that event. Here he opposes Saxon councils to Norman parliaments.

68. I.e., until Judgment Day. This is not a Fifth Monarchist statement but a claim that a rightly constituted commonwealth should endure perpetually.

69. I.e., there will be no House of Lords comprised of nobility and bishops.

70. See foreword to this tract.

71. An allusion to the considerable agitation for setting up a protector in England on the analogy of the doge of Venice. Richard Cromwell was sug-

gested for such a role, and Lambert and Monk were often suspected of desiring it.

72. See foreword to this tract. The House of Orange had also claim to the territory of Nassau, and its princes were officially known as Princes of Orange-Nassau.

73. Milton here reiterates the principal points at issue between Charles and his parliament in the years before the outbreak of war, and prophesies the perpetuation of such disputes if the monarchy were restored.

74. A fairly close paraphrase of the passage in *Politics,* III, 15, arguing that aristocracy is generally preferable to monarchy "providing only that a number of men equal in virtue can be found."

75. Milton here appeals to the Aristotelian principle earlier recorded in his *Commonplace Book,* that the "form of the state [is] to be fitted to the peoples disposition" (*Yale Milton,* I, 420).

76. 1 Sam. viii 5–18.

77. 1 Sam. ii 12–17.

78. 1 Sam. viii 18. See above, note 32.

79. Lands formerly owned by the king and the bishops had been awarded to Commonwealth supporters, who could expect to lose them without recompense when they were again claimed by their original owners.

80. *pacification:* the secret Engagement Charles signed with Lord Lauderdale and the other Scottish Commissioners on December 26, 1647, in which he agreed to have the Covenant confirmed by Parliament, to establish Presbyterianism in England for three years, and to suppress the Independents, in return for confirmation of his control of the militia and his veto over Parliament. Just a few months after this negotiation the second civil war broke out. *Cambridge Modern History,* IV (New York, 1906), pp. 346–47.

81. The Royalist pamphlets heaped insult and derision upon the Rump, the army, and notable Commonwealthsmen, among them Milton. Some of the titles reveal their tone: William Collinne, *The Spirit of the Phanatiques Dissected* (March 24, 1660); *The Rump Served in with a Grand Sallet* (March 1, 1660); Roger L'Estrange, *No Blinde Guides, in Answer to a Seditious Pamphlet of J. Milton's . . .* (April 20, 1660).

82. Bacchus is often shown in a chariot pulled by panthers or tigers, as in Titian's painting *Bacchus and Ariadne.*

83. The preaching tub was a makeshift pulpit set up in the streets by ignorant "mechanic" preachers; the sweating-tub was used in treatment of venereal disease. By this wordplay Milton throws up to the Presbyterians that by repudiating the sectaries and associating with the Royalists they have chosen for themselves very strange yoke-fellows.

84. I.e., the Presbyterians had been actors in the five-act "play" of the rebellion through the third act, although at that point (the regicide) they lost control of the course of action.

85. Prince Rupert (1619–82), son of Elizabeth, Queen of Bohemia, and Frederick V, Elector Palatine, was a nephew to Charles I, a redoubtable leader of cavalry charges, and later commander of Charles' fleet.

86. Royalist landholders were declared delinquents by the Long Parliament and their estates were seized, but by act of Parliament, January 30, 1644, they could retain their estates by compounding, that is, paying a sum of money set by the Parliament.

87. An encouragement to Lambert and the Fifth Monarchy men, then in arms. See foreword to this tract.

88. The royalist faction, as defeated enemies, are said to be deprived of their right of suffrage.

89. This is somewhat disingenuous, for the rest of the pamphlet shows clearly that Milton knows he is speaking to a small remnant.

90. William Camden (1551–1623), *The History of the Most Renowned and Victorious Princess Elizabeth* (London, 1688), pp. 17–18, 317–77, testifies to Elizabeth's care of religion and the established church, and to her suppression of dissent, noting, for example, her assumption of power over the church through an act "for Restoring the Crown of *England* to its former Jurisdiction in matters Ecclesiastical."

91. An allusion to Charles II's upbringing, his sojourn in France, and his attachment to the Spanish on whose part he had fought in Flanders.

92. The restored Long Parliament published the Covenant again on March 5, 1660 (*Commons Journal,* VII, 862).

93. *Eikon Basilike,* ch. xxvii; *Eikonoklastes,* ch. xxvii.

94. From the time of the revolt against Spain the lack of centralized power hampered the Netherlands in the conduct of war and international affairs; just recently, the failure of some provinces to support their admirals had contributed to the Dutch loss of the Naval War to England.

95. In 510 B.C. Cleisthenes ended civil strife by creating tribes, each of whom might elect its demarch or mayor, and provided for local control over the districts and smaller towns.

96. Milton suggests that the plagues were a visitation of God punishing the evils of monarchy; since 1625 there had been no great epidemic in England.

97. Perhaps the idol queen is Hathor, the Egyptian Aphrodite. See the story of the Hebrews' desire in the desert to return to Egypt to enjoy the "cucumbers, and the melons, and the leeks, and the onions, and the garlick" (Num. xi 5).

98. In this passage, Milton defends the Commonwealth cause and its traditional name from such scurrilous treatments as Prynne's *Winding Sheet for the Good Old Cause* (1660), or, *A Coffin for the Good Old Cause* (1660).

99. Jer. xxii 29.

100. Cf. Ezekiel's vision of the dry bones which revive as he preaches to them, interpreted as the symbol of the House of Israel re-established by God in peace and glory and sanctity (Ezek. xxxvii).

101. The common metaphor for backsliding, drawn from the story of the Israelites who, fearful that they could not overcome the pagan tribes inhabiting the Promised Land, sought someone to lead them back to Egypt (Num. xiv 4).

THE HISTORICAL WRITINGS, THE COMMONPLACE BOOK, AND THE STATE PAPERS

EDITED BY J. MAX PATRICK

Summaries with extracts of:

The History of Britain, composed ca. 1646–ca. 1666, published 1670, including the digression or *Character of the Long Parliament*

A Brief History of Moscovia, written ca. 1648, published 1682

The Commonplace Book, 1630?–1665?

Literae Pseudo-Senatus, 1676

Republican Letters, 1682

Letters of State, 1694

The Skinner and Columbia Manuscripts and other State Papers, composed 1649–1660

THE HISTORY OF BRITAIN.

THAT PART ESPECIALLY NOW CALL'D ENGLAND.

FROM THE FIRST TRADITIONAL BEGINNING, CONTINU'D TO THE NORMAN CONQUEST. COLLECTED OUT OF THE ANTIENTEST AND BEST AUTHOURS THEREOF BY JOHN MILTON.

London, Printed for *J. M.* for *James Allestry* at the *Rose* and *Crown* in St. Paul's Church-Yard, MDCLXX.

INCLUDING THE DIGRESSION OR

CHARACTER OF THE LONG PARLIAMENT.

Milton began *The History of Britain* about 1646, probably completing a draft of Books I and II before February 1648, and of Books III and IV about a year later when he became the Council's Secretary for Foreign Tongues. About August 1655 he returned to his private studies, presumably to carry the work up to his own times, as he originally intended. However, he stopped at the Norman conquest. The date when he completed Books V and VI is uncertain. It is not unlikely that he made some revisions in all six books before the first edition appeared in 1670. In its final form, the history amounted to an explanation by analogy of why the Revolution, the Puritan Reformation, the Commonwealth, and the Protectorate of the 1640s and 1650s failed. But Milton may well have conceived the idea of the *History* about 1642–44 in the flush of his enthusiasm for the Revolution. Then, as he wrote in *Areopagitica,* he felt justified in stating that "by all concurrence of signs, and by the general instinct of holy and devout men . . . God is decreeing to begin some new and great period in his Church, ev'n to the reforming of Reformation it self: what does he then but reveal Himself to his servants, and as his manner is, first to his English-men . . . [?]

Methinks I see in my mind a noble and puissant Nation rousing herself like a strong man after sleep . . . as an Eagle muing her mighty youth, and kindling her undazl'd eyes at the full midday beam." Perhaps Milton's original intention was, accordingly, to record something like the biblical history of God's first chosen people, the Jews, by writing about his other chosen people, the English, dealing with their mighty youth, examining their successes and failures, drawing the lessons from them and applying them to the seventeenth century, and, hopefully, culminating the story with England's achievement of Christian liberty and the Reformation reformed. If so, the events of the 1650s and 1660s must have caused Milton to change his mind and, consequently, to recast what he had written optimistically, making his account an explanation of failure rather than a hymn to success and glory, but still mindful of similarities between the histories of God's chosen peoples.

If there is no clear evidence that Milton did significantly revise his *History* before publishing it in 1670, there is likewise no clear evidence that he did not do so. What is certain is that in 1642 he envisaged writing optimistically about England's past. In *The Reason of Church-Governement,* he expressed his resolution "to be an interpreter and relater of the best and sagest things among mine own Citizens throughout this Iland in the mother dialect. That what the greatest and choycest wits of *Athens, Rome,* or modern *Italy,* and those Hebrews of old did for their country, I . . . might doe for mine . . . content with these British Ilands as my world, whose fortune hath hitherto bin, that if the Athenians, as some say, made their small deeds great and renowned by their eloquent writers, *England* hath had her noble atchievments made small by the unskilfull handling of monks and mechanicks." Milton's epics and *Samson Agonistes* were the chief products of this aspiration, but his *History of Britain* was a closely related product, particularly so inasmuch as he had once planned to center his major epic around King Arthur. Recognition that Arthur's historicity was doubtful and that treatment of scriptural themes could transcend Virgil and Homer led to the epics and left the eloquent glorification of England's "noble atchievments" to be treated in a prose history which would sift the errors out of standard sources and properly interpret "the best and sagest things" in Britain's past and present. But it would seem that the events of Milton's own times led him to shift his emphasis: he would still exalt noble achievements, but his main aim became minatory—to point a warning finger at the reasons why the inhabitants of Great Britain had failed in the past to create a free, godly, responsible, successful society, and by direct statement and analogy to indicate what might and eventually what did cause the seventeenth-century revolution to end in calamity, as he viewed it.

There is a possibility that Milton wrote more than the extant six books of the *History* and that the *Character of the Long Parliament*, which has survived and has been called a *Digression* originally intended for inclusion in Book III, was actually intended for a later book. It was not included in the 1670 printing or in the improved and augmented version based allegedly on "a Copy corrected by the Author himself," which John Toland published in *A Complete Collection of the Historical, Political, and Miscellaneous Works of John Milton* (3 vols.; Amsterdam, 1698). In 1738 this version was reprinted in two volumes which were prefaced by Thomas Birch's account of Milton, and early in Book III, Birch inserted a "Digression" which had been published in 1681 as *Mr. Milton's Character of the Long Parliament and Assembly of Divines in 1641* (a questionable date). With somewhat different wording this *Character* occurs in a seventeenth-century manuscript owned by Harvard University; its text and that of 1681 are printed with George Philip Krapp's edition of the *History* in the *Columbia Milton*, X 1–325, 385–86, and XVIII, 247–55, 514–16. A summary of the *Character*, based directly on the Harvard manuscript, is introduced into the account of Book III below. A definitive edition of the *History* and *Character* by French Fogle is forthcoming in the *Yale Milton*.

Milton's interest in history was aroused at St. Paul's School, furthered at Cambridge, and systematically developed in his reading after graduation. His *Commonplace Book* and almost everything else that he wrote are colored by this interest. And he was no mean historian: his choice of information from such sources as Bede, Gildas, and Geoffrey of Monmouth is marked by critical common sense; and his use of the historical works of Stowe, Holinshed, Camden, and the like shows discrimination and independence. The extracts from the *History* given below are taken from the 1670 edition.

The *History* begins, in cadences reminiscent of Sir Thomas Browne, by considering why it is that the deeds of some ages are unknown or obscured by fables, "Whether it were that the use of

Letters came in long after, or were it the violence of barbarous inundations, or they themselves at certain revolutions of time, fatally decaying, and degenerating into Sloth and Ignorance; whereby the monuments of more ancient civility have bin som destroy'd, som lost. Perhaps dis-esteem and contempt of the public affairs then present, as not worth recording, might partly be in cause. . . . What ever might be the reason, this we find, that of *British affairs,* from the first peopling of the Iland to the coming of *Julius Caesar,* nothing certain, either by Tradition, History, or Ancient Fame hath hitherto bin left us. That which we have of oldest seeming, hath by the greater part of judicious Antiquaries bin long rejected for a modern Fable." Nevertheless these reputed tales may contain "reliques of somthing true" and therefore merit the telling over "be it for nothing else but in favour of our English Poets and Rhetoricians, who by thir Art will know, how to use them judiciously."

Though sure that "*Britain* hath bin anciently term'd *Albion,*" Milton doubts that Brutus was its founder. Nevertheless "we cannot so easily be discharg'd" of this tradition "as the due and proper subject of Story." Accordingly Milton relates it, including the account of King Leir and the "plain dealing" Cordelia. "Now might be seen a difference between the silent, or down-right spok'n affection of som Children to thir Parents, and the talkative obsequiousness of others." Cordelia ruled her land for five years in peace until her sisters' sons, "not bearing that a Kingdom should be govern'd by a Woman, in the unseasonablest time to raise that quarrel against a Woman so worthy," made war against her. Milton thus acknowledged that in some instances a female could be worthy of ruling a nation, just as he acknowledged in *Doctrine and Discipline* that a husband could subject himself to the superiority and authority of a wife who was more rational than he. However, critics point to the attacks on government by women in the *History of Britain* and cite Milton's grudging admission that Martia was remembered for having "excell'd so much in wisdom, as to venture upon a new Institution of Laws," to which he adds that she ruled during her son's minority, "and then, as may be suppos'd, brought forth these Laws, not her self, for Laws are Masculin Births, but by the advice of her sagest Counsellors; and therein she might do vertuously, since it befell her to supply the nonage of her Son: else nothing more awry from the Law of God and Nature, than that a Woman should give Laws to Men." On the other hand Milton tells how Convenna, mother of two sons bout to battle each other, threw herself between them and reconciled them.

At the beginning of Book II, Milton returns to the theme of fame and mutability and soon connects them with history:

> he whose just and true valour uses the necessity of Warr and Dominion, not to destroy but to prevent destruction, to bring in liberty against Tyrants, Law and Civility among barbarous Nations, knowing that when he conquers all things else, he cannot Conquer *Time*, or *Detraction*, wisely conscious of this his want as well as of his worth not to be forgott'n or conceal'd, honours and hath recourse to the aid of Eloquence, his freindliest and best supply; by whose immortal Record his noble deeds, which else were transitory, becoming fixt and durable against the force of Yeares and Generations, he fails not to continue through all Posterity, over *Envy, Death,* and *Time,* also victorious.

The following account of the Roman conquest is often spirited and usually discriminating: thus Milton rejects the notion that the Druids were philosophers and exposes them as "factious and ambitious" men who fought over the office of archpriest and failed to restrain their people from lewd lives. He objects to the Roman historians' accounts of Boadicea as the Briton's chief commander "as if in *Britain* Woemen were Men, and Men Woemen." And he declines to follow such historians by inventing set speeches for such persons as Boadicea, particularly in their accounts of her battle against the Romans: "the truth is, that in this Battel, and whole business, the *Britans* never more plainly manifested themselves to be right *Barbarians.*"

Nevertheless, Milton inclines to credulity about the early appearance of Christianity in Britain, finding it "most probable" that a British king was "the first of any King in *Europe,* that we read of," to embrace Christianity, and that "this Nation" was "the first by publick Authority" to profess it—"a high and singular grace from above, if sincerity and perseverance went along, otherwise an empty boast." Indeed, Milton inclines to credit Gildas' assertion that Christianity was known in England in the time of Tiberius. But when the end of Roman domination in Britain is reached, Milton laments that he must now depend upon those "dubious Relaters" of civil matters, the monks who, in matters of religion were "blind, astonish'd, and strook with superstition."

Book III begins with an observation "that the late civil broils . . cast us into a condition not much unlike" to what the Britains wer in when Roman rule ceased. By comparing "that confus'd Anarch with this intereign, we may be able from two such remarkable turn of State . . . to raise a knowledg of our selves both great an weighty, by judging hence what kind of men the *Britans* generall are in matters of so high enterprise." It is important for a nation t know itself rather than be puffed up with "vulgar Flatteries an Encomiumns."

The Romans being gone, the British lacked "the wisdom, the vir tue, the labour, to use and maintain true libertie," so that the shrank "more wretchedly under the burden of their own libertie than before under a foren yoke." Then came those "half-naked Bar barians," the Scots and Picts, killing, wasting, and destroying "From these confusions arose a Famin, and from thence discord an civil commotion" and divisions in the church. "Lies and falsities and such as could best invent them, were only in request. Evil wa embrac'd for good, wickedness honour'd and esteem'd as virtue." A a protection against the invaders, the Britains invited in the Saxons "a barbarous and heathen Nation, famous for nothing else but rob beries and cruelties. . . . So much do men through impatienc count ever that the heaviest which they bear at present, and t remove the evil which they suffer, care not to pull on a greater as if variety and change in evil also were acceptable. Or whethe it be that men in despair of better, imagine fondly a kind of refuge from one misery to another."

The Harvard manuscript of the Digression indicates that it should follow here. Although it is probable that Milton finally himself de- cided to exclude it from the *History*, it is useful to treat it at this point, if only because it helps to emphasize his view that the deeds and men of one period throw light on those of another; also because it illuminates his conception of a kind of consistency in the inhabit- ants of Great Britain, which was largely due, in his opinion, to its climate; and because it throws light on Milton's view of God's role in human affairs. (Quotations from the Digression are based on the Harvard manuscript.)

The Digression begins with a problem of comparative history. Other nations, both ancient and modern, strove hazardously for lib- erty and, gaining it, "soo enobl'd thir spirits, as from obscure and small to grow eminent and glorious commonwealths." How, then, is one to account for the fact that the Britains, "having such a smooth occasion giv'n them to free themselves as ages have not afforded, such a manumission as never subjects had a fairer, should let it pass through them as a cordial medcin through a dying man without the least effect of sence or natural vigor"? And this gives rise to a related question: after twelve ages and more God drew a near parallel "betweene their state and ours in the late commotions"; why was it that those who gained control of the civil government in all its forms were unable

> to hitt so much as into any good and laudable way that might show us hopes of a just and well amended common-wealth to come? . . . they had armies, leaders and successes to thir wish; but to make use of so great advantages was not thir skill. To other causes therefore and not to want of force, or warlike manhood in the Brittans, both those and these lately, we must impu[te] the ill husbanding of those faire opportunities, which migh[t] seeme to have put libertie, so long desir'd, like a brid[le] into thir hands.

Rightly used, this liberty might have made the ancient Britains happy; but the same kind of defects, vices, and miscarriages brought seventeenth-century Englishmen,

> after many labours, much blood-shed, and vast expence, to ridiculous frustration. . . . For a parlament being calld, and as was thought many things to redress, the people with great courage and expectation to be now eas'd of what discontented them chose to thir behoof in parlament such as they thought best affected to the public good, and some indeed men of wisdome and integritie. The rest, and to be sure the greatest part, whom wealth and ample possessions or bold and active ambition rather than merit had commended to the same place, when onc[e] the superficial zeale and popular fumes that acted their new magistracie were cool'd and spent in them, straite every one betooke himself, setting the common-wealth behinde and his private ends before, to doe as his owne profit and ambition led him. Then was justice delai'd and soone after deny'd, spite and favour determin'd all: hence faction, then treacherie both at home and in the field, ev'ry where wrong and oppression, foule and dishonest things commited daylie, or maintain'd in secret or in op'n. Some who had bin call'd from shops and warehouses without other merit to sit in supreme councel[s] and committies, as thir breeding was, fell to hucster the common-wealth; others did thereafter as men could sooth and humour them best: so that hee onely who could give most, or under covert of hypocritical

> zeal insinuate basest enjoy'd unworthylie the rewards of learning and fidelitie, or escap'd the punishment of his crimes and misdeeds.

Their votes, instead of repealing bad laws brought new taxes. The faithfullest supporters of the cause were slighted or tossed from one committee to another.

To reform religion divines were called, but not by any ecclesiastical rule. They seized college posts for themselves, practiced plurality and wanted to "set up a spiritual tyrannie by a secular power to the advancing of thir owne authorit[ie] above the magist[r]ate." Between them and their disciples "there hath not bin a more ignominious and mortal wound to faith, to pietie, nor more cause of blaspheming giv'n to the enimies of god and of truth since the first preaching of reformation." Seeing the ineffectiveness of the politicians and the hypocrisy of the churchmen, the people

> became more cold and obdurate than before; som turning to leudness[,] som to flat atheisme. . . . Thus they who but of late were extolld as great deliverers, and had a people wholy at thir devotion, by so discharging thir trust as wee see, did not onely weak'n and unfitt themselves to be dispencers of what libertie they pretented, but unfitted also the people, now growne worse and more disordinate, to receave or to digest any libertie at all. For stories teach us that libertie sought out of season in a corrupt and degenerate age brought Rome it self into further slaverie. For libertie hath a sharp and double edge fitt onelie to be handl'd by just and vertuous men, to bad and dissolute it become[s] a mischief unwieldie in thir own hands. neither is i[t] compleatlie giv'n, but by them who have the happi[e] skill to know what is greivance and unjust to a people; and how to remove it wiselie; that good me[n] may enjoy the freedom which they merit and the bad the curb which they need. But to doe this and to know these exquisit proportions, the heroic wisdo[m] which is requir'd surmounted far the principle[s] of narrow politicians: what wonder then if the[y] sunke as those unfortunate Britans before them[,] entangl'd and oppress'd with things too hard and generous above thir straine and temper. For Britain (to speake a truth not oft spok'n) as it is a land fruitful enough of men stout and couragious in warr, so is it naturallie not over fertil of men able to govern justlie and prudently in peace; trusting onelie on thir Mother-witt, as most doo, and consider not that civilitie, prudence, love of the public more than of money or vaine honour are to this soile in a manner out-landish; grow not here but in minds well implanted with solid and elaborate breeding; too impolitic els and too

crude, if not headstrong and intractable to the industrie and vertue either of executing or understanding true civil government. Valiant indeed and prosperous to winn a field, but to know the end and reason of winning, unjudicious and unwise, in good or bad success alike unteachable. For the sunn, which wee want, ripens witts as well as fruits; and as wine and oyle are imported to us from abroad, so must ripe understanding and many civil vertues bee imported into our minds from forren writings and examples of best ages: we shall else miscarry still and com short in the attempt of any great enterprise. Hence did thir victories prove as fruitless as thir losses dangerous, and left them still conquering under the same grievances that men suffer conquer'd, which was indeed unlikely to goe otherwise unless, men more than vulgar, bred up, as few of them were, in the knowledge of Antient and illustrious deeds, invincible against money, and vaine titles, impartial to friendships and relations had conducted thir affaires. But then from the chapman to the retaler many, whose ignorance was more audacious than the rest, were admitted with all thir sordid rudiments to beare no mean sway among them both in church and state. From the confluence of all these errors, mi[s]chiefs, and misdemeanors, what in the eyes of man cou[ld] be expected but what befel those antient inhabita[nts] whom they so much resembl'd, confusion in the end[.] But on these things and this parallel having anou[gh] insisted, I returne back to the storie which gave matter to this digression.

So ends the portion omitted from the seventeenth-century editions of *The History of Britain*. Returning to his main narrative, Milton tells of increasing ruin, "Wherin we have heard the many miseries and desolations brought by divine hand on a perverse Nation; driv'n, when nothing else would reform them, out of a fair Country into a Mountanous and Barren Corner, by Strangers and Pagans. So much more tolerable in the Eye of Heav'n is Infidelity profess't, than Christian Faith and Religion dishonour'd by unchristian works."

In Book IV, Milton tells how the Saxons became Christians and relates their "scatterd story," which he had to pick out here and there inasmuch as Bede preferred "Legends of Visions and Miracles" to "civill matters." "Yet from hence to the *Danish* Invasion it will be worse with us, destitute of *Beda.*" Rather than rely on "obscure and blockish Chronicles" or imitate the conjectures made by Huntington and Malmesbury, Milton chooses to "represent the truth naked, though as lean as a plain Journal." Suffice it here to pass over his list of calamities to Ecbert's conquest of the whole island in the year 828, at which point Book V begins.

> The summe of things in this Iland, or the best part therof, reduc't now under the power of one man; and him one of the worthiest, which, as far as can be found in good Authors, was by none attain'd at any time heer before unless in Fables; Men might with some reason have expected from such a Union, peace and plenty, greatness, and the flourishing of all Estates and Degrees: but far the contrary fell out soon after, Invasion, Spoil, Desolation, slaughter of many, slavery of the rest, by the forcible landing of a fierce Nation; *Danes* commonly call'd . . . the same with *Normans;* as barbarous as the *Saxons* themselves were at first reputed, and much more; for . . . these unsent for, unprovok'd, came only to destroy. . . . God had purpos'd to punish our instrumental punishers, though now Christians, by other Heathen, according to his Divine retaliation; invasion for invasion, spoil for spoil, destruction for destruction. The *Saxons* were now full as wicked as the *Britans* were at their arrival, broken with luxury and sloth, either secular or superstitious. . . . What longer suffering could there be, when Religion it self grew so void of sincerity, and the greatest shews of purity were impur'd?

In the accounts of the reigns of Ecbert, Ethelwolf, Ethelbald, etc., which follow, it comes as a relief to find Milton admiring Alfred for "all virtuous emploiments both of mind and body . . . no man more patient in hearing causes, more inquisitive in examining, more exact in doing justice, and providing good Laws, which are yet extant; more severe in punishing unjust judges or obstinate offenders . . . no man than hee more frugal of two pretious things in mans life, his time and his revenue; no man wiser in the disposal of both." His noble mind "renderd him the miror of Princes." Concerning Edgar, Milton notes two faults and expresses some wonder "how they were so few, and so soon left, he coming at 16 to the Licence of a Scepter; and that his vertues were so many and so mature, he dying before the Age wherin wisdome can in others attain to any ripeness: however, with him died all the *Saxon* glory. From henceforth nothing is to be heard of but thir decline and ruin under a double Conquest." In order not to blur or taint the praises of their former actions and well-defended liberty, Milton decided that the relation of this decline and conquest would be more than enough for his sixth and last Book.

From the account given of the Danes, the following comments may be extracted here. Concerning Canute's career, Milton observes, "it is a fond conceit in many great ones, and pernicious in the end, to cease from no violence till they have attain'd the utmost of thir ambitions and desires; then to think God appeas'd by thir seeking to bribe him with a share however large of thir ill-gott'n spoils, and then lastly to grow jealous of doing right, when they have no longer need to do wrong." And on Canute's demonstration to sycophants that the ocean would not obey him, Milton comments that it was so evident a truth that "unless to shame his Court Flatterers who would not else be convinc't, *Canute* needed not to have gone wet-shod home."

In connection with Edward the Confessor, Milton notes that his wife Edith was "commended much for beauty, modesty, and, beyond what is requisite in a woman, learning. *Ingulf,* then a youth . . . was sometimes met by her and pos'd, not in Grammar only, but in Logic." There is only brief passing reference to "the Tyrant *Macbeth.*"

The *History* ends with the Norman conquest, made possible because the clergy lost good literature and religion and the great men, given to gluttony and dissolute life, made prey of the common people and spent all they had in drunkenness, "attended with other Vices which effeminate mens minds. Whence it came to pass, that they carried on with fury and rashness more than any true fortitude or skill of War." As a result, William had an easy conquest. "*And as the long-suffering of God permits bad men to enjoy prosperous daies with the good, so his severity oft times exempts not good men from thir share in evil times with the bad.*"

The conclusion is abrupt: "If these were the Causes of such misery and thraldom in those our Ancestors, with what better close can be concluded, than here in fit season to remember this Age in the midst of her security, to fear from like Vices without amendment the Revolution of like Calamities?"

Apparently this last sentence was written in a time of security, possibly in the midst of Cromwell's Protectorate but more probably shortly before the *History* was published in 1670; as the longer satires of Milton's friend Andrew Marvell reveal, the times had plenty of vices, and a revolution involving calamities like those which overcame the ancient and mid-seventeenth-century inhabitants of Britain was not unlikely to break out.

For Milton the cure lay not only in the practice of true religion but in the proper training of statesmen. Neither opportunistic politicians nor tradesmen called to sit in supreme councils would suffice; what were needed were "men more than vulgar, bred up . . . in the knowledge of Antient and illustrious deeds, invincible against money, and vaine titles, impartial to friendships and relations," as he stated in the Digression. And it is noteworthy that the production of such statesmen was the aim of the program which he set forth in *Of Education*.

The *History* and Digression have received considerable scholarly attention. Noteworthy are the following:

Constance Nicholas, *Introduction and Notes to Milton's History of Britain,* Illinois Studies in Language and Literature, Vol. 44 (Urbana, Ill., 1957).

Charles H. Firth, "Milton as an Historian," *Proceedings of the British Academy,* III (1907–8), 227–57.

Harry Glicksman, "The Sources of Milton's *History of Britain,*" *Wisconsin Studies in Language and Literature,* XI (1920), 105–44.

J. Milton French, "Milton as Historian," *PMLA,* L (1935), 469–79.

On the authenticity of the Digression, see Appendix B in Zera S. Fink, *The Classical Republicans* (Evanston, 1945).

A BRIEF HISTORY OF MOSCOVIA
London, 1682

subtitled, MOSCOVIA: OR, RELATIONS OF MOSCOVIA, AS FAR AS HATH BEEN DISCOVER'D BY ENGLISH VOYAGES GATHER'D FROM THE WRITINGS OF SEVERAL EYE-WITNESSES; AND OF OTHER LESS-KNOWN COUNTRIES LYING EASTWARD OF RUSSIA AS FAR AS CATHAY, LATELY DISCOVERED AT SEVERAL TIMES BY RUSSIANS.

"The Authour's Preface" and a brief account

According to the publisher's Advertisement, "This Book was writ by the Authour's own hand, before he lost his sight. And sometime before his death dispos'd of it to be printed." According to Milton's Preface, which he probably composed sometime in the 1660s or early 1670s, he wrote the book "many years hence . . . at a vacant time": this was probably between 1645 and mid-January 1649. A definitive edition by George B. Parks is forthcoming in the *Yale Milton.*

THE AUTHOUR'S PREFACE

The study of Geography is both profitable and delightfull; but the Writers thereof, though some of them exact enough in setting down Longitudes and Latitudes, yet in those other relations of Manners, Religion, Government and such like, accounted Geographical, have for the most part miss'd their proportions. Some too brief and deficient satisfy not; others too voluminous and impertinent cloy and weary out the Reader; while they tell long Stories of absurd Superstitions, Ceremonies, quaint Habits, and other petty Circumstances little to the purpose. Whereby that which is usefull, and onely worth observation, in such a wood of words, is either overslip't, or soon forgotten: which perhaps brought into the mind of some men, more learned and judicious, who had not the leisure or purpose to write an entire Geography, yet at least to assay something in the description of one or two Countreys, which might be as a Pattern or Example, to render others more cautious hereafter, who intended the whole work. And this perhaps induc'd *Paulus Jovius* to describe onely *Muscovy* and *Britain.* Some such thoughts, many years since; led me at a vacant time to attempt the like argument; and I began with *Muscovy,* as being the most northern Region of *Europe* reputed civil; and the more northern Parts thereof, first discovered by English Voiages. Wherein I saw I had by much the advantage of *Jovius.* What was scatter'd in many Volumes, and observ'd at several times by Eye-witnesses, with no cursory pains I laid together, to save the Reader a far longer travaile of wandring through so many desert Authours; who yet with some delight drew me after them, from the eastern Bounds of *Russia,* to the Walls of *Cathay,* in several late Journeys made thither overland by *Russians,* who describe the Countreys in their way, far otherwise than our common Geographers. From proceeding further other occasions diverted me. This Essay, such as it is, was thought by some, who knew of it, not amiss to be published; that so many things remarkable, dispers'd before, now brought under one view, might not hazard to be otherwise lost, nor the labour lost of collecting them. J.M.

The main text is divided into five chapters, followed by a list of sources, "being all either Eye-witnesses, or immediate Relaters from such as were." The nature of the contents suggests to George B. Parks[1] that Milton may have intended the work to be useful as a guide to ambassadors. The opening "brief description" tells of the cold barrens of the north and, characteristically of Milton, mentions how the first mariners to arrive there from England found twenty monks in St. Nicholas Abbey, "unlearned . . . and great drunkards: their Church is fair, full of Images and Tapers." But Milton also mentions "Rose Island, full of damask and red Roses, Violets, and wild Rosemary," grass, seasons, the construction of boats, fairs, the salting of swans, geese, ducks, and partridges for winter provision, the number of houses in various towns, wild animals, and like specific details as far as he has been able to ascertain them, especially information about where the English are resident or trading. "*Mosco*

[1] "The Occasion of Milton's *Moscovia,*" *SP*, XL (1943), 399–404.

. . . is reputed to be greater than *London* with the Suburbs, but rudely built, their Houses and Churches most of Timber, few of Stone, their Streets unpav'd." The Emperor's Palace "neither within, nor without is equal for state to the King's House in *England* but rather like our Buildings of old fashion with small Windows, some of Glass, some with Latices, or Iron Bars."

Milton's special interests are revealed in his choice of material. Thus he seldom mentions a monastery without also mentioning the poverty, ignorance, or savagery of the people thereabout. Inevitably he relates that the Emperor "exerciseth absolute power." Sometimes he notes features more or less admirable: for example, that a rich man who is no longer able to serve the public interest willingly surrenders everything he has to the ruler and accepts a small living pension. "They have no Lawyers, but every man pleads his own Cause, or else by Bill or Answer in writing delivers it with his own hands to the Duke; yet Justice by corruption of inferiour Officers is much perverted." Systematically but briefly revenues, military matters and the like are treated. As for religion,

> They follow the *Greek* Church, but with excess of Superstitions; their service is in the *Russian* Tongue. They hold the Ten Commandments not to concern them, saying that God gave them under the Law, which *Christ* by his death on the Cross hath abrogated . . . yet for Whordom, Drunkenness and Extortion none worse than the Clergy. . . .
>
> When there is love between two, the Man among other trifling Gifts, sends to the Woman a Whip, to signify, if she offend, what she must expect. . . . Upon utter dislike, the Husband divorces; which Liberty no doubt they receiv'd first with their Religion from the *Greek* Church, and the Imperial Laws. . . . They have no Learning, nor will suffer to be among them; their greatest friendship is in drinking; they are great Talkers, Lyars, Flatterers and Dissemblers. They delight in gross Meats and noysom Fish; their Drink is better. . . . But there is no People that live so miserably as the Poor of *Russia*. . . .

Similarly factual accounts of Siberia, Tingoesia, and other countries follow; then a history of Moscovian dukes and emperors, and a particularized account of English voyages to Russia by the northeast and of English embassies. "The discovery of *Russia* by the northern Ocean, made first, of any Nation that we know, by *English* men, might have seem'd an enterprise almost heroick; if any higher end than the excessive love of Gain and Traffick had animated the design." Nevertheless, things profitable to knowledge resulted, "as good events ofttimes arise from evil occasions."

The account is an example of Milton's wide-ranging interests, especially in geography and history and of what in many respects was the most important intellectual ambition of the better minds of the seventeenth century—the sifting of fact and scientific truth from fiction, myth, error, and superstition. Inasmuch as Milton seems to have considered the possibility of producing a series of such works on different countries, the history of *Moscovia* suggests also something of what the nature of Milton's contribution to English prose literature might have been had not the revolutionary struggle diverted his pen to serve the causes of liberty and Protestantism.

A NOTE ON MILTON'S *COMMONPLACE BOOK*, 1630?–1665?

Milton's *Commonplace Book* of notes based on his general reading of about ninety authors seems to have been given by one of his amanuenses, Daniel Skinner, to Sir Richard Graham, Viscount Preston (1648–59), sometime after Milton's death. In 1874 this bound manuscript volume was found in the library of a descendant of a brother of the Viscount. Alfred J. Horwood's edition of it was published in 1876 with numerous errors which were largely corrected in a revised edition issued in 1877, *A Common-place Book of John Milton* (Camden Society, New Series XVI). Meanwhile, in 1876, the Royal Society of Literature published one hundred copies of a "facsimile" or autotype based on the original—a careful copy, not a photographic reproduction of the manuscript. In 1938 the complete text accompanied by translations into English of passages in foreign languages appeared in Volume XVIII of the *Columbia Milton.* In 1953 Volume I of the *Yale Milton* printed all the English entries along with translations of the others (unfortunately without their originals) in an edition by Ruth Mohl, amply annotated. She was largely successful in tracing references to their sources, in identifying the editions used by Milton, and in dating many of the entries, thus adding considerable to the discoveries set forth by James Holly Hanford.[1]

Milton is known to have kept at least one other commonplace book to which he refers as a "Theological Index" or "Another Index"; but it has not been found. The surviving one is divided into the conventional triple form—moral or ethical, domestic or "economic," and political. It reveals his many-faceted interests, the development of his mind, his scholarly methods and attitudes, his ideas, and his ideals. But the fact that Milton noted an idea is no guarantee that he agreed with it. The following quotations are

[1] "The Chronology of Milton's Private Studies," *PMLA*, XXXVI (1921), 231–314.

selected from passages written in English, with an occasional bracketed note about entries in other languages. In most cases, only the topic headings such as "Moral Evil" and "Of Virtue" are given here: the reader should keep in mind that Milton's practice was to follow each heading with illustrative and critical passages garnered from a variety of sources, often with comments of his own. All these topic headings are given below, in their original order, to serve as a guide to the contents of the *Commonplace Book;* but only a very sparse sampling of the main contents is given, merely enough to indicate the nature and significance of the collection and to point to its relevance for Milton's other prose works. The original consists of about 15,000 words and should be consulted in Ruth Mohl's edition in the first volume of the *Yale Milton* along with the Latin as provided in the *Columbia Milton.* Ellipses indicate that part of the material under a heading has been omitted. The punctuation and capitalization of the original have been modified for clarity; references to sources have been shortened and regularized.

ETHICAL INDEX

Moral Evil. Of the Good Man. Of Virtue. Avarice.

Gluttony . . . Whether lawfull, disputed with exquisite reasoning (Sidney, *Arcadia*). King Edgars law against drunkennesse (Stowe), which Englishmen are said to have learned of the Danes in his days (Holinshed).

Of Courage . . . The cause of valour a good conscience, for an evil conscience, as an English author noteth well, "will otherwise knaw at the roots of valour" like a worm "and undermine all resolutions" (Robert Ward, *Animadversions of Warre,* 1639).

Of Duels. Of the Knowledge of Literature. [See the quotations below in the notes on *Areopagitica,* 1641 ed., p. 10.]

Of Curiosity. [According to a Latin note, the Emperor Constantine wisely urged that questions about God which human reason finds difficult to understand should be suppressed in silence because they might cause schisms in the church if they became known to the people.]

Of Poetry. Of Music. Consultation. Of Lying. Of Theft. Of Keeping Faith.

Of Justice . . . A just woman, but farre more renouned was the lady of Sir Stephen Scroope who by threatening to forsake her husband unlesse he would discharge his lieutenantship of Ireland justly reclaim'd him and made him a worthy man (Campion, *History of Ireland*).

Of Flattery: Read King Kanuts act by the sea side and answer to flatterers in his life.

Of Reproof. Of Evil Speaking.

ECONOMIC INDEX

Of Food. Of Conduct.

Marriage (See *Of Divorce*): [In a series of Latin entries Milton cites Eusebius and other church fathers concerning marriages of the apostles and various bishops; then Milton continues in English:] and the Preists of England before the conquest . . . forbidden to marry by Anselme; much condemn'd therfor by an old writer Hen. Huntington (Holished); see also the absurd articles of the other synod, p. 34. See also Matthew Paris against forbidding marriage to the clergie (Speed). [Other entries treat polygamy and marriage to one of another religion.] The discommodities of mariage. See Chaucer marchants tale, and the wife of Baths prologue. [According to a Latin entry based on John Selden's *Uxor Hebraica*, the earliest Christian ministers had no right to share in marriage contracts. Milton comments that popes and pontiffs sought profit and power from such matters and adopted some pagan customs accordingly.]

Concubinage. Of the Education of Children [see *Of Education*, ed. Hartmann, above].

Of Divorce. [In Latin entries Milton cites Sarpi's history of the Council of Trent to assert that divorce was transferred to ecclesiastical courts because the canonists thus gained riches and power. He refers to Sarpi's treatment of divorce problems and assertion that public marriage rites were introduced many centuries after the apostles. (Professor Mohl dates these entries 1641–1643?) Other entries state that marriage cases belonged to civil magistrates before the clergy; that Charlemagne divorced his wife without giving a reason; that Matthew of Paris thought divorce permissible for the religious differences of the partners if the orthodox partner wanted it—not merely if one of the two deserted the other. Milton then instances divorces by famous men for reasons such as ugliness, sterility, natural impediments, and conduct.]

Of Slaves.

Of Marriage: To forbidd Polygamy to all hath more obstinat rigor in it than wisdom. . . .

Divorce. [A Latin note, dated 1643–45? by Mohl, says that divorce should be allowed because physicians and nearly all others acknowledge that physical intercourse without love is cold, unpleasing, unproductive, harmful, bestial, and abominable according to Sinibaldus, *Geneanthropeia.* Milton comments that it is unendurable that either partner or at least an innocent one should be bound against his or her will by so monstrous a fetter.]

Riches. Poverty. Alms. Of Usury.

POLITICAL INDEX

The State . . . The form of state to be fitted to the peoples disposition; some live best under monarchy, others otherwise, so that the conversions of commonwealths happen not always through ambition or malice, as among the Romans who, after thire infancy were ripe for a more free government than monarchy, beeing in a manner all fit to be Kings; afterward growne unruly, and impotent with overmuch prosperity were either for thire profit or thire punishment fit to be curb'd with a lordly and dreadfull monarchy; which was the error of the noble Brutus and Cassius who felt themselves of spirit to free an nation but consider'd not that the nation was not fit to be free; whilst forgetting thire old justice and fortitude which was made to rule, they became slaves to their own ambition and luxurie. . . .

Love of Country.

Laws . . . Alfred "turn'd the old laws into english" (Stowe); I would he liv'd now to rid us of this norman gibbrish. . . . Edward the Confessor reduc't the laws to fewer, pick't them, and set them out under name of the common law (Holinshed). Lawyers opinions turn with the times for private ends (Speed) . . . Kings of England sworne to the laws . . . at thire crowning. . . .

Customs of Foreign Nations.

King . . . [According to a Latin note, kings hardly recognize themselves as mortals or understand what pertains to man except on the day when they are made rulers or the day they die. On the first of these occasions they feign humanity and gentleness to capture the popular vote. On the other, faced by death and their evil deeds, they confess the truth—that they are wretched mortals.] . . . The clergie commonly the corrupters of kingly authority turning it to tyrannie by thire wicked flatteries even in the pulpit. . . . The first original of a King was in paternal authority, and from thence ought patterne himselfe how to be toward his subjects (Smith).

Subject.

Gentleness . . . Prohibition of books not the wisest cours . . . and indeed wee ever see that the forbidden writing is thought to be a certain spark of truth that flyeth up in the faces of them that seek to chok and tread it out, wheras a book autorized is thought to be but the language of the time" (Bacon). Prohibition of books when first us'd. The storie therof is in the Councel of Trent Book 6 strait from the beginning. . . . [A Latin entry on how God's glory may be served by adversaries' books cites De Thou's relation how Spanish theologians published a Protestant translation of the Bible though concealing the translators' names.]

The Tyrant. The King of England. Courtiers. Political Adroitness.

Of Laws, Dispensations from them, and Indulgences. [According to a Latin entry, dispensations from man-made laws are permissible because of the imperfections of the lawmaker; but dispensations have no place in God's laws because nothing is hidden from him.]

Liberty. Nobility. Severity. King. Of Religion, to What Extent it Concerns the State. Various Forms of Government. Property and Taxes. Official Robbery or Extortion (See *Pope* . . . in Another Index). *Plague. Athletic Games.*

Public Shows. [Latin entries cite church fathers' condemnations but assert that plays on sacred subjects rightly produced have real value.]

Of Military Discipline. Of War. Of Civil War. Of Allies. Of Sedition. Of Besieging a City and Of a City Besieged. Tyrant. Of Navigation and Shipwrecks.

LITERAE PSEUDO-SENATUS ANGLICANI, 1676
MILTON'S REPUBLICAN-LETTERS, 1682
LETTERS OF STATE, WRITTEN BY MR. JOHN MILTON, 1694
THE SKINNER AND COLUMBIA MANUSCRIPTS and other State Papers

On March 13, 1649, the Rump Parliament's newly appointed Council of State designated a Committee to consider England's former alliances with foreign states. Since external affairs involved a variety of languages, especially Latin, the Council swore in John Milton as Secretary for Foreign Tongues on March 22 or 23. He was more often called Latin Secretary. The position was a distinguished one: Roger Ascham had served in it from 1553 to 1568, and Erasmus had filled a similar post. Milton's immediate predecessor (later an assistant) was George Rudolph Weckherlin; but his exclusive right to publish Cicero and other authors in Latin as a means of supplementing his salary was not extended to Milton, whose annual remuneration began at £288/13/6½. In the *Second Defense* he explains that he never canvassed for preferment or made use of his friends for it: he took the position at the invitation of the Council. It gave him a chance to play an important, in some senses a heroic, role by applying his knowledge of history, politics, geography, languages, and rhetoric in the service of England and Protestantism. It was, perhaps, a step toward that pleasure which he described in *Prolusion VII*—"a pleasure with which none can compare—to be the oracle of many nations, to find one's home regarded as a kind of temple, to be a man whom kings and states invite to come to them, whom men from near and far flock to visit."

The post was one in a grand European tradition. The writing of State Papers, particularly official letters, was an art with established conventions and formularies. A nation's civilization and worth were partly judged by the quality of its public documents—so much so that when few Englishmen had mastery of polished Latin, Henry VII imported Polidore Vergil to ensure that his letters to foreign princes were couched with Ciceronian felicity.

In the traditional letter there were three main divisions: (a) the protocol, consisting of invocation, superscription, inscription, and salutation; (b) the main text, consisting of prologue, promulgation, narration, disposition, and conclusion; and (c) the tailpiece, consisting of date and seal. As usual Milton exploited these conventions flexibly, making no use of an invocation (such as *In nomine sanctae et individuae Trinitatis*). In the prologue or preamble, especially in the earliest letters, he tended to be traditional, reminding even near enemies of old friendship and alliances. Such an emphasis on English governmental continuity and the assuming that treaties and commercial arrangements made under the monarchy were still in force helped to give respectability to the new English republic whose regicide governors were conscious of their precarious power.

For the Miltonic letters of state there are three main sources, all based on copies which Milton kept in his own possession. The most authoritative of these is *Literae Pseudo-Senatus Anglicani* (Letters of the English Pseudo-Parliament): in 1676 two almost identical editions were published in the Netherlands. Their contents are partially duplicated, with some additional letters, in the Skinner manuscript (written by Daniel Skinner, now in the Public Record Office) and the Columbia manuscript, once owned by Sir Thomas Phillipps (now in Columbia University Library). An inaccurate English version, *Milton's Republican Letters,* 1682, was followed in 1694 by a more reliable but not entirely trustworthy translation made by Milton's nephew, Edward Phillips. Some of the letters and also the treaties with which Milton was connected occur in a variety of manuscripts, separate editions, and printed collections: see the accounts in Volumes XIII and XVIII of the *Columbia Milton.* A number of the originals delivered to foreign governments have been discovered, especially by Maurice Kelley, in foreign archives.

Numerous drafts and copies, in English and Latin, of Miltonic state letters written during the Commonwealth period were recently discovered.[1] Though calendared in the Thirteenth Report of the Historical Manuscripts Commission in 1891, these had been overlooked by Miltonists. These Nalson Papers, borrowed from official

[1] J. Max Patrick, in *Seventeenth-Century News,* XVIII (summer-autumn 1960), 23–26.

sources by John Nalson, are now the property of the Duke of Portland and are on deposit in the Bodleian Library with photostats in the House of Lords Library. Copies of some of them as well as a few further drafts of letters also occur among the Baker manuscripts in Cambridge University Library, the Tanner manuscripts in the Bodleian, the transcripts of Dutch archives in the British Museum, and the Letter Book of the Council of State. An edition based on all the sources mentioned above is being prepared by the present editor for publication in the *Yale Milton.*

These new finds and some of the originals discovered abroad reveal that quite a few of the texts preserved by Milton and hitherto regarded as authoritative were semifinal versions: apparently it was not always possible or convenient for him to have copies made for his personal files.

Typical of Milton's letters are a classical vocabulary, subtle and diplomatic phrasing, avoidance of abrupt transitions, consistent decorum and politeness, and brilliantly persuasive rhetoric. On these grounds such a letter as 170A[2] may be rejected as definitely not composed by Milton. His characteristics may be seen in Letter 2,[3] *Perspecta nobis,* addressed to Hamburg on January 4, 1650. It shows how he diplomatically colored harsh facts. Though the Hamburgers professed neutrality, they had failed to punish the English Royalists who attacked the parson of the Merchant Adventurers there and had likewise failed to prosecute those who kidnapped several of that company's most prominent merchants. Moreover, the Hamburgers were allowing Montrose to gather an army in their city and were abetting English nationals in resisting the official Engagement to be loyal to the Commonwealth. Yet Milton manages to dignify this partiality as conspicuous neutrality which he twists into good will by sheer rhetoric. Cleverly he contrasts England's former doubtful condition with her present success under a government which he represents as being firmly in control. Thus by rhetorical assumption he glosses over the increasing troubles with Scotland, opposition to the Engagement, and numerous other uncertainties at home. Behind this veil of diplomacy Milton was trying to put pressure on Hamburg, but he handles matters with finesse. Having noted that in the past the Hamburger's conduct was *perspecta,* that is, well remembered because it was tried and carefully noted, he indicates

[2] *Columbia Milton,* XIII, 642.
[3] Ibid., p. 2.

that the Senate's present conduct leaves something to be desired, is contrary to what is done in the best Protestant countries, and is likely to arouse retaliation. He adroitly conceals the fact that not a few of the English merchants in Hamburg sided with the Royalists or at least sought to avoid identification with Parliament. Delicately Milton suggests that loyal English nationals are being prevented by one or other of the senators—only one or two—and hints that the English government knows the identity of these impeders. Then by blaming "certain Scottish individuals," he provides the Senate with a means of extricating themselves from an intolerable situation without losing face.

This diplomatic adroitness must not be credited solely to Milton. The evidence available suggests that the nature of his work was as follows. The Council of State assigned to him some of the day-to-day correspondence but chiefly the task of helping to prepare the most extremely important letters addressed to sovereign states. The Council or one of its committees would give him a general outline of what they wished said or a preliminary draft. Milton would then compose the letter, sometimes in consultation with a political expert like Henry Marten. The letter would then be submitted for approval or suggestions in Committee, Council, and Parliament. He would then incorporate any changes, usually retaining his semifinal draft, and would then submit the final version to be copied, signed, and despatched abroad. The earlier drafts which survive show that in final versions Milton, though faithful in substance to what the Council suggested, reduced prolixity, eliminated vulgarity and commercial particulars, and elevated the tone. The authenticity of a letter attributed to him may in part be judged by its efficiency and succinctness. He typically indulges in a minimum of mere polite verbosity. He knows how to be oblique but refrains from beating about the bush. In contrast, many of the state letters received from abroad, particularly those from German states, are written in pretentious jargon and sound like a long-winded Lutheran preacher's imitation of Polonius. In letters which are clearly of his own composition, Milton ruthlessly pares away needless phrases: his characteristic letters are organic unities, brilliantly integrated, richly significant.

Even when the letters do not seem to be very important, they are packed with allusions and implications. In the case of the early correspondence with Hamburg, most of the documents and background information available to Milton has survived, especially the reports sent to London by Richard Bradshaw who was Pamela's rival in epistolary fecundity. With great care and tact Milton echoes phrases in the letters being answered and refers to specific matters in terms which, though general, are unmistakably clear. His Latin uses both an interplay of overtones and verbal gymnastics reminiscent of phrases like "gnashing for anguish" in the battle scenes of *Paradise Lost*. Indeed, it is tempting to look for parallels between the rhetoric of the epic and that of the state letters. For example, the first Miltonic letter to Spain, *Antonium Ascum virum*, February 4, 1650, shows some similarity to the first speech of the Father in *Paradise Lost*, III. Both God and the Council of State present their case to "suitable judges of human affairs." The "unspeakable utterances of expatriates and fugitives in Spain" are paralleled by the "glozing lies" of Satan. The authors of the letter point to "the atrocious illegal acts" of their opponents which forced resort to arms by the virtuous and ultimate defeat of the evildoers; the Father similarly blames the war in heaven on those who freely chose to abuse freedom and right and to ordain their own fall. He justifies himself with reference to his "high decree" in a manner not unlike the Council's appeal to its published writings. Neither Deity nor Council proves its case: in both instances it is rhetorically assumed and dogmatically stated as almost self-evident.

The ninth letter in the *Columbia Milton* illustrates how the range of the state letters extended beyond statecraft. It concerns the plight of Jane Puckering, a wealthy orphaned ward whose misfortunes must have reminded Milton of those of the Lady in *Comus*. In 1649 a fortune-hunter, Thomas Welsh, ravished her away to Flanders and forced her into an alleged marriage contract. A complex of intrigues followed. The English navy, with the complicity of the local governors, sent in a kind of commando raid whose members whisked her into a nunnery. Appeals and counterappeals were made to the King of Spain (who was ruler of Flanders), and his representatives. The Jesuits and even the Papal Nuncio were dragged into the case; and Milton and the Council composed a letter of protest (part of it, newly translated, is given here).

To the Most Serene Prince Leopold, Archduke of Austria and Governor of the Belgian Provinces under King Philip.

Reports have reached us that Jane Puckering the maiden heiress of an illustrious and opulent family, while still under the tutelage

> of guardians because of her youth, was kidnapped not far from a house where she happened to be staying near Greenwich and was immediately taken from the hands and embraces of her friends and carried off to Flanders in a vessel readied for that purpose by the contrivances of one Welsh who by fair and foul means has tried everything, even the terror of threatened death, to force this wealthy girl to marry him. As soon as this news reached us, along with no little clamor of serious complaints concerning this atrocious and unheard-of villainy, we decided to apply some remedy and directed certain men to negotiate with the governors of Nieuport and Ostend (for the unfortunate girl is reported to be landed in that vicinity) about rescuing this free-born maiden from the clutches of her abductors. Out of singular kindness and zeal for decency, both governors lent aid toward the relief of the captive maid who had been feloniously hurried from home. To escape the violence of those brigands by any means available, she has been placed in a convent of nuns as a sequestered person awaiting further proceedings. To extricate her from it, Welsh has instituted an action at law in the ecclesiastical court of the Bishop of Ypres concerning a marriage contract with him. However, since both the abductor and the abducted are our nationals, since the crime was perpetrated within our dominion (as abundantly appears from the sworn testimony of witnesses), and since the extensive inheritance lies within our territories (It is the bait for which the kidnapper chiefly gapes), we accordingly deem that the whole inquest and judgment of this case devolves only upon us. Therefore let him come here, that man who calls himself the husband or betrothed, and let him present his case and claim custody of her whom he alleges to be his legal wife. . . .

The letter goes on to ask for the girl's return not only as a favor but as something required by common humanity and "that sense of honor, in good and brave men, which defends the honor and chastity of that sex." This is Milton's characteristic note, though perhaps a little more melodramatic than usual.

An example of a more typical letter is printed below for the first time; *Ad ea omnia* was sent by Parliament to the Senate of Hamburg on April 2, 1649. A Latin draft of it in Henry Marten's hand, with corrections in Milton's autograph was discovered in the Marten-Loder manuscripts in the Brotherton Library of the University of Leeds in 1952 by C. M. Williams. (Our thanks are due to him and to the Library for permission to publish it.) The final version seems to have been burned in 1849.

Illustri et magnifico civitatis Hamburgensis Senatui Amicis nostris Charissimis Salutem.

Magnifici Viri, Amici charissimi.

Ad ea omnia quae per hosce annos in asseranda libertati pertulimus mala haud levissimum accessit hoc quod non adversis duntaxat hostium telis domi peteremur, sed foris etiam pessimis obstractatorum calumniis. Qui proelio imbelles post turpem fugam, quod armis non poterant maledicendo efficere se posse sperantes invidiam in nos quam possunt maximam apud vicinas nationes concitare nituntur. Unde multis in locis ubi incerti atque improbi rumores judicia hominum alioqui forte saniora occupavere, mercatores nostros aliosque cives, siquis communi patriae libertati impensius paulo studere existimantur, injuriose tractari accipimus. Neque hoc praetermittere debemus perlatum ad nos esse immunitates etiam eorum, ac privilegia, quae in urbe vestra diu obtinuerunt, intercidi nuper atque infringi; quae quidem nos inter summas has temporum difficultates rata habuimus, vestrisque civibus sarta tecta praestitimus; quodque magis liberum religionis exercitium intra aedes societatis hactenus concessus impediri, supplicationes ob res a nobis prospere gestas intercidi, hostibus idem concedi, siquod forte incommodum nobis datum est. Adfertur etiam tres quosdam sicarios ab Joanne Cocrano Scoto apud suos perduellionis reo, apud nos olim seditionum administro, ut creditur immissos, superiore aliquo jejunii die ministrum ad contionem euntem adortos esse; quem et ibi trucidavissent, si, quos intenderant in eum sclopos, ignem concepissent, aut non a suis mature subventum esset. De his apud Vos conqueri negotiatores nostros non dubitamus. Cum itaque nostrorum injurias ad nos pertinere perspicuum sit, causam eorum commendatam habeatis rogamus; siquid solitarum immunitatum immunitam esse ostenderint. Neque patiamini audocissimorum hominum scelera impune esse; id enim a vobis enixe postulamus, et dignitatis Vestrae haud parum interest, ut ne hostes Reipublicae tantam sibi licentiam in Civitate libera summant. Nobis interim summa diligentia cavebitur, ne amicitia quae inter nos tam vetusta est offensione ulla interrumpatur. Quod et de vestra pariter aequitate ac prudentia nobis pollicemus. Valete.

Milton in his own hand capitalized the *A* in *Amicis,* crossed out *armis* and replaced it with *telis,* replaced *mercatorum familiae* with *societatis,* added *idem,* substituted *negotiatores* for *mercatores,* and made other slight changes. A translation follows.

To the Illustrious and Magnificent Senate of the City of Hamburg, our Cherished Friends, Greeting.

Magnificent Men, Cherished Friends.

To all those evils which we have endured throughout these years in securing our liberty, not the least addition has been that we were being attacked not only by the weapons of enemies in our homeland but also by the worst calumnies of detractors abroad. Some men who are unable to wage war after their base retreat, hoping to effect by lies what they were not able to do by arms are trying to arouse the greatest possible hatred of us among neighboring nations. Accordingly, we understand that in many places where confused and unreliable rumors have taken possession of men's judgments which otherwise would have been sound, our merchants and others who are our citizens are being treated illegally if they seem to be overzealous for the general liberty of our country. And we must not neglect to mention that, according to what we have heard, the immunities and privileges which they have long held as established in your city have lately been cut off and restricted. Despite the very great difficulties of the times we have regarded these advantages as valid, and we have extended solid protection as a roof over your citizens. Therefore all the more do we object because the free exercise of religion, hitherto permitted within the buildings of the Company is being impeded; and we complain because celebrations for our military successes are cut off, though they are not denied to our enemies if we happen to receive a setback.

It is also brought to our ears that a certain trio of assassins sent, it is believed, by John Cochrane, a Scot charged with treason among his countrymen and formerly accessory to rebellion among us, attacked the minister when he was going to his congregation on one of the most recent fast days; and they would have killed him right there if the weapons they trained on him had fired or if help had not been promptly forthcoming from his friends. We have no doubt that our merchants are making complaints to you about these matters. Since unlawfulness to our citizens is clearly our concern, we ask you to consider their legal position if they show that their traditional immunities have been truncated. As we do not allow the crimes of the most brazen of men to go unpunished, so we ask the like earnestly of you; for it is hardly consonant with your dignity if such enemies of a state take such license to themselves in a free city.

In the meantime we shall most diligently take care that the friendship so long established between us is not broken by any offense. And this we promise in return for both your fairness and your prudent foresight toward us. Farewell.

THE FAMILIAR LETTERS, 1627–1666

EDITED AND TRANSLATED BY JOHN T. SHAWCROSS

Foreword

Selected Familiar Letters

FOREWORD

The tradition of letter writing inherited by Milton's age developed specific varieties and conventions which people today do not observe in the same way. As in all rhetoric, the basis for every schoolboy's education through the seventeenth century, letters were to be both *utile* (instructive) and *dulce* (delightful). The three main varieties may be called *paraenectic, epideictic,* and *informative,* although they are not mutually exclusive.

(a) The *paraenectic* attempted to persuade the recipient to a course of action or a point of view by precept (or logical argument). Letters written in this tradition (which we may classify as *deliberative*) would be addressed to one's peers or inferiors; for example, Milton's letters to his former students Richard Jones and Richard Heath. (b) The *epideictic* attempted to persuade the recipient to a course of action or a point of view by example of the addressee, and thereby it was frankly complimentary. Letters written in this tradition (which we may call *demonstrative*) would be addressed to one's peers or superiors; for example, Milton's letters to his former tutors Alexander Gill and Thomas Young. The *epideictic* was heightened in language and tone, in comparison with the *paraenectic.* (c) The *informative* letter was not a specific type with traditional attributes, but simply a business letter written for a specific reason or circumstance; for example, Milton's letters to John Bradshaw or Bulstrode Whitlocke. The informative letter particularly was usually encased in compliment. Underlying the epistolary tradition is decorum, the demand that the form and style of a piece of writing be appropriate to its recipient, subject, and purpose.

Basically, there were two styles of epistolary writing: the plain and the graceful. Although letters were supposed to reflect a dialogue between writer and recipient, they were obviously more studied and were supposed to observe certain requirements. A letter should abound in glimpses of character; it could not be too long and might even have to be terminated somewhat abruptly (compare

Letter 3 here); it was to present "the heart's good wishes in brief" (as Demetrius expressed it), simple subjects given in simple terms and its "ornament" was to derive from bits of friendly advice, such as from philosophic proverbs or classical or biblical allusions.

The plain style employed current and familiar diction; its language was lucid, vivid, and natural; it was to avoid ambiguities and to use resumptive repetition (*epanalepsis*), thereby ensuring understanding. The graceful style tended to compress thought and language by a not entirely natural arrangement of words, by figures of speech and comparisons, and by a greater use of proverbs; it was concerned most with charming expression and a heightened tone. These styles were not prescribed for the three main varieties of letters, but the plain style was commonly used in the informative and paraenectic letter and the graceful in the epideictic and sometimes the paraenectic.

Structurally, a letter followed the dictates of rhetoric as far as it could: there was an exordium, or introductory statement complimenting the recipient; then the major section setting forth the main idea and the argument or example or information establishing that idea; and finally the peroration, or farewell with perhaps a brief restatement of the letter's main concern.

Thirty-one personal letters written by Milton in Latin were published by Brabazon Aylmer, with seven college prolusions, under the title *Joannis Miltonii Angli, Epistolarum Familiarium Liber Unus,* in May 1674. Ten additional letters have been discovered, and thirty-three to him are known. Those from Milton and twenty-seven to him are given in the *Columbia Milton* in Volumes XII and XVIII. Letter XLVII in the Columbia edition, dated October 20, 1651, formerly thought to be written to Milton by Hermann Mylius, is rather to George Weckherlin, a colleague of Milton's; but an additional letter from Mylius has been found, dated October 25, 1651. Five letters from Henry Oldenburg have appeared since the Columbia edition, the dates of which are ca. June 1656; December 28, 1656; July 7, 1657; October 4, 1657; and December 12, 1659. These six letters are printed by J. Milton French in *The Life Records of John Milton* (New Brunswick, 1949–58) under those dates. Columbia gives original languages and translations. The *Yale Milton* includes, under the editorship of Alberta and W. Arthur Turner, new, annotated translations of twenty-six letters from Milton and twenty-six to him in Volumes I–IV. The remainder are to appear in succeeding volumes.

A selection of fifteen letters is included in the present edition in new, annotated and literal translations by the editor. Letters 6 and 10, in English, are from manuscript, with all abbreviated forms silently expanded. The rest are translated from the Latin (with some Greek phrases) of the 1674 edition, except for Letter 9 which exists in holograph. Chosen for their significance for a study of Milton's biography, ideas, and other works, they range from the earliest (1627) to the latest (1666). Other letters, both to and from Milton, are referred to in the notes. Recipients include friends (Diodati, Dati), teachers (Young, Gill), students (Heath, Ranelagh—neither included here), foreign governmental associates (Oldenburg, Van Aizema), and business associates (Bradshaw, Whitlocke—the latter not included here). Subjects include personal activities, writings, political matters, friends, etc.

Dating of the letters resting only on Aylmer's printing has frequently proved unreliable: the dates attached, or their interpretation, are particularly questionable because Milton's method varies and because we cannot be sure whether Milton or his correspondents were consistently using English or European style (a ten-day difference existing between them in the seventeenth century).

LETTER 1[1]

TO THOMAS YOUNG,[2] HIS TEACHER

Although I had resolved within me (most excellent teacher) to send you a certain short letter, composed at night in metrical numbers, I nevertheless did not think I had done enough until I had written besides another with an unfettered pen; for that unparalleled and singular gratitude of my mind which your merits dutifully claim in me was not to be put to the test in that cramped type of speaking, straitened by fixed feet and syllables, but in free discourse, rather on the contrary, if it can be fashioned, in an Asiatic exuberance of words. Although, in truth, to express sufficiently how much I owe you were a work far greater than my strength, even if I should plunder all the arguments which Aristotle[3] and which that logician of Paris[4] collected, even if I should exhaust all the springs of eloquence. You rightfully complain (as you justly can) that my delivered letters to you are very few and very short; but I really do not grieve for my failing in so delightful and so desirable a duty so much as I rejoice and almost exult at their holding me in a place in your friendship which can urge frequent letters from me. But although I have not written to you in more than three years,[5] I pray that you not ascribe it to worse reasons, but in view of your wonderful good nature and sincerity, that you deign to explain it in milder terms. For I call God as witness how much I honor you as a father, even with what singular reverence I have always followed you, and how much I have feared to disturb you with my writings. First, certainly, I am concerned that since nothing else commends my letters, their rarity may. Next, since I am graced by a most powerful longing for you, I always think you near, and speak to you and look at you as though you were present, and soothe my sorrow (as commonly occurs in love) with a certain vain fancy of your presence, I really fear that as soon as I should consider sending a letter to you, it would suddenly come into my mind how far the distance of earth you are separated from me; and so the pain of your absence, now almost lulled, would grow harsh again and shatter the sweet

Asiatic: elaborate, rhetorically ornamented prose style.

dream. The Hebrew Bible,[6] your very pleasant gift, I received long ago. I have written these lines at London[7] among trifling city diversions, not, as I am accustomed, surrounded by books: therefore if anything in this letter has been less pleasing, it shall be compensated by another more persevering, as soon as I have returned to the haunts of the Muses.[8]

London, March 26. 1627.[9]

NOTES

1. So numbered in the 1674 edition (pp. 7–9), Columbia, and Yale.

2. Milton's tutor in 1618–20 (?), Young (1587?–1655) was exiled to Hamburg in 1620 as pastor to the English merchants there, apparently because of his refusal to subscribe not only to articles concerning faith and the sacraments in the Thirty-Nine Articles of the Anglican church, but also to those concerning rites and ceremonies. (See Milton's *Elegia Quarta,* which accompanied this letter, especially lines 87–94.) He visited England in March–July 1621 and around January–April 1625; upon his return in 1628, he became vicar of St. Peter and St. Mary in Stowmarket, Suffolk. He was the TY of "SMECTYMNUUS" and perhaps introduced Milton to the pamphleteering war with *Of Reformation* (ca. May 1641), connected with Young by Alfred Stern, *Milton und seine Zeit* (Leipzig, 1877–79), II, 57, and Arthur Barker in *MLR,* XXXII (1937), 517–26.

3. In the *Organon.*

4. Peter Ramus (1515–72), in *Dialecticæ partitiones,* whose ideas were expounded in Milton's *Artis Logicæ* (1672). Whereas Aristotle was largely empirical, Ramus was essentially syllogistic.

5. No communication prior to the present letter has been found. In *Elegia Quarta* Milton berates himself as "justly reproved as tardy, and confesses his offence, and is ashamed to have forsaken his duty" (lines 59–60).

6. This has not been found.

7. The letter was written the day after Easter when Milton was at home from Cambridge.

8. Milton may not have actually written upon returning to Cambridge; no letter is known.

9. The year is given as "1625" in the first edition, but see William R. Parker's argument in *MLN,* LIII (1938), 399–407. The relation to *Elegia Quarta* (1627) is primary in redating.

LETTER 2[1]

TO ALEXANDER GILL[2]

I received your letter[3] and, what marvellously delighted me, your really sublime verses,[4] everywhere redolent of truly poetical majesty and Virgilian genius. I knew of course how impossible it would be for you and your genius to divert your mind from poetical affairs and to remove those more heavenly animated frenzies and the celestial and sacred fire in your inmost breast,[5] since (as Claudian [wrote] about himself)[6] your "heart breathes forth Phoebus in his entirety." And so if you have not fulfilled your promises to yourself, I here praise your (as you assert) inconstancy; I praise, if such it is, your depravity; moreover, for me to be made by you the judge of so magnificent a poem, I no less glory in, and account to my honor than if the contending gods of music themselves had come for my judgment, which they fable happened once upon a time to Tmolus, native God of the Lydian mountain.[7] I do not really know whether I should congratulate Henry of Nassau more on the capture of the city or on your verses: for I think this victory has brought forth nothing more illustrious or more celebrated than your short poem. Assuredly, when we hear you sing the favorable successes of the allies on such a resounding and triumphal trumpet, how great a poet we shall flatter ourself, if by chance our affairs,[8] at last more prosperous, should demand your congratulatory muses. Farewell learned sir, and may you know by the fame to be had my utmost thanks to you for your verses.

London, May 20. 1630.[9]

NOTES

1. So numbered in the 1674 edition (pp. 9–10) and Columbia, but Letter 4 in Yale.

2. Milton's teacher and friend, Gill (1597?–1644?) was the son of the master of St. Paul's School. He ran afoul of the government after drinking a toast to John Felton, assassin of the Duke of Buckingham, at Trinity College, Oxford, in September 1628. Further remarks on James and Charles and a poem caused him to be fined by the Star Chamber in November and to be remanded to prison, from which he was freed in December. He received a full pardon two years later. Probably soon after he became an usher (assistant) at Thomas Farnaby's school.

3. Not extant.

4. "In Sylvam-Ducis," which celebrated the capture of Hertogenbosch by Frederick-Henry of Nassau in September 1629, during the Thirty Years' War.

5. Apparently Gill had resolved in 1628 not to write further since his recent poem on Felton had got him into difficulties.

6. *De raptu Proserpinae,* I, 6. Phoebus Apollo was the god of poetic inspiration and music.

7. Midas, King of Phrygia, was given ass's ears for judging Pan, patron of shepherds and thus of rustic melody, superior to Apollo. Tmolus, a mountain in Lydia (Phrygia), is equated with Midas and cited as a god in Ovid's *Metamorphoses,* XI, 146–93.

8. Perhaps a reference to *Elegia Septima* and the Italian poems written presumably around May 1630 or so.

9. The year is given as "1628" in the first edition, but see Eugenia Chifos' discussion in *MLN*, LXII (1947), 37–39. The reference to Gill's poem is primary in redating. The letter was written from London because the plague had closed Cambridge from April 17, 1630, through December.

LETTER 3[1]

TO THE SAME

In my former letter[2] I did not so much answer you, as avert my turn in answering; and so I silently promised that another would be following soon, in which I should reply at somewhat greater length to your most friendly challenging; but even if I had not promised this, it must be confessed that this in one way or another is your most distinguished right; for I think that each of your letters cannot be balanced except by two of mine, or if it be charged more exactly, not even by a hundred of mine. Behold included with this letter that matter about which I wrote somewhat more obscurely, on which I was first laboring with great effort,[3] hindered by the shortness of time, when your letter reached me: for a certain fellow of our house, who was going to respond in the philosophical disputation at this academic assembly, by chance entrusted to my puerility[4] the verses to be composed on questions according to annual custom, he himself having long before passed trivial nonsense of that kind and being more intent on serious things. It is these, given over to type,[5] that I have sent you, since I knew you to be the keenest judge of poetical matters and the most honest judge of mine. Because if you will deign to send me yours again, there will certainly be no one who will be better chosen for them, I grant, who will more properly judge in proportion to their merit. Indeed whenever I remember your almost constant conversations with me (which even in Athens itself, in the Academy itself, I seek and long for), I think immediately, not without sorrow, of how much reward my absence has cheated me, who never left you without a manifest increase of knowledge and growth, quite as if I had been to some

Same: Alexander Gill; see Letter 2, note 2.
fellow: Fellow of the College, normally an M.A. and a tutor.
Academy: i.e., Cambridge and its university, English equivalents of the school where Plato taught.

emporium of learning. And doubtless among us, as far as I know, is hardly anyone who, almost unskilled and unlearned in philology and philosophy alike, does not fly away to theology unfledged,[6] quite content to touch that lightly also, so much as is hardly enough for sticking together a trifling speech by any method and as it were sewing it together with worn-out patches from here and there: indeed it may be feared lest that priestly ignorance of a former age may by degrees attack our clergy.[7] And so, since I shall certainly discover almost no companions in study here, I should turn my attention directly to London, except that I am planning to withdraw during this summer vacation to a profoundly literary leisure, and, as it were, to hide myself in the bowers of the muses.[8] But since you already do this from day to day, I think it to be almost a crime to interrupt you longer with my noise at present. Farewell.

Cambridge, July 2. 1631.[9]

NOTES

1. So numbered in the 1674 edition (pp. 10–12) and Columbia, but Letter 2 in Yale.

2. This is apparently lost; it cannot be Letter 2 given here.

3. Perhaps the reconstruction of what occurred is that Milton sent verses as mentioned in Letter 2, which Gill criticized; Gill's reply included further verses and a poetic challenge; and Milton acknowledged receipt of this letter during June, mentioning "obscurely" what he was then working on. This work, included with the present letter, is usually identified as *Naturam non pati senium* (and sometimes as *De Idea Platonica*).

4. This is probably only in contrast to the age of the older Fellow.

5. They may have been printed simply for distribution at the Great Commencement, which frequently offered such "trivial nonsense"; these, if extant, would constitute Milton's earliest "printed" work.

6. Milton's disdain for his fellow students is well documented, e.g., in the *Apology for Smectymnuus* (1642).

7. I.e., the Anglicans as opposed to the Roman Catholic priests roughly during the fifteenth century, after Wycliffe and before England's break with the Papacy under Henry VIII. "Degrees" puns on their attainment of masters' and theological degrees.

8. Since he considers "retiring," the "bowers of the muses" cannot be Cambridge as some have supposed. Perhaps it is Hammersmith to which his family moved ca. 1631. This retirement is referred to in *Prolusion VII* (see pp. 15–16, of the present edition), which further indicates the inadequacy of Cambridge as the "bowers of the muses," and accords with Tillyard's dating of *L'Allegro* and *Il Penseroso*.

9. The year is given as "1628" in the first edition, but see my reconsideration in *ELN*, II (1965), 350–55. Platonic elements, the interpretation of Milton's words, and the relationship in time to other biographical events are primary in redating.

LETTER 4[1]

TO THOMAS YOUNG

On looking at your letter,[2] most excellent preceptor, this alone struck me as superfluous, that you assert an excuse for slowness in writing; for, though nothing could strike the senses as more desirable to me than your letters, how could I or ought I to hope that you might have so much leisure from serious and more sacred things as to have time always to answer me, especially since that is a matter entirely of kindness, and least of duty? That I should suspect that you had in truth forgotten me, your so many recent favors to me by no means allow. For I do not see that you would dismiss to oblivion one laden with so many kindnesses. Having been invited to your country place, as soon as spring has come to maturity, I will gladly come, to engage in the delights of the season, and not less of your conversation, and will withdraw myself from the city noise for a little while to your Stoa of the Iceni, as to that most celebrated porch of Zeno[3] or the Tusculan[4] estate of Cicero, where you, with moderate means but truly regal spirit, like some Serranus or Curius,[5] placidly reign in your little field, and, contemner of fortune, hold as it were a triumph over riches themselves, ambition, pomp, luxury, and whatever the throng of men admire and are confounded by. But, as you have deprecated the blame of slowness, I flatter myself that you will pardon me again for this haste, for since I had put off this letter to the last, I have preferred to write a few ill words, and those a little more clumsily, than nothing. Farewell, much to be respected Sir.

Cambridge, July 21. 1631.[6]

Thomas Young: see Letter 1, note 2.
maturity: i.e., sometime after June 22, the summer solstice.
Stoa: pun on "stoa" (porch) and *Stow*market, Young's parish.
Iceni: ancient inhabitants of Britain around Suffolk.

NOTES

1. So numbered in the 1674 edition (pp. 12–13) and Columbia, but Letter 3 in Yale.
2. The letter from Young is not extant.
3. Zeno was the Greek Stoic philosopher who taught from his "stoa" in Athens. Milton hints also that Young must needs be stoical about his curacy, so removed from the city and so frugal of livelihood.

4. Tusculum was a summer residence of Roman nobles fifteen miles southeast of Rome.

5. Consuls of Rome in the third century B.C. M. Atilius Regulus (Serranus) was reputed to have asked to be relieved of duty against the Carthaginians to care for his farm, and M. Curius Dentatus was renowned as a model of simplicity and frugality.

6. The year is given as "1628" in the first edition, but see my discussion in *ELN*, II (1965), 350–55. The time element in the exchange of letters mentioned here is primary in redating.

LETTER 5[1]

TO ALEXANDER GILL

If to me you had presented gold, or preciously embossed vases, or whatever of that sort mortals admire, it would certainly shame me never to have repaid you in return, as much as it might be equated by my abilities. Since you have bestowed upon me such charming and graceful hendecasyllabics the day before yesterday,[2] how much more precious is that indeed than deserved gold, you have made me so much the more troubled by what costly item I should repay the kindness of such a pleasant favor. At hand, indeed, were some things of my own of this kind,[3] but which I should in no way rate worthy of sending in a contest of equality of gift with yours. I send, therefore, what is not exactly mine, but also that truly divine poet's, this ode of whom, only last week, with no deliberate intention certainly, but from I know not what sudden impulse before daybreak, I was rendering, almost in bed, to the rule of Greek heroic verse:[4] so that, it is clear, relying on this assistant, who surpasses you no less in theme than you excel me in art, I should have something that might appear to approach a balancing of accounts. If anything should occur which should satisfy your opinion of my verses less than you are used to, understand that, since I left your school, this is the first and only thing I have composed in Greek—occupied, as you know, more willingly in Latin and English matters. For whoever spends study and labor in this age on Greek writing runs a risk that he sings for the most part to the deaf. Farewell, and expect me on Monday (if God will) in London among the booksellers.[5]

Alexander Gill: see Letter 2, note 2.
truly divine poet's: David, supposed author of the Psalms.
since I left your school: i.e., since 1624.
Monday: December 8, the day before his birthday.

Meanwhile, if indeed you have the influence of friendship with that Doctor, the annual President of the College,[6] so that you can promote our business, take the trouble, I pray to approach him very quickly in my behalf. Again, farewell.

From our suburban residence, Decemb. 4. 1634.

suburban residence: Hammersmith.

NOTES

1. So numbered in the 1674 edition and Columbia, but Letter 4 in Yale.
2. These "hendecasyllabics" are unknown; his collected verse, *Parerga,* had been published in 1632.
3. These do not survive.
4. The Greek paraphrase of Psalm cxiv.
5. The London booksellers were located in St. Paul's Churchyard. Gill was to be appointed high master of St. Paul's School upon his father's death in November 1635.
6. Milton's references have not been identified. Taking the language literally, Alberta and Arthur Turner (*Yale Milton,* I, 322, note 5) suggest that the doctor of divinity may have been Thomas Worral, rector of St. Botolph, Bishopsgate and president of Sion College in 1634. Milton's remarks have not been sufficiently considered in evaluating his "studious retirement" from 1632 through 1637; the words may indicate that a clerical career was still a possibility. The institution also served as a guild of parochial clergy.

LETTER 6[1]

Sr,[2] besides that in sundry other respects I must acknowledge me to proffit by you when ever wee meet, you are often to me, and were yesterday especially, as a good watch man[3] to admonish that the howres of the night passe on (for so I call my life as yet obscure, and unserviceable to mankind) and that the day with me is at hand wherin Christ commands all to Labour while there is light.[4] which because I am persuaded you doe to no other purpose then out of a true desire that god should be honourd in every one; I therfore thinke my selfe bound though unask't, to give you account, as oft as occasion is, of this my tardie moving;[5] according to the præcept[6] of my conscience, which I firmely trust is not without god. yet now I will not streine for any set apologie, but only referre my selfe to what my mynd shall have at any tyme to declare her selfe at her best ease.[7] But if you thinke, as you said, that too much love of Learning is in fault, and that I have given up my selfe to dreame away my yeares in the armes of studious retirement like

Endymion with the Moone as the tale of Latmus goes,[8] yet consider that if it were no more but the meere love of Learning, whether it proceed from a principle bad, good, or naturall[9] it could not have held out thus Long against so strong opposition on the other side of every kind, for if it be bad why should not all the fond hopes that forward Youth and Vanitie are fledge with together with Gaine, pride, and ambition call me forward more powerfully, then a poore regardlesse and unprofitable sin of curiosity should be able to with hold me, wherby a man cutts himselfe off from all action and becomes the most helplesse, pusilanimous and unweapon'd creature in the world, the most unfit and unable to doe that which all mortals most aspire to either to be usefull to his freinds, or to offend his enimies. Or if it be to be thought an naturall pronenesse there is against that a much more potent inclination inbred of which about this tyme of a mans life sollicits most, the desire of house and family of his owne, to which nothing is esteemed more helpefull then the early entring into credible employment, and nothing more hindering then this affected solitarinesse. and though this were anough yet there is to this another act if not of pure, yet of refined nature no lesse available to dissuade prolonged obscurity, a desire of honour and repute, and immortall fame seated in the brest of every true scholar which all make hast to by the readiest ways of publishing and divulging conceived merits[10] as well those that shall as those that never shall obtaine it. nature therfore would præsently worke the more prævalent way if there were nothing but this inferiour bent of her selfe to restraine her. Lastly the Love of Learning as it is the pursuit of somthing good, it would sooner follow the more excellent and supreme good knowne and præsented and so be quickly diverted from the emptie and fantastick chase of shadows and notions to the solid good flowing from due and tymely obedience to that command in the gospell set out by the terrible seasing of him that hid the talent.[11] it is more probable therfore that not the endlesse delight of speculation but this very consideration of that great commandment does not presse forward as soone as may be to underg[oe] but keeps off with a sacred reverence, and religious advisement how best to undergoe not taking thought of beeing late so it give advantage to be more fit, for those that were latest lost nothing when the maister of the vinyard came to give each one his hire.[12] and heere I am come to a streame head copious enough

fond: foolish.
forward: immodest. *fledge:* furnished, implying maturity.
credible: creditable.
immortall: eternal, but also heavenly. See also Letter 8 and *Lycidas*.
præsently: immediately.

to disburden it selfe like Nilus at seven mouthes into an ocean, but then I should also run into a reciprocall contradiction of ebbing and flowing at once and doe that which I excuse my selfe for not doing preach and not preach.[13] yet that you may see that I am something suspicio[us] of my selfe, and doe take notice of a certaine belatednesse in me I am the bolder to send you some of my nightward thoughts some while since[14] (because they com[e] in not altogether unfitly) made up in a Petrarchian stanza which I told you of[.]

after the stanza.[15]

by this I beleeve you may well repent of having made mention at all of this matter, for if I have not all this while won you to this, I have certainly wearied you to it. this therfore alone may be a sufficient reason for me to keepe me as I am least having thus tired you singly, I should deale worse with a whole congregation, and spoyle all the patience of a Parish. for I my selfe doe not only see my owne tediousnesse but now grow offended with it that has hinderd m[e] thus long from comming to the last and best period of my letter, and that which must now cheifely worke my pardon that I am

Your true and unfained freind.

period: pun on "punctuation point" and "sentence."

NOTES

1. Found in the Trinity manuscript in two drafts (fol. 6v and 7r), it was printed in Columbia (both drafts), as Letter XXXVIII, and Yale, as Letter 5. Its dating has usually depended upon the inclusion of *Sonnet 7* in the first draft (1632 or, for some, 1631) and upon the starting of the manuscript (1631–33, depending on the date assigned *Arcades*). However, more recently a date ca. September 1637 has been argued; see my articles in *MLN*, LXXV (1960), 11–17; *PBSA*, LIV (1960), 293–94; and *MLQ*, XXIV (1963), 21–30.

2. Thomas Young (see Letter 1, note 2) is conjectured as the recipient by William R. Parker in *TLS* (May 16, 1936), p. 420.

3. Compare "So thou, O son of man, I have set thee a watchman unto the house of Israel; therefore thou shalt hear the word at my mouth, and warn them from me" (Ezek. xxxiii 7), "The watchman said, The morning cometh, and also the night" (Isa. xxi 12), and the eleventh hour of Matt. xx 6.

4. John ix 4: "I must work the works of him that sent me, while it is day: the night cometh, when no man can work." Compare Milton's *Sonnet 19:* "Doth God exact day labour, light deny'd, / I fondly ask."

5. This was perhaps ca. September 1637 when Milton seems to have begun to remove himself from his "prolonged obscurity" and "studious retirement."

6. Indicating that he had thought out and planned his retirement beforehand.

7. A word implying for Milton a time when relaxation against the evils of the world is possible. "Best ease" would suggest at Judgment.

8. Beloved by Selene (the Moon), Endymion, a shepherd on Mount Latmos in Caria, was cast into a perpetual sleep so that she could descend each night to embrace him. The image equates his studious obscurity with the darkness of ignorance dispelled only by borrowed light.

9. "Bad" or "good" principles would proceed from man; a "natural" one, from God.

10. If the arguments referred to in note 1 are sound, Milton was probably working on a revision of *Comus* to be published within six months.

11. See Matt. xxv 24–30, and especially, "Take therefore the talent from him, and give it unto him which hath ten talents." Milton referred to the parable again in *Reason of Church-Government*, p. 35 ("those few talents which God at that present had lent to me"), and in *Sonnet 19*, lines 3–6.

12. See Matt. xx 1–16, and especially, "Take that thine is, and go thy way: I will give unto this last, even as unto thee . . . So the last shall be first, and the first last: for many be called, but few chosen."

13. I.e., address a congregation like a preacher but be most ineffectual in doing so, because, as he says below, of wearying them with his tediousness. The sentence shows that he has decided against a clerical career by this time, but that it is not yet far in the past, and that he is not quite certain of a specific career, with numerous avenues for activity still open. The image of the streamhead reinforces note 5.

14. "Ago"; the phrase suggests the lapse of a few years between the writing of the "nightward thoughts" and the letter.

15. *Sonnet 7*, which muses upon a concern of the letter: Milton's lack of accomplishment or even direction for accomplishment.

LETTER 7[1]

TO CHARLES DIODATI[2]

Now at length I see plainly what you are doing: you are vanquishing me finally by obstinate silence; because if it is so, bravo! have that little glory, behold! I write first. However, if at any time this matter should really come into contention why neither has written to the other in between times, beware you think that I shall not be by many respects[3] the more excused: manifestly so indeed, as one by nature slow and lazy to write, as you properly know; while you, on the other hand, whether by nature or by habit, are wont not unwillingly to be drawn into literary correspondence of this sort. It makes also for my favor that I know your mode of studying to be so arranged that you repeatedly breathe in between,

respects: partibus, punning on the meaning "parts" (genitals).
slow and lazy: ὀκνηρός . . . γράφειν, punning on the meanings "cowardly" "to use a pencil."
by habit: consuetudine, punning on the meaning "intercourse."

visit your friends, write much, sometimes make a journey, whereas my genius is such that no delay, no rest, no care or thought almost of anything, diverts me until I reach where I am being driven, and complete, as it were, some great period of my studies. Wholly hence, and not from any other cause, believe me, is it that I indeed more slowly approach discharging my offices spontaneously; in replying to such, O our Theodotus, I am not a very dilatory person; nor have I ever been guilty of not closing any letter of yours by another of mine in due turn. How is it that, as I hear, you have returned letters to the bookseller, to your brother too rather frequently, either of whom could, conveniently enough, on account of their nearness,[4] have been responsible for those to me, if there had been any? What I complain of, however, is that, whereas you had promised that you would be sojourning with us when you departed from the city, you did not keep your promises: if you had even once thought of your neglect of those promises, a necessary subject for writing would not have been wanting. And this which you possess, deservedly, as I see it, I have been waiting to declaim. What you will contrive in answer you will see for yourself. But meanwhile, how is it with you, I pray? Are you all right in health? Are there in those parts any young learned people with whom you can associate with pleasure and chat, as we were accustomed? When do you return? How long do you intend to tarry among those hyperboreans?[5] I wish you answer me these questions one by one: but since you know not only now that your affairs are in my heart, cherish likewise that, in the beginning of autumn, I turned off from a journey in order to see your brother for the purpose of knowing what you were doing. Lately also, when it had been by accident conveyed to me in London by some one that you were in town, without delay as if by storm, I hastened to your chamber; but that was the vision of a shadow![6] for nowhere did you appear. Wherefore, if you can without inconvenience, fly hither more swiftly, and fix yourself in some place, which location will proffer

reach: pervadam, punning on the meaning "penetrate."
studies: studiorum, punning on the meaning "desires, zeal"; compare "mode of studying" before.
spontaneously: also meaning "wantonly, superfluously."
Theodotus: "god-given," a Greek form of "Diodati."
your brother: John Diodati.
learned people: erudituli, "those experienced in love."
accustomed: consuevimus, punning on the meaning "to cohabit with."
hyperboreans: those living in the north.
autumn: around the end of September.
chamber: cellam, punning on a room in a brothel.

me a more pleasant hope to become able somehow or other at least sometimes to exchange visits, though I wish you were as much our neighbor in the country as you are in town. It will be according to the love of God! I would say more about myself and my studies, but would rather in person;[7] and now tomorrow we[8] are to return to that country-residence of ours, and the journey so presses that I have hardly thrown this together on the paper in haste. Farewell.

London: November 2, 1637.[9]

NOTES

1. So numbered in Yale, but Letter 6 in the 1674 edition (pp. 14–16) and Columbia.

2. Charles Diodati was the boyhood friend to whom Milton addressed *Elegia Prima, Elegia Sexta,* and at least *Sonnet 4* of the Italian poems, and who was subject of *Epitaphium Damonis*. Letter 8 is also addressed to Diodati; and two of his letters to Milton in Greek are extant in British Museum Add. MS 5016*, folios 5, 71 (usually dated spring 1626? and 1625? respectively). Diodati (1609?–1638) attended St. Paul's School before Milton; matriculated at Trinity College, Oxford, on February 7, 1623; received a bachelor's degree on December 10, 1625, and a master's on July 8, 1628; and was incorporated at Cambridge in 1629 when Milton received his bachelor's degree. He was at the Academy of Geneva from April 16, 1630, to September 1631 as a theology student, returning to England to study medicine. At the time of this letter he was probably just going into his own practice, having studied with his well-known father, Theodore. He died while Milton was in Italy, perhaps of the plague; he was buried at St. Anne's, Blackfriars, London, on August 27, 1638, as was his sister Philadelphia less than three weeks before. See Donald C. Dorian, *The English Diodatis* (New Brunswick, 1950), for a full biography.

3. There are many similar puns; the more significant ones are indicated.

4. The family house (and shop) in Bread Street (not far from booksellers in St. Paul's Churchyard or the parish of St. Anne's, Blackfriars) was maintained, although Milton and his father lived in Horton, Bucks, regularly, his mother having died there the previous April.

5. Where Diodati was or exactly what he was doing is unknown. Chester has been suggested as location but apparently only because he had stayed there in 1626.

6. Pindar, *Pythian Odes,* VIII, 95. (The annotations in the volume of Pindar owned by Harvard have been rejected as Milton's by Maurice Kelley and Samuel Atkins in *SB,* XVII [1964], 77–82.)

7. He was anxious to tell Diodati of his plans for immortality; see Letter 8 and note 5.

8. This perhaps indicates that he was accompanied rather than the formal plural form often used by one person. If so, his father (now seventy-four years old) may have come down to tend to affairs concerned with Sir Thomas Cotton's suit against him.

9. The 1674 edition gives the month as "Septemb."; but the Turners argue that Milton may have dated this and the next letter "IX" (that is, "2.IX.1637"), which was erroneously interpreted by the printer as the ninth month New Style rather than Old Style.

LETTER 8[1]

TO CHARLES DIODATI

While other friends generally in their letters think it enough to express a single wish for health, I see now how it is that you bestow the same salutation so often; for, to those mere wishes which were formerly all that you yourself and as yet others could convey, you would now have me understand, evidently, as an addition to increase your art and moreover all your medical force.[2] For you bid me be well six hundred times, well as I wish to be, well as I can be, and so forth even more superlatively. Verily it is proper that lately you have been made the distributing steward of health, though you squander the whole store of salubrity; or, doubtless, health itself ought now to be your parasite, since you behave like a king and command her to be obedient. I therefore congratulate you, and pronounce that it is therefore necessary to return you regards on a double account, as of friendship so also of an excellent profession. I did indeed, since it had been so agreed, long expect your letters; yet, in fact, never having received any, I did not, believe me, on that account allow my old good-will toward you to cool in the least; rather that same excuse for delay which you used in the beginning of your letter I had anticipated already in my own mind that you would offer, and that rightly and consistently with our relationship. For I would not wish true friendship turn on balances of letters and salutations, all which may be false; but that it should rest on both sides in the deep roots of the mind and sustain itself, and that begun by sincere and sacred respects, though mutual courtesies should cease, yet it should be free from suspicion and blame all life long; toward which fostering this letter is not so much written as much as a living recollection of virtues on both sides. And besides, should you have persisted in not writing, there would be that which could supply obligation; your worth writes me in your place, and inscribes true letters on my inmost senses, your foolish candor writes me, and your love of good; your genius also, by no means an every-day one, writes me and commends you to me more and more. Do not, therefore, be unwilling, having reached that tyrannic citadel of medicine, to display those terrors to me, as if you wished to demand back your six hundred healths from me, to all but one, by a little reason

Charles Diodati: see Letter 7, note 2.

raised step by step, if by chance (which God at any time forbid) I should become a traitor to friendship, and remove that terrible battery which you seem to have trained on my neck that it shall not be lawful to be ill without your good leave. For, lest you should threaten too much, it is impossible indeed that I should not love those like you. What besides God has resolved concerning me I know not, but this at least: He has instilled in me, if indeed any one, a powerful love of the beautiful. Not with so much labor, as the fables have it, is Ceres said to have sought her daughter Libera[3] as I am accustomed day and night to explore this idea of the beautiful, just as for a certain beautiful image, through all the forms and countenances of things (for many are the shapes of divine things)[4] and to follow as I am led on by some sure signs. Hence it is that, when any one scorns what the vulgar believe in their depraved estimation of things, and dares to feel and speak and be that which the highest wisdom throughout all ages has taught to be best, to that man I attach myself immediately by a kind of need, wherever I find him. If, whether by nature or by my fate, I am so adjusted that by no effort and labor of mine am I myself strong enough to rise to such an honor and height of praise, nonetheless, that I should always cherish and look up to those who have attained that glory, or happily aspire to it, neither gods nor men, I trust, have prohibited. But now I know you wish to have your curiosity satisfied. You anxiously ask many questions, even as to what I am thinking of. Listen, Theodotus, but let it be in your ear, lest I blush; and allow me for a little while to talk more loftily with you. You ask what I am thinking of? So may the good God help me, of immortality![5] And in fact what am I doing? Growing my wings and meditating flight; but as yet our Pegasus raises himself on very tender pinions. Let me be lowly wise! I will now tell you seriously what I am thinking of: to migrate into some inn of the lawyers[6] where there is a pleasant and shady walk, because there there is a more convenient habitation among a number of companions, if I wish to remain at home, and a more suitable headquarters if I choose to make excursions to any place. Where I am now, as you know, I live obscurely and cramped. Of my studies[7] also I shall apprise you. I have by continuous reading brought down the affairs of the Greeks as far as to the time when they ceased to be Greeks: I have long been occupied by the obscure business of the Italians under the Longobards, the Franks, and the Germans, to that time when liberty was granted them by Rodolph, King of Germany; from that period it will be better to read separately what each city produced by its own war. But what are you doing? How long will you hang over domestic matters as a son of the family, forgetting your town companions? Unless this step-motherly war be more hostile indeed[8] than the Dacian or the Sarmatian, you will certainly have to hasten so as to come to us at least for winter-quarters. Meanwhile, if it can be done without trouble to you, I beg you send me Justiniani, the historian of the Venetians;[9] I will, on my word, see that it is properly guarded against your arrival, or, if you prefer, that it is sent back to you not very long after. Farewell.

London: November 23, 1637.[10]

Dacian, Sarmatian: Eastern European peoples, hostile to Rome.

NOTES

1. So numbered in Yale, but Letter 7 in the 1674 edition (pp. 17–20) and Columbia.

2. Diodati seems to have just begun medical practice.

3. Ceres, goddess of growing vegetation, sought her daughter, Proserpina, goddess of fertility, for nine days after Pluto had abducted her to Hades. Proserpina was identified with Libera, a rustic deity of fertility and wine; Milton's citation thus emphasizes freedom of restraint in his pursuit of the beautiful. Ceres' persuasions of the gods to allow Proserpina to return to earth for eight months of the year indicates the hoped-for success of Milton's seemingly difficult pursuit.

4. A final comment in Euripides' *Alcestis, Andromache, Bacchae, Helen,* and *Medea.*

5. The editor has argued for this as the period of Milton's decision to become a poet as a life work in *MLQ,* XXIV (1963), 21–30. *Lycidas,* which is clearly conceiving immortality, was being written at the time of this letter.

6. This would not be particularly to study law; such residence was commonplace.

7. In *Prolusion VII* he had spoken of the joy "given to the mind that soars through the histories and geographies of every country observing the condition and changes of kingdoms, nations, cities, and peoples" (p. 20 of the present edition). He has progressed during his "studious retirement" systematically through these histories up to ca. the thirteenth century. His further remarks suggest that he had already read and perhaps had already made entries from items 1–9, 14, 17–22, 26–28 (Eusebius, Socrates Scholasticus, Procopius, Sulpicius Severus, Evagrius, Sigonius, Prudentius, Clement, Cyprian, Ignatius, Justin Martyr, Cedrenus), in the *Commonplace Book* (hereafter *CPB*), as numbered by James Holly Hanford in *PMLA,* XXXVI (1921), 251–314. These are dated 1635–37? or 1637–38? by Ruth Mohl in the *Yale Milton.* On the same basis, items 10–13, 15–16, 23–25 (Gregoras Nicephoras, Cantacuzenus, Dante, Boccaccio, Ariosto, Tertullian) may have been made around this time or a little later, before his trip abroad. These are dated 1637–38? by Miss Mohl.

8. Diodati's father married (date unknown) a woman named Abigail, who did not get along with her step-children.

9. Bernardo Giustiniani, *De origine urbis Venetiarum rebusque ab ipsa gestis historia* (Venice, 1492). The work does not appear in the *CPB.*

10. The 1674 edition gives the month as "Septemb.," but see Letter 7, note 9.

LETTER 9[1]

TO CHARLES DATI,[2] NOBLEMAN OF FLORENCE.

With how great and what new pleasure I was filled, my Charles, conveyed unexpectedly by your letter, since it is impossible for me to describe it adequately, I wish you may in some degree understand at least from the anguish without which any great delight of men is hardly granted. For, while running over that first part of your letter, in which elegance certainly contends nobly with friendship, I should have called it in truth unmixed joy, the rather because I see how friendship conquers labor to yield you. Immediately, however, when I came upon that passage where you write that you had sent me three letters before, which I now know to have vanished, then, in the first place, that sincere gladness began to be infected and disquieted with a sad regret, and presently something graver springs up, by which I am accustomed to despair very frequently my own position: those of our neighborhood whom, by chance, or some others of valueless habit, necessity has cemented to me, whether by accident or by law, those who in no other respect are commendable sit daily with me, weary me, even, by Hercules, plague me to death as often as it pleases them,[3] whereas those whom habits, disposition, studies, had becomingly united as friends, are now almost all denied me, either by death or by most unjust separation of places,[4] and are so quickly for the most part snatched from my sight that it is necessary for me to dwell in a perpetual solitude, for the most part. As to what you say, that from the time of my departure from Florence you have been anxious about my health and always mindful of me, I truly congratulate myself that each has an equal and mutual feeling, which discerning in one alone I was perhaps adjudging to my credit. Very sad to me also, I will not conceal from you, was that departure, and it planted there stings in my soul which now stick there deeper, as often as I think with myself that I relinquished against my will and with such complete separation so many companions as well as such good friends and so obliging in one city, far off indeed, but nevertheless most dear. I call to witness that tomb of Damon,[5] always to be sacred and solemn to me, by whose death adorned with grief and lamentation crushed, till I desired to take refuge in what comforts I could, and to breathe again a little—nothing else relieves me more agreeably than the most pleasant memory of your whole being, and I recall you to mind in detail. This you must have read yourself long before, if that poem[6] reached you, as now first I hear from you. I had very carefully caused it to be sent, in order that, however small of talent, even in those few little verses, introduced in the manner of an emblem, it would be by no means obscure testimony nevertheless of my love towards you.[7] Besides, I believed that by this means I should attract either you or others to write; for, if I wrote first, it would be necessary to write either to all, or if I displayed preference to any one, I feared that I should incur the reproach of others who learned of it, with the hope that very many there would still be alive who might certainly lay claim to this attention from me. However, you first of all, both by this most friendly call of your letter, and now by your thrice-repeated attention of having written, have freed me of my obligation to you, with the complaint of answering long ago the interchanges of the rest. There was, I confess, an additional cause for that silence in that most turbulent state of our Britain, subsequent to my return home, which caused my mind to turn shortly afterwards from protecting my studies to defending life and fortunes, by whatever necessary means. What withdrawal to literary leisure could you suppose given one among so many waging battle of the citizenry, slaughters, flights, seizures of goods? Yet, even in the midst of these evils, since you request to be informed about my studies, I have brought to public view not a few things in my native language;[8] which, were they not written in English, I would willingly send to you, to whose opinion I attribute very much value. The part of the poems which is in Latin I will send shortly, since you wish it; and I would have done that spontaneously long ago, but that, on account of what remarks are made most harshly against the Pope of Rome in some pages,[9] I had a suspicion they would be less agreeable to your ears. Now I beg of you that how much indulgence you were wont to give, I say not to your own Dante and Petrarch in the same case, but with singular politeness to me, as you know, to be free to speak among you, the same you will obtain (for of yourself I am sure) from my other friends whenever I may be speaking of your religion in my own way. I am reading with pleasure your description of the exequies to King Louis,[10] in which I recognize both your style—not that pertaining to the crossroads and dedicated to merchants which you jest lately to be practising, but that eloquent one, welcomed by the Muses—and the chief of Mercurial men. It remains that we agree on some method and plan by which henceforth our letters may be able to pass to and fro on both sides by a sure route. This does not seem very difficult, when so many of our merchants have frequent and abundant negotiations with you, and whose couriers run backwards and forwards every week, and whose vessels sail from this place to that not much less oftener. I shall commit this charge, rightly I hope, to the bookseller James, or to his master, my very familiar acquaintance.[11] Meanwhile farewell, my Charles; and to Coltellini, Francini, Frescobaldi, Malatesta, Clementillo the younger,[12] and whoever else you know feels most kindly to me, and, finally, to the Gaddian Academy,[13] you will give the best salutations in my name. Again farewell.

London: April 21, 1647.[14]

NOTES

1. Letter 10 in the 1674 edition (pp. 28–32) and Columbia, Letter 11 in Yale; the holograph of this letter is owned by the New York Public Library.

2. Dati (1619–76), writer and savant, belonged to the Academia del Cimento and the Academia della Crusca in Florence. Milton met him while in Italy. A commendatory poem from him prefaces the 1645 *Poems,* and there are letters dated November 1, 1647 (manuscript in the New York Public Library), which answers Milton's, and December 4, 1648 (British Museum Add. MS 5016*, folios 9–10). Milton refers to Dati in *Epitaphium Damonis* and *Defensio Secunda.*

3. Perhaps he refers to such as his nephew John Phillips, the students he tutored, the financial difficulties with his wife's family, and the criticisms of his views on divorce.

4. He was separated from many of the friends, such as Diodati and those whom he had met while abroad. Probably, too, his father's death a month before was on his mind.

5. Charles Diodati, who died while Milton was abroad.

6. Milton's elegy to his lost friend, *Epitaphium Damonis.* It was published separately ca. 1640; see my article in *SB,* XVIII (1965), 262–65.

7. Milton recalled that when he was in Florence "Dati and [Antonio] Francini taught their beech trees my name / and both were noted for their songs / and learning, both of Lydian blood" (*Epitaphium Damonis,* 136–38). His statement is direct (thus not "obscure proof"), yet symbolic in referring to them as Tuscan shepherds singing the praises of Milton on their pipes.

8. Eleven prose tracts and the 1645 *Poems* (half in English). The Latin poems may have been printed separately; there is a special title page and separate pagination. See Harris F. Fletcher, *John Milton's Complete Poetical Works* (Urbana, Ill., 1943), I, 150.

9. In the Gunpowder Plot poems.

10. *Esequie della Maestà Christianiss: di Luigi XIII. il Giusto, Re di Francia e di Navarra . . .* (Florence, 1644).

11. Neither of these has been identified.

12. Members of the Florence litterati, the first three mentioned in *Defensio Secunda,* p. 84, as acquaintances during Milton's European sojourn. Antonio Malatesti wrote fifty sonnets called *La Tina* in September 1637 and presented

them to Milton, according to the title page of an eighteenth-century (or later) publication. See French, II, 375–76. Chimentelli may be the same as Clementillo, cited in *Defensio Secunda*. Six Italian sonnets from Milton to Chimentelli were reported by Thomas Hollis in 1762 as reposing in the Laurentian library in Florence; they have not been found.

13. The "Gaddian Academy" was the Svogliati Academy in Florence, where Milton read Latin poetry in September 1638 and March 1639.

14. The manuscript dates the letter the third day after Easter, which would mean April 20.

LETTER 10[1]

My Lord,[2]

But that it would be an interruption to the publick, wherein your studies are perpetually imployd, I should now and then venture to supply this my enforced absence[3] with a line or two, though it were my onely busines, and that would be noe slight one, to make my due acknowledgments of your many favours, which I both doe at this time and ever shall; and have this furder which I thought my parte to let you know of, that there will be with you to morrow upon some occasion of busines a Gentleman whose name is Mr. Marvile;[4] a man whom both by report, and the converse I have had with him, of singular desert for the state to make use of; who alsoe offers himselfe if there be an imployment for him. His father[5] was the Minister of Hull and he hath spent foure yeares abroad in Holland, ffrance, Italy, and Spaine,[6] to very good purpose, as I beleeve, and the gaineing of those four languages; besides he is a scholler and well read in the latin and Greeke authors, and noe doubt of an approved conversation, for he com's now lately out of the house of the Lord ffairefax who was Generall, where he was intrusted to give some instructions in the Languages to the Lady his Daughter. If upon the death of Mr. Wakerly[7] the Councell shall thinke that I shall need any assistant in the performance of my place (though for my part I find noe encumberance of that which belongs to me, except it be in point of attendance at Conferences with Ambassadors, which I must confesse, in my Condition I am not fit for) it would be hard for them to find a Man soe fit every way for that purpose as this Gentleman, one who I beleeve in a short time would be able to doe them as good service as Mr. Ascan.[8] This my Lord I write sinceerely without any other end then to performe my dutey to the Publick in helping them to an able servant; laying aside those Jealosies and that æmulation which mine owne condition might suggest to me by bringing in such a coadjutor; and remaine,

My Lord
your most obliged and faithfull servant ffeb. the 21.
John Milton 1653.

NOTES

1. Letter XLIII in Columbia, Letter 22 in Yale; manuscript in hand of amanuensis in Public Record Office, SP Dom 18/33, p. 75. Also in this amanuensis' hand are transcriptions of *Sonnets 11–14*, corrections in *Sonnets 15–17* and *On the Forcers of Conscience*, and a heading for *Sonnet 13*, second draft in Milton's hand, all in the Trinity manuscript. (The *Columbia Milton*, XII, 403, is incorrect in assigning Letter XLI to Whitlock, dated February 12, 1652, to this scribe.)

2. John Bradshaw, president of the Council of State, who died October 31, 1659. Milton probably presented him copies of *The Tenure of Kings and Magistrates* (in Exeter Cathedral Library) and *Defensio Secunda* (through Marvell). Bradshaw willed £10 to Milton in a codicil, dated September 10, 1655 (Prerogative Court of Canterbury, Pell 549).

3. This would be as a result of his blindness, after at least February 1652.

4. Andrew Marvell was friendly with Milton from at least the early 1650s onwards, Edward Phillips asserting that when Milton was imprisoned in 1660, Marvell, as a member of Parliament from Hull, "acted vigorously in his behalf" (*Letters of State*, p. xxxvii). He may have aided in making *Defensio Secunda* better known in France; see Letter 13, note 8. His often quoted "On *Paradise Lost*" prefaced the second edition in 1674. Mrs. Anne Sadleir, Cyriack Skinner's aunt, wrote to Roger Williams (manuscript in Trinity College, Cambridge, R.5.5) that Marvell had helped Milton finish "that most accurssed Libell," which seems to refer to the "book that he wrot against the late King" (i.e., *Eikonoklastes*). If true, perhaps it was this activity in 1649 which recommended Marvell to Thomas, Lord Fairfax, as tutor to Fairfax's daughter at Nun Appleton House in Yorkshire during 1651–52. Marvell and Skinner were acquaintances. Marvell's appointment as assistant Secretary for Foreign Tongues seems not to have been made until September 2, 1657. A copy of a letter from Marvell to Milton, dated June 2, 1654, is extant in the British Museum, Add. MS 4292, fol. 264.

5. Andrew Marvell's father was also named Andrew, a clergyman and master of the alms-house at Kingston upon Hull, Yorkshire; he drowned in 1641.

6. From 1642 through 1646, perhaps as a tutor.

7. George Weckherlin, undersecretary of state (1624–41) and Secretary for Foreign Tongues (1644–49), was recalled to assist Milton in March 1652 after he had retired. He was succeeded by John Thurloe on December 1, 1652, and died on February 13, 1653.

8. Anthony Ascham, envoy for the Cromwell government, who was murdered in Spain in 1650. Philip Meadows seems to have been named assistant on October 17, 1653; Peter or Nathaniel Sterry was appointed on September 8, 1657, as a substitute for Meadows, who was also a governmental agent, but he seems not to have served.

LETTER 11[1]

TO LEONARD PHILARAS,[2] ATHENIAN.

As I have been from boyhood a worshipper of all of Greek name, and of your Athens chiefly (if nothing else), so I have always been most convinced at the same time by this, that that city would some time or other bestow a noble recompense for my affection toward her. Nor, in truth, has that ancient genius of your most noble country failed my prophecy, for to me it has presented you, an Athenian brother and a most loving friend. As I was known to you by writings only, and you yourself separated by place, you have addressed me most courteously through correspondence; and, coming afterwards unexpectedly to London, and visiting one unable to see, even in that calamity on account of which I am more distinguished to no one, and possibly more contemptible to many, you honor the same with kindness. As you have, therefore, advised me that I should not give up all hope of recovering my sight, and that you have a friend and patron in Paris, the physician Thevenot,[3] the most particularly eminent oculist, and that you will consult him about my eyes, provided you receive from me that from which he will be able to understand the causes and symptoms of the malady, I will do, to be sure, what you advise, that I may not perchance seem to refuse assistance offered providentially from whatever source. It is ten years, I think, more or less, since I felt my sight getting weak and dim,[4] and at the same time my spleen; and all my viscera were oppressed and distressed by wind: in the morning, if I began, as usual, to read anything, I felt my eyes at once pained inwardly; I avoided reading, thereupon to be refreshed after moderate bodily exercise. When I looked at a candle, a kind of iris was seen to encircle it. Not very long after, a mist appearing in the left part of my left eye (for that eye became clouded some years before the other) was snatching away all objects which were lying on that side. Objects in front also, if I perhaps closed the right eye, seemed smaller. With the other eye also failing perceptibly and gradually through approximately three years, I observed, some months before because my sight was entirely decayed, that objects, though I myself was not moving, all seemed to swim, now to the right, now to the left. Inveterate mists now seem to have settled in my entire forehead and temples, which weigh me down and depress me the most with a kind of sleepy heaviness in the eyes, especially from meal-time continually to evening; so that not seldom there comes into my mind the description of the Salmydessian seer Phineus in the Argonautics:[5]

> and a dark stupor enveloped him
> and he thought the earth reeled beneath his feet,
> and he lay in a strengthless trance, speechless.

But I should not omit that, while yet a little sight remained, when first I lay down in bed, and turned myself to either side, there used to shine out an abundant light from my shut eyes; then, my sight growing less from day to day, colors, correspondingly duller, would burst out with force and a certain noise from within; but now, as if with its clearness extinct, it is an unmixed blackness, or set apart, as if inwoven with an ashy color, it is wont to pour itself forth. Yet the darkness which is perpetually to be seen, by night as well as by day, seems always nearer to a whitish than to a blackish, and when the eye rolls itself, there is admitted, as through a small chink, a certain little bit of light. And so, whatever ray of hope also there may be no shine forth from this physician, still as in a case incurable, I prepare and compose myself thus;[6] and I often think this, that since many be the days of darkness, as the Wise Man[7] warns, destined for everyone, my darkness hitherto, by the singular kindness of the Divine Will, amid rest and studies, and the voices and greetings of friends, has been much milder[8] than that deathly one.[9] But if, as is written, "Man shall not live by bread alone, but by every word that proceedeth out of the mouth of God,"[10] which is to say, to what purpose does anyone not rejoice in this in the same way: to be capable of seeing, not by his eyes alone, but sufficiently by God's leading and providence? Verily, while He looks out for me, He provides for me; because He does, he guides me and leads me forth as with His hand through my whole life;[11] truly I shall have willingly bid my eyes rest from work,[12] since it has seemed best to Him. And to you, my Philaras, whatever may befall, I now bid farewell, with a mind not less brave and steadfast than if I were Lyncaeus.[13]

Westminster: Septemb. 28, 1654.

NOTES

1. Letter 15 (pp. 39–42) in the 1674 edition and Columbia, Letter 24 in Yale.

2. Philaras, a Greek, was an envoy of the Duke of Parma at Paris from 1640 to 1654. Milton seems to have learned of him from M. Augier, an agent for the Cromwellian government. Philaras sent Milton his portrait with a biographical sketch, and later they apparently met. Letter 12 (June 1652) in the 1674 edition is addressed to him also, and his praise of the *Defensio Pro Populo Anglicano* is mentioned in *Defensio Secunda*, p. 129. This may be the letter from Milton

which Augier's secretary reported to John Thurloe (Bodleian MS Rawlinson A.13, fol. 246) as being seized in Paris (ca. April 23, 1654) when Philaras was ousted by the Count of Riva.

3. François Thévenin; see James Holly Hanford's discussion in the *Bulletin of the Medical Library Association*, XXXII (1944), 23–34.

4. His sight began to fail in autumn 1644; he was blind in the left eye by 1650, and totally blind before February 1652. He describes his blindness in *Paradise Lost*, III, 22–26, in terms of "a drop serene" (*gutta serena*), total blindness, or "dim suffusion," partial blindness. But his eyes were "clear / To outward view of blemish or of spot" (*Sonnet 22*); compare *Defensio Secunda*, p. 42. William B. Hunter, Jr., re-examines the psychosomatic relationships of Milton's blindness in the *Journal of the History of Medicine and Allied Sciences*, XVII (1962), 333–41.

5. *Argonautica*, II, 203–5. Phineus was stricken with blindness for having unerringly foretold Zeus' sacred will. (Cf. Milton's statement in *Sonnet 22* that he had lost his eyes for having overplied them "in liberties defence.") Phineus is also referred to in *Paradise Lost*, III, 36.

6. When read rightly, *Sonnet 19* manifests his total adjustment.

7. Ecclesiastes, the Preacher (cf. Eccles. xii 9). "Truly the light is sweet, and a pleasant thing it is for the eyes to behold the sun: But if a man live many years, and rejoice in them all; yet let him remember the days of darkness; or they shall be many" (Eccles. xi 7–8).

8. Compare *Sonnet 19* ("who best / Bear his mild yoak, they serve him best") and Matt. xi 29–30 ("Take my yoke upon you, and learn of me . . . For my yoke is easy and my burden is light").

9. At Judgment Day as Eccles. xii describes it. Verse 1 is echoed in *Paradise Lost*, VII, 25–27, and Verse 2 in *Sonnet 22*.

10. Matt. iv 4. Ecclesiastes had admonished, "Cast thy bread upon the waters: for thou shalt find it after many days" (xi 1); and "The words of the wise are as goads" (xii 11).

11. "For all this I considered in my heart even to declare all this, that the righteous, and the wise, and their works, are in the hand of god" (Eccles. ix 1).

12. "The dayspring from on high hath visited us, To give light to them that sit in darkness and in the shadow of death, to guide our feet into the way of peace" (Luke i 78–79).

13. One of the Argonauts, Lynceus had such keen eyesight that he could see through the earth.

LETTER 12[1]

TO LEO VAN AIZEMA[2]

It is gratifying that you retain thus far the same remembrance of me as the good will you very politely showed before by once and again visiting me while you resided among us. In regard to the book on divorce which you write you have given to someone to be turned into Dutch,[3] I would rather you had given it to be turned into Latin: For I now know by experience among those books how the vulgar are accustomed to fish out opinions not yet common. I wrote sometime ago, in fact, three tracts on that subject: the first in two books, in which The Doctrine and Discipline of Divorce (for that is the title of the book) is contained throughout; another which is called Tetrachordon, and in which the four chief passages of scripture concerning that doctrine[4] are explicated; the third, Colasterion, in which a certain sciolist[5] is answered. Which of these tracts you have given to be translated, or what edition, I do not know: for the first of them was published twice, and was much more enlarged in the later edition. If you have not been made aware of this already, or if I understand that you desire anything else from me, such as sending you the more correct edition or the rest of the tracts, I shall do it carefully and with pleasure. For there is nothing at present that I wish changed in them or added. Therefore, if you keep to your intention, I earnestly wish for myself a faithful translater, for you all things favorable.

Westminster: Feb. 5, 1654.[6]

NOTES

1. Letter 16 in the 1674 edition (pp. 42–43) and Columbia, Letter 25 in Yale. The letter answers Aizema's written from The Hague on January 29, and found in British Museum Add. MS 5016*, fol. 8.

2. Aizema was ambassador to England from Hamburg and the Hanse towns from ca. February to ca. August 1652. Sometime during this period he visited Milton.

3. The "book on divorce" is probably *Doctrine and Discipline of Divorce*, although Milton says he does not know which Aizema means. Whichever it is, no Dutch translations are known.

4. Gen. i 27–28; Deut. xxiv 1–2; Matt. v 31–32; and 1 Cor. vii 10–16.

5. The title of the pamphlet is, in part: "Colasterion: A Reply To a Nameles Answer Against The Doctrine and Discipline of Divorce. Wherein The trivial Author of that Answer is discover'd. . . . Answer a Fool according to his folly, lest hee bee wise in his own conceit." The "Nameles Answer" was published, according to Thomason's dating, on November 19, 1644.

6. Milton's residence was in Petty France, Westminster, at this time. The year date is legal style.

LETTER 13[1]

TO HENRY OLDENBURG[2]

I am glad you have arrived safe at Saumur, the goal of your travel, as I believe:[3] for you are not mistaken that the news would be most particularly agreeable to me; who both esteem you for your own merit, and know the cause of the undertaking of the journey to be so honorable and praiseworthy. On the other hand what you have heard, that so infamous a high-priest[4] has been called to instruct so illustrious a church, I had rather any one else had heard it in Charon's[5] boat than you in that of Charenton: for it is strongly to be feared that whoever thinks to reach heaven at any time under such detestable auspices will be duped a whole world out of the way. Woe to that church (only God avert the omen) where such ministers please, principally through the ears, whom the church, if it truly wishes to be called reformed, would more justly eject than elect to office. Because you have shared my writings with no one unless requested,[6] you have indeed done well and judiciously, not in my opinion alone, but also in that of Horace:[7]

> Err not by zeal for us, nor on our books
> Draw hatred by impetuous action.

A certain learned man, a friend of mine,[8] sojourned last summer at Saumur. He wrote to me that the book[9] was sought after in those parts: I sent only one copy; he wrote back that some of the learned with whom he had shared it had been pleased with it more than with anything else. Except that I thought I should be doing a pleasing thing for them, I should have spared you trouble by all means and myself expense. Truly,

> If by chance my heavy load of paper chafes you,
> Cast it aside rather than, because you are bid suffer,
> Throw off the saddles rudely.[10]

To our Lawrence,[11] as you bade, I have delivered greetings in your name: for the rest, there is nothing which I should wish you to do or trouble yourself about before you as well as your pupil are in suitably good health, and may you return to us as soon as possible with such wishes fulfilled.

Westminster: Aug. 1, 1657.

Charon: the boatman transporting the dead across the Styx.
a friend of mine: Andrew Marvell.

NOTES

1. Letter 24 (pp. 55–57) in the 1674 edition and Columbia.

2. Henry Oldenburg was emissary from Bremen to Cromwell's government from ca. mid-1653 through ca. mid-1656, when he became a student at Oxford. He was friendly with Milton and with at least some of Milton's pupils—Edward Lawrence, Cyriack Skinner, and Richard Jones, Earl of Ranelagh. Letters 14 (July 6, 1654), 18 (June 25, 1656), and 29 (here given as Letter 14) in the 1674 edition were also addressed to Oldenburg; copies of letters from Oldenburg

to Milton (ca. June 1656; December 28, 1656; July 7, 1657; October 4, 1657; December 12, 1659) are extant in the Royal Society (MS I, ff. 9, 11, 22v–23r, 30, 61).

3. As tutor-companion to Ranelagh, Oldenburg had embarked on a four-year trip abroad ca. May 1657, apparently because of Ranelagh's dissoluteness and tendency to intemperateness. Letter 25 in the 1674 edition written to Ranelagh on the same day as this to Oldenburg says: "As long as you detain yourself there, you will be in port; at other times guarding yourself against sandbanks, rocks, and the songs of the Sirens. But, in whatever manner you think to enjoy yourself, I should not wish you to thirst too much for Saumurian wine. . . ." Saumur, on the Loire, was the seat of Protestantism in France; white wine is a major industry.

4. Alexander More, Milton's antagonist during the 1650s, was appointed minister at Charente in western France in the middle of 1657, as Oldenburg reported to Milton in his letter of July 7, 1657.

5. Oldenburg had written that after he returned to Paris from a meeting in Charente, he received confirmation of More's appointment by return boat. Milton puns on the closeness between "Charontis" and "Charentonis."

6. Oldenburg had remarked: "These people are of such a nature that whoever knows how to relate something to their ears and to soothe their emotions by the pandering of words easily has the power to gain favor among them. . . ."

7. Horace, *Epistles*, I, xiii, 4–5. Horace had sent a copy of the first three books of *Odes* to Augustus by one Vinnius Asina; with mock anxiety he advises the bearer how to present the gift.

8. This "friend" is identified as Andrew Marvell by Elsie E. Duncan-Jones, *TLS*, December 2, 1949, and July 31, 1953; the letter is not extant.

9. Since Oldenburg mentions Milton's "last" book written against More, the reference is to *Pro se Defensio contra Alexandrum Morum Ecclesiasten*, published August 8, 1655. He says that if he had shown the people a copy of the book, "I should surely stir up the most certain hatred against myself; and I should probably draw away the fewest from their insane zeal for More."

10. Horace, *Epistles*, I, xiii, 6–8. The "saddles" were especially used on asses.

11. Edward Lawrence, son of Henry Lawrence, Lord President of Cromwell's Council of State, was a member of Parliament; *Sonnet 20* is addressed to him. He died shortly after this letter was written.

LETTER 14[1]

TO HENRY OLDENBURG

The indulgence which you ask for your silence you will give rather to me, whose turn, if I remember, to answer it was. Assuredly dimished affection towards you does not make me guilty of the neglected duty, for of this I should wish you to be fully persuaded, but either employments[2] or domestic cares[3] prevented me, or per-

Henry Oldenburg: see Letter 13, note 2.

haps the sluggishness of writing itself. As you wish to know, I am truly as healthy, with God's help, as I am accustomed to being: as to compiling the history of our political troubles, which you seem to urge, I am far from doing: for they are worthier of silence than of commemoration. There is need not of one to compile a history of our troubles, but of one who can happily settle the troubles themselves;[4] for, with you, I fear lest, amid these civil discords, or rather madnesses, we shall seem to the enemies of liberty and even religion, allied just recently, excessively suitable; in truth they have not therein inflicted a severer wound on religion than we ourselves did long before by our crimes.[5] But God, as I hope, on His own account and for his own glory, which is now being attacked, will not allow the counsels and assaults of the enemy to succeed by their own determination, whatever disorders kings and cardinals meditate or fabricate. Meanwhile, for the Protestant Synod of Loudun, which you write is shortly to meet,[6] I wish it—what has never befallen any synod yet—a happy result, not a Nazianzenian one;[7] moreover, the result will be happy enough for it at this time, if it decree nothing else than to expel Morus. Concerning my posthumous adversary,[8] as soon as it appears, I also ask you to inform me as soon as possible. Farewell.

Westminster: December 20, 1659.

NOTES

1. Letter 29 (pp. 62–63) in the 1674 edition and Columbia. Milton answers Oldenburg's letter of December 12, 1659.

2. Milton had written and published *A Treatise of Civil Power* (February 1659) and *Considerations Touching the Likeliest Means to Remove Hirelings* (August 1659) recently.

3. His second wife, Katherine Woodcock, had died on February 3, 1658, and their daughter on March 17, 1658, leaving Milton with the care of the three surviving children of Mary Powell—Anne (now thirteen), Mary (now eleven), and Deborah (now seven).

4. He was to write *The Readie and Easie Way to Establish a Free Commonwealth* in the following February in a further futile effort to retard the Restoration. Charles' Roman Catholic connections created great alarm; Oldenburg remarked that "it is feared that [the Spanish and French] may join arms for the extermination of those who march in defense of liberty and the purer religion."

5. The avarice and rapine that have shared the land both during and after the civil wars. "May the cultivation of peace and justice take the place of all wars and of injustice" was Oldenburg's wish.

6. Meeting at Anjou from November 10, 1659, to January 10, 1660, the synod found Alexander More, Milton's antagonist, innocent of charges of heresy and immorality, and restored him to a pastorate in Paris. Oldenburg specifically cited this part of the synod's agenda.

7. Oldenburg had recalled St. Gregory of Nazianzus' observation "that he had never seen a good outcome to any synod, and that the evils of the church

had acquired increases rather than decreases in assemblies of this sort." Gregory (ca. 329–90), restored as patriarch by the First Council of Constantinople in 381, made the comment in a letter to Procopius, the Prefect of the City, when summoned to a synod in 382. (See *Sancti Patris Nostri Gregorii Nazianzeni, Theologi, Opera* [Cologne, 1690], I, 814, Letter 55.)

8. Claude de Saumaise (Salmasius), who died in 1653, had condemned the English regicides in *Defensio Regia pro Carolo I* (1649); Milton's *Pro Populo Anglicano Defensio* was written as a reply. Oldenburg reported that a defense of Salmasius was then in press at Dijon; it appeared in 1660 as *Claudii Salmasii ad Johannem Miltonum Responsio.*

LETTER 15[1]

TO THE VERY DISTINGUISHED GENTLEMAN, PETER HEIMBACH,[2]

Councillor to the Elector of Brandenburg.

If, among so many deaths of my countrymen, in a year of such heavy pestilence, you believed chiefly from some rumor, as you write, that I also had been carried off, it is no wonder. For that rumor among your people is not displeasing, be it understood, if men were anxious for my safety because of it, for I consider it to be a sign of their goodwill towards me. But by the blessing of God, who had provided for my safe return in the country,[3] I am still alive and well; I trust I am not useless for any duty that remains to be performed by me in this life.[4] After so long an interval[5] for me to have come into your mind is truly very pleasant; although, from your exuberant expression of the matter, you seem to show some suspicion that you have rather forgotten me, seeing that you are astonished, as you say, at the marriage of so many different virtues in me. Certainly I should dread a too numerous progeny from so many marriages, if it were not known that virtues are nourished and flourish most in straitened and hard circumstances; and yet of those one has not very prettily imparted to me the esteem of hospitable reception. For what you call policy, I would prefer you call loyalty to one's country, who, having enticed me with her fair name, has almost expatriated me, so to speak. The chorus of the rest, however, sings clearly in harmony. One's country is wherever it is well. I shall conclude, first procuring this from you, that if you find anything incorrectly written down or not punctuated, you will impute it to the boy who has taken it from my dictation, being utterly ignorant of Latin, so that I was forced, while dictating, not without misery, to spell out each of the letters completely. Meanwhile I am glad that your merits as a man whom I knew as a youth of extraordinary hope have promoted you to so honorable a place in your Prince's favor; and I desire and hope for you all prosperous things. Farewell!

London, August 15, 1666.[6]

NOTES

1. Letter 31 (pp. 65–66) in the 1674 edition and Columbia. It answers a letter from Heimbach on June 6, 1666 (British Museum Add. MS 5016*, ff. 6–7).

2. Peter Heimbach, who may have in part owed his governmental appointment to Milton's recommendation through Henry Lawrence, minister to Holland, had known Milton from at least mid-1656. A copy of the 1645 *Poems* had been presented to him with an inscription citing Heimbach as poet, orator, philosopher, and lawyer. Letters 20 (November 8, 1656) and 27 (December 18, 1657) in the 1674 edition were also written to him. In the first he is addressed as "the most accomplished youth" and in the second, as "the most accomplished man."

3. His friend and sometime amanuensis, Thomas Ellwood had arranged for him to stay at Chalfont St. Giles, Bucks, from ca. June 1665 to ca. February 1666.

4. The duty of writing "to inbreed and cherish in a great people the seeds of vertu . . . [and] to celebrate in glorious and lofty Hymns the throne and equipage of Gods Almightinesse, and what he works, and what he suffers to be wrought with high providence in his Church" (*Reason of Church-Government*, p. 39) had been discharged with *Paradise Lost*, finished by 1665.

5. Perhaps there had been no communication between them since the end of 1657.

6. Milton was living in Jewin Street at this time.

CHRISTIAN DOCTRINE, DE DOCTRINA CHRISTIANA, 1640–1673?

EDITED BY J. MAX PATRICK

Foreword

Summary of *Christian Doctrine*

FOREWORD

In 1823 a packet inscribed "To Mr. Skinner, Merchant," was found among the state papers in London. Part of its contents was a three-volume Latin compilation by John Milton, *De Doctrina Christiana,* consisting of 745 numbered pages, 196 of them copied by Daniel Skinner from the opening sections (no longer extant) of the original manuscript; the remaining 549 pages are the surviving portion of that original; they are largely in the hand of Jeremie Picard, but there are interpolations and corrections added by others, including Skinner. The latter had intended to publish the work in Amsterdam, but finding the printer reluctant, and being warned against publishing so dangerous a work, Skinner surrendered it to Sir Joseph Williamson, with the result that it found its way into official repositories. The date when Milton began its composition, apparently basing it in part on an earlier systematic compendium of theology, is uncertain; however, it seems to have reached the stage of a fair copy in 1658–60, apart from changes which Milton dictated later. He seems to have regarded it as a completed work, but he obviously had no intention of excluding from it any further insights into Holy Scriptures which the Holy Spirit might inspire, for he conceived of the interpretation of the Bible as a dynamic process.

In 1825 the Latin text and a translation by Charles Sumner were published by the Cambridge University Press, and his English version was also printed in Boston, Massachusetts. The Latin was reprinted at Braunschweig in 1827. A revised translation by Sumner was included in the Bohn edition of Milton's *Prose Works,* edited by J. A. St. John (1843–53). Volumes XIV–XVII of the *Columbia Milton* contain a re-editing of Sumner's texts made by James Holly Hanford and Waldo Hilary Dunn. A new edition and translation are being prepared for the *Yale Milton* by Maurice Kelley and John Carey.

The following summary account of *Christian Doctrine* derives from Sumner's rendering and from the Latin as printed in the *Columbia Milton.* Except in passages put into quotation marks, no claim to precise translation is made here. The account is intended as a guide to this controversial treatise and little more. Inevitably, selection and condensation misrepresent the careful wording of the original. Milton's usual method is to state a definition or proposition and to follow it with a series of scriptural citations to document the key words of the definition or proposition. Most of this scriptural documentation has been omitted below, despite the fact that for Milton it was the very heart of his treatise. In the account given below, the focus is on his own statements, his none too frequent comments and observations, and on those aspects of *Christian Doctrine* which are of chief interest to students of Milton and his works. Readers should use this account as a springboard to the full text. They should also remember that a selective digest of a lengthy work in Latin can hardly do justice in another language to the niceties of controversial theology and its special vocabulary.

Book I of *Christian Doctrine* deals with knowledge—knowledge of the Father, Son, and Holy Spirit, as well as of the nature of the church. Book II treats the more practical matter of the worship of God. Since this worship involves fulfillment of three classes of duty —duties toward God (chs. i through vii), duties of man toward himself (chs. viii through x), and duties of man toward his neighbor (chs. xi through xvii)—the emphasis of Book II is clearly ethical.

Some of the features of *Christian Doctrine*, which scholars and others have found of particular interest or significance, and some of the controversies to which it has given rise may be mentioned here. Milton's professed aim is to base what he teaches solely on the Bible. On the whole he does so, but sometimes he reasons not only from scriptural statements but from history, semantics, first principles, and the universal agreement of mankind. Occasionally he complements a position by noting that it is held by some theologians; frequently he re-enforces an attack on some doctrine by emphasizing that it is a Roman Catholic one. He clearly expected that most of his readers would be Protestants, but the fact that he wrote in Latin indicates that he hoped for a European as well as a British audience. His attitude toward the scholastic divines and their niceties in academic and theological disputation is almost unvaryingly disparaging. Nevertheless, he had been trained in scholasticism himself, and so had most of his intended contemporary readers. As a result, while on the one hand he denounces scholastic reasoning as merely human, particularly when it probes into speculations and distinctions where the Bible is, or seems to Milton to be, less precise than the scholastic speculations, he nevertheless involves himself in not a few logical distinctions and niceties. Presumably in such cases he would claim that there is a difference between true and false reasoning. But it must be remembered that, as in all his major works, Milton was trying to persuade his readers; and persuasion involves adjustment to the mentality of those who are to be persuaded. If they think scholastically and if scholastic reasoning is likely to lead them to accept what he holds to be true, he is obviously willing to accommodate his arguments to what he regards as their limitations.

In one respect Milton was handicapped by his attempt to base what he taught exclusively on the Holy Scriptures, for—on the ground of Scripture, of course—he held that of the two religious guides, the written word and the Spirit, the latter is the more reliable. He acknowledged that the text of the Bible is corruptible, indeed, that some New Testament passages occur in only some of the original versions and vary in wording when they do occur; but he had faith that the Spirit which enlightens the believer is incorruptible. Therefore, Milton contended, Scripture is not "to be interpreted by the judgment of man, that is, by our own unassisted judgment, but by means of the Holy Spirit who was promised to all believers" (Book I, ch. xxx). However, it is obviously sometimes difficult for an inspired interpreter of the Bible to persuade others to accept his conclusions, especially because they may be at a different stage of spiritual understanding. Milton's task, accordingly, is to take advantage of illuminations of the Spirit within him and to make his interpretations persuasive to readers by providing scriptural documentation and by adjusting his comments and interpretations to their understanding.

In making such adjustments he was to some extent following a precedent set in the Holy Scriptures. Milton explains the biblical doctrine of accommodation in Book I, chapter ii: the words of the Bible are God's accommodation to the limited capacities of human understanding: he has expressed himself sufficiently and as clearly as is proper for mankind. Hence Milton's advocacy of refraining from probing speculatively, especially by scholastic reasoning, into what God has apparently chosen not to reveal. It is man's duty to comprehend as best he can what is stated in the Bible. Aided by the divine illumination within the believer, he can discover a great deal. But it is best to be content with God's formulations. Milton shows a noticeable reluctance to go beyond what Scripture states about certain matters. Thus he finds no scriptural warrant for the orthodox doctrine of the Trinity, insists on taking literally the reiteration that God is numerically one, and denies that one can be three. On the other hand, he finds clear scriptural authority for the mystery of Christ's dual nature.

According to Milton's interpretation, the Son was the first of God's creations: "Of His own will, God created, or generated, or produced the Son before all things," within the limits of time, and imparted to the Son as much as he chose of the divine nature and the divine substance itself. But Milton cautions that care must be taken not to confound the substance with the whole essence. Equating *essence* with *hypostasis* or individual existence, he asserts that God's essence, the very nature of God, can pertain only to one hypostasis or person who is exclusively the Father. Without contradicting that nature the Father cannot share equally with another person such attributes as unity and infinity and omnipotence. The generation or begetting of the Son was supernatural, and Milton does not presume to probe deeply into the process, preferring to keep as far as possible to biblical terminology. Creation having begun with the generation of the Son, "God the Father produced everything that exists by His Word and spirit, that is, by His will," the Word here being the Son working as a secondary agent at the will of the Father, and the spirit being the divine power rather than any person, according to Milton. He finds no biblical support for the orthodox doctrine that heaven, the material universe, and everything in them were created out of nothing. In his view they were produced out of confused and formless matter which had proceeded at some previous time from the Father. This original matter was intrinsically good, was a substance derived from the Father who is the fountain of every substance, and was the chief productive stock of every subsequent good. In the act of what is ordinarily called "the creation," this raw matter was "adorned and digested into order by the hand of God . . . it merely received embellishment from the accession of forms." In short, the Son, acting at the will of the Father, imposed form on the matter which had proceeded from the Father. Milton seems to have thought of the production of the Son himself as a similar process on a higher level in the scale of being—as a kind of birth whereby a distinct, separate, and inferior person issued, emanated, spirated, and proceeded from the Father, made out of his substance (or substance that had proceeded from him), and endowed with as much of his nature and the gift of his attributes as he chose to give and was able to give without contradicting himself. Scholars dispute over Milton's exact meaning and are generally less willing than Milton was to be content with imprecision of knowledge about a process which is largely incomprehensible to man's limited intellect even in the accommodated language of Scripture and the alternatives afforded by Milton's resort to synonyms. Like Adam at the end of *Paradise Lost* Milton recognized that, with what God revealed, man had his "fill of knowledge," as much as "this Vessel can contain," beyond which it is "folly to aspire."

Consistent with this realistic humility Milton follows the Bible where it is definite and explicit even in matters which modern readers try to explain away; for example, God's punishing descendants for the evils of their ancestors and groups or nations for the faults of individuals (Book I, chs. xi). But the very brevity and lack of comment on some subjects such as witches and witchcraft suggests the possibility that Milton may have cherished some hesitations about orthodox views on them without being able to reach any clear conclusions.

On the other hand, in some matters, especially divorce, he was ready enough to interpret the letter in the light of what he held to be the Spirit or in the light of "right reason" and to contend that the union of man's highest faculties is more essential to marriage than mere carnal conjunction.

Milton's self-restraint about probing into forbidden or at least not explicitly revealed knowledge is perhaps most noticeable in his treatment of the Holy Spirit. As he shows, "the Spirit" is a term used in both Testaments with many different meanings. He makes some effort to sort these out but in many instances simply preserves the biblical phrasing and refrains from interpreting it.

Milton also has great regard for what the Bible does not say. Thus, finding no condemnation of polygamy, he decides that God approves of it. In this instance the reader may wonder why Milton did not decide that in spirit, if not in the letter, the Bible favors monogamy. He sticks to the fact that there are approved examples of it in Scripture and does not presume—perhaps does not want—to go beyond that fact. Yet on other matters he is more willing to move to descriptive comments—for example, his observation that since its original institution, marriage, as a remedy against incontinency, has become somewhat secondary.

Perhaps the chief importance of *Christian Doctrine* is the light it throws on Milton's other works. The distinction drawn in Book I, chapter xi, between the two parts of sin—evil concupiscence and the act itself—is useful for understanding the nature of the Fall in *Paradise Lost*. So is Milton's explanation in Book I, chapter xii, of what God meant when he told Adam and Eve that death would be the penalty if they ate the fruit: "death," according to Milton, refers not merely to the death of body and soul at the end of a man's life (another of Milton's unorthodox ideas), but includes all the evils that tend toward it—guiltiness, shame, loss of innate righteousness, slavish subjection to sin, etc. It is obviously important for readers to remember Milton's tendency, in treating such ideas as "the creation" and "death," to adjust them to fit the Bible (or his interpretation of it), even though such adjustments change the ordinary meanings of those terms.

The account of renovation and regeneration in Book I, chapters xvii–xviii, is significant for understanding Samson's development in *Samson Agonistes*. And the account of the virtues in Book II illuminates interpretation not only of him but also of characters in the other major poems; thus it is possible to view the Lady in *Comus* as an exemplar of the special virtues which are connected with man's duty toward himself; and Book II, chapters ix–x, and Book II, chapter iii, throw special light on Samson. Even as early a work as *Lycidas* finds echoes in the imagery of wolves in Book I, chapter xxxi.

Many years ago when it was suggested that Milton might have lied about seeing Galileo in Italy, a prominent scholar arose and declared that he would rather die than think that Milton would tell a lie. Though scholarship has demonstrated that there is no good reason for accusing Milton of lying about Galileo, it is interesting to note his defense of certain kinds of falsehoods and deceptions in Book II, chapter xiii. Recognizing that there are numerous instances of deceptions practiced by worthy men in the Bible, Milton acknowledges the validity under some circumstances of resorting to falsehood in order to confer positive benefits on another, particularly by doing him a service against his will. This defense of functional and beneficial deception is obviously a key to his resort to rhetoric and to his arguing in his opponents' terms in his propagandist works. This portion of *Christian Doctrine* is thus helpful for understanding the purpose and method of his passionate advocacy, and also throws light on his literary artistry. Also of literary importance, in Book I, chapter xxx of *Christian Doctrine,* is his explanation of how to read and explicate Scripture—an explanation which is readily adaptable to how to read and explicate his own works. And in this connection his treatment of parables, irony, and the like in Book II, chapter xiii, should not be overlooked.

No foreword and summary account is sufficient to indicate adequately how important *Christian Doctrine* is for students of Milton. They should consult not only the full text but also the brilliant treatment of it and relevant scholarship provided in Maurice Kelley's *This Great Argument: A Study of Milton's* De Doctrina Christiana *as a Gloss upon* Paradise Lost (Princeton, 1941; repr. Gloucester, Mass., 1962). Kelley exposes serious faults in Arthur Sewell's *A Study of Milton's* Christian Doctrine (London, 1939), but it is still worthy of consideration. Even more caution needs to be observed in reading Denis Saurat, *Milton, Man and Thinker* (New York, 1925). But there are some fine insights in Walter C. Curry, *Milton's Ontology, Cosmology, and Physics* (Lexington, Ky., 1957).

Controversies over particular aspects of *Christian Doctrine* are numerous. See, for example, the articles by William B. Hunter, Jr., J. H. Adamson, and Maurice Kelley on Milton's "Arianism" in *The Harvard Theological Review,* LII–LIV (1959–61); also Hunter's treatment of Milton's theological vocabulary in the same journal (LVII [1964], 354–65), and, by the same author, "Milton on the Incarnation: Some More Heresies," *JHI,* XXI (1960), 349–69. All these articles are ably discussed by Barbara Kiefer Lewalski in the sixth chapter of *Milton's Brief Epic: The Genre, Meaning, and Art of "Paradise Regained"* (Providence, 1966).

CHRISTIAN DOCTRINE

JOANNIS MILTONI ANGLI DE DOCTRINA CHRISTIANA EX SACRIS DUNTAXAT LIBRIS PETITA DISQUISITIONUM LIBRI DUO POSTHUMI:

CONCERNING CHRISTIAN DOCTRINE COMPILED SOLELY FROM THE HOLY SCRIPTURES IN TWO POSTHUMOUS BOOKS BY THE ENGLISHMAN JOHN MILTON

(The product of many years of study and compilation, *Christian Doctrine* seems to have been largely completed by 1660 apart from various refining changes introduced later. It was first published in 1825. The following is a summary.)

THE PREFATORY ADDRESS

On the model of St. Paul's epistles, *Christian Doctrine* begins with a salutation: "John Milton, Englishman, to all the churches of Christ and to all who profess the Christian Faith throughout the world, peace and recognition of the truth, and eternal salvation in God the Father and in our Lord Jesus Christ."

According to Milton, his treatise is derived solely from the Bible; it is needed because other works of its kind contain specious reasoning, misconstructions of Scripture, and hasty deductions. He has discovered far more than he had expected to find that needs reformation in accordance with the Bible and hopes that his best possession will have a candid reception: it will be more illuminating than disturbing; in any case, 1 Thess. v 21 orders us to test all things. Readers should suspend uncertain opinions until scriptural evidence convinces them. He addresses himself to the learned or at least those who have a mature understanding of the Gospel. The right to sift every doctrine and to write about it according to one individual persuasion is of great importance to Christian libert; otherwise, force and tyrannical man-made laws prevail. Reader should test doctrines by scriptural testimonies before branding them as heretical: only what contradicts the New Testament may properly be called heresy.

BOOK ONE: FAITH, OR THE KNOWLEDGE OF GOD

CHAPTER ONE: DEFINITION OF CHRISTIAN DOCTRINE AND ITS PARTS

Christian doctrine is what Christ disclosed in various ages concerning the nature and worship of God in order to promote God's glory and man's salvation. Christ was not known under that name in the beginning. What he revealed cannot be derived from philosophers or man-made laws but only from Scripture under guidance of the Holy Spirit. The two parts of Christian doctrine are faith—knowledge of God, that is, what is to be habitually believed, not the habit of believing—and love—the worship of God.

CHAPTER TWO: GOD

God has imprinted so many unquestionable tokens of himself on the human mind and has left so many apparent traces of himself throughout nature that no sane individual can be ignorant of his existence. The order and purposiveness of everything in the world testify that a supreme, efficient power existed before it and ordained it for a specific purpose. Some pretend that nature or fate is this supreme power; but the word "nature" implies birth or origination due to some pre-existent agent and properly means either the essence of a thing or the general law which is the origin of everything, under which everything acts. And fate can be nothing but a decree from some almighty power.

Those who attribute the creation of everything to nature necessarily associate chance with it as a joint divinity, thus substituting two, often opposing, sovereign rulers for one God. Visible proofs, verified predictions, and wonderful works have compelled all nations to believe that either God or some evil power presides over the world's affairs; but it is inconceivable that evil could be supreme over good; therefore God exists. Indeed, his existence is proved by conscience or right reason in men. Without God there would be no distinction between right and wrong. No one would follow virtue or be restrained from vice unless conscience or right reason convinced men that they are accountable to a God for their actions. The Scriptures prove the same; and also the dispersion of the Jews because of their sins, as God forewarned them: their scattered condition is living testimony of God's existence and the Bible's truth.

Nature and reason alone are insufficient for correct ideas about God. To know him as he really is transcends man's powers. In the Bible God has made as full a revelation of himself as our minds can conceive: he accommodates himself to our capacities and shows us how we should conceive of him. Therefore, we should not fly beyond what we can understand or indulge in subtleties beyond what the Bible states. In it we learn that his attributes are truth, possession of a most simple essence which admits of no compound, immensity, infinity, eternity, immutability, incorruptibility, omnipresence, omnipotence, and unity. Numerous passages, especially the First Commandment, plainly state that he is one God in the ordinary sense of numerical unity. Nothing should be said of him which is inconsistent with that unity or which assigns to him attributes of unity and plurality at the same time. Vitality, intelligence, and will show his power and excellence. His prescience is so extensive that long before free agents or their thoughts are born he knows what their thoughts and actions will be.

CHAPTER THREE: THE DIVINE DECREES

By a general decree God ordained from all eternity, of his own free, wise, and holy purpose, whatever he willed or was to do. His foreknowledge is another name for his wisdom; in men's language, it is the idea of everything which he had in his mind before he decreed anything. But he did not decree all things absolutely; some things he left in the power of free agents, independent of necessity. It is impossible that he would have fixed by necessary decree what we know is in the power of man. Since God decreed that man would be a free agent, it remained with man to decide whether he would stand or fall: the consequences were contingent upon man's decision and God did not necessitate them. The future events which he foresees are *certain* to happen but will not *necessarily* happen, for his prescience is intransitive and cannot influence what is foreknown. Since God foreknew that Adam would fall of his own free will, that fall was *certain* but it was not *necessary*. So God's foreknowing that the Israelites would turn to strange gods did not predestinate them to do so.

CHAPTER FOUR: PREDESTINATION

Before the foundation of the world God foresaw that man would fall of his own accord and, out of pity, he predestinated all believers to eternal salvation. This predestination to salvation is called election and is the only sense in which "predestination" is used in the Bible. Its object was not simply man as a being who was going to be created but man as a being who was going to fall of his own accord.

God did not decree grace or any other mode of reconciliation for man independently of Christ's sacrifice. Predestination is the effect of God's mercy, love, grace, and wisdom in Christ and should be attributed to those qualities in the Father rather than to his absolute and secret will.

Scripture offers salvation equally to all, in the Old Testament for obedience, and in the New for faith. Throughout the Bible this offer is uniformly conditional. God's predestinating us "in Christ" is on condition of faith in Christ: only those who believe are chosen. God rejects only the disobedient and unbelieving, excluding no one from salvation until he has rejected the offers of sufficient grace. Thus the sin of the individual is the primary cause of reprobation. The reprobation lies not so much in the divine will as in the obstinacy of those who refuse to repent while it is in their power to do so.

CHAPTER FIVE: THE SON OF GOD

Milton alleges that if he were a member of the church of Rome, "which requires implicit obedience to its creed in all points of faith," he would have acquiesced from education or habit in the doctrine of the Trinity; but he recognizes only the Bible as the rule of faith.

On the basis of Scripture, Milton grants that the Father and the Son are different persons and that the Son existed in the beginning under the name of the Logos or Word: he was the first of the whole creation; afterwards all things in heaven and earth were made by him. But Milton finds no proof in the Bible that the Son was generated from all eternity. His generation, like his priesthood, kingly power, and resuscitation from the dead, was owing to the Father's will and decree. It was in God's power not to beget the Son; if he had begotten a coequal, he would have impaired himself. He made the Son of his own substance; but that does not mean that the Son is coessential with the Father. If the Son were coeval and coessential with the Father and of the same numerical essence, they would be one person and the title of Son would be inappropriate. The Son was begotten within the limits of time, as "this day" in Psalm ii 7 and Acts xiii 33 makes clear. He was, as the Bible states, "the first born of every creature" (Rom. viii 18) and "the beginning of the creation of God" (Rev. iii 14). The Father imparted to him as much as he pleased of the divine nature and of the divine substance; but we must be careful not to confuse this substance with the whole essence. No more than this is revealed in the Bible concerning the generation of the Son. Anyone who wants to be wiser than this becomes foiled in his pursuit of wisdom, tangled in sophistry, and involved in darkness.

According to Milton, Christ's being called "God" several times in the Bible gave rise to the hypothesis that the Son is essentially one with the Father though personally and numerically another. Milton contends that this is a strange hypothesis, contrary to reason if one essence is represented as both simple and compound, and contrary to the First Commandment if "one" and "two" have the same meaning for God and man. Inasmuch as the term "god" is applied to kings and princes in the Bible, there is no need to violate reason if the same term is applied to Christ. Accordingly Milton urges men to cease hypothesizing about sacred matters. They should follow exclusively what Holy Scripture teaches which is, according to him, that there is one true, independent, supreme God and that he is numerically one, as human reason, the common language of mankind, and his people the Jews have considered him to be. In evidence, Milton cites and discusses numerous scriptural passages, with particular emphasis on 1 Cor. viii 4–6, John x 29 and xiv 28.

CHAPTER SIX: THE HOLY SPIRIT

"Scripture is silent with regard to the nature of the Spirit, in what manner it exists, or whence it arose; which is a caution to us not to be overhasty in our conclusions on the subject." Milton notes that in the Bible "the Spirit" is a term variously used for God, Christ, the person of the Holy Spirit, God's power, the light of his truth, a divine impulse transmitted through Christ or some other channel, God's spiritual gifts, the donation of the Holy Spirit, or a symbol of that person. After citing what the Son said about this Holy Spirit and discussing many texts, Milton concludes that as a person the Holy Spirit was created by God's free will before the world but later than the Son: being sent by the Father and the Son, the Spirit is dependent upon them and inferior to them and gives only what he receives from them.

CHAPTER SEVEN: CREATION

The Father, by means of his Word, the Son acting as a secondary agent, and by means of his spirit or divine power (not the personal Holy Spirit), produced everything that exists, not out of nothing but out of pre-existing matter which proceeded from God himself and which, though it was confused and formless at first, was nevertheless good because of this origin. Creation consisted in digesting and giving form to this matter. Because it originated in an eternal, incorruptible God, it cannot be altogether annihilated.

Things invisible—that is, the angels and the heaven of the blessed—were apparently formed before the creation of things visible—that is, the material universe and everything in it; and the apostasy of some of the angels seems to have taken place before the foundations of this world were laid. Man's body and soul were given their first existence when he was created. Being made in the image of God, man was given natural wisdom, holiness, and righteousness. Without extraordinary wisdom, man could not have given names to the whole animal creation with such sudden intelligence (Gen. ii 20).

CHAPTER EIGHT: GOD'S PROVIDENCE OR GENERAL GOVERNMENT OF THE UNIVERSE

The general government of God is that by which the Father regards, preserves, and governs the whole creation with infinite wisdom and holiness according to the conditions of his decree. Since man's spontaneous fall, God preserves men and things only as regards their existence, not their primitive perfection. Though his government extends to voluntary actions, there is no infringement on the liberty of the human will. He exercises his providence by allowing sin to exist, by withdrawing his grace, and by impelling sinners to sin by hardening their hearts and darkening their understandings; however, he does not compel the innocent to act wickedly; and it is only after a man has conceived sin that God influences his will so that it operates good for others or punishment for himself. God eventually converts every evil deed into an instrument of good, contrary to the expectation of sinners, and thus he overcomes evil with good.

God's ordinary providence (commonly called nature) is that by which he upholds and preserves the immutable order of causes appointed by him in the beginning. By his extraordinary providence either he or someone empowered by him produces effects contrary to the usual order of nature. Such miracles manifest his power, confirm faith, and take away all excuse for unbelief.

CHAPTER NINE: THE SPECIAL GOVERNMENT OF ANGELS

Like man in his original state, the good angels are upheld by their own strength, not by God's grace. They stand around His throne as ministering agents. They praise God and are obedient to him in all respects, and their ministry relates especially to believers: thus there are numerous examples of angels present at religious assemblies of believers. It seems probable that some of them are appointed to preside over nations, kingdoms, and particular districts. Sometimes they are sent as messengers of divine vengeance to punish the sins of men and destroy cities and nations. Michael is their leader. They know some things by revelation, some by means of their excellent understandings; but there is much of which they are ignorant. The evil angels are those who revolted of their own accord before the fall of man. They are reserved for eternal torment; but they are sometimes allowed to wander through the earth, the air, and heaven itself to execute God's judgments. Their knowledge is great but tends to increase their misery. They also have their prince and retain their respective ranks.

CHAPTER TEN: THE SPECIAL GOVERNMENT OF MAN BEFORE THE FALL, INCLUDING THE INSTITUTIONS OF SABBATH AND MARRIAGE

Having placed man in Eden with everything necessary for happiness, God commanded man not to eat the fruit of a certain tree under penalty of death if he disobeyed. The command was a test of obedience, for the act forbidden was an indifferent one. The tree of knowledge of good and evil was named from the outcome of eating it: since Adam tasted it we know not only evil but we know good only by means of evil. For it is by evil that virtue is chiefly exercised and shines with greater brightness.

Though God hallowed the Sabbath to himself and dedicated it to rest, Scripture does not say that its institution was made known to Adam or that any commandment to observe it was given before the delivery of the Law on Mount Sinai.

Marriage was instituted, if not commanded, at the creation and it consisted in the mutual love, society, help, and comfort of husband and wife, though with a reservation of superior rights to the husband. This most intimate connection of man with woman was ordained by God for the purpose either of the procreation of children or of the relief and solace of life. Gen. ii 24 is not a law or commandment but states what would have been an effect or natural consequence of that union in the perfect state of man: the passage is intended only to account for the origin of families.

Noting that there is a most dangerous tendency in religion to account as sin what is not such in reality, Milton considers what the Bible says about polygamy and decides that it is not forbidden there. He observes that it is the divine precepts themselves that are obligatory, not the consequences deduced from them by human reasoning.

Milton cites texts to show that God is specially concerned to make marriage prosperous and happy. The consent of living parents should not be wanting; but the mutual consent of the parties themselves is naturally the first and most important requisite: there can be no love or good will, and consequently no marriage, without mutual consent. The consent must be free from fraud. The parties should agree in matters of religion and should exercise benevolence, love, help, and solace mutually. Since Adam's fall, the provision of marriage as a remedy against incontinency has become somewhat secondary. Marriage is not a command binding on all, but only on those unable to live chastely without it. It is honorable in itself and forbidden to no order of men.

Being a most intimate union, marriage should not be lightly dissolved; but good will, love, help, comfort, and fidelity on both sides are the essential form of marriage; and if the essential form is dissolved, the marriage itself is virtually dissolved. God joins only what is suitable, good, and honorable: he has not made provision for unnatural and monstrous associations pregnant with dishonor, misery, hatred, and calamity. "It is not God who forms such unions, but violence or rashness or error or the influence of some evil genius." "God in His just, pure, holy law has not only permitted divorce on a variety of grounds but has even ratified it in some cases and enjoined it in others." Christ's words in Matt. xix 8 were meant for the Pharisees, not as a general explanation of divorce. God even extended the benefit of laws of divorce to those who He knew would abuse them through the hardness of their hearts, thinking it better to bear with the obduracy of the wicked than to refrain from alleviating the misery of the righteous or allow the institution itself to be subverted. And "can anyone who understands the spirit of the Gospel believe that it denies what the law did not scruple to concede either as a right or an indulgence to the infirmity of human nature?"

God ordained that marriage should be indissoluble for man in his state of innocence in Paradise before the entrance of sin into the world; but He permitted its dissolution after the Fall to prevent the innocent from being exposed to perpetual injury from the wicked. This permission forms part of the law of nature and of Moses and is not disallowed by Christ. It is a flagrant error to convert a gospel precept into a civil statute and to enforce it by legal penalties.

CHAPTER ELEVEN: THE FALL OF OUR FIRST PARENTS; SIN

Sin is the transgression of the law, either of that rule of conscience which is innate and engraven upon the mind of man, or of the special command of God. The sin common to all is the one which our first parents, and in them all their posterity, committed when they cast off obedience to God and tasted the forbidden fruit. This sin originated in the instigation of the devil and in the liability to fall with which man was created. It was most heinous, for it included every sin that can be named. It comprehended distrust in the divine veracity, credulity in the assurances of Satan, unbelief, ingratitude, gluttony, excessive uxoriousness in the man, a want of proper regard for him on Eve's part, insensibility to the welfare of their offspring, parricide, theft, invasion of the rights of others, sacrilege, deceit, presumption in aspiring to divine attributes, fraud in the means employed, pride, and arrogance.

Milton observes that universally the penalty incurred by the violation of sacred things attaches not only to a criminal but to his posterity and that God in such passages as Exod. xx 5 declares that this is the method of his justice. Milton explains the principle behind this justice as follows: God foresaw that infants, though guiltless of actual sin, would grow up similar to their sinful parents if they were allowed to live; others, though smitten for crimes of their ancestors, are justly obnoxious for sins of their own. Accordingly, in Lev. xxvi 40, Neh. ix 2, and numerous other texts, the penitent are enjoined to confess not only their own sins but those of their fathers. Subjects are also afflicted for the sins of their rulers or a nation for the iniquity of an individual.

Personal sin is that which each man commits personally, apart from the common sin.

There are two parts, gradations, divisions, or modes of sin: (1) evil concupiscence, which is the desire to sin, and (2) the crime itself, the act of sin which is commonly called "actual sin." It is called "actual sin" because it usually consists in some act, though it may also be incurred by words and thoughts and even by omission of good actions. However, sin is not properly an action, for in reality it implies defect. Every act is good in itself; properly speaking not the act itself but its irregularity, its deviation from the line of right, is what is evil. Therefore the act itself is not the matter of which the sin consists; it is only the "subject" in which the sin is committed.

CHAPTER TWELVE: THE PUNISHMENT OF SIN

The punishment of sin is death, and under that term as used in Scripture all evils that tend toward death are included; for mere bodily death did not follow Adam's sin immediately. Accordingly, theologians treat four degrees of death. The first includes all the evils that came immediately after the Fall before bodily death: guiltiness, terrors of conscience, pollution of the whole man, and consequent shame. The second degree, spiritual death or loss of divine grace and innate righteousness, took place at the moment of the Fall. It consists of obscuration of right reason, deprivation in part of righteousness and liberty to do good, and that slavish subjection to sin and Satan that constitutes a sort of death of the will. However, some remnants of the divine image and original excellence remain in the understanding, and enough liberty of will remains for man to perform indifferent actions and good works.

CHAPTER THIRTEEN: THE DEATH OF THE BODY

The third degree of death is that of the body. All nature is also subject to mortality because of the Fall. Inasmuch as God did not except any part of man from the punishment of death, it follows that the whole man—body, soul, and spirit—dies. The fourth degree of death is the punishment of the damned, death eternal.

CHAPTER FOURTEEN: MAN'S RESTORATION AND CHRIST AS REDEEMER

The restoration of man is the act by which the Father, through Jesus Christ, delivers man from sin and death to a far more excellent state of grace than that from which he fell. In this restoration are comprised the redemption and renovation of man. By the act of redemption, Christ, in conformity to the Father's eternal counsel and grace and in the fullness of time, voluntarily redeemed all believers at the price of his own blood. Even before man repented, God showed his grace by promising that one from the woman's seed would bruise the serpent's head.

Christ is the only redeemer and mediator. As redeemer, his nature is divine and human. The incarnation by which he, being God, took human nature and was made flesh without ceasing to be numerically the same as before is the greatest mystery of our religion, and it is frequently spoken of as a mystery in Scripture in contrast to the lack of mention there of a mystery of the Trinity. Since the incarnation is such a mystery, we should not assert anything rashly concerning it on mere grounds of philosophical reasoning. It is enough to know that the Son of God assumed human flesh, that he is called both God and man in the Scriptures, and that he was in reality both God and man: the mode of union is unknown to us; and it is best to be ignorant of whatever God wills should remain unknown. That the Son remains one Christ is a matter of faith; whether he retains a twofold will and understanding is a point on which Scripture is silent and into which, accordingly, we need not enquire. The subject of his two natures is too profound a mystery to warrant any positive assertions respecting it.

The efficient cause of Christ's conception was the Holy Spirit, according to Matt. i 20 and Luke i 35, "by which words," says Milton, "I am inclined to understand the power and spirit of the Father Himself."[1]

CHAPTER FIFTEEN: THE OFFICE OF THE MEDIATOR, AND HIS THREEFOLD FUNCTIONS

At the special appointment of the Father, Christ voluntarily performed and continues to perform on man's behalf everything needed for obtaining reconciliation with God and eternal salvation. In this mediatorial office, he functions as prophet, priest, and king. As prophet, he instructs his church in heavenly truth and declares his Father's will, thus externally promulgating divine truth and internally illuminating man's understanding. As priest, he once offered himself to the Father as a sacrifice for sinners and he always intercedes for us by appearing in God's presence for us and by rendering our prayers agreeable to him. As king, Christ governs and preserves the church, chiefly by an inward law and spiritual power, and he conquers its enemies. As long as there is occasion for him to mediate, he will carry out these functions.

[1] Compare *Paradise Lost*, XII, 368–69: "A Virgin is his Mother, but his Sire / The Power of the most High."

CHAPTER SIXTEEN: THE MINISTRY OF REDEMPTION

Christ discharged his mediatorial office by his humiliation and by his exaltation. As God-man, he voluntarily submitted himself to the divine justice, in life and in death enduring everything requisite for man's redemption. Then, having triumphed over death and having laid aside the form of a servant, he was exalted to immortality and highest glory partly by his own merits and partly by the Father's gift, for the benefit of mankind. There were three degrees in this exaltation: his resurrection from the dead, his ascension into heaven, and his sitting on the right hand of God—a Hebraism signifying that he was exalted to a place of power and glory next to the Father. His divine and human natures both suffered in his humiliation and both participated in his exaltation. He made complete reparation for *all* mankind.

CHAPTER SEVENTEEN: MAN'S RENOVATION, INCLUDING HIS CALLING

Renovation is the change by which a man who was formerly cursed and obnoxious to the divine wrath is brought into a state of grace. The mode of a man's renewing is either natural or supernatural. The natural mode influences only the natural affections; it includes the calling of the natural man and the consequent change in his character. Calling is either general or special. God's general calling is his inviting all mankind in various ways to knowledge of the true deity. Special calling invites particular men, both elect and reprobate, in preference to others. Calling partially renews the natural mind and will of man so that he is led to seek a better knowledge of God and is altered for the better. A man thus enlightened is endued with power to will what is good and to act freely. But God's calling and the consequent change in the natural man do not ensure salvation unless a man is also regenerate.

CHAPTER EIGHTEEN: REGENERATION

Supernatural regeneration restores man, more completely than before, to the use of his natural faculties, that is, the power to form right judgment and to exercise free will. The Word and the Spirit operate so that the old man is destroyed and the inward man is regenerated after God's image: the whole man, body and soul, is sanctified for the service of God and the performance of good works. The external cause of this regeneration is Christ's death and resurrection.

CHAPTER NINETEEN: REPENTANCE

The effects of regeneration are repentance and faith. Repentance precedes faith and is the gift of God; by it the regenerate man sees that he has sinned, detests and avoids evil, humbly turns to God, and earnestly strives to follow righteousness. Chastisement often helps to cause repentance, but God limits it and strengthens us to endure afflictions.

CHAPTER TWENTY: SAVING FAITH

Saving faith is a complete persuasion which is operated in the regenerate through God's gift so that, on the authority of the promise, we believe that what he promised in Christ is ours, especially the grace of eternal life. Properly speaking the seat of faith is in the will, not in the understanding. From faith, hope arises, a sure expectation of those future things which are already ours in Christ.

CHAPTER TWENTY-ONE: INGRAFTING IN CHRIST AND ITS EFFECTS

Ingrafting in Christ occurs when believers are planted in him by the Father; that is, they are made partakers in Christ and meet for becoming one with him. The effects of ingrafting and regeneration are newness of life and increase. Newness of life or living unto God is also called self-denial. The new life brings comprehension of spiritual things and love of holiness. Comprehension of spiritual things is a condition of mind which God produces; by it natural ignorance is removed from those who are ingrafted in Christ, so that, enlightened by God's teaching, they know everything requisite for eternal salvation and the true happiness of life. Love, or charity, arises from the sense of the divine love which is shed in the hearts of the regenerate so that those who are ingrafted in Christ become dead to sin and alive again unto God and brings forth good works spontaneously and freely—for our co-operation is required.

The increase which is operated in the regenerate either is absolute, that is, an increase, derived from the Father, of the gifts received by regeneration and ingrafting in Christ; or the increase is relative, that is, to some degree in the power of the regenerate themselves.

Though perfection is not to be expected in this life, we should strive for it: hence the struggle in the regenerate between the flesh and the spirit. Those who are strenuous in this conflict, who struggle against the world and Satan and who labor to attain perfection in Christ are frequently called perfect and blameless and without sin in Scripture, though they are really imperfect; sin, though still dwelling in them, does not reign over them.

CHAPTER TWENTY-TWO: JUSTIFICATION

Relative or internal increase refers either to the Father only or to the Father and Son conjointly. The first of these is called justification and adoption. Justification is the gratuitous purpose of God whereby men who are regenerate and ingrafted in Christ are absolved from sin and death by Christ's satisfaction and are accounted just in the sight of God not by the works of the Law but through faith. As far as men are concerned, justification is gratuitous; but insofar as Christ is concerned, it is not gratuitous: Christ took our sins upon himself by imputation and paid the ransom, thus effecting their expiation of his own accord and at his own cost. Man, paying nothing on his part, but merely believing, receives the imputed righteousness of Christ as a gift. Finally, the Father, appeased by this propitiation, pronounces the justification of all believers. "A simpler mode of satisfaction could not have been devised, nor one more agreeable to equity." We are justified by faith without the works of the Law but not without the works of faith: a living and true faith cannot be without works, though these may differ from works of the written law. This interpretation "affords no countenance to the doctrine of human merit, inasmuch as both faith itself, and its works, are the works of the Spirit, not our own." Because our faith is imperfect, works which proceed from it cannot be pleasing to God except insofar as they rest upon his mercy and are sustained by that foundation alone. When a man is said to be perfect and just in God's sight, this is to be understood according to the measure of human righteousness and as compared to the righteousness of others; or it may mean that such a man was endued with an undissimulating, sincere, upright heart.

CHAPTER TWENTY-THREE: ADOPTION

Adoption is the act by which God adopts as his children those who are justified through faith. In one sense all men are by nature sons of God, the author of their being; but the particular sense meant here is that of adopted children. Adoption makes them heirs of God through Christ. They are sons of God by a new generation, by an assumption of a new nature, and by a conformity to his glory. From this adoption is derived liberty, a privilege known to Abraham's descendants even under the law of bondage: "in the spirit of this liberty they did not scruple even to infringe the ceremonies of religion when observing those ceremonies would have been inconsistent with the law of love."

CHAPTER TWENTY-FOUR: UNION AND FELLOWSHIP WITH CHRIST AND HIS MEMBERS, WITH CONSIDERATION OF THE MYSTICAL OR INVISIBLE CHURCH

The increase of the regenerate, considered with reference to the Father and Son conjointly, consists in our union and fellowship with the Father through Christ the Son, and our glorification after the image of Christ. The fellowship which arises from this union consists in a participation, through the Spirit, of the various gifts and merits of Christ. From this fellowship with Christ arises the mutual fellowship of the members of Christ's body (which they call the communion of saints), and from this union and fellowship of the regenerate with the Father and Christ and among themselves results the mystical body, which is called the invisible church, of which Christ is the head. Since the body of Christ is mystically one, the fellowship of his members must also be mystical, not confined to time or place but composed of individuals of widely separated countries in all ages since the world's foundation.

CHAPTER TWENTY-FIVE: IMPERFECT GLORIFICATION; THE DOCTRINES OF ASSURANCE AND FINAL PERSEVERANCE

Imperfect glorification is the state of men who, being justified and adopted by the Father, are filled with consciousness of present grace and excellency and expectation of future glory to such an extent that their glory is already begun. Regeneration and increase are accompanied by confirmation or preservation in the faith, which is also the work of God. These three, considered as proximate causes on the part of God, and their effects (faith, love, etc.) considered as proximate causes on the part of man, or as acting in man, produce assurance of salvation and the final perseverance of the saints. Such are the beginnings of glorification. Its perfection is not attainable in the present life.

CHAPTER TWENTY-SIX: THE MANIFESTATION OF THE COVENANT OF GRACE; THE LAW OF GOD

Having considered renovation as far as it is developed in this life, we now trace its manifestation and exhibition in the covenant of grace. God declared this covenant when he stated that he would put enmity between the serpent, or Satan, and the seed of Eve. This covenant was exhibited in the Mosaic law and in the Gospel. The law of Moses was a written code of many precepts intended for the Israelites alone, with a promise of life to those who obeyed the code and a curse on those who disobeyed it; its purpose was that they, being led thereby to acknowledge the depravity of mankind (including their own), might have recourse to the righteousness of the promised savior; and that they and, in the course of time, all nations might be led under the Gospel from the weak, servile rudiments of this elementary institution to the full strength of the new creature and a manly liberty worthy of the sons of God. But the Law was imperfect: what neither it nor its observers could attain has been attained by faith in God through Christ. The promise of the Law extended only to happiness in this life, that of the Gospel to eternal life.

CHAPTER TWENTY-SEVEN: THE GOSPEL AND CHRISTIAN LIBERTY

The Gospel is the new dispensation of the covenant of grace; far more excellent and perfect than the Law, it was first announced obscurely by Moses and the prophets; afterwards it was announced in the clearest terms by Christ himself and his apostles and evangelists; and since then it has been written in the hearts of believers and is ordained to continue even to the end of the world: it contains a promise of eternal life to all those in every nation who shall believe in Christ when he is revealed to them and a threat of eternal death to those who shall not believe. On the introduction of the Gospel or new covenant through faith in Christ, the entire Mosaic law was abolished: as a law of commandments contained in ordinances, it cannot justify; it is a source of trouble and subversion to believers; it even tempts God if we try to perform its requisitions; it has no promise attached to it, or, to speak more properly, it takes away and frustrates all promises, whether of inheritance, adoption, grace, or of the Spirit; nay, it even subjects us to a curse—therefore, it must necessarily have been abolished. However, the sum and essence of the Law is not abrogated, for its purpose is attained in that love of God and our neighbor which is born of the Spirit through faith: the end for which the Law was instituted, namely the love of God and our neighbor, is thus by no means to be considered as abolished. The injunctions of the Law are now written in the hearts of believers with this difference, that in certain precepts the Spirit seems to be at variance with the letter of the Law whenever we can more effectually consult the love of God and our neighbor by departing from the letter. Thus in Mark ii 27, Christ said that the sabbath was made for man, not man for the sabbath.

Christian liberty results from the Gospel's abrogation of the law of servitude—though, strictly speaking, liberty is the peculiar fruit of adoption and, as such, was not unknown in the time of the Law: see Chapter xxiii. But it was not possible for man's liberty to be perfected or fully manifest before the coming of Christ our deliverer; therefore, liberty must be considered as belonging in a special manner to the Gospel, and as consorting with it because truth is principally known by the Gospel and because the Gospel's peculiar gift is the Spirit.

Through Christ our deliverer, Christian liberty looses us, as by enfranchisement, from the bondage of sin and consequently from the rule of law and of man, to the intent that, being made sons instead of servants and perfect men instead of children, we may serve God in love through the guidance of the spirit of truth. Hence we are freed from the yoke of human judgments and even more from civil decrees and penalties in religious matters. Nay, we must withstand the opinions of the brethren themselves if they are influenced by motives unworthy of the Gospel. A weak believer should not judge rashly the liberty of a Christian brother who has stronger faith than his own; rather, the weaker should all the more willingly give himself up to be instructed. But neither this reason nor pretended consideration for weaker brethren warrant edicts of the magistrate which constrain believers or in any way deprive them of their religious liberty. When a magistrate takes this liberty away, he takes away the Gospel itself and indiscriminately deprives both the good and the bad of their privilege of free judgment.

CHAPTER TWENTY-EIGHT: THE EXTERNAL SEALING OF THE COVENANT OF GRACE

Our next subject is the sealing of the covenant of grace, or its representation under certain outward signs. Under the law of Moses, it consisted in circumcision and the passover; under the Gospel, in baptism and the Lord's supper. These ceremonies, particularly the last two are known as sacraments, a sacrament being a visible sign ordained by God by which he sets his seal on believers in token of his saving grace or of the satisfaction of Christ, and by which we testify faith and obedience to God with a sincere heart and a grateful remembrance. In baptism, the bodies of believers are immersed in running water to signify their regeneration by the Holy Spirit and their union with Christ in his death, burial, and resurrection. Infants are not to be baptized, for they are incompetent to enter into a covenant or to pronounce a vow. Let the church, therefore, receive infants which come unto her, after the example of Christ, with imposition of hands and benediction, but not baptism.

The Lord's supper is a solemnity in which Christ's death is commemorated by the breaking of bread and pouring of wine: both of these elements are tasted by each communicant, and the benefits of Christ's death are thus sealed to believers. Consubstantiation and, above all, the papistical doctrine of transubstantiation are irreconcilable with reason and common sense, with the habits of mankind, with the testimony of Scripture, with the nature and end of a sacrament, with the analogy of baptism, with the ordinary forms of language, with the human nature of Christ, and with the state of glory in which he is to remain until the day of judgment. Sacraments are not absolutely indispensable: many have obtained the gifts of the Spirit through the word and faith alone. We nowhere read in Scripture of the Lord's supper being distributed to the first Christians by an appointed minister—only that they partook of it in common, frequently, and in private houses. Confirmation, penance, extreme unction, orders, and marriage are not sacraments. Marriage is not even a religious ceremony: it is a purely civil compact and its celebration in no way belongs to the ministers of the church. In any case, sacraments ought to be imparted equally to all believers.

CHAPTER TWENTY-NINE: THE VISIBLE CHURCH

The visible church is the assembly of those who are called by God, whether they are regenerate or not. The tokens of the visible church are pure doctrine, the proper external worship of God, genuine evangelical love, and a right administration of the seals of the covenant. Because Christ is the head of the mystical and visible church, no one but he has the right or power to preside over it. No authority may be found in Scripture for an earthly head in the person of Peter or a succession of Roman pontiffs. The keys of heaven were not committed exclusively to him. In any case, what proof have we that privileges given to him are continued to his successors, or that these successors are the Roman pontiffs?

The universal visible church consists of ministers (persons appointed by divine commission to perform various offices in the church of Christ) and all those people who openly worship the Father through Christ anywhere, whether alone or with others. Extraordinary ministers are persons (prophets, apostles, evangelists, and the like) inspired and sent on special missions by God to plant or reform the church by means of writing or preaching. Any believer endowed with the necessary gifts is competent to act as an ordinary minister and to administer baptism.

CHAPTER THIRTY: THE HOLY SCRIPTURES

The writings of the prophets, apostles, and evangelists, composed under divine inspiration, are the Holy Scriptures. The books usually subjoined to those recognized as canonical by the orthodox [that is, by Protestants] and known as apocryphal are by no means of equal authority with the others and may not be adduced as evidence in matters of faith. The use of Scriptures is prohibited to no one: they are adapted for the daily hearing or reading of all classes and orders of men; and they are plain and perspicuous in all things necessary to salvation and are adapted to the instruction even of the most unlearned by means of diligent and constant reading. The liberty of investigating Scripture thoroughly is granted to all; but it is to be interpreted by means of the divine illumination of the Holy Spirit, not by man's unassisted judgment. In itself Scripture possesses clarity and is sufficient for its own explanation, especially in matters of faith and holiness. How foolish, therefore, is it for theologians to persist in darkening religion's most momentous truths by intricate metaphysical comments, stringing the useless technicalities and empty distinctions of scholastic barbarism! It is only to those who perish that the Scriptures are obscure.

No passage of Scripture is to be interpreted in more than one sense; however, in the Old Testament this sense is sometimes a compound of the historical and typical. The requisites for public interpretation of Scripture as laid down usefully by theologians are knowledge of languages; inspection of the originals; examination of the context; care in distinguishing between literal and figurative expressions; consideration of cause and circumstances, antecedents and consequences; mutual comparison of texts; and regard to the analogy of faith. Attention must also be paid to anomalies of syntax. No inferences are to be allowed except those which follow necessarily and plainly from the words themselves: otherwise we may receive what is not written for what is written, the shadow for the substance, the fallacies of human reasoning for the doctrines of God. Our consciences are bound by the declarations of Scripture, not by the conclusions of the various schools of philosophers. Since every believer has a right to interpret the Scriptures for himself, inasmuch as he has the Spirit for his guide and the mind of Christ is in him, public interpretations can be useful to him only to the extent that they are confirmed by his own conscience. No visible church or magistrate should impose interpretations on us. If professed believers disagree about what Scripture means, it is their duty to tolerate such a difference until God reveals the truth to all. Scripture is the sole judge of controversies—or, rather, every man is to decide for himself through its aid and with the guidance of the Spirit of God. The church cannot be the rule or arbiter of that on which it is itself founded.

Under the Gospel, we have an external Scripture—the written Word—and an internal one—the Holy Spirit, written in the hearts of believers. The text of the Bible may be corrupted and, in fact, does vary in different manuscripts, transcripts, and editions; but the Spirit cannot be corrupted; neither is it easy to deceive a man who is really spiritual. The Mosaic law was handed down in an uncorrupted state; the remaining books of the Old Testament, particularly the historical ones, though they seem to contradict themselves in chronology, are regarded as doctrinally sound. But the New Testament has come to us through the hands of many persons who were subject to various temptations; nor have we any copies in the authors' handwriting by which to correct the errors of others. It is hard to conjecture why Providence committed the New Testament writings to such uncertain guardianship unless he intended to teach us by this circumstance that the Spirit is a more certain guide than the Bible.

When acquiescence in human opinions or obedience to human authority is exacted in matters of religion in the name of the church or the Christian magistrate from those who are individually led by the Spirit of God, the effect is that of imposing a yoke not on man but on the Holy Spirit. And we are expressly forbidden to pay any regard to written or unwritten human traditions in Deut. iv 2; Prov. xxx 6; Rev. xxii 18–19; Isa. xxix 13–14; Matt. xv 3, 9; Gal. i 8; 1 Tim. vi 3; Tit. i 4; 1 Tim. i 4; and Col. ii 8. Moreover, in matters of this nature, we cannot trust implicitly the opinions of our forefathers or of antiquity. Even to the venerable name of our mother church itself we are not to attach any undue authority unless we understand by this expression the mystical church in heaven.

CHAPTER THIRTY-ONE: PARTICULAR CHURCHES

A particular church is a society of persons who profess the faith, are united by a special bond of brotherhood, and are organized in the best way for edification and the mutual communion of the saints. The ordinary ministers of a particular church are presbyters (also called bishops) and deacons. In the early church, bishops and presbyters must have been the same. Some presbyters were set apart for teaching, some watched over the discipline of the church, and in particular instances these functions were combined. A deacon's duty is to administer to the temporal wants of the church in general and, in particular, of the poor, the sick, and strangers. Widows of the church are associated with deacons in the performance of their duty. The choice of ministers belongs to the people, and each minister should undergo a special trial before being admitted to office. It is exemplary, noble, and honorable for a minister to follow the example of our Lord and to render unpaid service to the church; however, some recompense is both reasonable and sanctioned by the law of God and the declarations of Christ and his apostles. Ministers should look for necessary support of life not from the edicts of the civil power but from the spontaneous good will and liberality of the church. If the Christian religion depends for its existence on no firmer supports than wealth and civil power, how can it be more worthy of belief than the Mahometan superstition? To exact stipendiary payments, to bargain for them, to extort them under civil edicts, or to resort to legal processes for ecclesiastical allowances is the part of wolves. In these days there are many who like wolves and unlike good shepherds seek out more abundant pastures for themselves. They ought to live on their own private resources, by the exercise of some calling, by some industry, as did the prophets. The only persons who should be regarded as the people of the church are those who are well informed in Scripture doctrine and are able to try any teacher or groups of teachers by the rule of Scripture and the Spirit. The people are warned not to take delight in vain teachers. Every church, so constituted, is to be considered integral and perfect no matter how small its numbers; as regards its religious rights it has no superior on earth. But particular churches may communicate with each other and co-operate for the general welfare. However, Milton finds no trace of councils in the Scripture.

The enemies of the church are various, but all of them will be destroyed. The greatest of them is called Antichrist. Their frauds and persecutions are various, and we are enjoined to flee from persecution except where flight would not be conducive to the glory of God. There are appropriate consolations for the persecuted.

CHAPTER THIRTY-TWO: CHURCH DISCIPLINE

Discipline is the bond that holds a particular church together. It consists in agreement among the church members to fashion their lives according to Christian doctrine and to regulate everything in their public meetings decently and with order. It is prudent and pious to solemnize the formation or re-establishment of a particular church by a public renewal of the covenant. Similarly, when an individual unites himself to a particular church, he should covenant with God and the church to conduct himself so as to promote his own edification and that of his brethren. This covenant ought properly to take place in baptism. In church gatherings each individual should, in turn, be authorized to speak, prophesy, teach, or exhort, according to his gifts; the apostles did not ordain that an individual should have the sole right of speaking from a higher place.

The Bible enjoins women to keep silent in church.

The administration of discipline (called "the power of the keys") was not committed exclusively to Peter or his successors or specifically to any individual pastor, but to the particular church collectively.

Every man is subject to the civil power in matters properly civil; it has dominion only over the body and external faculties of man; and it punishes even those who confess their faults. Only members of the church are subject to the ecclesiastical power, and that only in religious matters; ecclesiastical power is exercised exclusively on the faculties of the mind; and the ecclesiastical power pardons all who are penitent. It is highly derogatory to the power of the church to suppose that her government cannot be properly administered without the intervention of the civil magistrate.

CHAPTER THIRTY-THREE: PERFECT GLORIFICATION, INCLUDING THE SECOND ADVENT OF CHRIST, THE RESURRECTION OF THE DEAD, AND THE GENERAL CONFLAGRATION

Perfect glorification is effected in eternity. Its fulfillment and consummation will commence from the period of Christ's judgment and the resurrection of the dead. When he will come is known only to the Father. When he comes, the dead will rise and the living will be suddenly changed. Christ with the saints, arrayed in the Father's glory and power, will judge the evil angels and all mankind. Each individual will be judged according to the measure of illumination which he has enjoyed. Coincident with Christ's second coming, his glorious reign on earth with the saints will begin. His kingdom of grace (also called the kingdom of heaven) began with his first advent, but his kingdom of glory will not begin till his second advent. After the expiration of a thousand years, Satan will rage again and assail the church at the head of an immense confederacy of its enemies; but he will be overthrown by fire from heaven and condemned to everlasting punishment.

After the evil angels and chief enemies of God have been sentenced, judgment will be passed on mankind: then the wicked will be punished and the righteous will have perfect glorification, that is, eternal life and perfect happiness arising chiefly from the vision of God. Our glorification will be accompanied by the renovation of heaven and earth and of all things therein adapted to our service or delight, to be possessed by us in perpetuity.

BOOK TWO: THE WORSHIP OF GOD

CHAPTER ONE: GOOD WORKS

The true worship of God consists chiefly in the exercise of good works—those which men perform by the Spirit of God working in them through true faith, to the glory of God, the assured hope of their own salvation, and the edification of their neighbors. The essential form of good works is their accordance with faith, not their accordance with the decalogue; for it is faith that justifies, not observance of the Mosaic law. The true essential form of good works is conformity with the unwritten law of the Spirit which the Father gave men to lead them into all truth. What the Papists call works of supererogation are clearly impossible. Men's good actions are not their own but the acts of God working in them: hence the vanity of human merits.

CHAPTER TWO: THE PROXIMATE CAUSES OF GOOD WORKS

God is the primary cause of good works. The proximate causes are good habits, the virtues which comprise our whole duty to God and man. The general virtues of wisdom and prudence belong to the understanding. By wisdom we seek and learn God's will and govern our actions accordingly. Opposed to wisdom is folly—ignorance of God's will, false conceit of wisdom, prying into hidden things (as did Adam and Eve, contrary to God's command), and merely human or carnal wisdom. By the virtue of prudence we discern what is proper to be done under varied circumstances. The general virtues of sincerity, promptitude, and constancy belong to the will. Sincerity (also called integrity and a good conscience) consists in acting rightly on all occasions with sincere desire and hearty determination of mind. Contrary to sincerity are evil conscience—more properly called the individual's consciousness of his own evil, and also evil thoughts and hypocrisy. The virtue of promptitude is the alacrity which excites us to act with a ready and willing spirit: its opposites are precipitancy and the forced or unspontaneous discharge of duty. Constancy is the virtue of undeviatingly persevering in determination to do right; its opposites are inconstancy and obstinacy in error or in a wrong purpose.

CHAPTER THREE: THE VIRTUES WHICH BELONG TO THE WORSHIP OF GOD

Special virtues are those which pertain to a particular branch of duty—duty toward God or toward man. Our duty toward God relates to his immediate worship or service. Internal worship consists in acknowledging the one true God and in cultivating devout affections toward him. Opposed to it are atheism and polytheism. Devout affections toward God are love, trust, hope, gratitude, fear, humility, patience, and obedience. By the love of God we prefer him above all and desire his glory; an effect of this love is trust in God, whereby we wholly repose on him: opposed to such trust are distrust, overweening presumption, carnal reliance, and trust in idols. Hope is the certain expectation that God's promises will be fulfilled; opposed to it are doubt and despair. By gratitude we acknowledge God's goodness in conferring benefits on creatures so unworthy as we are; opposed to it are ingratitude toward God and the bestowing on idols or on created things of the gratitude which we owe him. By fear of God we reverence him as the supreme Father and Judge, and dread offending him above all things. By humility we acknowledge our unworthiness in his sight; opposed to humility are pride toward God, and false or superstitious humility. By patience we acquiesce in God's promises through confident reliance on his providence, power, and goodness, and by it we bear inevitable evils with equanimity recognizing them as his dispensation sent for our good; opposed to patience is impatience under the divine decrees—a temptation to which the saints themselves are sometimes liable. By obedience we put God's will as the paramount rule of our conduct and serve him alone; its opposite is disobedience.

CHAPTER FOUR: EXTERNAL WORSHIP

External worship, or true religion, is the invocation or adoration of God in the form and manner prescribed by him, and the sanctification of his name in all of life's circumstances. Invocation includes supplication and thanksgiving, and oaths and the casting of lots. Supplication is the act, under the guidance of the Holy Spirit, of reverently asking God for lawful things for ourselves or others through faith in Christ. The Lord's Prayer was intended rather as a model of supplication than as a form to be repeated verbatim: set forms of worship are superfluous, for with Christ as our master and the Holy Spirit to assist us, we have no need of human aid. Indeed, our prayers need not always be audible: silent mental supplication, whispers, and even groans in private prayer may suffice. The offer of prayers may be solitary or in company, but should be made with understanding: hence the impropriety of public prayer in an unknown tongue. Vain repetitions and empty words are to be avoided. The Bible enjoins no particular posture of the body in prayer. In accordance with 1 Cor. xi 4, which was written when covering the head was a token of subjection, it was usual for men to pray or prophesy with heads uncovered. Now that covering the head has become a token of authority and uncovering it of submission, it is the custom with most churches, in compliance with the spirit of the Law, to worship God uncovered, but to prophesy covered in token of the authority with which the speaker is invested. All places are equally suitable for prayer, and also all times. We are commanded to pray for all mankind, even our enemies, but not for any whom we know certainly to be past remedy (Jer. vii 16; cf. xiv 11–12; John xvii 9; and 1 John v 16). We are even commanded to call down curses on the enemies of God and the church, on false brethren, and grievous offenders against God or even against ourselves. Supplications offered in a spirit of faith and obedience will be heard, but believers are not heard when what they seek is contrary to their own good or God's glory. Sometimes even the prayers of unbelievers prevail with God, for he is kind to all and occasionally grants even the requests of devils. Sometimes he complies with our prayers in anger, as he did when the Israelites asked for flesh (Num. xi 18 ff.) and for a king (Hos. xiii 11).

Prayer is assisted by fasting and vows. In a religious fast a man abstains not so much from eating and drinking as from sin, so that he may devote himself more closely to prayer. In ancient times various inflictions were added to fasting for the mortification of the body, in conformity with the customs of those nations. A vow is a promise to God respecting some lawful matter solemnly made to testify readiness to serve him or to express gratitude to him. But we must be careful not to debar ourselves or others from things which God intended for our use, such as meat or drink, except when the exercise of our liberty may be a stumbling-block to any of the brethren; the same rule applies to marriage. Vows of voluntary poverty are superstitious. Impious vows are not binding. Sacrilege is the non-performance of a vow or the appropriation to private use of things dedicated to God. Addresses to God, especially returning thanks with gladness for divine benefits, are frequently accompanied by singing and hymns in honor of the divine name.

CHAPTER FIVE: OATHS AND THE LOT

An oath calls God to witness the truth of what we say, with a curse on ourselves should it prove false. If we observe an oath extorted compulsorily by a robber or the like, the sin is doubled: we should acquit ourselves of an obligation which dishonors God instead of entangling ourselves more deeply in the bonds of iniquity. In casting lots we appeal to God to explain doubts and decide controverted questions. The objection that on successive repetitions the result is not invariably the same has no force inasmuch as God, when tempted by importunate enquiries, as in the instance of Balaam (Num. xxii 12, 20), does not uniformly return the same answers.

Idolatry is the making, worshiping, or trusting in idols whether considered as representations of the true God or a false one. The cherubic images over the ark are not to be accounted idols, however. To discharge some civil duty, it is lawful for a true believer to be present at idol-worship, but as far as possible such duties should be avoided. The invocation of angels and saints is forbidden: the subterfuges by which the Papists defend the worship of them are truly frivolous. Invocation of devils and practice of magical arts are also forbidden. But, as appears from the divinely appointed star of Bethlehem and the journey of the Wise Men, all study of the heavenly bodies is not unlawful or unprofitable.

CHAPTER SIX: ZEAL

An ardent desire of hallowing the name of God, together with an indignation against whatever tends to the violation or contempt of religion, is called zeal. Its opposites are lukewarmness, ignorant or imprudent zeal, too fiery zeal, and hypocritical and boastful zeal. The name of God should be hallowed both in word and deed. We should make consistent and, when necessary, open profession of his worship, even to martyrdom.

CHAPTER SEVEN: THE TIME FOR DIVINE WORSHIP, WITH CONSIDERATION OF THE SABBATH, LORD'S DAY, AND FESTIVALS

Previous to the Mosaic law, public worship was not confined to any definite place; under the Law it took place in the synagogues and temple; under the Gospel any convenient place is proper. We do not know the time of public worship before the Law; under the Law it was the sabbath or seventh day. Under the Gospel this has been revoked and no particular day has been appointed in its place.

CHAPTER EIGHT: DUTIES TOWARD MEN AND THE GENERAL VIRTUES WHICH BELONG TO THEM

The virtues connected with our duty toward man are those owed to himself and those owed to his neighbor, and they are either the general virtues of love and righteousness, or special virtues. The love of man toward himself consists in loving himself next to God and in seeking his own temporal and eternal good. Opposed to this is perverse hatred of self, loving self more than God, and despising a neighbor in comparison to self. Righteousness toward ourselves consists in proper self-government, including the entire regulation of the internal affections (love and hatred, joy and sorrow, hope and fear, and anger), the discriminating pursuit of external good, and the resistance to, or patient endurance of, external evil.

CHAPTER NINE: THE FIRST CLASS OF SPECIAL VIRTUES CONNECTED WITH MAN'S DUTY TOWARD HIMSELF

The special virtues have reference to bodily gratifications or to possessions which enrich and adorn life. The virtue which prescribes bounds to bodily gratification is temperance, and under it are comprehended sobriety (abstinence from immoderate eating and drinking), chastity (temperance as regards the unlawful lusts of the flesh), modesty (refraining from obscenity of language or action and from anything inconsistent with the strictest decency of behavior in reference to sex or person), and decency (refraining from indecorum or lasciviousness in dress or personal appearance). Moderation in enjoying temporal possessions is manifested in contentment, frugality, industry, and a liberal spirit—liberality being a temperate use of our honest acquisitions in the provision of food and raiment and the elegancies of life. The virtues especially appropriate to high station are lowliness of mind and magnanimity—opposites of arrogance, desire of vain glory, boasting, glorying in iniquity and misdeeds, an ambitious spirit, pride, and pusillanimity.

CHAPTER TEN: THE SECOND CLASS OF VIRTUES CONNECTED WITH MAN'S DUTY TOWARD HIMSELF

The virtues exercised in resistance to, or endurance of, evil are fortitude and patience; their opposites are timidity and rashness; impatience and an effeminate spirit; hypocritical patience, and stoical apathy.

CHAPTER ELEVEN: THE DUTIES OF MAN TOWARD HIS NEIGHBOR AND THE VIRTUES COMPREHENDED UNDER THOSE DUTIES

We next consider the same virtues as exercised toward our neighbor. Charity toward our neighbor consists in loving him as we love ourselves. Love toward him is absolute, comprising humanity, good will, and compassion, or reciprocal, comprising brotherly love and friendship.

CHAPTER TWELVE: THE SPECIAL VIRTUES OR DUTIES WHICH REGARD OUR NEIGHBOR

Discharge of our special neighborly duties includes regulation of our actions and affections as concerns a neighbor. His internal good is consulted by regard to his safety and honor; his external, by concern for his good name and worldly interests. Under this class of virtues are comprehended innocence, meekness, and placability.

CHAPTER THIRTEEN: THE SECOND CLASS OF SPECIAL DUTIES TOWARD OUR NEIGHBOR

We consult our neighbor's good name by showing him due respect in our deportment, conversation, and speaking about him, and by avoiding anything which might injure him causelessly in the opinion of others. We should avoid falsehoods; but parables, hyperboles, apologues, and ironical modes of speech are not falsehoods; for their object is not deception but instruction. In the proper sense of the word "deceit," no one can be deceived without being injured at the same time; accordingly when, instead of injuring a person by a false statement, we confer positive benefit on him or prevent him from inflicting or suffering injury, we are doing him a service against his will; and it is not deceit. Stratagems for purposes of war, though coupled with falsehood, are lawful because, where we are not under an obligation to speak the truth, there can be no reason why, when occasion requires it, we should not utter even what is false. Milton adds, "I do not see why this should be more allowable in war than in peace, especially in cases where, by an honest and beneficial kind of falsehood, we may be able to avert injury or danger from ourselves or our neighbor." In short, the scriptural denunciations against falsehood refer only to violations of truth which are derogatory to God's glory or injurious to ourselves or our neighbor. In such passages we are commanded to speak the truth; but to whom? —not to an enemy, not to a madman, not to an assassin, but to our neighbor, that is, one to whom we are connected by the bonds of peace and social fellowship. If it is to our neighbor only that we are required to speak the truth, it is evident that we are not forbidden to utter what is false, when necessary, to such as do not deserve that name. Nothing is prohibited in the Ninth Commandment but what is injurious to our neighbor; it follows that a falsehood productive of no evil to him, if prohibited at all, is not prohibited by that commandment. Hence, we are justified in acquitting all those holy men who, according to the common judgment of theologians, must be convicted of falsehood; for example, Abraham in Gen. xxii 5; Joseph in Gen. xlii 7 ff.; the Hebrew midwives in Exod. i 19 ff.; Moses in Exod. iii; and Jonathan in 1 Sam. xx 6, 28.

At considerable length Milton treats veracity and candor and the allied virtues of simplicity, faithfulness, gravity, taciturnity, courteousness, urbanity, freedom of speech, the spirit of admonition, and, as is his usual method with virtues, their opposites. By freedom of speech he means speaking the truth with boldness.

CHAPTER FOURTEEN: THE SECOND CLASS OF SPECIAL DUTIES TOWARD OUR NEIGHBOR (CONTINUED)

The virtues by which we promote the worldly interests of our neighbor are integrity and beneficence. Integrity is abstaining from the property of others. All transactions of purchase and sale, letting and hire, lending and borrowing, keeping and restoring deposits are included under commutative justice. In treating loans, Milton considers the differences of opinion about usury and decides that it is not in itself reprehensible; otherwise God would not have allowed the Israelites to lend upon usury to strangers (Deut. xxiii 20); moreover, if it is lawful to receive profit for the use of cattle, lands, houses, and the like, why not also for the use of money? Under the Gospel usury is to be condemned only when it is taken from the poor, when its sole object is gain, and when it is exacted without regard to charity and justice, even as any other species of lucrative commerce carried on in the same spirit would be equally reprehensible and equally entitled to be called by the Hebrew word which signifies "a bite." Milton proceeds to treat moderation, beneficence, liberality, magnificence, and gratitude.

CHAPTER FIFTEEN: THE RECIPROCAL DUTIES OF MAN TOWARD HIS NEIGHBOR, ESPECIALLY PRIVATE DUTIES

Private duties are partly domestic, comprehending the mutual duties of husband and wife, parent and child, brethren and kinsmen, master and servant. Milton illustrates these with copious scriptural citations and little comment.

CHAPTER SIXTEEN: THE REMAINING CLASS OF PRIVATE DUTIES

The principal virtues of duties exercised toward strangers are almsgiving and hospitality. These are illustrated from Scripture.

CHAPTER SEVENTEEN: PUBLIC DUTIES TOWARD OUR NEIGHBOR

Public duties are political and ecclesiastical. Under the political ones are comprehended the obligations of the magistrate and people to each other and to foreign nations. It is especially the magistrate's duty to encourage religion and the service of God, to protect it, but not to force religion upon the people. Joshua xxiv 15 and Psalm cv 14 show that kings are forbidden to exercise violence against religious persons in any matter whatever; therefore, much more are they forbidden to force the consciences of such persons in the matter of religion itself. In our own times, Christians are often persecuted or subjected to punishment for matters which are purely controversial or which are left by Christian liberty to the judgment of each believer or which are not expressly treated in the Gospel. Since the ecclesiastical minister is not entitled to exercise absolute authority over the church, much less can the civil magistrate claim such authority. Undoubtedly, as the kingdom of Christ is not of this world, so it is not sustained by force or compulsion which are the supports of earthly rule. The outward profession of the Gospel ought not to be made a matter of constraint. As to the inner parts of religion (faith and liberty of conscience), these are beyond its power, being in their nature matter of ecclesiastical discipline alone, and being incapable of being affected by the determinations of human tribunals. Moreover, it is absurd and impious to compel the conscientious to adopt a religion which they do not approve, or to constrain the profane to bear a part in that public worship from which God has interdicted them.

The opinion that obedience is due to the commands not only of an upright magistrate but also to the commands of a usurper, even when they are contrary to justice, has no basis in Scripture. But I am far from denying that it may be the part of prudence to obey the commands even of a tyrant in lawful things or, more properly, to comply with the necessity of the times for the sake of public peace as well as personal safety.

There seems no reason why war should be unlawful now, any more than in the time of the Jews; nor is it anywhere forbidden in the New Testament.

Public ecclesiastical duties consist in the reciprocal obligations of ministers and of the church considered collectively and individually.

[illegible] SEVERITY OF SOME [illegible] TOWARDS GOD [illegible]

[illegible] political and [illegible] Under [illegible] political [illegible] one of [illegible] the [illegible] people [illegible] especially the [illegible] and [illegible] Christians are often persecuted [illegible] subjected to punishment for matters which are purely [illegible] conscience [illegible] in the [illegible] believes [illegible] treated in the Gospel [illegible] absolute authority [illegible] church [illegible] the civil magistrate [illegible] kingdom of Christ is not of this world [illegible] the Gospel [illegible] liberty [illegible] to compel [illegible] which they do not approve [illegible]

[illegible] not only [illegible] but also to the commands of [illegible] it may be the part of prudence [illegible] lawful [illegible]

[illegible]

[illegible]

BIBLIOGRAPHY[1]

EDITIONS

Except for a few recently discovered items such as the state letter to Hamburg which is printed here for the first time, all of Milton's prose works, in English and in Latin, accompanied by translations, are included in the Columbia Milton—*The Works of John Milton,* gen. ed., Frank A. Patterson, 18 vols. in 21 (Columbia Univ. Press, 1931–38). The English prose works and translations of the Latin ones are being published in the Yale Milton—*Complete Prose Works of John Milton,* gen. ed., Don M. Wolfe: 4 vols. out of a projected 8 have appeared (Yale Univ. Press, 1953–). The Yale texts are more nearly definitive than the Columbia ones and are accompanied by explanatory annotations. Copious selections of the prose are included in *Milton's Prose,* ed., Malcolm W. Wallace, World's Classics (1925); *The Student's Milton,* ed., Frank A. Patterson (Columbia Univ. Press, 1933); *John Milton: Prose Selections,* ed., Merritt Y. Hughes (Odyssey Press, 1947); *Milton's Prose Writings,* ed., M. Burton (Everyman's Library, rev. ed., 1958); *John Milton: Complete Poems and Major Prose,* ed., Merritt Y. Hughes (Odyssey Press, 1957).

BIBLIOGRAPHIES, GUIDES AND HANDBOOKS

David H. Stevens, *Reference Guide to Milton from 1800 to the Present Day* [i.e., through 1928] (Univ. of Chicago Press, 1930); Harris F. Fletcher, *Contributions to a Milton Bibliography, 1800–1930* (Univ. of Illinois Studies, 1931); Calvin Huckabay, *John Milton: A Bibliographical Supplement, 1929–1957* (Duquesne Univ.

[1] Other relevant works are cited in the Forewords and Footnotes. For titles connected with Milton's poetry, see the Bibliography in *The Complete English Poetry of John Milton,* ed., John T. Shawcross (1963).

Press, 1960); E. N. S. Thompson, *John Milton: A Topical Bibliography* (Yale Univ. Press, 1916); *The Cambridge Bibliography of English Literature* (1941), I, 463–73, and its *Supplement* (1957), V, 225–37. For Milton scholarship since 1957, see the annual volumes of the English Association, *The Year's Work in English Studies;* Modern Humanities Research Association, *Annual Bibliography of English Language and Literature;* Modern Language Association, *PMLA,* May issues; "Recent Literature of the English Renaissance," *Studies in Philology.*

To keep abreast of current scholarship, see the reviews and abstracts in *Seventeenth-Century News* and *English Abstracts.* There is a selective list of editions and scholarship of all periods in James Holly Hanford, *Milton,* Goldentree Bibliographies (Appleton-Century-Crofts, 1966). There is a survey guide to editions and scholarship, with summaries and opinionative commentary, covering all periods, in *Milton Literature* by J. Max Patrick and John R. Mulder (Educational Guidelines, Inc., paper, and Facts on File, Inc., clothbound, 1967). There are brief accounts of the prose works in Edward S. LeComte, *A Milton Dictionary* (1961) and James Holly Hanford, *A Milton Handbook,* 4th ed. (1946). Frank A. Patterson and French Fogle, *An Index to the Columbia Milton* (1940) serves as a concordance to the prose works.

CULTURAL CONTEXT AND HISTORICAL BACKGROUND

Don Cameron Allen, *Doubt's Boundless Sea: Skepticism and Faith in the Renaissance* (Johns Hopkins Univ. Press, 1964); Herschel Baker, *The Wars of Truth* (Harvard Univ. Press, 1952); Émile Bréhier, *The History of Philosophy: The Seventeenth Century* (Univ. of Chicago Press, 1966); Douglas Bush, *English Literature in the Earlier Seventeenth Century* (rev. ed., Oxford Univ. Press, 1962), *The Renaissance and English Humanism* (Univ. of Toronto Press, 1939, repr. 1941), *Classical Influences in Renaissance Literature* (Harvard Univ. Press, 1952); W. G. Crane, *Wit and Rhetoric in the Renaissance* (1948); Morris W. Croll, *Style, Rhetoric, and Rhythm: Essays,* ed., J. Max Patrick et al (Princeton Univ. Press, 1966); Godfrey Davies, *The Early Stuarts* (Oxford Univ. Press, 1937); Zera S. Fink, *The Classical Republicans* (Northwestern Univ.

Press, 1945; repr. 1962); Joseph Frank, *The Levellers* (Harvard Univ. Press, 1955); George Peabody Gooch, *English Democratic Ideas in the Seventeenth Century* (Cambridge Univ. Press, 1908; rev. ed., 1927); H. J. C. Grierson, *Cross Currents in English Literature* (1929; repr. 1966); William Haller, *Tracts on Liberty in the Puritan Revolution*, 3 vols. (Columbia Univ. Press, 1935), *The Rise of Puritanism* (Columbia Univ. Press, 1938), *Liberty and Reformation in the Puritan Revolution* (Columbia Univ. Press, 1955); Christopher Hill, *Society and Puritanism in Pre-Revolutionary England* (1964); Samuel Kliger, *The Goths in England* (Harvard Univ. Press, 1952); Francis R. Johnson, *Astronomical Thought in Renaissance England* (Johns Hopkins Univ. Press, 1937); Lawrence A. Sasek, *The Literary Temper of the English Puritans* (Louisiana State Univ. Press, 1961); F. S. Siebert, *Freedom of the Press in England* (Univ. of Illinois Press, 1952); John Tulloch, *Rational Theology and Christian Philosophy in England in the Seventeenth Century*, 2nd ed., 2 vols. (Edinburgh, 1872); A. S. P. Woodhouse, *Puritanism and Liberty* (London, 1938); George Yule, *The Independents in the English Civil War* (Cambridge Univ. Press, 1958); Perez Zagorin, *A History of Political Thought in the English Revolution* (London, 1954).

SCHOLARSHIP ON MILTON AND HIS PROSE WORKS

Herbert Agar, *Milton and Plato* (Princeton Univ. Press, 1928; Oxford Univ. Press, 1931); Arthur Barker, *Milton and the Puritan Dilemma, 1641–1660* (Univ. of Toronto Press, 1942, 1956), "Christian Liberty in Milton's Divorce Pamphlets," *MLR*, XXXV (1940), 153–61; J. B. Broadbent, "Milton's Rhetoric," *MP*, LVI (1959), 224–42; Robert R. Cawley, *Milton and the Literature of Travel* (Princeton Univ. Press, 1951); William M. Clyde, *The Struggle for the Freedom of the Press* (Oxford Univ. Press for St. Andrews Univ., 1934); George N. Conklin, *Biblical Criticism and Heresy in Milton* (King's Crown Press, 1949); Walter C. Curry, *Milton's Ontology, Cosmogony, and Physics* (Univ. of Kentucky Press, 1957); Roy Daniells, *Milton, Mannerism, and Baroque* (Univ. of Toronto Press, 1963); *Eikon Basilike*, ed., Philip A. Knachel (Cornell Univ. Press for the Folger Shakespeare Library, 1966); Fred Emil Ekfelt, "The Graphic

Diction of Milton's English Prose," *PQ*, XXV (1946), 46–69; Ronald David Emma, *Milton's Grammar* (The Hague, 1964); G. Blakemore Evans, "The State of Milton's Text: The Prose, 1643–48," *JEGP*, LIX (1960), 497–505; Michael Fixler, *Milton and the Kingdoms of God* (London, 1964); Harris F. Fletcher, *The Use of the Bible in Milton's Prose* (Univ. of Illinois Press, 1929); J. Milton French, "Milton as Historian," *PMLA*, L (1935), 469–79; Allen H. Gilbert, "Milton's Defense of Bawdry," *SAMLA Studies in Milton*, ed., J. Max Patrick (Univ. of Florida Press, 1953); W. E. Gilman, *Milton's Rhetoric* (Univ. of Missouri Press, 1939); John B. Gleason, "The Nature of Milton's *Moscovia*," *SP*, LXI (1964), 640–49; William Haller, "Before *Areopagitica*," *PMLA*, XLII (1927), 875–900, "Milton and the Protestant Ethic," *JBS*, No. 1 (1961), pp. 52–57, "Hail Wedded Love," *ELH*, XIII (June, 1946), 79–97; Kathleen Hartwell, *Lactantius and Milton* (Harvard Univ. Press, 1929); Nathaniel Henry, "Milton's Last Pamphlet: Theocracy and Intolerance," pp. 197–210 in *A Tribute to George Coffin Taylor*, ed., Arnold Williams (Univ. of North Carolina Press, 1932); John F. Huntley, "*Proairesis, Synteresis*, and the Ethical Orientation of Milton's *Of Education*," *PQ*, XLIII (1964), 40–46.

John Illo, "The Misreading of Milton" [*Areopagitica*], *Columbia University Forum*, VIII (1965), 38–42; Thomas Kranidas, *The Fierce Equation: A Study of Milton's Decorum* (The Hague, 1965); Ida Langdon, *Milton's Theory of Poetry and Fine Art* (Yale Univ. Press, 1924); Martin A. Larson, "Milton and Servetus," *PMLA*, XLI (1926), 891–934, "Milton's Essential Relationship to Puritanism and Stoicism," *PQ*, VI (1927), 201–20; Barbara Kiefer Lewalski, "Milton: Political Beliefs and Polemical Methods, 1659–60," *PMLA*, LXXIV (1959), 191–202, "Milton on Learning, and the Learned-Ministry Controversy," *HLQ*, XXIV (1961), 267–81; Joshua H. Neumann, "Milton's Prose Vocabulary," *PMLA*, LX (1945), 102–20; Marjorie H. Nicolson, "Milton and Hobbes," *SP*, XXIII (1926), 405–33; C. A. Patrides, *Milton and the Christian Tradition* (Oxford Univ. Press, 1966; Harry F. Robins, *If This Be Heresy: A Study of Milton and Origen* (Univ. of Illinois Press, 1963); Malcolm M. Ross, *Milton's Royalism* (Cornell Univ. Press, 1943), *Poetry and Dogma* (Rutgers Univ. Press, 1954); Irene Samuel, *Plato and Milton* (Cornell Univ. Press, 1947); Denis Saurat, *Milton: Man and Thinker* (1944; repr., London, 1946); Howard Schultz, *Milton and Forbid-*

den Knowledge (Modern Language Association, 1955); George F. Sensabaugh, *That Grand Whig, Milton* (Stanford Univ. Press, 1952), *Milton in Early America* (Princeton Univ. Press, 1952); James H. Sims, *The Bible in Milton's Epics* (Univ. of Florida Press, 1962); Sigmund G. Spaeth, *Milton's Knowledge of Music* (Princeton Univ. Library, 1913; Ernest Sirluck, "Milton's Political Thought: The First Cycle," *MP*, LXI (1964), 209–24; D. T. Starnes and Ernest W. Talbert, "Milton and the Dictionaries," *Classical Myth and Legend in Renaissance Dictionaries* (Univ. of North Carolina Press, 1955).

Kester Svendsen, *Milton and Science* (Harvard Univ. Press, 1956), "Science and Structure in Milton's Doctrine of Divorce," *PMLA*, LXVII (1952), 435–45; James E. Thorpe, *Milton Criticism* (1950); E. M. W. Tillyard, *The Miltonic Setting* (Cambridge Univ. Press, 1938, 1947, *Studies in Milton* (1951); Richard M. Weaver, "Milton's Heroic Prose," *The Ethics of Rhetoric* (1953, 1963); Robert West, *Milton and the Angels* (Univ. of Georgia Press, 1955); George Whiting, *Milton's Literary Milieu* (Univ. of North Carolina Press, 1958), *Milton and This Pendant World* (Univ. of Texas Press, 1958); Don M. Wolfe, *Milton in the Puritan Revolution* (1941).

J. MAX PATRICK received his B.A. degree from the University of Toronto and his B.Litt. and D.Phil. degrees from Oxford University. He is Professor of English in the Graduate School of Arts and Science, New York University. His publications include *Hugh Peters: A Study in Puritanism; Francis Bacon; The Quest for Utopia;* and *The Complete Poetry of Robert Herrick,* in the Anchor Seventeenth-Century Series. Professor Patrick is the General Editor of the Anchor Seventeenth-Century Series and Editor of *Seventeenth-Century News.*

ARTHUR M. AXELRAD received his B.A. degree from Brooklyn College and his M.A. and Ph.D. degrees from New York University. He has written articles and reviews for *Seventeenth-Century News,* and was Abstracts Editor until 1965. He is an Assistant Professor of English at California State College at Long Beach.

EVERETT H. EMERSON studied at Dartmouth, Harvard, and Duke. He reviews books regularly for *Seventeenth-Century News,* and has written articles on Milton and Calvinism and a study of John Cotton. He is the Secretary of the Modern Language Association Conference of Scholars on Colonial American Literature, and is Professor of English at the University of Massachusetts.

THOMAS R. HARTMANN received his B.A. and M.A. degrees from St. Thomas College, and his Ph.D. degree from New York University. Since 1959 he has been Assistant Editor of *Seventeenth-Century News,* to which he has contributed many articles and reviews. He is an Assistant Professor at Brooklyn College.

WILLIAM B. HUNTER, JR., received his B.A. degree from Princeton and his M.A. and Ph.D. degrees from Vanderbilt University. He is secretary of the Milton Society of America and author of *The Complete Poetry of Ben Jonson,* in the Anchor Seventeenth-Century Series. He is Professor of English at Macalester College.

BARBARA KIEFER LEWALSKI received her B.A. degree from Kansas State Teachers College, and her M.A. and Ph.D. degrees from the University of Chicago. Her previous publications include *Milton's Brief Epic: A Study of Paradise Regained.* She is Professor of English at Brown University.

JOHN R. MULDER received his Ph.D. degree from the University of Michigan. He is Associate Editor of *Seventeenth-Century News* and co-author with Professor J. Max Patrick of a guide to Milton scholarship to be published shortly. He is Assistant Professor at New York University.

JOHN T. SHAWCROSS received his Ph.D. degree from New York University. A member of the editorial board of *Seventeenth-Century News,* he is also treasurer of the Milton Society of America. His publications include *The Complete English Poetry of John Milton* and *The Complete Poetry of John Donne,* both in the Anchor Seventeenth-Century Series. He is Professor of English at the University of Wisconsin.

The Anchor Seventeenth-Century Series presents the major—and significant minor—texts in English of the Seventeenth Century in authoritative and inexpensive editions. Prepared especially for Anchor Books by a distinguished group of American and Canadian scholars, these newly edited texts meet the highest standards of scholarship and readability. Each volume incorporates the latest textual and critical discoveries, and the series as a whole is designed to provide a reliable access to the literature of the Seventeenth Century.